MOON HANDBOOKS®

NEW MEXICO

Albuquerque International Balloon Fiesta

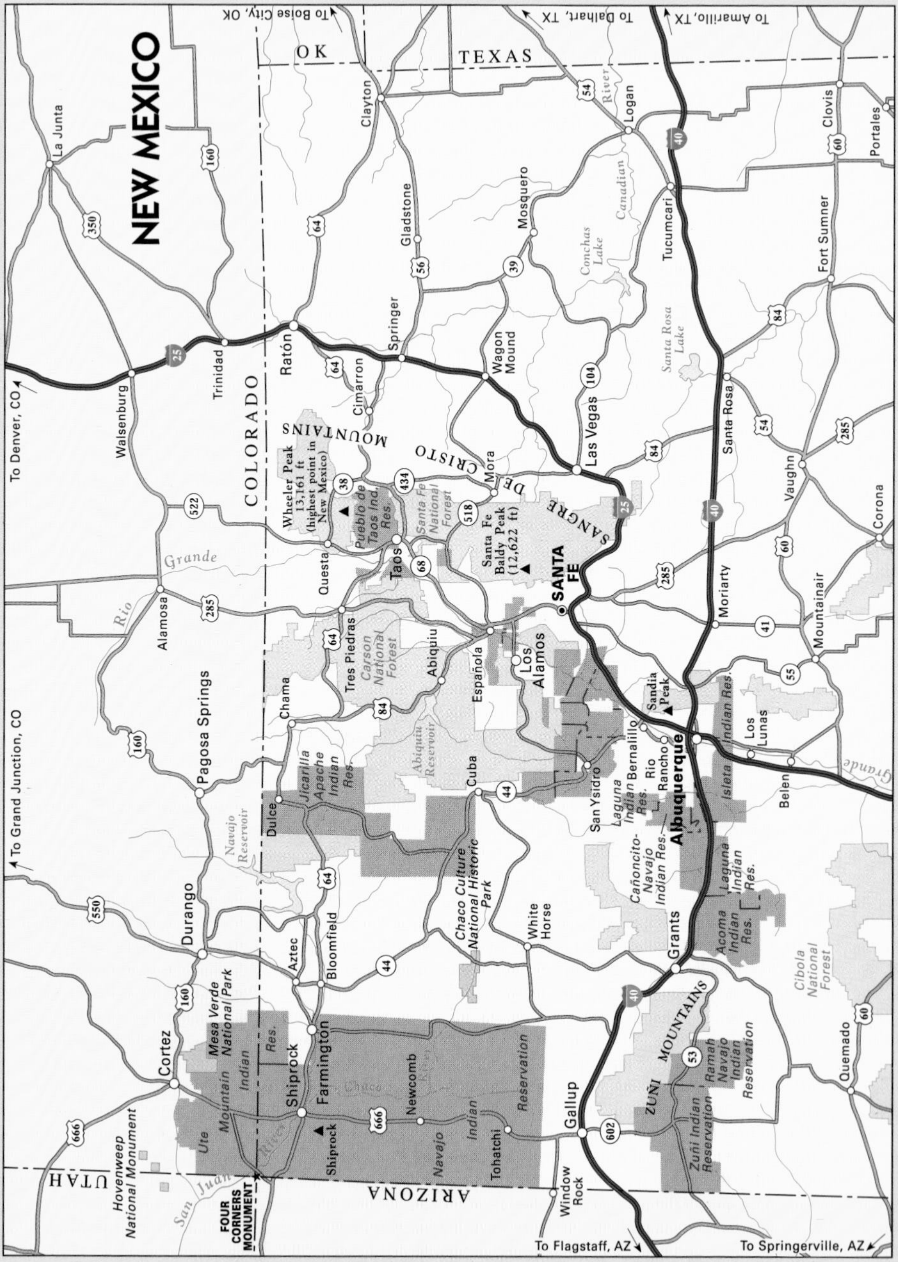
NEW MEXICO
COLORADO
UTAH
ARIZONA
OK
TEXAS
To Denver, CO
To Grand Junction, CO
To Boise City, OK
To Dalhart, TX
To Amarillo, TX
To Flagstaff, AZ
To Springerville, AZ
La Junta
Walsenburg
Trinidad
Alamosa
Pagosa Springs
Durango
Cortez
Hovenweep National Monument
Mesa Verde National Park
Ute Mountain Indian Res.
FOUR CORNERS MONUMENT
Shiprock
Farmington
Aztec
Bloomfield
Newcomb
Tohatchi
Navajo Indian Reservation
Gallup
Window Rock
Chaco Culture National Historic Park
White Horse
Dulce
Jicarilla Apache Indian Res.
Navajo Reservoir
Chama
Tres Piedras
Carson National Forest
Abiquiu
Abiquiu Reservoir
Cuba
Española
Los Alamos
SANTA FE
Santa Fe Baldy Peak (12,622 ft)
Santa Fe National Forest
Taos
Pueblo de Taos Ind. Res.
Questa
Wheeler Peak 13,161 ft (highest point in New Mexico)
SANGRE DE CRISTO MOUNTAINS
Mora
Cimarron
Ratón
Springer
Wagon Mound
Clayton
Gladstone
Mosquero
Las Vegas
Logan
Tucumcari
Conchas Lake
Canadian River
Santa Rosa Lake
Santa Rosa
Fort Sumner
Clovis
Portales
Vaughn
Corona
Moriarty
Mountainair
Sandia Peak
Bernalillo
Rio Rancho
Albuquerque
San Ysidro
Laguna Indian Res.
Isleta Indian Res.
Los Lunas
Belen
Cañoncito-Navajo Indian Res.
Laguna Indian Res.
Acoma Indian Res.
Grants
ZUÑI MOUNTAINS
Ramah Navajo Indian Reservation
Zuñi Indian Reservation
Cibola National Forest
Quemado
Rio Grande
San Juan River
Chaco River

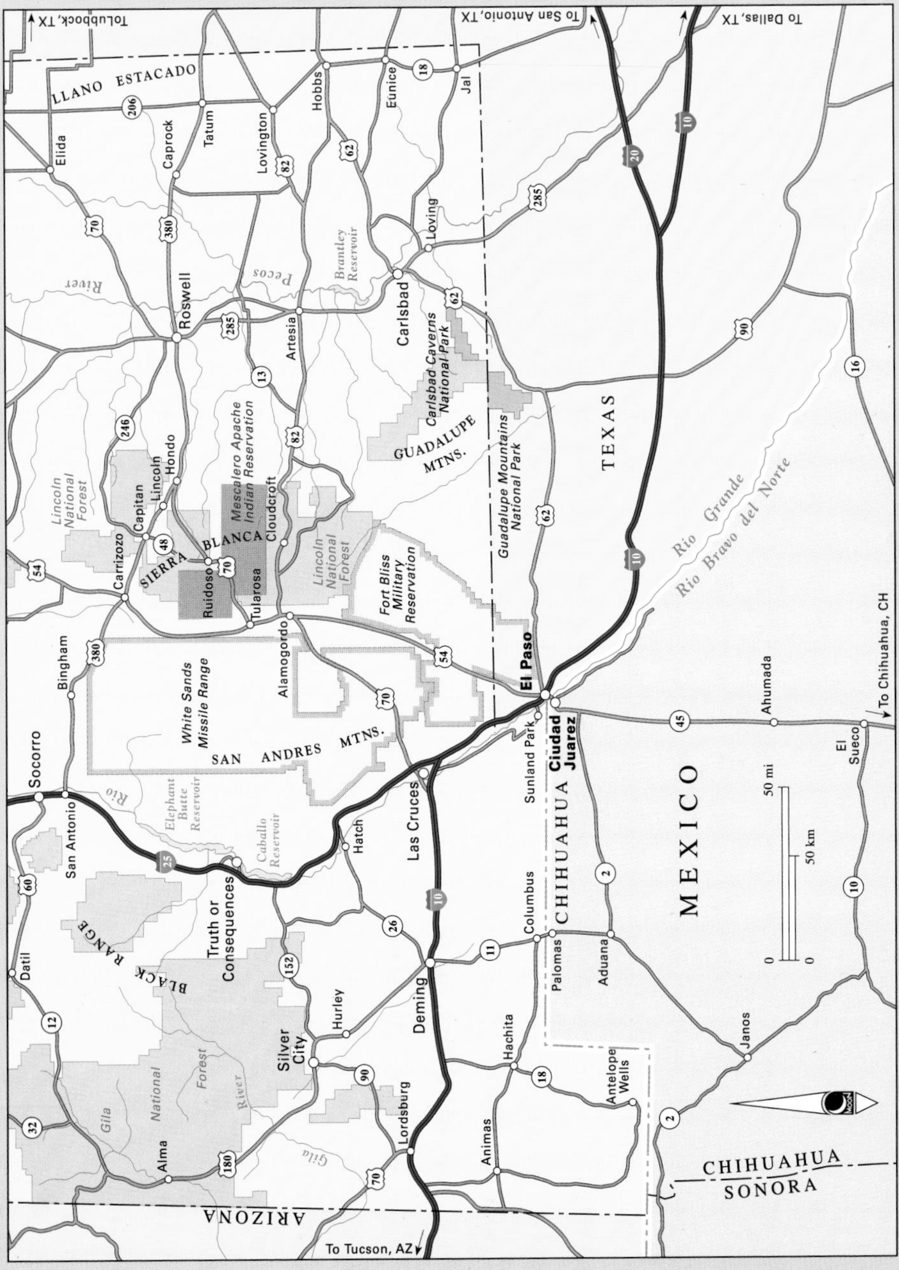

To Lubbock, TX
To San Antonio, TX
To Dallas, TX
LLANO ESTACADO
Elida
Caprock
Tatum
Lovington
Hobbs
Eunice
Jal
Loving
Brantley Reservoir
Pecos River
Roswell
Artesia
Carlsbad
Carlsbad Caverns National Park
GUADALUPE MTNS.
Guadalupe Mountains National Park
TEXAS
Mescalero Apache Indian Reservation
Lincoln National Forest
Capitan
Lincoln
Hondo
Carrizozo
SIERRA BLANCA
Ruidoso
Tularosa
Cloudcroft
Alamogordo
Fort Bliss Military Reservation
El Paso
Ciudad Juarez
Sunland Park
Rio Grande
Rio Bravo del Norte
Bingham
White Sands Missile Range
SAN ANDRES MTNS.
Socorro
San Antonio
Elephant Butte Reservoir
Caballo Reservoir
Truth or Consequences
Hatch
Las Cruces
BLACK RANGE
Datil
Silver City
Hurley
Deming
Columbus
Palomas
CHIHUAHUA
Aduana
Ahumada
El Sueco
To Chihuahua, CH
MEXICO
50 mi
50 km
Gila National Forest
Gila River
Alma
Lordsburg
Hachita
Animas
Antelope Wells
Janos
CHIHUAHUA
SONORA
ARIZONA
To Tucson, AZ

storm over the Jemez Mountains

© STEPHEN METZGER

MOON HANDBOOKS®

NEW MEXICO

SIXTH EDITION

STEPHEN METZGER

AVALON
TRAVEL

Moon Handbooks New Mexico
Sixth Edition

Stephen Metzger

Published by
Avalon Travel Publishing
An Imprint of
Avalon Publishing Group, Inc.

Please send all comments, corrections, additions, amendments, and critiques to:

Moon Handbooks New Mexico

Avalon Travel Publishing
1400 65th Street, Suite 250
Emeryville, CA 94608, USA
email: atpfeedback@avalonpub.com
www.moon.com

Printing History
1st edition—1989
6th edition—May 2003
5 4 3 2

ISBN: 1-56691-580-5
ISSN: 1543-6187

Editor: Rebecca K. Browning
Series Manager: Kevin McLain
Copy Editor: Karen Gaynor Bleske
Graphics Coordinator: Deb Dutcher
Production Coordinator: Darren Alessi
Cover Designer: Kari Gim
Interior Designers: Amber Pirker, Alvaro Villanueva, Kelly Pendragon
Map Editor: Olivia Solís
Cartographers: Mike Morgenfeld, Ben Pease, Mark Stroud, Carol S. Seigel
Proofreader: Erika Howsare
Indexer: Karen Gaynor Bleske

Front cover photo: © John Elk III

Distributed by Publishers Group West

Printed in United States by Worzalla

About the Author

Stephen Metzger

© GINA METZGER

Steve Metzger first traveled through the Southwest as a child, when each summer his father took the family to visit his hometown of Prescott, Arizona. Steve recalls sitting in the rear-facing third seat of the tan '65 Plymouth station wagon as desert miles rolled beneath the car's tires and, with his brother Rick, recognizing the landscape from their favorite western movies and television shows. He remembers being struck by the desert's harsh beauty and the squalor of the people who eked out livings selling frybread from roadside lean-tos (though it would be many years before he would actually use the words "squalor" and "eke" in sentences of his own making).

These early road trips set the tone for his love of travel, and when he graduated high school, he lit out for the Colorado Rockies, where he truly thought he'd be able see it rain fire in the sky.

After realizing that working ski lifts for $1.60 an hour held little hope for a future of continued travel, he returned to California, where he attended Marin Community College, Lake Tahoe Community College, and Chico State, earning both bachelor's and master's degrees in English. He has spent the last 20 years traveling—from the Sangre de Cristo mountains of northern New Mexico to the French and Italian Alps—as well as writing, teaching, and raising a family. In addition to the three books he has written for Avalon Travel Publishing *(Moon Handbooks New Mexico, Moon Handbooks Santa Fe-Taos,* and *Moon Handbooks Colorado),* he has written for the *San Francisco Chronicle* and for several magazines. He has also published poetry and short fiction in literary journals and is a member of the English and American studies departments at California State University, Chico.

When he is not writing, traveling, or teaching, Metzger enjoys spending time with his family—wife Betsy and daughters Hannah and Gina—and their two yellow Labs, Nellie and Toby. He still loves to return to the Southwest of his childhood, where he has a broader appreciation of that land with which he fell in love so long ago. Sometimes, toward the end of a John Ford western in his American studies classes, if he looks closely enough, he sees that old Plymouth wagon bringing up the rear of the charging cavalry, and two young boys, wide-eyed and grinning in the back seat.

For Hannah Rose—Vaya con los dioses

Contents

SPECIAL TOPICS

SOUTH-CENTRAL NEW MEXICO 162

SPECIAL TOPICS

SOUTHEASTERN NEW MEXICO 189

SPECIAL TOPICS

RESOURCES 329

Maps

MAP SYMBOLS

═══	Divided Highway	◉	State Capital	⛳	Golf Course
═══	Primary Road	○	City/Town	⛷	Ski Area
═══	Secondary Road	★	Point of Interest	▲	State Park
=======	Unpaved Road	•	Accommodation	ʌ	Campground
-------	Trail	▼	Restaurant/Bar	)(	Mountain Pass
✈	Airport	▪	Other Location	▲	Mountain
				≋	Waterfall

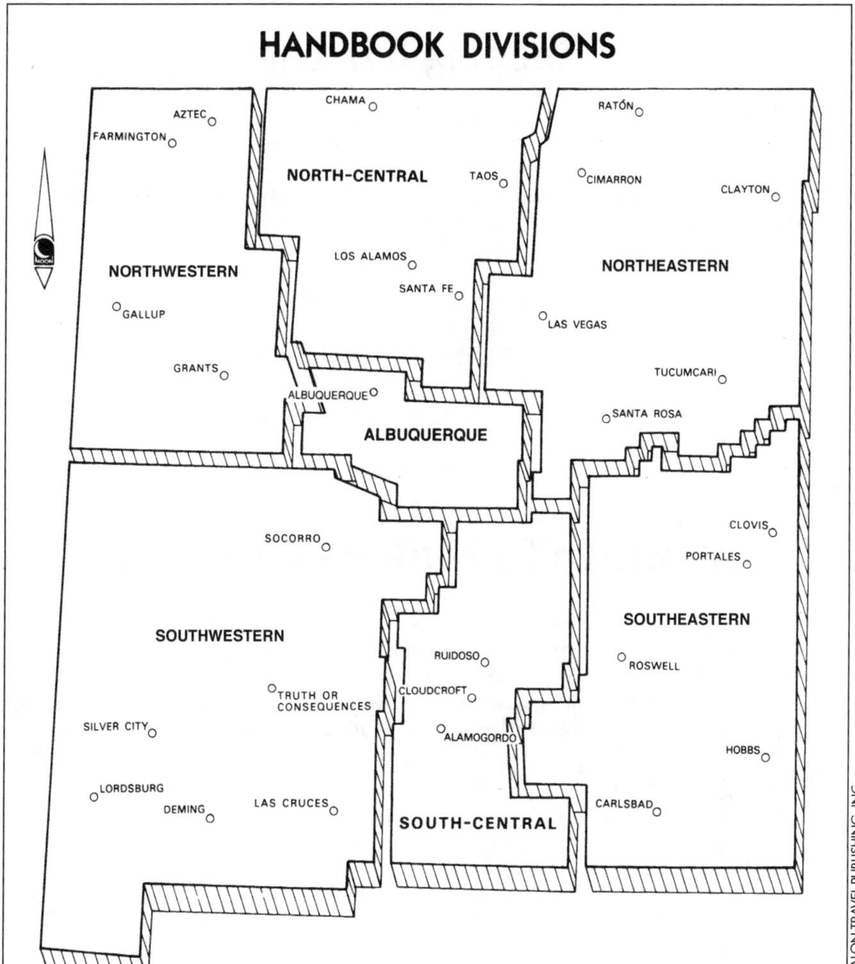
HANDBOOK DIVISIONS
AZTEC
FARMINGTON
CHAMA
NORTH-CENTRAL
TAOS
RATÓN
CIMARRON
CLAYTON
MOON
NORTHWESTERN
LOS ALAMOS
SANTA FE
NORTHEASTERN
GALLUP
LAS VEGAS
GRANTS
TUCUMCARI
ALBUQUERQUE
SANTA ROSA
ALBUQUERQUE
CLOVIS
SOCORRO
PORTALES
SOUTHEASTERN
SOUTHWESTERN
RUIDOSO
ROSWELL
TRUTH OR CONSEQUENCES
CLOUDCROFT
SILVER CITY
ALAMOGORDO
HOBBS
LORDSBURG
DEMING
LAS CRUCES
CARLSBAD
SOUTH-CENTRAL

Keeping Current

Although we strive to produce the most up-to-date guidebook humanly possible, change is unavoidable. Between the time this book goes to print and the moment you read it, a handful of the businesses noted in these pages will undoubtedly change prices, move, or even close their doors forever. Other worthy attractions will open for the first time. If you have a favorite gem you'd like to see included in the next edition, or see anything that needs updating, clarification, or correction, please drop us a line.

Moon Handbooks New Mexico
Avalon Travel Publishing
1400 65th Street, Suite 250
Emeryville, CA 94608, USA
email: atpfeedback@avalonpub.com

New Area Code for New Mexico?

As *Moon Handbooks New Mexico* went to press, the New Mexico Public Regulations Commission and the Federal Communication Commission were debating the implementation of a new area code—575—for New Mexico. The affected areas would include Albuquerque, Los Alamos, and Santa Fe, and some of the surrounding communities. The most current information suggests that this change will occur in June 2003, at the very earliest. If and when the change does occur, callers will be informed via recorded message any time they call the existing 505 area code.

Preface

More than 20 years ago, I was living in Barcelona, Spain, teaching English at a small private college. Three of my students were young professional photographers who happened to be in business together, and they were studying English for one reason: they wanted to go to New Mexico to shoot. Now, I'm not sure any one of them could have pinpointed New Mexico on a map of the United States, but they all shared a dream of traveling there. *"La luz,"* they would say, poring over pictures of the high desert. "The light."

Shortly afterward, I saw New Mexico for the first time myself and knew exactly what they meant. It was a late afternoon in summer. Betsy and I crossed over from Arizona on I-40, drove through Gallup, and headed toward Albuquerque. In the distance, dark storm clouds moved monstrously across the sky, streaked with fierce rain. But there between the Zuñi and Navajo Reservations, on the high desert east of the city, sunlight danced on mesa-sides, softened red-rock canyons, and brightened the greens of the piñons and junipers; a quiet, almost eerie glow swept the landscape, and the rain still looked a long way off.

We pulled off the highway, got out of the car, and were surprised by the wind, warm and soft. A tumbleweed rolled by. We walked a few hundred feet from the road, found the dead discarded skin of a snake, stood quietly watching the storm. The air around us was electric, almost palpable.

Soon we felt large drops of rain on our bare arms, saw dark spots appear on the earth. We stood for a moment, strangely and unexplainably reverent, then dashed for the car. Once inside, we laughed, dried our faces, sat and watched the storm, its front as well defined as a bulkhead. Finally, we got back on the highway—an inch deep now in water—and headed for Albuquerque.

Within minutes we broke through the back side of the storm, and there was that light again—intense, vivid, otherworldly. I thought about Indian ceremonials, Sun, Cloud, and Rain dances, and I came closer than I ever had to understanding them. The sun as a god? Why not?

I don't know if Xavi, Estevan, and Sergi, my photographer friends, ever made it to New Mexico. I don't know if they've had a chance yet to see the light that so moved them in photographs. But when I see it, I think of them. You were right, guys: *La luz es mágica.*

After supper I walked on a dirt road in the twilight, through a gate and into a field, with towering trees and Taos Mountain on one side and Taos Plain falling away on the other, clear to the Ranchos and the ranges beyond. I was rapt, remembering that four hundred years of history had passed by here, was quiet, hearing the whisper of ghosts around me, was content to be one link in an endless chain.

Lawrence Clark Powell,
from *Southwest Review,* 1957

Allons! The road is before us! It is safe—I have tried it—my own feet have tried it well—be not detain'd! Let the paper remain on the shelf unwritten, and the book on the shelf unopen'd! Let the tools remain in the workshop! Let the money remain unearned! Let the school stand! Mind not the cry of the teacher! Let the preacher preach in his pulpit! Let the lawyer plead in the court, and the judge expound the law. Camerado, I give you my hand!

Walt Whitman,
from *Leaves of Grass*

Introduction

The Land

With a 10,000-foot topographical relief—from 2,840 to 13,160 feet—New Mexico claims a remarkably diverse landscape, including sections of the Rocky Mountains, the Great Plains, and the Colorado Plateau, as well as six of the world's seven life zones. Fifth-largest state in the country—behind Alaska, Texas, California, and Montana—New Mexico encompasses 122,666 square miles, tilting gradually downward from north to south like a giant wedge of cheese.

During the first part of the Paleozoic era (570 million to 245 million years ago), much of New Mexico was submerged beneath a shallow sea. Toward the end of that era, during the Permian period, New Mexico's first mountains rose from the flat seabed, which explains the occurrence of marine fossils in the state's high country, as well as in the sandstone and limestone formations of the desert. Southeastern New Mexico's Permian Basin, once a vast inland sea, contains large deposits of salt, gypsum, and potash, and its perimeters are marked by mountain ranges that were at one time huge organic underwater reefs. By the Mesozoic era (245 million to 65 million years ago), New Mexico was a tropical swampland, and throughout that era's three periods—the Triassic, Jurassic, and Cretaceous—dinosaurs sloshed through the increasing

© STEPHEN METZGER

Take the Sandia Tram into the clouds for a stunning view of the surrounding valley.

vegetation, and the waters teemed with fish, turtles, and other marinelife.

The Cenozoic era (beginning 65 million years ago) brought the beginning of the landscape we see today. The inland seas had receded, leaving a thin crust of earth which during the next 60 million years heaved and uplifted, forming great mountain ranges. Volcanic activity throughout the state, but particularly in the northeast, further disrupted the earth's surface. By the beginning of the Pliocene epoch, about five million years ago, New Mexico was a land of lakes, rivers, and marshes, and large mammals, such as elephants and camels, roamed the grasslands. Tiny prehistoric horses also wandered the plains of Pliocene New Mexico.

Off and on during the Pleistocene epoch, starting less than two million years ago, much of northern New Mexico was covered by giant glaciers, at times reaching as far south as Ruidoso. Finally, the ice receded for good, and perhaps as early as 20,000 years ago, humans first appeared in New Mexico. Nomadic hunters, most likely still en route south after having crossed over from Asia, tracked mammoths, mastodons, ground sloths, and antelope across the eastern New Mexico plains.

The Mountains

Though New Mexico's dominant mountains are of course the Rockies, along with their subranges, the Sangre de Cristos and San Juans, scores of separate mountain ranges are scattered throughout the state. Because New Mexico tilts north to south, the northern mountains are generally higher, with several peaks over 10,000 feet. In the south, the ranges are smaller and lower but often more dramatic, steep flanks rising sharply from valley floors, serrated ridges scraping the sky. The Organ Mountains just outside Las Cruces are a striking example of this type of small range, fierce in its pitch to the heavens. Mostly aligned north to south, other New Mexico mountain ranges include the Jemez west of Santa Fe, the Whites and Sacramentos near Ruidoso, the Mogollons, Elks, and Piños Altos north of Silver City, and the Manzanos and Sandias south and east of Albuquerque.

Colorado Plateau

Ranging from 5,000 to 8,000 feet above sea level, the Colorado Plateau is a huge, uplifted landmass stretching across much of northern New Mexico and Arizona, as well as Colorado and

LOUISE FOOTE

Dinosaurs such as the *Tyrannosaurus rex* were once common in much of New Mexico.

Utah. In places the plateau's rim is clearly visible, and in others the rise is much more gradual. State Highway 44 angles northwest just north of Albuquerque, climbing slowly onto the Colorado Plateau. In northeastern New Mexico, between Clayton and Cimarron, volcanoes have burst through the plateau's crust, and cinder cones are scattered about the horizon. Through the years, the western Colorado Plateau was home to various Native American civilizations, and the area is dotted with uncountable numbers of ruins, from tiny shelters to huge pueblos, such as Pueblo Bonito at Chaco Canyon.

The Desert

It's no wonder, actually, that a lot of people believe New Mexico to be all flat and dry. After all, many travelers passing through stay right on the interstates, which with a few exceptions pass through some of New Mexico's most desolate areas. Interstate 40, following old Route 66 through the Southwest, slices from Gallup to Tucumcari—a pretty barren stretch most of the way. Although near Grants the road passes just south of 11,301-foot Mt. Taylor, one of the Navajos' sacred mountains, and not too far east of there it rises between the Sandias and Manzanos, it'd still be easy to think of this part of New Mexico as nothing but desert. Same with I-25 south of Albuquerque. Pretty dry and pretty flat out there.

And there's no mistaking it: New Mexico *is* a dry state. This of course has been a problem for New Mexicans and passers-through as long as there have *been* New Mexicans and passers-through. For everyone from the Anasazi of the Four Corners area to modern alfalfa farmers in the southeast, from the cattle drivers of the 19th century to modern RV drivers heading from Albuquerque to Carlsbad, water has always been a prime concern. Visitors to Acoma Pueblo today can see the Indians' precious natural cisterns in the mesa top, and even the most cursory attention to Southwestern Indian mythology will point to the importance of water in the tribes' histories.

New Mexico's real desert is in the south, though—the northern Chihuahua and Sonora Deserts, where the elevation drops to around 3,000 feet. Those who've driven across the state on I-10 understand. Carlsbad, Las Cruces, Deming—each receives fewer than 15 inches of rainfall per year. And the vegetation shows it. Although you don't see the saguaro cactus in New Mexico that you do in Arizona, you do see other desert flora: ocotillo, mesquite, sage, and yucca.

The Rio Grande

The Rio Grande, or Great River, is one of the Southwest's most important waterways, and without it, a large part of New Mexico would simply be uninhabitable. From its headwaters on the eastern side of the Continental Divide in southern Colorado the Rio Grande gathers momentum quickly, and by Taos it's a raging current, popular with white-water rafters. From north of Taos to just south of Española, the Rio Grande carves a narrow gorge deep into the basalt and sandstone of the Colorado Plateau. Once down on the plain the river slows, broadens, and is characteristically silty, depositing sediment along

© STEPHEN METZGER

The Rio Grande carves into the Colorado Plateau north of Santa Fe.

the valley floor. Eventually, the great river leaves New Mexico near Las Cruces and then defines the Texas-Mexico border to Brownsville, where it spills into the Gulf of Mexico.

For thousands of years, the Rio Grande has both attracted and provided for people in New Mexico. Two thousand years ago, large populations of Indians were farming its banks between Albuquerque and Socorro, diverting water onto fields of corn, beans, and squash. Later, as the pueblo populations were developing, the tribes built their cities near the river, again relying on it to irrigate their crops. Irrigation from the Rio Grande continues today, with several dams—most notably Elephant Butte—built along the lower river and supplying farmers with much-needed water.

Still, the river is undependable. Even with the dams regulating its course and helping to keep its banks from overflowing, the river maintains a personality all its own. Its tributaries, the Rio Chama, the Rio Puerco, the Jemez—as well as the thousands of arroyos, one minute dry under a relentless summer sun, the next raging with the water of a flash flood—combine to keep the river always testing its banks, taking small detours here and there, and ultimately making sure anglers, farmers, rafters, and other river-watchers stay on their toes. (See also Climate in the Albuquerque chapter.)

Flora and Fauna

New Mexico's multifarious geography makes it home to a great mosaic of plants and animals—from the mesquite, creosote, horned toads, and rattlesnakes of the desert to the aspen, spruce, bighorn sheep, and elk of the mountains. The first humans in New Mexico saw an even more varied range of wildlife than we see today. In fact, it was spear points found embedded in the fossilized remains of animals long extinct that led anthropologists to many of their modern theories of the first human habitation in the New World. Saber-toothed tigers, ground sloths, mastodons, and woolly mammoths were all once important to primitive New Mexicans' survival. Until the end of the 19th century, American bison, grizzly bears, and wolves were also prominent in the area—although today, the only ones you'll see are in zoos. The pronghorn, one of the species that has survived human development of the Southwest, has been common in the area for more than 10,000 years; travelers watching the grasslands around Gallup, Clayton, Deming, Roswell, and many other towns will likely see small herds of pronghorn grazing in the distance (they tend to be a little skittish and rarely get very close to the road).

Roadrunners

Some of New Mexico's plants and animals have become so familiar they're recognizable to almost everyone. The state bird, the roadrunner, appears on postcards, T-shirts, and coffee mugs and in kids' coloring books—almost always in caricature. A lot more people see silly likenesses of roadrunners than see the birds themselves.

Yet if you keep your eyes open in your travels, there's a pretty good chance you'll see the real McCoy. From the backyards of suburban Albuquerque to the outback of the boot-heel, the roadrunner is actually a rather friendly critter, happily taking handouts from humans (although its natural diet consists of insects, small rodents, and reptiles, including rattlesnakes). Though the roadrunner is not generally considered a game bird, some Mexican *curanderos* (folk healers) claim its meat can heal tuberculosis, boils, and leprosy.

A member of the cuckoo family and known to ornithologists as *Geococcyx californianus,* the roadrunner is also called the chaparral cock, medicine bird, lizard bird, and, by the Mexicans, *paisano, churca,* and *correcamino.* These long-legged, long-billed birds are brown, allowing them to blend into their desert surroundings, and a full-grown roadrunner can reach nearly two feet in length from its ragged crest to its scraggly tail (which is roughly half its length). Of course, the roadrunner's speed is one of its most well-known features; using its tail as a sort

BOB RACE

the roadrunner, New Mexico's state bird

of rudder, a roadrunner in full flight (perhaps from Wile E. Coyote) can attain speeds of 20 miles per hour.

NEW MEXICO'S LIFE ZONES

Six of the world's seven life zones (the "Merriam" system, based on elevation and rainfall) occur in New Mexico, and though many of the state's plants and animals can be found in two or more, most individual species find a favorite niche in just one zone.

Lower Sonoran Zone

Much of the lower quarter of New Mexico—including Las Cruces, Alamogordo, and Carlsbad—is in the Lower Sonoran Zone (below 4,500 feet). This huge expanse of dry flatlands is home to prickly pear, cholla, mesquite, creosote, yucca, and saltbush, while cottonwood, olive, and cedar trees grow near the waterways. Hikers in these areas, particularly in the dry, sandy parts, should keep their eyes open for snakes: diamondbacks and prairie rattlers are common enough that you should wear protective boots, and when you hear that distinctive hiss, allow plenty of room to walk around. Watch, too, for scorpions, centipedes, and tarantulas; their venom is poisonous and affects different individuals to varying degrees of severity.

Six of the world's seven life zones (the "Merriam" system, based on elevation and rainfall) occur in New Mexico.

Other reptiles are common in the Lower Sonoran Zone, including many varieties of lizard, as well as nonvenomous snakes, such as the gopher snake. Rodents, such as squirrels and mice, live throughout the Lower Sonoran, although they most often burrow into underground holes to protect themselves from the harsh desert sun.

A number of larger animals can be found in this zone as well, including the javelina, or collared peccary, a member of the hippopotamus family resembling a wild boar. Small herds of these animals can be seen rooting in the southwestern corner of the state, particularly in the boot-heel. Other animals found in this zone are deer, pronghorn, and mountain lion.

Upper Sonoran Zone

Most of New Mexico falls in the Upper Sonoran Zone (4,500–6,500 feet), including much of the northern two-thirds of the state and many of the southern mountain areas. Many of the animals found in the Lower Sonoran Zone are also found in the Upper, while the flora changes significantly—although some of the desert grasses and cacti, such as grama grass and cholla, grow in both zones. The creosote, yucca, and mesquite begin to be replaced by piñon, juniper, and oak, and, in the upper reaches, by ponderosa pine.

The Upper Sonoran Zone is also used extensively for ranching. In fact, in recent years, environmentalists have begun to grow concerned with the problems of overgrazing; ranchers have let sheep and cattle virtually destroy not only private rangelands but vast public lands as well.

During the late 1990s, environmentalists and ranchers continued to battle over legislation limiting public-lands grazing. In 1997, environmentalists won a significant victory when 2,000 head of cattle were removed from public lands. And while environmentalists became more "mainstream" in hopes of accomplishing their goals—including running for and winning public office—they also received death threats for their efforts. The first years of the new millennium will be extremely important in these areas, as grassroots organizations such as Gila Watch, as well as larger groups such as the Sierra Club, continue to go head to head with the powerful cattle and banking industries, which have long controlled these lands.

Transition Zone

The ponderosa pine, which just begins to appear on the high slopes of the Upper Sonoran Zone, grows increasingly prominent in New Mexico's Transition Zone (6,500–8,500 feet). Much of north-central New Mexico, as well as the higher reaches of many of the state's mountain ranges (such as the Mogollons), are in this zone, where in addition to the ponderosa you'll find oak, juniper, spruce, and Douglas fir. The increased precipitation and cooler climate support a wider range of wildlife than is found in the desert. Rodents (squirrels, chipmunks, and porcupines) are very common, as are larger mammals (mule and whitetail deer) and game birds (quail and wild turkey). Travelers willing to get away from the highly populated areas, particularly those hiking into the backcountry, have a chance to see black bears, elk, and mountain lions.

This is also wildflower country, and from late spring through fall many of the woodland meadows are vibrant with columbine, New Mexico groundsel, and pennyroyal.

Canadian Zone

Ponderosas begin to thin out and give way to spruces, firs, and aspens in the Canadian Zone (8,500–9,500 feet). The snowfall and cold weather make for a much harsher climate, and though deer and elk are found here, they usually migrate to lower, more hospitable elevations in the winter.

Covering less than 2 percent of New Mexico, the Canadian Zone occurs in Ruidoso's White Mountains, the Mogollons, the Jemez, and the San Juans, and in parts of the Sangre de Cristos between Las Vegas and the Colorado border.

Hudsonian Zone

The heavy snowfall and short growing season of the Hudsonian Zone (9,500–12,000 feet) combine to make these slopes off-limits to all but the hardiest of plant and animal life. Elk, bighorn sheep, and mountain goats, plus marmots and small rodents, can be seen in the summer. During the colder months, the boughs of bristlecone pine, blue spruce, and subalpine fir stand snow-laden, until dry winter winds whip them clean and the snow falls to the cold white ground in billowy puffs. With the warmer days, animals return

BOB RACE

mountain lion

to forage on the fungi, fed by the moisture of the melting snow, while birds, such as the water pipit, flit from branch to fallen log feeding on freshly hatched insects.

Alpine Zone

Occurring only on New Mexico's highest peaks—Wheeler, for one, and some of the others in the Enchanted Circle area—the Alpine Zone (higher than 12,000 feet) is mostly above timberline, and the ground is rocky and inhospitable. Wildflowers, such as forget-me-nots and buttercups, appear during the brief summer, while pikas (small, hamsterlike animals) and marmots scamper over rocks and around the bases of the few remaining bristlecone pines.

History

THE FIRST NEW MEXICANS

Until about 40 years ago, anthropologists believed that humans first arrived in the New World about 2,000 years ago. However, thanks in part to several early-20th-century discoveries in the Southwest, particularly in New Mexico, modern anthropological theory now holds that the first humans most likely passed through the New Mexico area at *least* 20,000 years ago on their way south after having crossed over from Asia.

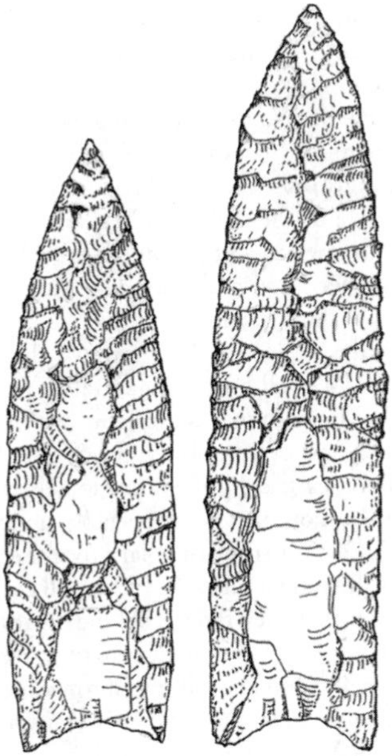

BOB RACE

Clovis points

Although recent finds in Central and South America have contributed to contemporary theories of the New World's first human habitation, the discoveries in New Mexico turned anthropology on its ear by proving beyond doubt that humans had come across from Asia at least 8,000 years earlier than previously thought. Sort of an Olduvai Gorge of the New World, New Mexico provided scientists with evidence that primitive hunters had stalked the plains of the Southwest in quest of animals that have been extinct for more than 10,000 years.

Sandia Man

Evidence of the earliest-known inhabitants of New Mexico was discovered in a cave in the Sandia Mountains just north of Albuquerque. Although it wasn't until 1936 that news of the find reached the anthropology department at the University of New Mexico, the discovery had actually been made nine years earlier by Boy Scouts innocently exploring a small cave.

What the Scouts had found was the claw of a giant ground sloth; what trained anthropologists found was a layer of datable yellow ochre, scrapers and spear points, hearths of two fireplaces, and scorched ceilings—but not a single human or animal bone. The tools, though, suggest people were living in, or at least passing through, the Sandias 12,000 years ago. The spear points tell us they killed animals, most likely to eat, and the scrapers tell us they probably skinned the animals for their furs.

Folsom Man

Two years before the Boy Scouts discovered the evidence of Sandia Man, George McJunkin was riding his horse along Dead Horse Gulch in northeastern New Mexico when he came across some bones and flint points unlike any he had ever seen. News of his find reached the University of Denver, and scientists from that school and many others headed for the site. Ultimately, they determined the bones to be from a postglacial subspecies of bison, long extinct, and the spear points, two to three inches long, had clearly been used to kill the animal.

Since then, Folsom points have been found across the plains of eastern New Mexico and southeastern Colorado, proof that Folsom Man wandered in large numbers throughout the area 10,000 years ago. Blackwater Draw near Clovis, one of the richest archaeological sites in the country, has provided evidence that these primitive hunters once stalked giant ground sloths, three-toed horses, woolly mammoths, mastodons, pronghorn, and deer. Another type of spearhead—the Clovis point—has also been discovered at Blackwater, suggesting nomads were in this area perhaps 2,000 years before Folsom Man.

Early Rio Grande Civilizations

Two thousand years ago, Indians were farming the banks of the Rio Grande from Socorro to Albuquerque. Using techniques that had spread north from Mexico and Central America, they farmed corn, beans, and squash, made baskets, and lived in primitive shelters along the river's shores. So fertile was this land and so successful were these early farmers that scientists believe the area actually experienced overcrowding.

Eventually, some of the Indians left the river area. By A.D. 800, splinter groups had begun to build pit houses and establish small communities on both sides of the Rio Grande—communities that would later develop into the highly sophisticated pueblo civilizations. Ancestors of the Indians who built Abo, Gran Quivira, and Quarai Pueblos east of the river most likely were refugees from the Rio Grande.

Anasazi

Although anthropologists also refer to the early Rio Grande farmers as Anasazi (of the Basketmaker period), the term is most often used to describe the Indians who thrived in the Four Corners area from about A.D. 800 to 1300. The Anasazi (actually a Navajo word, probably best translated as Enemies of Our Ancestors) were a peaceful people—farmers and potters—and highly religious. Their huge adobe and stone pueblos are thought today to have been culture and trade centers, and evidence suggests that they traded with other native peoples as far west as the Pacific Ocean and south deep into Mexico. Their pueblos—three- and four-story apartment-style buildings—often contained up to 400 rooms, some of which were living quarters, some of which were used to store grain. Also characteristic of the pueblos were kivas (ceremonial meeting places), built partially underground and round to symbolize the womb of Mother Earth.

The largest of these ancient "cities" exists in ruins at Chaco Culture National Historic Park about midway between Gallup and Farmington. Ruins of large Anasazi pueblos are also found near Aztec, northeast of Farmington, and at Bandelier National Monument just south of Los Alamos. In addition, thousands of smaller Anasazi ruins are scattered about the Four Corners area of the Colorado Plateau. Some have been discovered and excavated; some have been left alone. Thousands more are thought to be as yet undiscovered.

By the end of the 13th century, the Anasazi pueblos had all been abandoned. The exodus has been attributed to drought, overcrowding, disease, and even raids by newcomers (the arrival of the Apache and Navajo loosely coincides with abandonment of the pueblos), although no one knows for sure just what drove the Anasazi from their great cities. It is generally assumed, though, that they filtered southeast toward the Rio Grande and that they were the ancestors of the Pueblo Indians whom Coronado encountered when he arrived in New Mexico in 1540. Today's Acoma, Zuñi, Sandia, Jemez, Taos, and other Pueblo tribes are most likely descendants of the great Anasazi culture.

SPANISH CONQUEST

The Spanish Arrive

Although Francisco Vásquez de Coronado is generally credited (blamed?) with being the first European to arrive in New Mexico, as well as with bringing the horse to the New World, his visit was actually preceded by those of other Spaniards 13 years earlier. In 1527 a Spanish ship sank off the coast of Florida (some sources say Texas), and four survivors spent nine years traveling west across the continent. They eventually reached the Gulf of California and then headed south, until they arrived in the village of Culiacán. There they told stories of what they had seen (or heard about, or imagined): seven huge cities whose houses were made of turquoise and gold, the Seven Cities of Cibola.

Antonio de Mendoza, the viceroy of New Spain (as Mexico was called until 1821, when it became independent of Spain), was intrigued with the men's stories and promptly dispatched an exploring party to head north and verify them. The group was led by Fray Marcos de Niza, a missionary who'd previously guided expeditions to Central and South America. In 1539 de Niza arrived at Hawikuh (one of the Zuñi pueblos), erected a cross, and claimed the land for Spain. Still thinking the adobe pueblos were the fabled golden cities of Cibola, the Spanish began almost immediately to make plans to conquer the Indians. The first step was to send an army: Coronado would be its leader, de Niza its guide.

In the winter of 1540, Coronado led 300 soldiers, 225 of them on horseback, up from Compostela, New Spain. An eager and well-appointed army, if a somewhat inexperienced one, the troops consisted not only of Spaniards but of Portuguese, Italians, and even a Frenchman, a German, and a Scot. In July, the army arrived at Hawikuh, and, though it was clear the adobe pueblo was no golden city, they attacked the Zuñis, who surrendered to the armored soldiers within an hour.

Disappointed that they hadn't found at Zuñi the riches they sought, Coronado and his men soon headed east. They approached Tiguex Pueblo, on the Rio Grande near present-day Bernalillo, in September and quickly subjugated the defenseless Indians. The men spent the winter of 1540–41 on the Rio Grande, attempting to convert the tribe to Christianity. In April, the army left Tiguex for Quivira, another city they'd heard about, stopping en route at Pecos Pueblo, just east of present-day Santa Fe. Finally, after marching east for nearly 40 days, they began to think the golden cities might not really exist. They returned to Tiguex, and in April 1542 headed south for New Spain, or Mexico. Coronado's expedition had failed.

A number of attempts to colonize the area that is now New Mexico took place in the late 16th century, but it wasn't until 1598 that the government of New Spain financially endorsed a colonizing party. In January of that year, Don Juan de Oñate led a group of perhaps 400 soldiers, priests, and settlers, as well as cattle and horses, up the Rio Grande, claiming the land for Spain as he went. In July, he arrived at San Juan Pueblo, near the confluence of the Rio Chama and Rio Grande, where he set up headquarters, proclaimed himself first governor of New Mexico, and began working to convert the Indians.

During the next few months, Oñate and his men explored the area and invaded several pueblos, and in October a small contingent traveled west to Acoma, Zuñi, and Hopi country. In December Oñate was attacked by Acoma Indians, who killed 13 Spaniards, including Juan de Zaldivar, Oñate's nephew and lieutenant. In retaliation, the Spanish killed thousands of Acomas, throwing some off the cliffside, cutting the feet off others, and taking many more into slavery.

Ultimately, Oñate's colonizing expedition did not fare well. The soldiers and settlers were dissatisfied with the harsh climate. In 1607 Oñate resigned as governor of New Mexico and returned to Mexico City, where he was charged with mistreating the natives and not respecting his own men, particularly the expedition's priests. In 1608, Oñate's resignation was accepted, and he was fined and banned from New Mexico for good.

In 1607 Don Pedro de Peralta was appointed governor of New Mexico, and in the spring of that year he moved the Spaniards' headquarters south and began work on La Villa Real de la

Santa Fe de San Francisco de Asis, or Santa Fe. For the next 70 years, the Spanish continued to colonize New Mexico, baptizing Indians and building missions at the pueblos. The Indians took to Christianity in varying degrees. Some felt it didn't conflict with their own religious beliefs and actually subscribed to both pagan and Christian doctrine. Others felt that Christianity was oppressive, especially in the hands of the Spaniards, many of whom tortured and murdered those who wouldn't convert. By the middle of the 17th century, although thousands of Indians had been converted, there had also been much resistance and several bloody battles.

The Pueblo Revolt

By the 1670s, the Pueblo people were growing increasingly angry with both the Spaniards' presence on their land and the Spaniards' intolerance of native religious beliefs. The Spanish burned kivas, destroyed ceremonial objects, and in 1675 flogged nearly 50 Pueblo religious leaders for practicing "witchcraft." Finally, the natives had had enough.

One of the flogged Pueblo Indians was Popé, a member of the San Juan tribe, who after his punishment fled north to Taos. There he worked to organize other Pueblo leaders and tribes in a sophisticated rebellion against the Spanish. In August 1680 a group of runners—with knotted ropes signifying the exact day of the revolt—notified the various pueblos that the time had come. Originally scheduled for August 13, the rebellion was moved up to August 10, the day of the Feast of San Lorenzo, after the Indians realized the Spanish had learned of the revolt.

Collectively, the northern Pueblo tribes rose up and fought their conquerors. They burned missions, destroyed crops, and killed priests, farmers, and entire families, finally driving survivors to Santa Fe, which lay under siege for nine days. On August 21, the Spaniards made their break. As the rebelling Indians watched from mesas and hillsides, about a thousand Spaniards, low on food and supplies, headed downriver toward El Paso. Along the way, they picked up scattered groups of other settlers, as well as converted Indians.

Meanwhile, the rebelling Pueblo Indians had moved into Santa Fe, where they occupied the Palace of the Governors and began to eradicate all traces of Spanish occupation. They ceremoniously burned governmental records and documents and destroyed crosses and other Christian icons. However, the movement was not strong enough to hold together once the Spanish had been driven out, and in short time, factionalism began to splinter the Indians. Fewer than 10 years later, many had returned to their pueblos, while a handful remained in Spanish-built houses in Santa Fe.

Reconquest

Between 1688 and 1692, several groups of Spanish missionaries attempted to reclaim New Mexico for the crown. It wasn't until August 1692, though, that Don Diego de Vargas, the wealthy new governor and *capitán-general* of New Mexico, marched up the Rio Grande from El Paso and rather easily reconquered the first Indians he encountered. On September 13, after passing many burned and abandoned pueblos, de Vargas gathered his army outside the walls of Santa Fe and convinced the Indians inside to pledge their loyalty to Spain. However, the other pueblos still had to be reconquered.

For the next four years, de Vargas attacked New Mexico's northern pueblos one by one, meeting more resistance at some than at others. The Jemez people, for example, were very distrustful of the returning Spanish and fought hard against reconquest. Zia and Santa Ana Pueblos, on the other hand, quickly submitted to de Vargas and actually joined in battles against the Jemez and others. Finally, in the summer of 1696, all the pueblos had been reconquered—only after, however, the longest and most successful uprising of Native Americans against colonists.

Spanish Colonial Period

New Mexico remained under Spanish rule for the next 125 years, the Spaniards gradually populating more and more of the Rio Grande Valley between Taos and Isleta. Though the Pueblo Indians had been pretty much subjugated and felt powerless against Spanish colonization, the

Comanches, Apaches, and Navajos began an aggressive series of raids—on the Spanish and their converts.

For the most part, though, this was a relatively quiet time for New Mexico, with farmers and ranchers living on isolated land grants. It was also a time when the first real class distinctions began to appear in New Mexican societies: between the large landowners and those who worked the land. The grants in the mountainous northern part of the state tended not only to be smaller than those on the lower plains, but they also were kept under the possession of the crown. Families farmed small plots of land for sustenance only, while they developed isolated mountain communities in which marriages between Indians and Spanish were common. To this day, some of these northern communities remain so isolated from the outside world that their customs and language bear more resemblance to those of 18th-century Spain than they do to other areas of New Mexico.

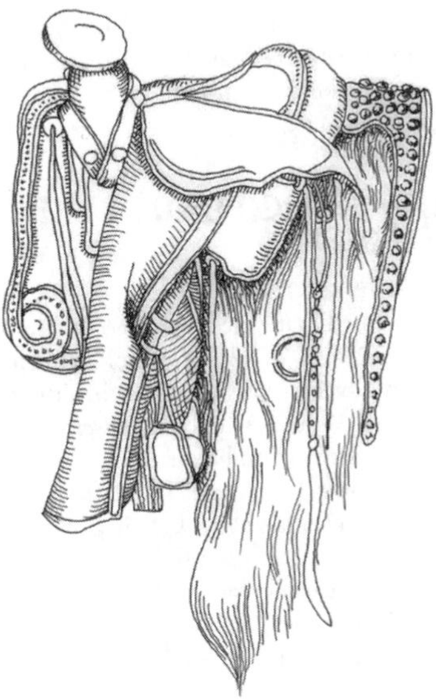

LOUISE FOOTE

Mexican fiesta saddle

UNDER MEXICAN RULE

Mexican Independence

By the early 1800s, Spain was no longer the great world power it had been for the three previous centuries, and its grip on the New World was rapidly weakening. Meanwhile, the fledgling United States, seeing the potential for trade in the area, had its eye on New Mexico.

In September 1821 Mexico won its independence from Spain, and the first week of 1822 saw great celebrations from Mexico City to Santa Fe, by then home to 6,000 people. Almost immediately, the United States and New Mexico began vigorous trading, with pack trains departing regularly from Missouri for Santa Fe. Thus was born the Santa Fe Trail.

The Mexican Republic

Things were not a whole lot different under Mexican rule than they were under Spanish, except that the governor, who was both military and civil head, had to answer to Mexico City instead of Madrid. And even though the government was now headquartered much closer, New Mexico was still a much-neglected northern outpost, its military forces poorly supplied and underfinanced. In attempts to bring revenues to the area, New Mexico governors often imposed large taxes on United States imports.

Between 1821 and the late 1870s, New Mexico's rambunctious capital, Santa Fe, continued to grow and develop, thanks largely to the bustling Santa Fe Trail. Now that Americans were trading with Mexicans, Santa Feans began to be exposed to a people and a lifestyle that until then had been completely foreign. Mountain men brought furs and hides from the northern Rockies, and "prairie schooners" carried cotton, medicines, furniture, tobacco, spices, and musical instruments. Santa Fe, the town at the end of the trail, had a reputation for wild dance halls, gambling saloons, and brothels, and in the 1820s and '30s trade increased from $15,000 to $1 million a year.

Indian attacks on settlers continued throughout this time. Comanches and Jicarilla Apaches raided Santa Fe–bound wagon trains on New

Mexico's northeastern plains. This ultimately led to the building of Fort Union near Las Vegas, where the Cimarron Cut-off reconnected with the main Santa Fe Trail. Gila Apaches vigorously defended their homeland in the southwestern part of the state.

NEW MEXICO UNDER THE AMERICANS

An American Territory

The United States declared war on Mexico on May 13, 1846. In June, General Stephen Watts Kearny advanced on Santa Fe, and although the governor, Manuel Armijo, had assembled 6,000 troops, his army fled before Kearny even arrived in the capital. On August 18, 1846, Kearny entered Santa Fe, raised the U.S. flag in the central plaza, and offered protection to the New Mexicans as long as they swore allegiance to the new government. On May 30, 1848, the Treaty of Guadalupe Hidalgo was signed, which ceded to the United States a large chunk of land running from Texas west to California, including northern New Mexico. Five years later, the $10 million Gadsden Purchase added to American lands a large chunk of southern New Mexico and Arizona. New Mexico Territory was now formally the property of the United States.

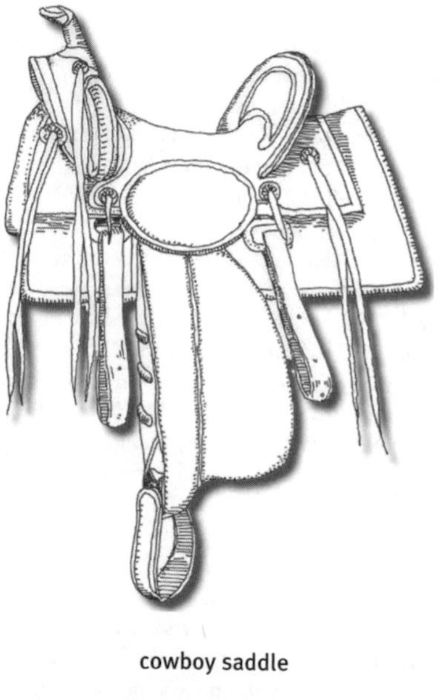

DAVE HURST

cowboy saddle

But Wait, Didn't the Land Still Belong to the Indians?

Of course it did, insofar as Native American philosophy allowed for land "ownership" at all. And even though the United States now owned this land on paper, the native peoples still considered it theirs. The Pueblo tribes for the most part had acquiesced and were quietly going about their ways in their small villages—farming; making baskets, pottery, and jewelry; performing ceremonial dances; and attending Catholic Mass. The Navajos, Apaches, and Comanches, however, weren't so willing to submit, in part because they had been more nomadic in the first place and would not be happy confined to small parcels of land.

So along with the land that the United States government got with the Treaty of Guadalupe Hidalgo and the Gadsden Purchase, it also got New Mexico's Indians, a good many of them quite fed up with how they'd been treated. The United States, though, was a little more aggressive in dealing with the "Indian problem" than the Spaniards and Mexicans had been. In one of the most famous and embarrassing moments in U.S.-Indian relations, U.S. troops, led by Kit Carson, destroyed the homes, crops, and livestock of "uncooperative" Navajos, murdered those who wouldn't submit to them, and forced the starving survivors—mostly Navajos, but some Mescalero Apaches as well—to walk nearly 300 miles from the Gallup area to Bosque Redondo near Fort Sumner, where they could be "concentrated." The Long Walk began in March 1864, and by the end of that year 8,000 Native Americans were imprisoned along the Pecos River on the harsh prairieland of northeastern New Mexico. In 1868, the Navajos signed a treaty granting them the land they now occupy in the Four Corners area, the largest Indian reservation in the United States.

Meanwhile, the Apaches, led by Geronimo, were waging war against the encroaching Anglo settlers. In 1886, Geronimo was promised a reservation, but instead his people were put on a train for Florida, where many died imprisoned in a federal fort. Finally, Geronimo was returned to Fort Sill, Oklahoma, where he was put on exhibit; he died there in 1909.

The Iron Horse

One of the biggest influences on the development and settlement of New Mexico was the railroad. In the late 1870s and early 1880s, railroad tracks began to be laid across the state, linking isolated towns and communities. Almost overnight, the wagon trains and stagecoaches disappeared, replaced by the powerful locomotive. For the first time people, cattle, food products, ore, and other items could be transported quickly and reliably across the vast expanses of New Mexico Territory. In addition, the new industry brought thousands of jobs to the area, with stations needing to be built about every 100 miles. From Gallup to Ratón, Las Cruces to Santa Fe, the railroad significantly changed the landscape of New Mexico and the lifestyles of its people.

Statehood

New Mexico was admitted to the Union on January 6, 1912. It's one of the country's peculiar ironies that one of the first states to be settled by Europeans was one of the last to be given state status: Remember that New Mexico was colonized nearly a quarter century before the Pilgrims landed on Plymouth Rock. Why was it admitted so late? In part, because of its location. First a Spanish and then later a Mexican outpost, New Mexico (along with its neighbor, Arizona, admitted at about the same time) was a long way from the commercial and political centers of the country. It also lacked some of the natural resources of a state such as California, which, admitted in 1850, promised not only gold but great natural harbors and fertile fields for farming. Yet there's perhaps another reason New Mexico was admitted so late. The state, settled by the Spanish, is naturally largely Hispanic, and many New Mexicans of Spanish descent feel it might have been admitted sooner had its people more closely resembled the fair-skinned settlers of the East Coast. On top of that, many New Mexicans were at best only vaguely familiar with the English language, and even today it's the second language of a great percentage of the population.

New Mexico and the Bomb

In the fall of 1942, Robert Oppenheimer and U.S. General Leslie Groves drove from Albuquerque to Los Alamos. No stranger to New Mexico, Oppenheimer had spent long days in his youth riding horseback in the Sangre de Cristo Mountains, where his family had a summer home, and he knew the state's isolated location would provide the security necessary to secretly research nuclear energy in the race with the Germans for the atomic bomb. Appointed director of the project, Oppenheimer was largely responsible for the 100 scientists working in secrecy on the Pajarito Plateau above Santa Fe, as well as for the project's success.

On July 16, 1945, at Trinity Site in the Tularosa Basin northwest of Alamogordo, the world's first atomic bomb was detonated. William L. Laurence, hired as official scribe for the experiment, wrote,

> ***It was like the grand finale of a mighty symphony of the elements, fascinating and terrifying, uplifting and crushing, ominous, devastating, full of great promise and great foreboding.***

Light from the blast could be seen in Gallup, Los Alamos, Albuquerque, and much of the rest of New Mexico.

Thus was launched New Mexico's love/hate relationship with the nuclear age. In a sense, atomic energy has been very good for the state, bringing industry and jobs; I-25 between Las Cruces and Denver is known as the "Nuclear Corridor" because of the disproportionate number of nuclear energy-related defense-industry contracts awarded to companies located there. Los Alamos Labs and Sandia Labs in Albuquerque are at the forefront of defense-industry and high-tech computer research.

Not without a price, though. Los Alamos, for example, is having problems dealing with the waste produced in the labs. One solution has been to bury the stuff. The Waste Isolation Pilot Plant (WIPP) is in the early stages of a 35-year project that proposes ultimately to bury 38,000 shipments of nuclear waste—from Los Alamos and other nuclear plants around the country—in salt beds deep beneath the ground 26 miles southeast of Carlsbad; the first shipment arrived from Idaho on March 26, 1999. This is scary enough without the thought of how to *get* it there. In addition to questioning the safety of actually burying the waste, environmentalists around the country are deeply concerned about the routes: interstate and U.S. highways through large towns and cities, including Albuquerque, Grants, and Roswell.

New Mexico's Citizen Soldiers

In addition to the atomic bomb, New Mexico claims at least a couple of other important contributions to World War II. The 200th and 515th regiments of the United States Coast Artillery—also known as the New Mexico Brigade—played important roles in the Pacific Theatre, and both units suffered extreme casualties not only in battle but in the infamous Bataan Death March in the spring of 1942. The soldiers' stories and heroism are honored at the Bataan Memorial Museum in Santa Fe (1050 Old Pecos Trail, 505/474-1670; see the Santa Fe chapter for more information).

Also, as recently dramatized (some say trivialized) in the recent film *Windtalkers,* Navajo and other Indian "code talkers" used their native languages to help confuse the Japanese during World War II, contributing significantly to American success in the Pacific. For more information on how Native Americans language skills were used in major American conflicts, from World War I to Vietnam, go to website: www.lapahie.com/NavajoCodeTalker.cfm.

The Population Boom

Between 1940 and 1980, New Mexico's population tripled; roughly 1.5 million people live in the state today, a third of them in Albuquerque. Of course, the Sun Belt is its own attraction, and many people come to the Southwest for the climate, warm and dry year-round. More and more, though, people are migrating to New Mexico for its industry, relatively novel in the state. In addition to Sandia and Los Alamos labs, computer-chip plants and other electronics-industry plants are sprouting like weeds. Computer companies are packing up and moving wholesale from California's Silicon Valley to the Rio Grande Valley, where land is considerably cheaper.

And to accommodate the workers, Albuquerque is building homes and apartments like there's no tomorrow. Look to the hills west of town, where the houses of Rio Rancho, a modern suburb of Albuquerque, sprawl across the plateau; this little "suburb" is actually the state's fourth-largest city, behind Albuquerque, Santa Fe, and Las Cruces. But there still isn't enough housing to go around. Many electronics-industry and other high-tech workers are transferred to Albuquerque and put up in temporary housing while they have homes built for them. This of course means apartments. Lots of apartments—from the high-rent, high-security digs in Albuquerque's Northeast Heights section to standard off-base military units near Kirtland Air Force base to run-down duplexes and fourplexes close to downtown.

And Albuquerque's not alone in the boom. Las Cruces, Alamogordo (with nearby Holloman Air Force Base), Santa Fe, and other New Mexico towns are beginning to feel the pressures of growth. Chief among the many concerns of this growth is an adequate water supply. Always in short supply in the desert, water is increasingly not only a matter of informal concern but is also at the center of lawsuits and negotiations pitting farmers against developers, ranchers against environmentalists, and government agencies against resort owners. And the boom's far from over. Word's out that land is still relatively inexpensive here, that the possibilities for outdoor recreation are virtually endless, and that the sun shines almost every day. Can you blame folks for packing up and moving here?

Economy

New Mexico's economy—and its economic history—is as diverse as the land itself. From the ancient trading networks of the Anasazi to the high-tech computer-chip labs in Rio Rancho, from 1950s'-era uranium mines in the Gallup area to the airbases scattered about the state to the tourism in Taos—a lot of different industries have contributed and continue to contribute to the state's economy.

And still, New Mexico is not a wealthy state. One vital resource necessary for the smooth flow of income has always been scarce; the state has precious little water. For millennia farmers have depended on the rains, and they have often been frustrated. Though irrigation has made water supplies more consistent, growers still rely on nature and the skies. As recently as 1996, New Mexico was the victim of a devastating drought that affected farmers in the east, ski-resort operators in the north, and vacationers throughout the state; most public lands were closed well into summer, when the monsoons finally came.

In addition, the state's pueblos and reservations have long experienced poverty nearly Third World in its scope. In large part because the land on which the pueblos sit is so inhospitable, unemployment rates of 50 percent are not rare. Some of the tribes have been more successful than others in harnessing what few resources they have. The Mescalero Apaches, for example—whose reservation in the White Mountains offers far more opportunities for economic development than do most of the pueblos—own and operate a ski resort and a large convention/vacation complex near Ruidoso. Many of the tribes are also making some headway with other ventures, such as casinos. Yet the fact remains that chronic poverty has exacted a heavy toll on the hopes and spirits of a large percentage of the state's Native American population.

Additionally, the state was hit hard by the defense-industry reductions of the 1990s after the collapse of the Soviet Union and the end of the Cold War. Between 1991 and 1997, in fact, when bases across the country were routinely shut down or "realigned," New Mexico lost 8,500 defense-related jobs.

Conversely, parts of the state experienced a boom of sorts beginning in the early 1990s. Computer-industry manufacturers such as Intel, Signetics, Honeywell, and Siemens provided work for thousands of New Mexicans. By 2000, the state's computer industry was employing roughly 30,000 people. The 1990s also saw the proliferation of casinos, owned and mostly operated by Native Americans. As the 1990s wound down, the casinos were employing between 5,000 and 6,000 people and netting between $300 million and $400 million annually.

But longtime residents know booms can be short-lived. The uranium mines that once promised to bring prosperity to northwestern New Mexico are now little more than museums and memories, and many of the mom-and-pop restaurants and motels that once thrived along busy Route 66, for example, have been shut down by the franchises—Days Inns, Motel 6s, Cattle Barons, and McDonald's—that now dot I-40. In many towns the outlying areas near the freeway off-ramps and franchises are far busier than the downtown areas. In addition, in the late 1990s and early 2000s, many New Mexico manufacturers, including Levi-

BOB RACE

Strauss and Sara Lee Corporation's L'Eggs (a panty-hose maker based in Las Cruces) shut their doors, and some of the high-tech firms, in reaction to a declining economy and sinking oil prices, reduced their labor forces. On the other hand, in 2000, Rio Rancho's Intel and Phillips Semiconductors announced large capital expansions that would increase the number of workers, and the state of New Mexico began renovating Albuquerque's I-25 (north-south) and I-40 (east-west) intersection, a project estimated to employ thousands round-the-clock for the next several years.

Meanwhile, New Mexicans everywhere continue to look to the skies. Farmers in the south and east pray for the rain they desperately need to water their cotton, peanuts, wheat, and chiles, while a good snowfall year will make it more likely that a Taos bed-and-breakfast will manage to keep its head above water.

The People

Much has been made of New Mexico's multicultural heritage. Volumes have been written about the contributions of the state's people of American Indian, Spanish, and Anglo descent. Erna Fergusson's excellent book, *New Mexico, A Pageant of Three Peoples,* examines the state's drama in terms of its major players, showing how the three ethnic groups combine to create an intricate and unique population, as complex yet interdependent as the landscape itself. A living example of the whole's being greater than the sum of its parts, New Mexico's population truly is a pageant, the people tracing their lineage to colorful and important ancestors—the local Indians to the Anasazi, Hispanics to Oñate, and Anglos to the area's first cowboys, miners, and railroaders.

Lately, too, New Mexico has seen large influxes of other ethnic groups. Blacks, Mideasterners, and Asians, finding the land hospitable and the citizens relatively tolerant, are moving to the cities—particularly Albuquerque—in larger and larger numbers. Which only serves to make the state better. While the tapestry of the people of New Mexico grows more and more complex, it also grows stronger and more beautiful to gaze upon.

NATIVE PEOPLES

New Mexico's Indians are basically from three major groups: Apaches, Navajos, and Pueblos. Of the three, the Pueblos have been in the area the longest; most likely they are the descendants of the Anasazi who were farming the Rio Grande Valley more than 2,000 years ago and who later built the huge pueblos at Chaco Canyon, Aztec, and Bandelier. The Navajos and Apaches arrived much later, probably not long before the Spanish.

The Pueblo Indians

New Mexico's Pueblo Indians live in 19 pueblos (self-contained villages) in the northern part of the state, mostly near the Rio Grande. These highly religious people take great pride in their ancient customs. Ceremonials, including dances, parades, and games, occur regularly throughout the year, often in conjunction with the feast days that honor the pueblos' patron saints. Most Pueblo people have adopted Christianity, which, they feel, is not incompatible with their native beliefs. Christian doctrine, insofar as it implores its followers to "Love thy neighbor," etc., gracefully complements traditional Pueblo religion, although historically this acceptance hasn't worked both ways. Missionaries, in attempting to force the Pueblos to accept Christ, often burned kivas and even murdered those who refused to convert.

Pueblo Indians are known for their exquisite pottery, which varies significantly from tribe to tribe. The Santa Clara tribe, for example, is famous for its polished black-on-black pots, while Acoma pottery is characteristically white or gray, decorated with black or red geometric designs and stylized animals. The Pueblos are also well respected for their gorgeous jewelry. Zuñi coral, turquoise, and silver necklaces and bracelets are stunning in their detailed workmanship.

The Navajos

Anthropologists believe that the Navajos arrived in the Southwest between A.D. 1000 and 1600, most likely around 1450. After centuries of conflict with both the Spanish and the Americans, the Navajos in 1868 were finally concentrated on the 25,000-square-mile (about the size of West Virginia) reservation in the Southwest's Four Corners area. In the early 20th century, the Navajos formed a General Council to negotiate leases on their oil-rich land, and the tribe still derives much of its revenue from these leases; more than 300 are in effect today. Also important to the economy of the tribe (the largest in the country, with about 200,000 members) are timber, grazing (cattle and sheep), and ore (coal and uranium).

A living example of the whole being greater than the sum of its parts, New Mexico's population truly is a pageant, the people tracing their lineage to colorful and important ancestors.

Navajo silversmiths are some of the most respected in the world; their ornate silver and turquoise necklaces, belt buckles, watchbands, and other jewelry fetch high prices and are often imitated. The Navajos are also admired for weaving—their rugs, with brilliant reds and intricate patterns reflecting ancient traditions, are favorites among collectors.

Other than the oil and gas beneath it, Navajo land has little in the way of natural resources, and many Navajos have a difficult time surviving. Unemployment rates and poverty are sky-high. Disease and alcoholism run rampant through Indian villages and families. Self-esteem is often miserably low. Fortunately, tribal traditions remain alive and vital. Dances and other ceremonials can breathe new life into individuals, families, and communities. In 1989 Gallup-area Navajos organized a fund-raising walk to Santa Fe, revenues from which went to antialcoholism Indian health services.

The Apaches

A more nomadic people than the Pueblos or the Navajos, the Apaches fought stubbornly against encroaching Spanish and American settlement in the Southwest—thus their reputation as fierce

COURTESY OF NEW MEXICO DEPARTMENT OF TOURISM/MARK NOHL

Colorfully outfitted dancers from Zuñi Pueblo in western New Mexico prepare to perform.

and ruthless warriors. In truth, the Apaches were a relatively peaceful people—farmers, hunters, gatherers—but still highly protective of their people, land, and customs.

Today, fewer than 4,000 Apaches live on two reservations in New Mexico. The Jicarillas have nearly 800,000 acres in the northern part of the state between Chama and Farmington, and the Mescaleros have about 450,000 acres in the White Mountains south of Ruidoso. Both the Jicarillas and the Mescaleros are enterprising people, owning and operating resort lodges, selling timber, raising cattle, and making money from fees for fishing and hunting licenses. In addition, the Jicarilla derive substantial income from oil and natural gas leases.

Because of the government's eradication of the Apaches, little is left of their culture, save for language and social structure, although attempts are being made to revive some of the traditional crafts. Dolls, beadwork, coiled baskets, buckskin clothing, and cradleboards are beginning to reappear, and travelers can sometimes find these items at gift shops on the reservations, particularly at the Mescaleros' Inn of the Mountain Gods and the Jicarilla Inn in Dulce.

NATIVE TONGUES

With its multicultural heritage and population, New Mexico is naturally a multilingual state. In Las Cruces, for example, I was listening to a baby-boomer rock radio station that featured bilingual jokes. One of the disc jockeys was giving the other a "Spanish lesson" so that the latter could impress his date. He wanted to know how to tell her the meal she had cooked was very good. *Su comida,* he was taught to say, *tiene el sabor de la comida del perro* (basically, "this food tastes like dog food"). First of all, it's fascinating that enough of this station's listening audience is at least bilingual enough to understand the joke, and second, presenting Spanish this way, on an otherwise-English station, validates what to many is a "second" language, providing a subtle yet comical rebuttal to the highly offensive English-only movement.

Another example is equally instructive. I was eavesdropping on a party of teachers at a restaurant in Farmington one afternoon as they talked about an advertisement for a job opening. One of the men said,

> ***They were looking for someone who was bilingual, so I applied. I learned later they meant English and Navajo.***

The Pueblo Indians add a host of tongues to the state's multilingual mix. Though they're most likely all descendants of the Anasazi, they speak five distinct languages: Keresan (Acoma, Cochiti, Laguna, San Felipe, Santa Ana, Santo Domingo, and Zia Pueblos), Tiwa (Isleta, Picuris, Sandia, and Taos), Tewa (Nambe, Pojoaque, San Ildefonso, San Juan, Santa Clara, and Tesuque), Towa (Jemez), and Zuñi (Zuñi).

On the Road

Sight-Seeing Highlights

Nearly palpable textures of blue, thunderheads that cast dancing shadows on distant mesas, electrical storms and sunsets so intense the heavens seem literally ablaze—no pun intended, but the New Mexico sky is without question one of the highlights of any visit to the state. It's certainly one of the memories that will remain with you long after your socks are back in drawers and your suitcases and backpacks back in closets. In fact, it's most likely what you'll find yourself talking about as you try to recapture for friends your trip to one of the most magical areas of the United States.

If you're like most visitors to New Mexico, you won't be able to stay as long as you'd like, so how can you get the most out of your visit? Good question. In fact, one that travel writers themselves constantly grapple with. I've found over the years that I can more easily answer that question if I rephrase it slightly: What, as specifically as possible, do I want to *do* on this trip? Or, what *type* of trip do I want this to be? Am I primarily interested in sight-seeing? In meeting the people? In exploring the history? In recreation? Is there anything I definitely don't want to miss?

Once I've answered those questions as best I can, my trip begins to focus itself. Then everything else falls into place. All of which is a rather roundabout way of saying, Dear Reader, you're pretty much on your own. *You've* got to make some decisions; you've got to set priorities. Nonetheless, because I've had the good fortune to spend a heck of a lot of time in New Mexico and to explore not only its major tourist areas

© STEPHEN METZGER

The open road calls—Highway 84 near Abiquiu.

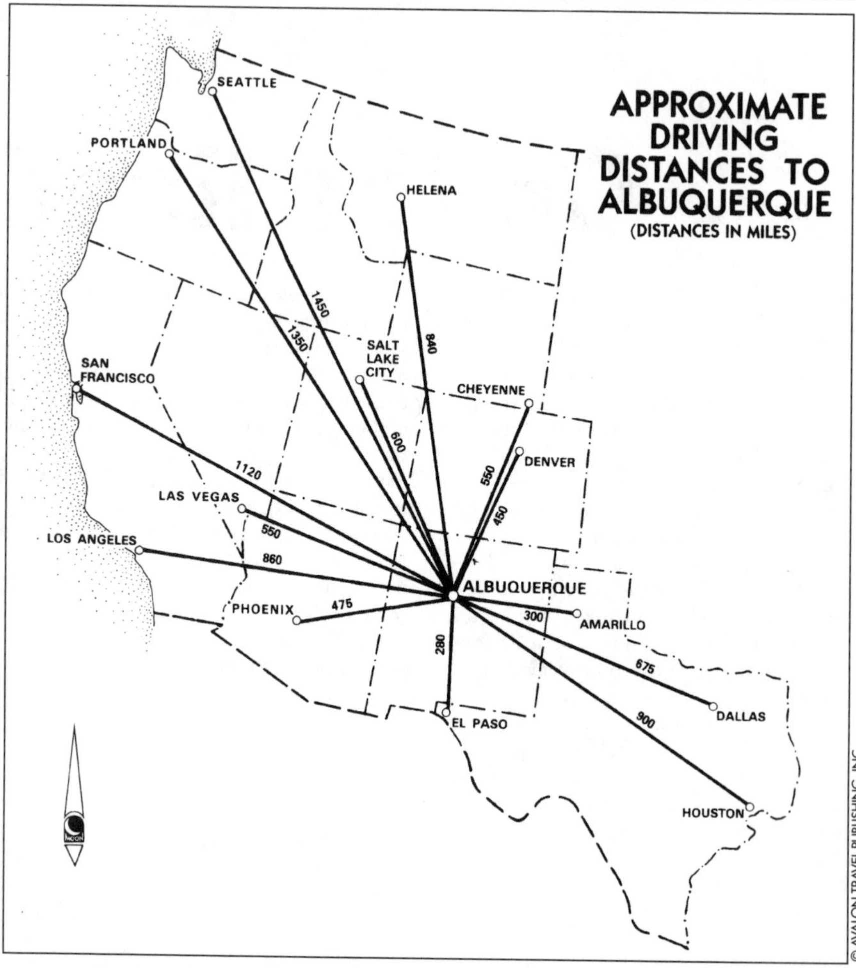

but its back roads as well, I can help out. Allow me to make a few suggestions.

THINGS TO SEE

Santa Fe: The city manages to offer in encapsulated form much of what you'll find throughout the state. You'll want to explore the historic plaza area, visit the old churches, wander into the myriad museums, galleries, and gift shops, where you can buy authentic Native American jewelry, sandpaintings, pottery, and rugs. Linger over a margarita and a plate of authentic New Mexican food.

Taos: Be sure to visit **Taos Pueblo,** which, along with Acoma Pueblo west of Albuquerque, is one of the oldest continually inhabited villages in North America. Visit Taos's art galleries and historic museums; drive north to **Rio Grande Gorge,** where Highway 64 crosses over the Rio Grande.

Albuquerque: You'll also want to spend some time exploring Albuquerque. The **Old Town**

area offers excellent opportunities not only to shop for authentic Native American artwork but to visit historic sites to get a sense of what the town was like in the 18th century. In addition, within walking distance of Old Town are several excellent museums that will provide perspectives on the area's history, natural history, and economy. Just north of Old Town, the **Indian Pueblo Cultural Center** should be on your must-see list. There you'll learn all about the people of New Mexico's 19 Native American pueblos. Head west to visit **Acoma Pueblo,** a New Mexico wonder. And if you're in Albuquerque in October, don't miss the **Albuquerque Balloon Fiesta,** the world's largest hot-air balloon event, drawing participants and spectators from around the world.

Nearly palpable textures of blue, thunderheads that cast dancing shadows on distant mesas, electrical storms and sunsets so intense the heavens seem literally ablaze—no pun intended, but the New Mexico sky is without question one of the highlights of any visit to the state.

New Mexico's ruins are also fascinating. Though perhaps the most spellbinding is **Chaco Culture National Historic Park,** its remote location and dirt-road access make getting there a real commitment. Nearly as impressive is **Bandelier National Monument,** just west of Santa Fe, where you wander among the homes and ceremonial sites of ancient Anasazi cliff dwellers. Other ruins worth visiting are **Pecos National Monument; Salinas National Monument,** particularly the Gran Quivira unit; **Coronado State Monument;** and **Aztec Ruins National Monument.**

Note: These ruins, and thousands of the petroglyphs and pictographs, are on public land. They belong to all of us, to *you.* They also belong to something larger, more difficult to define: our collective humanity, our collective past, our future. *Do not deface Indian ruins or prehistoric art. Do not attempt to remove anything from these sites.* It is not only ethically and morally wrong, but it is illegal. If you see anyone defacing or otherwise tampering with or vandalizing these works, report the offender to the appropriate local agency so that law enforcement can be dispatched; phone numbers are provided under the separate listings that follow.

In addition to these sites and ruins, some of New Mexico's roads and highways themselves are legitimate attractions, offering unsurpassed scenery and glimpses into the state's past. If you have time, take the back road to Taos, through **Chimayó, Truchas, Las Trampas,** and **Ranchos de Taos.** The **Enchanted Circle,** an 85-mile loop north of Taos, circles Taos Pueblo and Mt. Wheeler, the highest peak in New Mexico, and takes you up into aspen-and-fir forests and across broad mountain meadows, past ski and fishing resorts and along tumbling mountain streams, before dropping back onto the Taos Plateau. Other wondrous routes in the state include **Highway 84** from Española through Abiquiu to Chama, **Highway 64** from Taos to Farmington, **Highway 70** across the Mescalero Apache Reservation and through the White Mountains, and **Highway 180** north along the western flank of Gila National Forest.

THINGS TO DO

Though it's natural to want to relax on vacation, it'd be a shame in New Mexico not to take advantage of all the things the state offers to *do,* things that'll keep you busy, things that'll make your trip that much more memorable, and, finally, things that'll help you burn off some of that genuine New Mexican food. First off, New Mexico's **snow skiing** ranks as some of the best in the country. **Taos Ski Valley,** a world-class resort famous for its high percentage of expert runs, regularly racks up rave reviews in national ski magazines and is unquestionably one of the Rockies' finest ski areas. In addition, some of the smaller, lesser-known ski areas, including **Ski Apache, Santa Fe Ski Area, Red River Ski Area,** and **Sandia Peak Ski Area,** offer fine snow and challenging runs. On top of that, the state's

EVENTS

A list of all the annual events in New Mexico would be a book in itself. From county fairs and rodeos to art festivals and Indian ceremonials, there's nearly always something going on. Following is a calendar of some of the highlights. Check locally for exact schedules and tourist information—especially in the case of Native American ceremonies.

January 1, 6, 7: ceremonial dances at most pueblos
January 22–23: Feast Day at San Ildefonso Pueblo
February 2: dances at Picuris and San Felipe Pueblos
Easter: dances, footraces, parades at many pueblos
May 1: Feast Day at San Felipe Pueblo
May 3: footraces and Corn Dance at Taos and Cochiti Pueblos
mid-May: Gathering of Nations Pow Wow, Albuquerque
late May through mid-June: Taos Spring Arts Celebration
June 6: Rain Dance at Zuñi Pueblo
June 24: dances at Cochiti, San Juan, and Taos Pueblos
late June: New Mexico Arts Fair
early July: opening of Santa Fe Opera
July 4: fireworks, parades, ceremonials throughout the state
late July: Spanish Market in Santa Fe
early August: Old Lincoln Days in Lincoln
August 10: Feast of San Lorenzo at Acoma, Cochiti, and Laguna Pueblos
August 12: Santa Clara Pueblo Feast Day
mid-August: Indian Market in Santa Fe
mid-August: Inter-tribal Ceremonial in Gallup
late August: Great American Duck Races in Deming
Labor Day: Fiesta de Santa Fe
September 2: San Estevan Feast Day at Acoma Pueblo
September 4: Feast Day and Harvest Dance at Isleta Pueblo
mid-September: State Fair in Albuquerque
September 30: footraces at Taos Pueblo
October 3–4: Feast of St. Francis at Taos and Nambe Pueblos
early October: Albuquerque Kodak International Balloon Fiesta
November 12: dances at Jemez and Tesuque Pueblos
December 12: dances and processions at Taos, Jemez, Nambe, and Pojoaque Pueblos
December 24: dances, torchlight parades, luminarias at Acoma Pueblo, Ranchos de Taos, and around the state
December 24–29: dances, processionals, and evening Masses at most pueblos

sprawling national forests and backcountry areas offer excellent **cross-country skiing** for every level.

Come summertime there's even more to do, and New Mexicans like to take full advantage. From **fishing** to **mountain biking, horseback riding** to **white-water rafting,** to simply **hiking** leisurely through pine forests or over piñon-covered hillsides, New Mexico will satisfy.

THINGS TO EAT

A confession: Each time I approach New Mexico, whether on vacation or a research mission, it's not the skiing or hiking I'm looking forward to, nor is it wandering through the Indian ruins and the wonderful shops and galleries. It's not the museums or the pueblos.

It's the food.

From the world-renowned restaurants in Santa Fe to the tiny holes-in-the-wall in every little town you'll pass through, New Mexico offers dishes that will not only make any vacation better but will also very likely change the way you cook and order in restaurants the rest of your days. Be sure to try a **breakfast burrito** and some **blue-corn pancakes** (probably not at the same meal!), a bowl of **green-chile stew** made from fresh local chiles, a **green-chile hamburger, blue-corn chips** and fresh **salsa,** a plate of ***carne adovada,*** (a delicious marinated-and-then-baked pork dish usually served with red beans and flour tortillas) some **enchiladas** stuffed with cheese, chicken, or beef and topped with red or green chiles; and after dinner, top it all off with a **sopaipilla** (a pillowy pastry) filled with honey.

And then wander outside, under that wildly sprawling palette. Recall the day's visit to the ruins and the friends you made. Breathe deeply, filling your lungs with as much of that Southwestern sky as they'll hold. And in this way, take New Mexico with you.

A word of caution: Although must urban-area New Mexico restaurants offer no-smoking seating areas, many outside the larger towns and cities do not. Don't be surprised when, in Tucumcari, Hobbs, or even in Taos, you chomp into a scrumptious burrito or take that first shovelful of green-chile stew only to have some courtesy-challenged neighbor light up a smoke at a nearby table.

Outdoor Recreation

For as little precipitation as New Mexico gets, it offers a surprisingly huge array of outdoor recreation, much of which relies on the state's lakes and rivers, as well as on the snow that falls in the high mountain regions. Windsurfing, fishing, water-skiing, white-water rafting, kayaking, cross-country and Alpine skiing—all are immensely popular with New Mexicans, who are no slouches when it comes to getting outdoors. In fact, many New Mexicans claim that's what keeps them in the area: no matter where you are, a lake, campground, trout stream, golf course, ski slope, or hiking trail is just a short drive away.

Hiking, Backpacking, and Camping

New Mexico takes special pride in its state park system, with dozens of diverse locations scattered about the state. Most offer overnight camping and flush toilets, and many have hot showers. Generally, the parks are very well maintained and often include self-guided nature trails and visitors centers. Day use is $4, and overnight camping starts at $8 a night, for a primitive site ($4 extra each for electrical and sewage hookups.

In addition to New Mexico's more than 45 state parks, the state has thousands of square miles of national forest, scores of Forest Service campgrounds, and huge tracts of protected wilderness areas, off-limits to motor vehicles but begging to be explored by hikers and backpackers. You'll also find scores of private campgrounds throughout New Mexico, many equipped for RVs.

For more information on New Mexico's state parks, write **New Mexico State Park and Recreation Division,** Villagra Building, P.O. Box

1147, Santa Fe, NM 87504-1147, or phone 888/NMPARKS (888/667-2757). You can also get up-to-date information from the division's website: www.emnrd.state.nm.us/nmparks.

For information on New Mexico national forests, write **USDA Forest Service,** Region 3, Albuquerque, NM 87102, or call 505/842-3292.

Bicycling

The Southwest has definitely not let the cycling boom pass it by. Whether it's touring or mountain biking, human-powered two-wheeling is getting more and more popular in New Mexico. In the north-central section of the state, particularly, you'll see cyclists working out on back roads and pumping up steep mountain passes. Several roads in the Albuquerque area are especially popular, including the Turquoise Trail to Santa Fe and the frontage road along I-40 East.

New Mexicans have jumped on the mountain-bike bandwagon, and the miles and miles of trails through the state's national forests are perfect. Check at district ranger offices for trail maps and restrictions. An excellent source of information for mountain bikers is the nonprofit **International Mountain Bicycling Association.** For lists of shops and companies offering tours and races, visit its website: www.imba.com. New Mexico's state IMBA representative is Charles Ervin at bicycles@twowheeldrive.com.

Another good source for information on bicycling in New Mexico is the **New Mexico Touring Society,** P.O. Box 1261, Albuquerque, NM 87103-1261, 505/237-9700, website: www.swcp.com/~russells/nmts.

Most bike shops also are happy to point you toward a good ride.

Hunting and Fishing

Except for saltwater fishing, New Mexico offers just about every kind of recreational angling you can imagine. Troll for striped bass in Elephant Butte Lake, cast barbless-hook dry flies for catch-and-release trout in the San Juan River, doze in your lawn chair beside Bluewater Lake while you wait for a catfish to bite, or jig through the ice for dinner-size trout on El Vado Reservoir.

New Mexico also offers excellent hunting opportunities, for both large game—elk, deer, bighorn sheep, black bear, and antelope—and

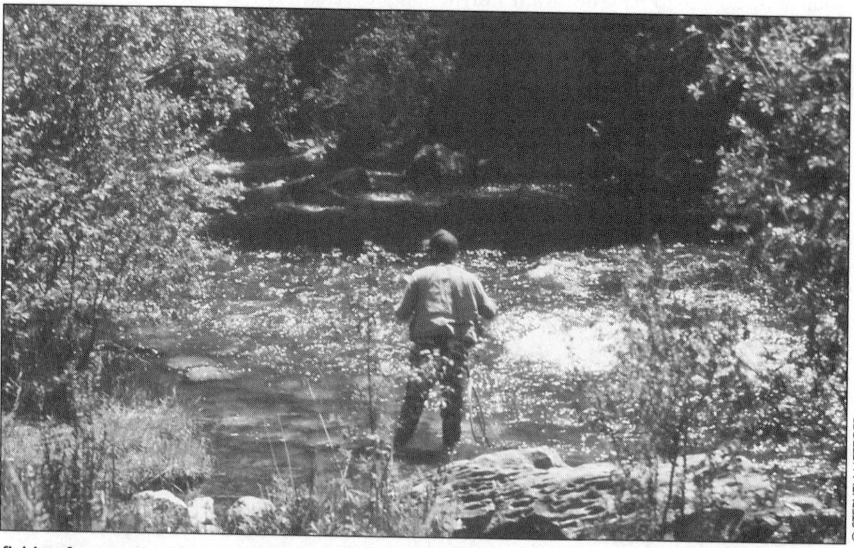

© STEPHEN METZGER

fishing for trout in the Pecos Wilderness Area, near Santa Fe

small game and birds—rabbit, squirrel, grouse, quail, and turkey.

For information on hunting, fishing, and license fees in New Mexico, write the **New Mexico Department of Game and Fish,** 1 Wildlife Way, Santa Fe, NM 87507, phone 505/476-8000, or visit the website: www.gmfsh.state.nm.us.

Rafting and Windsurfing

These are two of New Mexico's fastest-growing sports. Several Santa Fe and Taos outfitters lead half- to three-day rafting expeditions down many Southwest rivers. Especially popular are trips down the Rio Grande and Rio Chama. Summer afternoons when the winds whip up, the brightly colored sails of windsurfers and sailboats can be seen on Storrie Lake near Las Vegas, Cochiti Lake southwest of Santa Fe, and El Vado Reservoir near Chama. Regattas are held regularly.

Skiing

Because of the dry desert air of the Southwest, the snow that falls on the mountains of New Mexico is some of the best in the country. The Sangre de Cristo Mountains, a subrange of the southern Rockies, are well known for their light powder and deep drifts, and Taos Ski Valley, in the heart of these mountains, is known to cognoscenti as one of the world's best ski resorts. With an unusually high percentage of advanced and advanced-intermediate runs, Taos is the favorite of some of the best skiers in the country.

In addition to Taos, though, New Mexico claims a handful of other excellent downhill areas: Ski Apache, in the White Mountains outside Ruidoso; Santa Fe Ski Area, just minutes from the capital; Sandia Peak Ski Area, in the Sandia Mountains overlooking Albuquerque; and Red River and Angel Fire in the Sangre de Cristos north of Taos. Several smaller ski areas around the state—near Cloudcroft, Los Alamos, and south of Taos—are excellent local and day-use areas.

New Mexico is also a veritable haven for cross-country skiers. With its thousands of miles of national forest, as well as a handful of private areas specifically developed for Nordic skiing, New Mexico welcomes those who'd rather ski quietly off into the woods than stand in lift lines after spending more than $30 for a ticket. Cross-country skiers will find excellent terrain in the Jemez Mountains south of Los Alamos, Santa Fe National Forest north of the capital, the Enchanted Circle area north of Taos, the woods near Chama, and many other areas around the state.

For more information on skiing in New Mexico—from reservations to up-to-the-minute snow reports—visit the website: www.skinewmexico.com.

Arts

To some, New Mexico and art are nearly synonymous. From Anasazi and Mimbres pottery to contemporary oil paintings, sculpture, and photography, art has helped define this region for thousands of years. Santa Fe and Taos, particularly, are legitimate artists' colonies, recognized worldwide for the museum-quality work produced and sold there. In addition, some of the tiny, lesser-known towns, such as Chimayó, produce weavings, jewelry, woodcarvings, and other wares that draw collectors and dealers from around the world.

In Santa Fe, you can visit galleries where world-class artists display their paintings and sculptures. You can arrange tours to studios to watch the artists at work. The capital's annual Spanish and Indian Markets, Gallup's Inter-tribal Ceremonial, and Taos's three-week Spring Arts Festival offer visitors chances to buy pieces directly from the artists. At the State Fair and the Arts and Crafts Fair in Albuquerque, booth after booth is chock-full of juried pieces. In fact, nearly every town in the state has an annual art fair, where gorgeous Southwestern art is displayed and sold, while most pueblos have gift shops that sell high-quality pottery, jewelry, rugs, kachinas, and sandpaintings by Native American artists. In addition, the sidewalks of the plazas in Albuquerque and Santa Fe are lined with Indians selling their wares spread on blankets.

COURTESY OF MUSEUM OF INDIAN ARTS AND CULTURE, SANTA FE/DUANE ANDERSON

Museum of Indian Arts and Culture, Santa Fe

Literature

New Mexico is a land steeped in literature. From Pueblo emergence myths and Spanish folk tales to contemporary fiction, the land and the stories of the people who live on it are virtually inseparable. Of particular interest is the 20th-century fiction that has come out of the state: modern New Mexico novelists and short-story writers are weaving into their work Native American mythology and legend, as well as Spanish colonial folklore.

Taos writer John Nichols has been one of the most successful of New Mexico's scribes. His novels, combining realism, magic, and social commentary, take readers into the fantastic realm of his wonderful characters. His best book, *The Milagro Beanfield War,* was made into a movie—directed by Robert Redford—with Sonia Braga, Daniel Stern, and rock singer Ruben Blades.

In the Pulitzer Prize–winning *House Made of Dawn,* American Indian writer N. Scott Momaday tells the story of a scarred World War II veteran from Jemez Pueblo who unsuccessfully attempts to sort out the discrepancies between the two worlds in which he's forced to live; ultimately he falls back on tribal heritage and tradition in a last-ditch effort to make some sense of who he is. Leslie Marmon Silko's novel *Ceremony* deals with the same theme, although her main character is more successful than Momaday's, in part because as he relearns the importance of ritual and ceremony, he also re-embraces the female side of his personality, crucial to the Native American idea of the "whole" person. Silko has also written numerous short stories, such as "Yellow Woman," based on Pueblo myth.

Fans of the murder mystery will love Tony Hillerman's whodunits. Hillerman, an ex-UPI reporter and UNM journalism professor, takes you from Zuñi Pueblo and the Navajo Reservation to Chaco Canyon, the Smithsonian Institution, and federal offices in Washington, D.C., as he follows his Navajo police officers Jim Chee and Joe Leaphorn on the trails of murderers, pothunters, and other evil characters. Although

TONY HILLERMAN'S NAVAJO DETECTIVE NOVELS

The hand lay palm up, and the wind had drifted a little sand against it, and even to Listening Woman's sensitive touch, it felt like nothing more than a little stick. And so she tapped her way, still calling and muttering, down the path toward the place where the body of Hosteen Tso lay sprawled beside his overturned rocking chair—the Rainbow Man still arched across his chest.

Tony Hillerman, from Listening Woman

I will tell you something about stories, [he said]

They aren't just entertainment.

Don't be fooled.

Leslie Marmon Silko, from Ceremony

It'd be easy to dismiss Albuquerque author Tony Hillerman's novels as simple stories, classic whodunits whose only distinction is their setting. Indeed, like most novels of the genre, they'll keep you turning pages, right up till the last one, as you work to second-guess the detectives—Navajos Jim Chee and Joe Leaphorn—and try to solve the mysteries yourself.

But there's a lot more going on in these books. First of all, Hillerman is no slouch when it comes to research, and his accurate depiction of Indian landscapes, people, ceremonies, and ways of life have won him the deep respect of Southwest Native Americans, particularly the Navajos, who use his books in their tribal schools and who awarded him the Navajo Tribe's Special Friend Award. And the respect is clearly mutual. Hillerman refuses to glorify the Indians about whom he writes, but nor does he dwell on the reservations' poverty and squalor, though in confronting the ugly side of reservation life head-on and honestly he helps us see past stereotypes to the complex realities of modern Indian life.

COURTESY OF TONY HILLERMAN

Tony Hillerman

One of the joys of reading Hillerman novels is in learning about the customs and social norms of the characters who populate them. In *The Ghostway,* we learn that Navajo tradition dictates that the dead be buried with their boots on the wrong feet, so evil spirits will have a difficult time following their footprints to the afterlife. In *A Thief of Time* and *Talking God,* we learn about the beliefs and superstitions associated with sacred burial sites, where spirits guard not only bones but pieces of pottery, and anyone disturbing them is asking for *trouble.*

Hillerman was born in 1925 and raised in Oklahoma, in a town called

(continued on next page)

TONY HILLERMAN'S NAVAJO DETECTIVE NOVELS (cont'd)

Sacred Heart, about 70 miles from Oklahoma City. Because of the poor conditions of the local public school, Hillerman attended a Catholic boarding school for Pottawatomi and Seminole Indian girls. He got a degree in journalism from the University of Oklahoma in 1946 and a master's degree in English literature in 1966. According to Michael Parfit, writing in the December 1990 *Smithsonian* magazine, Hillerman was always at odds with the "city kids" from nearby Konowa, who knew how to use telephones and whose homes had indoor plumbing. "I was 21 years old before I made my first telephone call," Hillerman told Parfit. Since then Hillerman has always felt a sense of "us versus them" in the world, and this is a theme he has carried into his novels.

Hillerman joined the army during World War II and was sent to France, where he broke both legs and won Bronze and Silver Stars. When he returned, he went into journalism, working for many magazines and newspapers (including stints as a UPI reporter in Oklahoma City and Santa Fe, as well as executive editor of the *New Mexican*). He also spent 15 years at the University of New Mexico, as professor and chair of the journalism department and as assistant to the president. His first mystery novel, *The Blessing Way*, was published in 1970. Since then, he has written more than a dozen more; he's also written several nonfiction books, penned introductions to many others, and collected and edited some of the finest writing on New Mexico (*The Spell of New Mexico;* see Suggested Reading). Hillerman's detective novels have been on the *New York Times* best-seller list several times; he won the Edgar Allan Poe Award, France's Grand Prix de la Littérature Policière, and the Silver Spur Award for best novel set in the West; and he has served as president of the Mystery Writers of America.

Hillerman's other Southwest mystery novels include *Dance Hall of the Dead, People of Darkness, The Fly on the Wall, The Dark Wind, Skinwalkers, Coyote Waits, Sacred Clowns, The Wailing Wind, Hunting Badger, The First Eagle,* and *The Fallen Man.*

fun and entertaining reading, Hillerman's books are not to be taken too lightly. His research is meticulous, and he depicts his Indian characters with accuracy and love. In addition to the Navajo Tribe's Special Friend Award, Hillerman has won the Mystery Writers of America's Edgar Allan Poe Award and France's Grand Prix de la Littérature Policière.

Poetry is also becoming important in New Mexico, with several Hispanic and Native American poets being recognized nationally for their work. Simon Ortíz, N. Scott Momaday, Jimmy Santiago Baca, Paula Gunn Allen, Leslie Marmon Silko, and others are drawing from their Southwest experiences and adding a new voice to contemporary poetry. And not all of it is pretty as it often realistically depicts the pain and squalor of contemporary life on the pueblos and in the barrios.

Bookstores throughout the state, particularly in Albuquerque, Santa Fe, and Taos, are recognizing the renewed interest in Southwest regional literature and holding regular readings. Local poets and fiction writers read short passages from their work to small gatherings, where they also usually sign and sell their books.

Accommodations

New Mexico's travelers' accommodations run the full gamut from backcountry campgrounds to bed-and-breakfasts, roadside motels to high-rise hotels with valet parking. Even the most remote towns usually have an inexpensive motel or two, and you're rarely far from a state park, most of which provide overnight camping starting at $8. New Mexico's main tourist towns—Albuquerque, Santa Fe, and Taos—have wide ranges of lodging possibilities, including RV campgrounds, inexpensive motels, and luxury hotels. Generally, it's cheaper to stay on the outskirts of town, although you'll sacrifice the convenience of central-location lodging.

Campgrounds

Camping is the least expensive way to bed down in your travels through New Mexico. With nightly fees ranging from free to about $28 (for some of the more costly RV sites), the state's campgrounds are generally well maintained, safe, and comfortable. State park campgrounds, widely scattered throughout New Mexico, usually provide running water, modern restrooms with flush toilets, sheltered sites, electrical hookups, and kids' playgrounds. Keep in mind, though, that many of these parks, especially those in the south, are in some pretty hot and deserty areas, and though some provide shelters for shade, the summer sun can be brutal. Scores of national forest campgrounds are found throughout the state, particularly in the mountains near Silver City, Cloudcroft, Santa Fe, Las Vegas, and Taos.

For more information on New Mexico's state parks, write **New Mexico State Park and Recreation Division,** Villagra Building, P.O. Box 1147, Santa Fe, NM 87504-1147, or phone 888/NMPARKS (888/667-2757). You can also get up-to-date information from the division's website: www.emnrd.state.nm.us/nmparks. For information on camping and campgrounds in New Mexico's national forests, write **USDA Forest Service,** Region 3, Albuquerque, NM 87102, or call 505/842-3292. A good website offering general information on New Mexico camping, as well as links to other useful sites, is accessible at camping.about.com/blaastNM.htm.

Note: When camping in New Mexico, stay away from arroyos. A perfectly blue sky can cloud up in minutes, and sudden storms can turn dry creekbeds to raging rivers before you can say "flash flood."

BOB RACE

Bed-and-Breakfasts

Although often a bit on the pricey side ($60–150 a night), bed-and-breakfasts are one of the best ways to experience New Mexico. Many Spanish colonial haciendas and 19th-century Victorians have been recently converted to bed-and-breakfasts, and the small inns generally provide intimate and personal service, with a true feel of New Mexico's past. Santa Fe and Taos alone offer dozens of bed-and-breakfast possibilities. Contact the **New Mexico Bed and Breakfast Association,** P.O. Box 2925, Santa Fe, NM 87504-2925, 800/661-6649, website: nmbba.org. You can also get information and make reservations at **Bed and Breakfasts Online** at the website: www.bbonline.com/nm. The **Taos Association of Bed and Breakfast Inns** lists more than two dozen different inns in the Taos area alone. For information or reservations, visit the website: www.taos-bandb-inns.com.

HOTEL AND MOTEL CHAINS

If you've been on the road at all in the United States in the last few years, you've noticed the amazing proliferation of chain lodging—from Motel 6s to Super 8s to all the Inns (Holiday, Ramada, Comfort, Days . . .). Even many of the ol' Best Westerns have been upgraded and remarketed in recent years; the familiar yellow-crown signs that once rose comfortably into the low skylines of twilight have been replaced by modern deep-blue signs with stylized red crowns and electronic marquees advertising sports bars and exercise rooms. Most of these lodges offer competitive rates; clean, quiet rooms; and a known quantity in terms of price, amenities, and general quality. Unfortunately, they've also helped further the depersonalization of small-town America; the colorful little mom-and-pop places can't compete.

Following is a list of some of the common hotel and motel chains, their approximate rates for a room for two, and what you can expect them to provide. In general, you can count on a swimming pool, laundry facilities, television with a movie channel, free local phone calls, free morning coffee, and a choice of smoking or no-smoking rooms. Many offer discounts to members of various groups and clubs: the American Automobile Association, American Association of Retired Persons, military employees, and others. Always ask.

Refer to this information later on in the book when you come across a listing for one of the chains below.

Best Western, 800/528-1234. Best Westerns are individually owned and vary considerably in size and appearance—from roadside motels to downtown high-rises. They all must meet strict standards, however, and you are generally assured of quality and comfort. I stay at them frequently, as I know they'll be clean and quiet and the service dependable and friendly. Most have pools; many have restaurants on the premises. Rates generally range $50–75, slightly higher in the larger towns.

Days Inn, 800/DAYS INN (800/329-7466). Consistently comfortable and clean, though without much personality. Most have pools; no restaurants. Doubles are usually about $50–55.

Holiday Inn, 800/HOLIDAY (800/465-4329). Generally the most upscale of the lodges listed here. Each has a restaurant, lounge, pool, and meeting facilities. Doubles are generally in the $70–130 range.

Holiday Inn Express, 800/HOLIDAY (800/465-4329). Scaled-down versions of Holiday Inns, these lodges offer continental breakfasts, and most have pools. Rates run $55–100.

Motel 6, 800/4-MOTEL-6 (800/466-8356). Cookie cutter, but comfortable. Small pool; bathrooms with shower stall but no tub. This chain is extremely popular, and rooms fill up quickly. Oftentimes the No Vacancy sign goes up well before nightfall. Doubles are $35–50.

Ramada Inn, 800/2-RAMADA (800/272-6232). Varying from urban high-rises to smaller-town motels, Ramadas all offer restaurants, lounges, and meeting rooms and are reliably comfortable and clean. Doubles are usually $45–80.

Super 8, 800/800-8000. Consistently clean and quiet. Rates run $45–60.

Hotels and Motels

After a long hot drive across the desert, a clean bed in an air-conditioned room often seems like paradise. Relatively inexpensive, rooms in New Mexico hotels and motels range from $25 for a double in one of the motel metropolises such as Gallup or Tucumcari to $150 and up for a room for two in a downtown Santa Fe or Albuquerque hotel.

Remember that prices vary from season to season. Generally, summer is the high season, although in towns such as Taos, where winter-sports enthusiasts descend in hordes, prices go up at Christmas and remain high throughout the ski season.

In Albuquerque, a city stretching at the seams, experts on public safety recommend getting a room in a good hotel rather than trying to save a few bucks on a cheaper room. Most Albuquerque hotels provide free shuttle service to the airport, and a trolley runs between the Old Town plaza and the major hotels.

Food and Cooking

One of the best things about visiting New Mexico is eating the native food. Almost every restaurant—whether its tables are carved wood with linen napkins on them or chipped Formica with catsup bottles, whether its specialty is seafood or lox and bagels—will have somewhere on its menu a selection of tamales, burritos, sopaipillas, and chile stews.

One of the best things about visiting New Mexico is eating the native food. Almost every restaurant will have somewhere on its menu a selection of tamales, burritos, sopaipillas, and chile stews.

Start with a margarita or a good Mexican beer, a basket of chips, and a bowl of salsa; then try a green-chile burrito and a sopaipilla (and of course another margarita or beer). Or, if you're really brave, try New Mexican food to start your day: a breakfast burrito (chile, eggs, cheese, and beans wrapped in a flour tortilla) will definitely clear your head and sinuses, although you may not be the most popular traveling companion afterward, especially if you're in a car with the windows rolled up.

Often mistakenly called "Mexican food," *New* Mexican dishes, though similar, actually belong in a separate category. An integral ingredient in much of the state's cuisine is the red or green chile ("chili" is actually the correct spelling, but most New Mexican cooks and food writers prefer to spell it with an "e"). New Mexican chile stew, for example, uses chiles instead of the red beans typically associated with the dish. Grown in large numbers in fields along the Rio Grande in the southern part of the state (Hatch bills itself "The Chile Capital of the World," and New Mexico leads the country in chile production), red and green chiles vary in degrees of spiciness, although you'll rarely find one as hot as the notorious Mexican jalapeño. Ask your waiter which is hotter: one day it'll be the red, the next the green, depending on the specific time and place the peppers were harvested.

The beans served with New Mexican meals also set the state's food apart from Mexican cuisine. Unlike the mushy refried beans (frijoles) usually accompanying Mexican dishes, New Mexican meals typically include the dark pink or purple pinto beans. Take a spoonful, pour them onto a flour tortilla, and roll them up inside.

Sopaipillas are another characteristically New Mexican food. Most commonly served as a side dish, either with your meal or for dessert, a sopaipilla is a small, pillow-shaped bread/pastry, deep-fried and served hot, usually with honey. Sopaipillas are also sometimes served stuffed—with chiles, onions, beans, cheese, and/or meat.

Travelers who really want to experience the cuisine of the Southwest should also sample Native American food. Indians at roadside stands near pueblos and on the reservations often sell frybread, a deep-fried bread usually cooked over

RECIPES

Jim Fish's Green Chile Stew

2–3 lb. beef, goat, venison, chicken, turkey, or any combination
2–3 cans of beer
3 large onions
1 tsp. cumin seed
pinch of oregano
5–6 garlic cloves
salt and pepper
pinch of sage
2 lb. green chiles
a few small red potatoes (optional)

The day before serving, cover meat with beer and simmer for 3–4 hours. Let cool in liquid. The next day, shred the meat into the liquid. Add onions, cumin, oregano, garlic, sage, and chiles. Salt and pepper to taste. Bring to boil and simmer for about an hour. If you use the potatoes, put them in the same pot about 45 minutes before serving, and let them steam. Serve with cornbread and salad.

Jim Fish's Cornbread

3/4 cup whole wheat flour
2 1/2 tsp. baking powder
3/4 tsp. salt
2 eggs
1/4 tsp. butter
1 cup milk
1–2 tsp. sugar
1 1/4 cups yellow (or blue) stone-ground corn meal

Put butter in 10-inch cast iron skillet, place in oven, and set oven to 425°F. Mix eggs and milk. Mix dry ingredients in a large bowl. Add eggs and milk. When butter is melted, pour about one-third into batter. Mix with a few rapid strokes. Pour batter into skillet (with the rest of the butter). Bake until golden brown (25–30 minutes).

Beth and Dorothy's Black Bean Soup—New Mexico–Style

Note: this is *very* hot.
2 1/2 cups beans
5 pints water
1 tsp. salt
hamhock, beef, or chicken broth (amount will determine soup's consistency)
1 clove garlic
3 jalapeño peppers
1/4 large onion
black pepper

Soak beans overnight in water (or boil for 2 minutes and then let sit for 1 hour). Add other ingredients, bring to boil, and simmer for 2–3 hours.

Salsa
2 tomatoes, medium-sized
1 Bermuda onion, medium-sized
1 clove garlic
1/2 tsp. salt
2 or more green chiles

Use fresh chiles (roasted, peeled, and seeded) or frozen or canned chiles. Chop the chiles, tomatoes, and onions very fine. (Don't lose the juice of the tomatoes!) Mash the garlic with the salt. Mix well. Add more chiles to suit your taste. Allow flavors to blend at least an hour before using. Store in refrigerator or freezer. Use on tacos, eggs, hamburgers, or as a dip for chips. Makes about 1 pint.

(From *New Mexico Magazine*'s *The Best from New Mexico Kitchens,* 1978.)

Sopaipillas
2 cups flour
2 tsp. baking powder
1 tsp. salt
2 tbsp. lard
1/2 cup water
shortening for frying

Sift dry ingredients together. Work in lard and lukewarm water to make a soft dough. Chill in refrigerator. Roll out dough on a floured surface to about 1/4-inch thickness. Cut into 3-inch squares. Deep fry in hot lard (or vegetable shortening) at 400°F a few at a time. Brown on each side and drain on paper towels. Serve piping hot. To eat, poke open and pour in honey or slather with honey butter.

(From *New Mexico Magazine*'s *The Best from New Mexico Kitchens,* 1978.)

Don's Perfect Margarita
5 ice cubes
3 oz. gold tequila
2 oz. Triple Sec
2 oz. lime juice (bottled is best, although in a pinch frozen will suffice)
1 tbsp. margarita salt
1 lime

Mix ice, tequila, Triple Sec, and lime juice in blender. Rub the rims of two glasses with a wedge of lime. Dip glasses into margarita salt. Pour, and enjoy.

an open fire, for about $1 a loaf. You can find Navajo tacos, served open-faced on a thick puffy tortilla or piece of frybread, at some restaurants in Indian country and often at food booths at county fairs and arts and crafts shows.

New Mexico's Wineries

In a way it's perfectly appropriate that New Mexico—with its ancient history—should be developing a wine industry. After all, wine production is one of the oldest industries known to humankind. In fact, the world's first civilizations began when nomadic hunters turned to agriculture and settled into semipermanent communities. And anthropologists believe that some of the first crops grown were intended ultimately for fermentation, among them grapes and barley.

Though in terms of production and reputation, New Mexico's wine industry is small compared to that of California's Napa Valley, it's nonetheless worth keeping an eye on, as new vineyards and wineries appear frequently and, more important, the wines get better. By the early 2000s, nearly 30 wineries were scattered about the state, from the fertile fields of the Las Cruces area to the rolling southern Sangre de Cristo Mountains near Taos. And as more and more wineries open, more and more tourists are adding winetasting to their New Mexico itineraries. In addition, each year a number of wine festivals offer opportunities to sample the wares of the various wineries and to learn more about this fascinating and rapidly growing industry. Among them: the **Mesilla Valley Wine Festival,** in Las Cruces on Memorial Day weekend (505/646-4543); the **Santa Fe Wine Festival** in Santa Fe in mid-June (505/646-4543); and the **New Mexico Wine Festival at Bernalillo** on Labor Day weekend (505/867-3311).

The largest concentration of New Mexico wineries is in the area of the Rio Grande Valley between Albuquerque and Velarde (about midway between Santa Fe and Taos)—quite convenient, considering this is the main corridor for tourist travel in the region. Albuquerque wineries include **Anderson Valley Vineyards,** 4920 Rio Grande Blvd. NW, 505/344-7266, and **Gruet Winery,** 8400 Pan American Freeway NE, 505/821-0055. **Santa Fe Vineyards** is just north of Santa Fe on the road to Taos; you'll find its tasting room at 235 Don Gaspar in Santa Fe, 505/982-3474.

One of the state's newest and most intriguing wineries is **Anasazi Fields** in Placitas, about 15 minutes north of Albuquerque. Anasazi Fields's grower and vintner Jim Fish specializes in handmade, oak-aged wines made from domestic cherries, wild and ornamental plums, apricots, peaches, crabapples, raspberries, and four varieties of grapes. Fish's fruit wines are dry, not sweet like most fruit wines, thanks to a higher degree of fermentation, a grape-wine finish, and oak aging. They are designed, he says, "to be enjoyed with fine foods, good music, and dear friends." The winery is open Saturday 10 A.M.–5 P.M., Sunday noon–5 P.M., and other days by appointment. To get there, take Exit 242 north at Bernalillo and take Highway 165 east six miles to Placitas; continue for another quarter mile to Camino de Los Pueblitos, where you'll turn left. The entrance will be on your left just where the road bends sharply to the right. For information, phone 505/867-3062 or write Anasazi Fields, P.O. Box 712, Placitas, NM 87043.

For a brochure and map of New Mexico wineries, or for more information on New Mexico wines, contact **New Mexico Wine Growers Association,** P.O. Box 30003, Dept. 3AE, Las Cruces, NM 88003-0003, 505/646-4543.

Alcohol Regulations

The legal drinking age in New Mexico is 21. Alcohol is not sold in stores between midnight Saturday and noon Sunday, although you can get alcohol in restaurants with your meals during that time.

Transportation

Although several companies offer tours of New Mexico—from Indian ruins to modern art museums—and the major tourist areas provide excellent public transportation, you're better off with your own rig. Remember that it's a long way between places you'll want to see, and you'll enjoy the luxury of capricious stops—whether for rest, for water, or to explore a ruin or town not on your itinerary.

MILEAGE MAP OF NEW MEXICO

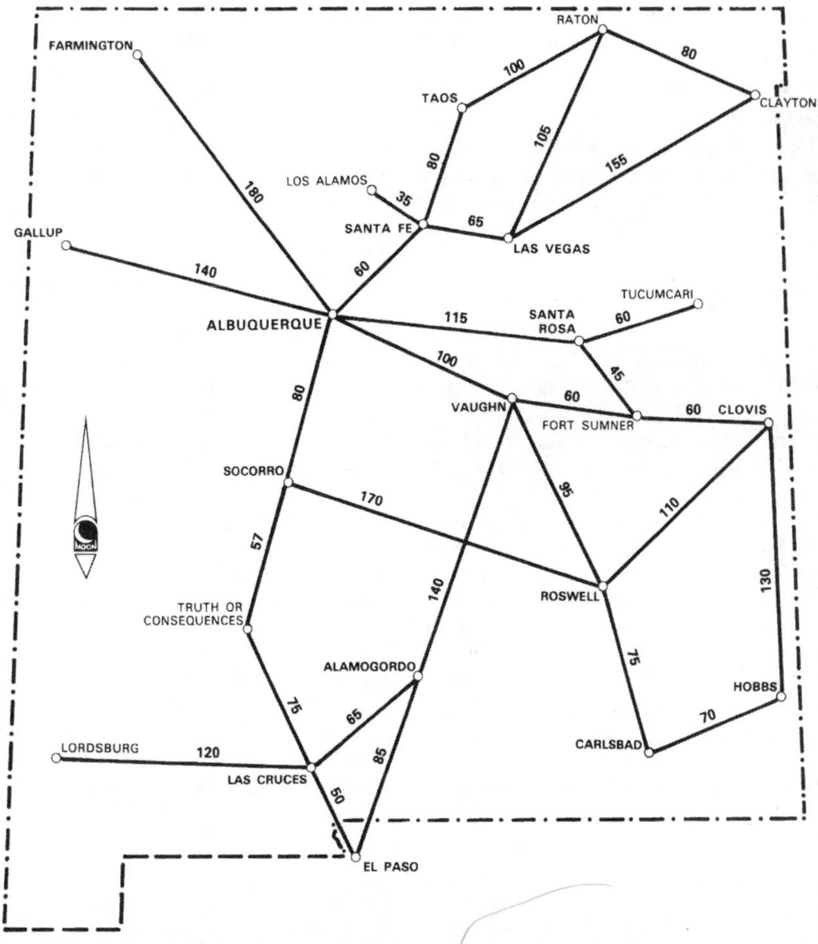

ON THE ROAD

New Mexico by Air

Most major airlines fly into Albuquerque International Airport, and from there, Mesa Air services much of the rest of the state, including Santa Fe, Roswell, Alamogordo, and Carlsbad. To book a flight into Albuquerque, contact your local travel agent, or book it yourself on one of the numerous travel websites; for information and reservations on Mesa, phone 800/MESA-AIR (800/637-2247).

You'll find rental cars available at New Mexico's airports. Several "rent-a-wreck" companies have started up in New Mexico, offering completely reliable cars in slightly worse cosmetic shape than those offered by the major chains.

By Car

This is the best way to see New Mexico. Unless you drive across I-40 from Gallup or Tucumcari to Albuquerque, up I-25 from Las Cruces to Santa Fe, and then up the back roads to Taos, you'll never really appreciate how vast and diverse this state is. For the most part, the roads are excellently maintained and make driving painless and easy.

In the summer, you'll be better off with air-conditioning, especially if you plan to head south to Carlsbad or Las Cruces. In the winter, carry snow chains. And year-round, it's always a good idea to have a good map with you. Most bookstores have map departments stocked with detailed maps of specific parts of New Mexico. One particularly good source is **Dumont Maps and Books of the West,** 235 Don Gaspar, Santa Fe, 505/982-3474; phone for hours of operation. You can also get maps from the New Mexico **Tourism and Travel Division** of the Economic Development and Tourism Department, 505/827-0291 or 800/545-2040. Obvious but often overlooked map sources are local phone books. Most include detailed maps, often very well annotated. Finally, the American Automobile Association publishes excellent and up-to-date road maps of the state as well as tour books with detailed listings of accommodations and some attractions. Check your local phone book.

By Rail

Although New Mexico is often associated with railroad travel (from the heyday of the Atchison, Topeka, & Santa Fe), these days the rails are used much more for freight than for passengers. At press time, **Amtrak** had recently received a "stay of execution" and was still providing passenger service to New Mexico. The Sunset Limited barrels through the southern part of the state with stops in Lordsburg and Deming, and the Southwest Chief crosses from Gallup to Albuquerque, up to Santa Fe, then up through Las Vegas and Ratón. Some New Mexicophiles claim this is the *only* way to get here. For information on Amtrak, call 800/872-7245, or visit its website: www.amtrak.com.

By Bus

A couple of bus lines, including **Greyhound** (website: www.greyhound.com) provide bus service throughout New Mexico, from Hobbs to Farmington. Although modern buses are generally air-conditioned and comfortable and offer a classic way to see the country and meet the people along the way, long-distance bus rides can take their toll. Use the bus to get from town to town, not to explore the state's many widespread attractions.

Organized Tours

Gray Line Tours, 505/542-3880 or 800/256-8991, has available a wide range of tours of the state, including to ruins and festivals, and **Rojo Tours,** 505/474-8333, leads tours to Taos and Taos Pueblo, Chaco Canyon, "O'Keeffe Country," and Santa Fe art studios and sculpture gardens. The company also offers a Rio Grande Valley Artisans and Pueblo Tour.

Shopping and Money

Souvenirs of your trip to New Mexico can include anything from tacky T-shirts and rubber tomahawks to quality art—poetry, painting, jewelry, Navajo rugs—running thousands of dollars. Most of the major tourist areas—Santa Fe, Taos, Old Town Albuquerque—are home to dozens of gift shops, galleries, and boutiques. You can also buy from the state-licensed street vendors, whose work is guaranteed authentic and is usually of the highest quality. Generally, prices are competitive, although it's still a good idea to shop around for comparison.

Among the most popular crafts and art: turquoise and silver jewelry, kachina dolls, sandpaintings, pottery, and weavings. Two good places to visit before heading out on shopping adventures are Albuquerque's Turquoise Museum—where you can get a feel for the different grades and types of turquoise—and Indian Pueblo Cultural Center, which provides an overview of the distinctions among the pottery styles of the different pueblos. In addition, Bien Mur, a gift shop on the north end of Albuquerque (off Tramway), sells high-quality pottery, jewelry, and other artwork from the pueblos.

BOB RACE

Money Matters

New Mexico state **sales tax** is 6 percent, which is also added to all lodging charges. In addition, many local governments have supplemental taxes ranging from 2 to 6 percent. Plan on **tipping** restaurant servers 15–20 percent of your bill; motel/hotel housekeepers a couple of bucks a night; and hotel/airport baggage handlers $.50 to $1 a bag. Remember that most service help is grossly underpaid and that while overtipping a buck or two probably won't make much of a dent in your budget, it might make a difference in what and how well a struggling single parent feeds his or her child the next day.

Automated-teller machines (ATMs), though ubiquitous in the more populated parts of the state, won't be as easy to come by in the smaller desert and mountain communities. Don't venture into the "outback" assuming you're going to be able to get cash at the drop of a sombrero. On the other hand, traveling with large amounts of cash isn't smart, either.

Staying Healthy

Traveling anywhere requires certain precautions, and New Mexico is no exception. The main thing to be aware of here is the weather: The harsh summer sun can severely burn exposed skin and desiccate unprepared travelers, sudden rainstorms can turn highways to rivers, and winter storms can quickly blanket roads, making them slick and difficult to navigate. If you're traveling in New Mexico in the summer, carry plenty of water; you can never have too much. An ice chest is ideal for keeping drinks and food cool. If you plan to get out and hike around at all, make sure your skin is protected; a hat with a wide brim is a good idea, as is a good strong sunscreen. Don't worry about your tan; your health is more important, and a sunburn is not only painful, but long-term exposure to the sun can lead to skin cancer.

Winter travelers should always carry snow chains. Skiers heading into the Sangre de Cristos, the Jemez, or the White Mountains need to remember how suddenly winter storms can blow in. Also, obey all chain-control restrictions. They're there for *your* safety.

Motorists should also carry both first-aid kits and tool kits in their cars. First-aid kits should include Band-Aids, gauze, medical tape, insect repellent, lip balm, and some form of pain pills. You should carry a spare blanket, flathead and Phillips screwdrivers, adjustable wrench, jack, booster cables, shovel, and a good spare tire.

In addition, be aware of the following specific afflictions and climate-caused maladies that could mar your visit. Understanding these problems and taking the appropriate precautions will greatly increase the chances of staying healthy while exploring the state. Much of the following information was taken from the American Medical Association's *Encyclopedia of Medicine.*

Sunburn

Sunburn is most common in fair-skinned people and most likely to occur *at high elevations,* where a thinner atmosphere naturally blocks fewer ultraviolet rays. Skiers and other winter-sports enthusiasts should be especially careful, as the sun's reflection off the snow doubles the effect of harmful rays. Even on cloudy days, much of the sun's ultraviolet energy still penetrates.

The two best ways to prevent sunburn are gradual exposure (increasing each day) and application of a sunscreen with a high sun-protection factor (SPF). Available at pharmacies, sporting goods stores, and even grocery stores, sunscreens with a high SPF (15 or higher) should be applied liberally and often. Treatment for sunburn includes the application of any of several available lotions and ointments; particularly effective are those with aloe. Severe cases may require medical treatment.

Dehydration

Dehydration is the result of a drop in the body's water level and often a corresponding drop in the level of salt. Being at higher altitudes can cause an increase in dehydration. Symptoms include severe thirst, dry lips, increased heart and breath rate, dizziness, and confusion. Often the skin is dry and stiff; what little urine is passed is dark. When salt loss is heavy, there will also be headaches, cramps, lethargy, and pallor. Severe cases of dehydration can result in coma.

To prevent dehydration, you must replace the three (or more) quarts of water your body loses every 24 hours to perspiration and urination. Even in moderate temperatures and climates, you should be cautious and drink more than you probably think you need; a good rule of thumb is to drink enough water to keep the urine pale. Treatment for dehydration includes fluid and salt replacement—in severe cases delivered intravenously.

Altitude Sickness

Also known as mountain sickness, altitude sickness most commonly affects mountain climbers, hikers, and skiers who ascend too rapidly to heights above 8,000 feet. Caused by a reduction in atmospheric pressure and a corresponding decrease in oxygen, altitude sickness alters the blood chemistry and affects the nervous system, muscles, heart, and lungs.

Symptoms of altitude sickness include headache, nausea, dizziness, and impaired mental abilities. In severe cases, fluid buildup in the lungs leads to breathlessness, coughing, and heavy phlegm. Untreated, these symptoms can lead to seizures, hallucinations, and coma. Delays in treatment can even lead to brain damage and death.

The best way to prevent altitude sickness is to ascend *gradually* to elevations above 8,000 feet. Take a day or two for each 2,000–3,000 feet. Victims of altitude sickness should return to lower elevations immediately; if necessary carry them. If available, pure oxygen can be administered (ski patrollers usually keep oxygen tanks handy).

Giardia

Giardia, or giardiasis, is an infection of the small intestine caused by the single-celled parasite *Giardia lamblia.* Giardia is spread by direct personal contact with another's stool or by contaminated food or water; the latter should be of particular concern to hikers and backpackers. In remote high-country areas, clear-running stream water can be contaminated by wild animals carrying the parasite.

Symptoms of giardia usually begin one to three days after the parasite has entered the system and include violent diarrhea, gas, cramps, loss of appetite, and nausea. To avoid contracting giardia, always wash your hands before handling food, and *do not* drink stream or lake water without first boiling or purifying it. Purifying with either iodine (in liquid, tablet, or crystal form) or with a .1 micron water filter is sufficient. If using a powdered drink mix to cover the taste of iodine, wait to add it until after the allotted treatment time, as the ascorbic acid (vitamin C) can interfere with the purification process. Check sporting goods stores and mountaineering shops for water-purification kits.

Hypothermia

Hypothermia, usually caused by prolonged exposure to cold, occurs when body temperature drops below 95°F. At that point, the body is unable to generate enough warmth to sustain itself. Elderly people and children are most prone to the condition, which is characterized by a slowed heart rate, puffiness, pale skin, lethargy, and confusion. In severe cases, breathing is also slow. Taking the proper precautions can go a long way toward prevention; wear warm clothing, including gloves and a hat, eat high-carbohydrate foods often, and drink plenty of fluids.

Hypothermia requires immediate medical attention, and victims are often treated in intensive-care units of hospitals and warmed under controlled conditions. While awaiting medical assistance, move the victim to a warm place, remove wet clothing, and replace it with a warm blanket; have another person join and hold the victim beneath the blanket and, if possible, give the victim something warm (not hot) to drink. *Do not* let the victim walk, do not rub the skin or apply direct heat, and do not give the victim alcohol.

ON THE ROAD

CRIME AND PUBLIC SAFETY

In previous editions of this book, I've felt a responsibility to include information on crime and public safety. I've talked at length with police officers in major cities, asking them to recommend ways travelers can avoid being victims of crime. Their answers have been pretty standard and shouldn't surprise veterans of the road: don't leave valuables in motel or hotel rooms or in plain sight

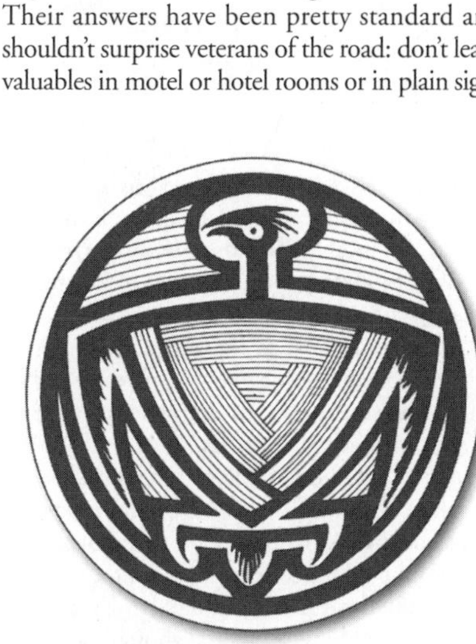

BOB RACE

A NEW MEXICO QUIZ

How much do you know about New Mexico? Are you a *novicio* or *experto,* Tucumcari tenderfoot or Mesilla master? Answers to all of the following questions can be found in *Moon Handbooks New Mexico;* the answers to the quiz appear at the end of the North-Central New Mexico chapter.

History

1) When did the first humans appear in New Mexico, and who were they?
2) From what language do we get the word "Anasazi," and what does it mean?
3) When did the Anasazi "disappear"? Why? Where did they go?
4) What's a kiva?
5) What's unique about Mimbres pottery?
6) When did the Spanish first arrive in New Mexico? What were they looking for?
7) When was Santa Fe founded?
8) What was the Pueblo Revolt?
9) How long was New Mexico under Mexican rule?
10) What was the Long Walk?
11) When was Fort Union built and what was its primary purpose?
12) When was New Mexico admitted to the Union?
13) When and where was the world's first atomic bomb detonated?

Geography and Geology

14) Of the 50 U.S. states, where does New Mexico rank in size?
15) Where are New Mexico's highest and lowest points, and what are their elevations?
16) Where are the Sandia Mountains? What's their highest point?
17) Where are the headwaters of the Rio Grande?
18) What are the names of New Mexico's two deserts?

on car seats; park and walk in well-lighted areas; travel with companions, especially if you're a woman; ask local hotel and motel employees for the safest route to your restaurant; report suspicious activity—in short use common sense.

Pretty decent advice, I always thought. And pretty responsible of me to have my readers' safety in mind and to try to help them navigate sometimes-seedy urban areas.

But recently, while exploring the stark beauty of Colorado's Four Corners area, alone on a gorgeous summer-stormy day on a remote bluff overlooking McPhee Reservoir near Cortez, I was assaulted myself. Fortunately, it wasn't as bad as it could have been, and though rattled, I was really none the worse for wear.

It was, however, a heck of a wake-up call, and it got me wondering to what degree the rise in the national crime rate was reflected in the country's wilderness areas. So when I got back to California, I phoned a half dozen or so Forest Service representatives, trying to get a feel for the rise in crime, if any, on public lands. Most agreed that crime was up, but they were understandably vague in their answers. "Lots of theft from parked cars," one told me. "Don't leave valuables inside." Another told me boaters at McPhee should make sure to lock up their boats, and to keep an eye on them at night; boats have been stolen from their moorings, only to turn up several days later in another arm of the lake.

19) After which U.S. presidents are New Mexico counties named?

People

20) How many people live in New Mexico, and what portion live in Albuquerque?
21) How many Indian pueblos are within the state's borders?
22) How many distinct languages occur within the pueblo tribes?
23) Who was New Mexico's most famous outlaw? Who killed him? (Bonus: Who played them in the Sam Peckinpah film?)
24) Who was almost single-handedly responsible for the 20th-century revival of Pueblo pottery?
25) Who is the author of well-known mystery novels that take place on Zuñi and Navajo Reservations?
26) What famous British author lived in Taos in the 1920s?
27) Who was New Mexico's most famous artist, and where did he or she live?
28) In what hotel can you find the Ronald Reagan Room?

Tourism and Recreation

29) Where are the state's largest concentrations of museums?
30) Where's the best place to scuba dive in New Mexico?
31) Where are you most likely to bump into Madame Butterfly?
32) What is the state's most famous underground attraction?
33) What is the major agricultural industry of Portales?
34) What is unique about Acoma Pueblo?
35) Where is the Atomic Energy Museum?
36) What is New Mexico's state bird?
37) Where are New Mexico's best chile peppers grown, and when is the best time of the year to buy them?

But is crime on public lands actually increasing? Yes, according to Debra Shore in an article in *Outside* magazine. In fact, Shore says crime on public property doubled in the first half of the 1990s, and indications are that the increase will continue. Why? In part, it's simply because of the larger numbers of visitors to these areas. But it's also a result of federal-level budget cuts, which in turn means less law enforcement. According to Shore, the country's national parks alone attracted more than 273 million visitors in 1994, up nearly 70 million from the mid-1980s. Yet there are 39 fewer law-enforcement officers. A total of 541 million acres (national park and forest, plus BLM land) is patrolled by 3,600 officers, or, as Shore points out, "about one officer for every 150,000 acres." By the late 1990s, the country's national parks were attracting nearly 300 million visitors a year. The number continues to rise while law enforcement decreases.

In the article, Shore singled out 16 national parks, forests, monuments, and recreation areas where crime was high enough to merit extraordinary caution. Among them: Joshua Tree National Monument (California), Lake Mead National Recreation Area (Nevada), Daniel Boone National Forest (Kentucky), and Big Bend National Park (Texas). The crimes? Murder, drug trafficking, sexual assault, and theft, as well as less-serious offenses such as fighting (over the harvesting of extremely valuable mushrooms in Oregon's Deschutes National Forest, for example) and the general mischief (bottle throwing, destruction of public property) of rowdy drunks who are all of 16.

And what about assault, particularly sexual assault? How often does it happen, and nearly happen? How many assaults are not reported and thus can't be factored into the equations? I'm not sure. And I don't think there's any way to find out. I do know this, though: my own private wilderness is no longer what it once was. I will be more cautious on public land, less likely to travel alone. And, sadly, I will raise my two daughters to think of the wilderness not only as a refuge *from* the dark side of humanity, but also a potential refuge *for* it.

The price, as William Blake would say, of experience.

Communication and Information

A good rule of thumb for all travelers is to communicate. That is, let folks know where you're going and when you expect to be back. If you're heading into remote areas, it's especially important to let someone know your intended route and schedule so if you don't return on time they can come looking for you or at least report you missing. If you don't have friends or relatives to keep apprised of your travels, let someone at your lodge, hotel, or bed-and-breakfast know your plans. And if you're heading out into the backcountry, be sure to stop in at the nearest ranger station; most have forms or books specifically intended to keep track of visitors.

Important Phone Numbers

Dial 911 in emergencies. A dispatcher will send police, an ambulance, or a fire truck.

All of New Mexico is in the **505 area code,** and from out of state this prefix should be dialed. (As of press time, there was talk of adding area code 575; if and when such a change occurs, callers will be informed via recorded message when they dial area code 505.) To reach the main office of the New Mexico **State Police,** dial 505/827-9000. For information about **road and weather conditions,** phone 505/827-9300.

For information about camping, fishing, and hunting on the Navajo Indian Reservation, write **Navajo Fish and Wildlife Department,** P.O. Box 1480, Window Rock, AZ 86515, or phone 602/871-5338. The number for the **Jicarilla Apache Tourism Office** is 505/759-3255, and for the **Mescalero Apache** it's 505/671-4494.

For information, brochures, and maps of New Mexico, phone the New Mexico **Tourism and Travel Division** of the Economic Development and Tourism Department at 505/827-0291 or 800/545-2040.

Northwestern New Mexico

Introduction

Soft red-rock cliffs and canyons, mesas rising dramatically from valley floors, desolate badlands where dinosaurs once roamed, massive lava flows, Anasazi ruins, Navajo cowboys, sheepherders, and silversmiths—northwestern New Mexico seems at times surreal, like a Sam Shepard play with a Salvador Dali set. Drive through in the late afternoon—when the desert sun plays tricks with the eye, distorting canyon walls and making mesas float on far horizons, when a storm appears from nowhere and sudden cracks of thunder and bolts of lightning unnerve the sky and a torrential rain turns roads to rivers—and you'll understand why the land is sacred to the Indians and has been for nearly 2,000 years.

The first signs of human habitation in the area are grinding stones, spear points, and atlatls from the Early Basketmaker Period (A.D. 1–450). Anthropologists know little about these early Anasazi, as they apparently had no pottery, and much of their basketry didn't survive the harsh desert elements. By around 450, though, the Indians were beginning to experiment with pottery, had moved out of caves, and were constructing crude round pit houses. Between 750 and 1100, the Developmental Pueblo Period, the Anasazi were building the great villages for which they are so well known. Although they no longer occupied the pit houses, they retained their early homes' round shape for their kivas, the partially buried ceremonial chambers that symbolized the womb of Mother Earth. Each pueblo had at least one kiva, and some of the larger ones had as many as half a dozen.

The 12th century saw a tremendous growth in the sophistication of the Anasazi pueblos. The masonry and reinforcement of the walls and ceilings were improved,

© STEPHEN METZGER

The San Juan River offers boating, fishing, and swimming in otherwise arid country.

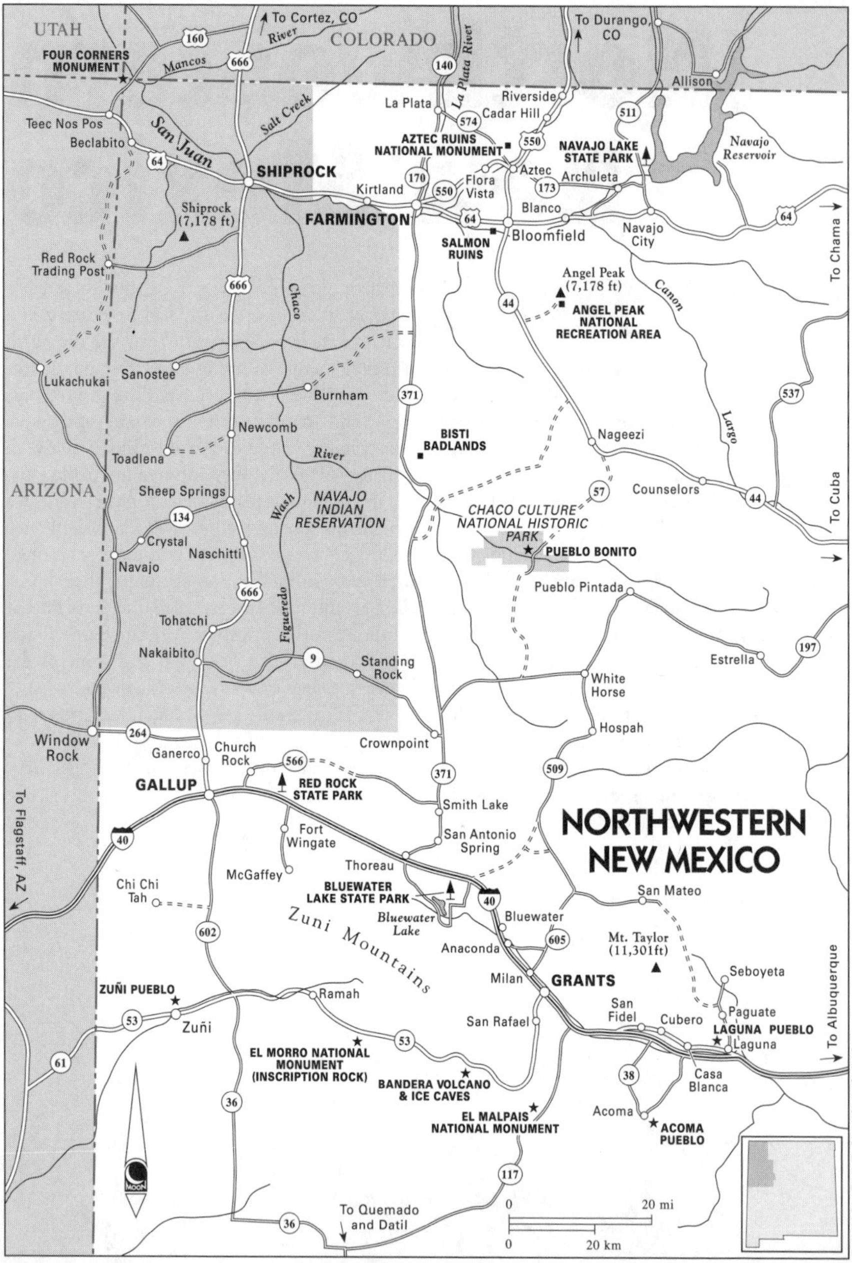

NORTHWESTERN NM

HIGHLIGHTS

Acoma Pueblo: tours of mesa-top pueblo; also museum and shopping

Aztec Ruins: outlier of Chaco Canyon civilization; only completely reconstructed Great Kiva in the country

Chaco Canyon: camping, hiking, sight-seeing at ruins of ancient Anasazi "city"

El Malpais National Monument: ancient lava flow

El Morro National Monument: sight-seeing and hiking at Inscription Rock and site of ancient pueblo

Inter-tribal Ceremonial (Gallup): Indian festival with rodeos, art and jewelry displays, and a parade

Navajo Lake State Park: fishing, camping, boating, and swimming

Navajo Reservation: country's largest Indian reservation—sight-seeing and shopping

Shiprock: bizarre basalt rock formation, central to Navajo mythology

Zuñi Pueblo: sight-seeing and shopping

allowing later pueblos to reach as high as four stories, with hundreds of rooms housing perhaps as many as 5,000 people. The center of the late 12th-century culture was at Chaco Canyon, but thousands of "outlier" pueblos, smaller villages connected to Chaco and each other by trade routes, dotted the Colorado Plateau of northwestern New Mexico.

Around 1200, the Anasazi began to abandon their pueblos. Though many of the structures were occupied again later—by Mesa Verdeans, for example, who came down from southern Colorado—the great Chacoan Anasazi civilization left its homes, and culture, behind. Most likely, these were the ancestors of modern Pueblo Indians, including the Zuñi, Acoma, and others scattered throughout the Rio Grande Valley.

Probably around 1450, Athapascan tribes began to filter into New Mexico from the north: they would divide eventually into two groups, the Apaches and the Navajos. The Apaches comprised several different bands, and most of them continued southward, eventually settling in the areas around present-day Silver City and Ruidoso. The Navajos, however, remained in northwestern New Mexico and northern Arizona.

When the Spanish arrived in northwestern New Mexico in 1540, they found not the great cities of gold they'd heard about, but various groups of Pueblo Indians living for the most part peacefully among themselves. Coronado and his soldiers and missionaries invaded Zuñi Pueblo in midsummer of that year, quickly subdued the inhabitants, and camped at the pueblo for six months while they explored the countryside.

In 1598, Oñate's colonizing party also marched through northwestern New Mexico and in 1599 battled the Indians at Acoma Pueblo. In 1605, on his return from the Gulf of California, Oñate passed by Inscription Rock (at what is today El Morro National Monument) and carved a record of his visit.

From the early 17th century until the late 19th, Indians resisted the settling of their territory—some more aggressively than others. The Navajos, particularly, fought to protect their land and in 1864 were finally defeated. That spring, 3,000 of the remaining Indians—weakened and bedraggled—were rounded up and forced to walk the 300 miles from Fort Wingate, near Gallup, to Fort Sumner.

Today, the Navajo tribe is the largest in the country. Though plagued with the problems—particularly alcoholism and unemployment—typical of a people whose land, pride, and spirit have been exploited and stolen, the Navajos remain strong. They maintain a number of energy and irrigation projects in the Farmington area and in Gallup sell their exquisite jewelry and fine rugs and blankets to tourists passing through on I-40.

Unfortunately, I-40 is all many travelers see of this part of New Mexico. They jam from Flagstaff to Albuquerque, and then maybe turn north toward Santa Fe or Taos, and never take time to explore this northwestern corner. Their loss, I guess. But still, when you see country such as that around Aztec, the lush San Juan River

Basin, and the fingery blue inlets of Navajo Lake, when you wander the ancient Anasazi cities of Chaco Canyon, when your breath is taken away by the mystically floating Shiprock, a basalt monolith sacred to the Navajo, you'll be glad you followed the road less taken.

Gallup

Interstate 40 cuts a meandering swath across the United States from Southern California to North Carolina. Through the Southwest, I-40 follows the old Route 66, a highway deeply ingrained into the American psyche—John Steinbeck's and the Joads' "Mother Road," a favorite of song-writers from Will Rogers to Merle Haggard, and, if you recall from the mid-'60s, the best place around to "get your kicks." Though I-40 is in many places miles from the old route, as well as from many of the small towns and businesses that had depended for years on passers-through

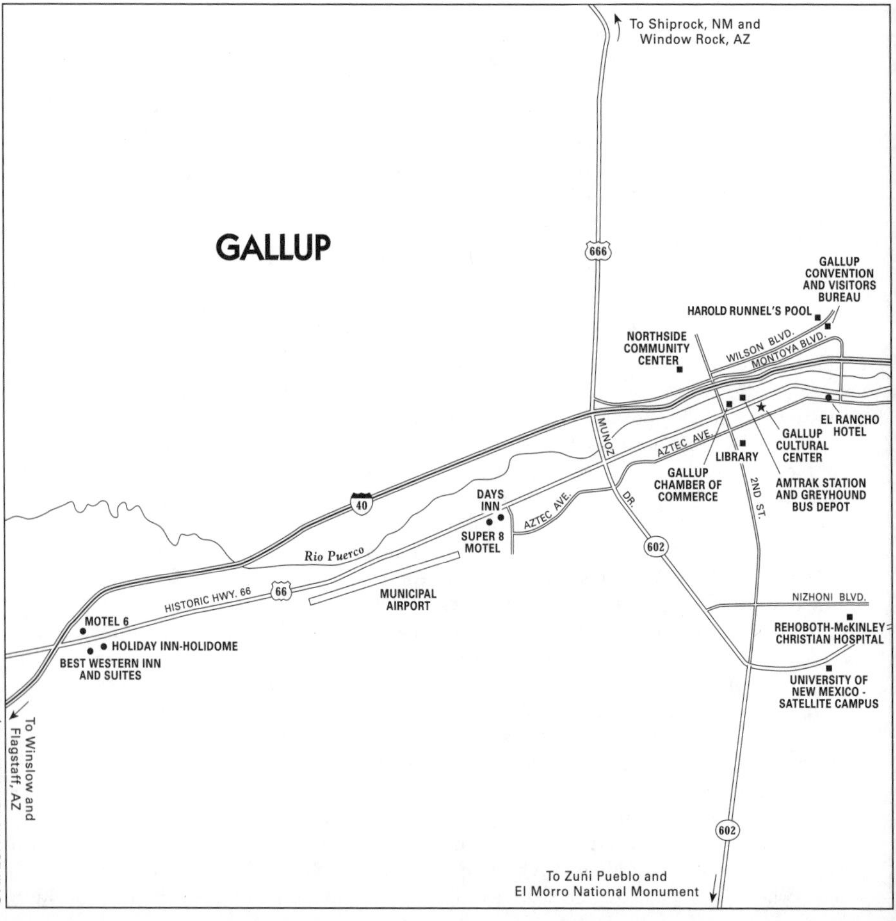

for their very existence—and though the Burma-Shave billboards and Phillips 66 signs are long gone—this road is still a classic American artery, with a character and soul all its own.

The Border to Gallup

As you cross the border from Arizona, you'll be struck by two things: the gorgeous, soft red rock of the Rio Puerco and the scores of bright yellow billboards advertising cigarettes and Indian jewelry—all "At Least 50% off!" Welcome to New Mexico. Actually, your first glimpse of the state here is quite appropriate.

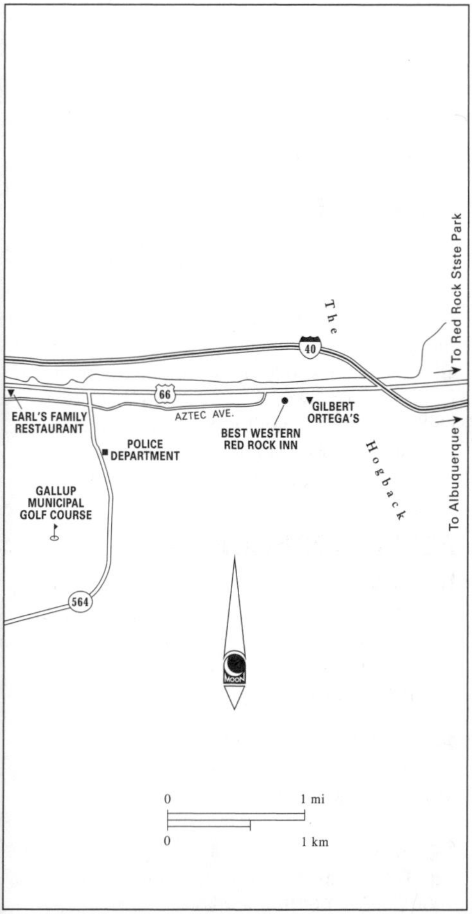

This 25-mile stretch between the Arizona border and Gallup is a sort of microcosm of much of the rest of New Mexico: hauntingly beautiful mesas and plains, leather-skinned Navajo cowboys in old Chevy pickups, an endless and breathtaking big sky, and the tacky entreaties for the tourist dollar.

Gateway to Indian Country

Billing itself as the "Gateway to Indian Country," Gallup (pop. 19,200) is a bustling trade center for Navajo and Pueblo Indians, as well as for tourists passing through northern New Mexico on I-40. The main drag through town—old Route 66—is marked by miles and miles of economy motels (rooms starting at around $25 a night), high-profile Indian gift emporiums, and pawnshops with barred and dirty windows.

Relying largely on tourism for its survival, Gallup is famous throughout the world for its annual Inter-tribal Ceremonial, for which Native Americans from around the country come to show and sell their wares and to take part in the various rodeos and parades. Situated about midway between the borders of the massive Navajo Reservation to the north and smaller Zuñi Reservation and Pueblo to the south, this really is the heart of Indian country. And if the landscape tugs a bit on some vague memory and seems somehow familiar, if you imagine Indians appearing over a distant hill, chances are you *have* seen it before: through the years, the area has been a favorite of Hollywood directors, who've filmed dozens of Westerns here, with the black-hatted, the white-hatted, and the headdressed exchanging bullets and arrows in the bouldery red-rock canyons.

So even though the inevitable tourist schlock does sometimes invade the hardened land and seductive mood of Gallup, rest assured that a stop here is as decent an introduction to New Mexico as you're going to get.

History

Gallup was nothing more than a one-saloon stop on the Westward Overland Stage until 1879, when the Atchison, Topeka, & Santa Fe Railroad came close to the area and opened it up for coal exploration. The town was officially founded that year, and builders pushed the railroad through to town in 1881. Coal, found in large deposits in the area, attracted settlers to Gallup, and the town was incorporated in 1891; it was designated the seat of the newly formed McKinley County in 1901. In the early part of the 20th century, Gallup was a hub of Navajo wool and piñon-nut trading.

The area continued to be a major supplier of coal well into midcentury, and the work in the mines attracted immigrants from throughout Europe. After World War II, though, when oil replaced coal as the country's major heat and energy source, Gallup's mines were closed.

SIGHTS

Red Rock State Park

From 1922 until 1978, the Inter-tribal Ceremonial took place in Gallup proper; in 1979, the festivities were moved to nearby Red Rock State Park (three miles east of Gallup on I-40). This hauntingly austere sandstone park features towering red cliffs eroded by centuries of wind and rain to soft and gently curving mounds uplifted from the grassy desert floor. Anasazi archaeological sites (dating A.D. 300–1200), including several petroglyphs and pictographs, dot the 640-acre park. A small **museum** (admission free; $1 donation appreciated) features displays of the area's history, the pottery—both ancient and modern—of local Indians, a large collection of kachina dolls, Hopi baskets, Apache masks and clothing, tack and saddles from previous Ceremonials, and paintings by former Gallup resident Lloyd Moylan, who took part in the WPA's Federal Art Project and depicted in his oils all the beauty that is the Southwest: the Indians, the landscape, and the sky.

Red Rock State Park has both a large arena for rodeos and a smaller amphitheater for Indian dancing. Dances are nightly Memorial Day through Labor Day (admission $4, free for kids under five). Those wishing to stay right at Red Rock can set up tents or hook up motorhomes at the park's campground (tent sites go for $8, hookups $12–16). A small general store and post office are in the historic Outlaw Trading Post, built in 1888. Horses may be boarded at the park's stables.

Red Rock State Park is open year-round, and the museum is open Monday–Friday 8:30 A.M.–4:30 P.M. (summer hours may vary; call ahead). For more information, contact Red Rock State Park, P.O. Box 10, Church Rock, NM 87311, 505/722-3829.

Gallup Cultural Center

This small, recently opened center focuses on the history and prehistory of the Gallup area, including exhibits highlighting Native American contributions and the development of the railroad—appropriate given that the center is in the restored Atchison, Topeka, & Santa Fe Railroad Station (1927). You'll also find a small theater, showing instruction videos, and a café. The center is at 201 E. Hwy. 66, and admission is free. Open daily Memorial Day through Labor Day 9 A.M.–9 P.M., closing at 6 P.M. the rest of the year. Call 505/572-7534 for more information.

University of New Mexico

Roughly 1,500 students attend the Gallup campus of the University of New Mexico, which offers the first two years of UNM's coursework (degrees are not given, and students must finish their work at the Albuquerque campus). Courses in the Navajo language are among those offered. Take a drive up to the campus, high on a bluff above town. The view of downtown Gallup, the east-west ribbon of I-40, and the surrounding area will help you get your bearings.

ACCOMMODATIONS

Under $50

You'll find plenty of small mom-and-pop and franchise motels in Gallup in this price range, in large part because of the numbers of truckers who pass through looking for some no-frills shuteye. Chain lodging in Gallup includes a **Days Inn,** 1603 W. Hwy. 66, 505/863-3891; **Super 8 Motel,** 1715 W. Hwy. 66, 505/722-5300; and **Motel 6,** 3306 W. Hwy. 66, 505/863-4492.

$50–100

The **El Rancho Hotel** in downtown Gallup, 1000 E. Hwy. 66 (Business Loop 40), 505/863-

9311 or 800/543-6351, is one of the most colorful lodges in the Southwest. Built in 1937 by R. E. Griffith, brother of film director D. W. Griffith, the hotel, billed as "the World's Largest Ranch House," quickly became a home away from home for Hollywood celebrities working on the many movies filmed in the area—among them *Texas Rangers, The Hallelujah Trail, The Big Carnival, The Streets of Laredo,* and *Colorado Territory.* Remodeled in 1988 by local jewelry entrepreneur Armand Ortega, the El Rancho is a classic example of sprawling Southwestern architecture, its high-ceilinged lobby decorated with huge chairs and couches with colorful wool covers, a monstrous stone fireplace, and beautiful Navajo rugs over a heavy-tiled floor. A stairway—itself looking like something out of *High Chaparral* or *Johnny Guitar*—leads to the second floor, where the walls of a railed balcony are adorned with signed black-and-white glossies of the stars who've stayed there: Wallace Beery, Jimmy Stewart, Kirk Douglas, Henry Fonda, Mae West, Lee Marvin, and James Cagney, to name a few.

Although the 110 rooms at the El Rancho are numbered, they're better known by the names of the people who've bedded down in them. You can stay in the W. C. Fields Room, the Marx Brothers Room, the Katharine Hepburn Room, even the Ronald Reagan Room.

Among the franchise inns in this price range are the **Red Rock Inn Best Western,** 3010 E. Hwy. 66, 505/722-7600; **Best Western Inn and Suites,** 3009 W. Hwy. 66, 505/722-2221; and the **Holiday Inn-Holidome,** 2915 W. Hwy. 66, 505/722-2201.

For RVers, a **KOA** campground is just west of town on Highway 66, 505/863-5021. Sites with hookups run about $20. Camping is also available at **Red Rock State Park** three miles east of town on I-40, 505/722-6196. Primitive sites are $8, and RV sites with hookups are $12–16.

MORE PRACTICALITIES

Food

In addition to the glut of fast-food chains represented in Gallup, mostly on Highway 66 through town, there are a handful of classic small-town, lower-profile places by which locals swear and that have been attracting passers-through for decades. A favorite is **Earl's Family Restaurant,** 1400 E. Hwy. 66, 505/863-4201. Here you can get good American food—chicken, ribs, etc.—as well as excellent New Mexican food, including green-chile stew, in a casual, down-home atmosphere. Lunches run $5–10 and dinners $6–13. Open daily.

The **El Rancho Restaurant** in the El Rancho Hotel, 505/863-9311, also serves good down-home meals at reasonable prices. Traditional American breakfasts are served daily 6–11 A.M. and start at $3 for hotcakes and go to about $9 for steak and eggs. For a taste of the regional cuisine, try the breakfast taco or a Navajo taco. In addition to the everyday selections of steaks, seafood, and barbecued pork, beef, and chicken, El Rancho offers daily specials, highly recommended, especially if they're New Mexican. Expect to pay $6–8 for sandwiches and specials, $10–15 for dinner plates. The restaurant is open daily till 10 P.M.

For more traditional, steak-and-seafood fare, try the **New Mexico Steakhouse,** in the Best Western Inn and Suites, 3009 W. Hwy. 66, 505/722-2221. Entrées will run you $8–20. Open daily for dinner.

Shopping

Approaching Gallup, you're assaulted by the scores of billboards offering "incredible" deals on Indian crafts and jewelry; most claim at least 50 percent discounts. Though the majority of the shops are legitimate, comparison shopping will usually save you money. You can also buy from individual artists and salespeople, although the Federal Trade Commission and the Gallup Chamber of Commerce recommend dealing only with reputable dealers (the chamber has a complete listing) and insisting on a certificate of authenticity. The gift shop in the **El Rancho Hotel,** 1000 E. Hwy. 66, offers exquisite local wares, including jewelry, rugs, and paintings. Also check out **Gilbert Ortega's,** 3306 E. Hwy. 66; 505/722-6666, a popular and long-standing shop. You'll also find good deals on Native American wares in Window Rock (Arizona), about 23 miles northwest of Gallup (take Highway 666 north and watch for the turnoff to Window Rock).

For other shopping needs, JCPenney, Wal-Mart, Sprouse-Reitz, and Safeway all have stores in Gallup on West Highway 66.

Recreation

Golfers can drive on over to 700 Old Zuñi Rd. to the **Gallup Municipal Golf Course,** 505/863-9224. Two community swimming pools—the **Northside Community Center** pool and **Runnells**—keep Gallupians and passers-through from wilting in the often harsh summer heat.

Annual Events

In 1922, a small group of Gallup businessmen organized a handful of local Indians and invited them to dance and show their crafts at an exhibit at the McKinley County Fair. Today, the annual **Inter-tribal Ceremonial,** which Will Rogers once called "The Greatest American Show," is still going strong. In fact, it's Gallup's main tourist attraction, with Navajo, Zuñi Pueblo, Hopi, Crow, Kiowa, Comanche, and Cheyenne people among the thousands from throughout the West who come to Gallup to dance, compete in crafts shows, and take part in the rodeo. During the Ceremonial, which traditionally runs four days in early- to mid-August, Gallup is packed with In-

COURTESY OF NEW MEXICO DEPARTMENT OF TOURISM/GARY ROMERO

the annual Inter-tribal Ceremonial

dians—both Ceremonial participants and spectators—and tourists, who browse the crafts displays by day and whoop it up at the rodeo by night. Saturday morning's parade attracts as many as 25,000 to the streets of Gallup. Note: Every bed and floor space in Gallup is spoken for long before the Ceremonial. Make reservations early, at least by June.

The annual Intertribal Ceremonial is Gallup's main tourist attraction, with Navajo, Zuñi Pueblo, Hopi, Crow, Kiowa, Comanche, and Cheyenne people among the thousands from throughout the West who come to Gallup to dance, compete in crafts shows, and take part in the rodeo.

As an adjunct to the Inter-tribal Ceremonial, the Gallup Chamber of Commerce, Red Rock State Park, and the Ceremonial Association present **Indian dances** every night of the summer, Memorial Day through Labor Day, downtown at the Amtrak depot. Among the dances performed: the Eagle, Rainbow, and Buffalo Dances. (Note: Only certain "social" dances can be performed for the public. A great many other dances can be done only within a religious context and are not for the eyes of outsiders.) The nightly dancing begins about 7:30, and admission is free. Phone 505/863-4131 or 800/242-4282 for more information.

Gallup attracts thousands of visitors each year to its Lions Club–sponsored rodeo, the **Western Jubilee Week/Red Rock Rodeo,** held the third weekend in June. The festivities include a parade downtown and a rodeo out at Red Rock State Park. The rodeo, which draws some of the best riders in the Southwest to compete for $40,000 in prize money, includes a special "kids' rodeo," an old-timers' roping competition, a parade, country music and Indian dances, and the selection of the obligatory rodeo queen. Profits from Western Jubilee Week go to various charities, including scholarships, health projects, and youth activities. Small admission price for adults and children six to 12. Phone 505/722-3829 for more information.

The Gallup **Film Festival** is held every October and focuses on the films and filmmakers that have paid tribute to the Southwest on the silver screen. The four-day festival often includes appearances by some of the producers and directors of the festival's featured films. In addition to the "classics" (*Lonely Are the Brave,* for example, with Kirk Douglas, filmed in Albuquerque and the Sandia Mountains), the festival also screens documentaries on migrant farmworkers and Native Americans.

Every winter (usually in early December), Gallup sponsors the **Red Rock Balloon Rally** at Red Rock State Park. More than 100 balloons compete in races and demonstrations of navigational skills. Winners are awarded Indian jewelry and sandpaintings. Spectators are advised to wear warm clothes. More information is available at 505/722-3829.

Phone the Gallup Convention and Visitors Bureau at 800/242-4282 for information on these and other regular Gallup-area events.

Information and Services

The **Gallup Convention and Visitors Bureau** is on the north side of town at 701 Montoya. Phone the bureau at 505/863-3841 or 800/242-4282, or write P.O. Box 600, Gallup, NM 87305, to have information on Gallup sent to you. You can also get information, and order a visitor packet, from the bureau's website: www.gallupnm.org. The bureau-affiliated Indian Country Council also is a good source of information, particularly for Native Americana throughout northwestern New Mexico. Visit the website: www.indiancountrynm.org.

The **Gallup Chamber of Commerce** also has a small visitors center right downtown next to the Amtrak station. Stop in and pick up a copy of *The Indian Trader* for stories on historic Gallup traders, profiles of contemporary artists, listings of current events, and directories of trading posts and galleries; it's published monthly. There's also a small room with displays dedicated to Navajo Code Talkers, Navajos who used their native language to help secure

American intelligence during World War II. The **Gallup Public Library** is at 115 W. Hill Ave., 505/863-3692.

Rehoboth-McKinley Christian Hospital is at 901 Red Rock Dr., 505/863-6832. Phone the Gallup Police Department at 505/722-2231 and the state police in Gallup at 505/863-9353.

Transportation

If you're flying in, **Mesa Air,** 800/MESA-AIR (800/637-2247), has passenger service to Gallup from Albuquerque and Phoenix. The **Amtrak** station is at 201 E. Hwy. 66, 505/863-3244. The **Greyhound** bus depot is at 105 S. Dean, 505/863-3761.

Driving and Public Safety

For years Gallup had the dubious distinction of being nicknamed "Drunk City." Its alcohol-related death rate was five times the national average, and until the early 1990s, Gallup police were arresting nearly 30,000 drunks annually. Travelers were advised to drive especially carefully in town, and, if possible, to avoid driving altogether on Friday and Saturday nights.

Thankfully, Gallup was well aware of its problem and took steps to deal with it. Specifically, in February of 1989, partially in response to the tragic death of a three-month-old infant in a drunk-driving accident, hundreds of people walked from Gallup to Santa Fe to meet with lawmakers and to lobby for help. Later that year, the county was given $300,000 to fund an alcohol-crisis center; additionally, the county voted to increase the alcohol-excise tax and to close drive-up liquor windows (liquor dealers filed suit, and the windows weren't closed until 1992). In 1991, McKinley County became the first county to lower the driving-under-the-influence level to .08 percent, and in 1992 the Robert Wood Johnson Foundation awarded the Northern New Mexico Council of Governments a $3 million "Fighting Back" grant to mobilize the communities to reduce alcohol abuse. Within months, there was a drop in drunk-driving arrests and alcohol-related fatalities. By 1998, Gallup's alcohol-crisis had become a national model, and that same year, the governor signed a bill closing all the drive-up liquor stores in the state, citing McKinley County's success.

Gallup is still a long way from earning the nickname "Abstinence City," but things have improved dramatically. In 2000, there were only 17,000 arrests for drunkenness, down nearly half from the old days. And the people have planted over 10,000 trees as symbols of the journey they've undertaken and to remind them of how far they still have to go—the trees also serve as a reminder of those who have paid the price along the way.

Vicinity of Gallup

NAVAJO INDIAN RESERVATION

Gallup is just a few miles south of the massive Navajo Reservation (15 million acres, most in Arizona). With a population of about 200,000, the Navajo Nation dwarfs all other tribes in the area. The Navajos are known for their silver and turquoise jewelry, as well as for their rugs, woven from the wool of sheep tended by Navajo sheepherders.

Hubbell Trading Post National Historic Site

Although across the border in Arizona, Hubbell's is worth a visit by those passing through the Gallup area. The oldest continuously operated trading post on the Navajo Reservation, Hubbell's was founded in 1878 by John Lorenzo Hubbell, a New Mexican by birth, who befriended the Navajos after their internment at Fort Sumner. At the visitors center, silversmiths and weavers demonstrate their skills; both scheduled and self-guided free tours are offered. Take Highway 191 north from I-40 at Chambers, Arizona, then Highway 264 one mile west. Open daily 8 A.M.–6 P.M. except holidays. For more information, call 602/755-3475.

I-40 EAST

Fort Wingate

Twelve miles east of Gallup on I-40, this fort today is used primarily as a weapons storage site, although it does boast a far more colorful past. In 1860, Fort Fauntleroy, named for U.S. General Thomas Turner Fauntleroy, was established where Wingate now stands (called Shashbito, or Bear Springs, by the Navajo). When Fauntleroy resigned his commission to join the Confederate Army, it was renamed Fort Lyon, then renamed again in 1866, this time after Captain Benjamin Wingate, a Union soldier killed in one of New Mexico's two major Civil War battles, the Battle of Valverde. After the war, the fort was used as a base for archaeological and ethnological expeditions until 1914, when it sheltered 4,000 Mexican troops fleeing Pancho Villa in northern Mexico. Fort Wingate is not open to the public except on occasion, when special tours are offered.

Bluewater Lake State Park

This is an isolated fishing, boating, sailing, and camping spot about midway between Gallup and Grants. Turn off I-40 at Exit 63 and wind seven miles on Highway 412 up into the piñon-covered bluffs and over the ridge to Bluewater Lake. During the spring, winter (Bluewater Lake is popular for ice fishing), and fall, anglers take some good-sized German brown trout out of Bluewater Lake, and summer produces some catfish the size of P.T. boats. The state park charges a $4 entrance fee and an $8 (per night) camping fee. Sites with hookups are available for $12–16, and restrooms are equipped with hot showers. A kids' playground has a swing set, merry-go-round, and jungle gym.

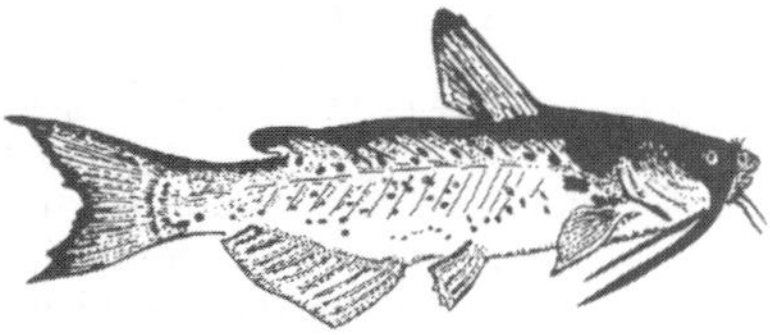

LOUISE FOOTE

Lots of big channel cats like this one lurk in Bluewater Lake.

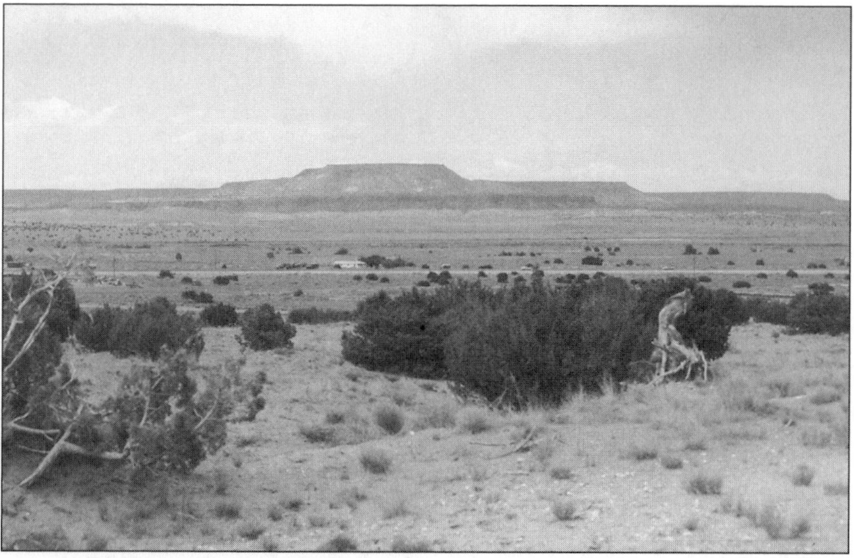

© STEPHEN METZGER

barren Navajo country between Gallup and Grants

NORTHWESTERN NM

HIGHWAY 53 EAST

The back route (via Highway 602 and Highway 53) from Gallup to Grants is a lot longer than the interstate. But if you've got the time (driving without stopping will take you at least twice as long as the one-hour interstate cruise), there are big payoffs. First of all, it's a whole lot prettier. You wind through rolling piñon-covered hills, grassy flatlands (keep your eyes peeled for antelope playing in the distance), and centuries-old lava flows with rock formations that look like something off an early sci-fi film set. In addition, go this way and you're traveling with history: Highway 53, known as the "Ancient Way," follows the old Zuñi-Acoma trade route and was used by Coronado in 1540. Plus, there's a whole lot to do along the way. You could easily spend a full day meandering the back way from Gallup to Grants—stopping to shop for Indian jewelry, to hike through ancient ruins, and to wander through bizarre, almost lunar, lava landscapes.

Zuñi Pueblo

Thirty-four miles south of Gallup on Highway 602 and then 10 miles west on Highway 53, Zuñi is the largest of New Mexico's 19 pueblos (pop. 8,000). The pueblo was built on the ruins of the ancient site of Halona, one of the Seven Golden Cities of Cibola that drew Coronado to the New Mexico area in 1540. Although the Zuñi were under a decree from Spain's King Ferdinand to adopt Roman Catholicism, they continued performing their ceremonial dances. Visitors to Zuñi Pueblo today can view Zuñi dancers adhering to centuries-old rituals, although the full extent of the dances' cultural and social significance is lost to most non-Indians, even those who are students of Native American beliefs and religions. One of the most important and best-known ceremonies is the all-night Shalako dance (which figures in Tony Hillerman's *Dance Hall of the Dead*) in late November or early December. Visitors are prohibited.

The Zuñi are known for their fine needlepoint, inlay, and turquoise jewelry, which you can find for sale on the pueblo often at better prices than in shops in surrounding towns and the major cities. Additionally, the Zuñi people speak a language unrelated to those of the other pueblo tribes; some anthropologists attribute this to the possibility that the Zuñi are the de-

ceremonial Zuñi masks

© DOVER PUBLICATIONS

scendents of the Mimbres people—not the Anasazi—which would make them linguistic descendents as well.

The Zuñi Museum and Heritage Center is open Monday–Friday, 9 A.M.–5 P.M.; phone 505/782-4403 for information on the museum or visiting the pueblo. You can also arrange private tours of the pueblo and artists' studios at the center.

Our Lady of Guadalupe Mission was originally built by the Spanish in 1629, destroyed in the Pueblo Revolt of 1680, rebuilt, then destroyed again in the mid-17th century, and finally rebuilt again in 1969.

Visitors to the pueblo can buy Zuñi jewelry and pottery at a number of small stores in the center of town, including the **Shiwi Trading Post,** open daily 9 A.M.–7 P.M., as well as at the tribe-owned **Pueblo of Zuñi Arts and Crafts** (phone 505/782-5531 for information and hours of operation). Zuñi silver is exceptional, and the jewelry is typically of silver, turquoise, mother-of-pearl, and coral. The pottery is characteristically white or light-colored and adorned with a highly stylized bird, plant, or deer.

For a nominal fee, you can buy a permit to take photographs. At Zuñi, as at all pueblos, obey the local rules and laws and respect the people who make them.

Lodging is available at the pueblo at **The Inn at Halona,** 23 Pia Mesa Rd., 800/752-3278, website: www.halona.com. The eight rooms run $50–100, breakfast included.

El Morro National Monument

El Morro (Spanish for The Bluff or The Headland) has been a customary stop for passers-through since prehistoric times, when Indians carved petroglyphs in the huge cliffs. The first "modern" inscription was left in 1605, when Don Juan de Oñate carved into the sandstone a record of his visit, translated as:

> ***Passed by here the Adelentado Don Juan de Oñate from the discovery of the Sea of the South [the Gulf of California], the 16th of April, 1605.***

Through the centuries, countless other visitors carved their names and messages in the sandstone, and El Morro became known as much for its inscriptions, the majority of which are from the 18th and 19th centuries, as for its natural beauty. (Of course, federal law and common courtesy prohibit inscribing or carving of any kind by modern visitors.) Atop El Morro is a partially excavated Anasazi pueblo, abandoned long before the Spanish arrived. Allow a couple of hours to wander from the museum in the visitors center along the foot of the cliff where the inscriptions are, then up to the ruins on the mesa. Along the way, you'll find the views spectacular—not only of the distant mesas and mountains, but of the fields of wildflowers: Rocky Mountain beeplants (which the Navajo use for salad greens), Colorado four o'clocks, and Hooker's evening primroses.

The visitors center (with a museum displaying tools and pottery from the pueblo) is open daily 9 A.M.–7 P.M. Memorial Day through Labor Day, and 9 A.M.–5 P.M. the rest of the year (closed Christmas Day). Trails close an hour earlier. Admission is $3 per person for a seven-day pass. A small campground (small fee for camping mid-May through mid-October) has pit toilets and well water, and the sites are nicely secluded among the juniper trees.

To get to El Morro National Monument, take Highway 53 about 30 miles east from Zuñi or 50 miles west from Grants. (Note: Highway 53 leaves Grants heading south but bends west after about 10 miles.) For more information, write El Morro National Monument, Rt. 2, Box 43, Ramah, NM 87321, or call 505/783-4226.

Bandera Volcanic Crater and Ice Caves

About 20 miles past El Morro, heading east toward Grants, you'll come to the Ice Caves and nearby Bandera Volcanic Crater. Privately owned but open to the public, the cave is in a volcanic chamber, where cool temperatures (31°F) guarantee perpetual ice on the cave floor and in its crevices. The cave was first shown to Coronado by the Zuñis, and in recent history local farmers got all the ice they needed from the cave floor.

A 300-yard trail leads from the parking lot over

the lava—through oak, juniper, and ponderosa—to the 75 steps that descend into the caves.

A real judgment call here: If you need some fresh (and cool!) air, and feel like hiking out over the lava, go ahead. But what you'll see is nothing more than a slab of green (from the algae) ice about 30 feet square on a cave floor. You might be disappointed. In any case, bring a sweater if you plan to linger.

A separate trail—this one 1.5 miles long—leads about halfway up the flank of 5,000-year-old, 450-foot-high Bandera Volcano. Another judgment call: if you've been to Capulin Volcano or spent much time at all exploring New Mexico, there's a risk you'll come away yawning.

Admission to the caves/volcano is $8, slightly less for kids five to 12. For information, phone 888-ICE-CAVE (888/423-2283), or visit the website: icecaves.com.

Grants

In 1950, Paddy Martinez, a Navajo sheepherder from the Grants area, stumbled upon an odd-looking rock. It was yellow. Unlike anything he'd ever seen. Martinez turned the rock over to authorities and in so doing became, in effect, the founding father of the "Uranium Capital of the World."

Grants (pop. 12,000) is a small town on the hillside north of I-40 about halfway between Gallup and Albuquerque. Known more for what it's near than what it is, Grants is a low-key little town, its main drag lined with fast-food franchises and gas stations. Yet it's surrounded by some of the most important and fascinating sights and attractions in New Mexico, including El Morro and El Malpais National Monuments, Acoma Pueblo, Mt. Taylor, and Chaco Culture National Historic Park.

History

The history of Grants dates to 1872, when Don Jesus Blea settled here and called his new home Los Alamitos (The Little Cottonwoods). In 1881, the Grant brothers, from Ontario, Canada, founded a railroad stop here, and the town became known as Grants Camp. Officially named "Grants" in 1935, the town hit boom times in the early 1940s, with the discovery of oil at Hospah field at nearby Ambrosia Lake.

After Paddy Martinez discovered the yellow rock, though, Grants took on a whole new tenor. Anaconda Company, the first among many, opened a huge uranium mine near Grants, the Jackpile Mine, and the town grew by leaps and bounds. Later, as the uranium industry slacked off, so did the local economy, although things picked up again in the 1970s, when the Grants area was the source of half of all uranium oxide mined in the United States.

SIGHTS

New Mexico Mining Museum

This fascinating museum, designed to replicate an underground uranium mine, displays historical mining equipment, dioramas, and local Indian artifacts. Individual tours are self-guiding, and the displays include ore carts, blasting caps and wires, ventilation tubes, vertical passages between levels, and the mine shaft itself. However, groups (15 maximum) can arrange guided tours, on which tour leaders offer firsthand accounts and sometimes anecdotal explanations of the mine and equipment. The museum is at 100 Iron Street. Memorial Day through Labor Day, hours are Monday–Saturday 9 A.M.–6 P.M., Sunday noon–3 P.M. Open the rest of the year Monday–Saturday 9 A.M.–4 P.M. Admission is $3; no charge for kids eight and under. Guided group tours are an additional $10 per group. For more information, call 505/287-4802 or 800/748-2142.

El Malpais National Monument

Serving as a boundary between the Acoma and Zuñi "cultural provinces," El Malpais (The Bad Country or The Badlands) is a broad and windswept land of ancient lava flows, ice caves, and sprawling forests of pine and aspen. Indians from the surrounding pueblos, having long used the land as a religious refuge, most likely find humorous the Spanish moniker "badlands."

Surrounding the 114,000-acre national monument is the 262,000-acre El Malpais National Conservation Area (NCA). Together, the parks encompass a geologically unique landscape. La Ventana (The Window), for example, New Mexico's best-known natural arch, is a wind-sculpted, water-eroded wonder carved out of sand dunes 150 million years ago.

Additionally, two parcels of land (totaling 102,000 acres) within the NCA have been officially designated Wilderness Areas. **West Malpais Wilderness Area** is mostly open prairie and includes "Hole-in-the-Wall," a 6,000-acre *kipuka*—an island of grassland surrounded by lava. Pronghorn can often be seen grazing and romping in the flats. **Cebolla Wilderness Area** is more rugged, with hawks and eagles nesting among the mesas, cliffs, and hills. At the **El Malpais Information Center,** 505/783-4774, 23 miles south of Grants on Highway 53, you can pick up maps and detailed information on hiking, camping, and exploring the monument. Open year-round 8:30 A.M.–4:30 P.M.

PRACTICALITIES

Accommodations

Grants has about two dozen motels and several campgrounds. The most accessible motels are at the east end of the main drag through town (Santa Fe Avenue) at the junction with I-40. Among them are a **Comfort Inn,** 1551 E. Santa Fe Ave., 505/287-8700; a **Holiday Inn Express,** 1496 E. Santa Fe Ave., 505/285-4676; and a **Best Western Inn and Suites,** 1501 E. Santa Fe Ave., 505/287-7901 (all $50–80). The **Motel 6,** Exit 85, 505/285-4607, will run you about $45 for two.

Downtown, you'll find several blocks of small, locally run motels with doubles running $40–60. Among the nicer ones is **Sands Motel,** 112 McArthur (a block north of Santa Fe Avenue), 505/287-2996.

RVing

The **Grants Cibola Sands KOA,** a quarter mile south of Grants on Highway 53, 505/287-4376 or 888/264-5229, has complete hookups, laundry and shower facilities, a grocery store, and a recreation room. RV sites are about $25. Campers and tenters are also welcome. **Lavaland RV Campground,** at the east Grants exit from I-40, 505/287-8665, also has complete hookups and facilities. RV sites and tent sites are about $18. (Note: Lavaland isn't the kind of place where you'd want to set up and stay. More a spot to crash before getting back on the road, this campground is stark and barren and quite close to the constant rattle and hum of the freeway.)

Food

Not surprisingly, Grants is home to more than a few excellent Mexican restaurants. Last time through I had the carne adovada burrito ($5; excellent) at Monte Carlo, 721 W. Santa Fe Ave., 505/287-9250. Open daily 7 a.m.–10 p.m. Another good bet is El Cafecito, 820 E. Santa Fe Ave., 505/285-6229 (open Monday–Friday 7 a.m.–9 p.m., closing at 8 p.m. weekends. A popular lunch and dinner house, La Ventana, 110½ Geis St., 505/287-9393, serves steaks, prime rib, seafood, and Mexican food. Open Monday–Saturday 11 a.m.–2 a.m.

The **New Mexico Steakhouse,** at Best Western Inn and Suites, 1501 E. Santa Fe Ave., 505/287-7901, serves steak, seafood, pastas, and salads, nightly 5 P.M.–9:30 P.M.

You'll also find a McDonald's, Kentucky Fried Chicken, Godfather's Pizza, and other fast-food franchises in Grants.

Recreation

The Grants golf course is at **Zuñi Mountain Country Club,** 505/287-2666, and is open to the public. The Grants **municipal swimming pool** is at 554 E. Washington, 505/287-7927. Call for hours.

Information and Services

The Grants/Cibola **Chamber of Commerce,** 100 N. Iron, 505/287-4802 or 800/748-2142 (at the New Mexico Museum of Mining), is a helpful source for tourists and those considering relocating to the area. The chamber aggressively markets both Grants and nearby Milan, with brochures containing information for tourists as well as for those looking to relocate. Visit its website: www.grants.org. The Grants branch of New Mexico State University offers a variety of classes leading to a two-year associate degree, as well as various classes in personal development. The **Grants Public Library** is at 525 W. High St., 505/287-7927.

Cibola General Hospital, 1212 Bonita Rd., 505/287-4446, has a 24-hour emergency room. The number for the Grants Police Department is 505/287-4404, and the state police can be reached at 505/287-4141.

Transportation

Bus depots for both **Greyhound,** 505/285-6268, and **Trailways,** 505/287-3490, are in downtown Grants at 1801 W. Santa Fe Avenue. There is also a small municipal airport, 505/287-4700, although the closest passenger service (Mesa Air) is in Gallup or Albuquerque.

Vicinity of Grants

ACOMA PUEBLO

About a half-hour drive southeast from Grants, Acoma Pueblo is one of the true wonders of New Mexico, an experience not to be missed. Built on a sandstone mesa rising 357 feet above the plain, as a safeguard against other raiding tribes, Acoma Pueblo was once home to several thousand Indians, although only a few hundred remain on the mountain today. The pueblo was most likely built around the middle of the 12th century and is, with Taos Pueblo, one of the two oldest continually inhabited settlements in the United States.

Coronado first saw Acoma in 1540 and was taken, as is today's visitor, by the pueblo's unique mesa-top location. He wrote:

> ***One of the strangest ever seen, because the city was built on a high rock. The ascent was so difficult that we repented climbing to the top. The houses are three and four stories high. The people are of the same type as those in the province of Cibola [Zuñi] and they have abundant supplies of maize, beans, and turkeys.***

In 1598, most of New Mexico's Pueblo Indians submitted to the Spanish, although they soon became distrustful and attacked the party of Don Juan de Zaldivar, who had come to Acoma for cornmeal. In retaliation, Don Juan de Oñate and 70 of his men attacked and overtook the pueblo; once inside, they murdered 70 Acoma men, throwing their bodies over the cliffside. The young girls of the pueblo were sent to Mexico to be sold as slaves, and the other women, as well as all males between 12 and 25, were kept as servants of the Spanish who stayed in New Mexico. Oñate's soldiers then cut one foot off each Acoma man over the age of 25 and sentenced each to 20 years of forced labor.

Acoma was the last pueblo to surrender to the Spanish after the Pueblo Revolt and Reconquest. In December 1858, the Acoma, along with six other Pueblo tribes, formally applied to the United States government for land rights. Typically, their requests were initially largely ignored, although several years later President Lincoln listened to the ideas and complaints of the tribal representatives and gave each tribe a silver-headed cane, inscribed (the only variation being the pueblo name):

> *A. Lincoln*
> *Prst. U.S.A.*
> *Acoma*
> *1863*

Acoma governors still consider this cane a badge of office and pass it on ceremoniously to their successors each January after elections.

Touring Acoma Pueblo

Tours of Acoma Pueblo begin at the visitors center at the bottom of the mesa, where a van takes small groups to the top. The walking tour, led by an Acoma guide, takes about an hour and wanders the city's ancient streets, past vendors selling jewelry, pottery, frybread, and soda pop, and into the San Estevan del Rey Mission (still in use today) at the top of the hill.

Be sure to have your tour guide point out Enchanted Mesa. This steep-sided mesa across the plain from Acoma is said to be the ancestral home of the Acoma people, who grew crops on the valley floor. According to legend, one day the ancient Acomas were working their fields when a sudden rainstorm washed away the access to the mesa top. A girl and her mother were stranded up top, and instead of staying alone on the mesa and starving, they leapt off the cliff to their deaths.

At the end of the tour, the hardy in your group can take the 10-minute walk back down. It's steep and tough going at times, with steps and handholds carved into the cliffside, but it's a good way to view pre-road travel up the mesa. A museum at the visitors center documents the pueblo's history with examples of ancient pottery and tools. A gift shop sells pottery and jewelry, as well as souvenirs and knickknacks, and Acoma Indians often set up booths in the parking lot to sell their wares. Tours of the pueblo are offered every 30 minutes, daily 8 A.M.–5 P.M. in fall and winter, 8 A.M.–7 P.M. in spring and summer. Cost is $9 for adults and $8 for children. Camera permits are $10.

Acoma is closed to the public July 10–13, the first weekend of October, and Easter weekend.

To get to Acoma Pueblo, take I-40 east from Grants to Exit 96 and follow the road signs. From Albuquerque, take Exit 102.

For more information, write Pueblo of Acoma, Box 309, Acoma Pueblo, NM 87034, or phone 505/552-6604. You can also visit its website: www.puebloofacoma.org.

Annual Events

Acoma celebrates several saint's days with feasts and rooster pulls (see Glossary): San Juan's Day, June 24; St. Peter and Paul's Day, June 29; Santiago's Day, July 25. On September 2, San Estevan's Feast accompanies the Harvest Dance. Christmas festivals are held December 25–28 at San Estevan del Rey Mission Church. Cameras are usually not allowed on special days.

Note

Even given Acoma's published schedule, it's a good idea to double-check before visiting. Call the tribal office at 505/552-6604.

CHACO CULTURE NATIONAL HISTORIC PARK

Chaco Canyon is one of North America's true wonders. Though today nothing more than crumbling ruins in a dry canyon 30 miles from the nearest paved highway, between A.D. 1000 and 1100 Chaco was the social, economic, and religious center of the most complex and sophisticated society north of Mexico. With an intricate network of roads and trading systems connecting to smaller, outlying settlements (called "outliers" by archaeologists), some as far as 100 miles away, Chaco Canyon was home to 13 separate "cities" supporting perhaps as many as 5,000 people.

First seen by non-Indians in 1849 (the Washington Expedition—a military group doing topological surveys), Chaco wasn't seriously excavated until nearly the turn of the 20th century. Richard Wetherill, leader of the Hyde Exploring Expedition, worked at Chaco 1896–1900 and was eventually murdered (under still-mysterious circumstances) near one of the pueblos. In 1907, Chaco Canyon National Monument was established, then given National Historic Park designation in 1980, extending the park to 33 sites outside the canyon.

Although there is some evidence (grinding stones and spear points) that Chaco Canyon was inhabited by Anasazi from the Early Basketmaker Period (A.D. 1–450), it wasn't until the Modified Basketmaker Period (450–750) that the people became firmly rooted in the area and began to build housing structures. By the 500s, Chacoans were constructing pit houses and kivas, as well as the first aboveground storage bins (for the corn they were growing), usually with walls and roofs made from brush and mud. Several of the sites in Chaco Canyon exhibit this kind of architecture.

By the Developmental Pueblo Period (750–1100), the Anasazi of the Chaco area were reaching their full stride. Pit houses had been replaced by communal dwellings—at first simple

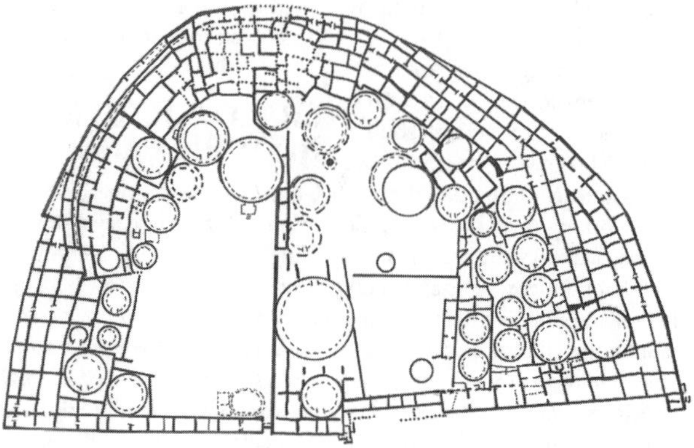

LOUISE FOOTE

an artist's sketch of Pueblo Bonito, once home to a thriving community of Anasazi Indians

single-storied, flat-roofed structures made of rock, mud, and vertical poles. By the end of the period, homes were being built atop each other, the classic black-on-white and distinctly Anasazi pottery was being produced, and cotton textiles had been introduced. All the while, the people continued to grow corn on the valley floors and improve their crude irrigation techniques.

The Classic (or Great) Pueblo Period (1100–1300) saw Chaco blossom not only into a highly sophisticated grouping of pueblos—some four stories high—but also into a booming trade center for the entire Four Corners area, as well as for much of the rest of the Southwest and even down into Mexico. In fact, shells from the Pacific have been found at Chaco, as have remains of birds (scarlet and green macaws) native only to southern Mexico. The architecture of the pueblos themselves has been divided by archaeologists into three different phases: the Bonito, the Hosta Butte, and the McElmo, defined by the shapes and sizes of the structures and by the manner in which the stone and mud were used.

The Bonito Phase saw the construction of enormous pueblos, probably thoroughly preplanned and often shaped like a "D" or "E," surrounding important plazas or courtyards. The Hosta Butte pueblos were typically smaller, apparently haphazardly added onto and built with thinner stones than the Bonito pueblos. Pueblos built in the McElmo style were different still, constructed by relative newcomers to Chaco who had emigrated south to the canyon from the San Juan region. These were larger than the Hosta Butte pueblos but not nearly as huge or sophisticated as the Bonito. They were most often square, multistoried, and built without central plazas.

By 1200, Chaco had been almost completely abandoned. No one knows why such an advanced civilization, evidently faring quite well, would suddenly decide to hit the road, although several theories have been advanced. One holds that since the abandoning of Chaco coincides roughly with the arrival in the Southwest of the Athapascans (Apaches and Navajos) from the north, the Anasazi were driven from Chaco. Recent anthropology tends to discount this, though, in part because without the horse (not brought to the New World until the 16th century) to help in raids and getaways, invaders would have had a difficult time against civilizations as advanced as Chaco. Another common theory has been that a severe drought, which plagued the Southwest in the late 13th century, dried up fields and drove Chaco farmers in search of more fertile land. This, too, has largely been discounted of late: concrete evidence shows that Chaco was abandoned before the drought struck.

Still another theory is that Chaco was an outpost of Mexico's Toltec Empire, which fell at the same time Chaco did. If that was the case, Chaco was abandoned not because the canyon itself failed to be fruitful but because the people could no longer rely on trade from the south.

Finally, recent archaeology suggests that Chaco might have been abandoned because of a combination of lack of human foresight and environmental wrath: Chaco's valley floor is actually quite small, barely seven miles from one end to the other. It's quite possible the land was becoming farmed out, that torrential rains following short periods of drought (two or three seasons) simply washed arable land away. This, combined with the problems that typically attend a city bursting at the seams—disease, unrest, and internecine hostilities—most likely led to Chaco's downfall; the civilization simply grew up and passed on.

But where'd they go?

As the Anasazi left, they dispersed, living in small groups and ending up in different parts of the Southwest. Possibly the Acoma, Hopi, and Zuñi are all descendants of Chaco Canyon Anasazi. So too, perhaps, are the many Pueblo Indians of the Rio Grande Valley. No one knows for certain. What we do know is that for the most part, the Chacoans left most of their technology in the canyon. The masonry, architecture, and irrigation systems of this sophisticated civilization were never matched by its descendants.

Visiting the Park

Just getting to Chaco can be an adventure. The park is about midway between Grants and Farmington, and whether you come in from the north or the south you've got a good 45-minute dirt-road ride through canyons and cattle fields and along arroyos and mesa-sides before you find yourself on the luxury of the park's pavement (the road in from the north is the better of the two). The nearest town is 60 miles away, and there's no lodging, gas, food, or repair service in the canyon.

Once at the park, you'll find a visitors center with a museum, film-viewing room, and small bookstore. From there a one-way road circles up one side of the canyon and down the other, with parking lots at the various pueblos along the way. Most of the pueblos are short, easy walks—100 yards or so—from the parking lots, although three are off the road and accessible only by two- to five-mile (round-trip) hikes. The most impressive is the famous Pueblo Bonito, which once stood four stories high and contained 600 rooms and 40 kivas. The walk to Pueblo Bonito is one of the shortest and easiest. Also check out New Alto and Pueblo del Arroyo.

Ideally, a visitor would spend days at Chaco, camping and hiking into the various ruins, but plan on a minimum three or four hours in Chaco Canyon to explore the different pueblos and petroglyph sites you can drive to. Also, allow yourself some time to wander around the museum before heading out to the ruins. The pottery, tools, and jewelry from the pueblos, along with the dioramas of the villages, explanations of different pottery and masonry styles, and chronology of excavation, will familiarize you with the culture and prepare you for what you'll see. The 25-minute film *Anasazi,* a dramatization of prehistoric life in the Four Corners area, and the hourlong *Chaco Legacy* are shown regularly throughout the day. *Sundagger,* a film about nearby Fajada Butte and its possible connection to Chaco solstice celebrations, lasts 25 minutes and is shown on request.

Chaco Canyon Visitors Center is open daily 8 A.M.–6 P.M. Memorial Day through Labor Day and 8 A.M.–5 P.M. the rest of the year; the ruins are open sunrise to sunset. Entrance fee is $4, or $8 per carload.

Camping

The National Park Service maintains 47 sites at **Gallo Campground** near Chaco Canyon Visitors Center. Sites are $10 a night, with a seven-night maximum; the campground is usually full by

3 P.M. and is first-come, first-served. No firewood available; flush toilets but no showers. No trailers longer than 30 feet.

Two group campgrounds (accommodating up to 30 people each) are available at Gallo, with notice; phone 505/786-7014.

Getting There

From Gallup or Grants take I-40 to Thoreau (pronounced "threw") and take Highway 371 north. Two miles north of Crownpoint, turn right and follow the signs to the Chaco Canyon turnoff. From there, it's a 20-mile dirt road (allow about another 45 minutes or so) to the park. From Farmington, take Highway 64 east to Bloomfield, then Highway 44 southeast to the junction with Highway 57, or to Highway 45 at Nageezi and then south. The roads are well marked. For road conditions, phone 800/432-4269.

Because Chaco's so isolated, you'll probably want to bring an ice chest with food and drinks. You can stock up at the small Thoreau Shopping Center or markets in Farmington or Bloomfield.

Chaco Information

For more information, phone 505/786-7014 or check the website: www.nps.gov/chcu.

OTHER SIGHTS NEAR GRANTS

Crownpoint

This town, on the way to Chaco Canyon from Thoreau, is at the eastern border of the Navajo Indian Reservation and is the headquarters of the Eastern Navajo Nation. Best known for its regular auctions of Navajo rugs, Crownpoint swells several times a year with weavers and traders alike. Auctions are held at Crownpoint Elementary School. To get there, turn west off Highway 371 at the Crownpoint turnoff, and then watch for the cars (or ask someone in Crownpoint—the streets don't have names). For information, contact the **Crownpoint Rug Weavers Association** at 505/786-7386 or visit its website: www.mte.addr.com/rug-auction.

Mt. Taylor

Take Highway 547 (Lobo Canyon Road) from Grants to the highest peak in the area, 11,301-foot Mt. Taylor, an extinct volcano, which the Navajo call Dzil Dotlizi, or Turquoise Mountain. Marking the traditional Navajo world's southern border, Mt. Taylor is also one of their four sacred mountains, and it is spiritually significant to nearby Pueblo Indians as well. Two campground/picnic areas on the road up the mountain—**Lobo Canyon** and **Coal Mine**—offer interpretive nature trails and views of the mountain and surrounding region. The last five miles, leading to 11,026-foot La Mosca Peak Lookout, are unpaved and recommended for four-wheel-drive vehicles and hikers only.

Laguna Pueblo

Laguna is a strangely picturesque pueblo, and a pulloff/rest stop on I-40 allows travelers to view the village from a distance: the San José de Laguna Church standing tall on the hillside surrounded by several hundred squatting houses, their squalor and sadness heartbreakingly typical of so many natives' homes.

This is the newest pueblo in New Mexico, as well as one of the least homogenous. It was founded in 1699 by small groups that had wandered from Santa Domingo and Cochiti Pueblos, and the blood of many modern Lagunas is descended from Acoma, Zuñi, San Felipe, Zia, Oraibi, Sandia, and Jemez Indians, as well as from whites who moved onto the pueblo in the late 19th century.

In the 1870s, the Anglo Marmon family moved onto the pueblo, built a mill, and, with a handful of Protestants, including Dr. John Menaul, tried to move the Indians away from their traditional customs. The Marmons, a descendant of whom is writer Leslie Marmon Silko (see Suggested Reading), went so far as to write a "constitution" that would govern the Indians. Eventually, two of the pueblo's kivas were ripped out, and the Lagunas who refused to "modernize" hit the road in what pueblo historians call the Laguna Break.

Except on ceremonial days, there's not a whole lot to see at Laguna, save for the San José de Laguna Church, built in 1699. The interior, the work of Indian craftspeople, is colorfully decorated with symbols typical of Native American mythology—sun, moon, stars, rain, and rainbow.

Ceremonial dances are held in Laguna Pueblo on June 24 (San Juan's Day), August 10 (Corn Dance), September 19 (Harvest Dance and celebration in honor of the pueblo's patron saint, St. Joseph), and December 24 (Christmas Eve Dance). The annual **All-Indian Baseball Tournament** is held at Laguna each September, with tribes from pueblos around the state competing for top honors. Laguna Pueblo is open to the public during daylight hours, although no photography, or any other kind of recording, is allowed.

To get there, take the Laguna Pueblo exit from I-40. For information, write Box 194, Laguna Pueblo, NM 87026, 505/552-6654. You can also get information by visiting website: www.indianpueblo.org/ipcc/lagunapage or website: www.newmexico.org/culture/pueblo_laguna.html.

Four Corners Area

Four Corners is the only place in the United States where the borders of four different states meet. New Mexico, Arizona, Utah, and Colorado all touch here, and the spot is commemorated by an inlaid slab of concrete and a small visitors center.

This is the heart of Indian country. The Navajo, Ute, and Hopi tribes all lay claim to land nearby—the Navajo and Mountain Ute Reservations abut here, and the Navajos, particularly, count the country around the Four Corners area as among its most sacred. As you drive through, you can see why: It's a haunting and strangely beautiful land, miles and miles of barren plains marked by sudden mesas, red rock, and bizarre sandstone cliffs, crumbling and melting away like alien landscapes in a Steven Spielberg film. The hills, dotted with juniper and piñon pine, roll away like the soft waves of an ocean current to meet the deep sky on a far horizon.

At Four Corners Monument, you can get down on all fours and put each one of your limbs in a different state.

Four Corners Monument

A stone slab marks the precise spot where the four states' borders meet, and tourists gather for the requisite photo opportunity (pose on all fours—a foot in Arizona, a foot in Utah, a hand in Colorado, and a hand in New Mexico, and bring a slide of *that* back to show your friends . . .). Indians, all of whom are licensed, have booths set up near the parking lot and sell jewelry, pottery, sandpaintings, and snacks and refreshments. Maps, brochures, and drinking water are available at the small visitors center, and there are porta-toilets in the parking lot. The monument is open daily from about sunrise to sundown; entrance is $2.50 per vehicle. For information, phone 505/871-6647.

TOWN OF SHIPROCK

Named for the rock formation 15 miles southwest of town, Shiprock was founded in 1903 as the headquarters for the Northern Navajo Indian Agency and served in that capacity until 1938, when all subagencies were consolidated at Window Rock, Arizona. Shiprock today is a thriving center for Navajo trading, business, and health care. A uranium-processing facility nearby provides work for local tribe members.

The Northern Navajo Fair

Shiprock has sponsored this well-known festival every fall for nearly 90 years. The fair attracts Indians from throughout the Four Corners area, many of whom dress in traditional tribal garb. Among the highlights are a rodeo and exhibits featuring classic Navajo jewelry and weaving—rugs, blankets, and clothing.

Shiprock

This bizarre rock formation rising 1,500 feet from the desert floor is sacred to the Navajos, who call it Tse Bida'hi (Winged Rock). According to legend, early Navajos were attacked by another tribe, and they took refuge on the rock, which sprouted wings and carried them to safety from the evil threat below. Another myth has Spider Woman (the grandmother/goddess/creator of many Navajo stories) rescuing a slayer of monsters from the top of Shiprock. Drive out just before sundown, and watch how it seems to hover eerily just above the horizon. (Although climbers may salivate at the thought of getting out the ropes or freeclimbing the steep sides of Shiprock, they had better stay in their vans. This is a sacred landmark, folks, and strictly off-limits.)

SHIPROCK TO GALLUP

Highway 666 drops due south out of Shiprock, slicing through the east end of the Navajo Indian Reservation, and arrives in Gallup 90 miles later. This route passes just east of the huge basalt "Winged Rock"; Tribal Route 13 leads to its base (climbing is not allowed on the rock). Between Shiprock and Gallup you'll see a number of other impressive monoliths, which, like Shiprock, are the cores of long-gone volcanoes.

To the east of Highway 666 is Chaco Canyon (see Chaco Culture National Historic Park, above), although the only way to get there from this road is to cut off on Tribal Route 9, which begins its meandering path to Highway 57 about 15 miles north of Gallup. Across the desolate plain are hundreds, perhaps thousands, of ancient Anasazi ruins, many of which were "outliers" of Chaco and connected by road to the central core of cities. A handful of short roads spur off Highway 666, most leading to Navajo homes or tiny communities.

Washington Pass

Highway 134 cuts west off Highway 666 just north of Sheep Springs and climbs through the Chuska Mountains before crossing into Arizona and rolling down into Window Rock, headquarters of the Navajo Nation. The pass through the mountains was named for Colonel John Washington, a U.S. soldier in the area in the late 1840s negotiating peace settlements with the Navajos. During the talks, a battle broke out between the soldiers and the Navajos, and one of the Navajos' most respected leaders, Narbona, was killed and scalped.

In recent years, Navajos have lobbied to have the name of the pass changed. They believe the name should reflect the history of people of the area rather than that of the U.S. Army. One group, based at Navajo Community College in Shiprock, wants the name changed to Narbona Pass. Other Navajos simply want the name of the pass returned to its original, Beeshlichi'ii Bigiizh (Copper Pass).

Canyon de Chelly National Monument (Arizona)

Just over the border into Arizona are some of the best-preserved Anasazi ruins in the Southwest, including pit houses from A.D. 500 and cliff dwellings from 1100–1300, as well as Navajo hogans. Access to the 26-mile-long canyon is provided by hiking trails, horseback, and jeep tours. Take Highway 134 west to Tribal Route 12, then go north on 12 to Tribal Route 64 south. For information, write Box 588, Chinle, AZ 86503, or phone 928/674-5500. Or check the monument's website: www.nps.gov/cach.

FARMINGTON

From Shiprock to Farmington, Highway 64 follows the San Juan River, rolling through the fertile and cultivated river valley past cornfields and fruit orchards. The small town of Fruitland, about halfway between the two towns, was settled by Mormons in 1877 and is therefore a bit of an anomaly out here on the edge of the Navajo Reservation (whose border is just east of Shiprock).

Farmington (pop. 36,000; elev. 5,395 feet), near where the Animas and La Plata Rivers empty into the San Juan, is known as Three Rivers to some of the neighboring Indians, although the Navajos call the town Tohta, or Among the Rivers. Farmington's origin was as a cattle and "farming town," but its economy today relies on a number of other nearby industries, including coal, electric power—generated by the Four Corners Plant—and the Navajo Indian Irrigation Project.

Among the eclectic array of Farmington-area attractions are horse racing, the Connie Mack baseball tournament, a balloon festival, and some of the finest trout fishing in the Southwest.

History

The first whites to settle in the Farmington area arrived in the mid-1870s, when they drove cattle into the area; by the late '70s, the valley was already being cultivated and irrigated for peach and walnut trees. From then until the turn of the last century, when the town was incorporated, it was the subject of several Indian land disputes and the site of a number of rowdy shoot-'em-ups—including an 1880s stereopticon show in the Farmington schoolhouse that failed to impress local cowboys, who shot at the screen until the frightened and humiliated showman jumped out a window.

Gateway Park Museum and Visitors Center

A city-operated museum at 3041 E. Main, 505/599-1174, includes a strong collection of pioneer-era artifacts from northwestern New Mexico. Exhibits vary throughout the year. There's also a gift shop with books, toys, and games with local and/or educational focuses, and souvenirs. Hours are Monday–Saturday 9 A.M.–5 P.M. and Sunday noon–5 P.M. Admission is free.

In addition, the **E3 Children's Museum and Science Center,** at 203 W. Orchard, includes giant wall puzzles, a bubble machine, and a special microscope with a three-inch viewer among its variety of hands-on displays for kids. Open Wednesday–Friday noon–5 P.M., Saturday 10 A.M.–5 P.M. Admission is free. For more information or to reserve special tours, phone 505/599-1425.

Accommodations

Farmington has a wide range of motels, from super-economy digs to midrange inns to several newer upscale franchise hotels all the way to, well, a cave. Let's start there: **Kokopelli's Cave Bed & Breakfast,** 206 W. 38th St., 505/325-7855, is a real honest-to-goodness cliff dwelling, albeit one that dates only from 1980, when it was blasted out of the side of the mountain and set up as living/working quarters for a local geologist. The 1,650-square-foot cave, 280 feet above the La Plata River, now serves as a bed-and-breakfast and features a

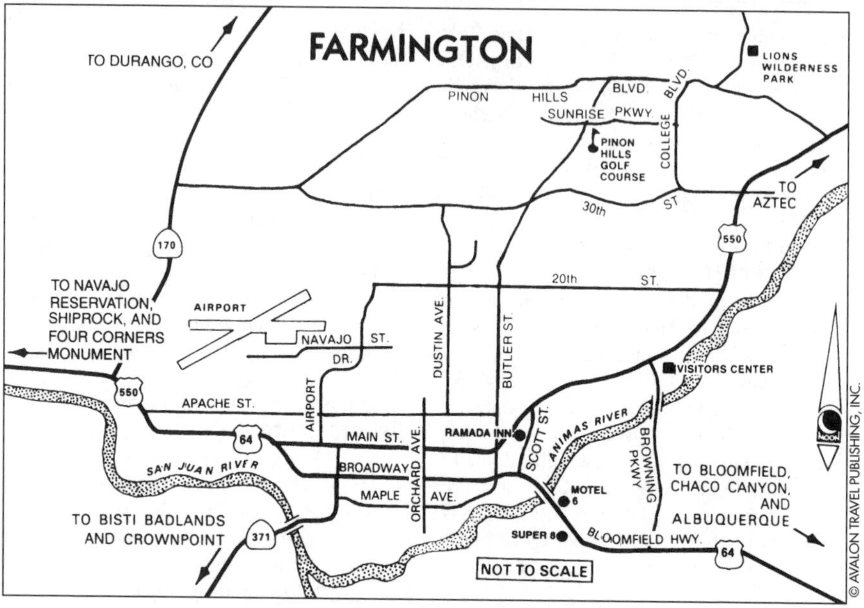

"waterfall shower," a replica of an Anasazi kiva, and access by ladder. The "digs" rents for $200–250 a night for two. For more information, and some pretty amazing photos, check out its website: www.bbonline.com/nm/kokopelli/index.

Those interested in something a bit more conventional might try one of several franchise inns downtown. The following are conveniently located at the junction of Highways 550, 64, and 371: a **Ramada Inn,** 601 E. Broadway, 505/325-1191; a **Holiday Inn,** 600 E. Broadway, 505/327-9811; a **La Quinta Inn,** 675 Scott, 505/327-4706; and the **Best Western Inn and Suites,** 700 Scott, 505/327-5221. All of the above will run $50–100.

There are a **TraveLodge** downtown at 510 Scott, 505/327-0242, and a **Motel 6** just a half mile west of the downtown area at 1600 Bloomfield Hwy., 505/326-4501 (both under or around $50). Across the street at 1601 Bloomfield Hwy. is the **Super 8,** 505/325-1813 (also under or around $50).

RVing

The **KOA,** 1900 E. Blanco Blvd. in Bloomfield, 505/632-8339, has full hookups starting at about $25, as well as showers and a laundry room. Tent sites are slightly less.

Food

You'll find a wide array of dining possibilities in Farmington—fast-food franchises, pizza parlors, and fancy steak-and-seafood restaurants. A local breakfast tradition is **Sonya's Cookin USA,** 2001 Bloomfield Hwy., 505/327-3526, where huge and excellent servings of *huevos rancheros* and more traditional American dishes run $4–8. Open every day, also for lunch and dinner.

La Fiesta Grande, 1916 E. Main, 505/326-6476, is another deservedly popular spot serving terrific Mexican food at very reasonable prices: lunch specials run $4–6, dinners $6–10. The recently renovated (1998) **Clancy's Restaurant,** 2703 E. 20th St., 505/325-8176, serves an eclectic array of burgers, enchiladas, and fish and chips for $5–9. Open daily for lunch and dinner.

3 Rivers Eatery and Brewhouse, 101 E. Main, 505/324-2187, is a classic brew pub, serving burgers, salads, pastas, and other pub grub, as well as the requisite beers brewed on location. The brewhouse also makes its own sodas for the kids and other nonimbibers. Entrées run $8–16. **KB Dillon's Bar and Grille,** 101 W. Broadway, 505/325-0222, has an all-you-can-eat salad bar and dinners—steak, prime rib, veal, and seafood—running $12–25. Farmington's also been **Outback Steakhoused,** at 4921 E. Main, 505/324-2122. Dinner served daily, $8–22.

Most of the nicer hotels downtown have dining rooms with good food, including the Best Western Inn and Suites, and the Holiday and Ramada Inns.

For those who'd rather eat on the run, Farmington also has two McDonald's, a Domino's Pizza, three Pizza Huts, and a couple of KFCs.

Recreation

The San Juan River, especially the stretch between Bloomfield and Navajo Dam to the east, offers some of the finest trout fishing in the state. Several restricted stretches directly below the dam attract fly casters from throughout the Southwest. For information about Farmington-area fishing, stop in at **Zia Sporting Goods,** 500 E. Main, 505/327-6004. You'll find plenty of sporting equipment (camping, fishing, hunting) and friendly advice. You can also take a guided trip on local waters from a number of outfitters. Among the most convenient are the lodging-fishing packages offered by the Best Western Inn and Suites. Guides pick up guests at the hotel and take them to some of the best holes on San Juan, with prices starting at about $185 per person. For more details or to make reservations, go to website: www.newmexico-innandsuites.com/pages/farm-fishing.html. The Farmington Convention and Visitors Bureau has a complete listing of area guides and outfitters.

Farmington is also close to some of the best snow skiing in the United States. Colorado's southern Rockies, from Durango to Gunnison, get lots of fine light powder that blankets meadows and hangs heavy on the boughs of pines and cedars—whether your bag is Nordic or Alpine skiing, southern Colorado has more than enough to satisfy, *without* the crowds of Vail, Beaver Creek, and Aspen. Zia Sporting Goods carries a full line of ski equipment.

Citivan Golf Course, 505/599-1194, is maintained by the Farmington city government and is open to the public. Farmington's newest course, opened in 1989, is **Piñon Hills Golf Course.** Phone 505/326-6606 for information and tee times. **Hidden Valley Country Club,** 505/334-3248, is in Aztec and open to nonmembers.

Outdoor Theater

Throughout the summer, the sandstone outdoor amphitheater in Lions Wilderness Park, two miles north of town on College Boulevard, offers a range of theater. Optional preshow Southwestern dinner. Phone 800/448-1240 for more information.

Annual Events

The **Apple Blossom Festival** every April features a dance, parade, and melodrama. In May, the **Farmington International Balloon Festival** includes races and navigational competitions, and the nationally known **Connie Mack World Series Baseball Tournament** is played in late August. For information on these and other events, contact the Farmington Convention and Visitors Bureau.

In September, the two-day **Totah Festival** celebrates both Native American and early pioneer contributions to the Four Corners area. Included are Navajo rug exhibits and auctions, and Indian dancing. Write General Chairman, Totah Festival, 901 Fairgrounds, Farmington, NM 87401, or call 505/599-1169.

Information and Services

The Farmington **Convention and Visitors Bureau** is at 3041 E. Main, 505/326-7602 or 800/448-1240. Call or stop by for friendly advice on what to do and see and where to stay in the area. It also has a thorough and helpful website: www.farmingtonnm.org. The Farmington **public library** is at 100 W. Broadway, 505/327-7701.

Complete hospital services are available at San Juan Regional Medical Center, 801 W. Maple St., 505/325-5011. Phone the Farmington Police

Department at 505/327-0222, and the state police in Farmington at 505/325-7547.

Transportation

Passenger service to Farmington is provided by **Mesa Air,** 800/637-2247 or 505/326-3336 (from Colorado Springs, Denver, Albuquerque, and major New Mexico cities); **America West Express,** 800/235-9292 or 505/326-4494 (from Phoenix, Flagstaff, Bullhead City, and Kingman, Arizona; and Fresno, Palm Springs, and Santa Barbara, California); and **United Express,** 800/241-6522 or 505/326-3216 (from Denver, Cortez, and Grand Junction, Colorado).

The **Trailways** bus depot is just off Main Street at 101 E. Animas, 505/325-1009. **Avis,** 505/327-9864, **Budget,** 505/327-7304, and **Hertz,** 505/327-6093, rent cars at the Farmington airport.

VICINITY OF FARMINGTON

Navajo Reservation

With about 200,000 members, the Navajo is the largest Indian tribe in the United States, its 15-million-acre reservation sprawling over much of the Four Corners area. The largest chunk of the reservation occupies most of northeastern Arizona, with a small area spilling over into northwestern New Mexico and southern Utah. Its eastern border is just a couple of miles west of Farmington, extending north to Colorado and south nearly to Gallup.

Visitors are welcome on the reservation, and Navajos are a bit more amenable to being photographed than are some of the other Southwestern Indians (although they're also known to be a bit more savvy and may charge a small fee; at any rate, always ask permission first). Since 1938, the Navajo tribe has been headquartered in Window Rock, Arizona. For more information about visiting the reservation, write **Navajoland Tourism Office,** P.O. Box 663, Window Rock, AZ 86515, or phone 520/871-6436 or 520/871-7371. You'll also find lots of useful information at website: www.newmexico.org/culture/res_navajo.html.

Bisti Badlands

With its huge mushroom-shaped spires (called hoodoos) and red, olive-green, and bone-white

pronghorn antelope

cliffs, the harsh and desolate Bisti Badlands—and the nearby De-Na-Zin—afford the traveler views of some of the most bizarre landscapes this side of Tycho Crater.

Sixty-five million to 70 million years ago this area was lush with vegetation, and dinosaurs sloshed through the swampland. For nearly 100 years, paleontologists and geologists have been studying fossils taken from the area, and the rich sandstone and shale have yielded important information about early marinelife, the dinosaurs' disappearance, and the transition to dominance by terrestrial mammals. Before the white man arrived, this brutal land was important to both the Ute and Navajo Indians, the Navajos claiming it as sacred burial land and using the earth's natural colors as pigments for their sandpaintings.

More recently, whites have claimed this land—and not only scientists interested in studying its role in the history of the planet. But why would such a lunar landscape be of interest to outsiders, who generally don't believe in the spiritual value of land itself?

That's right. It's rich in natural resources. Bisti Badlands sits atop billions of tons of recoverable coal, and the area's been a prime target of strip-mining interests. Thankfully, the 1984 federal San Juan Basin Wilderness Preservation Act protects the nearly 4,000-acre Bisti area, as well as another 27,000 acres to the west, including the De-Na-Zin and the 2,720-acre "Fossil Forest." Officially designated a BLM Wilderness Area, Bisti Badlands is home to numerous species of reptiles, small mammals, and raptors, including the bald eagle and prairie falcon.

To get to Bisti Badlands, take Highway 371 south from Farmington about 40 miles and watch for the road signs.

BLOOMFIELD

Bloomfield (pop. 6,500; elev. 5,400 feet) is a small crossroads town 13 miles east of Farmington. Relying largely on the area's natural resources—coal, natural gas, and petroleum—as well as on the fertility of the San Juan Basin, Bloomfield's economy is based on energy production, ranching, and farming. Though today Bloomfield is a quiet little community—a gas or snack stop for tourists en route to Anasazi ruins or trophy trout streams—the town boasts one rowdy past, starring gunfighters and rustlers and lawmen gone bad.

History

First settled in the mid-1870s, in the 1880s Bloomfield was home base for the infamous rustlers, the Stockton Gang. Port Stockton, the gang's patriarch, arrived in the Bloomfield area after having fought in the Lincoln County War, allegedly with 15 notches already carved on his gun. Because he was so good with his sidearm, Stockton was made a lawman, but even the authority vested in him could not persuade him to use his piece for the good. During his short stint as a peace officer, Stockton allegedly shot and wounded a barber who had accidentally cut Stockton while shaving him. He also crashed a party to which he was not invited, using his six-gun for an invitation and dancing all night with it slung on his hip.

By the turn of the last century, Bloomfield had mellowed, and its residents had turned from rustling and shoot-outs to farming and ranching. In 1906, the Citizen's Ditch and Irrigation Company reclaimed 6,000 acres of the San Juan River and used the water to irrigate fields of grains, beans, and fruit. The Bloomfield Irrigation District, which took over the old irrigation company in 1911, is still in operation.

Salmon Ruins and Heritage Park

One of the "outliers" of Chaco Canyon 50 miles to the south, Salmon Pueblo, according to studies of the rings in roof beams, was probably constructed between 1088 and 1095. The original pueblo was built in the shape of a "C," 430 feet long along the back wall and two stories high. The village contained 250 separate rooms roughly surrounding the plaza and a Great Kiva.

The Chacoans who lived in Salmon Pueblo were farmers, growing corn and squash and supplementing their diets with wild plants and the meat of rabbit, deer, and elk. Although the original builders inhabited Salmon Pueblo only for about 60 years, other less-advanced Indians moved into it after the Chacoans left in the mid-1100s.

© STEPHEN METZGER

Salmon Ruins

In the late 1800s, George Salmon homesteaded the area around the ruins and protected it from vandals and treasure hunters. You can see the remains of his home and outbuildings today as you wander through the ruins, which were named for him. In 1969, San Juan County bought the land on which the ruins sit, and the county's residents passed a $275,000 bond for the construction of the San Juan County Archaeological Research Center and Library. Most of the excavation of Salmon Ruins was done between 1972 and 1978, and the half million artifacts taken from the site are housed at the research center, many of them in the museum.

The park and ruins are open to visitors daily 9 A.M.–5 P.M.; November–March, Sunday hours are noon–5 P.M. Admission is $3 for adults, discounts for kids and seniors. Start at the museum, where pottery, bone tools, and a drawing of the original pueblo are displayed. If you have time, take a look at the short film on the Anasazi, which paints an excellent portrait of the people who inhabited Salmon Pueblo and Chaco Canyon. From the museum, a short (400-yard) trail winds down past cottonwood trees and rabbit bushes to the ruins, only about a third of which have been excavated.

To get to Salmon Ruins, take Highway 64 two miles west from Bloomfield. The parking lot is on the south side of the highway. For more information, write San Juan Archaeological Research Center at Salmon Ruins, 975 Hwy. 64, Farmington, NM 87401, or call 505/632-2013.

Practicalities

The main concentration of the area's motels, restaurants, and services is in Farmington, 13 miles west on Highway 64 (see above). In Bloomfield, the **Bloomfield Motel,** 801 W. Broadway (Highway 64, one block west of the junction with Highway 44), 505/632-3383, has doubles in the $50 range. There's also a **Super 8,** 505/632-8886, right downtown at the junction of Highway 64 and Highway 44 ($50–70). The **Bloomfield KOA campground,** 1900 E. Blanco, 505/748-2807, has RV sites with full hookups for about $24 for two people and tent sites for $15—including hot showers.

VICINITY OF BLOOMFIELD

Angel Peak National Recreation Area

This dry, desolate, and seldom-used recreation area is named for the odd-shaped rock formation that towers above its 10,000 acres. Known to the Indians as Tsethl Gizhi, or Rock on Top of Two Prongs, and also known over the years as Twin Angels and Lost Angels, Angel Peak dominates this BLM-maintained badlands, which 40 million years ago was a huge inland sea and in the 17th and 18th centuries was known to the Spanish as El Nacimiento (The Birthplace).

You won't have to fight for a campsite here. I was at Angel Peak late one Saturday afternoon in July and not one site was occupied. It was almost eerie—stunted juniper dotting the soft gray and orange cliffs and dramatically carved canyons, rocky dirt trails wandering off into the wispy tumbleweeds, still under the hot afternoon sun, and not a soul in sight. The perfect place to be alone with your thoughts.

The well-maintained gravel road to Angel Peak NRA is about 15 miles south of Bloomfield off Highway 44. A mile in, you'll come to a small picnic area and lookout. The first campground is four miles from the main road, and the largest campground, with the best sites, is at the end of the road, seven miles in. Neither the picnic area nor the campgrounds have running water, and only a few of the sites have shelters (there's no natural shade). Pit toilets only. No fee. Watch for the road signs and the turnoff on the east side of the highway.

Chaco Culture National Historic Park

An ancient settlement of 13 separate Anasazi villages, including the immense Pueblo Bonito, Chaco Canyon was the cultural center for a vast network of prehistoric Indian communities and is the most important archaeological site in New Mexico. (See Vicinity of Grants, above.)

Angel Peak stands stark above the badlands.

Aztec and Vicinity

Aztec (pop. 5,800 "and six old soreheads"; elev. 5,686 feet) is one of New Mexico's true jewels. Over a mile high in elevation and straddling the Animas River in the fecund San Juan River Basin, Aztec is green and vibrant and in the heart of some of the prettiest country in the Southwest.

The town itself is not really typical of New Mexico. Unlike the sleepy treeless neighborhoods and adobe homes so common to the rest of the state, Aztec's streets are tree-lined and hilly, its homes of wood and brick—part Midwestern, part Victorian.

Truly a town with a sense of humor, Aztec takes great pride in its "soreheads." In 1969, the Aztec Chamber of Commerce erected a sign identifying the town: "Welcome to Aztec, Home of 4,000 Friendly People and 6 Old Soreheads." An immediate hit with the townspeople, the sign led to the election of six specific soreheads, who posed for the weekly *Independent Review* with bags over their heads and their backs to the camera. For the next 18 years, the identity of the original soreheads was a mystery, although scores of Azteckians claimed to have been among the six elected.

During Aztec Fiesta Days in 1987, the sorehead tradition was revived: six new soreheads were elected and, after they'd ridden down Main Street with bags over their heads, were debagged and identified. The tradition continues, with six new soreheads elected each year. Only the number of friendly people has changed.

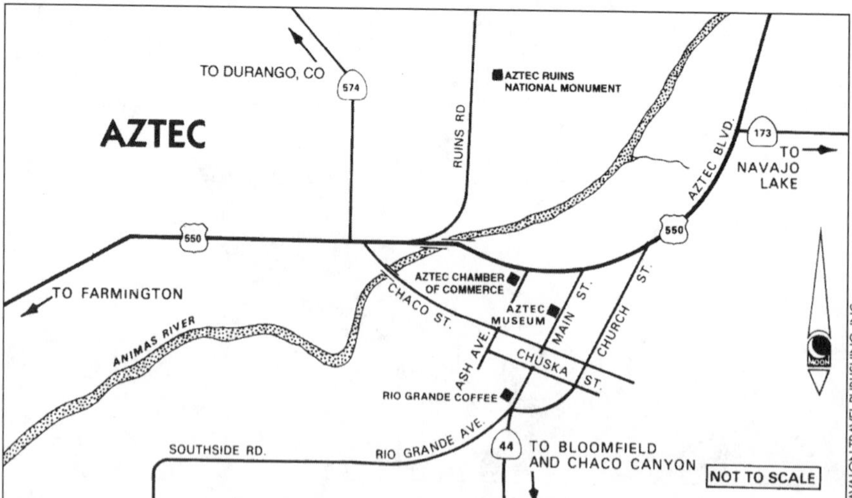

History

In the mid- to late 19th century, the Aztec area was popular among fur trappers, who by 1876 had completely wiped out the beaver population in the Animas, San Juan, and La Plata Rivers. The town, named for the ruins of Aztec Pueblo, was laid out in 1890 and in 1897 became the seat of San Juan County, formed by the partitioning of Rio Arriba County, now adjacent to the east. Since the turn of the century, Aztec has continued to prosper, partly because of the produce grown in its fertile fields and partly because of the many tourists who come for the nearby fishing, rafting, and water- and snow skiing, and to see the vast remains of the Anasazian Aztec Pueblo.

SIGHTS

Aztec Museum and Pioneer Village

This historical museum complex at 125 N. Main St. in downtown Aztec displays structures and artifacts from throughout the area's history. Among the exhibits are a small church, schoolhouse, general store, tools and pottery from pueblo ruins, early government documents and medical records, an old wooden oil-drilling rig (circa 1920), and a primitive telephone switchboard, as well as scores of historical photos. The museum also features traveling exhibits from the Smithsonian Institution, New Mexico and Colorado universities, and various other museums and archaeological societies. Summer hours are Monday–Saturday 9 A.M.–5 P.M.; the rest of the complex opens at 10 A.M. Admission is $2 for adults, $1 for kids. Mid-June through mid-September, the Pioneer Players perform a "High Noon Shoot-out" (at noon, natch). For more information, write Aztec Museum, 125 N. Main St., Aztec, NM 87410, or phone 505/334-9829.

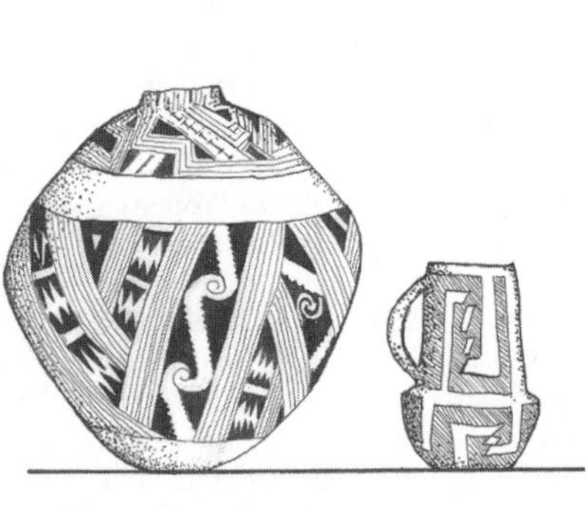

BOB RACE

typical Anasazi pottery

Aztec Ruins National Monument

This is among the most well-preserved and best-reconstructed of all the Anasazi villages and is part of the three-pueblo cultural chain that includes Chaco Canyon to the south and Colorado's Mesa Verde to the north.

First recorded in 1776 by the Dominguez-Escalante Expedition, which passed by the ruins on its way to the Pacific, Aztec was thought by early settlers to have been part of Mexico's great Aztec empire. In truth, the pueblo was built in the 11th or 12th century by Chacoan Anasazi Indians, who had lived in pit houses and smaller pueblos in the area for hundreds of years.

Resembling Pueblo Bonito at Chaco Canyon, Aztec was a three-story, "E"-shaped structure with hundreds of individual rooms, dozens of kivas, and one Great Kiva in the central plaza. Like Chaco, Aztec was abandoned by the end of the 12th century, lay deserted for several decades, and was repopulated and added onto in the mid- to late 13th century by less-advanced people migrating south from Mesa Verde. By 1275 or so, though, the Mesa Verdeans had left Aztec as well, and the pueblo probably lay virtually untouched until the mid-19th century, when Anglos began to settle the area and scientists started taking an interest in early Southwestern cultures.

In 1878, when anthropologist Lewis H. Morgan began investigating the ruins, he found nearly a quarter of the pueblo's original stones missing—most had been removed by settlers who used them for building. In 1916, Aztec Pueblo became part of the American Museum of Natural History, and in 1923 it was given national monument status. Most of the excavation at Aztec was done between 1916 and 1934 by Earl H. Morris, who completely reconstructed the pueblo's Great Kiva.

© STEPHEN METZGER

Aztec Ruins National Monument

Today, Aztec is one of the most important ruins in the Southwest, and its Great Kiva is the only one that has been reconstructed. Walk out into the pueblo, crawl through tiny doorways that connect the rooms, and then climb down into the covered Great Kiva. More so even than Chaco, Aztec provides an opportunity to imagine what it must have been like in New Mexican villages 350 years before the Spanish came and 400 before Columbus arrived on the East Coast.

Be sure to allow some time to wander around the museum in the visitors center. In addition to a film that gives an excellent overview of the Anasazi culture (explaining their emergence from the "other world" and the symbolism of the kiva), you'll find excellent displays of artifacts from the pueblo—bone jewelry, textiles, pottery, and basketry—as well as an exhibit of a warrior burial and a diagram and textual explanation of Aztec's excavation.

Memorial Day through Labor Day, the ruins are open daily 8 A.M.–6 P.M. (till 5 P.M. the rest of the year). In the summer, park rangers offer frequent but irregularly scheduled talks about the ruins and the Anasazi people. Adjacent to the visitors center is a grassy, wooded picnic area. Admission is $4; no charge for kids 16 and younger. To get to the pueblo, take Ruins Road north from Highway 550 just west of downtown Aztec.

For more information, write Aztec Ruins National Monument, P.O. Box 640, Aztec, NM 87410, or phone 505/334-6174. You can also visit the monument's website: www.nps.gov/azru.

Historical Tour

A walking tour of downtown Aztec includes a number of buildings on both the National Register of Historic Places and the New Mexico State Register of Cultural Properties. Among the tour's showpieces—most of which are on Main and Church Streets—are the Citizens Bank Building (1903) at 105 S. Main, the Odd Fellows Hall (1903), 107 S. Main, and one of the town's early jails (1912), 125 N. Main. For a map and complete descriptions of the various structures, stop in at the Aztec Chamber of Commerce, 110 N. Ash, or the Aztec Museum Complex, 125 N. Main.

PRACTICALITIES

Accommodations

The nicest lodge in town is the **Step Back Inn,** 103 W. Aztec, 505/334-1200, where the 40 good-sized rooms are named after 19th-century Aztec-area settlers and decorated in Victorian style. Doubles run $50–70.

Miss Gail's Inn, 300 S. Main, 505/334-3452 or 888/534-3452, is a bed-and-breakfast in the historical part of town—located, in fact, in Aztec's first hotel. Each of the eight rooms has a private bath. You can also get rooms at **El Aztec Motel,** 221 S. Main, 505/334-6300, and the **Enchantment Lodge,** 1800 W. Aztec, 505/334-6143. Both are around $50 for two.

Twenty-two miles west, Farmington has a wide range of motels and inns (see Four Corners Area, above). Camping is available at nearby **Navajo Lake State Park** (see below).

Food

The **Aztec Restaurant,** 107 Aztec Blvd. NE, 505/334-9586, is a local favorite for hearty down-home meals and Mexican specialties. Breakfasts run about $4–8, sandwiches are $4–7, and dinners range from $6 (burger, enchiladas) to $12 (rib-eye steak). Another good bet is the **Rio Grande Coffee Company Atomic Espresso,** 122 N. Main, 505/334-0109, where you can get espresso drinks and bagels. The little restaurant also serves soups, salads, and quiche for lunch (till 3 P.M. weekdays, 2 P.M. weekends).

Recreation

Aztec prides itself on its proximity to some of the Southwest's best country for recreational sports. The San Juan River just east of town offers excellent trout fishing, both to the earnest fly caster and to the less serious angler—who'd rather sit on shore in a lawn chair, pulling on a cold one while a night crawler does the grunt work. Several posted stretches of the San Juan below Navajo Dam are open to artificial lures with single, unbarbed hooks only. Most of the rest of the river is free of bait restrictions. Several local sporting goods stores stock not only quality equipment but excellent advice as well: try **Handy Bait and Tackle Shop,** 504 Aztec Blvd., Aztec, 505/334-9114, and **Abe's Motel and Fly Shop** at Navajo Dam, 505/632-2194. Book guided trips through **Four Corners Guide Service,** 505/632-3566 or 800/669-3566, website: www.4cornersguideservice.com. Full-day float trips are $225 for one, $275 for two.

The cool waters of Navajo Lake, east of Aztec, offer boating, water-skiing, fishing, and swimming—welcome respite from the sometimes-cruel summer heat of the Four Corners area. Aztec is also close to some excellent snow skiing, both downhill and cross-country. Just 15 miles south of the Colorado border, Aztec is a gateway to southern Rocky Mountain Alpine skiing. To the east, the Carson National Forest and the area around Chama abound with miles and miles of cross-country ski terrain.

Annual Events

Aztec's **Fiesta Days** in early July typically include a rodeo, parade, mariachi band, and bicycle race.

Information and Services

The Aztec **Chamber of Commerce** runs a very nice welcome center at 110 N. Ash, a block south of Aztec Boulevard on the west end of town. It's got scads of information on the Four Corners area, including maps, literature on parks and ruins, and a complete list of campgrounds and motels. Phone the Aztec Chamber of Commerce at 505/334-9551. The **Aztec Museum** at 125 N. Main also dispenses literature on the area. You can also get information from Aztec's website: www.cyberport.com/aztec, or email the chamber at aztec@cyberport.com.

The nearest hospital to Aztec is the San Juan Regional Medical Center, 801 W. Maple St., Farmington (22 miles west), 505/325-5011. The Aztec Police Department is at 201 W. Chaco, 505/334-9456 or, in emergencies, 505/334-6101. Call the state police in Farmington at 505/325-7547.

Transportation

The nearest airport to Aztec is Farmington Municipal, 22 miles west. **Mesa Air,** 800/MESA-AIR (800/637-2247), provides passenger service.

The **Farmington bus depot** is at 111 N. Allen, 505/325-1009.

VICINITY OF AZTEC

Navajo Lake State Park

After their internment at Fort Sumner, the Navajo Indians in 1868 signed a treaty with the United States government that returned to them a portion of their Four Corners homeland area and promised each family 160 acres of farmable land. Nearly 100 years later, in 1963, Navajo Dam was completed on the San Juan River; for the first time, thanks to the Navajo Indian Irrigation Project (made possible by the dam), the Indians were finally able to farm in the area.

In addition, the dam provided a huge increase in recreational possibilities in the area. Navajo Lake State Park, created a year after the dam was finished, encompasses nearly 18,000 square acres of land and 13,000 acres of water, home to rainbow and brown trout, kokanee salmon, black bass, bluegill, and crappie. The lake is extremely popular during the summer, when folks flock to the cool waters to escape the desert heat (in the winter, hardy ice fishermen drill holes through the lake's frozen crust and fish from lean-tos and trucks). A 3.5-mile stretch of the San Juan River below the dam is also part of the park and boasts some of the best trout fishing in the Southwest. Be sure to check local regulations, as several stretches along here are "catch-and-release" only and restricted to artificial lures with single, unbarbed hooks.

A number of campgrounds are scattered around the dam and lake. One of the nicest is **Cottonwood Canyon Campground,** although the three-mile sandy dirt road in is rutted and nasty and often washed out in places. Once there, though, you'll appreciate the shaded spots among the red-rock cliffs and gnarled juniper. Day use is $3, and camping is $6.

Abe's Motel and Fly Shop, 505/632-2194, has an RV park with full hookups. Sites go for about $12.

Information

For information about Navajo Lake State Park, phone 505/632-2278. For information about

San Juan River from Navajo Lake State Park

boating and fishing in the area, stop in at Abe's or other sporting goods stores in Aztec. For New Mexico state fishing regulations, write New Mexico Department of Game and Fish, 1 Wildlife Way, Santa Fe, NM 87507, or phone 505/476-8000.

Albuquerque

Introduction

With a population of about 450,000, Albuquerque (elev. 5,200 feet) is home to a third of all New Mexicans. And although the state capital is Santa Fe, an hour north, Albuquerque is really New Mexico's big gun. This is where the state's businesses are headquartered—from banks to microchip manufacturers. It's also home to the 24,000-student University of New Mexico; Albuquerque International Airport, the largest in the state; Sandia Laboratories, with 7,700 workers one of the Southwest's single largest employers; the Albuquerque Dukes, Triple-A farm team of the L.A. Dodgers; Kirtland Air Force Base; and enough museums, galleries, and gift stores to keep you exploring the city for weeks.

Sprawling at the junction of two major interstates—40 and 25—and along the shores of the Southwest's major waterway—the Rio Grande—Albuquerque is a potpourri of places and people and perspectives. Contiguous or close by are sleepy neighborhoods and bustling city thoroughfares. Centuries-old historical districts and modern high-rises. Small markets and huge shopping malls. Squalid apartment complexes and elite housing developments. Mountain bikes and Range Rovers. Mexicans, Laotians, and Southern Californians, and, of course, cowboys and Indians.

Unfortunately, many visitors to Albuquerque never penetrate the city's skin. They pass through on I-40, maybe stay at a Holiday Inn, spend a few hours walking around Old Town, buy a T-shirt and a few postcards, take a photograph of

© SL DUTCHER

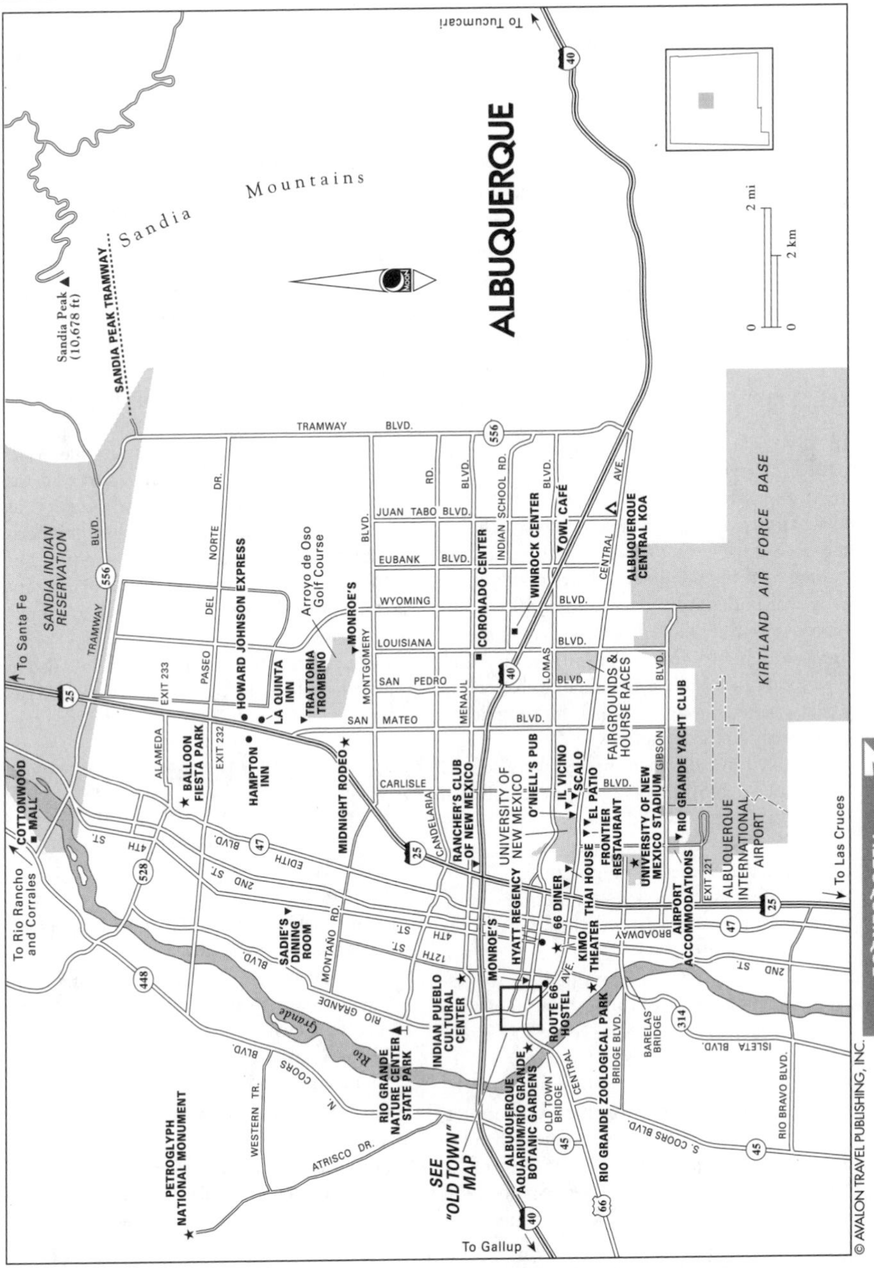
ALBUQUERQUE
Sandia Mountains
Sandia Peak (10,678 ft)
SANDIA PEAK TRAMWAY
SANDIA INDIAN RESERVATION
To Santa Fe
To Tucumcari
To Rio Rancho and Corrales
To Gallup
To Las Cruces
TRAMWAY BLVD.
JUAN TABO BLVD.
EUBANK BLVD.
WYOMING BLVD.
LOUISIANA BLVD.
SAN PEDRO BLVD.
SAN MATEO BLVD.
CARLISLE BLVD.
MONTGOMERY BLVD.
MENAUL BLVD.
INDIAN SCHOOL RD.
LOMAS BLVD.
CENTRAL AVE.
GIBSON BLVD.
PASEO DEL NORTE DR.
ALAMEDA
CANDELARIA RD.
MONTAÑO RD.
EDITH BLVD.
4TH ST.
2ND ST.
12TH ST.
RIO GRANDE BLVD.
BROADWAY
ISLETA BLVD.
RIO BRAVO BLVD.
S. COORS BLVD.
N. COORS BLVD.
WESTERN TR.
ATRISCO DR.
BRIDGE BLVD.
BARELAS BRIDGE
OLD TOWN BRIDGE
EXIT 233
EXIT 232
EXIT 221
Rio Grande
Arroyo de Oso Golf Course
COTTONWOOD MALL
BALLOON FIESTA PARK
HAMPTON INN
HOWARD JOHNSON EXPRESS
LA QUINTA INN
TRATTORIA TROMBINO
MONROE'S
MIDNIGHT RODEO
CORONADO CENTER
WINROCK CENTER
OWL CAFÉ
ALBUQUERQUE CENTRAL KOA
RANCHER'S CLUB OF NEW MEXICO
UNIVERSITY OF NEW MEXICO
O'NIELL'S PUB
IL VICINO
SCALO
EL PATIO
FRONTIER RESTAURANT
THAI HOUSE
66 DINER
HYATT REGENCY
KIMO THEATER
ROUTE 66 HOSTEL
SADIE'S DINING ROOM
INDIAN PUEBLO CULTURAL CENTER
RIO GRANDE NATURE CENTER STATE PARK
ALBUQUERQUE AQUARIUM/RIO GRANDE BOTANIC GARDENS
RIO GRANDE ZOOLOGICAL PARK
PETROGLYPH NATIONAL MONUMENT
SEE "OLD TOWN" MAP
FAIRGROUNDS & HOURSE RACES
UNIVERSITY OF NEW MEXICO STADIUM
RIO GRANDE YACHT CLUB
AIRPORT ACCOMMODATIONS
ALBUQUERQUE INTERNATIONAL AIRPORT
KIRTLAND AIR FORCE BASE
0 2 mi
0 2 km
© AVALON TRAVEL PUBLISHING, INC.

ALBUQUERQUE

an Indian silversmith or Hispanic weaver, and then get back in the Buick for the trip across the desert. But if you're willing to poke around a bit—to explore the city's backstreets and dusty secondhand bookstores and wander through the historical and prehistorical sites just minutes from downtown—you'll get a much better feeling for Albuquerque. And when you leave, you'll take with you a sense of having gotten to know a complex and multifaceted personality.

***Today, Central Avenue is still a major crosstown artery, providing glimpses of an America few remember and most have only seen in old black-and-white photos and movies such as* The Grapes of Wrath.**

HISTORY

In 1540, when Coronado first passed through the Albuquerque area, the Rio Grande Valley looked much different than it does today. During the intervening years, the waters of the great river have eroded the floodplain, the river's level has dropped dramatically—more than 50 percent in the last century alone, largely because of the increased demand for irrigation—and Albuquerqueans have built levees and dug channels to direct the water away from their housing developments and office buildings.

What Coronado encountered were several thousand Pueblo Indians living peacefully on land their ancestors had farmed for 15 centuries. The Rio Grande, something the Indians had neither the desire nor the ability to tame, simply ran its course—sometimes mild, sometimes angry, always providing water for the Indians' crops.

In 1706, the town of Alburquerque was established by a group of Spanish families who had been granted land by King Felipe V of Spain. Acting Governor Francisco Cuervo y Valdes moved from Bernalillo, 30 miles north, to be with the colonists and assist them in founding their home—which they named Villa de San Felipe de Alburquerque in honor of the Duke of Alburquerque and viceroy of New Spain, Don Francisco Fernandez de la Cueva Enrique.

Albuquerque (the first "r" was dropped in the last half of the 19th century, after the Americans took over) soon became an important stop on the Old Chihuahua Trail (the Santa Fe-to-Mexico extension of the Santa Fe Trail), and because of its location on the largest waterway in the Southwest, it immediately began to attract settlers. By 1800, Albuquerque was home to more than 1,000 people, most of whom lived near the original settlement in small adobe houses clustered around the church, San Felipe de Neri, and the town's central plaza (today the center of Albuquerque's Old Town).

During the middle part of the 19th century, Albuquerque became an important military outpost. In 1880, the railroad came to town, helping establish it as a shipping destination for many of the goods sent from the East Coast, as well as a point of embarkation for Southwest goods being sent east, including livestock, pelts, lumber, minerals, and ore.

The University of New Mexico was founded in 1889, establishing the city as one that took its education seriously. In the early part of the 20th cen-

HIGHLIGHTS

Albuquerque International Balloon Fiesta (October): largest hot-air balloon festival in the world

Indian Pueblo Cultural Center: shopping, museum, Indian dancing

New Mexico State Fair (September): arts and crafts, rodeos, food, livestock and agriculture competitions

Old Town Albuquerque: shopping, sight-seeing, museums, restaurants

Salinas National Monument: ancient pueblos and Spanish missions

Sandia Mountains: hiking, camping, sight-seeing, snow skiing, aerial tramway

Turquoise Trail: ghost towns, shopping, sight-seeing, museums

HERE'S ADOBE IN YOUR EYE

One of the charms of north-central New Mexico is the abundance of adobe-style structures. Homes, hotels, haciendas, even banks and office buildings are made of adobe, although the latter are often *adobe-style,* or made of modern plaster or stucco and painted to resemble adobe.

The Spanish word *adobe* actually comes to us by way of Arabic, in which *atob* means sun-dried brick. Before the Spanish arrived in the New World, Native Americans were using mud to build their homes and pueblos, whether on cliffsides or in secluded canyons, using a method known as "puddling": wet slabs of mud 8–10 inches thick set in place and, when dry, topped by subsequent layers. When the Spanish arrived, they introduced adobe *blocks,* sections preformed in wooden molds that could be carried and stacked more easily.

Until the arrival of the railroad, door and window openings in adobe structures were relatively small. With the railroad, though, came increased trade, and by the end of the 19th century, adobe buildings often included glass, as well as lumber shipped from distant mills.

Today, it's often difficult to tell Territorial adobe from a modern imitation. One thing's for certain, though, and that is that adobe is clearly the most natural architectural style in northern New Mexico, with homes and haciendas dotting the rolling hills and blending into the landscape as perfectly as it is possible for a man-made structure to do.

tury, as tuberculosis patients flocked to the Southwest, Albuquerque built numerous sanatoriums; today, both the university and the medical industry are major Albuquerque-area employers.

In 1926, the federal government officially recognized the cross-country chain of highways—connecting Chicago and Los Angeles, Lake Michigan and the Pacific—as U.S. Route 66. An important American icon, Route 66 passed through Albuquerque along what is now Central Avenue. Today, Central Avenue is still a major crosstown artery, providing glimpses of an America few remember and most have only seen in old black-and-white photos and movies such as *The Grapes of Wrath:* old motels and diners, movie theaters and pawnshops, dime stores and hat stores, and street corners lined with off-duty soldiers and homeless Indians, shoe salesmen and high-heeled ladies.

Nearly 300 years after its founding, Albuquerque is still a hub of activity and transportation; the people here seem always on the go. Though a cross-country highway no longer cuts through downtown, two major cross-country interstates (I-25 and I-40) pass over and through it. In fact, so well used is that north-south intersection that, in 2000, a major renovation was begun that is expected to ease the congestion the late 20th century saw; it is estimated to employ thousands for the next several years.

Meanwhile, several major boulevards continue to be jam-packed with fast-paced motorists (folks book through this town) from sunup to sundown. From Old Town down by the river to the thoroughfares up toward Northeast Heights, Albuquerque is a city on the move.

CLIMATE

One July, during a late-afternoon rainstorm, an Albuquerque teenager left her house for her job at a fast-food restaurant. She never made it. The north end of town, where she lived in a comfortable and sturdy home, had turned into a torrent of angry water. Streets that a half hour before had been bone dry were now four feet deep in water rushing madly from the Northeast Heights section—at the foot of the Sandia Mountains—toward the flatlands and valley carved millennia ago by the Rio Grande. Her car was found a quarter of a mile down the road from where she'd abandoned it, apparently stuck in water from Cottonwood Arroyo. Had she lived, she'd surely warn travelers about summer storms.

Just as summer brings the drama of the opera season to Santa Fe, it brings the drama of rainstorms to most of the state. And with that come the flash floods. Albuquerque, though developed and paved and fortified against the deluges, is far from immune. A highly localized storm can bring four, six, even eight inches of rain in a single hour to an area not much larger than a city block, while an area just a half mile away may be hit with nothing more than a few drops, or a fine spray—like the misty afterwash of a violent waterfall. Arroyos, dry 95 percent of the time, swell with rainwater that tears down hillsides and onto streets, themselves swelling with raging water two, three, four feet deep. All the while lightning cracks and thunder booms, like the fierce summons of wrathful gods.

Try not to go out when it's like that.

If you have to, be careful. Don't drive across moving water. Don't drive through water whose depth is uncertain. Stay away from arroyos. So dangerous is New Mexico's monsoon season that during these summer storms, the Albuquerque Police Department's "Operation Raft" is often put into effect—firefighters stand by with aquatic rescue equipment, specially designed to save people who have been swept into the city's arroyos.

Thankfully, these storms often break up as quickly as they hit. You'll be sitting windowside in a cozy diner watching the rain pelt the street under a darkening sky. You'll look away for barely a moment, and then when you look back, the storm has let up, the rain has stopped, and the sky is already beginning to clear. Within an hour, the rivers that have seized the streets have retreated. By morning, the only testimony to the storm's occupation will be the detritus strewn at street corners and the cottonwoods' dustless leaves, clean under the optimistic sky of the new day.

Winter, by contrast, can be quite mild. Though the heat of summer days often pushes the mercury up into the 90s, and winter nights in this nearly mile-high city can drop below freezing, there's still that desert sun to take the edge off the chill and keep the snow from sticking around for more than a few hours.

Just a few miles from town, though, the snow does stick. The Sandia Mountains, highest point of which is 10,678 feet, keep constant vigil over the city in their shadow, and those needing a snow fix can either take the aerial tramway on the northeast side of town or drive around the mountains' back side. Either way, you'll be a long way from the desert floor in a matter of minutes—skiing, snowshoeing, sledding, or just taking in the natural beauty of a New Mexico winterscape.

Sights

OLD TOWN

Why not begin your tour of Albuquerque where the city itself began, in Old Town? Here you can get a real taste of the city's past. Visit the old San Felipe de Neri church, built in 1706. Stroll through the grassy plaza, and explore the narrow backstreets lined with 300-year-old adobe homes (most turned to shops and boutiques).

Shopping at Old Town

Old Town offers you the complete range of shopping—from quality gift shops to tacky souvenir emporiums, from artists working in exclusive galleries to vendors selling jewelry on blankets spread on the sidewalk. In Old Town you can buy everything from T-shirts to turquoise, authentic Apache baskets and handwoven Navajo wool rugs to your-name-here coffee mugs, from scented candles to beaded "Indian" belts.

The first thing you need to know about Old Town is that parking ain't easy. If you're looking for a spot on the street—especially during the summer—you could circle the area for hours. Thankfully, a number of inexpensive

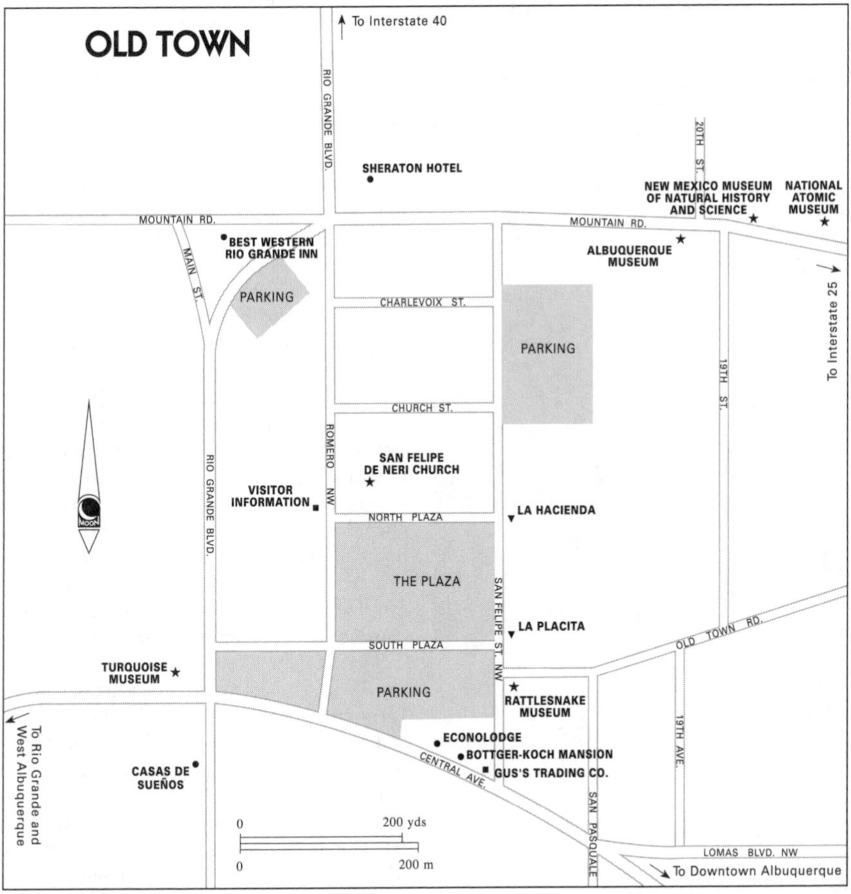

pay parking lots are nearby. Probably the best way to go is to park at the city lot at the Albuquerque Museum just off Mountain Road, where parking hourly and daily rates make parking easy and safe. From the parking lot, you enter Old Town the back way (it's all of a 50-foot walk) and pass a number of shops en route. (There are also city parking lots on the west side of Old Town off Rio Grande Boulevard.) See the map.

A good place to start your tour of the shops is at the Turquoise Museum, 2107 Central NW (half a block west of Old Town), 505/247-8650, where a knowledgeable staff will explain the different types and grades of turquoise and silver, to better prepare you for the massive amounts of the stuff you'll see—and to help you distinguish the good buys from the bad. Admission is $4, with discounts for kids, seniors, and groups.

Information at Old Town

An information booth is on Romero NW across from the church. You'll find information here not only on Old Town but on attractions, dining, and lodging throughout Albuquerque—including bus routes and schedules—and on the rest of New Mexico as well. Attendants will gladly answer any questions you have about where to go

COURTESY OF NEW MEXICO DEPARTMENT OF TOURISM/MARK NOHL

San Felipe de Neri church in Old Town, Albuquerque

and how to get there. Hours are Monday–Saturday 10 A.M.–5 P.M., Sunday 11 A.M.–5 P.M.

MUSEUMS NEAR OLD TOWN

New Mexico Museum of Natural History and Science

Tired of pueblos and Indian jewelry, mesas and burritos? Of Billy the Kid and arrowhead collections? Ready for a completely different kind of museum? Then head on down Mountain Road toward Old Town, and keep going until you see the life-sized dinosaur that stands guard in front of this terrific museum, one of Albuquerque's true treasures. This museum, with friendly and knowledgeable docents at every turn, provides an in-depth look at ol' Mother Earth, from the Big Bang 12 billion years ago to the 12,000-year-old Folsom hunters of eastern New Mexico. Along the way, you view models of DNA and read about its function, walk through a "live" volcano, stop at a theater for a narrated slide show of the creation of New Mexico's San Juan Basin, learn why New Mexico was once home to so many dinosaurs (during the Triassic period of 245–208 million years ago, the area was part of a floodplain with verdant tropical forests), and best of all, get a close-up view of dinosaur skeletons and life-sized dinosaur models that move and even bellow like the real ones must have. New Mexico's State Dinosaur, the *Coelophysis,* stalks one wall, while the *Quetzalcoatlus* soars high above the museum floor, its 35-foot wingspan stretching nearly from wall to wall.

Kids will love this place (my wife the teacher says, "It'd make a *perfect* field trip"), especially the dozens of hands-on displays. At some you pick up telephone receivers and listen to minilectures, and many of the fossils and dinosaur bones have signs that say Please Touch. The museum is open daily 9 A.M.–5 P.M., with slightly reduced hours of operation in September and January. Entrance is $5, less for kids and seniors; additional fees for entrance to the adjacent Lodestar Astronomy Center or the DynaTheatre.

The museum is also "rentable" for kids' birthday parties. For reasonable rates, you can have the Partysaurus Room on the second floor all to yourself, and the museum provides a hostess, tables, chairs, and cleanup. A tour of the museum is included.

The museum is at 1801 Mountain Rd. NW. For more information, write the New Mexico Museum of Natural History and Science, P.O. Box 7010, Albuquerque, NM 87194-7010, call 505/841-2800, or visit the website: museums.state.nm.us/nmmnh/nmmnh.html. For information on the theaters, phone 505/841-5950.

Albuquerque Museum of Art and History

Across the street from the Natural History Museum, this huge museum documents 400 years of New Mexico history with maps from old Spain (one showing California as an island), Spanish armor and helmets (where we learn that the practice of saluting a superior officer is probably a holdover from the days when a soldier had to raise his visor to show his face), blacksmithing

COURTESY OF THE NEW MEXICO MUSEUM OF NATURAL HISTORY AND SCIENCE/DAVID MANDEL

entrance to the New Mexico Museum of Natural History and Science

tools, sarapes, and blankets. One room is devoted to a revolving exhibit called *Asi Es la Vida (This Is the Life),* in which students from local grammar and high schools display their work. A theater in the museum shows films on Albuquerque's history, and you can get information about guided tours of nearby Old Town, which begin at the museum. You can also pick up brochures and maps for self-guided tours. Museum hours are Tuesday–Sunday 9 A.M.–5 P.M. The museum is at 2000 Mountain Rd. NW. Admission is $2 for adults, with discounts for kids and seniors; admission is free the first Wednesday of each month. For more information, call 505/243-7255.

National Atomic Energy Museum

This museum, just a little over an hour away from Los Alamos National Laboratories, where the atomic bomb was developed, is extremely educational and at the same time a bit disconcerting.

Once inside, you embark on a self-guided tour focusing on the development of atomic energy, particularly weaponry. On one wall is a copy of Einstein's letter to FDR informing (and warning) him of uranium's potential use. There are photos of Fermi and Oppenheimer hard at work on plutonium production, and of the secret projects throughout the country where much of the early research and testing took place. And as you wander through the displays you can't help but be a little saddened by it all, by the fact that the greatest intellects of the '30s and '40s were bent on producing something that would ultimately have the power to destroy the earth.

And then there are the bombs: "Little Boy" and "Fat Man." The former is a replica of the one dropped on Nagasaki, the latter of the one dropped on Hiroshima. Also displayed are the atomic bombs that came later: the Mark 6, Mark 7, Mark 17. You see how they became more graceful and streamlined, and you read about how they became more powerful and sophisticated.

The tour through the museum also takes you to several small screens, where you can view films of such events as the Pacific nuclear tests, such as the one that destroyed Eniwetok atoll. One display discusses the purposes of nuclear testing, while another explains the Limited Test Ban Treaty. Near the end of the tour are the *Energy Horizons* exhibits, where you can "compute your radiation dose" and read about the Waste Isolation Pilot Plant and how "safe and efficient" it is.

The museum also regularly shows the film *Ten Seconds That Shook the World,* usually at 10:30 A.M., 2 P.M., and 3:30 P.M. Newsreel clips from the '30s and '40s are included in a discussion of the development of atomic energy, culminating with the dropping of Little Boy and Fat Man and Japan's surrender. (Call the museum to double-check screening times.) The museum's outdoor display includes various missile systems, a 280 mm cannon, and the B-52, which you learn was used in atmospheric nuclear tests in the Pacific.

The Atomic Energy Museum, 1905 Mountain Rd., is open daily 9 A.M.–5 P.M., except New Year's Day, Easter, Thanksgiving, and Christmas. Admission is $3 for adults, $2 for kids. Note: after 32 years at Kirkland Air Force Base, the National Atomic Energy Museum is being housed in these temporary quarters while it awaits construction of its new digs nearby at Balloon Fiesta Park—expected to be completed by 2005 or 2006. Both sites are welcome changes from the formerly difficult-to-reach location.

For more information, or to arrange guided tours of the museum (for parties of six or more), call 505/284-3243.

American International Rattlesnake Museum

This small museum inside a gift shop just off the plaza, at 202 San Felipe NW, 505/242-6569, claims to have the world's largest collection of live rattlesnakes. It also carries lots of books and other publications on snakes and other reptiles, and on nature conservation and education in general. Open Monday–Saturday 10 A.M.–5 P.M. and Sunday 1 P.M.–6 P.M. Admission is $2 for adults, $1 for kids.

OTHER MUSEUMS

Indian Pueblo Cultural Center

At 2401 12th St. NW, one block north of I-40, this combination museum-gift shop-gallery-restaurant is an excellent place to introduce yourself to New Mexico's 19 Indian pueblos. Start downstairs in the museum. The first room is devoted to an overview of the Pueblo peoples, including discussions and flow charts of the three main Pueblo languages and many dialects. From there, you enter the prehistory room, which explains New Mexico's Indian civilizations from Clovis man to Spanish contact. Included are ex-

dancer at the Indian Pueblo Cultural Center

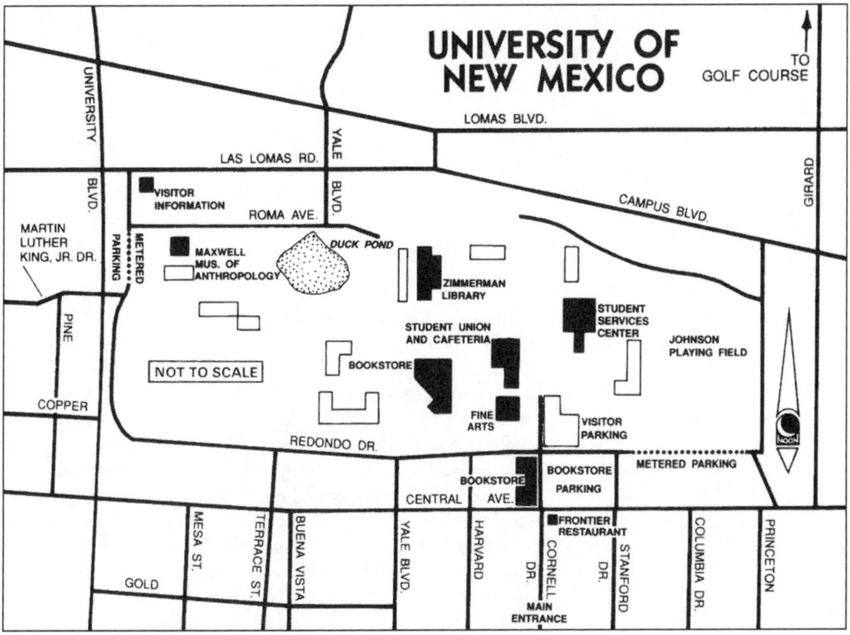

amples of Clovis and Sandia projectile points dating from 18,000 B.C., as well as a variety of dioramas and models of villages. The history room documents the Indians' time in New Mexico from Coronado (1540) until modern history. There are also explanations of tribal governments—both precontact and modern—and a look at pueblo life today, including a model of a "typical tourist," shorts and camera and all. Finally, a circular walkway takes you past a series of exhibits, explaining the history of each pueblo and displaying modern pottery, clothing, blankets, and tools.

Upstairs is an art gallery, featuring pottery and paintings by contemporary Pueblo artists, and a large gift shop, with everything from gimmicky ashtrays and salt-and-pepper sets to elegant alabaster sculptures with price tags as high as $2,000. There's also a huge selection of rugs, jewelry, sandpaintings, and kachina dolls. A restaurant serves typical Pueblo, Hopi, and Navajo cuisine (frybread, Navajo tacos, etc.) at reasonable prices. The center's hours are daily 9 A.M.–5:30 P.M., and the restaurant is open 7:30 A.M.–3:30 P.M. General admission to the museum, clearly the highlight of the center, is $4; seniors pay $3 and students $1. For more information, write Indian Pueblo Cultural Center, 2401 12th St. NW, Albuquerque, NM 87102, or call 505/843-7270 or 800/766-4405.

If you're around on a summer weekend, call ahead to get times for the Indian dances. Kids, especially, appreciate the demonstrations, although this is also an excellent opportunity for adults to get an introduction to various tribes' dancing styles and symbolism, and maybe even some mythology. The dances are held on the lawn in the courtyard of the center, and admission is free. (Indian dancers can also be hired for private parties and other functions. Contact the Indian Pueblo Cultural Center for more information.)

University of New Mexico Center for the Arts

Tucked away in a corner of the University of New Mexico's Fine Arts building, this little museum has

THE UNIVERSITY OF NEW MEXICO

Founded in 1889, this 25,000-student campus near downtown Albuquerque is the city's fourth-largest employer (9,500 employees) and the state's largest and most influential educational facility: included among UNM graduates are a third of the state's current legislators, lawyers, and physicians and a quarter of the state's teachers. With its adobe buildings and deep-green lawns, museums and concert halls, and its ethnically diverse student population lost in books beneath shade trees, chatting in the cafeteria, and scurrying to classes, UNM offers the visitor an excellent opportunity to wander among a vital and fascinating community.

UNM offers associate degrees in nine fields, bachelor's degrees in 137, master's in 133, and Ph.D.s in 69, as well as 12 educational-specialist certificates and degrees in law and medicine. Among the programs and departments for which the school is particularly highly regarded are anthropology, biology, environmental studies, Latin American studies, and nuclear pharmacy (75 percent of the state's pharmacists are graduates of UNM's school of pharmacology). The University of New Mexico's 1,200 full-time faculty members include professors recognized worldwide for their scholarship and contributions to their fields. Among them are the English department's Rudolfo Anaya (novelist), anthropology's Lewis Binford, and physics' Marlan Scully. The average student-to-instructor ratio is 16:1.

The prestigious UNM Medical Center (including the School of Medicine, the University and Carrie Tingley hospital, Children's Psychiatric Hospital, the Mental Health and Cancer Centers, and the Center for Noninvasive Diagnosis) sees more than 350,000 outpatients a year. In addition, the University of New Mexico Press, which publishes a wide array of scholarly books (about 50 titles), is recognized internationally as among the finest of university presses. The University of New Mexico has branch campuses in Gallup, Los Alamos, and Valencia County, and graduate centers in Los Alamos and Santa Fe.

Visiting UNM

Spending a few hours on the University of New Mexico campus is a wonderful way to enrich a visit to Albuquerque. Whether your bent is simply wandering around the sprawling lawns and shady patios or taking advantage of the marvelous cultural opportunities the university offers, or a little bit of both, you'll enjoy your visit. You'll find an array of art museums and galleries, a geology and meteoritics museum, the Southwestern Museum of Biology, and the Maxwell Museum of Anthropology. The school's library system is the largest in the state, with nearly two million books. The campus bookstore carries, in addition to thousands of textbooks stacked to the ceilings, books on New Mexico and the Southwest (including University of New Mexico Press titles) and a wide array of gifts, from UNM T-shirts to fraternity decals.

Begin your visit to the campus at the Visitor Information Center at 1700 Las Lomas SE (see map), where you can pick up brochures, gallery listings, concert schedules, and other materials. To get more information, write Public Affairs Department, Hodgen Hall 122, University of New Mexico, Albuquerque, NM 87131-0011. You can also call Public Affairs at 505/277-5813. Other useful numbers: Admissions, 505/277-2446; Zimmerman (general) Library, 505/277-5761; Maxwell Museum of Anthropology, 505/277-4404; University Art Museum, 505/277-4001; and University Operator, 505/277-0111.

an outstanding permanent collection of paintings, photography, and sculpture, as well as rotating temporary exhibits. The permanent collection includes fascinating mid-19th-century photography, 16th- to 18th-century Italian paintings, three Georgia O'Keeffe pieces that were gifts of her estate, and photos by Ansel Adams and Diane Arbus. Admission to the museum is free, although donations are gratefully accepted. Hours are Tuesday–Friday 9 A.M.–4 P.M., Tuesday evening 5–8 P.M., and Sunday 1–4 P.M. A small but well-stocked bookstore is at the entrance to the museum. The museum is adjacent to Popejoy Hall on Cornell Street, 505/277-4001.

Maxwell Museum of Anthropology

On the University of New Mexico campus, the Maxwell Museum has two sections. The first rotates a wide range of exhibits of anthropological interest, primarily of the Southwest, but from around the world as well: photos of ancient mud homes in Africa and India, for example. The second is made up of selections from the museum's own collection, including Apache masks and moccasins, a beaded medicine turtle, baskets, and cradleboards. Watch for the *People of the Southwest* exhibit, set up like an archaeological dig, highlighting historical cultures of the area. To get to the Maxwell Museum of Anthropology, take University Boulevard north from Central and watch for signs. Metered parking spaces are provided on campus near the museum for short-term parking. Hours are Monday–Friday 8 A.M.–5 P.M. Admission is free, but donations are gladly accepted. Phone 505/277-4405.

OTHER ALBUQUERQUE SIGHTS

Sandia Peak Tramway

Billed as the world's longest single-span tramway, the 2.7-mile 60-passenger Sandia Tram rises in 15 minutes from the deserty foothills on Albuquerque's northeast side to a lush and windy mountain peak 4,000 feet above. The views up top, of Albuquerque and the surrounding area, are absolutely spectacular. Take a late-evening tram, and watch the sun set from the viewing platform. Typically, summer storms in the valley mean billowy clouds building up at eye level, as the sky turns a vivid pink and the sun drops behind Cabezon Peak to the west.

You can also use the tram terminal as a starting

COURTESY OF NEW MEXICO DEPARTMENT OF TOURISM/DAN MONAGHAN

The Sandia Peak Tramway is an engineering marvel. The car climbs 4,000 feet in about 15 minutes, depositing riders at the top of Sandia Peak.

point for day and overnight hikes. Serious backpackers and casual mountain walkers alike will delight in the Sandias' many trails, and wildlife buffs will want to keep their eyes peeled for the many animals in the area—from the common rabbits and ground squirrels to the less-often-seen coyotes, bighorn sheep, and mountain lions.

Memorial Day through Labor Day, the tram runs Thursday–Tuesday 9 A.M.–10 P.M.; the rest of the year it runs Thursday–Tuesday 9 A.M.–8 P.M. and Wednesday 5–8 P.M. Cost is $14 for adults, $10 for seniors and kids 5–12 (discount with dinner at the High Finance Restaurant at the top; see Food, following).

During the winter, you can take the tram to the top of Sandia Peak Ski Area and spend the day on the slopes. Reduced fares are offered to "trammers" buying ski-lift tickets.

Notes: 1) The tram closes the first two weeks of November for annual maintenance. 2) Bring a sweater, as even if it's warm at the base, it's likely to be windy and cold up top, especially in the evenings.

For more information on the Sandia Peak Tramway or the High Finance Restaurant, call 505/856-7325. For more information on hiking in the Sandia Mountains, call the Sandia Ranger Station at 505/281-3304 or Cibola National Forest office at 505/275-5207. A 24-hour national forest road- and trail-conditions message can be reached by calling 505/842-3891.

Rio Grande Nature Center State Park

This is an excellent place to take the kids for an afternoon of exploring indoor nature exhibits and hiking through tangled river brush and along wandering riparian trails—in fact, you get so caught up in the natural world along the river, it's easy to forget downtown Albuquerque is just a few miles away. It's also one of the city's great bargains. A buck buys you entrance to the park (kids under six are free), where an introductory visitors center offers goodies sure to please nature lovers of all persuasions: an active cutaway beehive; a large window looking out on a pond, with sketches of what to look for (frogs, turtles); maps of bird migration routes; a display of the Sandia Mountains' five life zones; and a resource/reading room, with couches and copies of *National Geographic.* Field guides and binoculars can be borrowed from the visitors center and taken out into the park.

Once you've explored the visitors center, pick up one of the interpretive guidebooks and head out to the two trails. Each is about a mile long, and both wind out into the willows, tamarisks, cottonwoods, and cattail marshes. Watch for birds—more than 260 species spend at least part of their time here—as well as coyotes, beavers, and raccoons.

To get to the Rio Grande Nature Center, take Candelaria Road west until it dead-ends into the park, or take Rio Grande Boulevard north from Old Town and turn left on Candelaria. The center is open daily 10 A.M.–5 P.M. Picnicking is not allowed inside, but benches and shade are provided at the parking lot and are perfect for a pre-walk picnic. Admission is $1; kids six to 18 get in for $.50, and kids under six are free. For more information, phone 505/344-7240.

Petroglyph National Monument

This state and city park, on a volcanic escarpment on Albuquerque's west side, includes thousands of petroglyphs dating from A.D. 1000–1600, as well as five extinct volcanoes. Four short trails (the longest is about 200 yards) with points-of-interest markers wander up into the million-year-old lava flow, past bizarre ceremonial drawings and various representations of birds, animals, and people. The quality of the petroglyphs varies greatly, both in degree of preservation and skill level of artist (some look as if they might have gotten only a C+ at finals time: "Say, Thag, maybe you ought to think about switching over to the arrowhead department . . . "). Overall, the petroglyphs aren't quite as good as those at Three Rivers, on Highway 54 north of Alamogordo.

You'll find picnic tables at the base of the cliff, restrooms, and parking at each trailhead. The park is at 6900 Unser Boulevard. From I-40, take the Unser Bouelvard exit and go north three miles to the main visitors center. A second visitors center, Boca Negra Canyon, is five miles north from there; both visitors centers are open daily

8 A.M.–5 P.M. Entrance fee is $1 per car weekdays, $2 on weekends. For more information, phone 505/839-4429.

Albuquerque BioPark

This three-part complex includes the **Rio Grande Zoological Park,** the **Albuquerque Aquarium,** and the **Rio Grande Botanic Gardens** and collectively offers an impressive array of displays of flora and fauna from the Southwest and from around the world.

A visit to a zoo might not strike you as a typical New Mexican experience, but if you've got a free afternoon, you'll enjoy the diversion. First of all it's a clean zoo. No crappy, littered cages, and lots of nice shaded picnic tables and lawns (for humans). Second, this zoo is hip. Throughout are displays pointing out the plights of endangered species, and though the animals are by definition not in their natural environment, they are part of a captivity-bred program, so at least the critters haven't been kidnapped and forced to go from the wild to the cages.

The zoo covers 60 acres along the Rio Grande and is open Monday–Friday 9 A.M.–5 P.M., weekends till 6 P.M. Memorial Day through Labor Day. Admission is $5 for ages 13–63 and $3 for ages three to 12 and 64 and over. Kids two and under get in free. Strollers and cameras are available to rent, and food (hot dogs, nachos, giant pretzels, sundaes, etc.) is available inside at the Phoenix Plaza and Lobo Cafes. Take 10th Street south from Central; you can't miss it. Phone 505/764-6200.

The Albuquerque Aquarium and the Rio Grande Botanic Garden complex, which opened in late 1996, is a huge, $11 million project that includes a 500,000-gallon aquarium with a shark tank and simulated tidal flats and coral reefs; a 10-acre botanical garden that includes a 3,000-square-foot pavilion devoted to desert vegetation; and a separate walled garden replicating Renaissance Spanish and Moorish architecture and featuring cultivated flora.

The new complex, 2601 Central (at the intersection of Tingley), 505/764-6200, is open daily 9 A.M.–5 P.M., weekends till 6 P.M. Memorial Day through Labor Day. Admission is $4.50 for adults, $2.50 for kids.

Wildlife West Nature Park and Wildlife West Chuckwagon

This 122-acre interactive educational facility offers visitors the chance to view close-up much of the state's native flora and fauna. In addition to the animals that have been acquired from rehabilitation facilities—mule deer, raccoons, foxes, and turtles—the park's "habitat enhancement" efforts have led many wild animals to call the place home. Among these welcome interlopers are squirrels, skunks, porcupines, coyotes, prairie dogs, and various birds and reptiles.

A favorite site for school field trips, the park holds a birdwalk (just under a half mile long), a large pond with observation deck, a seven-acre deer paddock, a 200-seat auditorium, and a food-service area. In addition, bird-handling classes are offered for $20. Wildlife West Nature Park is operated strictly by grants, donations, and volunteers.

Admission to the park is $3 for adults, $2 for students and seniors. Summer hours are daily 9 A.M.–6 P.M. The rest of the year the park is open noon–4 P.M. To get there, take I-40 about 10 miles east from Albuquerque to Exit 187 (Highway 344); then take the frontage road west about a mile. For more information, phone 505/281-7655 or 877/815-9453. You can also reach the park at website: wildlife@swcp.com.

Coronado State Park and Monument

About 15 miles north of Albuquerque, along the high west bank of the Rio Grande, are the ruins of the Kuaua Pueblo. Coronado arrived here in 1540 and encountered a thriving population of Indians living in a multistory apartment-type pueblo. By the late 16th century, the Indians had abandoned their complex, perhaps going as far north as Taos, perhaps just moving to the nearby Sandia or Santa Ana Pueblos. The ruins of Kuaua are open to the public today, and though they're not as impressive as the Pecos or Quarai, for example (in part, because no mission walls tower over the crumbling adobe), they are worth visiting. A visitors center and museum at the state monument explain the Indians' lifestyle along the Rio Grande, as well as Coronado's expedition (you can actually try on a replica of a 16th-century Spanish steel breastplate and helmet). Out among the ruins, you can climb down inside a reconstructed kiva and see reproductions of the polychrome murals discovered inside. The monument is open daily 8:30 A.M.–5 P.M. May 1 through mid-September, and 8 A.M.–5 P.M. the rest of the year. Entrance fee is $4 per car. For more information, phone 505/867-5351.

The state park, adjacent to the monument, has camping facilities, and the adventurous can wade into the muddy Rio Grande. Costs are $4 for day use, $8 for a primitive campsite, with an additional $4 for hookups. The park has bathrooms with flush toilets and hot showers. To get to the park and monument take the Highway 44 exit from I-25 and go one mile west of Bernalillo. The ruins are on your right. For state park information, phone 505/867-5589.

Practicalities

ACCOMMODATIONS

Albuquerque has as wide a range of accommodations as you can imagine—from designer Holiday Inns to seedy motels that accommodate the illegal street trade, from classic old hotels with valet parking to Motel 6s. A few times a year it's of utmost importance to reserve a room well in advance. During the State Fair in September and the Balloon Fiesta in October, for example, if you haven't booked a room by early summer, you'll probably be plumb out of luck.

Remember also that Albuquerque is a big city, and there is crime. The Albuquerque Police Department's Crime Prevention Unit recommends not scrimping when it comes to lodging. Stay in a decent hotel, they say, one with a well-lighted parking lot and 24-hour desk service.

Under $50: Hostel

Generally the least expensive way to travel, and one of the best ways to meet fellow travelers, hosteling can be a real adventure, though it's not for everyone. The typical dorm-style accommodations, the chore(s) you'll be asked to do to offset the exceptionally low rates (under $20), and the socializing demanded by the lack of privacy can either suit your needs and moods or not. If they do, check out the **Route 66 Hostel,** 1012 Central NW, 505/247-1813, which offers dorm-style lodging as well as some private rooms, including use of kitchen facilities.

Under $50

Other than staying at a hostel, if you're really set on spending less than $50 on a night's lodging, you have two options, one recommended, the other not. First, the "not." Don't stay in one of the cheap motels downtown on or near the old Route 66. Despite recent urban-renewal projects, this area's still rather run down and not particularly "tourist-friendly." A better bet in that price range are the franchise motels, many of which are at the freeway exits especially on the outskirts of town. Naturally, these digs are about as generic as you can imagine—with very little in the way of amenities—but if all you're looking for is a good clean bed in a clean safe room, then this might be the ticket.

The classic generic motel, of course, is the Motel 6—believe me, I've stayed in many—and there are about a half dozen in the Albuquerque area. Among them: on I-40 on the west side at Coors Road (Exit 155), 505/831-8888; on I-40 on the east side (Exit 167), 505/294-4600; and on I-25 on the north side (Exit 232), 505/821-1472. For a complete list or to book a room online, go to website: www.motel6.com.

$50–100

Lodging in this price range is still the mostly generic franchise inns, though obviously a bit nicer and with a bit more amenities. You're likely to find exercise rooms, free continental breakfasts, inside corridors, and other bonuses. Among these lodges are several near the airport, including the **Best Western Airport Inn,** 2400 Yale,

505/242-7022; **Comfort Inn,** 2300 Yale, 505/243-2244; and **La Quinta Inn** 2116 Yale, 505/243-5500.

There's not much near Old Town Albuquerque in this price range, except an **Econo Lodge,** 2321 Central, 505/243-8475. On the other hand, there are scads of possibilities along Interstates 40 and 25. On the north end (Exit 231 from I-25) is another **La Quinta Inn,** 5241 San Antonio, 505/821-9000; a **Howard Johnson Express,** 7630 Pan American Freeway, 505/828-1600; and a **Hampton Inn,** 5101 Ellison, 505/344-1555.

$100–150

If you can afford to move into this range you're going to have a lot more to choose from, including a handful of very nice hotels within walking distance of Old Town and several distinctive bed-and-breakfasts.

One of Albuquerque's oldest and most colorful hotels is **La Posada de Albuquerque,** 125 2nd St. at the corner of Copper (one block from Central), 505/242-9090 or 800/777-5732. This was one of native New Mexican Conrad Hilton's first hotels, built in 1939, and it has all the charm and elegance of that era, combined with typical New Mexican design and architecture. La Posada offers both valet parking and free limo service to and from the airport. And though rooms aren't cheap, they're not as pricey as you might guess (though suites can run to $275). For a splurge after a number of grubby days on the road, La Posada just might be what the ol' doctor ordered.

The **Sheraton Old Town,** 800 Rio Grande Blvd., 505/843-6300 or 800/237-2133, is one of the closest hotels to Old Town and the nearby museums (five-minute walk). Extensively remodeled in 2001, the Sheraton is also about the highest-rise around (11 stories), its rooms offering views of Old Town, much of Albuquerque, and the surrounding area. Still another good bet is the **Best Western Rio Grande Inn,** 1015 Rio Grande Blvd. NW, 505/843-9500—also within walking distance of Old Town.

$150–250

In contrast to the prewar decor of La Posada, the **Hyatt Regency,** 330 Tijeras NW, 505/842-1234, is one of the city's most modern-looking hotels and offers 21st-century amenities and luxury to go with it, including valet parking. This downtown hotel is a favorite of business folk and conventioneers, so rates are actually less (sometimes under $100) on weekends.

Bed-and-Breakfasts: $100–200

Several dozen bed-and-breakfast lodges are scattered in and around Albuquerque, with quite a few conveniently located near Old Town. Just one block from the Old Town plaza is a long-standing favorite, the **Bottger-Koch Mansion,** 110 San Felipe NW, 505/243-3639 or 800/758-3639, with seven rooms (view them at website: www.bottger.com). Originally built in 1212, the mansion has been remodeled several times and is now one of the classiest and most convenient places to stay in the city. Nearby, and nearly as convenient, the **Casas de Sueños,** 310 Rio Grande SW, 505/247-4560 or 800/242-8987, offers 21 rooms, including some casitas (small, individual units).

Just north of Albuquerque, in the quietly historic village of Corrales, the **Chocolate Turtle,** 1098 W. Meadowlark Ln., 505/898-1800 or 800/898-1842, offers four nicely appointed and spacious rooms; rates include a full Southwest breakfast and the house specialty, chocolate-candy turtles, served every afternoon.

Camping and RVing

Albuquerque has been KOA'd twice; both offer pull-through sites for about $30 with full hookups. The **KOA Kampground North** is about 15 miles north of town just off I-25 in Bernalillo (555 Hill Rd.), 505/867-5227 or 800/562-3616. A very nice, tree-shaded campground, this KOA offers free pancake breakfasts to all guests. From the north, take the Bernalillo exit; from the south, take the Highway 44 exit toward Aztec and Cuba and follow the signs.

The **Albuquerque Central KOA,** 12400 Skyline NE, 505/296-2729 or 800/562-7781, is at the Juan Tabo south exit from I-40.

In west Albuquerque, pull-through sites with full hookups are available at **American RV Park**

of Albuquerque, 505/831-3545 or 800/282-8885, Exit 149 from I-40.

FOOD

As you'd expect, there are scores of restaurants in Albuquerque featuring excellent Mexican and New Mexican food, but neither is there a shortage of places dishing up fine cuisine from around the world—Thai, Indian, Italian, Vietnamese, Japanese, Native American, and more. And prices range just as broadly. You shouldn't have trouble finding any number of restaurants serving great meals for under $6, and if you want to splurge, there are some where dinner for two can set you back more than $100. Following is a small sampling of what you'll find.

Start Me Up

The downtown, university, and Old Town areas are all rife with places perfect for getting a jump on the day. You'll find coffee-and-pastry shops on seemingly every block, as well as the ubiquitous Starbucks (at last count, there were 10 in town).

My favorite breakfast spot in Albuquerque, though, is the **Frontier Restaurant,** at the corner of Central and Cornell (2400 Cornell), 505/289-3130. Open 24 hours, the Frontier is an ideal spot to check the pulse of Albuquerque's university crowd, the businesses that cater to it, and the city's post-punk street folk. The frontier specializes in good cheap breakfasts (try a homemade cinnamon roll), as well as lunch and dinner.

Lunch and Dinner near Old Town

Several restaurants on and near the plaza cater to Old Town visitors; in general their food is good and authentic. On weekends and busy days throughout summer reservations are a good call.

Right on Old Town Plaza in a structure built in 1706, **La Placita Dining Rooms,** 208 San Felipe NW, 505/247-2204, is a pleasant place to rest after wandering around the gift shops and museums. Several individual dining rooms (which truly separate the smoking and no-smoking sections) and period decor give diners a genuine sense of 18th-century territorial New Mexico. And the food isn't bad at all. I had a green-chile chicken burrito that was hot enough to send beads of sweat from my forehead dripping onto the detective novel I was reading. A very good sign. Those interested in something tamer can order from the American-food section, featuring burgers, salads, shrimp, and steaks; entrées run $6–16.

Another popular Old Town eatery is **La Hacienda,** at 302 San Felipe just off the plaza, 505/243-3131. Lunch offerings are sandwiches ($5–9) and Mexican plates ($6–10). For dinner, steak and seafood are in the $10–18 price range, while Mexican plates run $8–12. Reservations are a good idea on weekends and in summer.

For upscale dining in Old Town, try **Maria Teresa,** 618 Rio Grande, 505/242-3900. In a National Historic building dating from the 1840s, Maria Teresa serves traditional New Mexican dishes, as well as steaks, seafood, pastas, and salads, with lunch running $8–12 and dinner $12–25.

Near Downtown and the University

For authentic New Mexican food at excellent prices, try **El Patio,** at 142 Harvard SE, across Central from the University of New Mexico, 505/268-4245. A small, cozy restaurant, with tables both inside and on the patio outside, this place specializes in *chiles rellenos, burritos, fajitas, and, a personal favorite, carne adovada,* with complete dinners running $5–10. À la carte items, including *rellenos* and stuffed sopaipillas, cost $3–5. Weather permitting, outside diners are serenaded by a low-key Spanish guitarist.

The two **Monroe's** restaurants, at 1520 Lomas Blvd. NW, 505/242-1111, and 6021 Osuna NE, 505/881-4225, are small diner-style New Mexican restaurants that have been serving some of the best food for the best prices in town since 1962. The sopaipillas, about the size of a small station wagon, are excellent. A favorite among locals, especially families, Monroe's serves breakfast, lunch, and dinner seven days a week. House specials (*huevos rancheros,* Mexican pizza, the "Guaco-taco Plate," and green-chile hamburgers) are served for both lunch and dinner. In addition to rice-and-bean dinner plates (blue-corn enchiladas, tamales, *chile rellenos,* and combos), Monroe's also serves burgers and sandwiches, as well as desserts (flan, sundaes, and pies); carry-out available.

For good old-fashioned American fare, try the **66 Diner,** 1405 Central NE (between the university and downtown), 505/247-1421. This neon neo-diner, complete with soda fountain, serves "Blue Plate Specials" nightly (spaghetti and meatballs, fried catfish), burgers and sandwiches, and a variety of desserts, malts, and shakes. Saturday and Sunday mornings, the 66 serves breakfast 8–11 A.M. Try the blue-corn hotcakes or the fresh fruit and yogurt. Open daily for lunch and dinner. Another retro diner is the **Owl Cafe,** 800 Eubank (at the I-40 exit), 505/291-4900. A direct descendant of the legendary Owl Cafe in San Antonio (New Mexico), the Owl serves burgers, sandwiches, meatloaf, and other American food, as well as the green-chile burgers for which it's famous. Breakfast, lunch, and dinner daily.

If you'd like to wash your meal down with something more interesting than the conventional Coors or margarita, stop in at **Il Vicino Wood Oven Pizza and Brewery,** 3403 Central, 505/266-7855, an Italian-style bistro that brews its own beer (and root beer) and offers a wide variety of interesting and inexpensive wines. Salads, pastas, and wood-fired pizzas run $6–10.

Other Nearby Dining

One of my favorite Albuquerque restaurants is **Sadie's Dining Room,** 6230 4th NW (about three miles north of Old Town), 505/345-5339. This busy place is a local tradition, having recently moved to this location from inside the bowling alley down the street. The food here is excellent, and the portions huge. Burritos, stuffed sopaipillas, and enchilada dinners run $8–11, although you can order à la carte and be guaranteed plenty of *comida.* You can also get burgers, steaks, and other dishes less traditionally local.

The **High Finance Restaurant,** 505/243-9742, offers a very different kind of "dining experience"—at the top of the tram at Sandia Peak. It may take saving your pennies and pesos, 'cause the place isn't cheap ($15–40), but the views of Albuquerque and the valley, the distant mountains, the clouds rolling in at eye level, and the sunsets are unbeatable. Appetizers run $5–9 and include deep-fried zucchini, shrimp, and scallops with lime and chiles, and escargots. Main dishes vary from traditional steaks and seafood to chicken and pasta dishes to Mexican. Specialties include veal fettuccine, scallops, prime rib, and Alaska crab legs. The High Finance menu also has child's plates, including small steaks, large hot dogs, and fries. Choose from an excellent wine list, but be careful: remember, you're 4,000 feet above Albuquerque and 10,000 feet above sea level.

To get to the High Finance, follow the signs from Tramway Boulevard to Tramway Loop. Open daily for lunch and dinner. Trams leave every 20–30 minutes, with return departures announced over loudspeakers in the restaurant.

If you feel like working up an appetite before dinner, you can also drive up the back side of the Sandias to Sandia Crest and hike three miles along the ridge to the restaurant.

Be sure to bring your camera and a sweater. Dress code here is "anything goes," and you see everything from hiking shorts to suits and gowns. Reservations are a good idea, not only to save you the few bucks off the fare, but because the restaurant is popular and gets awfully crowded.

A Bit of a Drive, but Worth It

For local color, a sense of history, and excellent New Mexican food, **Rancho de Corrales,** on Corrales Road in Corrales, 505/897-3131, is hard to beat. The hacienda in which the restaurant is built dates to 1801 and has a history rife with adultery, jealousy, and murder (read about it on the menu). Today, the restaurant is a quiet getaway from the hustle and bustle of downtown Albuquerque, with little hint of its scandalous past. Several dining rooms—the original rooms of the home—as well as an enclosed patio, provide a varied decor. Specials include enchiladas, stuffed sopaipillas, *flautas,* and burritos ($7–10). Steaks and seafood are also served, with prices a bit higher ($8–14). The Rancho's nightly live entertainment usually features a guitarist and vocalist. Wine, beer, and cocktails. Closed Monday.

The **Luna Mansion,** 505/865-7333, is south of Albuquerque in Los Lunas, in a Southern

Colonial-style adobe mansion built in 1881. Serving Sunday brunch as well as dinner five days a week (Wednesday–Sunday), this is a popular spot for Albuquerque folks looking to get out of the city. The restaurant features gourmet American, New Mexican, and continental cuisine, with fresh seafood specials, and has the most thorough wine list in the area. Take I-25 about 20 miles south to Los Lunas and follow the signs to the restaurant.

Near the Airport

The **Rio Grande Yacht Club,** 2500 Yale SE, 505/243-6111, serves a wide range of fresh seafood in a setting that tries to make its customers feel as if they're eating in Key West. Open for lunch and dinner daily. The **Village Inn,** in the parking lot of the Best Western Airport Inn on Yale SE, 505/243-5476, is open 24 hours a day, except midnight Sunday to 6 A.M. Monday.

Ethnic Foods

For Italian food in Albuquerque, check out **Trattoria Trombino,** 5415 Academy, 505/821-5974, which a respected friend claims is the best in town. The restaurant serves lunch Monday–Friday and dinner nightly, specializing in lighter versions of traditional Italian fare. Entrées—veal, pastas, seafood, and poultry—are in the $8–12 range. Another popular Italian restaurant is **Scalo, Northern Italian Grill,** 3500 Central SE, 505/255-8781, specializing in pastas, grilled meats, and fish. Open Monday–Saturday for lunch, Monday–Sunday for dinner.

For Thai food, check out the **Thai House,** 106 Buena Vista SE, 505/247-9205, where authentic (hot!) dishes are served at reasonable prices. Closed Sunday.

When the Boss Is Buying

One of the Albuquerque area's most upscale New Mexican restaurants is the **Prairie Star,** on Jemez Canyon Dam Road in Bernalillo, 505/867-3327. Adjacent to the new Valley Grande Golf Course, the restaurant offers a wonderfully pastoral rural setting, with views of the Sandia Mountains and the fertile Rio Grande Valley. Though new by Albuquerque standards—compared to restaurants 100 years old—the Prairie Star has already earned a solid reputation for itself among locals, tourists, and food critics. Indeed, *Albuquerque Monthly,* in a recent "Best of Albuquerque," wrote that the restaurant's name is "too modest. . . . It should be called the Prairie Five-Star," and the Albuquerque *Journal* said it's "the New Mexico experience your out-of-town relatives long for." Serving Tuesday–Sunday, the Prairie Star specializes in innovative New Mexican foods, such as trout topped with pine nuts, shrimp in a tequila sauce, and chicken grilled with local herbs and spices. Desserts might include green-chile ice cream and white-chocolate mousse served with berry purees.

Another upper-end favorite, where folks swear you'll find the city's best steaks, is **The Great American Land and Cattle Company,** 1550 Tramway NE, 505/292-1510. A long-standing Albuquerque tradition, this no-nonsense steakhouse specializes in good ol' American red meat. Hefty slabs of steak are accompanied by sides of beans and cole slaw, served family-style in buckets at your table. Expect to pay $60 and up for two, with drinks. The restaurant is open for dinner daily.

Another high-end eatery—one of the most elegant restaurants in town—is the **Rancher's Club of New Mexico,** in the Hilton Hotel at 1901 University Blvd., 505/884-2500. Dinner for two could easily run $75–100, but those who've eaten the food swear by it. Let me know what it's like. Open for lunch Monday–Friday, dinner daily, and Sunday brunch.

Eat Cetera

Looking for a place to hang out on a rainy afternoon, or some night after a movie? Try the **Double Rainbow,** 505/255-6633, at 3416 Central SE. This European-like café specializes in delicious gourmet ice creams and sorbets, desserts, and various coffee drinks, including espressos and cappuccinos. Weight-watchers beware, though: you'll find the display case of cheesecakes, carrot cakes, and lemon tortes tough to pass up. A huge newsstand with magazines varying from *Out* to *American Cowboy* to *Rolling Stone,* and cozy tables both inside and on the sidewalk outside, make the Double Rainbow an ideal place to hole up alone or to get to know someone better. The Double Rainbow also serves sandwiches, such as New York–style Reubens and mesquite-smoked turkey, for $2.95–4.50. For the noncaffeiners, there's a large selection of Italian sodas, mineral waters, and juices.

Following on the successful heels of Albuquerque's downtown Double Rainbow, a second store has opened at 4501 Juan Tabo NE, 505/275-8311. Attracting a much different crowd (Northeast Heights yuppies), the new Double Rainbow is much larger than the downtown store and equally successful. I stopped in one Wednesday evening around 9 and the place was packed. By the time I'd downed a bowl of French vanilla ice cream and lingered over a decaf, there was a line 20-deep waiting for tables.

Buffalo skulls along the high walls near the ceiling and along the stairway to the balcony have glow-in-the-dark eyeballs.

Grocery Stores and Markets

The grocery store chain with the widest selections and best prices in Albuquerque is **Smith's,** of which there are a half dozen or so. **Furr's** stores, also scattered about the city, have good selections too. **Wild Oats** at 6300 San Mateo NE (corner of Academy) and at 11015 Menaul NE, 505/275-6660, are upscale, yuppie/health-food grocery stores specializing in exotic and health-oriented produce, grains, meats (range-fed), and fish. Wild Oats also stocks health supplements and has one of the city's best selections of wines and beers, including many from microbreweries around the country. Open seven days a week. There are also Wild Oats stores in Santa Fe, at 1090 St. Francis and 1708 Llano.

For fresh, locally grown produce, check out the **farmers' market** on Tuesday and Saturday mornings on Central just west of the intersection with Pennsylvania.

ENTERTAINMENT

This is a big city, and there's a lot going on almost every night: gallery openings, big-name rock concerts, film series, semi-pro baseball games, open-mike nights, square dancing, stand-up comedy, and just about everything you can imagine. Both the Albuquerque *Tribune* and *Journal* publish extensive listings of what's going on where, as well as reviews and recommendations. Check also the UNM paper—the *Daily Lobo*—available free around town and offering detailed listings of who's playing where, from the smaller clubs to larger concert venues.

If you're looking for a place to spend a distinctly New Mexico night on the town, try the **KiMo Theatre** on Central in downtown Albuquerque. Built in 1927, this oddly ornate theater looks as if it were designed by a Pueblo Indian architect with art deco leanings (or maybe an art deconian who'd fallen in love with the Southwest and pueblo architecture). Its interior has the rounded corners and peach-beige hues typical of Southwest homes, and its beams and walls are painted with various Indian symbols. Buffalo skulls along the high walls near the ceiling and along the stairway to the balcony have glow-in-the-dark eyeballs. The KiMo, whose name is from the Tiwa meaning Mountain Lion or King of its Kind, books a wide variety of entertainment—from kiddie movies and cartoons on Saturday to internationally acclaimed modern dance and ballet troupes, from poetry readings featuring both local and imported talent to New Age performance artists. The KiMo regularly features well-known musicians, especially those in the folk tradition. The KiMo is sponsored in part by a grant from the Inter-Arts program of the National Endowment for the Arts. For more information and schedules, write KiMo Theatre, 419 Central NW, Albuquerque, NM 87102, or call 505/848-1370. You can also get up-to-date information from its website: www.cabq.gov/kimo. (By the way, even if you're not interested in seeing any of the KiMo's shows, head on down and take a look inside—open weekdays 9 A.M.–5 P.M. You'll probably never see anything like it again.)

Among the city's popular nightspots is **Midnight Rodeo,** 4901 McLeod NE, which often books big-name rock and country bands and also offers country-dance lessons. **O'Niell's Pub,** 3211 Central, 505/256-0564, features live Irish music.

SHOPPING

Although Old Town (see Sights, above) is where most Albuquerque visitors do the majority of their shopping, there are Indian jewelry, pottery, and other gift shops sprinkled generously around town. As in Old Town, they run the gamut from trinkety tourist traps to classy shops; you can usually tell the difference the minute you walk in the door.

For one of the city's finest and most authentic selections of Indian jewelry, pottery, basketry, sculpture, and other art, check out **Bien Mur Indian Market Center,** on the Sandia Reservation just north of town, 505/821-5400. You'll find a wide range of wares and prices here, and a conspicuous lack of the schlock found at other "trading posts." The salespeople are knowledgeable and helpful, too—they'll explain, for example, the difference between a Hopi bracelet and a Navajo copy—and you won't find the pressure here that you do elsewhere. Hours are Monday–Saturday 9 A.M.–5:30 P.M., Sunday 11 A.M.–5 P.M. Take the Tramway exit from I-25 and go east a half mile, or take Tramway from east Albuquerque toward I-25 and watch for the signs.

The gift shop at the **Indian Pueblo Cultural Center,** 2401 12th St. NW, has a wide selection of work—from sandpaintings, to kachinas, to pottery—from the various pueblos, as well as useful background information on the art and, oftentimes, the artists.

Another good place to shop for Native American crafts is **Gus's Trading Co.,** 2026 Central SW, 505/843-6381, where you'll find good prices on sandpaintings, jewelry, pottery, and other items.

Albuquerque has no shortage of mega-malls, either. **Coronado Center,** at the corner of Louisiana and Menaul, is home to more than 140 shops, anchored by five department stores: Broadway, Mervyn's, Sears, Foley's, and May D & F. From See's Candy to the Gap to Waldenbooks, the stores are pretty much identical to what you'll find in a large mall in Los Angeles, Minneapolis, or any other city in the country. But the wide array of shops, laid out on two levels and attractively decorated with many plants and skylights, makes the Coronado Center not only a delight for die-hard shoppers, but a tolerable place for the I-hate-malls contingent to pass a hot or rainy afternoon.

Winrock Center, just down the street (at Louisiana and I-40), has undergone a major makeover and is now competing with Coronado for the city's shoppers. Among its more than 100 shops and businesses, Winrock has three department stores (Dillard's, Marshalls, and Wards), two banks (Sunwest and First National), and a hotel, in addition to its other mall-type shops.

The **Cottonwood Mall** on the west side of Rio Rancho opened in July 1996. It offers 130 stores including four major department stores. A "theme" mall, this one is decorated in Albuquerque Balloon; upside-down hot-air balloons hang from the ceiling.

RECREATION

In the sunny Rio Grande Valley at the foot of the Sandia Mountains, and with the Jemez, Manzano, and Sangre de Cristo mountain ranges nearby, Albuquerque is in the heart of some of the finest recreation in the Southwest. Hiking, skiing (downhill and cross-country), golfing, cycling, camping, fishing—it's all here, or nearby. And Albuquerqueans take advantage of it. On weekends, they haul out their clubs, bikes, kayaks, tents, and fishing poles and head for their favorite spots. This is a town that loves its outdoors.

Cycling

Albuquerque's a big city and not exactly a cycler's utopia, but if you avoid certain streets and take advantage of some of the routes out on the edges of town, you should enjoy safe and scenic rides.

Streets to avoid on a bike: Central, Louisiana, Menaul, Montgomery, San Mateo, and Wyoming.

Streets that are better for crossing town: 2nd

Street, Alvarado, Claremont, Comanche, Constitution, Rio Grande, Santa Clara, and Stadium.

In addition, the city has constructed a number of bike paths through town. For an *Albuquerque City Bicycle Map,* call the Parks and Recreation Department at 505/768-3550.

Cycling outside the City

Once at the outskirts of Albuquerque, you've got some excellent rides to choose from (many riders take their bikes by car to a parking lot on the edge of town and ride from there). One popular route begins at the east end of town, at I-40 and Tramway (you can park your car at the shopping center, on the south side of I-40). Take the frontage road east to Highway 14 and head north. At the Sandia Crest junction, you can either turn left and wind your way up the steep road to the top of the mountain or continue north. The road to Sandia Crest is beautiful but difficult—14 miles of serious ascent; this is for experienced riders. If you continue north, you'll pass through rolling hills and, depending on how far you go, several picturesque old towns, where you can stop for lunch or just browse around (see the Turquoise Trail under Vicinity of Albuquerque, below). If you want, you can even go all the way to Santa Fe (72 miles), although again this is suggested for experienced riders only.

Or you can turn south at the Highway 14 junction (the new number of 14 South is 337) and go down through Tijeras and into the Manzano Mountains. This is one of the prettiest routes in the state, although it begins with a fairly extended uphill grade. Once on the ridge of the Manzanos, though, the riding gets easier, and you'll pass through a number of small towns. Should you get as far as Mountainair, you'll be able to ride into some fascinating Indian ruins (see Salinas National Monument and Manzano Mountains State Park under Vicinity of Albuquerque, below).

New Mexico has about two dozen bicycle clubs, roughly half of which are based in Albuquerque. Tours, including the Tour of the Rio Grande Valley, are held annually in town and throughout the state. For more information on cycling organizations, tours, races, or cycling in the state visit website: www.cabq.gov/bike.

Reminders: obey all traffic signs and signals—they weren't designed only for cars; use hand signals to let other riders and motorists know what you're doing; don't pass on the right; watch for cars pulling out, and make eye contact with drivers whenever possible; don't weave between parked or stopped cars; use a light at night; keep both hands ready to brake; wear a helmet.

Mountain Biking

With the Sandia Mountains so close, Albuquerque is a natural for mountain bikers. Be careful, though: some of the trails are restricted to hikers only. For more information, stop by any of the local bike stores, including those listed above, or the information booth at the Elena Gallegos Picnic Area (see below).

Hiking and Climbing

Albuquerque's position at the foot of the Sandia Mountains, butting up against the Cibola National Forest, affords city folk hundreds of miles of excellent hiking within a half-hour's drive of most parts of town. A good place to start is **Elena Gallegos Picnic Area** off Tramway, just north of the intersection with Spain Road NE. Look for the sign on Tramway, and then follow the paved road for 1.5 miles to the picnic area. (Entrance fee is $1 a carload.) From there, a number of trails wander up into the Sandias, and you'll be surprised how quickly you find yourself in the sticks, even though the city is still virtually at your feet. The trails vary in degrees of difficulty and length; the longest and most difficult is eight miles to the crest. The ranger at the gate (open 8 A.M.–8 P.M.) will gladly point you in a suitable direction.

The picnic sites are broadly scattered about the grounds and afford privacy as well as good views of the city and the Sandias. One sheltered two-table site is available for large groups (by reservation only—call 505/873-6620), and the bathrooms are wheelchair-accessible.

The back side of the Sandia Mountains offers excellent hiking as well. Take the Sandia Crest Trail road from Highway 14 North and

NEW MEXICO STATE FAIR

The New Mexico State Fair, held each year during the middle two weeks of September, is one of the state's premier events. Attendance consistently ranks in the top six state fairs nationally, and the State Fair Rodeo is the largest of its kind in the world. Other attractions include the midway carnival, with more than 100 rides and concessions; the Albuquerque Downs racetrack, featuring some of the fastest quarter horses and thoroughbreds in the Southwest; an extensive concert schedule, starring nationally known and local artists; as well as all the other things that bring throngs to state fairs: livestock and agricultural exhibits and competitions, food, artistic and cultural exhibits, food, educational and commercial exhibits, food, and perhaps the biggest draw of all—wonderful, sumptuous, varied, and delectable food.

For the past several years, the New Mexico State Fair has attracted more than one million visitors during its two-week run—not bad when you consider the entire state has only about a million and a half residents. State Fair management has worked hard to provide safety and comfort for all those who visit. Security people are everywhere, and they are as smiling and helpful as they are serious about their jobs. Comfort and rest areas are easy to find and well maintained. There are even special changing areas for the diapered visitors and their parents.

And for those mamas willing to let their babies grow up to be cowboys, the New Mexico State Fair Rodeo is a great place for them to start a-ridin' and a-ropin'. Top cowboys and cowgirls mosey on over to the Tingley Coliseum nearly every night the fair is in session for the big-money pro-rodeo competition. Besides the steer-wrestlin' and barrel-racin' events, each rodeo features a concert given by one of the nation's top performers of country and western music.

Fair visitors not attracted to the sights, sounds, and smells of the rodeo will not feel left out, however, for the nights offer more than one kind of entertainment. No state fair would be complete without the white-knuckled thrill of a roller coaster, Tilt-a-whirl, or Avalanche. Nor will any adventurous visitor to the New Mexico State Fair be denied ample opportunity to be spun, twisted, shook, rattled, and rolled. Out on the glittering midway are rides for those willing to risk them (and for those who find it fun just to watch). There, too, the fair-goer can pitch coins, toss darts, ogle the bearded lady and the two-headed calf ("It's alive, folks—step right up"), or try to fool the fellow guessing weights and ages over by the cotton-candy and caramel-apple stands.

Did someone mention food? Close your eyes and imagine: *chalupas,* frittatas, *suvlaki,* baklava, *chiles rellenos,* tempura, peanut pie, barbecued turkey legs, pizza, green-chile stew, frybread, the proverbial corn dog, and more, more, more. Thanks to New Mexico's varied ethnic

park at any of the picnic and camping areas along the way. You can also drive clear to the top of the mountain, where a three-mile trail leads to the restaurant at the top of the tram (take the tram back down if you can arrange to have someone meet you at the bottom).

For more information about hiking in Sandia National Forest, phone the Sandia Ranger Station at 505/281-3304.

The Sandias also offer a chance to hike into prehistory. In 1927, a group of Boy Scouts discovered a cave in the north Sandias that was later excavated by University of New Mexico professor Frank Hibben. Hibben and his staff discovered flint points and scrapers—although no human or animal remains—and in so doing dramatically changed the scientific community's view of when humans first came across the Bering Straits to North America: at least 8000 B.C.

Today, you can hike up to Sandia Man Cave and look out at the Rio Grande Valley, imagining what it must have been like 10,000 years ago. Take I-25 north from Albuquerque to the Placitas exit, and go east about eight miles. The pavement ends shortly after the town of Placitas, and a good dirt-and-gravel road continues up into the mountains. Stay on the dirt road for 2.5 miles, until you come to a small parking lot on

cultures, gastronomic excess is everywhere you look. The secret here is don't eat too much of any one thing at any one time. Nibble your way around the world as you stroll around the fair. Don't expect to walk off *all* those calories, though.

While the food is everywhere all the time, and the evenings are given to rodeos and roller coasters, mornings are the best times to visit the exhibits along Main Street. One important stop is the Indian Arts building. Here you'll find Pueblo Indian jewelry, pottery, weavings, and sandpaintings—some of the finest of their kind in the world, and almost everything is for sale. Also check out the Red Barn, where 4-H kids from around the state have assembled a heartwarming collection of typical farm animals. These are more than chickens and ducks and pigs; they're mama chickens with their baby chickens, mama ducks with their baby ducks, and mama pigs with their baby piggies—every one cuter than the last. Even in New Mexico, some city kids get their first looks at farm animals at the State Fair.

Just off Main Street at the west end of Heritage Avenue, you'll find the Indian Village and Villa Hispania, two other important stops. Both feature more superb ethnic food, as well as arts, crafts, music, and dancers. And either is a good place to find a shady spot in which to lean back, kick off your shoes, and relax for a while. There's no need to hurry; the rest of the fair will wait. You'll still have plenty of time to watch the quarter horse cutting competition at the Horse Arena, see the blue-ribbon orchids in the Flower Building, and watch the ponies run at the racetrack. There'll even be enough time for a wedge of hot apple pie smothered with tangy cheddar cheese at the Asbury Cafe. Mmmmm . . . Did someone mention food?

Getting There

The New Mexico State Fairgrounds, in the northeast quadrant of Albuquerque, are bordered on the south by Central Avenue, the north by Lomas, the east by Louisiana, and the west by San Pedro. Enter the main parking areas through Gate 8 or 9 off Louisiana or Gate 1 off Central. There are fees for parking (about $5), and admission runs $6–10. Children 12 and under are admitted free of charge. Gates are open 8 A.M.–midnight daily.

For further information, phone 505/265-1791.

Contributed by Jeff Everist, an outdoors writer based in Northern New Mexico.

your left. The trail is carved for about half a mile along a rocky cliffside until just below the cave, where a steel spiral staircase takes you from the end of the trail to the cave's entrance. As caves go, this isn't much: about eight feet high and 30 feet deep, with plenty of clever, modern-day graffiti (I doubt it was Thag who inscribed "Eat me" on the ceiling). But as an important archaeological site, Sandia Cave is worth the short drive and hike.

For more information on hiking in the Albuquerque area, pick up a copy of *Hiking Trails in the Sandia and Manzano Mountains,* by Kay Matthews. This handy book includes detailed descriptions of hikes (ranging 1.712 miles) throughout the mountains, maps of the area, suggestions for how to prepare for your hikes (what to wear and take), as well as discussions of the mountains' geology, fire restrictions, etc. Short sections on cross-country ski trails in the Sandias complete the book.

Folks interested in getting a little more vertical than the average hiker does should look into **New Mexico Mountain Club,** 505/277-3366, which offers a range of instruction and guided climbs in the area. You can also get information on hiking and climbing in the Sandias and other areas by stopping by **REI,** 1095 Mountain NW, 505/247-1191, near Old Town Albuquerque.

ALBUQUERQUE INTERNATIONAL BALLOON FIESTA

Pilatre de Rosier and Marquis d'Arlandes may not have been the Orville and Wilbur Wright of their time, yet they did achieve a somewhat obscure notoriety on November 21, 1783. That day, after a test flight piloted by a lamb, a rooster, and a duck, 40,000 people watched the two men rise 3,000 feet into the skies above Versailles, France, during history's first recorded untethered, manned balloon flight. And while de Rosier and d'Arlandes didn't exactly become household names, they no doubt fared better than the barnyard trio, whose names went totally unrecorded and whose fame didn't last beyond a banquet held later that evening.

More than 200 years later, hot-air ballooning has become an increasingly popular sport around the world—particularly in Albuquerque, New Mexico. For nine days each October, balloon enthusiasts gather in Albuquerque, and hundreds of brightly colored balloons rise at once into the early morning skies against the backdrop of the Sandia Mountains. It's a time when superlatives and adjectives are overused and fall short. The Albuquerque International Balloon Fiesta, "The Big One" (both are registered trademarks by which the fiesta's known), is billed as the most photographed event in the world.

More than a million people pay to get into the launch area, while thousands more watch from afar. Hundreds of balloons fly, and more than 1,000 pilots register for the event. People come from all over the world to join in the fun. Spectators have ample opportunity to view and photograph balloons filling and rising all around, or to buy souvenirs, extra film, and food from the many vendors.

Pilots and crews come to fly the famous "Albuquerque box," winds that blow the balloons in one direction near the ground and in the opposite direction at higher altitudes. This way balloons can go up, travel a few miles, rise a bit higher, and be blown back to where they started. Fliers also appreciate Albuquerque's mile-high altitude, which boosts their air time-to-fuel consumption ratio. And the mild fall weather rarely disappoints either the balloonists or the folks who come to see them.

Albuquerque has established a 77-acre Balloon Fiesta Park about a half mile west of Washington Street between Paseo Del Norte and Alameda Boulevard. Admission is about $5 per person per event; kids are free. Parking is free. RV parking is available for a nominal fee. Traffic can be heavy at times and is strictly regulated. Be sure to inquire locally before heading out. Most balloons launch between 7 and 9 A.M., depending on winds, weather, and event scheduling, and many people arrive as early as 5 A.M. to watch the balloonists setting up their rigs.

As if that weren't enough, balloonists often need extra help with launching, chasing, and pack-

This is an excellent camping, backpacking, fly-fishing, and cross-country skiing outfitter with a knowledgeable staff and good selection of maps, outdoor books, and related literature.

Camping

The mountains near Albuquerque abound in campgrounds, although on weekends during summer you'll most likely have to battle with the crowds for sites. The green and piney Jemez Mountains, northwest of the city, provide several gorgeous areas in the Santa Fe National Forest. Take I-25 north to Bernalillo, Highway 44 west, then Highway 4 northwest through Jemez Springs (see Vicinity of Los Alamos in the North-Central New Mexico chapter). Southeast of Albuquerque, Cibola National Forest in the Manzano Mountains offers a number of small campsites along Highway 337. Take I-40 east to Tijeras and then Highway 337 south toward Mountainair.

Fishing

You'll find a lot of excellent fishing within a couple of hours of Albuquerque. Fly casters head up to the Pecos River (see Pecos Wilderness Area in the North-Central New Mexico chapter) or to several

© STEPHEN METZGER

ing up their gossamer crafts, and it's possible to join in the fun by volunteering to be a crew member. At a special tent set up at the balloon park, willing hands are linked with those in need of them. If you're helpful enough (and lucky), you might even be given a ride yourself. For while being there certainly guarantees a good time, being part of it all is even better. Remember that day in Versailles? Forty thousand watched, but only two went aloft . . . not counting dinner guests. For more information on the Albuquerque Balloon Fiesta, phone 888/422-7277 or check out the website: www.aibf.org.

Contributed by Jeff Everist, an outdoors writer based in Northern New Mexico.

of the rivers and small streams in the Jemez Mountains (see Los Alamos in the North-Central New Mexico chapter). If they've got a couple of days and are willing to drive a bit farther, serious anglers work the trophy-quality San Juan River (see Aztec and Vicinity in the Northwestern New Mexico chapter). Lake anglers pack their boats with bait and beer and light out for a day at Elephant Butte Lake State Park (see Truth or Consequences in the Southwestern New Mexico chapter).

Golfing

Albuquerque has several golf courses open to the public, including **Arroyo Del Oso,** which has won awards from both *Sports Illustrated* and *Golf Digest.* The course is at 7001 Osuna; phone 505/884-7505 for greens fees and reservations. The area's newest course is the **Valle Grande,** on Santa Ana Pueblo just outside Bernalillo (about 20 miles north of the city), 505/867-9464. This beautiful course offers a magnificent setting at the foot of the Sandias and nestled in the fertile Rio Grande Valley. Other Albuquerque golf courses include: **Ladera Golf Course,** 3401 Ladera Dr. NW, 505/836-4449; **Los Altos Golf Course,** 9717 Copper Ave. NE, 505/298-1897; **Puerto**

Del Sol Golf Course, 1800 Girard Blvd. SE, 505/265-5636; and the two **University of New Mexico** courses: south, 505/277-4546, and north, 505/277-4146.

Skiing

Albuquerque's blessed with a midsized ski resort right in its backyard. Sandia Peak Ski Area has four chairlifts, two surface lifts, and 20 runs, and snowmaking on a quarter of its slopes (in case 150 inches of snowfall a year isn't enough). Hours are 8:30 A.M.–4:30 P.M. daily. To get to Sandia Peak, take I-40 east of Albuquerque to Tijeras, then take Highway 14 six miles north to the turnoff at San Antonito; the road is well marked. You can also get to the slopes by taking the Sandia Peak Tramway on the east side of town. Take Tramway Loop to the well-marked turnoff, then Tramway Road to the base of the tram. For more information, phone 505/296-9585.

The Sandia Mountains also provide excellent opportunities for cross-country skiers. Recently, Sandia Peak Ski Area has begun offering cross-country lessons. Kay Matthews' book, *Hiking Trails in the Sandia and Manzano Mountains,* includes a section on Nordic skiing in the Sandias, with excellent detailed descriptions and maps of a half dozen trails.

Albuquerque's cross-country skiers also head up toward the Santa Fe National Forest, either to the Jemez Mountains near Los Alamos or the Sangre de Cristo Mountains northeast of Santa Fe (see the North-Central New Mexico chapter). You'll also find cross-country ski trails in Cibola National Forest off Highway 337 southeast of Albuquerque.

Ballooning

This town's nuts about hot-air balloons, hosting each fall the largest balloon festival in the world (see the special topic Albuquerque Balloon Fiesta). The following companies offer balloon rides to the public: **Affordable Hot Air Balloons,** 505/864-9400 or 800/840-9449; **Braden's Balloons Aloft,** 505/263-0254; and **Rainbow Ryders,** 505/823-1111 or 800/725-2477.

The most thorough website for information on ballooning in Albuquerque is that of the **Albuquerque Aerostat Ascension Association** at website: www.hotairballooning.org. You can also phone the organization at 505/263-0222 (information on clubs, retailers, events, etc.).

ANNUAL EVENTS

Something's happening in Albuquerque nearly every weekend, in fact, nearly every day, and to stay on top of things you need to read the local newspapers (the *Tribune* or *Journal* or any of the convention and visitors bureau brochures and publications). The two big events of the year, though, are the **Albuquerque International Balloon Fiesta** and the **New Mexico State Fair.** The Balloon Fiesta, largest in the world, every October attracts balloonists and spectators from nearly every state and many different countries. The State Fair, held in September, also attracts huge crowds, and Albuquerqueans look forward to it year-round (for a description of both events by Albuquerquean Jeff Everist, see the respective special topics in this chapter).

Other important annual events in Albuquerque: **Gathering of Nations Pow Wow**—Indian dance competitions, arts and crafts displays and sales (mid-April; phone 505/836-2810); **Albuquerque International Air Show**

and Trade Expo—vintage planes and flying exhibits (mid-June; phone 505/247-4800); **New Mexico Arts and Crafts Fair**—huge array of wares by juried artists, working demonstrations, live entertainment, and a variety of ethnic food (late June; phone 505/884-9043); **New Mexico Wine Festival**—with tastings, food, live entertainment, and a juried art show (September; phone 505/867-3311; **Southwest Arts Festival**—more than 150 juried entrants from throughout the country (November; phone 505/821-1313).

For a complete, month-by-month listing of events and contact numbers, go to website: www.itsatrip.org/visitors/events.

INFORMATION AND SERVICES

Information

Albuquerque's superb **library** system includes a separately housed special collections department at 523 Central NE that concentrates on genealogy and New Mexicana, to which a separate room is devoted. With its Southwestern decor, high ceilings, and cozy chairs, this is an excellent place to kick back and browse through rare books, limited and first editions, and various perspectives and interpretations of New Mexico history. Call the main branch for hours. The main branch of the Albuquerque library is downtown at 501 Copper Ave. NW, 505/768-5150. Open Monday, Wednesday, Friday, and Saturday 9 A.M.–5:30 P.M., Tuesday and Thursday 12:30–9 P.M., closed Sunday and holidays. Short-term visitors to Albuquerque can get a library card and check out books the same day.

The recently remodeled and enlarged **University of New Mexico Bookstore,** on the UNM campus, 505/277-5451, has the best selection in town of books on New Mexico and the Southwest, as well as on archaeology, anthropology, and Indians. Special sections are devoted to Hispanic literature and to books published by the highly regarded UNM press.

For one of the best travel-book selections in town, check out **Book Works,** 4022 Rio Grande, 505/344-8139, which carries Moon Handbooks and other, less-revered guidebook publishers.

Albuquerque's listener-supported radio station **(KUNM)** is a good source for what's going on in the area (Albuquerque, Los Alamos, and Santa Fe). In addition, KUNM offers the syndicated *All Things Considered* on National Public Radio. Tune to 89.9 FM.

The **Albuquerque Convention and Visitors Bureau,** 20 1st Plaza (on Copper between 2nd and 3rd), 505/842-9918 or 800/284-2282, publishes a huge array of literature—brochures, pamphlets, and full-blown magazines—about the city. Open Monday–Friday 8 A.M.–5 P.M. The bureau also has satellite information centers scattered about the city: at Albuquerque International Airport (lower level), at Cottonwood Mall (open daily till 6 P.M.), and in Old Town at Plaza Don Luis on Romero NW. For electronic information, visit the bureau's website: www.abqcvb.org.

You can phone the **New Mexico Department of Tourism** at 800/545-2040.

Services

As a destination for tubercular patients in the early part of the century, Albuquerque has a recent history of excellent medical care, with a number of hospitals and urgent-care clinics. The University of New Mexico Hospital, 505/843-2111, provides long-term and emergency medical care; the Emergency Department is at 2211 Lomas Blvd. NE. Albuquerque's Presbyterian Hospital chain has three facilities in the city: at Central and I-25, 505/841-1234 or 505/841-1111 for emergencies; on Constitution near Wyoming, 505/291-2000 or 505/291-2121 for emergencies; and at San Mateo and I-25, 505/823-8000 or 505/823-8080 for emergencies.

If you're traveling through Albuquerque and need nonemergency medical assistance, you can call a physician-referral service or call and speak directly to a nurse. For quick and easy medical assistance in Albuquerque, phone the Lovelace Health Hotline at 505/262-3000 (or 800/366-3401, statewide).

The Albuquerque Police Department is downtown at 401 Marquette NW, 505/768-1986. In emergencies, dial 911.

CRIME AND SAFETY

A lot of Albuquerque women won't walk alone in the city at night. Anywhere. And these women aren't timid; these are intelligent, strong-willed, and courageous women. Friends of mine who live in the city shake their heads and say, "No way," when asked if they'd be comfortable alone in Albuquerque after dark.

Albuquerque is a small town grown large quickly, and in many ways it's still trying to catch up with itself. It also straddles the junction of two major interstate arteries, so it's both an obstacle and a target along the stolen-car and drug-trafficking routes. It's also home to more than half a million people.

But is it safe? Many women, women who love the city, say no, at least not at night. Officers at the Albuquerque Police Department's Crime Prevention Unit don't exactly agree. "If you're careful," they say, "and use your common sense, most areas of Albuquerque are safe." First, they advise, pick a good hotel. Check with the front desk to make sure the phone system works 24 hours a day and that dialing 911 won't get you a room on the ninth floor. They also recommend that you not leave valuables in hotel rooms or cars and that you park in well-lit areas. And when you're in public, "Keep your jewelry concealed. Wear necklaces inside your blouse, and turn diamond rings palmside." It's especially wise to be careful at the airport, where muggings, purse snatchings, and other assaults have occurred.

Though the department claims that most parts of Albuquerque are relatively safe, even at night, it suggests staying away from the "busy" part of Central Avenue. A former crime-prevention officer told me, "If you're looking for local talent, you might just end up running into one of our own ladies and getting hauled in by the vice squad."

You'll find most businesspeople in Albuquerque very helpful. They're proud of their city and want it to make a good impression on visitors. Hotel and motel clerks are usually more than happy to help out, let you use a phone, tell you the quickest (and safest) way to get somewhere. In addition, employees of 7-Eleven convenience stores are trained to assist in cases of emergency. Carry maps, avoid darkened areas, report suspicious activity to police or local business managers, and don't leave your Nikon in plain view on the backseat of your car. If you do go out at night, make every effort to find a companion—*before* you go.

TRANSPORTATION

Most major airlines fly into Albuquerque International Airport, and **Southwest,** 800/435-9792 or 505/831-1221, and **Mesa,** 800/MESA-AIR (800/637-2247), fly from Albuquerque to many of the smaller towns throughout the state and the Southwest. Most of Albuquerque's major hotels provide shuttle service to and from the airport.

Checker Airport Express, 505/765-1234 or 800/395-7680, and **American Limousine and Shuttle,** 505/877-7576, offer 24-hour shuttle service between the airport and all Albuquerque locations.

All the major chains rent cars in Albuquerque, including **Avis,** 505/842-4080 or 800/331-1212; **Budget,** 505/344-7196 or 800/527-0800; and **National,** 505/724-4500 or 800/227-7368. **Rent-a-Wreck** is at 500 Yale SE, 505/232-7552 or 800/247-9556.

The Albuquerque **bus station** is right downtown at the corner of Silver and 2nd Streets.

Getting Around

Albuquerque is a relatively easy city in which to get around. Remembering a few things will help keep you from getting lost. First, keep in mind that I-40 runs east-west across town and that I-25 runs north-south. Also remember that the Sandia Mountains are to the east and that the Rio Grande runs north to south on the west side of town—both are good landmarks. Finally, and most important, know that Albuquerque is pretty much laid out in grids; major streets run north-south and east-west. In fact, if you can remember just a few, as well as where they are in relation to where you're staying, you should be able to get around without too much risk of getting hopelessly lost.

Major east-west arteries (from the north end of town to the south): Montgomery, Menaul, Lomas, Central, and Gibson. Major north-south arteries (from the east of town to the west): Tramway, Juan Tabo, Eubank, Wyoming, Louisiana, San Mateo, University, Broadway, 4th Street, Rio Grande, and Coors (see maps).

Sun-Tran, Albuquerque's city bus line, offers extensive route coverage throughout the city, including stops at Old Town, the airport, Kirtland Air Force Base, and the University of New Mexico, as well as the city's business district. The fare is $.60. Phone 505/843-9200 for routes and information. If you're in a bigger hurry than a bus will allow for, Albuquerque's taxicabs are available 24 hours a day. Phone **Yellow-Checker Cab** at 505/842-5292 or **Albuquerque Cab Company** at 505/883-4888. Most hotels offer free shuttle service to and from Albuquerque International Airport.

Tours

If you'd rather leave the driving to someone else, you can arrange tours of Albuquerque, as well as much of New Mexico, through several different companies. **Rio Grande Super Tours,** 505/242-1325, and **Grayline,** 242-4998, conduct tours that include many of the city's main attractions, including the University of New Mexico, Petroglyph National Monument, the Rio Grande Nature Center, and Old Town. The half-day tours cost about $30. Smaller groups might want to look into **Taxi Tours of New Mexico,** 505/250-5146, where you can customize a tour or let your guide design one for you—for up to four people.

Vicinity of Albuquerque

The three central New Mexico counties of Bernalillo, Torrance, and Valencia are dominated by the sprawling city of Albuquerque, the broad Estancia Valley, the Manzano and Sandia Mountains, and the meandering Rio Grande, a fertile ribbon laid across the state's barren flatlands.

The Rio Grande (Great River) not only contributes in large measure today to the state's resources, irrigating fields and providing vast recreational possibilities, but it's also been the area's primary means of attracting and supporting human life for thousands of years. Two thousand years ago, large groups of people were living along the river's banks, growing corn and beans. So great were these pre-pueblo civilizations that the valley actually experienced overcrowding, and early in the first millennium small groups began filtering out. The inhabitants of Abo, Gran Quivira, and Quarai Pueblos on the east side of the Manzano Mountains southeast of Albuquerque were most likely refugees from the overpopulated Rio Grande Valley. Today, central New Mexico, like much of the rest of the state, recognizes the importance of its past civilizations, with monuments to several of the ancient pueblos.

RIO RANCHO

Sprawling on the low hills of Albuquerque's west side, Rio Rancho has grown, in less than two decades, from a tiny upscale bedroom suburb to the fourth-largest city in the state. During that same amount of time, Rio Rancho has added thousands of jobs to the local economy.

Most of these jobs, as well as most of the folks who've moved to Rio Rancho in the past decade or so, are in the computer technology field, making the city a sort of Silicon Valley of the high desert. Firms that have set up housekeeping in Rio Rancho include Intel Corp, Intuit, Taco Bell Accounting, Great American Stock Photographers, Days Inn, and Ramada Inn, as well as many other smaller companies.

One of the results of Rio Rancho's industry-linked growth is that the average age of the city's residents has dropped, while the average income and educational levels have risen. According to an article in *New Mexico Business Journal,* in 1980 17.5 percent of Rio Rancho's population was at retirement age or older. In 1996, it was less than 10 percent.

Last time I drove into Albuquerque, I came in

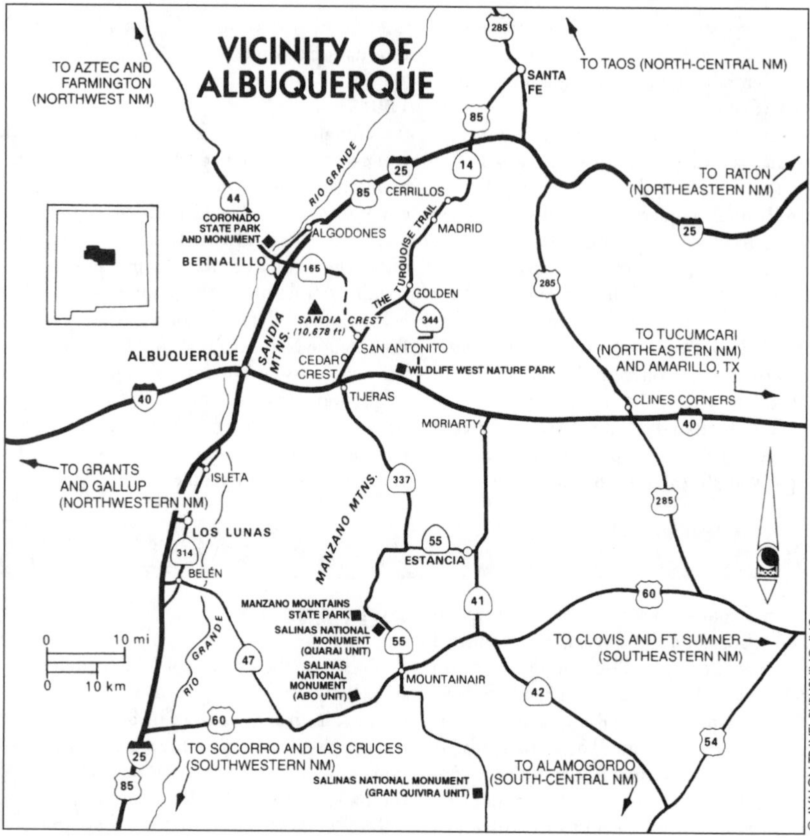

on Highway 44 from Farmington. I was surprised to see the Rio Rancho city limits sign even before I got to Bernalillo. I was even more surprised to see how far the development, not only of Rio Rancho but also of Bernalillo and Corrales, had encroached on the once-sleepy little valley. And though of course this development is good for the economy, blah, blah, blah, I was saddened to see the area losing some of its flavor. The Chile Hill Emporium, for example, long a low-key little gift shop and chile supplier (each fall we'd order 20 pounds sent to our Northern California home) had been taken over by Santa Fe's Jackalope, specializing in "folk art" and terracotta creations of every imaginable form, as well as in touristy souvenirs and knickknacks.

Then there's the new Cottonwood Mall, which opened in 1996. Construction of the mall completely transformed Rio Rancho and the west side of Albuquerque; thoroughfares were rerouted, creating general vehicular pandemonium for a while. But the mall—with more than 130 shops "anchored" by four large department stores and an entertainment center—is almost guaranteed to be successful: more than 400,000 people live within a 10-mile radius of it.

BERNALILLO

Bernalillo (pop. 6,100; elev. 5,100 feet) is a bustling little community about 18 miles north of Albuquerque whose facade belies its important

BOB RACE

past. Coronado stayed at the nearby Kuaua Pueblo when he passed through in 1540, and several haciendas in this area were occupied by Spanish settlers as early as the mid-1600s, thus predating the settling of Albuquerque by at least half a century.

Spanish settlers fled, however, in 1680, at the time of the Pueblo Revolt, but returned in 1692, when the Indians were reconquered. The town of Bernalillo was actually founded three years later, in 1695, by Don Diego de Vargas, then governor of New Mexico. Bernalillo thrived throughout the 18th and 19th centuries, and when the railroad came in the late 1800s, the main track passed right through town. In fact, if one of the major landowners in the area had not wanted so much money for his land, Bernalillo would have been home to the main switchyards and barns that ended up in Albuquerque. Through the next couple of centuries, Bernalillo was primarily a farming and livestock-shipping community, dwarfed by rapidly growing Albuquerque to the south.

In the mid-1990s, however, as housing tracts sprawled north and west of Albuquerque, blurring the lines and community distinctions between Bernalillo, Corrales, Rio Rancho, and Albuquerque, the area began to take off. Today Bernalillo's main street is lined with offices and galleries, and though you can still sense its slower-paced past—visible in the pastures and adobe barns crouched behind under-construction office buildings—the overriding feel is one of a once-sleepy town waking up in a pretty darned good mood.

And a Good Saloon in Every Single Town

Anyone searching out the real New Mexico ought to stop in at **Silva's,** on the west side of the main drag downtown (995 Camino del Pueblo). This small bar holds the oldest single-family-owned liquor license in the state; Felix Silva, grandfather of the current owner, started the business in 1932. Today, the place is part bar and part museum. Every square inch of wall space is covered with license plates, branding irons, saws, moonshine jugs, fishing creels, washboards, and hats. Yes, hats. Scores if not hundreds of baseball hats, cowboy hats, boaters, and every other kind imaginable, most of them looking as if they've been to hell and back. Each one was donated by the widow or other survivor of its original wearer, a now-dead Silva's patron. In fact, the brims on some of the hats are decorated with the birth and death dates of their owners ("Larry Rodriguez 1924–1967").

Sadly, the original Mr. Silva has joined his hatless former customers. One morning in April 1995, he walked in to work, poured a drink for a regular, then methodically laid his valued possessions—his wallet, his keys, and his gun—on the bar, walked into the bathroom, and died.

ALGODONES

Just north of Bernalillo and about halfway between Albuquerque and Santa Fe, Algodones is a small village dating from the 18th century that today reflects its Native American, Spanish, and Old West influences. Two hundred years ago, merchants passing between Mexico City and Santa Fe stopped here, and in the 19th century it was a Pony Express stop and then a Santa Fe Railroad depot.

A bed-and-breakfast inn here is worth special mention. **Hacienda Vargas** is in a 200-year-old, 5,000-square-foot ranch home in Algodones, with gardens, a hot tub, and seven large rooms with kiva fireplaces. The rooms go for $70–150 a night, including a full breakfast. For more information, write Pablo or Julia de Vargas, 1431 El Camino Real, P.O. Box 307, Algodones, NM 87001, phone 505/867-9115 or 800/261-0006, or visit the website: www.haciendavargas.com. To get there, take the Algodones exit from I-25 north of Bernalillo and go west to Highway 313 (El Camino Real).

The **Albuquerque North KOA** is one of the favorite RV campgrounds of some real seasoned travelers—my parents. They stayed here when visiting Albuquerque and loved it, lauding its views, peacefulness, and convenience. Sites with full hookups are about $30, tent sites about $22. Phone 505/867-5227 or 800/562-3616.

THE TURQUOISE TRAIL

If you're heading from Albuquerque up to Santa Fe and want to take the scenic route, or just prefer back roads over main arteries, take the longer but more picturesque Turquoise Trail. This route is cut along the back side of the Sandia Mountains (in fact, one spur winds to the top of Sandia Peak) and then rolls through undulating, cholla-rich hills and grassy plains before straightening out for the last few miles and jamming headlong into Santa Fe. Along the way, you pass through several old mining towns, all of which are worth stopping at and dawdling in. In fact, if you're not careful, these side trips could easily turn your hour-and-a-half scenic drive to Santa Fe into an enjoyable full-day exploration of old-time taverns and mining museums, boutiques, and pottery shops.

Take I-40 east from Albuquerque about eight miles to the Sandia Crest turnoff, then Highway 14 north. You'll pass through the small towns of Cedar Crest and Sandia Park and see San Antonito in the hills off to your right. About 12 miles up the road, you'll come to Golden, where gold was discovered in 1825 (the first discovery west of the Mississippi). Later, silver too was discovered in Golden, and at one time a single mine, the Cash and Carry Mine, employed 1,300 people. By 1893, the mines had all played out, and only about 100 people remained in the town. Golden's church was built in the 1830s, rebuilt in 1958, and is still in use today.

Madrid

Twelve miles farther, you'll come to Madrid (MAD-rid), where you'll definitely want to stop and look around. Madrid's heyday was from the late 19th century through the early 20th, when its mines were putting out huge quantities of coal. In 1928, Madrid mines produced 87,148 tons of anthracite and 97,562 tons of bituminous coal. When the railroad companies switched to diesel shortly after World War II, though, and natural gas replaced coal for other uses, Madrid's mines and most of its homes and shops were abandoned. In the mid-'70s, artists and craftspeople, many of whom were refugees from the 1960s, discovered Madrid, moved into some of the old miners' shacks, and refurbished the old stores into studios, boutiques, and gift shops.

Start at the Mineshaft Tavern (especially if it's around lunchtime). Here you can sit down with the locals over a beer and a burger, a plate of nachos, or, if you're feeling particularly brave, a buffalo steak. The Mineshaft, 505/473-0743, often features live music on weekends and holidays.

After you've reenergized at the Mineshaft, check out the **Old Coal Mine Museum** out back ($3). Here, you can venture down into an actual mine shaft, view a coal vein, and wander among the abandoned railroad equipment and mining tools. The last building on the short tour is the old Madrid jail, which, according to the map, was a "lively after-hours spot." For more information, phone 505/438-3780 or visit the website: www.turquoisetrail.org/oldcoalmine.

From there, walk north up the main road to the shops that line the boardwalk. You'll find beautiful earthenware, jewelry, and tapestries. Afterward, stop for an ice-cream cone at **The Depot,** a snack-and-curio shop inside an old Santa Fe boxcar.

Weekends, Memorial Day through Labor Day, Madrid's **Engine House Theatre** presents live melodrama. Phone 505/438-3740 for information or reservations. The season's plays are listed at the website: www.madridmelodrama.com.

Cerrillos

Continue north on Highway 14 to this last town on the Turquoise Trail. Though remembered mainly for its turquoise mines, including one that was owned by Tiffany Jewelers of New York, and for its high-quality turquoise, some of which found its way clear to Spain, the Cerrillos hills also held gold and silver. In fact, Thomas Edison once came to Cerrillos to test out an electromagnetic mining method (it didn't work). Although the town's mines produced until as recently as 50 years ago, the area was known for its fine turquoise long before Spanish contact, when the Indians mined the hills for gems. In the late 19th century, Cerrillos was of great economic importance to New Mexico and at one time supported 21 saloons and four hotels.

Today, Cerrillos feels like an old Mexican village at siesta time. Its unpaved streets are lined with old taverns, some open and some abandoned (sometimes it's difficult to tell which are which), general stores that sell everything from Mars bars to antique kitchenware, and pottery shops and studios. A souvenir shop at the far end of town sells cacti planted in old boots and shoes, gems and stones from the area (including Cerrillos turquoise), adobe bricks, cow skulls, and two-inch-square pieces of genuine (probably pronounced genu-INE) rattlesnake skin. A sign at the town's entrance claims that more than 12 motion pictures were filmed here, including the "well-known" Walt Disney movie, *The Nine Lives of Elfego Baca.*

MORIARTY

At the junction of I-40 and Highway 41, Moriarty (pop. 6,000) is the last decent-sized town westbound travelers will come to before hitting Albuquerque, about 35 miles west. Not much more than a main drag paralleling the freeway, Moriarty is a hub for farmers and ranchers working the Estancia Valley southeast of Albuquerque and the Galisteo area to the northeast.

The town was named for Michael Moriarty, an Iowan who settled here in 1887. The railroad came in 1903, and Moriarty has been a stop for east- and westbound trains ever since.

Moriarty Historical Museum

This small museum houses farming and ranching tools, testifying to Moriarty's agricultural past, as well as photographs of the old Moriarty house, a vacuum cleaner from 1915, a handwritten teacher's manual, and patchwork quilts. May 1–December 31, the museum, at 777 Central, is open Monday–Saturday 1–4 P.M.; the rest of the year it's open Tuesday, Friday, and Saturday 1–4 P.M. For more information, write the Moriarty Historical Society, 777 Central, Moriarty, NM 87035, or call 505/832-4764.

Accommodations and Food

The **Sunset Motel,** 501 Route 66, 505/832-4234, has decent doubles for under $50. Other motels in town include **Days Inn,** 505/832-4451, and a **Holiday Inn Express,** 505/832-6370, both at Exit 194 from I-40 and with doubles running $50–100. Good Mexican lunches and dinners are reasonably priced at **El Comedor** on Central, 505/832-4442 (you can't miss the sign).

Annual Events

The Moriarty area has been one of the nation's premier pinto bean–growing regions since the 1920s, and the town celebrates its poddy heritage every August at the National Pinto Bean Fiesta and Cook-off. Among the attractions: a parade featuring marching pinto beans, cooking competitions in which bean dips compete with bean cakes, and the "Queen Bean Contest," where past winners have dressed as burritos and cans of beans.

For more information about Moriarty's annual event, inevitably described as "a real gas," phone the chamber of commerce at 505/832-4087.

CLINES CORNERS

Clines Corners, 60 miles east of Albuquerque on I-40, advertises itself for 100 miles in every direction. Billboards promise souvenirs, T-shirts, authentic Indian jewelry, gas, hot coffee, and more. And Clines Corners definitely has all that. It also has snakeskin wallets, arrowheads, "New Mexico is for Lovers" coffee mugs—in short, a huge range of Southwest-flavor gifts, including some quality pottery and jewelry. But it's nearly axiomatic in New Mexico that the more billboards advertising a place the tackier it'll be, and Clines Corners is no exception. This is a tourist stop of the highest order: a minimart, cafeteria-style restaurant, gift shop spilling into several rooms, and two gas stations. The restaurant and gift shop are open daily 7 A.M.–8:30 P.M.

SALINAS NATIONAL MONUMENT AND MANZANO MOUNTAINS STATE PARK

Mountainair

Take Highway 337 and then Highway 55 about 45 miles south from Tijeras to Mountainair, where you'll find the visitors center and headquarters of Salinas National Monument (if not much else). The road winds along a broad ridge of the Manzano Mountains, rich with cottonwoods, juniper, and pine, through several small, general-store-only towns, and ends up in the little town, which bills itself as the "Gateway to Ancient Cities."

The town of Mountainair was founded in 1903, when the Atchison, Topeka, & Santa Fe Railroad decided to build the Belén Cut-off. Early settlers planted beans and corn, and Mountainair soon became the "Pinto Bean Capital of the World." A drought in the 1950s led to the selling of many of the area's farms, and ranching, still a major industry, began to flourish.

The Salinas National Monument visitors center and main office is on Highway 60 a block west of the intersection with Highway 55. Open daily 8 A.M.–5 P.M., the center displays art and artifacts, including examples of Pop Shaffer's folk art and architecture, and sells books of local and regional interest. For more information, call 505/847-2585.

The **Pueblo Cafe** in the historic **Shaffer Hotel,** 505/847-2888, serves American breakfasts, sandwiches for lunch, and Mexican dinners. Call to check hours of operation.

Salinas Pueblo Missions National Monument

This fascinating complex of three ancient pueblos and Spanish missions dates to the 12th century. The pueblos—Abo, Gran Quivira, and Quarai—are remarkably well preserved. The walls of the mission at Quarai climb three stories into the New Mexico sky, dwarfing the trees and

© STEPHEN METZGER

restoration at Gran Quivira

the handful of newer buildings scattered around it. The inhabitants of these pueblos, especially compared to their kin to the north, were weak and ill-armed, and the Spanish found them easy targets for conversion.

The Indians of the Salinas Valley were Tompiro- and Tiwa-speaking refugees from the Rio Grande area, where a population boom about 2,000 years ago had spurred large groups to seek homes elsewhere. Originally, these Indians built pit houses in the flat ground of the valleys, but by A.D. 1200 were at work constructing large apartment-type complexes on hillsides.

Tompiro Indians had finished construction on **Abo Pueblo,** nine miles west of Mountainair on Highway 60, by A.D. 1150 and had completely abandoned their valley pit houses. They lived in the pueblo for the next 450 years, farming peacefully, until the Spanish arrived in the late 16th century. By the late 1620s, the church of San Gregorio had been built alongside the pueblo, and most of the Indians had been converted to Christianity. There are picnic tables near the visitors center.

Twenty-six miles south of Mountainair on Highway 55, **Gran Quivira Pueblo** sprawls across a hilltop overlooking the flat Salinas Valley below. Still being excavated and reconstructed, the pueblo offers an impressive self-guided tour through 300 rooms, six kivas, and two churches (San Isidro and San Buenaventura). Originally called Pueblo de Las Humanas by the Spanish, Gran Quivira was abandoned in 1672, probably in part as a result of invading Apaches. The visitors center includes a bookstore, archaeological displays, and an audiovisual program.

Quarai Pueblo is eight miles north of Mountainair on Highway 55. Built about A.D. 1300, Quarai was settled by Tiwa-speaking Indians, who were converted in the early 1600s when the Spanish arrived. The church, Nuestra Señora de la Purísima Concepción de Curac, was built about 1630. Like many of the pueblos in the area, Quarai was a victim of Apache raiding parties, which terrorized the Indians and missionaries and probably eventually drove them to abandon the pueblo. The visitors center includes a model of the original pueblo mission, as well as displays of Indian ceremonial and missionary artifacts, including Spanish cookware and an original missionary's manual. Admission is free. You'll find a handful of picnic tables adjacent to the visitors center, as well as several down in a cottonwood grove next to the pueblo.

Each site has a small visitors center and picnic table. The three sites are open to the public free of charge Memorial Day through Labor Day 9 A.M.–7 P.M. and 9 A.M.–5 P.M. the rest of the year. For more information, phone 505/847-2585.

Manzano Mountains State Park

This is a quiet little campground 14 miles north of Mountainair on Highway 55, on a ponderosa pine–studded hillside looking out on the verdant valley below. Hiking trails are plentiful, but there's no drinking water. Entrance fee is $4 overnight camping is $8, $12 with hookups.

Information

For more information on Mountainair, Salinas National Monument, or Manzano Mountains State Park, write the **Mountainair Chamber of Commerce** at P.O. Box 595, Mountainair, NM 87036.

ISLETA AND BELÉN

Isleta

Isleta Pueblo, about 18 miles south of Albuquerque on I-25, is one of the oldest and largest pueblos in New Mexico, dating to the early 16th century and home today to about 3,000 people.

In 1629, the Spanish built a mission at Isleta and set about converting the tribe, which, compared to some of the more resistant groups, accepted Christianity fairly peacefully. Alonzo Garcia, lieutenant governor of New Mexico, was in Isleta in 1680 when the Pueblo Revolt broke out. Garcia, hearing reports that Santa Fe had been completely wiped out and Governor Otermin killed, immediately headed south, taking with him the Christianized Isletans, the Socorro-area Piro Indians, and most of the Spanish who'd settled in the region.

By 1692, only a handful of Indians were still

living at Isleta, many of whom were refugees from other Rio Grande–area pueblos. De Vargas, the new governor of New Mexico, took over Isleta that year, using the pueblo as his headquarters in his campaign to retake Santa Fe and to subdue the rebelling tribes between Isleta and Taos.

St. Augustine Church at Isleta is one of the oldest missions in the United States. The church's walls, high and white and Old Worldly, rise above the adobe shacks and homes that surround it. On the inside, the walls are decorated with paintings of Catholic saints. St. Augustine, open to visitors, is just a short drive from I-25. Take the Isleta Pueblo exit and follow the signs to the Indian Market Center; the church is at the north end of the main plaza.

Highway 314 runs south from Isleta to Belén, meandering along the sleepy shoals of the Rio Grande. A much prettier drive than I-25 just a few miles to the west, Highway 314 will pay you back in scenery what little you lose in time.

Belén

Belén (pop. 8,300), originally called Belem, or Bethlehem, was founded in 1741 by 24 Spanish families, who immediately began to farm the area, relying on the fertile riparian soil of the Rio Grande Valley. In the mid-1880s, the railroad came to Belén, and the train has since played an important role in Belén's economy and contribution to the south-of-Albuquerque area. Trains have been stopping in town for more than 100 years, delivering supplies and picking up export items—such as produce and hides—to be shipped around the country.

Between 1910 and 1939, passenger trains stopped at the Belén depot, and their customers dined at the Harvey House across the street, where they were served by "Harvey Girls" who lived upstairs. The Valencia County Historical Society's **Harvey House Museum** is in the original Harvey House Dining Room at 104 N. 1st St. in downtown Belén and features a re-created Harvey Girl bedroom, complete with white brass bed, washstand, and rocking chair. The museum is open Tuesday–Saturday 12:30–3:30 P.M. Phone 505/861-0581 for more information.

Lodging is available in Belen at the **Belén Best Western,** right downtown at 2111 Sosimo Padilla (Exit 191 from I-25), 505/861-3181. Doubles run $50–100.

For more information on Belén, write the **Belén Chamber of Commerce,** 712 Dalies Ave., Belén, NM 87002, or phone 505/864-8091.

Southwestern New Mexico

Introduction

Save for the Las Cruces/Mesilla area and the well-traveled stretch of I-25 from Socorro to the north Texas border, this is one of the least-visited parts of New Mexico. Including seven of the state's larger counties—Socorro, Sierra, Doña Ana, Luna, Hidalgo, Grant, and Catron—the southwestern corner of New Mexico encompasses about 28,000 square miles, or roughly a quarter of the state. Yet not many people get down here. Texans flock to south-central New Mexico—Ruidoso and the mountains of Lincoln National Forest—and summers see New Yorkers, Californians, Europeans, and Asians descending on the north state—Santa Fe and Taos. But the southwestern quarter remains wide open, primitive, and largely devoid of the motorhome convoys, Cadillacs, and tinted-glass Mercedes Benzes you see cruising much of the rest of New Mexico.

So of course the folks down here have mixed feelings about tourism. On one hand, you'll find aggressive chamber of commerce marketing and brochures boasting of excellent relocation opportunities. Yet on the other, people are skeptical of outsiders: Some of these southwesterners have been here for generations, and they *like* the fact that the world hasn't walked in on them and turned all their saloons into boutiques. Nor can you blame them. As you drive up Highway 180 through the rugged and piney

the town of Shakespeare in Southwestern New Mexico

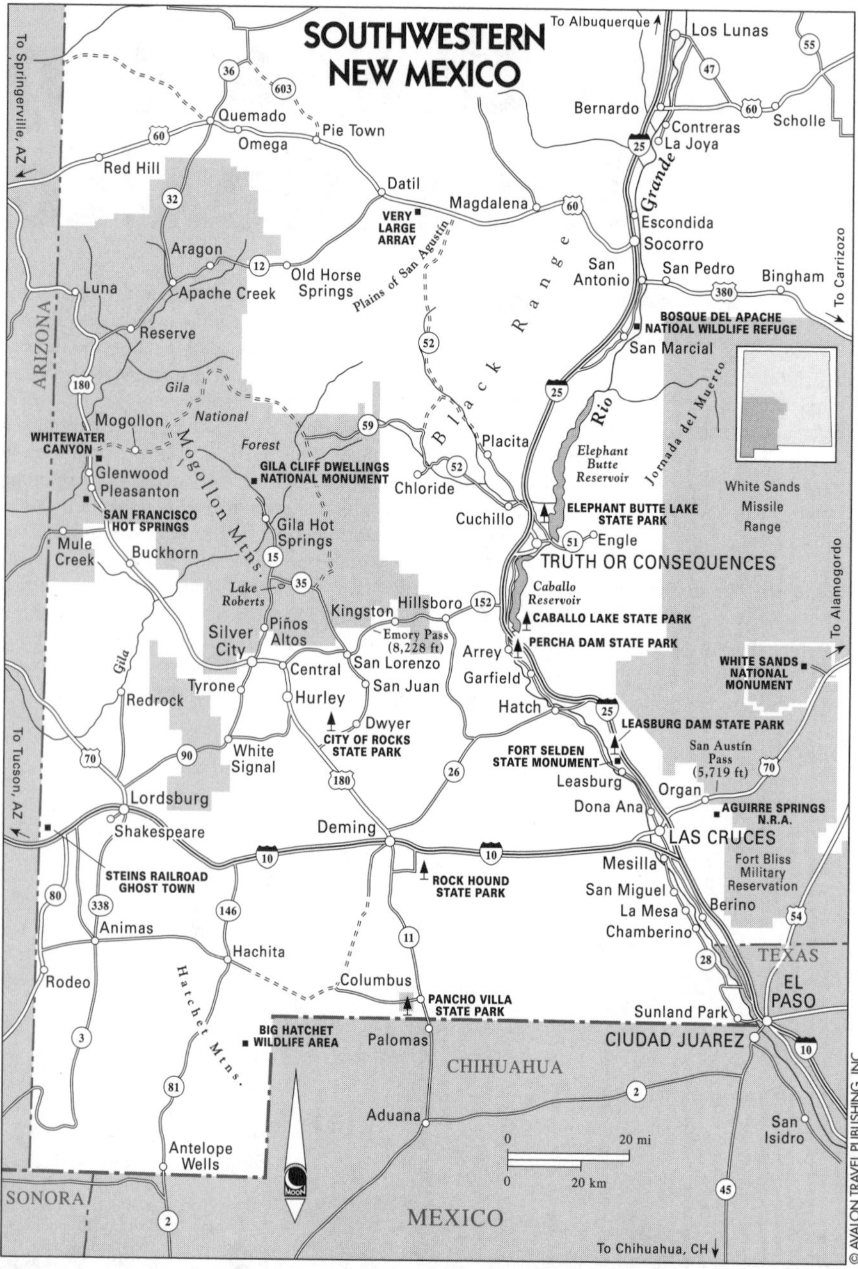

SOUTHWESTERN NM

Gila National Forest, or across Highway 90 and that wondrous landscape where desert, hill country, and mountain forest seem to blend into one endlessly stunning panorama, you appreciate the lonesomeness of the land, the quiet solitude of tiny towns dwarfed by gigantic mountain ranges, sprawling forests, and miles and miles of emptiness, broken neither by fence nor telephone wire. Yes, this is land that cleanses the soul, and too many people washing up would make for awfully dirty bath water.

Here you appreciate the lonesomeness of the land, the quiet solitude of tiny towns dwarfed by gigantic mountain ranges, sprawling forests, and miles and miles of emptiness, broken neither by fence nor telephone wire.

Until the Spanish came in the 16th century, this was—like all of New Mexico—Indian land. The Pueblos had farmed the fertile Rio Grande Valley for at least 1,500 years, and Apaches—though most likely having arrived from the north not long before the Spanish themselves—roamed the high country from the great river into what is now Arizona.

But things changed dramatically when the Spanish showed up. Though Coronado saw quickly that his "cities of gold" were not to be found, the priests who came with him—and those who came later with Oñate in 1598—saw just as quickly that there were souls here that needed saving: primitive people worshipping clouds, animals, and the earth itself. Heaven help us all!

The Rio Grande, the major geographic lineament of the Southwest, largely defined the Spaniards' route from old Mexico up to Santa Fe. Occasionally, though, the route along the river was difficult—broad and swampy in some places, narrow and steep-walled in others. About 15 miles north of Las Cruces, for example, where the Rio Grande Valley arcs to the west, early Spanish travelers left the river (near what was later to become Fort Selden) and cut due north. The Jornada del Muerto (Journey of the Dead), as this route became known, shortened the trip by several days, although it took travelers—many of whom died en route—into dry and barren desert, the domain of hostile Indians. The Jornada del Muerto rejoined the Rio Grande just south of present-day Socorro.

Today, driving through the wasteland basin of the Jornada, along Highway 380 between Carrizozo and San Antonio, you thank the gods you're in a car and not pulling a wagon or leading mules. You wave at occasional drivers coming the other way—allies in the lonesome emptiness. And you shudder at the irony of the name, Jornada del Muerto, for it was in this basin that the great demon of the 20th century first exploded into the world's consciousness, leaving in dying embers the last innocence of the human race: the first atomic bomb was detonated at "Trinity Site" southeast of Socorro (or Help), at the north end of the Journey of the Dead (what a long, strange trip it's been . . .).

But don't go thinking that the emptiness down there is all woe and despair. Quite the contrary. On the west side of the Rio Grande—west of Truth or Consequences and north of Silver

HIGHLIGHTS

Elephant Butte Lake: fishing, boating, camping

Gila Cliff Dwellings: fascinating lessons in prehistoric living—hiking and camping nearby

Gila National Forest and Wilderness Area: hunting, fishing, camping, backpacking, sightseeing

Mesilla (Las Cruces): historical museums, shopping, excellent restaurants

Mogollon and Shakespeare: ghost towns with abandoned 19th-century shops, homes, hotels (guided tours of Shakespeare)

Rio Grande: fishing, boating, bird-watching, sight-seeing

Silver City/Piños Altos: museums, Victorian homes, and rich mining heritage, gateway to Gila National Forest

Very Large Array: largest radio telescope in the world—visitors' facilities

City—you'll find some of the most remote and desolate country in the lower 48 states. Yet unlike the hot and sometimes hellishly barren deserts to the east, this is the country of the gods. In the spring or early summer, take a pack train into the Mogollon or Elk Mountains, fish the cascading streams of the high country, take deep breaths of that thin, pure air at 10,000 feet above sea level, and marvel at the distinctly blue sky colliding on the far horizon with the deep green of the mountain forests, waking now from a long snowy slumber.

If New Mexico is indeed a land of extremes, as author Tony Hillerman claims, then perhaps there's no better place to witness those extremities than the southwestern corner of the state. Here, you can spend a morning exploring the desert beauty of Columbus, yet be in Silver City—where Victorian homes cling to mined-out mountainsides—in time for an early dinner. You can wander one day the 17th-century streets and missions of Socorro or Mesilla and the next ponder the future of technology and the mind-boggling expanses of the universe at the Very Large Array, the most powerful radio telescope in the world. You can cross over into Mexico—at the border towns of Juárez and Palomas—and you can visit the only-in-America town of Truth or Consequences, named for, and pretty much devoted to, the radio and television show of the 1950s.

But whether your bag is fishing or rock-hounding, motorhoming or serious backpacking, high-tech or history, don't miss this often-overlooked corner of New Mexico. Just be sure to carry water.

Socorro

Socorro lies in the lush lowlands of the Rio Grande Valley about 80 miles south of Albuquerque. At the junction of I-25 and Highway 60 West, Socorro (pop. 9,000; elev. 4,600 feet) is also at the junction of the past and the future. Though many visitors to this little town today are simply passing through—stopping to gas up and fill their thermoses with coffee on the often-te-

© STEPHEN METZGER

San Miguel Mission, Socorro

dious drive between Las Cruces and Albuquerque—those who stop to explore find a unique blend of history and high-tech, from the centuries-old streets around the plaza to the world's largest radio telescope on the plains to the west.

California Street, the main drag through Socorro (Highways 85/60), is a typical small-town thoroughfare, lined with motels and fast-food joints. Unfortunately, this is all of Socorro most travelers see. Just a few blocks on either side, though, are vestiges of the town's colorful past, including the rebuilt San Miguel Mission and the central plaza, now a sleepy town park with a wide lawn, shade trees, and benches perfect for an afternoon snooze or crossword puzzle. Meanwhile, Socorro's New Mexico Institute of Mining and Technology and adjacent industrial park provide a solid economic base for the community, and the Very Large Array 50 miles west exemplifies perfectly New Mexico's position on the cutting edge of space-age technology, its giant "telescope" capturing and "photographing" radio waves emitted by stars and quasars in the far corners of the universe.

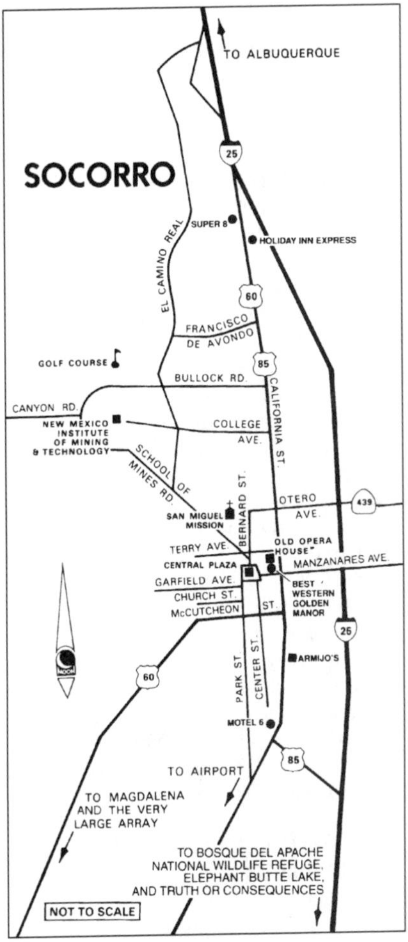

History

Socorro is one of the oldest towns in New Mexico, its history dating to 1615, when Franciscan priests began building the San Miguel Mission on what was then Piro Pueblo land. Naming the mission Nuestra Señora del Socorro (Our Lady of Help), the Franciscans set about converting the heathen Piros, who, unlike some of the more resistant tribes to the north, sided peacefully with the newcomers and soon began learning Old World methods of farming and worship. However, shortly after the mission was completed (in 1626), Apaches began raiding the Socorro settlement, and by 1680, when the Pueblo Indians—with the support of the Apaches—revolted against the Spanish, the Piros joined the refugee move south toward El Paso, and Socorro was abandoned.

For more than 100 years, Socorro—its mission burned, its homes looted—lay still and empty, a stark contrast to the fertile Rio Grande and riparian marshlands just a few miles east. In 1816, however, the Socorro Land Grant gave deed to the old town and surrounding territory to 21 families, who rebuilt the mission on the same site and resettled Socorro. Still, the relentless Apache raids continued, and it wasn't until the early 1880s, when the railroad was built and Socorro's population boomed, that they let up.

From the late 1880s until the turn of the last century, Socorro was a rowdy railroad and mining town. With the discovery of silver in the nearby hills, the town's population climbed to 5,000, and for many years Socorro served as a major shipping center for the area's silver, cattle, and flour, sent by rail to destinations throughout the country.

SIGHTS

Historic Walking Tours

The Socorro County Historical Society has outlined a thorough tour of old Socorro, which can be either walked in its entirety or broken up by a short drive between the two major historical centers—the downtown plaza area and an early residential section about three blocks away. Twenty-six different buildings and sites are included, and an annotated map helps you find your way around town. Among the buildings on the tour are the San Miguel Mission, built between 1819 and 1821 on the site of the original Franciscan mission (still in use today); the J. N. Garcia Opera House, built in 1886 and used for theater, opera, dances, and town meetings; the Val Verde Hotel (1919), which for many years served both railroad and early automobile tourists passing through Socorro; and the Hammel Brewery, which produced Illinois brand beer from Socorro's rowdy late 19th century until Prohibition. Pick up a free map of historical Socorro at the chamber of commerce, or write Socorro County Historical Society, P.O. Box 923, Socorro, NM 87801.

New Mexico Institute of Mining and Technology

Originally called the "School of Mines for Territorial New Mexico," the institute, like Socorro itself, has seen vital growth and prosperity as well as slump and abandonment. The college first opened its doors in 1889, when mining still played an important part in the area's economy. By World War II, though, with silver no longer being official tender and mining not as integral to the lifeblood of the area, the students had abandoned the campus, much as the Piros had abandoned Socorro 400 years before, and the school was used only as an army barracks. Then, in 1951, the college's name was changed to the "New Mexico Institute of Mining and Technology," an appellation that reflects its broader scope, and scholars replaced soldiers in the school's hallways.

Today, "Tech," as it's known in the area, specializes in physical and computer sciences, mathematics, and technical communication, offering degrees up to doctorates in geoscience, metallurgy and materials engineering, physics, petroleum engineering, and computer science. And with a $2 million-a-month payroll and 90 percent of its employees living in Socorro, the school is responsible for more than 70 percent of the town's cash flow.

The **Mineral Museum** in the Workman Center on the Tech campus displays nearly 10,000 examples of minerals from around the world. You can also explore the history and prehistory of Socorro County by viewing exhibits of fossils from plants and animals indigenous to the area. The museum is open Monday–Friday 8 A.M.–5 P.M.; no charge for admission. For more information, call 505/835-5420.

The Very Large Array

Although "Very Large Array" may be one of the most prosaic of names in a state otherwise given to creativity and color (witness Angel Fire, Truth or Consequences, and Shiprock), the name is, at least, appropriately descriptive. This is, in fact, a "very large array" of dish-shaped antennas (27 of them) laid out in the shape of a "Y" and connected to form a single large radio telescope for an astronomical observatory.

It's a stunning sight, really. There you are, out on the Plains of San Agustín, 7,000 feet in altitude, the high prairie grasses—dotted with cholla and juniper—seeming to stretch almost to forever, at least to where they finally meet the great sky, punctuated on summer afternoons by massive thunderheads. And suddenly in the distance you see them. Tiny at first. A "Y" of shiny white plates turned harmoniously to the heavens and arranged on railroad tracks.

But as you get closer, you realize these "plates" are anything but tiny. They're huge. Eighty-two feet across. A hundred tons. *Each.* (Including the stand and base, each antenna weighs 235 tons.)

The purpose of the VLA, the most powerful radio telescope in the world, is to photograph

© STEPHEN METZGER

Satellite dishes of the Very Large Array lend an odd touch of order to the desert.

light and radio waves emitted by other planets, stars (including our sun), and quasars (starlike objects resulting from explosions in distant galaxies). The antennas collect radio signals and send them to a central location, where the combined images achieve a dramatically high resolution and can be better studied. In the end, scientists at the VLA are learning a "very large amount" about the history and formation of the universe—some of the radio signals the VLA picks up were actually sent out billions of years ago.

Construction of the VLA began in 1974 and was completed in 1981. Total cost: $78.6 million. On the grounds is a fascinating visitors center, where photos are displayed, as are detailed exhibits explaining the intricacies of radio astronomy. You can also take a self-guided walking tour out among the antennas, computer room, and control buildings, where further displays are set up for visitors, and you can drive to a separate building where the antennas are assembled. The visitors center is free and open daily 8:30 A.M.–sunset.

The Very Large Array is about 50 miles west of Socorro on Highway 60. The turnoff is well marked. For more information, write Public Education Officer, National Radio Astronomy Observatory, P.O. Box 0, Socorro, NM 87801, or call 505/772-4255.

PRACTICALITIES

Accommodations

Most of Socorro's motels lie along California Street/Highway 85, the main drag and business loop off I-25; most offer lodging at the low end of the $50–100 range, although for under $50 you can still get doubles at the **Motel 6,** 505/835-4300, at the south end of town (take Exit 147).

The **Days Inn,** 505/835-0230, is at 507 N. California (about a block from Mission San Miguel). At the north end of town, and you'll find a **Holiday Inn Express,** 1100 N. California, 505/838-0556.

Food

In addition to the plethora of fast-food restaurants in Socorro is a handful of small, locally owned places, popular among locals and in-the-know passers-through. For good and relatively inexpensive Mexican and New Mexican food, try **El Sombrero,** 210 Mesquite, 505/835-3945, for excellent and reasonably priced specials (red and green chile dishes) and combos ($4–8). Open daily for lunch and dinner. Another longstanding favorite (first opened in 1918) is **Val Verde Steakhouse,** 203 Manzanares, 505/835-3380, where you can get steaks, seafood, and chicken dishes, as well as excellent Southwestern fare ($8–16).

Recreation

Socorro's public **golf course** is on the campus of the New Mexico Institute of Mining and Technology, 505/835-5335, and is the site of several annual tournaments. The city also has an Olympic-sized swimming pool open during summer; call 505/835-2052. About 70 miles south of Socorro, **Elephant Butte Lake** offers some of the best lake fishing in the state, as well as camping, boating, and water-skiing (see Truth or Consequences, following). For day hikes and bird-watching, check out **Bosque del Apache National Wildlife Refuge,** 18 miles south of town (see To Truth or Consequences, following). And if it's winter and you're in the Socorro area, keep in mind that the mountains of Ruidoso are barely an hour and a half away by car. There you'll find excellent Alpine skiing at **Ski Apache,** seemingly boundless glades and forests for Nordic skiing, and, for those less inclined (pun intended) to strap boards afoot, plenty of gentle (and not-so-gentle) hills for tubing and tobogganing (see Ruidoso and Vicinity in the South-Central New Mexico chapter and the Ski Apache special topic, also in the Ruidoso section).

Annual Events

For such a small town, Socorro has a chock-full calendar of events, from chamber of commerce dinner-dances to the County Fair and Rodeo. The biggest annual attraction is the four-day **Festival of the Cranes,** which attracts more than 15,000 birders and other outdoor lovers to Socorro (Bosque del Apache National Wildlife Refuge) late each November. The festival features workshops, seminars, bus tours, guided hikes, art exhibits, and dozens of other opportunities to learn about New Mexico's birds and other wildlife. Many are free; some require registration fees. For information, write Festival of the Cranes, Box 743-C, Socorro, NM 87801.

The New Mexico Institute of Mining and Technology **Science Fair** is held every April. Also on the Tech campus is the **Hilton Open Golf Tournament,** which tees off in June. Other annual events include the **Rockhounding Days** (late March); **San Miguel Fiesta** (August), with arts and crafts, outdoor dances, and a Fiesta Mass at the San Miguel Mission on Sunday; **Fat Tire Fiesta** (September); the **Socorro County Fair and Rodeo** (September); **49er Days** (October), with another golf tournament at Tech and historical exhibits at Socorro's old town plaza; **Enchanted Skies Star Party** (early October), with lectures, star viewing (with high-power telescopes), and a chuck-wagon dinner. In addition, Socorro's **Performing Arts Series** attracts musicians, dancers, acrobats, and magicians from around the world; recent participants have included rock bands and string quartets, the Chinese Golden Dragon Acrobats, and the Airmen of Note (the jazz ensemble of the U.S. Air Force). For more information on the Performing Arts Series, call 505/835-5525. For specific dates of the town's annual events, write or call the Socorro Chamber of Commerce.

Information and Services

The **Old Dana Book Store,** 203 Manzanares, 505/835-3434, carries books on the Southwest and other general-interest titles. The Socorro **Chamber of Commerce** is at 103 Francisco de Avondo; write P.O. Box 743, Socorro, NM 87801, call 505/835-0424, or visit the website: www.socorro-nm.com. The Socorro **public library** is at 401 Park SW, 505/835-1114.

Socorro General Hospital is on Highway 60 West and has a 24-hour emergency room, 505/835-1140. The Socorro Police Department is at 202 Fisher, 505/835-1150, and the Socorro office of the New Mexico State Police is north of town just off I-25, 505/835-0741.

Transportation

For information on bus service between Albuquerque and Socorro, phone **TNMO Bus Lines** at 505/835-1767. The depot is at 1007 S. California.

TO TRUTH OR CONSEQUENCES

I-25 continues its gentle arc south, paralleling the Rio Grande, often in sight through the low hills to the east. Don't be surprised at the number of cars you see pulling boats along this stretch: they're heading for Elephant Butte Lake, a true oasis in this mostly barren desert.

Bosque del Apache National Wildlife Refuge

About 18 miles south of Socorro is a different kind of oasis, and a veritable Eden for bird-watchers and nature lovers. This 57,000-acre refuge is home to 400 species of mammals, reptiles, and amphibians, while nearly 300 species of birds dwell here, either permanently or temporarily. Among the critters you're likely to see along the 15-mile drive through the refuge are deer, coyotes, snakes, ducks, egrets, cranes, and geese. Winter is an especially good time to visit, as migratory birds come down from the north to spend the cold season here along the Rio Grande. Recent winters have seen as many as 40,000 snow geese, 16,000 ducks, and 10,000 sandhill cranes. Even the endangered whooping crane has made its way to Bosque del Apache, thanks to a program begun in 1975 in cooperation with conservationists in Idaho: whooping crane eggs are placed in the nests of Idaho sandhill cranes, and the youngsters, not knowing they've been "adopted," join the sandhills when they head south for the Rio Grande.

In addition to the 15-mile loop through the refuge, you'll find a couple of viewing stands, several short walking trails, and three upland wilderness areas for extended day hikes. The refuge is open to the public from a half hour before sunrise to a half hour after sunset. The visitors center is open year-round, Monday–Friday 7:30 A.M.–4 P.M., weekends 8 A.M.–4:30 P.M. Entrance fee is $3 per vehicle.

To get to Bosque del Apache, take I-25 about 18 miles south of Socorro and watch for signs for the freeway exit (Exit 139). For more information, write Bosque del Apache National Wildlife Refuge, P.O. Box 1246, Socorro, NM 87801, or call 505/835-1828. The refuge also has an excellent website: southwest.fws.gov/refuges/newmex/bosque.html; it lists events, bird counts, and opportunities for volunteers.

Camping is available near Bosque del Apache at **Bosque Birdwatchers RV Park,** 1481 Hwy. 1, 505/835-1366.

While you're in the area, be sure to check out the **Owl Bar and Grill** in San Antonio, stopping at which, according to Bosque del Apache regulars, is almost a state law. Like its descendant in Albuquerque, this is a fun family place with lots of atmosphere and locally famous green-chile burgers. Hours are Monday–Saturday 8 A.M.–9:30 P.M., 505/835-9946.

Truth or Consequences

The first thing you'll want to know about Truth or Consequences (pop. 6,200; elev. 4,260 feet) is that it's not called Truth or Consequences. At least not by New Mexicans. It's "T or C." The second thing you'll want to know is that it wasn't always called T or C (*or* Truth or Consequences). Its original name was Springs of Palomas, which was changed to Hot Springs when Elephant Butte Dam was built.

Downtown T or C sits atop an apparently inexhaustible supply of hot mineral water—highly alkaline and nonlaxative—which gurgles to the earth's surface in eight wells and springs throughout town. Since prehistoric times, this water, ranging in temperature 98–115°F, has lured the bone-weary to the area for its restorative and curative powers. Between the 1880s and the 1930s, bathhouses and resorts were built around the springs, and though they are now somewhat run-down, they still attract arthritis patients and others afflicted with bone and muscle ailments, who come for "the cure." At some of the resorts, bathers can take advantage of whirlpools, saunas, and masseurs, as well as various nutrition and vitamin programs.

So, why "Truth or Consequences"?

Let's go back to 1950. That year, Ralph Edwards, host of the popular radio show, offered—to any town that would change its name to Truth or Consequences—a substantial bit of national publicity by way of a live, on-location show to be broadcast April 1 (April Fool's Day). The citizens of Hot Springs, New Mexico—or a majority of them, anyway: a series of elections was required to make it official—took the challenge. So, today, we have Truth or Consequences, a small resort town along the Rio Grande between Albuquerque and Las Cruces. We also have **Ralph Edwards Park** (a pleasant picnic area downtown on the Rio Grande), the annual Fiesta Days (featuring visits by Edwards himself), and an entire wing of a museum devoted to artifacts and mementos from Edwards's life and his contributions to the town. On a video shown in the Ralph Edwards Wing, an elderly Truth or Consequencian, caught up in the hoopla of Fiesta Days, looks into the camera and loudly proclaims:

> ***If there were more Ralph Edwards in this country, buddy, we wouldn't have to worry so much about the future.***

(I've always felt the same way myself . . .)

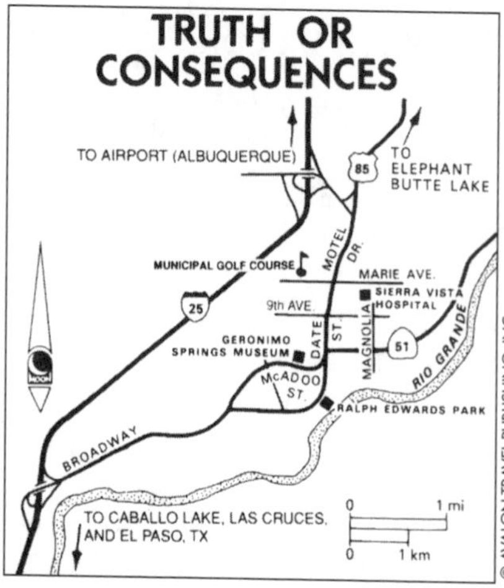

© AVALON TRAVEL PUBLISHING, INC.

SIGHTS

Geronimo Springs Museum

This little museum was dedicated during the 1972 Fiesta. Here, in addition to the Ralph Edwards artifacts, you'll find a fine exhibit of prehistoric Mimbres pottery, huge and beautifully displayed projectile point collections, early settler

© STEPHEN METZGER

entrance to Ralph Edwards Park in Truth or Consequences

artifacts—including saddles and barbed wire—U.S. Army uniforms dating from before the Civil War, assorted mining tools, and equipment from the construction of Elephant Butte Dam.

The Ralph Edwards Wing displays scrapbooks from Edwards's many visits to town, prize money from the show ($1 bills), and photos of Edwards from throughout his life, as well as photos of the celebrities who have joined him at Fiesta Days.

Geronimo Springs Museum is at 211 Main Street. Its hours are Monday–Saturday 9 A.M.–5 P.M. Cost is $2 for adults, with discounts offered to kids and seniors. There is also a small gift, book, and souvenir shop at the museum. For information, phone 505/894-6600.

Callahan's Auto Museum

This museum at 410 Cedar displays more than 20 vintage automobiles, including a Pierce-Arrow from the early 1920s and other rare cars. Hours are Monday–Saturday 10 A.M.–5 P.M. Admission is $3 per person or two people for $5. Phone 505/894-6900 for more information.

Elephant Butte Lake State Park

Although the many T or C hot springs, not to mention the incredible drawing power of Ralph Edwards, attract perhaps dozens of visitors to Truth or Consequences annually, many more come to the area for the recreation facilities offered by Elephant Butte Lake. The dam, construction on which was completed in 1916, was originally built to increase the irrigation in the valley. However, the lake has become a popular destination in its own right—for people from throughout the south and central part of the state who come for the water-skiing, fishing, and camping.

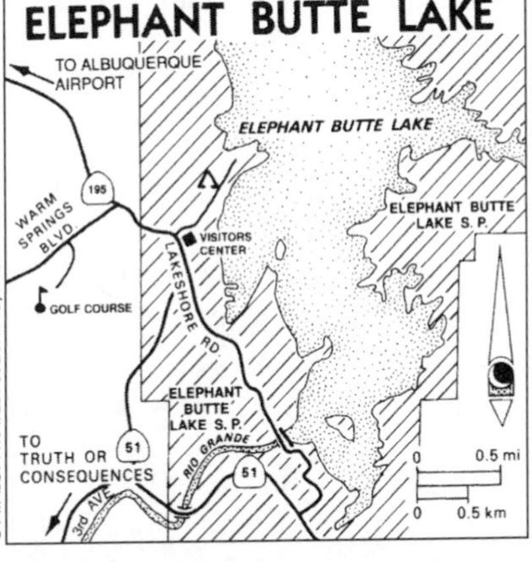

This large, multiuse recreational area was named for a rock formation said to resemble an elephant. Beneath the water's surface is the first pueblo seen by Don Juan de Oñate, who passed through the area in 1598 on his way to establish a capital for New Mexico. The park has several boat-launching ramps and a wide array of camping facilities. The visitors center displays exhibits of the dam's construction and photos of area wildlife, as well as models of fossils and bones discovered in the area, including the jawbones of a *Tyrannosaurus rex* and a stegmastodon (relative of today's elephant). Day use is $4, camping $8–12 a night. For information, phone 505/744-5421.

PRACTICALITIES

Accommodations

A number of motels along Truth or Consequences's main drag, especially on the north end, offer no-frills lodging. Among the nicer ones are **Ace Lodge Motel,** 1014 N. Date, 505/894-2151 (under $50); **Best Western Hot Springs Motor Inn,** 2270 N. Date, 505/894-6665; and **Super 8,** 2151 N. Date, 505/894-7888 (both $50–100).

Out by the lake is probably the nicest lodging in town, **Elephant Butte Quality Inn** on Highway 195, 505/744-5431. Amenities include tennis courts, nightly entertainment, and discounts at the golf course for guests ($50–100).

Camping

Though shade trees are rare in the Truth or Consequences area, a decent amount of camping is available. **Elephant Butte Lake State Park** has scores of sites; the ones with shelters are $10, and those without are $8. Hookups are an additional $4. A **KOA** campground south of town at Caballo offers tent sites (about $15) and RV sites (about $22 with full hookups) on Caballo Reservoir; phone 505/743-2811.

Truth or Consequences is also near the eastern border of the Gila National Forest, a camper's paradise. You can pitch your tent in one of the many developed campgrounds or hike in and boldly camp where no one has camped before.

Food

The **Clubhouse Restaurant** at the Elephant Butte Quality Inn on Highway 195, 505/744-5431, serves New Mexican and Mexican food, as well as steaks, seafood, and pastas ($8–18). In town, try **La Cocina,** 220 N. Date, 505/894-6499 (New Mexican and Mexican), or **Los Arcos,** 1400 N. Date, 505/894-2600 (steaks, seafood), both well regarded. There's also a **K-Bob's** at 2700 N. Date, 505/894-2127, where you can get steaks, seafood, chicken, and salads.

Recreation

The Truth or Consequences area offers an abundance of recreational opportunities. Anglers cast and troll the Rio Grande, Elephant Butte Lake, and Caballo Reservoir for black bass, striped bass, crappie, and catfish. Water-skiers, sailors, and windsurfers cruise the lake from dawn to dusk. Boaters can either launch from shore or from one of the three marinas on the south end of the lake. A guide service on Elephant Butte Lake offers fishing excursions (equipment included). Golfers choose between two different courses—the **Municipal Golf Course** at 700 Marie Ave., 505/894-2603, and the **Oasis Golf and Country Club** at Country Club and Stagecoach Roads, out by the lake, 505/744-5224.

Annual Events

T or Cians look forward to May and the annual **Fiesta Days,** when Ralph Edwards and assorted celebrities hold barbecues, public speeches, and a parade. A fiddle contest is held every October.

Information and Services

The T or C **Chamber of Commerce** has complete listings and prices of all the hot springs and spas in the area. For more information about Truth or Consequences, write the chamber at P.O. Box 31, Truth or Consequences, NM 87901, or call 505/894-3536 or 800/831-9487. In town, stop by its offices at 201 S. Foch Street. There's lots of information, too, at the chamber's website: www.truthorconsequencesnm.net. For more information on Elephant Butte Lake State Park, call 505/744-5421.

The small Sierra Vista Hospital is at 800 E. 9th Ave., 505/894-2111. The closest major hospital is Memorial Medical Center in Las Cruces, 505/522-8641. The number for the Truth or Consequences Police Department is 505/894-7111; for the sheriff it's 505/894-6617.

Transportation

Truth or Consequences is on I-25, a major north-south artery between El Paso and Denver. **Greyhound** offers passenger service to Truth or Consequences from Albuquerque to the T or C bus depot at 311 Broadway.

Truth or Consequences to Las Cruces

HIGHWAY 152 WEST

About 15 miles south of T or C, Highway 152 begins its winding way west, up out of the Lower Rio Grande Valley into Gila National Forest, up over Emory Pass, and then back down to Silver City. Though slow going, this route offers wonderful scenery—first through cottonwoods and the old towns of Hillsboro and Kingston, then up into the piñons and junipers of the Black Range—and is without doubt one of the state's roads less traveled.

Hillsboro

This shady little foothill town dates from the 1870s, when it was the center of a rich mining community that ultimately produced about $6 million in gold and silver. Among the many mines in the area was the Bridal Chamber, which until the silver crash of 1893 was one of New Mexico's most famous and productive mines. Today, travelers can stop in at the **S-Bar-X Saloon,** 505/895-5222, a funky little local hangout, proverbially voted best saloon and day trip from El Paso by the *El Paso Times.* Shoot a game of pool and knock back a cold one, or grab a burger at the adjoining **Jan's Cactus Cafe.** Bird-doggers will appreciate the restrooms, designated Pointers and Setters, with appropriate graphics.

CABALLO TO HATCH

The 75-mile stretch of I-25 between T or C and Las Cruces continues south along the Rio Grande, eventually rolling into the fertile Mesilla Valley. Along the way, you pass by a couple of state parks on the river (Caballo Lake and Percha Dam) as well as Fort Selden State Monument, and pass through New Mexico's prime chile-growing region.

Caballo Lake and Percha Dam State Parks

About 20 miles south of Truth or Consequences are two more Rio Grande state parks. Caballo Lake has two separate sites, one lakeside and one

© STEPHEN METZGER

good camping, picnicking, and fishing at Percha Dam State Park

SOUTHWESTERN NM

riverside, below the Caballo Reservoir Dam. The lake site has boat launching but not much shade or greenery, and the river site has trees and lawns. Percha Dam also has a nice lawn and shaded sites. Both Caballo Lake and Percha Dam offer camping, fishing, and picnicking, flush toilets, and showers. Fees are $4 for day use, $7 for camping ($8 for sheltered sites). Hookups are an additional $4. Phone 505/743-3942.

HATCH

Hatch's fertile riverside location has through the years been both bane and blessing. Bane because the Rio Grande has overflowed on occasion, causing havoc in the town. In fact, the town and several of its surrounding communities were once regularly threatened by rising waters, and Hatch was destroyed by a flash flood in 1921. With the construction of Elephant Butte, Caballo, and Percha Dams, though, the area was made relatively safe, and lately the water of the Rio Grande finds its way to fields more often than to streets.

Which is Hatch's blessing, as its fertile riparian soil makes it ideal for growing the hot peppers that make it the "Chile Capital of the World." Most Hatchians today work either in the chile industry or for White Sands Missile Base, which took over much of the land east of town in 1948.

If you're heading down I-25 to Las Cruces, stop in at Hatch and check out the tiny roadside chile shacks. You'll probably not find fresher and better-priced chiles and chile products anywhere. In late summer and fall, the tiny town about halfway to Las Cruces harvests its crop, and New Mexicans, from Lordsburg to Clayton, stock up. One of the first things you learn in New Mexico is that these chiles make the best stews, salsas, and *rellenos* on the planet. And there's no better way to buy them than from a roadside or parking-lot vendor, with cargo straight from the fields of Hatch.

Accommodations and Food

If you're heading south, you'll most likely want to go on to Las Cruces for lodging, although if you're too tired to drive any farther, or if you're dead set on staying in Hatch, there is one motel. The **Village Plaza Motel** at 608 Franklin, 505/267-3091, has good clean rooms for around $50. **Happy Trails RV Park,** right next door, 505/267-4522, offers sites with full hookups but little shade.

Not much here in the way of food for passers-through, either, though you might try **B and E Burritos,** 800 Franklin, 505/267-5191 (open Monday–Friday till 6 P.M. and on Saturday till 3 P.M.

Annual Events

The Hatch **Chile Festival,** the weekend before Labor Day, attracts chile fans and growers from throughout the southwestern part of the state. Festivities include a chili cook-off, parade, and fiddle contest.

Information and Services

Write the Hatch **Chamber of Commerce** at P.O. Box 38, Hatch, NM 87937.

The nearest hospital is Memorial General, 38 miles away in Las Cruces, 505/522-8641. The Hatch Police Department is at 104 Franklin, 505/267-3021. To reach the Doña Ana County Sheriff, call 505/526-6611 (Las Cruces).

SOUTH OF HATCH

Leasburg Dam State Park

About 20 miles south of Hatch, you'll come to this small park, named for Adolph Lea, who homesteaded a 160-acre tract in the southeast corner of the Fort Selden Reserve. With its proximity to the fort, the Lea ranch and community soon began "servicing" the soldiers, and before long conflicts arose between Selden's officers and Leasburg. Wrote the Fort Selden post surgeon in 1869:

> *The plague spot of the vicinity is the small settlement known as Leasburgh, where prostitutes and bad characters congregate at times when the troops of the garrison have money. All the venereal disease, which is by no means uncommon here, is directly traceable to this place."*

(Apparently Fort Selden wasn't into safe sex . . . .)

Today, numerous campsites are scattered among the cholla and creosote bushes (nothing grows taller than five feet or so, and there's no natural shade). Kids can entertain themselves at the playground and mini-adobe fort, and the park offers swimming and boating on the small lake formed by Leasburg Dam. Flush toilets and showers. Day use is $4, and camping is $8 ($10 with shelters for shade); add $4 for RV hookups. Phone 505/524-4068.

Fort Selden State Monument

Fifteen miles north of Las Cruces is Fort Selden State Monument and the ruins of Fort Selden. The fort was established in 1865 to guard the villages of Mesilla and Las Cruces against the Apache and as an outpost at the south end of the Jornada del Muerto. Until 1891, when the fort was decommissioned, it was used to protect wagon trains on the Camino Real. Douglas MacArthur lived here for two years of his childhood, while his father, Captain Arthur MacArthur, was commander.

A self-guided tour takes you out into the very weathered remains of the adobe fort, and a corresponding trail map points out officers' quarters, the hospital, etc. At the visitors center, a thorough display examines the fort's role in the history of the Mesilla Valley and the Jornada del Muerto through photographs, weapons, uniforms, and models and sketches of the fort in action.

On Saturday and Sunday afternoons June 1–September 1, hourly 11 A.M.–3 P.M., rangers clad in the dress of the day present *Hardtack and Black Powder*, a "demonstration of the uniforms, weapons, and equipage of the 19th-century U.S. Army." The show is also available for school groups and other organizations.

Fort Selden State Monument is open daily 8:30 A.M.–5 P.M. Admission is $2; kids 16 and under get in free. Take the Highway 185 exit from I-25 and watch for the signs.

For the detailed story of the fort, pick up *Fort Selden, New Mexico* for $3 at the visitors center. Phone 505/526-8911 for more information.

Las Cruces

A centuries-old hub of activity in the sprawling Mesilla Valley just an hour north of the Mexico border, Las Cruces (pop. 75,000; elev. 4,533 feet) is the seat of Doña Ana County. It's also home to both fascinating historic districts and brand-new malls, poverty-stricken Hispanics and Lacoste-clad college students, bustling street corners and indomitable mountain peaks just minutes from town.

The town's history dates to 1535, when the first Spaniards, led by Álvar Núñez Cabeza de Vaca, passed through the area. Later, in 1598, Oñate's expedition—including Spanish soldiers, missionaries, and colonists, also passed through on its way north (on this trip Oñate established the first capital of New Mexico at the pueblo of San Juan).

The Spanish called the native people they encountered in the Las Cruces area "Mansos," and no one is certain today whether these people were related to the Pueblo Indians farther north or to the Apache. At any rate, in 1630, Fray Alonso Benavides, after describing them as "robust people, tall with good features," recommended they be concentrated in a mission. In a short time, the tribe was destroyed—both through intermarriage with the Spanish, which blurred identity lines, and from exposure to smallpox and other diseases, which killed them off in huge numbers.

Once Oñate's trail had been blazed, the site of present-day Las Cruces became a much-used stopover for caravans heading north, and eventually the north-south route became known as El Camino Real (The Royal Route). The Las Cruces area proved a good resting and watering spot before Fort Selden just a few miles north, where the route veered northeast away from the river to the Jornada del Muerto (Journey of Death). El Camino Real was also the route the Spanish and converted Pueblo Indians took south in 1680 at the time of the Pueblo Revolt.

In 1787, a group of Mesilla Valley travelers came across the bodies of some oxcart caravan

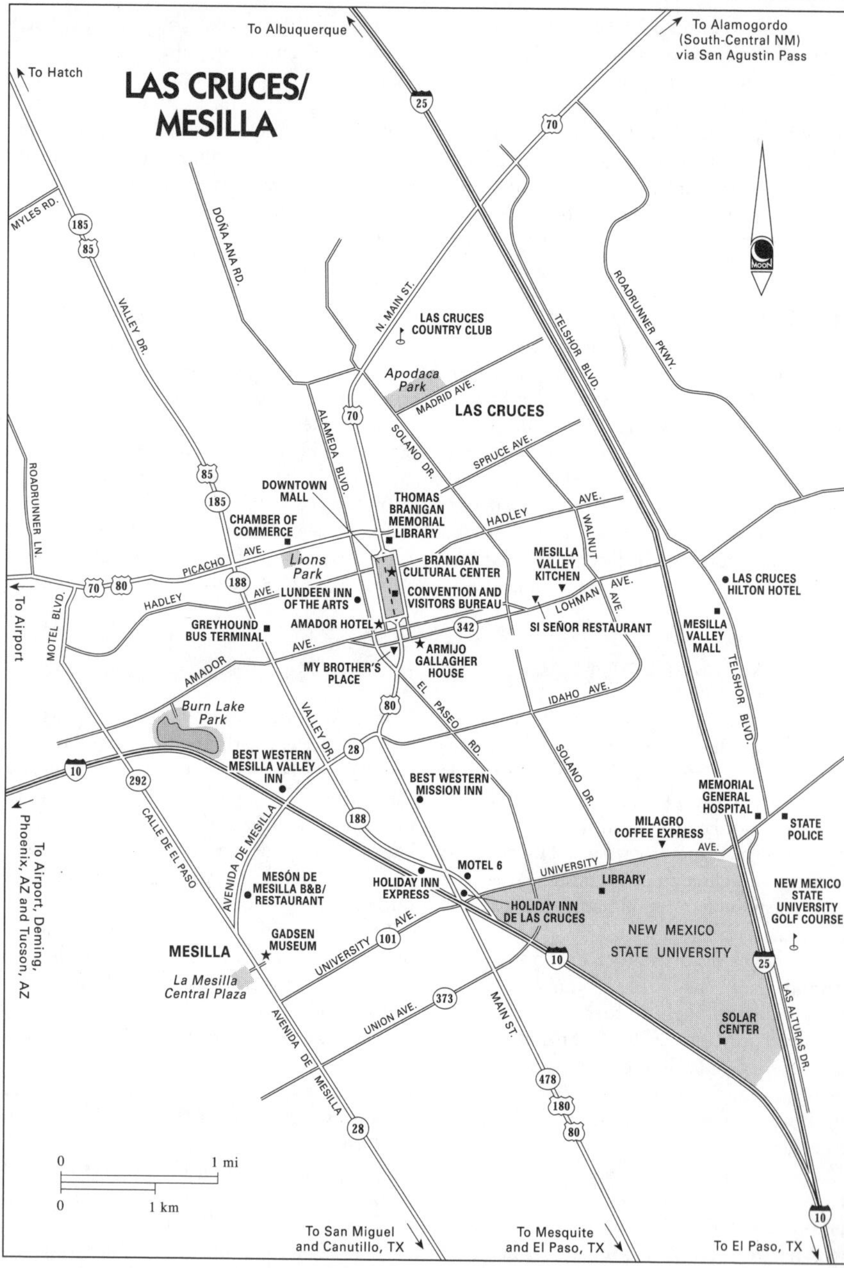
LAS CRUCES/
MESILLA
To Albuquerque
To Alamogordo
(South-Central NM)
via San Agustin Pass
To Hatch
MYLES RD.
DOÑA ANA RD.
VALLEY DR.
N. MAIN ST.
LAS CRUCES
COUNTRY CLUB
TELSHOR BLVD.
ROADRUNNER PKWY.
Apodaca
Park
MADRID AVE.
LAS CRUCES
ALAMEDA BLVD.
SOLANO DR.
SPRUCE AVE.
ROADRUNNER LN.
DOWNTOWN
MALL
THOMAS
BRANIGAN
MEMORIAL
LIBRARY
HADLEY
AVE.
WALNUT
CHAMBER OF
COMMERCE
PICACHO
Lions
Park
BRANIGAN
CULTURAL CENTER
MESILLA
VALLEY
KITCHEN
LAS CRUCES
HILTON HOTEL
To Airport
HADLEY
LUNDEEN INN
OF THE ARTS
CONVENTION AND
VISITORS BUREAU
LOHMAN
MOTEL BLVD.
GREYHOUND
BUS TERMINAL
AMADOR HOTEL
SI SEÑOR RESTAURANT
MESILLA
VALLEY
MALL
AMADOR
ARMIJO
GALLAGHER
HOUSE
MY BROTHER'S
PLACE
EL PASEO RD.
IDAHO AVE.
Burn Lake
Park
BEST WESTERN
MESILLA VALLEY
INN
BEST WESTERN
MISSION INN
MEMORIAL
GENERAL
HOSPITAL
STATE
POLICE
To Airport, Deming,
Phoenix, AZ and Tucson, AZ
CALLE DE EL PASO
AVENIDA DE MESILLA
MILAGRO
COFFEE EXPRESS
UNIVERSITY
AVE.
MOTEL 6
HOLIDAY INN
EXPRESS
LIBRARY
HOLIDAY INN
DE LAS CRUCES
MESÓN DE
MESILLA B&B/
RESTAURANT
NEW MEXICO
STATE
UNIVERSITY
GOLF COURSE
NEW MEXICO
STATE UNIVERSITY
GADSEN
MUSEUM
MESILLA
La Mesilla
Central Plaza
UNION AVE.
MAIN ST.
SOLAR
CENTER
LAS ALTURAS DR.
0
1 mi
0
1 km
To San Miguel
and Canutillo, TX
To Mesquite
and El Paso, TX
To El Paso, TX
© AVALON TRAVEL PUBLISHING, INC.

SOUTHWESTERN NM

© STEPHEN METZGER

The Organ Mountains rise like an old rusty saw above the Las Cruces desert.

drivers killed by Apaches. They erected crosses at the site in memorial. In 1830, some travelers from Taos were also attacked by Apaches. Crosses were erected in their memories, as well. From then on, the area where the crosses stood became known as La Placita de las Cruces (Little Place of the Crosses). Eventually, the name was shortened to Las Cruces.

Las Cruces became the county seat in 1852. A year later, the Gadsden Purchase (signed on the plaza in the village of Mesilla) redefined the Mesilla Valley, making it all property of the United States—before the purchase, all land west of the Rio Grande belonged to Mexico and all land east was claimed by the United States. In 1859, Father Manuel Chavez ordered construction of the town's first church, and in 1880 New Mexico State University (then the College of Las Cruces) first opened its doors. The railroad brought settlers and businesses to Las Cruces in large numbers in the 1880s.

As you approach this area today, your gaze is inevitably drawn to the striking mountain range just east of the city—peaks that rise 5,000 feet from the valley floor. These are the Organ Mountains, named for their pipelike spires and pinnacles that ascend heavenward in a jagged and narrow column. Often in late afternoon, the setting sun casts eerie light on the western slopes of the Organs, treating Las Cruces to a dazzlingly spectacular red curtain drawn to close the day.

White Sands Missile Range, over San Agustín Pass through the Organ Mountains, employs nearly 9,000 Las Cruceans. The city's second-largest employer is New Mexico State University, with about 4,000 workers.

SIGHTS

Las Cruces has two distinct historical districts, the **Mesquite** and the **Alameda Depot** areas, and it's quite proud of both. The Convention and Visitors Bureau can provide maps that pinpoint significant buildings and discuss their contributions to the history of the area. The **Amador Hotel,** on the corner of Amador and Water, was built in 1850, served as a brothel at one time, and is now home of the Doña Ana County Manager's Complex. Some of the rooms have been restored, and they display tools and clothing from the period. Open Monday–Friday 8 A.M.–noon and 1–5 P.M.; phone 505/525-6600. Also worth a visit is the **Armijo**

Gallagher House (now Pioneer Savings and Trust), built in the mid-19th century. The Armijo family has been important throughout New Mexico since 1695. Nestor Armijo, an early New Mexican businessman, bought the house in 1877 from its first owners, Bradford and Maricita Dailey, and immediately added a second story (which made it the first two-story house in Las Cruces). His appreciation for a variety of architectural styles—from Greek Revival to Victorian—can be seen today in the window moldings and parlor rooms. You can get a good sense of the old building by dropping in during banking hours.

New Mexico Museum of Natural History

The new and upscale Mesilla Valley Mall is the unlikely setting for this little museum. Exhibits have included *The Life of Caves, Fire, Dinosaurs* (on loan from the Museum of Boston), and *Jupiter and its Moons* (from the Smithsonian). Hours are Sunday–Thursday 10 A.M.–5 P.M., Friday 10 A.M.– 8 P.M., and Saturday 10 A.M.–5 P.M. To get to the Mesilla Valley Mall, take Lohman Street east from downtown; from the freeway, take the Lohman Street exit. Phone 505/522-3120 for more information.

New Mexico State University

This well-known agricultural college (team name: the "Aggies") also has a strong computer science department and one of the country's largest planetary observatories. The campus as well is one of the largest in the nation, dating to an 1880s land grant. The **University Museum** in Kent Hall at the corner of University Avenue and Solano Drive, 505/646-3739, has a rotating schedule of exhibits—usually focusing on historic and prehistoric Native American culture—a gift shop, and a bookstore. Open Tuesday–Saturday noon–4 P.M. The **library** is southern New Mexico's largest, with excellent special collections and photo archives. In summertime, the air-conditioned library is a wonderful place to get away from the heat for a while.

Branigan Cultural Center

This little library and museum in the Downtown Mall exhibits work by local artists as well as

© STEPHEN METZGER

San Albino Church, Mesilla

THE BUTTERFIELD STAGE ROUTE

This famous 19th-century mail and passenger stage route ran between St. Louis and San Francisco. Named for its engineer and contractor, John Butterfield, but known also as the Oxbow Route, it dipped south through Arkansas, Texas, and New Mexico. At one time, it employed 750 men and used more than 1,000 coaches, each pulled by a team of four or six horses. The 2,800-mile trip normally took 25 days and cost $100 to go west to east and $200 to go east to west.

The Butterfield Loop Trail is a modern-day route travelers can take that retraces parts of the old stage run and explores some of southwestern New Mexico's historic sites. Start in El Paso, Texas (the halfway point on the Butterfield Trail), and head north to Mesilla, west to Deming, and then south to Columbus, where you can walk across the border to Palomas and have lunch or dinner in a Mexican cantina (it takes dollars). Then head north again to Deming and west to Lordsburg and Shakespeare. Take Highway 90 north to Silver City and continue up into the Gila National Forest to the Gila Cliff Dwellings. Then head south again, back through the Mimbres River Valley, one of the last strongholds of Apache chiefs Victorio and Geronimo, past "City of Rocks," through Las Cruces, and back to El Paso (where your horse'll most likely need waterin').

photos and historical artifacts from Mesilla and Las Cruces. The center, at 500 N. Water, is open Tuesday–Friday 9 A.M.–5 P.M. and Saturday 9 A.M.–1:30 P.M. Phone 505/541-2155.

Mesilla

About three miles southwest from the center of Las Cruces, this is one of the highlights of a visit to the area. Once an Indian community atop a small hill (Mesilla means Little Table), the village was also a stop on the Butterfield Stage Route; in fact, La Posta, now one of the most famous restaurants in Las Cruces, was originally the stage station. The village's official beginnings were in 1850, when shortly after the Treaty of Guadalupe Hidalgo a number of people moved here to retain Mexican citizenship. The Gadsden Purchase three years later, however, made Mesilla the property of the United States anyway. In 1880, Billy the Kid's trial was held in Mesilla (although the resulting jail sentence was short-lived, as Billy escaped soon after—eventually to be killed by Pat Garrett in 1881 near Fort Sumner, New Mexico).

Originally across the Rio Grande from Las Cruces and connected by ferry (a flood changed the river's course in 1885), Mesilla is home today to a variety of colorful restaurants, galleries, gift shops, and museums. **San Albino Church** is one of the oldest missions in the Mesilla Valley, built in 1851 and reconstructed in 1906. It stands now at the end of the plaza, clean and stark against the sky, as though guarding still the tiny shops and old adobe.

The **Gadsden Museum** exhibits artifacts from Indian, Mexican, and early Anglo settlers. Open daily 9–11 A.M. and 1–5 P.M. Allow an hour for the guided tour. Admission is $2 for adults and $1 for kids 12 and under. For more information, call 505/526-6293.

San Agustín Pass

If you've come to Las Cruces from any direction but the east, and don't plan on heading that way to White Sands or Alamogordo, you at least ought to take a short drive over San Agustín Pass (5,710 feet) in the Organ Mountains. The road follows roughly part of the old Chisum Trail, and from the summit you can look west back to the Rio Grande snaking southward, Las Cruces, and the Mesilla Valley. Just over the pass to the east, look out to White Sands Missile Base: sometimes you can even see White Sands National Monument glistening in the Tularosa Basin. Park your car at the turnout and hike about 100 yards up to the scenic overlook for an even better view.

Organ Mountains Recreation Area

This rugged recreation area in the Organ Mountains due east of Las Cruces includes the **Aguirre Springs** and **Dripping Springs** National Recreation Areas. Nestled in the eastern foothills of the towering mountains among the huge boulders, yucca, and creosote, the area is an excellent place to get a sense of desert wildlife and geology. Aguirre Springs Campground has a couple of group picnic sites, with fire rings, grills, and pit toilets, and the trailheads of Pine Tree and Baylor Pass trails, which wind up into even more rugged and remote country. The Dripping Springs area, managed by the BLM and the Nature Conservancy, is named for a resort in the area originally built in the 1870s, which through the years hosted a number of famous and infamous Southwesterners (including Pancho Villa and Billy the Kid) and which is now scattered in ruins. La Cueva Picnic Area at Dripping Springs has 14 sites with tables and barbecue grills.

Caution: this is snake, scorpion, and tarantula land. We watched a jackrabbit bookin' full tilt through the bushes, and a few seconds later we came upon a tarantula the size of Liechtenstein. The dude snarled, reared back, and threw his front legs up into the air. We'd have run too, but it was easier just to roll our windows up and pray we had enough gas to get back to town.

To get there, take Highway 70 east from Las Cruces and watch for the signs. Note also that the road in is not recommended for trailers more than 22 feet long. For maps and more information, or to reserve one of the group sites, phone the office of the BLM in Las Cruces at 505/525-8228 or New Mexico's BLM headquarters in Santa Fe at 505/438-7400. You can also write the BLM at P.O. Box 27115, Santa Fe, NM 87502-7115.

On to Mexico

For folks in from the more northerly latitudes, Las Cruces is temptingly close to Mexico. El Paso is only an hour or so away, and the border town of Juárez is just across the river from there. A couple of things to keep in mind, though: 1) Your American car insurance is *not* good in Mexico, and if you get in an accident you could find

LOUISE FOOTE

tarantula, common in the Southwest desert

yourself in *mucho* trouble. Various places on the border offer short-term insurance for Americans crossing into Mexico. You can also get Mexico car insurance from many American agents in Las Cruces and El Paso. However, you *must* have both your registration and proof of American insurance. Without them, you won't be able to get even short-term Mexico insurance, and without insurance, you probably don't want to drive south of the border. 2) Though it's easy to get across the border *into* Mexico, it might not be so easy getting *out.* I've heard horror stories of people sitting in their cars for six hours and longer waiting for the line to move through Customs and Immigration. A turnaround is conveniently located just a few yards before the border, but once you're past there, it's a good chance you're going to have to wait in line to get back.

PRACTICALITIES

Accommodations

Las Cruces offers accommodations to suit just about every pocketbook. For under $50, you can find a handful of mom-and-pop motels, as well as a **Motel 6,** 235 La Posada Lane, 505/525-1010.

$50–100

One of the most distinctive lodges in the area is the **Lundeen Inn of the Arts,** a bed-and-breakfast with 20 guest rooms at 618 S. Alameda Blvd., 505/526-3326. In a century-old adobe, it has a wide range of antiques and quality art throughout. The rooms are named after prominent New

Mexican and Native American artists. For an impressive photo tour, check out the website: www.innofthearts.com.

The **Holiday Inn de Las Cruces,** 201 E. University, 505/526-4411, is worth a visit even if you're staying elsewhere. This is a beautifully appointed hotel, with an exotic lobby replete with indoor pool, hanging plants, antique couches, and tiled floors and walls. Across the lobby from the pool is the Pancho Villa Cafe, where the patio-style dining makes you feel you've been transported to old Mexico, or even to an Old World inn somewhere in the south of Spain. The Holiday Inn is also home to the Territorial Dining Room and the Billy the Kid Saloon.

Two Best Westerns also offer medium-priced lodging in Las Cruces. **Best Western Mission Inn,** 1765 Main St. near the I-10 exit, 505/524-8591, has large and comfortable rooms, with free coffee and morning paper (the *El Paso Times*) delivered to your room. **Best Western Mesilla Valley Inn,** 901 Avenida de Mesilla, 505/524-8603, is newer and nicer and has doubles running a tad higher, still under $100.

Another good bet is the **Las Cruces Hilton Hotel,** across from the Mesilla Valley Mall, the priciest of the town's fancier digs; phone 505/522-4300. There's also **Holiday Inn Express,** 2200 S. Valley, 505/527-9947.

$100–150

For a splurge—or just for something different—consider **Mesón de Mesilla** bed-and-breakfast, an old farmhouse-style inn on the road to Mesilla away from the traffic of downtown, 505/525-9212. Rooms here vary from basic quarters to the honeymoon suite, which includes champagne. All rates include a full breakfast in the elegant Mesón dining room. Call ahead to be picked up at the Las Cruces airport. Mesón de Mesilla is at 1803 Avenida de Mesilla as you drive from Las Cruces to Mesilla; watch for the signs. For more information, write P.O. Box 1212, Mesilla, NM 88046.

Camping and RVing

In addition to the camping at Aguirre Springs (see Organ Mountains Recreation Area, above) and Leasburg Dam (see South of Hatch, above), Las Cruces has a number of "improved" campgrounds and RV parks. **Siesta RV Camp,** 1551 Avenida de Mesilla (at the junction of I-10 and Highway 292), 505/523-6816, has 24-hour showers, a laundromat, small grocery store, and designated tent area. Full hookups are about $18 for two people.

Food

Las Cruces claims well over 100 restaurants, a large percentage specializing in Mexican and New Mexican food. You could easily spend a month or more checking out all the little holes-in-the-wall, sampling the enchiladas, burritos, *tacos al carbon,* and menudo. One of the oldest and most famous restaurants in town is **La Posta,** on the plaza in Mesilla, 505/524-3524; open Tuesday–Sunday for lunch and dinner. This exotic restaurant—once a stage stop on the old Butterfield Overland Route—has been written up in national magazines, and for nearly 50 years tourists have gone great distances out of their way to experience the food and atmosphere, as well as the 300-year-old building, with its Indian and South American gift shops, hanging plants, and birds in ceiling-high cages. Tamales, *chiles rellenos,* burritos, and huge plates of tacos range $6–12.

Also in Mesilla is the elegant **Double Eagle** restaurant, 505/523-6700. Upscale continental-style dinners include chicken Dijon, duck à l'orange, lamb chops, quail, and swordfish—priced at $12–24. Fancy desserts, such as cherries jubilee and parfaits, are $4–6. Open daily for lunch and dinner. Adjoining the Double Eagle is the lower-priced and not-as-fancy **Peppers,** 505/523-4999, specializing in local foods and produce. Tapas are served for both lunch and dinner and include soft tacos, blue-corn nachos, quesadillas, and blue-cornmeal fried oysters. Salads and New Mexican dishes are served for lunch. Dinners include salads, Mexican dishes, and steaks and seafood ($6–14).

For pure elegance, try the dining room at **Mesón de Mesilla,** 505/525-9212, where a chalkboard seafood menu changes daily, depending on what's biting (and getting caught in nets). Dinners are $16–24, and lunches run $8–14. It also serves an excellent Sunday brunch.

Another good Mexican restaurant is **Si Señor,** 1551 E. Amador, 505/527-0817, where combo plates and specials run $7–11. Open daily for breakfast, lunch, and dinner. Live mariachi music on weekends.

Walking distance from central Las Cruces, **My Brother's Place,** 336 S. Main, 505/523-7681, is a favorite of the downtown business set. Its large main room centers around a gurgling fountain, while a number of adjacent dining rooms (some nonsmoking) offer a cozy dining experience. Mexican and American entrées are $6–12. Open for lunch and dinner Monday–Saturday.

Pancho Villa Cantina and Cafe, in the delightful lobby of the Holiday Inn, serves both Mexican and seafood dinners for $6–8; phone 505/526-4411.

For a pastry or bagel and an espresso jolt, try the **Milagro Coffee Express,** 1722 E. University, 505/532-1042.

For a heartier breakfast, try the local favorite **Mesilla Valley Kitchen,** 2001 E. Lohman, 505/523-9311.

If you want to see what else is out there, pick up the Las Cruces "Restaurant Guide," published by the Convention and Visitors Bureau. You can also get a complete listing of Las Cruces–area restaurants at the website: www.lascrucescvb.org.

If you'd rather cook at home, and happen to be in town on a Wednesday or Saturday morning, stop by the downtown mall for the Las Cruces **Farmer's Market,** where you can pick up locally grown chiles, herbs, honey, and a wide range of produce, as well as crafts and novelties. For more information, phone 505/528-3276.

Entertainment

As you'd expect, the area around NMSU has pool halls and live-music venues to keep the students happy. If you want to kick up your heels to Tim McGraw, check out **Rodeo USA,** a county-and-western dance club at 170 W. Picacho, 505/524-5872. Authenticity guaranteed by the number of pickups in the parking lot.

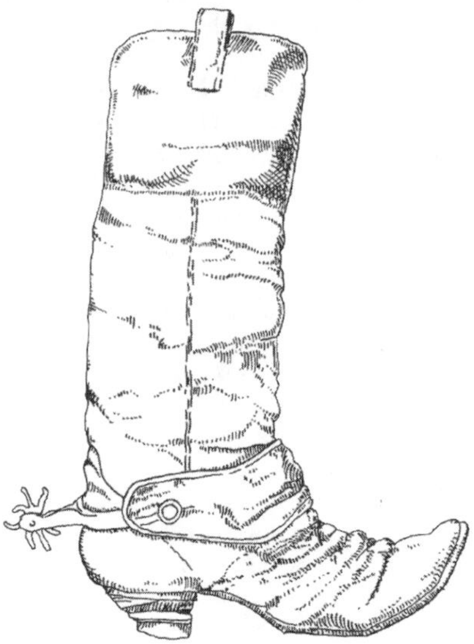

DAVE HURST

For something a little tamer, try **Billy the Kid Saloon** at the Holiday Inn, 210 University, 505/526-4411. Check out the Old West decor and order a shot from a waitress dressed like an old-time saloon girl (don't worry: firearms must be checked at the door . . .). Live music Monday–Saturday 8:30 P.M.–1:30 A.M.

In addition to the de rigueur multiplex theaters popping up in malls across the country and showing mostly United Artists releases, Las Cruces offers the New Mexico State University Film Series. For film listings, call 505/646-3235.

The ***Las Cruces Sun-News*** publishes the weekly entertainment guide *Que Pasa?,* which lists current "Hot Spots": what's showing, who's playing, etc. It's free at stores around town and most motels. You also should check out the ***Bulletin,*** an independent weekly distributed free in racks and at motels and restaurants around town. In addition to giving you a sense of what's happening around town in terms of entertainment, the *Bulletin* will also help you get a feel for the issues that are important to the folks who live here—always a good idea when visiting a town.

Shopping

If you're looking for gifts or souvenirs, head to Mesilla, where you'll find a dozen or so shops and galleries selling quality work. Wander around the plaza; mosey down the little side streets. A good place to start is at the **Mesilla Book Center** on the plaza in Mesilla. You can tell the minute you step into this place that it's a real bookstore: the shelves are in disarray, and though there is order to the books' display, you sense that the proprietors are more interested in *reading* than in flawless organization. You'll find books on everything from French impressionism to training your Great Dane, from traveling in British Columbia to improving your tennis serve. And, of course, *lots* of books of regional interest.

Next door to the Mesilla Book Center is **Del Sol Indian Rug Shop,** 505/524-1418, with a huge selection of handwoven rugs, blankets, and placemats, as well as Indian baskets, jewelry, and pottery, and assorted South and Central American boutique items. Open daily 10 A.M.–6 P.M.

The Galleria, a few steps down the street, kitty-corner from the church, has excellent paintings, woodcarvings, pottery, and ceramics. This is clearly a high-quality gift store, and its prices reflect that. Open Monday–Saturday 10 A.M.–5 P.M., Sunday noon–5 P.M.

For generic shopping, **Mesilla Valley Mall,** at the east end of Lohman, should satisfy all needs. Quite a bit nicer than the Downtown Mall, Mesilla Valley has a pet store, a JCPenney, a Beall's and other typical large mall–type shops. There's even a **Luby's Cafeteria** and a tavern—**O'Ryan's**—for those for whom a trip to the mall is just slightly less painful than Chinese water torture.

Las Cruces's two main north-south streets—Main and Water—flank the **Downtown Mall.** Wednesday and Saturday mornings, an open-air market is held here, with vendors setting up tables to sell local produce, baked goods, handmade jewelry, and various other knickknacks.

Recreation

The **Organ Mountains** east of Las Cruces offer miles of hiking and backpacking trails and, for the adventurous, numerous climbing opportunities, varying from easy to technical. For more information, call **The Frontier Shop** at 505/526-4786. You can fish the Rio Grande year-round, and Caballo and Elephant Butte Lakes to the north have even been known to yield a lunker or two on occasion.

Las Cruces has three **golf** courses, though two of them, Las Cruces Club, 505/526-8731, and Picacho Hills Country Club, 505/523-2556, are private. A public golf course on the grounds of New Mexico State University, 505/646-3219, is situated on a rolling hill overlooking town and in the shadow of the Organ Mountains, which loom nearby.

Las Cruces has more than 50 parks—although many are just small community and neighborhood numbers—to which the townsfolk head for softball, tennis, swimming, and barbecuing. **Apodaca Park,** at Madrid Road and Solano Drive, has a playground, two tennis courts, swimming pool, changing rooms, and restrooms. **Lions Park,** at the corner of Picacho and Melendres, has tennis and racquetball courts, picnicking, and swimming in Laabs Pool. Near I-10 off Amador Avenue, **Burn Lake Park** offers 25 acres of fishing, picnicking, and playground areas.

Annual Events

Fall's a good time to visit Las Cruces, as **The Whole Enchilada Fiesta,** including a hot-air balloon rally, takes place in late September or early October; phone 505/526-1968 for more information. The **Southern New Mexico State Fair,** 505/526-8179, is held here in early October, followed by the **New Mexico State Chile Championships** a couple of weeks later.

Information and Services

For more information about the Las Cruces area, contact the **Convention and Visitors Bureau** at 505/541-2444, or stop by the office at 211 N. Water. Visit one of the most thorough and helpful city sites in the state at website: www.lascrucescvb.org. To have tourist or relocation information sent to you, phone 800/FIESTAS (800/343-7827) or visit the website. The Las Cruces **Chamber of Commerce** is at 760 W. Picacho Ave., 505/524-1968. (For the

Hispano Chamber of Commerce, write P.O. Box 1686, Las Cruces, NM 88001.)

For more information about **New Mexico State University** and events there, call 505/646-0111.

The **Thomas Branigan Memorial Library** is at 200 E. Picacho Ave., 505/526-1045, and is open Monday–Thursday 10 A.M.–9 P.M., Friday–Saturday 10 A.M.–6 P.M., Sunday (September–May only) 1–5 P.M. The **New Mexico State University Library,** in Branson Hall, is open Monday–Thursday 7:30 A.M.–midnight, Friday 7:30 A.M.–9 P.M., Saturday 9 A.M.–5 P.M., Sunday noon–midnight.

Memorial General Hospital is on the east end of town just off I-25, 505/522-8641. The number for the emergency department is 505/521-2286. The main office of the Las Cruces Police Department is at 210 E. Picacho. For nonemergencies call 505/526-0795. The state police are on University Avenue; phone 505/524-6111.

Transportation

The **Greyhound** bus depot is at 415 S. Valley, 505/524-8518.

Mesa Air, 800/MESA-AIR (800/637-2247), has passenger service to Las Cruces International Airport, and **Las Cruces Shuttle Service,** 505/525-1784 or 800/288-1784, offers airport-hotel shuttles. Flying time between Albuquerque and Las Cruces is about one hour.

For route and fare information on Las Cruces's public transportation system, **Roadrunner Transit,** stop by the office at 1501 E. Hadley #A, or call 505/525-2500. Single-ride tokens cost $.50.

TO DEMING

Interstate 10 beelines west from Las Cruces through Tucson and Phoenix, eventually ending in Southern California, just a few feet from the beach near Los Angeles. Across the southwestern corner of New Mexico, I-10 parallels the Mexico border, staying within 30 miles most of the way. This is barren country, marked by long stretches of desert and occasional isolated mountain ranges, scree-flanked and barren themselves.

Rock Hound State Park

Forget for the nonce the usual public-property admonition to "Take only pictures; leave only footprints." At Rock Hound State Park, the rule doesn't apply. In fact, this park, as a recent Albuquerque *Tribune* article put it, is one "you can take with you." Here, rangers encourage visitors to take rocks they find—up to 15 pounds per person—for personal collections, to make jewelry, or to decorate the garden.

That's right. Rock Hound State Park—to go.

Established in 1965 and dedicated in June 1966, this little park, in the craggy desert uplifts that form the Little Florida Mountains, has been a favorite of rock and mineral buffs since the early part of the 20th century. These days, the park gets 45,000 visitors a year, most of whom come in the cool of winter, when the 29-site campground, among beautifully landscaped gardens of prickly pear, cholla, and bird of paradise, is often full. But according to park officials, even though many of these visitors do in fact take rocks from the park with them, the area's landscape has changed very little over the years.

The park's visitors include both casual and serious rock hounds, the latter hip to the agate, onyx, and opal often found just underground, sometimes lying right in view. Park officials claim anyone willing to do a little work can find something worthwhile (if not necessarily worth untold riches). Bring a pickax and shovel (the old army-surplus specials are ideal) and a good pair of hiking boots or shoes (the rock is loose in places and the hills steep) and head out into the park's 240 acres. Look for "nodules," round or oval rocks that when cracked open may contain agate or opal, or sometimes quartz crystal (these are called "Thunder Eggs").

The gates to Rock Hound State Park Campground are open daily 7:30 A.M.–sundown. Facilities include running water, flush toilets, and hot showers. Day use is $4 per vehicle, sheltered sites are $8, and electrical hookups are another $4.

About three miles across the valley from Rock Hound is **Spring Canyon,** a separate, day-use-only adjunct to the state park. Open Wednesday–Sunday 8 A.M.–8 P.M., Spring Canyon is a beautifully rugged area, with several picnic ta-

© STEPHEN METZGER

the only state park you can take with you

bles scattered amid the heavy vegetation at the bases of the huge monoliths of the Florida Mountains. A sheltered group site with six tables can be reserved for office and community functions.

To get to Rock Hound State Park (and Spring Canyon), watch for the signs just east of Deming. The park is south of the freeway. You can also get there by taking Highway 11 south from Deming and then a short road east into the mountains. From either direction, the route is well marked.

Deming and Vicinity

Deming (pop. 11,500; elev. 4,335 feet) lies halfway between Las Cruces and Lordsburg at a major junction along I-10. From here, Highway 180 shoots like a straight spoke northwest up into the mountains of Silver City, 50 miles away, while Highway 11 drops south just 30 miles to the Mexican border. Deming's twin claims to fame are its water, which is 99.9 percent pure, and its duck races (yes, you read correctly).

If you happen to be passing through Deming on the fourth weekend of August, you'll be just in time for the **Great American Duck Races** (GADR). The annual competitions were first held in 1979, when a handful of local merchants, bemoaning Deming tedium, decided duck races would bring some excitement to town. (Although stories of the origins vary somewhat, and my sources pleaded for anonymity, it seems likely that said businessmen had been drinking more than Deming's pure water when the idea surfaced.) Since those early days, the races' popularity has increased dramatically, and today a $7,500 purse draws as many as 400 entrants (ducks) and 30,000 spectators (human) from around the country. Among the weekend's festivities are the crowning of the "Duck Queen," something like a homecoming queen, and a "Darling Duckling," a cute local youngster (both human). The chamber of commerce even filmed a "Duckumentary," which tells the story of the races and spotlights some of the more, er, fowl moments of the festivities.

Through the years, the duck races have kept abreast of the political times. Soviet ducks were banned from competing while the army of their motherland occupied Afghanistan, and one of 1988's entrants was Michael DuQuackis. Among the trainer/owners returning each year is one Robert Duck (his actual name; you could look it up), who has had several winning ducks in recent races. To ensure that Duck and his competitors are playing by the rules, race officials are threatening to embark on a campaign of random drug testing. "Some of the ducks have been doing quack," said a Race Association member.

Deming's nonduck history dates to 1881, when the town was founded on a broad expanse of open prairie—the site where the Southern Pacific Railroad met the Atchison, Topeka, & Santa Fe. Just a little more than an hour west of Las Cruces (on desolate I-10), Deming is the seat of Luna County. The nearby mountains—Cooke's Peak to the north, the Floridas to the southeast, and Tres Hermanas (Three Sisters) to the south—have through the years been mined for gold, silver, copper, manganese, and onyx. The mines, except for the manganese mines in the Floridas, have long been abandoned.

The purest water and the speediest ducks? Who knows? Whatever the case, a stop in Deming just might be the perfect antidote to the tedium of the desert. Duck in when you start feeling daffy.

Deming Luna Mimbres Museum

The Luna County Historical Society runs this museum out of the old National Guard Armory building, a huge brick structure just a couple of blocks from Deming's main drag. During the early part of the 20th century, military troops recruited to help protect the U.S.-Mexico border were stationed here. The two-story museum is divided into several different rooms, and the pieces are displayed thematically. The Gilmore Quilt Room exhibits beautiful lace and quilts dating to 1847, the Military Room displays World War I and II weapons and uniforms, and the Doll Room—perhaps the most impressive of all—contains toys and more than 500 dolls from around the world. The museum also features an Indian Gallery, with Mimbres pottery and baskets from A.D. 550–1150, and other assorted Native American pottery and jewelry, as well as gems, minerals, fossils, and medical and dental equipment from the late 19th and early 20th centuries. The Deming Luna Mimbres Museum (including a small book and gift shop), 301 S. Silver St., is open Monday–Saturday 9 A.M.–4 P.M., Sunday 1:30–4 P.M. Admission is free; donations are accepted. For more information, write the Luna County Historical Society, P.O. Box 1617, Deming, NM 88031, or phone 505/546-2382.

PRACTICALITIES

Accommodations

Short-term digs in Deming are pretty much limited to RV parks and standard mid-Americana motels (except for the campground at Rock Hound State Park—see above), most of which you'll find on the east end of town and many of which offer doubles in the $50 range and under. I recommend the **Grand Motor Inn,** just east of downtown at 1721 E. Pine, 505/546-2631, or the **Mimbres Valley Inn Best Western,** also on the main drag at 1500 W. Pine, 505/546-4544. Doubles at both run $50–70. A very nice **Holiday Inn** sits alongside I-10 at Exit 85 on the east end of town, 4600 Motel Dr., 505/546-2661 (a bit more expensive at $50–100). The least expensive rooms are probably at the **Motel 6** at I-10 and Motel Drive, 505/546-2623 (under $50).

RVers can choose from about five different parks lined up on Highway 70/180 east of town. All offer nice sites with full hookups. Among them are **Dreamcatcher RV Park,** 4004 Motel Dr., 505/544-4004, and **Little Vineyard RV Park,** 2901 E. Motel, 505/546-3560.

Note: all of Deming's motels and RV parks are full during the Great American Duck Races. If you want a place to sleep then, make reservations well ahead of time.

Food

My favorite restaurant in Deming is **Si Señor,** right downtown at the corner of Silver and Pine (200 E. Pine), 505/546-3938. I ate there last time I passed through, and I'll eat there next time I do. This bustling but unassuming little place serves excellent examples of all the traditional Mexican dishes you'd expect, and the prices are very reasonable—most dinners are in the $6–9 range. Open daily.

I've also had good luck at the **Cactus Cafe** at the corner of Iron and Cedar (218 W. Cedar), 505/546-2458. The Cactus has a very good Mexican buffet (*chiles rellenos,* enchiladas, etc.), plus an excellent salad bar. Open daily 7 A.M.–8 P.M. **Fat Eddie's,** in the Holiday Inn, 505/546-2661, is an offshoot of the one first established in Las Cruces in 1977 and serves lunch and dinner.

In addition, on-the-go travelers can choose from among a handful of fast-food and franchise restaurants (Dairy Queen, K-Bob's, KFC, McDonald's) and several locally owned places.

Recreation

The **Rio Mimbres Country Club,** on the east end of town, 505/546-3023, offers both links and a pro shop, while the plains around Deming attract deer and quail hunters.

Annual Events

Besides the Great American Duck Races ("duck royalty pageant," outhouse races, tortilla toss), Deming does have other things going on regularly. The **Rockhound Roundup,** sponsored by the Deming Gem and Mineral Society, is held in March each year and features guided rock "outings," auctions, and judging seminars. Typically the event draws around 5,000 participants, 100 dealers, and hundreds of RVs from throughout the United States. All proceeds from the roundup go to Luna County charities and to high school scholarships. Write the Deming Gem and Mineral Society, P.O. Box 1459, Deming, NM 88031-1459, or phone 505/546-2674.

In early June, the chamber of commerce sponsors an arts and crafts fair, including refreshments and live entertainment. The **Southwestern New Mexico State Fair** is held in Deming every year in late September or early October and includes livestock competition, a rodeo, parade, and carnival. Information on the fair can be obtained by calling 505/546-2691. Finally, **Butterfield Trail Days,** in early July, commemorates the old Butterfield Stage line, founded in 1857. The two-day event is held at the county courthouse and features a parade, art show, trading post and flea market, and costume contests. Call the chamber of commerce for specific dates and more information.

Information and Services

The **Deming Visitors Center,** in the Deming/Luna County Chamber of Commerce building downtown at 800 Pine near the corner of Columbus, 505/546-2674, has lots of information on things to do and see in the area. Pick up a copy of *Desert Winds Magazine,* a free guide to the area published by the Tourism Development Committee. You'll also find lots of brochures—from weather profiles to retiree-recruitment literature—and, of course, information on the Great American Duck Races, including copies of the "Duckumentary" video (on sale for $15). The Deming **public library** is at 301 S. Tin Ave., 505/546-9202.

Deming's 52-bed Mimbres Memorial Hospital is at 900 W. Ash St., 505/546-2761. Larger and more complete facilities are just over an hour away in Las Cruces (Memorial General Hospital, 505/522-8641) and about 45 minutes away in Silver City (Gila Regional Medical Center, 505/388-1591). The Deming Police Department is on South Gold Avenue, 505/546-3011 (emergencies) and 505/546-8848 (nonemergencies). The local number for the New Mexico state police is 505/546-3481.

Transportation

Deming is just over an hour's drive west of Las Cruces, which is serviced by **Mesa Air,** 800/MESA-AIR (800/637-2247), and about 45 minutes from Grant County Airport in Silver City, also serviced by Mesa. **Greyhound,** 505/546-3881, has passenger service to Deming; the bus depot is at 300 Spruce. **Amtrak,** too, stops in Deming on its cross-country journey—the Sunset Ltd. heads west to Phoenix and Los Angeles and east through Dallas and Little Rock on its way to Chicago. Phone 800/872-7245 for more information.

COLUMBUS

Just a half hour south of Deming is one of the most historically fascinating areas in all of New Mexico. Although there's not a whole lot in Columbus today—in fact, it's nearly a ghost town—the place was once jumping with U.S. and Mexican soldiers, as the 13th Cavalry from nearby Camp Furlong battled Pancho Villa and 1,000 or so of his men. In fact, this battle marks the only time in U.S. history that the mainland was attacked by a foreign power. (See the special topic on Pancho Villa and his raid on Columbus.)

Established in 1891 just across the border from Palomas, Mexico, Columbus around the turn of the 20th century was a thriving community, supported largely by Camp Furlong: hotels, banks, drugstores, a theater, a school with 17 teachers, even a Coca-Cola bottling plant. When Camp Furlong shut down operations, the economy of Columbus rapidly went into the skids, and today the town is a lonely outpost in the dry flatlands of the southernmost reaches of the state, best known for Pancho Villa State Park, two small museums, and the port of entry from Mexico just a couple of miles to the south.

Pancho Villa State Park

New Mexico's most southerly state park is a stark and dry place, hardly a destination-type area—you'd have to be a serious student of turn-of-the-20th-century U.S.-Mexico history or someone who enjoys both solitude and emptiness to make this more than a short side trip from your travels through New Mexico, especially in the summer, when it's *hot.*

The 49-acre park has more than 60 campsites scattered around a desert botanical garden—including cholla, mesquite, bird of paradise, and creosote, and many varieties of desert flowers. There's very little shade, but you will find running water, hot showers, a dump station, and a visitors center, which houses a museum (open daily 8 A.M.–5 P.M.) displaying artifacts from the Pancho Villa conflict and showing a documentary film. Day use for the park is $4, campsites are $8, and electrical hookups another $4. Phone 505/531-2711.

Columbus Historical Museum

In the old Southern Pacific depot, the Columbus Museum exhibits early weapons, furniture, and clothing from the area. Summer hours are Monday–Thursday 10 A.M.–1 P.M. and Friday–Sunday 10 A.M.–4 P.M. Call ahead for off-season hours and to arrange group tours. Admission is free, although donations are gratefully accepted. Phone 505/531-2620.

Columbus Day Fest

This annual event is held the second Saturday in October in historic downtown Columbus. The day's events include a parade, game/food booths, street dance and entertainment. For more information, contact the Columbus Chamber of Commerce at 505/531-2663.

Mexico

Another reason to visit Columbus when you're in southwestern New Mexico is that it affords an excellent opportunity to drop into Mexico. Unlike at El Paso and Juárez east of Columbus, you won't have to wait for hours at the Customs line. Nope, things are pretty sleepy here in the border town of Palomas (Doves). In fact, we parked our car right at the border (avoiding the need for Mexican auto insurance) and walked across into Mexico for lunch. As in Columbus, there's not a whole lot here—a couple of restaurants and curio shops—but it's a wonderful experience to leave the States behind for a few hours and enter a different culture, even if it is just a border town, highly influenced by its powerful northern neighbor (your U.S. dollars are good, in fact *very* good, in Palomas).

Information

For more information on Columbus, contact the **Columbus Chamber of Commerce,** 201 Broadway #3, Columbus, New Mexico 88029-0365, 505/531-2663. You can also get information from the Columbus Historical Society by writing Box 562, Columbus, NM 88029, or by by phoning the museum at 505/531-2620.

PANCHO VILLA

PROCLAMATION
$5,000.00 REWARD
FRANCISCO (PANCHO) VILLA
ALSO $1,000. REWARD FOR ARREST OF
CANDELARIO CERVANTES, PABLO LOPEZ,
FRANCISCO BELTRAN, MARTIN LOPEZ
ANY INFORMATION LEADING TO HIS APPREHENSION WILL BE REWARDED.
CHIEF OF POLICE
Columbus
New Mexico
MARCH 9, 1916

Though Billy the Kid is perhaps New Mexico's archetypal outlaw—some historians branding him pure evil, others claiming he was simply a victim of the era's political corruptions—the name Pancho Villa evokes almost equal fear and regard. Born Doroteo Arango, Villa was a persona non grata of Mexico's Porfirio Díaz government, ostensibly because of his bank robberies and cattle thefts. Already wanted by government, Villa joined Victoriano Huerta's revolution against Díaz, although on June 4, 1912, after three or four battles with Huerta's forces, Huerta ordered Villa's arrest. Villa was imprisoned and sentenced to be shot, but he was reprieved by then-president Francisco Madero. He escaped from jail and crossed the border into the United States, then returned to Mexico in March 1913 and fought with Venustiano Carranzo against Huerta. After defeating Huerta, Carranza turned against Villa. Alvaro Obregón, then Carranzo's chief general, pursued Villa and his handful of troops throughout northern Mexico until late 1915, by which time Villa's forces were all but destroyed.

Shortly before dawn on March 9, 1916, Pancho Villa (sources variously claim his troops by then numbered from a mere 500 all the way up to 1,100), apparently in response to President Wilson's recognizing Carranza as Mexico's president, attacked the 13th Cavalry at Camp Furlong, New Mexico. Though the U.S. soldiers were outnumbered three to one, they succeeded in driving the Mexicans into retreat. Villa's men fled the camp to nearby Columbus, where they shot out shop windows, looted stores, and robbed and killed hotel guests. The Cavalry pursued Villa to Columbus and eventually killed nearly 250 of his men (18 Americans were killed in the raid, 12 wounded).

The next day, President Wilson ordered a "Punitive Expedition," to be commanded by General John "Blackjack" Pershing, to attempt to capture Villa or at least disband what was left of his troops. Pershing's expedition, using airplanes and trucks (the first time in history the United States ever used motorized vehicles in warfare), eventually chased Villa more than 500 miles back into his own country, dramatically reducing the numbers of Villa's troops, although Villa himself was never captured (he was, however, wounded by Carranza's men in March 1916). In February 1917, Pershing returned to Columbus, and Villa continued his battles against the Mexican government until he was assassinated on July 20, 1920.

Lordsburg and Vicinity

If the name "Lordsburg" rings a vague bell, you might be recalling the 1939 John Ford film *Stagecoach,* in which Ringo (John Wayne), Dallas (Claire Trevor), and several other unlikely characters are attacked by Geronimo and his band of Apaches en route from Tonto to Lordsburg. Of course, the U.S. Calvary arrive in time to run the savages off, and Dallas and Ringo make it safely to Lordsburg, where Ringo kills the Plummer brothers, and Ringo and Dallas make plans to marry, despite Ringo's learning of Dallas's status in Lordsburg as a former prostitute. Excellent movie.

About halfway between Deming and Lordsburg, in the low, undulating hills of the high desert, I-10 crosses over the Continental Divide. Lordsburg (pop. 3,500), situated in the empty Pyramid Valley, is a small town with a large Hispanic population and a laid-back ambience.

Though there are several stories about how the town got its name, most local historians believe it was named for Dr. Charles C. Lord, an army surgeon who, after the Civil War, moved to Tucson, where he became a prominent merchant and banker. Lord and a partner started a wholesale distributing company, delivering freight to much of what is today Arizona and New Mexico. One of their delivery destinations was a little nameless town west of Deming; when the freight handlers had a delivery there from Tucson, they shouted out "Lords," which morphed into "Lordsburg," and the name stuck.

Today, Lordsburg is the seat of Hidalgo County, New Mexico's "Boot-heel County," which is known nationwide for its geothermal resources. In fact, the United States Geological Survey, after recently discovering geothermal fluids in Hidalgo County's Animas Valley, south of Lordsburg, designated the area the "Lightning Dock Known Geothermal Resource Area." Temperatures up to 246°F have been documented in the shallow wells of the region, and more than 30,000 acres of public land have been leased for further study.

SIGHTS

Shakespeare

Don't come to the ghost town of Shakespeare—three miles south of Lordsburg—expecting to see one of the bard's comedies or tragedies, but do expect to learn something about history. The town's rambunctious past dates to 1856, when the first building was erected in the then-named town of Mexican Springs, although it wasn't until 1870, when silver in the hills brought prospective miners to the area in hordes, that the area saw a real boom. Renamed Shakespeare, after the Shakespeare Mining Company, which had staked a number of claims in the area, the town at that time hosted 3,000 people who roamed its streets, hotels, saloons, and brothels and lived in adobe houses, tents, and tiny hotel rooms. Abruptly, though, mining activity in Shakespeare subsided, and the town was all but abandoned. During the next 60 years, interest in Shakespeare's mines waned and ebbed, gradually dying out altogether, and in 1935 the entire town was purchased by the Hill family, which still owns the National Historic Site today.

Because the town is privately owned—in fact, the owners are Shakespeare's only residents—tours are offered far less frequently than had the state or federal government turned the place into a park or monument. Of course, this has its advantages. The tour guides actually grew up in the buildings they're taking you through, and they tell stories they were told as children—like the one about the hanging of Russian Bill and Sandy King in the Grant House Dining Room. They also dress in period clothing for the tour and do an excellent job helping visitors get a genuine feel for life on the frontier in the late 19th century.

Among the stops on the tour are the Stratford Hotel, where Billy the Kid allegedly once held a job as dishwasher; the town's assay office; the powder magazine; the blacksmith shop; the cemetery; and several saloons, including the Roxey Jay—once the fanciest in town, with a wood floor, mahogany bar, brass spittoons, and billiard and card tables (none of the finery remains).

The guided tours of Shakespeare take about 90 minutes; after the tour you're free to remain and wander back through town and out to the cemetery to check out the gravestones of the characters whose stories you've just heard. Special two-hour tours for groups of 12 or more can be arranged by calling ahead. Generally, scheduled tours are at 10 A.M. and 2 P.M. on Saturday and Sunday of the second and fourth weekends of every month. I'd highly recommend calling ahead, though, as tour days and times do vary (we happened to luck out and arrive just as a tour was starting, although the schedule we had indicated there would be no tours that weekend). Call 505/542-9034, or write Shakespeare Ghost Town, P.O. Box 253, Lordsburg, NM 88045. You can also get information at the website: www.shakespeareghostown.com. Admission is $3 for adults and $2 for kids 6–12, and all proceeds go toward further restoration of the town. From I-10, take the Main Street exit at Lordsburg (Exit 22) and turn south. Follow the signs 2.5 miles to Shakespeare.

Steins Railroad Ghost Town

The privately owned and recently renovated town of Steins was originally built in 1858 by the Butterfield Overland Mail Company. The town flourished in its heyday, and between 1905 and 1945 it was home to more than 1,000 people. Today, 10 buildings with artifacts and furniture from the 19th century are open to the public, affording glimpses into the Old West. Steins is open daily 9 A.M.–5 P.M., and admission is $2.50, with kids under 12 admitted free. To get there, take I-10 west from Lordsburg to Exit 3 (at Roadforks), and watch for the signs. For more information, write P.O. Box 2185, Roadforks, NM 88045, or phone 505/542-9791.

PRACTICALITIES

Accommodations

As you might imagine, Motel Boulevard (known as Railroad Avenue west of town) in Lordsburg is where you'll find most of the town's travelers' digs. The street parallels the Southern Pacific tracks, and most of the motels are on the east end of town. Two long-standing and reliable options are the **Best Western American Motor Inn,** 944 E. Railroad Ave., 505/542-3591, and the **Best Western-Western Skies Inn,** 1303 S. Main., 505/542-3535. Two newer lodges are a **Day's Inn,** 1100 W. Motel Dr., 505/542-3600, and a **Holiday Inn Express,** 1408 S. Main, 505/542-3666. All will run $50–100 for doubles.

The **Lordsburg KOA** is at 1501 Lead St. (take Exit 22 off I-10), 505/542-8003. Sites with complete hookups are about $25, and tent sites are $18.

Information and Services

Stop in at the **Lordsburg/Hidalgo County Chamber of Commerce** at 208 Motel Dr. for more information on the town and surrounding area (chamber-type brochures and a thorough Hidalgo County profile). You can also write 208 Motel Dr., Lordsburg, NM 88045, or phone 505/542-9864. The ***Lordsburg Liberal,*** published every Friday, includes listings of local events and is for sale for $.40 around the county.

The closest hospital to Lordsburg is the Gila Regional Medical Center in Silver City, about 45 miles northeast on Highway 90, 505/388-1591. The Lordsburg Police Department is at 206 Main St., 505/542-3505, and the state police are at Pyramid and 7th, 505/542-8827.

Transportation

The nearest airport with commercial passenger service (Mesa Air—800/MESA-AIR, or 800/637-2247) is the Grant County Airport south of Silver City on Highway 180, about an hour from Lordsburg.

SOUTH OF LORDSBURG

Known as the "boot-heel," that little square corner of New Mexico that drops into the Sonora Desert of Mexico is some of the most barren and sparsely populated land in the Southwest. Even Highway 81, which cuts south off I-10 between Deming and Lordsburg and ventures partway into the boot-heel, soon surrenders to the harshness of the desert floor, turning to dirt and meandering its way south to the Mexico border. On Highway 9, which cuts a narrow and seldom-traveled east-west ribbon just north of the boot-heel from Columbus to the Arizona border, you'll find just three "towns"—each with little more than a gravelly gas station. In short, this is land for those who like their solitude, or, more appropriately, one who likes *his* or *her* solitude.

Big Hatchet Wildlife Area

In the northeast corner of the boot-heel, just east of Highway 81, Big Hatchet's 105,000 acres of rugged juniper- and piñon-covered hills and mesquite- and creosote-blanketed plains are home to hawks, coyotes, deer, ring-tailed cats, foxes, mountain lions, badgers, and javelinas, as well as a closely watched herd of desert bighorn sheep. The area was reserved in 1926 as a refuge for the endangered sheep, and recent counts have the numbers at 90–100 (a drought in 1979 reduced the herd to 12).

Much of the state- and BLM-managed area is surrounded by private property, and ranchers hold the keys to the gates. The best public access is on the northeast side of the Hatchet Mountains. Coming south from Hachita on Highway 81, continue south on a dirt road where the pavement bends west (if you reach Hatchet Gap—the pass where Highway 81 crosses the mountains—you've gone too far). The area is completely undeveloped, but rewarding hiking awaits the adventurous. The view from the top of Big Hatchet Peak, reached by intermittent sketchy deer trails, is said to be one of the finest in southwestern New Mexico. For information about visiting Big Hatchet, call the BLM's Las Cruces office at 505/525-4341.

Silver City and Vicinity

Driving to Silver City (pop. 12,335; elev. 5,920 feet) from Lordsburg or Deming is a lesson in New Mexico's geographic extremes. From the dry and brown expanses of the desert to the moist and green forests of the mountains in under 45 minutes. And what a relief it is. Especially in the summer, when dry and brown also means hot, and moist and green also means cool (or at least cooler). In fact, Silver City, in the foothills of the Piños Altos Mountains at the south edge of the Gila National Forest, is actually just the beginning. A few miles north of town, where Highway 15 begins its winding, climbing way into the Mogollon Mountains and the depths of the forest, the scenery turns into some of the prettiest and lushest in all of New Mexico—easily rivaling even the better-known landscapes of the mountainous north state.

Silver City's downtown is of classic Victorian vintage, born of the mines that dotted the hillsides in the middle of the 19th century, and the town's streets, sidewalks, and buildings maintain that Wild West mining-town feel. Today, however, the town is defined more by Western New Mexico University (student population about 2,000) and the nearby wilderness areas than by roughnecks tearing in on Saturday nights to spend their wages on liquor and women—although some of the bars in Silver City still have reputations suggesting you might want to pass them by if, say, you're the type who likes little parasols in your drinks.

As you explore Silver City, you'll come across the "Big Ditch." Until the turn of the last century, this ditch was, literally, Main Street, but a series of floods between 1895 and 1906 gutted the road, leaving in its wake a 55-foot-deep canyon that today runs right through town. Among other things, this had the effect of turning some of Silver City's downtown buildings bass-ackwards: the storefronts—once facing Main Street—now face the ditch, and access is often from their back sides. In 1936, the ditch was lined with rock to decrease further erosion, and today "Big Ditch Park" includes picnic tables, walkways, and bridges across the ditch—definitely one of the strangest municipal parks you'll ever see.

Western New Mexico University is one of Silver City's showpieces, a 200-acre campus tucked on a hillside just above the downtown area.

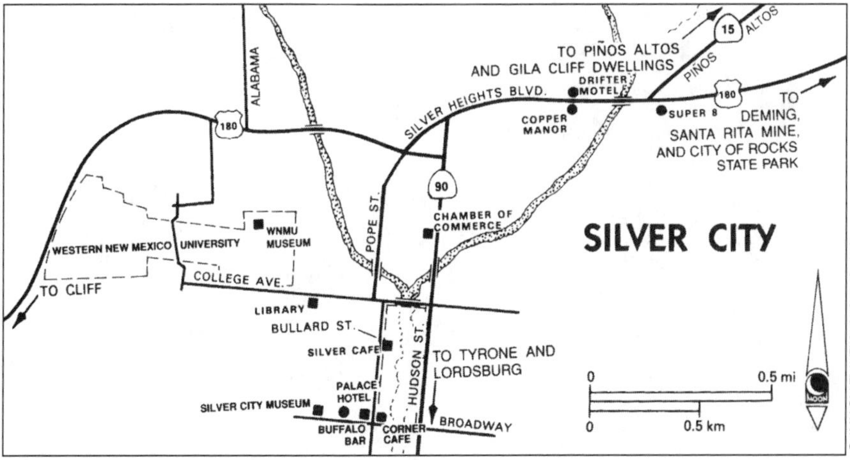

Founded in 1893 as New Mexico State Normal School (for training teachers), WNMU today has a wide liberal arts curriculum, and the school's stately buildings and rolling lawns add a degree of dignity to the town's character.

History

Originally, the Silver City area was in the heart of Apache country. First called La Cienega de San Vicente (The Marsh of St. Vincent—the place gets wet) by early Spanish settlers, the town began to lure Anglos shortly after the Civil War, when gold was discovered in the nearby hills. By 1870, silver had also been discovered—in more plentiful amounts than gold—and a number of claims were staked in the surrounding area, including the "Legal Tender" mine, just behind the present-day courthouse. Of course, this meant a huge influx of miners with their sights set on getting rich quick, and the town thrived, becoming in 1875 the official seat of Grant County. Still, until nearly the turn of the last century, Silver City was the victim of continuous raids by Apache warriors who refused to give up their homeland.

One of the more famous families to leave its mark on the Silver City area was the Antrims. Although scholars are divided on the subject, consensus pieces the Antrims' story together like this: William Antrim married Catherine McCarty in 1873 in Santa Fe. Among the witnesses at the wedding was McCarty's son, Henry. Antrim, looking to get rich, moved the family to then-booming Silver City, where he apparently spent more time in the goldfields than with his family. Although legend and song have young Henry McCarty killing his first man in Silver City at the age of 12, history disputes that. He was, however, first arrested here when, at the age of 15, McCarty held up a Chinese laundry. He was promptly thrown in the hoosegow, from which he soon escaped by climbing out through the chimney.

Henry stayed in Silver City, washing dishes at the Star Hotel, creating minor mischief, and, some say, reading. (Historians debate McCarty's level of literacy, some saying he couldn't read a word, others quoting friends who claimed he was "always reading"—from dime novels to police gazettes.) His mother died of consumption (tuberculosis) in 1874, and Henry probably left shortly thereafter.

Although some scholars say young McCarty first murdered in New York City in 1878, where he is said to have stabbed a policeman to death, most believe it was in Arizona in 1877, where he reportedly shot a blacksmith in a barroom dispute. He was arrested in Arizona, but escaped from jail once again, and it was then, historians believe, that he changed his name—to William Bonney.

MIMBRES INDIANS

At the same time the Anasazi were developing their highly complex civilizations (about A.D. 950–1200) in the northern part of the state, the Mimbres Indians, a branch of the Mogollon culture, were working away down here in the southwest along the banks of the Gila and Mimbres Rivers in what are now Grant, Luna, and Hidalgo Counties. An agricultural and devoutly religious people, the Mimbres left behind some of the most beautiful and intricate pottery in New Mexico—marked by its geometric designs and natural figures.

LOUISE FOOTE

Mimbres pottery: holes were cut in the bottom to release the pot's spirit.

Mimbres pottery, usually black (sometimes red) on white, is often found at gravesites, and pots have occasionally been found over skulls. Anthropologists believe the pottery was ceremoniously "killed," a hole poked in the bottom of each piece to release its spirit. It is from this pottery that we know what little we do about the Mimbres: archaeologists have discovered pieces that depict weddings, christenings, dancing, gambling, hunting, and children playing.

No one is certain why or exactly where the Mimbres went when they left southwestern New Mexico. Tree rings from the period, however, show evidence of an extended drought in the late 13th century, and it is commonly believed that the Indians migrated north in search of wetter climes for their crops. Most likely, they eventually assimilated into the Pueblo culture developing at the time between the Socorro and Taos areas.

He was killed by Pat Garrett near Fort Sumner in 1881, when he was 21. Henry McCarty, a.k.a. William Bonney, was better known, of course, as Billy the Kid.

Another famous Silver Citian is astronaut and moon-walker Harrison "Jack" Schmitt. Schmitt grew up here and is best remembered as the chief geologist on NASA's Apollo 17 flight.

SIGHTS

Silver City Museum

Specializing in "Frontier Victoriana," the Silver City Museum is in the old A. B. Ailman house, built in 1881. Ailman, one of Silver City's more successful citizens, originally came to town to try his hand at mining, did well at it, and later turned to banking.

The museum houses a large permanent collection of mining and household effects of early Silver Citians, in addition to ancient Indian (Mimbres) pottery and tools. A separate wing is set aside for rotating exhibits—most often thematically arranged items of historical significance from other old mining towns in the area, including models of the towns in their heydays.

In addition, the Silver City Museum includes a research center with extensive historical files, a photo archive, and a gift shop specializing in Southwest books. The museum also offers a lecture series, concerts, a Fourth of July Ice Cream Social, and a Victorian Christmas Evening.

The Silver City Museum is downtown at 312 Broadway and is open Tuesday–Friday 9 A.M.–4:30 P.M., Saturday–Sunday 10 A.M.–4 P.M. (closed Monday). Admission is free; donations are accepted. For more information on exhibits or scheduled events, write Silver City Museum, 312 W. Broadway, Silver City, NM 88061, or call 505/538-5921.

Billy the Kid Tour

If you're a real fan of the Kid, you might want to check out some of his old haunts. The self-guided tour starts at his boyhood home, just north of the Broadway Bridge on the east bank of the Big Ditch, then moves on to the site of the jail from which he escaped at age 15 (304 N. Hudson—now a Forest Service warehouse), and the Star Hotel (southwest corner of Hudson and Broadway), where Billy washed dishes and waited tables as a teenager. Other sites on the tour include Billy's mother's grave, his father's cabin in Glenwood, and the mine where his father worked. For more information and a map of the tour, stop by the Silver City-Grant County Chamber of Commerce at 201 N. Hudson.

Big Ditch Park

A tribute to Silver City's bizarre Big Ditch, testimony to what can happen when New Mexico's hard rains fall on over-grazed hillsides—floods at the turn of the last century turned Main Street into a 55-foot-deep ditch.

Western New Mexico University Museum

Western New Mexico University's collection of Mimbres pottery, dating to the 8th century, is the largest in the country and has been displayed at museums from Paris to Copenhagen to New York. The history of the school is also documented—in photos and various displays—and the animals of the area are exhibited in all their stuffed glory. Hours are Monday–Friday 9 A.M.–4:30 P.M. and Saturday and Sunday 10 A.M.–4 P.M. Take College Avenue to West, West north to 10th, then 10th up the hill to the museum. The museum's entrance is on the building's south side. Admission is free (donations appreciated). Phone 505/538-6386 for more information.

Old Tyrone/Phelps-Dodge Open Pit Mine and Mill

In 1912, the Phelps-Dodge Corporation bought land south of Silver City where copper had been mined since the 1870s. The company hired Bertram Goodhue, chief architect of the 1915 San Diego Exposition, to design a "company town," and Goodhue built Tyrone using Spanish Colonial architecture as his model. Tyrone, with its marble fountain, modern hospital, library, and houses with indoor plumbing, was completed in 1915 and at one time was home to more than 5,000 people. By 1928, though, demand for copper had decreased so much that Tyrone was abandoned, earning it the nickname "The Million Dollar Ghost Town." In the '30s and early '40s the site was a dude ranch, and today, old Tyrone is nothing more than the site of the open pit mine and mill, built in 1966 when the old buildings were razed. (Modern Tyrone, which you'll pass if you take Highway 90 from Silver City to Lordsburg, is seven miles north of the old town.) For a gander at the pit and mill, pull off Highway 90 on the south end of town between Broadway and Mill Streets and walk the 100 yards to the observation point. Free tours are offered weekdays by reservation. For information, phone the Silver City-Grant County Chamber of Commerce at 505/538-3785 or 800/548-9378.

PRACTICALITIES

Accommodations

The following motels in Silver City offer good clean rooms at reasonable rates (around $50): **Holiday Motor Hotel,** 3420 Hwy. 180 E, 505/538-3711 or 800/828-8291; the **Drifter Motel,** on the east end of town at 711 Silver Heights (Highway 90 and Highway 180), 505/538-2916 or 800/853-2916; the **Copper Manor;** and a **Super 8,** 1040 E. Highway 80, 505/388-1983, at the junction of Highway 180 and Highway 15.

If you'd rather stay downtown, check out the recently restored **Palace Hotel,** 106 W. Broadway, 505/388-1811, a classic Victorian built in 1882. The trade-off here for the central location is the possibility of noise from teenage cruisers; locals tell me of loud music late into the evening just below the windows of the Palace, particularly on Friday and Saturday nights. Doubles at the Palace go for $50–60.

Bed-and-Breakfasts

Very near the downtown area, **Carter House,** 101 N. Cooper, 505/388-5485, is both a bed-and-breakfast and American Youth Hostel. Built by local copper baron Theodore W. Carter in 1906 and restored between 1989 and 1992, the Carter House offers five bed-and-breakfast rooms, each with a private bath ($50–100), as well as dormitory-style lodging. For reservations or information on hostel rates, phone 505/388-5485, or write 101 N. Cooper St., Silver City, NM 88061.

If seclusion and uniqueness are what you're looking for, **Bear Mountain Lodge,** P.O. Box 1163, Silver City, NM 88061, 505/538-2538, is a must. Built in the 1920s as a home for emotionally disturbed boys and converted to a bed-and-breakfast in 1959, the Bear Mountain is a veritable New Mexico institution. Stay in one of the rooms in the two-story house itself, or rent one of the cottages, and take advantage of the ranch's 160 acres of piñony hills: hike, mountain bike, or go bird-watching—on your own or on a guided tour. The ranch has also been the site of several Elderhostel seminars. To get there, go west on Highway 180 about a half mile from downtown Silver City and turn north on Alabama. Continue for about three miles (Alabama becomes Cottage San Road) and turn left on Bear Mountain Road just past the first cattle crossing. The ranch is at the end of a half-mile, well-maintained dirt road.

Rooms and cottages for go for $120–180 a night. Get more information on rooms, special programs, and rates at the website: www.bearmountainlodge.com.

For a taste of Southwestern elegance with a French country flair, check out **The Cottages,** 2037 Cottage San Rd., the boyhood home of Apollo astronaut Harrison Schmitt. Built in 1939, this sprawling estate on 80 acres looks across the Continental Divide. Two suites in the main house and three separate cottages are available—three full meals included—all offering privacy and comfort. Rates for rooms in the house run $100–150, the cottages $150–200. For a brochure and more information, write P.O. Box 2562, Silver City, NM 88062, or phone 505/388-3000 or 800/938-3001. You can also get more information at the website: www.zianet.com/cottages

Camping and RVing

Silver City more than makes up for its paucity of motel rooms with its abundance of nearby campgrounds, as well as the spectacular camping and backpacking in the Gila Wilderness. You'll find a number of excellent campgrounds along Highway 15 between Silver City and Gila Cliff Dwellings. One of the nicest is the national forest's **Cherry Creek Campground,** a few miles past Ben Lilly Monument north of Piños Altos. Tall pines and lush ferns keep the dozen or so sites nicely concealed (no running water; pit toilets only). A couple of miles up the road, you'll come to **McMillen Campground,** also nicely shaded, with ferns, pines, and mossy hillsides keeping the area cool even on hot summer afternoons. At the end of the road (about 45 miles north of Silver City) are two more Forest Service campgrounds (see Gila Cliff Dwellings National Monument, following). South of Silver City, both tent camping and RVing are available at **City of Rocks State Park** (see East of Silver City, following).

More RV camping: the Silver City **KOA** campground is five miles east of town about a quarter mile south of Highway 180. RV sites with full hookups run about $22 for two people, while tent sites are about $15. April through October, you'd be wise to make reservations at least a couple of days ahead of your intended stay. Write Silver City KOA, HCR 88060, 11824 Hwy. 180 E, Silver City, NM 88061, or call 505/388-3351. In Piños Altos, the **Continental Divide RV Park,** 505/388-3005, offers RV sites for about $20 for two (an extra $2.50 for use of showers and dump station). Take Highway 15 north from Silver City about six miles.

Food

Silver City's range of restaurants is about as limited as its range of motels, although the few restaurants you'll find are quite good. Locals and tourists alike swear the best breakfasts in town are at the **Corner Cafe,** 505/388-2056, downtown at the corner of Bullard and Broadway, famous for its cinnamon rolls the size of Frisbees. Other breakfast specialties are the crepes, pancakes, and French toast. For lunch, the café serves a variety of sandwiches (turkey, club, and Reuben) and a "quiche of the day." Open Monday–Saturday 7 A.M.–4 P.M. and Sunday 8 A.M.–2 P.M. Just a few blocks up Bullard at the corner of 6th is the **Silver Cafe,** 505/388-3480, another local favorite, serving hot and authentic New Mexican food—chili, tacos, tamales, and burritos—for $2.50–3.50. The lunches are especially good. Open Monday–Saturday 7 A.M.–7:30 P.M. Still another excellent Mexican restaurant is the **Jalisco Cafe,** 103 S. Bullard, 505/388-2060, recommended for its fresh (daily) ingredients and healthful dishes. Hours are Monday–Thursday and Saturday 11 A.M.–8:30 P.M., Friday 11 A.M.–9 P.M.

A relative newcomer to Silver City, **Diane's Restaurant,** 510 N. Bullard, 505/538-8722, has quickly become popular throughout the area, the owner-chef having brought her Santa Fe–restaurant experience with her. Look for pastas and salads and grilled meats. Lunches (Tuesday–Friday) run $5–8, while dinner (Thursday–Saturday) entrées are in the $8–18 range. Diane's also serves brunch on weekends.

Entertainment

Las Vegas (Nevada) this is not. In Silver City, you won't find yourself having to choose between Robin Williams and Jay Leno. But there is the **Buffalo Bar,** one of the more, well, colorful watering holes in the area. On Bullard, a half block north of Broadway, this is where local miners come to drink, play pool, get rowdy, and, on Friday and Saturday nights, boogie to live rock 'n' roll. Definitely neither a family-oriented place, nor the kind of place you'd want to go for a relaxing drink in a quiet corner, the Buffalo draws the Hank Williams Jr. "All my rowdy friends have settled down" and-I'm-pissed-about-it crowd. Not that there's any danger of getting in a brawl, but as one woman told me when I asked her why she was holding her pool cue as if it were a weapon:

> ***It gets weird in here when you're with some dude, your husband's out of town, and your ex-husband's across the room.***

LOUISE FOOTE

collared peccary, or javelina

Occasionally, the Buffalo holds "College Night." You'd expect that things would get rowdy those nights as well, but Silver Citians say those are the nights to stay away—no alcohol is served as most of the students are underage.

The lounge at the **Drifter Motel** also has live music, generally country and western, every night but Sunday. Call 505/538-2916 for current information.

Recreation

As the gateway to Gila National Forest and Wilderness Area, Silver City is an outdoor lover's paradise. Whether for hunting (elk, mule deer, bighorn sheep, bear, mountain lion, javelina, and turkey), fishing (German brown, rainbow, and brook trout, bass, and catfish), day-hiking, backpacking, pack trips, or wildlife photography, the forests and mountains north of Silver City offer some of the best in the West. For information about hunting and fishing seasons, license fees, and other regulations, contact the **New Mexico Game and Fish Department,** 1480 N. Main St., Las Cruces, NM 88001, 505/524-6090.

Seventy-two-acre **Lake Roberts,** on Highway 35 just southeast of the Gila Cliff Dwellings, is a man-made lake nearly straddling the Continental Divide. The lake offers fishing and boating, and a number of fine hiking trails wander in the woods around the water and into the forest.

Silver City's **Scott Park Golf Course** in Scott Memorial Park has 18 holes. Phone 505/538-5041 for greens fees and hours.

Annual Events

In addition to its annual Fourth of July Frontier Days Celebration—with a parade, fireworks, and a dance—Silver City also sponsors Mining Days on Labor Day weekend. Celebrating its rich mining history, the town pulls out all the stops and offers stagecoach and pony rides, gold-panning demonstrations, ore-car loading, jack drilling, and golf and horseshoe tournaments. There are also a parade, a "Miner's Marketplace," and melodrama at the Buckhorn Saloon and Opera House in Piños Altos. For more information, write the Silver City-Grant County Chamber of Commerce.

Silver City is also the epicenter for a series of bicycle races held each June that attract hundreds of riders to thousands of dollars in prize money. The 22 events include road races, a 45-mile criterium in downtown Silver City, and four-mile time trials just outside town. Contact the chamber of commerce for specific dates and entry information.

Information and Services

The **Silver City-Grant County Chamber of Commerce** is one of the more ambitious in the state, publishing a wide assortment of maps and brochures on the area. Stop in at the office at 210 N. Hudson (Highway 90) and pick up a copy of *Four Historic Scenic Tours,* a wonderfully detailed listing of sites—from museums and town parks to hot springs and campgrounds—in the area around Silver City and Gila National Forest. The annually published *Silver City Grant County Magazine* is also available at the chamber. This free handy little guide includes articles on the area's history and current events, a community profile, and a detailed street map of Silver City. You can also contact the chamber by writing Silver City-Grant County Chamber of Commerce, 201 N. Hudson, Silver City, NM 88061, or by calling 505/538-3785 or 800/548-9378. It's also got a very thorough and user-friendly website: www.silvercity.org.

For information about **Western New Mexico University,** call 505/538-6106. The Silver City **public library** is at 515 W. College Ave., 505/538-3672.

Silver City's Gila Regional Medical Center is a full-service hospital at 1313 E. 32nd St., 505/388-1591. In nonemergencies, call the Silver City Police Department at 505/538-3723. The state police office is at 528 Hwy. 180 W, 505/388-1542.

Transportation

Silver City, up in the hills away from the main cross-country arteries, is serviced neither by bus nor train. **Mesa Air,** 800/MESA-AIR (800/637-2247), provides passenger service to Las Cruces and El Paso airports, and shuttle service is available between both airports and Silver City. Phone **Las Cruces Shuttle** at 800/288-1784 and **Silver Stage Line** at 800/522-0162.

EAST OF SILVER CITY

Santa Rita/Chino Open Pit Mine

This is the oldest active mine in New Mexico, having been worked as early as 1800. Originally a shaft mine, Santa Rita del Cobre (St. Rita of the Copper) was first staked by Lieutenant Colonel José Carasco and manned by convicts. The ore from Santa Rita was sent to Chihuahua, Mexico, and eventually to the Mexico City mint. Throughout the 19th century, ownership of the mine changed hands, and at one point Santa Rita was completely abandoned after repeated Apache raids.

By the late 1800s, most of the ore accessible by shaft had been mined, and in 1910 an open pit mine was begun, eventually swallowing the small town of Santa Rita. (Silver City's "Society of People Born in Space" celebrates people who were born in Santa Rita before it was the giant hole it is today. Annual reunions draw "space people" from all over the world.) The huge pit, by now more than 1.5 miles wide and 1,000 feet deep—a particularly gross example of the destruction of the earth for profit—can be seen from an observation point off Highway 152 about 15 miles east of Silver City (Highway 152 forks off from Highway 180 at Central, eight miles east of Silver City).

Kneeling Nun

Not one of the most breathtaking natural wonders in the Southwest, but the price is right. If you look hard enough and use your imagination, you might see a vague resemblance between a lone rock at the end of a bluff near the Santa Rita mine and a nun kneeling in prayer. The legend is that she is the stone incarnation of a Catholic nun, punished for falling in love with a Spanish soldier. Look to the south from Highway 152 near the mine.

City of Rocks State Park

This is one of those only-in-New-Mexico geologic oddities—huge rocks towering above the desert landscape, forming a maze of passageways with walls sometimes 50 feet high. In truth, the boulders are not "rocks" at all. Rather, they are the remains of a several-million-year-old lava flow—perhaps originating as far away as Albuquerque—that, as it cooled, condensed in areas known as "welded tuff." Although the flow was most likely covered later by other volcanic residue, through the years erosion, caused by wind and water, left only this 40-acre field of large, denser deposits, the monolith-type towers of the City of Rocks.

As you wander the "streets" of the city, watch for concave smooth spots in the flat areas of the rock—mortars where the Indians once ground corn.

At City of Rocks State Park, 505/536-2800, several dozen campsites are scattered among the towers, most of them nicely private. The restrooms are wheelchair-accessible and have flush toilets and hot showers. Fees for day use are $4, while camping is $8 (no electrical hookups or dump station).

To get to City of Rocks State Park, take Highway 180 toward Deming, then turn north on Highway 61. Watch for the turnoff on your left (right if you're coming north from Deming) and follow the signs to the park.

HIGHWAY 15 NORTH

Highway 15 climbs north out of Silver City and up into the Gila National Forest, through some of the state's most stunningly beautiful country, ending at the Gila Cliff Dwellings. Though you could drive straight to the cliff dwellings, visit them, and turn around to return to Silver City—taking about three hours—there's a whole lot more to see in the area, and you'd be wiser to give yourself an entire afternoon, or even the better part of a day, to poke around in the pines of the Gila region. (You could also spend weeks here—camping, hiking, horseback riding—in the Gila Wilderness; this is country that's hard to leave.)

Gila National Forest and Wilderness Area

Some of the most remote, rugged, and beautiful country in the Southwest, the Gila National Forest sprawls over nearly 3.3 million acres. The smaller, 30- by 10-mile unit between Lordsburg and Silver City is mostly rangeland, while the monstrous main unit stretches from Silver City north halfway to Gallup and from the Arizona border east almost to Truth or Consequences.

LOUISE FOOTE

wild turkey, common to Gila National Forest

LOUISE FOOTE

elk

Included in the wild country of the forest are a number of steep mountain ranges: the San Francisco, Black, Mogollon, and Diablos—mountains that Apache chiefs such as Geronimo, Cochise, and Mangas Coloradas once roamed with their warriors.

In 1924, a half million acres of the national forest—most of which embrace the Mogollon Mountains between Silver City and Reserve—were designated the nation's first wilderness area, and the Gila Wilderness today is still untamed and uninhabited—except by bear, deer, elk, beaver, bobcat, mountain lion (famous panther hunter Ben Lilly left a *few*), as well as antelope and wild turkey. A favorite of serious backpackers, hikers, and anglers, the Gila is also accessible by horseback, and a number of outfitters lead pack-train trips into the region. Local guides/fitters include **Gila Wilderness Expeditions,** 312 Double E Ranch Rd., P.O. Box 280, Gila, NM 88038, 505/535-2048, or **U-Trail the Gila Wilderness,** P.O. Box 66, Glenwood, NM 88039, 505/539-2426.

Permits are required to enter the Wilderness Areas of the Gila National Forest and can be obtained at any of the ranger stations. The Silver City district office is at 2915 Hwy. 180 E, 505/538-2771. You can also get information at the Gila Cliff Dwellings Visitors Center, 45 miles north of Silver City on Highway 15.

Piños Altos

The original seat of Grant County, Piños Altos (Tall Pines), seven miles north of Silver City, was founded in 1859 by miners returning from the California goldfields, who found color in nearby Bear Creek. Life was tough in the early days, though, with Apaches besieging early Piños Altians; in 1861, Cochise and Mangas Coloradas ran the first settlers out, and the miners didn't return until 1866, when operations resumed and Piños Altos was built into a good-sized community, with the requisite banks and saloons, and even an opera house.

Much of Piños Altos today has been restored, and like many of New Mexico's 19th-century settlements it is becoming a refuge for artists and artisans, who sell their work in studios and galleries in town. **Piños Altos Historical Museum** exhibits artifacts from the 19th-century heydays, and the opera house is open to visitors, with a display of historical photos from boomtown Piños Altos. For hours and information, contact the Silver City-Grant County Chamber of Commerce at 505/538-3785 or 800/548-9378.

On a hill on an unlikely backstreet in Piños Altos is **Hearst Church,** built in 1898 and financed by William Randolph Hearst (originally as a Methodist-Episcopal church). Today the adobe structure is home to the Grant County Art Guild, which displays local art and a small collection of mining equipment and other tools, wagons, and sleighs, including Pat Garrett's funeral hearse. Open summers only, with limited hours; phone the Silver City-Grant County Chamber of Commerce for information.

Just a couple of miles north of Piños Altos on Highway 15, you'll come to a parking lot, across the road from which is a short trail (150 feet) that leads to **Ben Lilly Monument.** According to *The Ben Lilly Legend,* by J. Frank Dobie, one of the Southwest's great novelists and scholars, Lilly was the last of the American mountain men, "the last of his tribe." Born on New Year's Eve, 1856, in Wilcox County, Alabama, Lilly was, by most accounts, the greatest mountain-lion hunter this country ever saw and, along with Davy Crockett, one of the two greatest bear hunters.

As with any figure of Lilly's proportions, it's dif-

© STEPHEN METZGER

Hearst Church, Piños Altos

ficult to separate the man from the myth. Stories abound about him, some believable, some not. For example, Lilly is said to have once leapt from his horse and wrestled to the ground a wandering steer, punched holes in its eyelids, and laced them shut with his shoestrings, claiming a blinded animal would not likely try to break from the herd. But Lilly was also in fact "chief huntsman" for Theodore Roosevelt's famous bear hunt to Texas in October 1907, and it was upon Roosevelt's return from this trip that "Teddy" bears became a national rage.

Lilly was also an early devotee of "natural" healing methods—such as kneeling over flaming horse manure and inhaling the smoke in order to cure his lungs, and he believed in what Dobie calls the "transference of characteristics": he preferred to eat mountain lion meat, which he felt would make him swift and graceful, instead of beef, which made him sluggish. Lilly spent his last years in New Mexico and Arizona, hiring out to local ranchers to kill the cats that were feeding on their stock. He died on December 17, 1936. The memorial looks out over the land that Lilly loved—rugged, wild, and uninhabited.

If you're in Piños Altos around dinnertime, stop in at the **Buckhorn Saloon,** 32 Main St., 505/538-9911. All its name implies, this Old-West bar and steakhouse serves huge meals in a virtual museum of a dining room (with an attached opera house). Entrées (burgers, seafood, beef) run $7–18. Open Tuesday–Sunday for dinner.

Gila Hot Springs

Thirty-eight miles out of Silver City, you'll come to Gila Hot Springs, where a small mom-and-pop gas station-grocery store sells camping and fishing gear, junk jewelry, and burgers. On the store's second story is a doll museum, called "Faerieland." Admission is $1. RV camping is also available, with sites with full hookups running about $18. Phone 505/536-9551 for more information.

Gila Cliff Dwellings National Monument

Although the pueblo cliff dwellings are probably the most impressive part of this national monument, several other types of homes—some occupied long before the cliff homes,

COUURESY OF NEW MEXICO DEPARTMENT OF TOURISM

ruins at Gila Cliff Dwellings National Monument

some occupied concurrently—are scattered about the land. The oldest is a pit house, most likely built between A.D. 100 and 400 by Mogollon people, the earliest inhabitants of the Gila River area and ancestors of modern-day Pueblo Indians. The ruins of a number of later, pre-pueblo houses have also been found near the cliff dwellings. Probably built around A.D. 1000, these homes were rectangular—unlike the pit houses, which were round—and were built completely above ground. The pueblos and cliff dwellings were built sometime after 1000 but had been abandoned by the early 1300s—archaeologists are still unsure exactly why.

The inhabitants of the cliff dwellings were primarily farmers, raising squash, corn, and beans. They supplemented their diets by gathering berries that grew nearby and occasionally killing a rabbit or deer. They were excellent potters, used cotton to make small blankets, and wove baskets, sandals, and clothing out of yucca and other native plants.

Visitors today can drive to the trailhead, where a one-mile round-trip hike (allow about one hour) leads to the cliff dwellings, 180 feet above the canyon floor. (Note: Highway 15 between Silver City and the cliff dwellings is not recommended for trailers more than 20 feet long.) Be sure to stop first at the visitors center for detailed pamphlets on the construction of the homes and the Indians who made them. You'll also find a small museum with a collection of pottery, baskets, and tools discovered in the area, as well as charts and diagrams explaining life on the cliffside in the 13th century.

Memorial Day–Labor Day, the cliff dwellings trail and visitors center are open 8 A.M.–6 P.M. The rest of the year, the trail is open 9 A.M.–4 P.M., and the visitors center is open until 4:30 P.M.. Boarding kennels are provided for pets, which are not allowed on the trail to the ruins.

Four Park Service campground are near the monument, and camping is free. For more information, call 505/536-9461.

To get to Gila Cliff Dwellings National Monument, take Highway 15 north from Silver City. Allow 90 minutes to two hours to get there, as the road is narrow and winding, snaking through canyons and along mountainsides, and wandering into dense forests of tall pine and fir. You can also get there via the Mimbres River Valley and Highway 35, the better route for those with bigger rigs and one that passes Lake Roberts and several improved Forest Service campgrounds. Admission is $3 for adults ($10 for family of four or more), and kids eight and under are admitted free.

Note: Though the trip from Silver City to the cliff dwellings might appear short on the map, this is no small commitment. By the time you add together an hour and a half to two (each way) to drive, an hour or so in the visitors center, and the half hour–plus (each way) hike from the visitors center to the dwellings, you're talking a good five or six hours.

Gila Country

Highway 180 rolls west out of Silver City, then curves slowly north, where it wanders into the Gila National Forest between the San Francisco and Mogollon mountain ranges. From there, it veers west again, crosses over into Arizona, and crawls northwest up toward Holbrook. Some 100 miles north of Silver City, Highway 12 tees into Highway 180 about 10 miles east of the Arizona border after having wound down from Datil, due west of Socorro on Highway 60. This drive, from Silver City up through the Gila National Forest to Socorro, offers the New Mexico traveler a wide array of scenery—from steep rock canyons and forested mountains to grasslands and high plateaus—and a number of the state's eclectic and off-the-beaten-track attractions—from the ghost town of Mogollon to the high-tech and visually arresting Very Large Array (VLA) outside Socorro. Along the way, you pass through some of New Mexico's most archaeologically rich country (the Gila National Forest is rife with Mogollon sites), as well as several classic one-horse towns—Cliff, Buckhorn, Pleasanton, Glenwood, Alma, Reserve. Each has little more than a gas station and small café, although in a couple—Glenwood, for example—you'll find small grocery stores, motels, and campgrounds or RV parks. Best to stock up, though—fill that ice chest with snacks, sandwiches, and plenty of beverages. These tiny towns are few and far between and the road long and lonesome.

© STEPHEN METZGER

the Catwalk at Whitewater Canyon

Between Silver City and Buckhorn (about 40 miles north), Highway 180 planes across grasslands and rolling hills dotted with tall yucca, the forested Mogollon and Piños Altos Mountains always in sight to the east. About 15 miles north of Buckhorn, the scenery improves dramatically as you enter Gila National Forest and begin to snake alongside the San Francisco River.

Shortly before Pleasanton (just inside the national forest) is **San Francisco Hot Springs,** where hot water gurgles out of the earth's depths and into the river. Crude dams and small rock walls have been built to isolate the hot water, and the result is a series of small pools perfect for relaxing and regenerating baths.

You'll find good camping here (no facilities), and the area, set off the highway at the bottom of a small canyon, is nicely isolated, given its location in one of the less populous parts of the state.

The hot springs make an ideal place to relax and rejuvenate, except when the ATV crowd shows up (mostly weekends) and turns a nice isolated spot into a noisy nightmare.

The turnoff to San Francisco Hot Springs, about one mile south of Pleasanton on Highway 180, is well marked; the one-mile dirt road is fine for all vehicles except oversized motorhomes and trailers.

GLENWOOD

Glenwood is a tiny resort town in the heart of the Gila National Forest about 60 miles north of Silver City. Once the site of a mine and mill, Glenwood today is known more as a base camp for hikers, hunters, anglers, and horsepackers heading into the Gila Wilderness—as well as for its proximity to Catwalk National Recreation Trail.

The Glenwood Trading Post, at the Chevron station in town, is open daily 7:30 A.M.–9 P.M. and sells basic groceries and camping supplies.

The Catwalk and Whitewater Canyon

If you can plan your visit to the Glenwood area so you're passing through around lunchtime, stop here at one of the nicest and most unusual picnic areas in the state. Whitewater Canyon is a steep and narrow box canyon just east of Highway 180 at Glenwood. At one time a hideout of Apache chief Geronimo, the canyon was later the site of substantial mining activity. But the canyon often dried up, and a four-inch pipe had to be run from up inside it down to its mouth where the processing mill was. Over the years, of course, the pipe needed repair, and the only access to its leaks was along the pipe itself—miners had to creep along the canyon wall balancing on the small pipe, which they nicknamed "The Catwalk." As more and more water was needed for the mill, the pipe was enlarged until it was 18 inches in diameter (and not as difficult to walk on). Then in 1913 the mill closed, and activity in Whitewater Canyon subsided. In 1961, the Forest Service built a steel catwalk up into the canyon, which today is part of the **Catwalk National Recreation Trail,** a short (30 minutes round-trip) hike up into the gorgeous canyon.

Take Catwalk Road out of Glenwood (north end of town) and follow the signs to the dirt parking lot. Several picnic tables are set in the shade of the sycamores and oaks beside the clear stream. The walk itself, though short, is rugged and steep in places (no wheelchair access here!), and you should wear hardy and comfy shoes or boots.

Accommodations

Los Olmos (The Elms) Guest Ranch, 505/539-2311, is a bed-and-breakfast sitting on eight acres of lawns and spreading elms and sycamores, its 14 small stone cabins (some sleeping up to six) isolated and individualized. Rates here are hard to beat: cabins run $60–150, including breakfast and dinner in the main lodge's "Chuck Wagon" dining room. Among the buildings on the grounds are the Antrim cabin, which Billy the Kid's stepfather owned and lived in while working nearby mines, and the original Catron County jail. For more information, write Los Olmos Guest Ranch, P.O. Box 127, Glenwood, NM 88039.

The **Crab Apple Cabins** are remodeled 1930s-era kitchenette cabins that sprawl across a large grassy meadow. All eight cabins—some sleeping up to six—are smoke-free. For a brochure, write P.O. Box 86, Glenwood, NM 88039, or phone 505/539-2400.

Information and Services

For more information on Glenwood and the surrounding area, write **Village of Glenwood,** NM 88039. For information on the Gila National Forest or Wilderness Area, call 505/388-8201 or 505/536-9461 (Gila Hot Springs).

The nearest hospital to Glenwood is Gila Regional Medical Center in Silver City, about 60 miles south on Highway 180, 505/388-1591. The state police office is also in Silver City, 505/388-1542.

MOGOLLON

Highway 159 barrels out of the Mogollon Mountains to meet Highway 180 about six miles north of Glenwood. Not recommended for night travel or for trailers more than 17 feet long, this is one steep road, winding sharply from the valley floor

© STEPHEN METZGER

"downtown" Mogollon

up into the densely forested mountains, along a narrow ridgetop, and down into the ghost of once-booming Mogollon, which lies quietly on the valley floor, the surrounding mountains dotted with both active and abandoned mines. (Although it's only 10 miles from Highway 180 to Mogollon, allow a good half hour, as most of the drive is switchbacks and steep grades.)

Mogollon is named for Don Juan Ignacio Flores Mogollon, governor of the New World's Spanish territory in the early 1700s. In 1870, Sergeant James Cooney, on a scouting expedition from nearby Fort Bayard, discovered silver in the area. Cooney kept his find under wraps, though, until his discharge a few years later, when he returned to stake his claim. Soon others followed, and the area became known as the Cooney Mining District, producing large amounts of silver and gold. Meanwhile, local Apaches, not taking kindly to the influx of miners, continually raided the mining settlements and in 1880 killed Cooney himself.

The Mogollon-area hills and creeks continued to account for much of New Mexico's gold and silver well into the 20th century, and at its peak (1912–15) it was providing more than $1 million a year in ore. By the end of World War II, however, activity had fallen off sharply, and Mogollon was abandoned, the few mines left in operation mostly worked by men staying in other nearby towns, such as Glenwood.

Mogollon today is a delightful portrait of the state's past, testimony to its architectural and geological diversity, and a prime example of New Mexico's several Lazaruslike ghost towns—in recent years, the little settlement has returned from the dead, resurrected by ambitious and enterprising artists, merchants, and carpenters.

Lodging in Mogollon is available at the **Silver Creek Inn,** HC 61, Box 306, Mogollon, NM 88039, 866/276-4882, website: www.silvercreekinn.com; it's in a historic building from the town's raucous past. Rates ($100–150) include full breakfast and dinner served to order.

Camping

The paved stretch of Highway 159 ends at Mogollon, but the road continues as dirt up into the mountains and deeper into the Gila National Forest. Three campgrounds at the **Willow Creek Recreation Area,** about 20 miles past Mogollon, offer private and quiet camping in the tall firs and pines alongside Willow Creek.

Information

For more information about Mogollon and the Gila National Forest and Wilderness area, write to the **Silver City-Grant County Chamber of Commerce,** 201 N. Hudson, Silver City, NM 88061, or call 505/538-3785 or 800/548-9378. You can also phone the Gila National Forest ranger station on North Silver Street in Silver City at 505/388-8201.

RESERVE

About 25 miles north of Mogollon, Highway 180 wanders west into Arizona, and the New Mexico traveler turns northeast onto Highway 12. From there, the road reaches northeast toward Albuquerque, passing through the tiny town of Reserve, the seat of Catron County, before dropping out of the Gila National Forest and onto the gently rolling Plains of San Agustín.

Founded in the 1860s by Mormon ranchers, Reserve (pop. 450) today is a classic blink-and-you'll-miss-it little town at the foot of the Tularosa Mountains. Originally three separate towns (Upper, Middle, and Lower San Francisco Plaza), Reserve has been famous since 1884, when it was the site of one of New Mexico's more well-known gunfights. Elfego Baca, a notoriously tough deputy sheriff from Socorro, was in town to keep rowdy cowboys in line. Eventually, Baca arrested a particularly belligerent cowboy from Texas. A Reserve lawman released the Texan, who, with several friends, decided to get revenge on Baca. After a 33-hour siege, during which Baca holed up in a small shack and killed three of the avengers, he was arrested for murder. Acquitted in Socorro of charges against him, Baca remained prominent in New Mexico law and politics (he was sheriff of Socorro, county clerk, and district attorney) until his death at the age of 80 in Albuquerque. (*The Nine Lives of Elfego Baca* is a movie filmed in Cerrillos, New Mexico, that tells the famous lawman's story through the eyes of the film's producer, Walt Disney.)

DATIL

From the late 1880s until shortly after World War I, this was prime cattle and sheep country, the now-quiet little towns bustling with cowboys and ranchers and the excitement of huge stock drives between Magdalena and Springerville, Arizona. This route is commemorated at Datil, near the junction of Highway 12 and Highway 60, by the **Hoof Highway Campground,** one of the spots at which wells were dug for watering cattle along this dry and desolate route. Camping is free here, and the sites, nestled among the fragrant piñon and juniper, offer expansive views across the broad Plains of San Agustín. The campground's pit toilets and well water—not to mention its out-in-the-boonies locale—guarantee at least some degree of the solitude that has drawn travelers to this high desert for centuries. Signs to the campground make it easy to find.

Highway 60 links Datil and Socorro, from the broad Plains of San Agustín down to the lush Rio Grande Valley due east. Along the way, you'll pass between the Datil and Gallinas mountains to the north and the Magdalenas to the south. Save for the typically majestic New Mexico landscapes and magic skies, which out in this desolate country seem even closer to the soul than usual, there are only a couple of points of interest out here: the **Very Large Array** (see Socorro, above) and the town of Magdalena.

MAGDALENA

There's a certain irony in this small town's appellation. Known in the late 19th century as one of the rowdiest frontier towns in the area, Magdalena (pop. 1,000) actually took its name from Mary Magdalene (whom Jesus supposedly cured of evil spirits), whose likeness was said to have been seen in a rock formation on a nearby hillside.

Like many of New Mexico's outpost towns, Magdalena saw a sudden rise in population and activity after the railroad came in 1884. For many years, in fact, Magdalena was the "end of the line," and cattle were unloaded here and driven west across the Plains of San Agustín and into Arizona. The old railroad depot today houses the city hall and library.

Be sure to stop in at **Evett's** on the north side of the main drag through Magdalena, 505/854-2449. This little soda fountain/restaurant/local hangout seems to be the social aorta of town. We stopped in on a Sunday afternoon, and the place was abuzz with leather-skinned ranchers sipping coffee from plain ceramic mugs and hormoney teenagers downing sodas and shakes and flirting with each other with reckless small-town abandon. There was even a group of bicyclists on a cross-country tour—their bikes parked outside—carbing up on monstrous piles of french fries. Evett's also serves burritos, chili, sandwiches, nachos, and a variety of salads.

The **Western Motel Bed and Breakfast and RV Park,** 505/854-2417, in a converted 1920 maternity hospital, offers a full range of accommodations options. Bed-and-breakfast rates run $50–100, depending on options (continental or full breakfast, spa use, etc.).

Magdalena to Carrizozo

The 30-mile stretch of Highway 60 between Magdalena and Socorro drops out of the mountains and into the Rio Grande Valley. From there, you can turn north toward Albuquerque or Salinas National Monument, or you can head south toward San Antonio and then east across the sprawling Chupadera Mesa to Carrizozo. From Socorro to Carrizozo is about 70 miles.

South-Central New Mexico

Introduction

Comprising just two counties, Otero and Lincoln, south-central New Mexico encompasses all the extremes found in the state—and nearly all the extremes found in North America. From the flat and barren Tularosa Basin and the spectacularly eerie White Sands desert to the lush and snowy forests of 12,003-foot Sierra Blanca, south-central New Mexico is a constant study in contrasts, not only geographical, but historical and cultural as well.

Beginning at a 100-mile east-west strip of Texas border and corridoring north another 300 or so miles, south-central New Mexico is largely desert, with a gorgeous series of mountain ranges—the Sacramentos, Whites, Capitans, and Jicarillas—rising like volcanic islands above a placid sea. (Indeed, on the west side of Lincoln County, a lava flow, El Malpais, cuts a dark and pitted path 40 miles long and five miles wide across the desert floor.) Between the Tularosa Basin and the area's high peaks, five of the world's seven biological life zones occur: Lower and Upper Sonoran, Transition, Canadian, and Hudsonian.

As early as 10,000 years ago, primitive people were living in, or least passing through, this part of New Mexico. Folsom Man, the first evidence of whom was actually discovered near the Colorado border, most likely hunted the plains of the Tularosa Basin and the lowlands east of the Sacramento Mountains. Geologists estimate that during Folsom Man's time, the snow and tree lines were about 1,000 feet lower than they are now. Also, what are now dry basins (or *bolsones,* Spanish for "purses") were once fertile valleys, with lakes and

©STEPHEN METZGER

Stop in for lunch at The Lodge in Cloudcroft—you might even see Rebecca, the resident ghost.

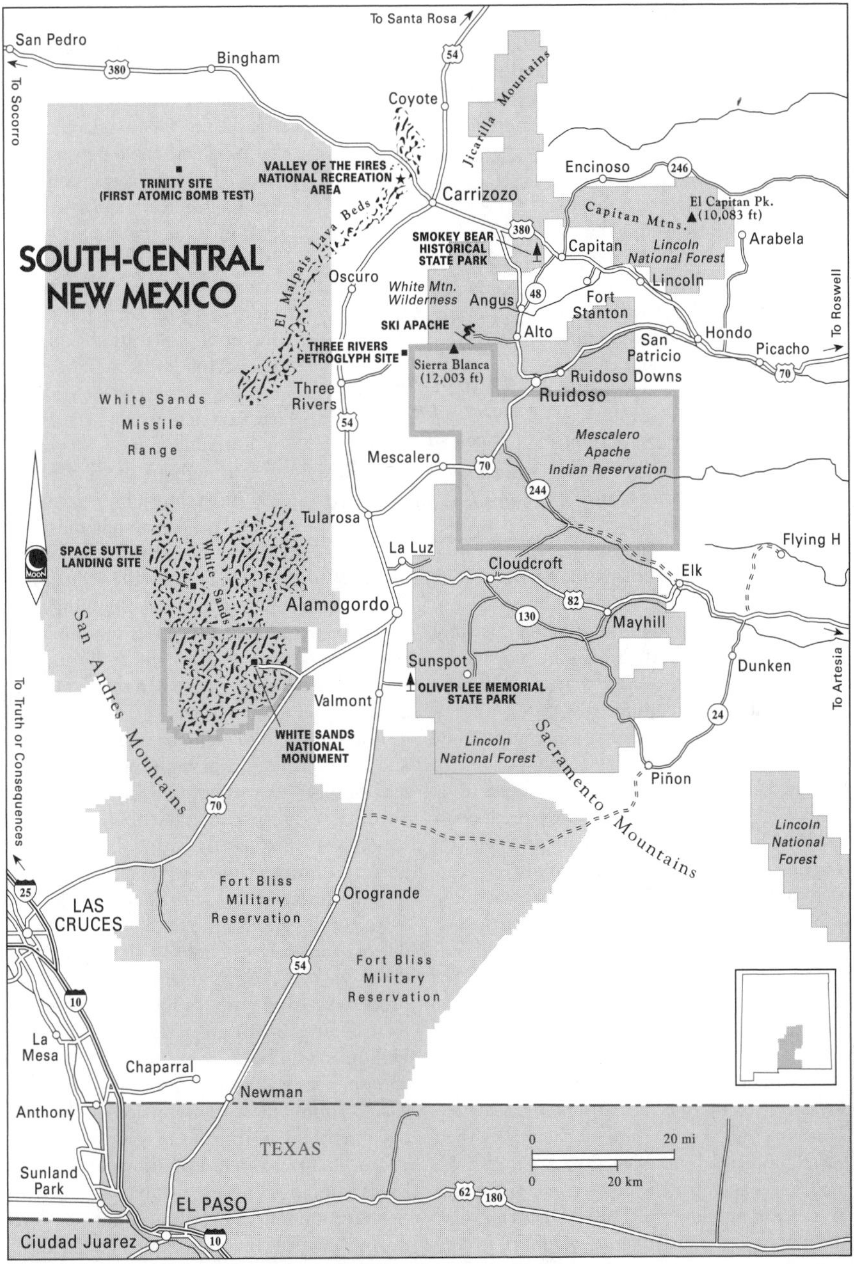
SOUTH-CENTRAL NEW MEXICO
To Santa Rosa
San Pedro
To Socorro
Bingham
380
54
Coyote
Jicarilla Mountains
VALLEY OF THE FIRES NATIONAL RECREATION AREA
TRINITY SITE (FIRST ATOMIC BOMB TEST)
Carrizozo
El Malpais Lava Beds
Encinoso
246
El Capitan Pk. (10,083 ft)
Capitan Mtns.
SMOKEY BEAR HISTORICAL STATE PARK
Capitan
Lincoln National Forest
Arabela
Oscuro
White Mtn. Wilderness
Angus
48
Fort Stanton
Lincoln
To Roswell
SKI APACHE
Alto
San Patricio
Hondo
Picacho
THREE RIVERS PETROGLYPH SITE
Sierra Blanca (12,003 ft)
Ruidoso Downs
70
Three Rivers
Ruidoso
White Sands Missile Range
Mescalero Apache Indian Reservation
Mescalero
244
Tularosa
SPACE SUTTLE LANDING SITE
White Sands
La Luz
Cloudcroft
Flying H
Elk
Alamogordo
82
130
Mayhill
San Andres Mountains
To Artesia
Sunspot
Dunken
OLIVER LEE MEMORIAL STATE PARK
Valmont
24
WHITE SANDS NATIONAL MONUMENT
Lincoln National Forest
Sacramento Mountains
Piñon
To Truth or Consequences
Lincoln National Forest
25
LAS CRUCES
Fort Bliss Military Reservation
Orogrande
Fort Bliss Military Reservation
10
La Mesa
Chaparral
Newman
Anthony
TEXAS
0
20 mi
0
20 km
Sunland Park
62
180
EL PASO
Ciudad Juarez

lush vegetation supporting the hunters' prey: mammoths, mastodons, four-toed horses, and wide-horned bison, as well as deer and antelope.

South-central New Mexico also served as a refuge for people abandoning the more fertile and highly civilized Rio Grande Valley to the west. As that area became more and more populated, perhaps to the point that it couldn't support all the people living there, small groups began to migrate out of the valley. "Fresnal Shelter," a cave in the foothills between Alamogordo and Cloudcroft, provided safeguard for Indian families as early as 1500 B.C. Later, between 1,500 and 1,000 years ago, ancestors of the Pueblo Indians built pit houses in the flatlands near present-day Three Rivers. Evidence of Indians in that area can be seen at the Forest Service's Three Rivers Petroglyph Site about midway between Carrizozo and Alamogordo. Alamogordo, too, is the site of prehistoric Indian settlements; archaeologists have discovered a handful of early-style pueblos in and around town.

On July 16, 1945, 60 miles northwest of Alamogordo, the world's first atomic bomb was detonated. The sky lit up, and the great mushroom cloud—the demonic icon of modern society—cast its first shadow on the land.

More recent history of south-central New Mexico is fraught with violence and storm. In the late 1800s, when the area was dominated by huge cattle spreads and range lords, battles over land and herds were fairly common. In July 1878, warring factions of merchants and cowboys battled for five days in what became known as the Lincoln County War. Among the participants: one Billy the Kid. And though the war itself was short-lived, the United States Cavalry, based at Fort Stanton, was called in afterward to patrol the town and nearby hills to keep violence from breaking out again.

The latter part of the 19th century also saw increased raids by Apache warriors. Resisting encroachment by farmers and ranchers upon their sacred homeland, the Mescalero Apache terrorized Anglo and Spanish settlers throughout these mountains and lowlands. In 1872, after a failed attempt by the United States government to concentrate a large number of the tribe near Fort Sumner (along with 8,000 Navajos), more than 400,000 acres of the White Mountains were set aside for them.

The railroad brought more settlers to the Southwest, and for the first time, work other than farming and ranching was available. The El Paso and Southwestern Railroad Company ran a spur line into the mountains east of Alamogordo so timbers could be transported to the valley floor for railroad ties. In 1899, the company built a vacation lodge in Cloudcroft for its employees, and tourism—which by the middle of the next century would be a major industry in the area—was born.

Throughout the first part of the 20th century, horse racing was a local passion among those who had settled in the rolling foothills of the White Mountains. By the 1930s, Ruidoso's summer race season was beginning to get national attention, and the races continue to attract pony fans from throughout the country; on weekends during race season there's rarely an empty motel room in town.

It was in 1945, though, that the most startling and unsettling chapter of south-central New Mexico's history was written. On July 16, 60 miles northwest of Alamogordo, the world's first atomic bomb was detonated. The sky lit up, and the great mushroom cloud—the demonic icon of modern society—cast its first shadow on the land.

Today, this area is still a focal point of modern defense and space technology. The White Sands desert west of the Sacramento Mountains is a proposed testing grounds for former president Ronald Reagan's Strategic Defense Initiative; Holloman Air Force Base, just outside Alamogordo, tests fighter jets and trains pilots; and Alamogordo's International Space Hall of Fame documents the history of the world's space programs, including demonstrations of the latest laser technology.

It's the mountains of south-central New Mexico, though, that attract the traveler. Rising sharply on the west and falling off more slowly to the

HIGHLIGHTS

Alamogordo Space Center: NASA museum, tours, and exhibits

Cloudcroft: camping, hiking, sight-seeing, outdoor sports

Lincoln: historical museums and tours

Mescalero Apache Reservation: hunting, fishing, golf, lodging facilities

Ruidoso: camping, hiking, outdoor sports, shopping, horse racing

Sierra Blanca Mountain: hiking, sight-seeing, snow skiing

Smokey Bear State Park: sight-seeing, museums, souvenirs (great for kids)

Three River Petroglyph Site: sight-seeing, camping

White Sands National Monument: sight-seeing, hiking, camping, tours

east, the Whites and Sacramentos are truly year-round playgrounds, enticing outdoor lovers from throughout the Southwest. Texans, particularly, have staked out these mountains, and many is the Ruidoso-area vacation home that has served as welcome refuge to generations of families fleeing the narcotic flatlands of West Texas.

When the weather's warm and the ground isn't covered with snow, anglers wade the tumbling streams and cast into alpine lakes for native and planted trout, day-hikers and backpackers wander the tall pines and firs of Lincoln National Forest and White Mountain Wilderness, golfers test their mettle against the mountains' thin air, and cyclists—both tourers and mountain bikers—work out with gorgeous forests and towering peaks as their backdrop.

Winter brings the snow to these mountains and with it the skiers, sledders, snowshoers, and tobogganers, as well as those who simply delight in a wintry landscape—pine boughs laden with puffs of soft snow and mountain meadows softened by December's gentle blanket. Ski Apache, the Mescalero-owned-and-operated ski resort high on the flanks of 12,003-foot Sierra Blanca just outside Ruidoso, and Ski Cloudcroft, a small, family-oriented area less than an hour from Alamogordo, offer excellent Alpine skiing, while the woods of Lincoln National Forest lure the cross-country crowd, those more interested in blazing their own trails through the pines than in riding chairlifts and following the crowds down the mountain. Winter evenings in Ruidoso, Cloudcroft, and the surrounding smaller mountain communities find fireplaces roaring and skiers warming their toes and sipping hot brandy after an exhilarating day on the slopes.

Because this part of the state offers such a wide array of climates—from the blistering valley heat of the White Sands desert to the cool breezes blowing through alpine valleys—travelers are advised to dress, or at least pack, accordingly. Even in the summer, when you're exploring the White Sands in shorts, and a sweater's the last thing on your mind, the White Mountains—just an hour away—could very likely be locked into a cold storm, with icy winds and incessant rains, or just the warm afternoon thundershowers that turn streets to creeks and roads to rivers. So go ahead and wear your shorts, but make sure you have a good water-resistant parka at hand. And carry lots of liquids to quench your thirst and ward off that desert heat. But remember, if you find yourself in the mountains, especially as the sun descends, a cup of hot soup or a steaming bowl of chili might be your best ally against the cool night air.

Carrizozo and Vicinity

Carrizozo, the sleepy seat of Lincoln County, has the feel about it of a town that time has passed by. In fact, given its size (pop. 1,200) and its junction location, rare is the traveler who does much more than that herself.

The town lies in a broad basin between the Sierra Oscuro and the Jicarilla Mountains, at the edge of El Malpais (The Badlands), a relatively recent and stunningly vivid lava flow. If you're traveling east-west, between Roswell and San Antonio, you drop onto the sweeping brown Carrizozo plain after winding through gorgeous green mountains and sensuous foothills. You're probably not going to be particularly taken with the town. If you're traveling north-south, between Albuquerque and Alamogordo, Carrizozo is little more than a place to release your cruise control for a few minutes before resuming your cross-country stride.

History

Carrizozo's past, like that of much of small-town New Mexico, is tied to the railroad: it was once the site of a roundhouse and repair shop. Carrizozo's heyday was 1910–20, when the town supported about 2,000 people. Unfortunately, a railroad strike in 1923 and, in following years, improvements in equipment—which meant less maintenance—led to a parting of ways for Carrizozo and prosperity.

Valley of Fires State Park

The Carrizozo Lava Flow, probably about 1,000 years old, is one of the youngest in the United States. Indian legend has it that the flow, called El Malpais by the Spanish, was once a valley of fire (actually, of course, that's fairly accurate).

Running north to south about five miles west of Carrizozo, the flow is 44 miles long, five miles wide, and up to 70 feet deep. Both the Indians and the Spanish steered clear of the harsh and rocky land, and Anglo ranchers had little luck grazing livestock in the sparse vegetation. Recently, biologists studying the flow have found that it supports a wide variety of wildlife, including deer, badgers, skunks, coyotes, ring-tailed cats, and rattlesnakes.

The state park at Malpais includes campsites (no natural shade), a self-guided nature hike, and a playground. Entrance fee is $4; overnight camping is $8 ($12 with hookups). Go five miles west of Carrizozo on Highway 380 and watch for the signs on your left.

PRACTICALITIES

Accommodations

Four Winds Motel, at the junction of Highways 380 and 54, 505/648-2356, has doubles in the $50 range. The **Sands Motel and RV Park** just south of town on Highway 54, 505/648-2989, has doubles for under $50, and you can park your RV for about $20, which includes hookups and cable TV.

Food

Four Winds Restaurant and Lounge at the junction of Highways 380 and 54, 505/648-2964, is open daily (hours are irregular) and serves breakfasts for $4–8, specializing in pancakes. Sandwiches, burgers, and roast beef at lunch range $5–8; Mexican dinners range $5–10 and steaks $10–15.

Recreation

The **Carrizozo Golf Course,** 505/648-2451, is a nine-hole course with a small pro shop. At the western border of Lincoln National Forest, the Carrizozo area offers abundant opportunities for hiking, backpacking, and camping. And if winter finds you in Carrizozo, you're within an hour's drive of the slopes of **Ski Apache,** just outside Ruidoso. Another ski area, **Ski Cloudcroft,** is less than two hours away. (For more recreation information, see Cloudcroft and Ruidoso and Vicinity, following.)

Information and Services

For more information about Carrizozo, write the **chamber of commerce** at P.O. Box 567, Carrizozo, NM 88301, or call 505/648-2732.

The closest hospitals are Gerald Champion Memorial Hospital in Alamogordo at 1209 9th St., 505/439-2100, and Lincoln County Medical Center in Ruidoso at 211 Sudderth Dr., 505/257-7381. Carrizozo Health Center, 710 E St., is open Monday–Friday 8 A.M.–5 P.M. Call 505/648-2317 or, after office hours, 505/648-2342. The nonemergency number for the police department is 505/648-2341. In emergencies, dial 911.

TO ALAMOGORDO

Highway 54 barrels south from Carrizozo and enters the Tularosa Basin, where the yucca-studded plain is flanked by the White and Sacramento Mountains towering just to the east and the San Andres Mountains standing stark and imposing to the west. Most of the San Andres range, as well as the western Tularosa Basin, is property of the U.S. government, which uses the land for missile and other sundry defense testing, and is strictly off-limits to unauthorized people.

Three Rivers Petroglyph Site and Picnic Area

About 36 miles north of Alamogordo off Highway 54, Three Rivers exhibits one of the largest collections of petroglyphs in the Southwest, as well as pit-house and pueblo ruins dating to A.D. 900. A 1,400-yard trail takes you from the picnic area up a rocky ridge, where you wind among the rocks and scramble over boulders, finding a seemingly endless number of petroglyphs (more than 5,000 have been counted). Some represent animals of the area (lizards, birds, and deer), some are of humans in ceremonial costume, and some appear to have connections to the heavens—perhaps they marked significant annual events. The site is unsupervised, and unfortunately, some of the petroglyphs have been vandalized: six- to 18-inch pieces are just plain missing from prominent drawings, while some have been "edited" (I doubt it was a 12th-century indigenous Mogollon artist who spelled out "George B., Houston" on that rock). The BLM's toll-free number to report vandalism is 800/NEIGHBOR (800/634-4426).

© STEPHEN METZGER

a few of the more than 5,000 petroglyphs at Three Rivers

Another trail leads to the partially excavated and reconstructed village. Here, you can view a pit house, an adobe house, and a multiroom adobe structure, which show the local tribe's progression in home construction.

Water and tables are available for campers and picnickers. Admission to the park is free. Watch for the sign at Three Rivers, and follow the paved road five miles east.

La Luz

This small town three miles north of Alamogordo is the oldest still-occupied settlement in the Tularosa Basin, having been founded in 1719 with the building of a Franciscan chapel. Today, the town is a quiet oasis of tree-lined backstreets and small galleries. **El Presidio Parque** is surrounded by the adobe walls of the old town and provides picnic tables in some of the basin's rare natural shade.

Alamogordo

Alamogordo (pop. 29,000; elev. 4,350 feet) is a bustling desert town nestled against the west slope of the towering Sacramento Mountains. Known for nearby White Sands National Monument and Alamogordo's own International Space Hall of Fame, Alamogordo (which means Fat Cottonwood) is the seat of Otero County and the largest town in the Tularosa Basin. It's also a large ranching and farming center—its irrigated fields sprawling north, south, and west—as well as home to Holloman Air Force Base, which tests guided missiles and pilotless aircraft.

In addition, Alamogordo is home to a branch of the Las Cruces–based New Mexico State University. The campus is attended by about 1,500 students, who can earn their first two years' credit there toward a four-year degree at the main campus.

As you visit or pass through Alamogordo, your attention will be quickly drawn to the town's di-

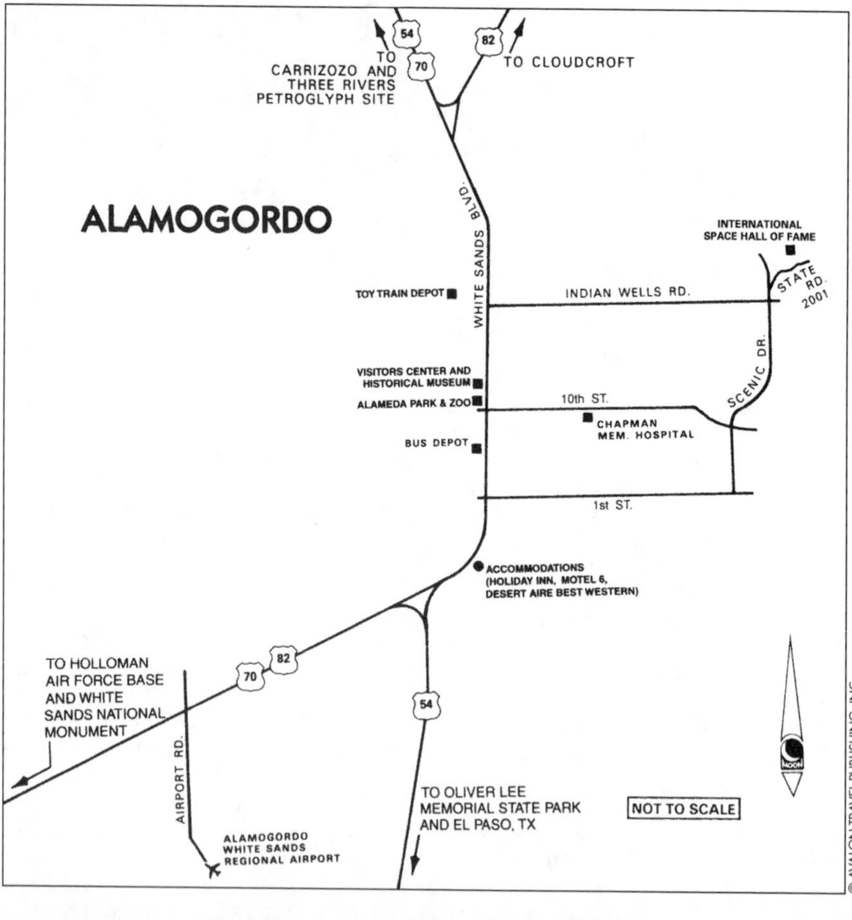

chotomous nature: clusters of garish fast-food franchises beside pretty public parks and lawns, and perhaps subtler but even more unsettling, the ever-present shadow of the space and nuclear age (the basin was chosen as a site for Reagan's "Star Wars" testing) contrasted with the area's fascination with its own simpler history.

History

The area around Alamogordo—both the desert sprawling westward and the mountains shadowing the town from the east—is rich in prehistoric sites, evidence that early humans once roamed these lands. Folsom Man is thought to have hunted in the area 10,000 years ago, and a cave between Alamogordo and Cloudcroft, known as the "Fresnal Shelter," housed Native American families 3,500 years ago. Sometime between 2000 and 1 B.C., early emigrants from the lush and highly populated Rio Grande Valley to the west were farming corn and squash and living in semipermanent dwellings in the area.

Between A.D. 600 and 1000, the inhabitants of the Tularosa Basin built pit houses near permanent water sources in the basin, and shortly after A.D. 1000 began constructing adobe pueblos, homes to increasingly complex societies. One such pueblo was actually within what are now Alamogordo's city limits, and two more were nearby. By 1350, all of these pueblos had been abandoned; some of the Indians may have moved just a little north, to the Las Humanas Pueblos, which were inhabited in the 16th century when the Spanish arrived.

About the time the pueblos of the Tularosa were being abandoned, the Apache arrived from the north (this is possibly more than coincidental, although no one is certain exactly why the Indians left the pueblos), and their various subgroups spread throughout southern New Mexico, Texas, and northern Mexico. The Mescalero (Eaters of Mescal) Apache settled in southeastern New Mexico, and for the next 600 years terrorized other Indian tribes, Spanish conquistadors and missionaries, and Anglo settlers and soldiers.

In the late 19th century, the Tularosa Basin consisted of huge cattle ranches; the Fall ranch alone covered 750,000 acres near Alamogordo. Many of the ranchers were at odds with each other, and several of their "disagreements" grew into outright hostilities. In some cases feuds and weeks-long sieges erupted, with gunfights and deaths from bullet wounds gaining national attention (see Lincoln, following).

Alamogordo, meanwhile, was the dream or "model city" of Charles Eddy, who bought the Alamo Ranch from Oliver M. Lee and subdivided 960 of its acres, attracting 4,000 new Alamogordians between 1898 and 1902. The El Paso and Northeastern Railroad, for which the newly founded Alamogordo was a division point, employed 300 people. Hundreds of others worked in the lumber industry, which, among other things, made the railroad ties that supplied the rest of the state.

In 1942, the U.S. Army began work on the Alamogordo Army Air Field, originally designed to train B-17 bomber crews. Three years later, on July 16, 1945, the face of Alamogordo, and the rest of the world, changed when a huge cloud mushroomed over Trinity Site in the Tularosa Basin northwest of Alamogordo. Humankind, in a perplexed mixture of consummate triumph and profound sorrow, gasped at the fiery spectacle—we had found the power to destroy ourselves.

SIGHTS

International Space Hall of Fame

Built on a hillside looking down on Alamogordo and across the Tularosa Basin to White Sands, the Space Hall of Fame is a four-story exhibit of the history of the world's (particularly the United States's and the Soviets') space programs. Visitors take the elevator to the top floor of "the Cube" (the 78-foot-high building that has won the New Mexico Arts Commission Award for new construction) and wind their way to ground level. Displays include models of the Apollo Command Module and NASA's planned space station, portable life-support systems, samples of "space food" (dehydrated corned beef, cheese spread, biscuits in cans, Graham Cracker cubes), photos of Earth taken from the moon, the history of satellites, and a look at early rocketry (much of which is from the early-20th-century Roswell, New Mexico lab). You can also sit down and play an interactive computer game, such as "Space-Tac-Toe," which allows you to mark your "X" only after you've answered correctly a space-trivia question. Hours are 9 A.M.–5 P.M.

Adjacent to the Space Hall of Fame is the **Clyde W. Tombaugh Dome Theater and Planetarium,** featuring IMAX films and laser-light shows as well as planetarium presentations. Phone 877/333-6589 for current films and presentations.

Admission to the Space Center ranges from $2.50 (Space Hall of Fame only) to $9 (Hall of Fame, theater, and planetarium). Senior citizen, military, and AAA discounts are offered. Wheelchairs and strollers are available. Take any of the major east-west streets east to Scenic Drive, and then go north to the Space Center (road signs make it easy to find). For more information, call 505/437-2840 or 800/545-4021.

White Sands National Monument

This is some of the strangest land you'll ever see: an ocean of rolling white sand dunes, in some places so pure you feel you're lost in a giant salt shaker. In others, stalks of lone yucca shoot up out of the wind-etched sand, like alien sentinels in a Frank Herbert novel.

The largest gypsum dunefield in the world, White Sands National Monument occupies 300 square miles of soft white sand, the dunes rising and changing with the prevailing winds—all surrounded by the desert of the Tularosa Basin and flanked by the Sacramento and San Andres mountain ranges.

The Tularosa Basin was formed with the uplifting of the Rocky Mountains (70 million years ago) and the subsequent settling of the Tularosa "crust" into a drainless basin. Over the eons, rainfall washed gypsum from the mountainsides, and the winds broke it up into grains of sand. This process is still occurring, and as a result, the dunes are still changing. The 16-mile loop through the park passes through the dunes in all their various stages—some are relatively flat, supporting significant plantlife; others are 60 feet high, with nothing growing in or on them. In some places, deep in the heart of the dunes, you can see nothing but the pure white of the driven sand. Hiking and playing in the sand is as much fun as playing in the snow, and you don't get cold or wet.

© STEPHEN METZGER

picnic shelters at White Sands National Monument

The visitors center, at the beginning of the loop, offers a fascinating introduction to the formation and history of the dunes, as well as to the plants and animals that live among them: spadefoot toads, hognose snakes, kangaroo rats, cactus wrens, ocotillo, cholla, and yucca.

Camping in the park is allowed only at the one primitive backcountry campsite, for which a permit and clearance from park headquarters are required. The visitors center has information about evening nature walks, as well as a gift shop with pottery, posters, jewelry, and souvenirs.

This is some of the strangest land you'll ever see: an ocean of rolling white sand dunes, in some places so pure you feel you're lost in a giant salt shaker.

Memorial Day through Labor Day, the visitors center is open 8 A.M.–7 P.M., and the dunes are open 7 A.M.–9 P.M. The rest of the year, the visitors center is open 8 A.M.–5 P.M. and the dunes 7 A.M.–sunset. Admission is $3. For recorded up-to-date information on White Sands, tune your AM radio dial to 1610 as you approach the park.

For more information, write White Sands National Monument, P.O. Box 1086, HAFB, NM 88330, or call 505/479-6124.

Oliver Lee Memorial State Park

Named for one of Alamogordo's prominent turn-of-the-20th-century cattle barons, this 180-acre park is at the mouth of Dog Canyon, 10 miles south of Alamogordo. Archaeological surveys of Dog Canyon, which slices dramatically up into the steep Sacramento Mountains, provide evidence that the area has been a campground for about 6,000 years: early humans took advantage of the year-round water in the canyon and also used the gap to travel from the desert floor up over the mountains. Mescalero Apaches also made good use of Dog Canyon's natural shelter and between 1849 and 1881 engaged in numerous skirmishes with the U.S. Cavalry.

In the early 1880s, Francois-Jean ("Frenchy") Rochas built a cabin at the mouth of the canyon, raising cattle and cultivating an orchard and vineyard in the valley below. Because Dog Canyon was the only year-round water supply in the area, Frenchy wasn't real popular with other local ranchers, and in 1894 he was found dead in his cabin with three bullets in his chest. (A coroner's jury hastily deemed Frenchy's death a suicide.) In 1905, Oliver Lee, who had worked with Frenchy to set up irrigation systems stemming from the canyon, took over the property and used it as a headquarters for his cattle holdings. At one time, Lee and his Circle Cross Cattle Company controlled a million acres of the surrounding valley. Lee served in the state legislature from 1918 to 1931 and died in 1941. Visitors can still see the remains of Frenchy's cabin from the park.

Oliver Lee Park features hiking up into Dog Canyon, as well as a campground with more than 40 sites and restrooms with showers and flush toilets. The visitors center displays Apache artifacts; many of Lee's and Frenchy's personal effects, including handguns and rifles; and U.S. Cavalry uniforms, weapons, and documents.

Entrance into the park is $3. Camping is $8, $12 with hookups. Take Highway 54 south from Alamogordo, and watch for the turnoff on your left.

Alameda Park and Zoo

Behind the Alamogordo Chamber of Commerce on White Sands Boulevard, this zoo exhibits more than 300 animals and birds from around the world, including eagles, llamas, and monkeys. Hours are daily 9 A.M.–5 P.M. except Christmas and New Year's Day. Admission is $2.20, with discounts offered to kids and seniors. For more information, write Alameda Park Zoo, 1321 White Sands Blvd., Alamogordo, NM 88310, or call 505/439-4290 or 800/826-0294; outside New Mexico, call 877/333-6589.

Tularosa Basin Historical Society Museum

This small history and pioneer museum is worth a visit, especially if you're planning to stop in at the Alamogordo Chamber of Commerce, which occupies the same building (at 1301 N. White Sands Blvd.). On display are Indian pottery and grinding implements, saddles and tack, 19th-century rifles and handguns, and a sampling of pioneer clothing. Also more recent stuff, such as early box cameras and a half dozen or so Edison home phonographs, complete with their huge bells. Hours are Monday–Friday 10 A.M.–4 P.M. and Saturday 10 A.M.–3 P.M. For more information, phone the chamber at 505/437-6120.

Toy Train Depot

Just north of the historical museum and visitors center, this will be of interest both to train buffs and to baby boomers remembering their days playing with the old Lionel and dropping smoke tabs into chimneys. The little museum, in an old depot right along the train tracks, displays scores of model trains and also offers real train rides through Alameda Park. The museum, at 1991 N. White Sands, is open Wednesday–Sunday noon–5 P.M., and train rides are offered 12:30–4:30 P.M. Admission price to each is $3. For more information, phone 505/437-2855.

Holloman Air Force Base

One of the duties of Holloman Air Force Base, about eight miles southwest of Alamogordo on Highway 70, is to provide contingency support for the space shuttle at White Sands Space Harbor. It's the home of the 49th Tactical Fighter Wing (F-15 fighters) and the 479th Tactical Training Wing. The base is completely self-contained, with shopping, a hospital, schools, a theater, and dental services for its 7,500 residents.

For information on Hollomon, phone 505/572-5406.

Trinity Site

Tours to the White Sands Missile Range Trinity Site, where the world's first atomic bomb was exploded, are offered by military police on the first Saturdays in April and October. The government claims that radiation levels at the site, though 10 times higher than at the "unbombed" surroundings, are safe for visitors. For more information contact the Alamogordo Chamber of Commerce. You can also get information on tour meeting times and places, well as on parking at the website: www.alamogordo.com/trinity.

PRACTICALITIES

Accommodations

Most of Alamogordo's motels are on the south end of town on White Sands Boulevard. Among them are a **Motel 6,** 251 Panorama Blvd., 505/434-5970, and the **All American Inn,** 508 S. White Sands, 505/437-1850 (both under $50). For $50–100, you can find clean and quiet rooms at **Holiday Inn Express,** 1401 White Sands, 505/437-7100, and the **Desert Aire Inn Best Western,** 1021 S. White Sands, 505/437-2110, where some of the suites have indoor spas ($50–100).

RVs can park at the **KOA Kampground** on the north end of town one block east of Highway 70 at 412 24th St., 505/437-3003. Rates are about $22 for two, including water and electricity. **Breezy Point RV Park,** two miles up Highway 82 toward Cloudcroft, has campsites and hot showers. Phone 505/434-0848.

Food

Like most American towns at major highway junctions, Alamogordo is rife with franchise fast-food restaurants: Wendy's, McDonald's, Pizza Hut, etc. If you're looking for something with a little more character, try **Maria's** at 604 E. 10th St., 505/434-4549—excellent authentic Mexican and New Mexican food for $5–8. A couple of other larger, higher-profile, and very popular Mexican restaurants include **Margo's,** 504 1st St., 505/434-0689, and **Ramona's,** 2913 N. White Sands, 505/437-7616. Both serve large quantities of excellent food with lots to choose from in the $6–12 range. For Italian food, try **Le Montichiari,** 2010 Pecan (corner of Indian Wells), 505/439-8071, where pastas, salads, and veal and chicken entrées run $8–13.

For something to stick to your ribs before you head out in the morning, try the **Waffle and Pancake Shoppe,** 950 S. White Sands, 505/437-0433, which serves, well, you know. . . . For an espresso dose, stop in at **Le Montichiari** (above), which opens at 9 A.M. daily, or at its sister restaurant, **Mastroddi's Espresso Cafe and Bagels,** 804 New York, 505/437-2323.

Recreation

Desert Lakes Golf Course is south of town off Highway 54, at 2351 Hamilton, 505/437-0290. The **Sacramento Mountains,** just east of Alamogordo, provide fishing and hunting, and you'll find some excellent snow skiing at **Ski Apache** (see the special topic in this chapter) and **Ski Cloudcroft,** both within 90 minutes of Alamogordo.

Annual Events

Every April and October, White Sands Missile Range conducts tours of Trinity Site (see above). In summer, White Sands National Monument is open till midnight during nights with full moons. The **Otero County Fair** is in August, and the **International Space Hall of Fame Induction** is the first Saturday in October. Holloman Air Force holds an open house in October. Call the chamber of commerce for exact dates.

Information and Services

The Alamogordo **Chamber of Commerce,** 1310 White Sands Blvd., has lots of information on visiting or relocating to the area. Contact the chamber at P.O. Box 518, Alamogordo, NM 88311-0518, 505/437-6120, or visit its website: www.alamogordo.com. The **public library** is at 10th and Oregon, 505/439-4140.

Gerald Champion Memorial Hospital is at 1209 9th St., 505/439-2100. The number for the city police is 505/439-4300; for state police, call 505/437-1313.

Transportation

Mesa Air, 800/MESA-AIR (800/637-2247), has passenger service from Albuquerque to Alamogordo White Sands Regional Airport. The **bus depot** is at 601 White Sands Blvd., 505/437-3050. The **Alamo/El Paso Shuttle,** 505/437-1472 or 800/872-2701, has regular service between Alamogordo and El Paso International Airport, including stops at Holloman Air Force Base. Call for schedules and rates. **Avis** is at 1401 White Sands Blvd., 505/437-3140.

Cloudcroft

The drive from Alamogordo up to Cloudcroft, which follows roughly the same route the old railroad line took, is one of the most spectacular in the southern part of the state. You climb rapidly and dramatically out of the hot and barren Tularosa Basin and find yourself quickly winding through forests and cool mountain air—from adobe and yucca to log cabins and pines in 20 minutes.

Cloudcroft is the kind of town proud New Mexicans point to when ignorant outsiders claim the state is all desert. In fact, if you were to open your eyes one fine summer morning and find yourself in Cloudcroft, you might swear you were in Alberta and that Lake Louise was just around the bend. Nestled at 8,640 feet among the pines and aspens of the Sacramento Mountains, Cloudcroft (pop. 750) is surrounded by the 215,000-acre Lincoln National Forest and lies just a few miles from the southern border of the 460,000-acre Mescalero Apache Reservation.

Cloudcroft's economy relies largely on tourism, with many eastern New Mexicans and West Texans heading for the area year-round. In the average winter, Cloudcroft gets around 75 inches of snow and is a popular ski town (Ski Cloudcroft, the southernmost ski resort in the state, is just outside of town), and in the summer the many camping, fishing, and hiking areas offer a welcome beat-the-heat getaway for lowlanders. Cloudcroft golfers tee off at the Lodge Golf Course, one of the highest golf courses in the United States (9,000 feet).

History

In the late 19th century, the El Paso and Southwestern Railroad ran a spur from Alamogordo up into the mountains so that lumber for railroad ties could be more easily transported down into the valley. At the end of this short line, which climbed 6,000 feet in just 27 miles, the railroad company in 1899 built a lodge as a getaway for railroad workers, their families, and El Pasoans. With a

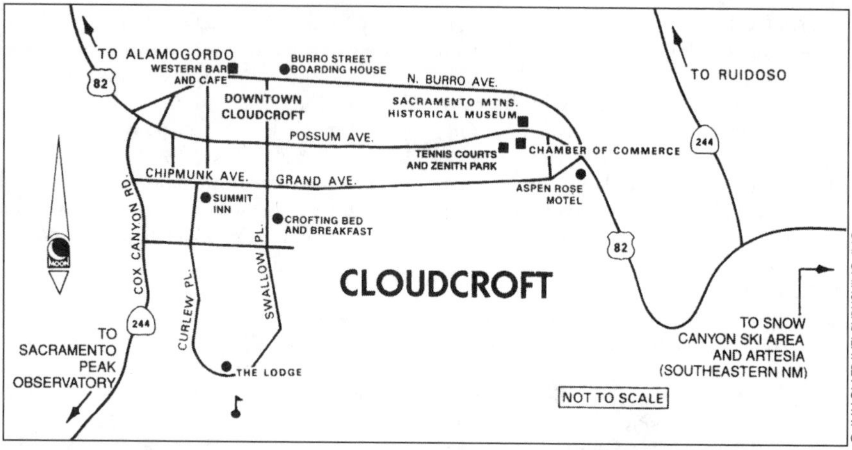

dancing pavilion, tennis, golf, bowling, billiards, a children's playground, and burro rides, the Lodge originally charged $3 per person for a weekend. It burned down in 1909 but was rebuilt in 1911 at a new location—high on a hillside overlooking downtown Cloudcroft. Among the guests who have stayed over the years at this elegant, Bavarian-style hotel are Pancho Villa, Clark Gable, and Judy Garland, who carved her name, under a drawing of a rainbow, on a wall in one of the Lodge's observatory towers.

Sacramento Mountains Historical Museum

This small museum on Highway 82 just east of downtown Cloudcroft displays artifacts from the area's history, including one of the best private arrowhead collections in the Southwest. Also on display are tools and domestic items from early Cloudcroft settlers and railroad workers—from kitchenware to dolls to musical instruments.

The museum's hours are irregular so it's best to call ahead: 505/682-2932. You can also get information on the museum from the Cloudcroft Chamber of Commerce at 505/682-2733. The chamber is right across Highway 82 from the museum.

Sacramento Peak Observatory

About 20 miles south of Cloudcroft, tucked away in the backwoods of the Sacramento Mountains, is a research center for monitoring solar activity and studying other stars in the galaxy. Though originally an Air Force facility, the center was taken over in 1976 by the National Science Foundation and the Association of Universities for Research in Astronomy. Since 1984 it has been a member of the National Optical Astronomy Observatories, with sister observatories at Kitt Peak, Arizona, and at Cerro Tololo, Chile. One of the telescopes rises from 20 stories underground to 13 stories above ground. The observatory grounds are open daily, and guided tours are offered Friday, Saturday, and Sunday at 2 P.M. June–August. Cost is $2 for adults, $1 for kids and seniors.

For tour hours or more information, phone 505/434-7003. Information and virtual tours are also available at the website: www.sunspot.noao.edu.

PRACTICALITIES

Accommodations

The Lodge, 505/682-2566 or 800/395-6343, is *the* place to stay in Cloudcroft, and prices are wide-ranging enough to make it affordable to most (and a splurge you'll thank yourself for later). Doubles start at $50–100, while parlor suites (for up to four people), some with wet bars, will run up to $250. The Lodge has an elegant dining room as well as a smaller lunch room and bar. Child care is available, and reservations are recommended. Write P.O. Box 497, Cloudcroft, NM 88317.

The Crofting Bed and Breakfast, 300 Swallow Dr., 505/682-2288, offers lodging in an early-20th-century Cloudcroft home; each room has a private bath, and guests can make use of kitchen facilities. Another option is the downtown **Burro Street Boarding House,** 608 Burro Ave., 505/682-3601.

Also in Cloudcroft, the **Summit Inn and Cottages** on Highway 82, 505/682-2814, offers kitchenettes, coffee, and juices. The **Alta Vista Motel,** 1605 Hwy. 82, 505/682-2221, has seven nicely appointed rooms. Both run $50–100.

The Cloudcroft area also has numerous cabins for rent, nightly, weekly, and monthly. For a complete listing, write the chamber of commerce.

Camping

Cloudcroft is surrounded by campgrounds, from primitive to RV-ready, and you can camp anywhere within Lincoln National Forest. **Pines Campground** is a Forest Service facility; 44 sites are hidden among the beautiful firs and pines, with pit toilets, drinking water, and picnic tables. No showers or hookups. Overnight fees are $8. Take Highway 82 east, then Highway 244 north. Just another couple of miles up Highway 244 are several other Forest Service facilities: **Apache, Saddle,** and **Silver** campgrounds charge $8 per night. **Deerhead Campground** on Highway 244 one mile south of Cloudcroft charges $8. For less primitive digs, try **Silver Springs Recreational Campgrounds** five miles northeast of Cloudcroft on Highway 244. Amenities include 38 sites (no drive-throughs) with RV hookups, a no-license-required trout pond, a tackle shop, and rental fishing equipment.

Food

The prices are high but the food's reputation is unsurpassed at **Rebecca's** at the Lodge, 505/682-3131. Appetizers (mushroom tempura, fresh spinach fettuccine) run $6–8. Entrées include steaks, fresh seafood, and *chateaubriand bouquetière* and range $15–22 (seafood prices vary according to catch and market price). Be sure to ask about Rebecca, the Lodge's "ghost," and watch for her in the darkened stairwells and hallways. The Lodge also serves lunch in an adjoining room. Try the quiche of the day, the fresh fruit plate, a sandwich, or a complete Mexican lunch.

Cloudcroft's 9,000-foot-high golf course

In addition, you'll find several cafés sandwiched between the gift shops and galleries in downtown Cloudcroft. Try the **Western Bar and Cafe,** on Burro Avenue, 505/682-2445, for Mexican and American lunch and dinner.

Shopping

Although very small, Cloudcroft supports a number of fine galleries and gift shops. Several shops specialize in Indian jewelry and pottery, while a handful of other small stores sell local ceramics and crafts. All are on Burro Avenue in Cloudcroft's tiny main business section, one block north of Highway 82.

Recreation

The Lodge's nine-hole golf course, at more than 9,000 feet above sea level, is one of the highest in North America. Greens fees are quite reasonable considering the course's reputation as one of the most scenic in the state. Call 505/682-2098 for greens fees and reservations. Nine miles southeast of Cloudcroft on Highway 24 is another nine-hole golf course, **Ponderosa Pines Golf and Country Club,** 505/682-2995.

Anglers can hole up at **Bear Canyon Lake.** Take Highway 244 from just east of town up to FSR 621. Note: even Cloudcroft propaganda classifies Bear Canyon Lake fishing as only "fair." Fishing is also available at Silver Lake north of Cloudcroft. If it's *fish* you're after and not fish*ing,* several lakes offer no-license, "limit guaranteed" angling.

Lincoln National Forest offers excellent opportunities for hikers—some of it true backwoods exploring, some of it tame and trailed. Check out the **Osha Trail,** a 2.5-mile loop that begins about one mile west of Cloudcroft. Look for the parking lot and trailhead on Highway 82 directly across from the old railroad trestle.

For wintertime activity, **Ski Cloudcroft** has one chairlift and one surface lift, 25 runs, lessons, rental equipment, and a ski school for kids ages four to seven. Weather permitting, it's open November–April. For more information, call 505/682-2333. The area also abounds in cross-country ski trails and snow-tubing.

Annual Events

The **Mayfair** is held every Memorial Day weekend in Zenith Park near the chamber of commerce offices and features arts and crafts, live entertainment, hay and horseback rides, and a barbecue. An adjunct to the Mayfair is the annual rodeo in Wimsatt Arena, seven miles east of Cloudcroft on Highway 82. Nearby High Rolls hosts the annual **Cherry Festival** the third weekend in June, spotlighting one of the area's premier crops—in pies, jams, and cider. The **July Jamboree,** first week in July, features arts and crafts, a horseshoe tournament, street dance, and bicycle tours. During the second weekend of September, Cloudcroft hosts **Railroad Days,** with railroad displays, hikes, and a "hobo breakfast" Sunday morning. The **Octoberfest and Aspencade,** first weekend in October, is also in Zenith Park and features local arts and crafts, entertainment, and guided Fall Foliage Tours through the trees and turning leaves.

Various festivities punctuate the **Christmas holidays,** from bonfires and caroling to ice sculpture, luminarias, and many events for the kids. Call the chamber of commerce for exact dates and times of any of Cloudcroft's annual festivities.

Information and Services

The folks at the **Cloudcroft Chamber of Commerce** are extremely knowledgeable about the Cloudcroft area and local goings-on, and they

love to talk Cloudcroft with visitors. The office is in the log cabin on Highway 82 on the east end of town. Stop in to say hi and to pick up the many hiking and camping maps, as well as a copy of the *Mountain Monthly*, a guide to the area and events. You can call the chamber at 505/682-2733 or visit its website: www.cloudcroft.net.

The nearest hospital is Gerald Champion Memorial Hospital in Alamogordo, 18 miles away; call 505/439-2100. The Cloudcroft police can be reached at 505/682-2101 (nonemergency) or at 911 in emergencies.

Transportation

Mesa Air, 800/MESA-AIR (800/637-2247), has passenger service between Albuquerque and Alamogordo. From there you can rent a car and be in Cloudcroft in half an hour. **Avis** is at 1401 White Sands Blvd., Alamogordo, 505/437-3140.

TO RUIDOSO

From Cloudcroft to Ruidoso, Highway 244 and Highway 70 snake through the 400,000-acre Mescalero Apache Reservation and some beautiful mountain scenery. In the summer, forests of tall pines open up to lush mountain meadows, dotted with grazing cattle and Appaloosa-borne Apaches. Ahead of you, Sierra Blanca—its darkly forested flanks giving way to an electric green above-timberline brush—towers omnipotently. In the winter, the mountain is covered deep in snow, its conical symmetry in dramatic contrast with the deep-blue sky.

Ruidoso and Vicinity

Snow skiing, hiking, fishing, camping, bicycling, horse racing and riding, historical tours, art galleries, verdant valleys, peaks towering far above the treeline, the gorgeous Mescalero Apache Reservation. Welcome to Ruidoso—an evergreen jewel in the White Mountains' rolling midlands. The scents of pines, cedars, and aspens, flameflowers, lupine, and scarlet penstemons mingle in the thin mountain air, while creeks, alive with snowmelt, trickle down hillsides toward clearwater lakes.

Naturally, few places in the world as nice as this go undiscovered. And Ruidoso (pop. 4,500; elev. 6,900 feet) isn't one of them. Nope. Folks know about this place. Although it doesn't get the masses that Taos and Santa Fe do, this little mountain town, an oasis surrounded by some of the most barren country this side of the Sahara, does see the tourists. Particularly from Texas. In fact, on any given weekend, the sidewalks of Ruidoso swell with visitors wandering in and out of gift shops, galleries, and little restaurants, and you're likely to see as many Texas as New Mexico license plates. In the summer, West Texans come up to Ruidoso to escape the heat, do a little golfing, fishing, hiking, and, especially, betting on the ponies. In the winter they come to snow ski—an inside joke has it that Ruidoso is Texas's only ski resort.

Promoting itself as a "year-round playground," Ruidoso (which you'll hear almost universally mispronounced as "Reodoso") lives up to its promise. In addition to the vast recreational possibilities, you can play at the racetrack, the bingo parlor, or the various nightspots in the area that feature live music and dancing. You can also entertain yourself for days wandering in and out of Ruidoso's many galleries and gift shops, which sell pieces varying from gimmicky schlock to museum-quality paintings and sculpture.

A word of caution: Don't pull into Ruidoso on a Friday or Saturday night, especially during ski or horse-racing season, hoping to find a choice of places to crash. You'll be lucky if you can find a bed at all, and you'll wish you'd been wise enough to phone ahead for reservations.

History

Ruidoso and Ruidoso Downs are actually two towns, nearly adjacent. Eventually named for the river that tumbles through town (the name means Very Noisy), Ruidoso was known as Dowlin's Mill, after the mill built on the river in 1853. It wasn't until the 1930s and '40s, though, that

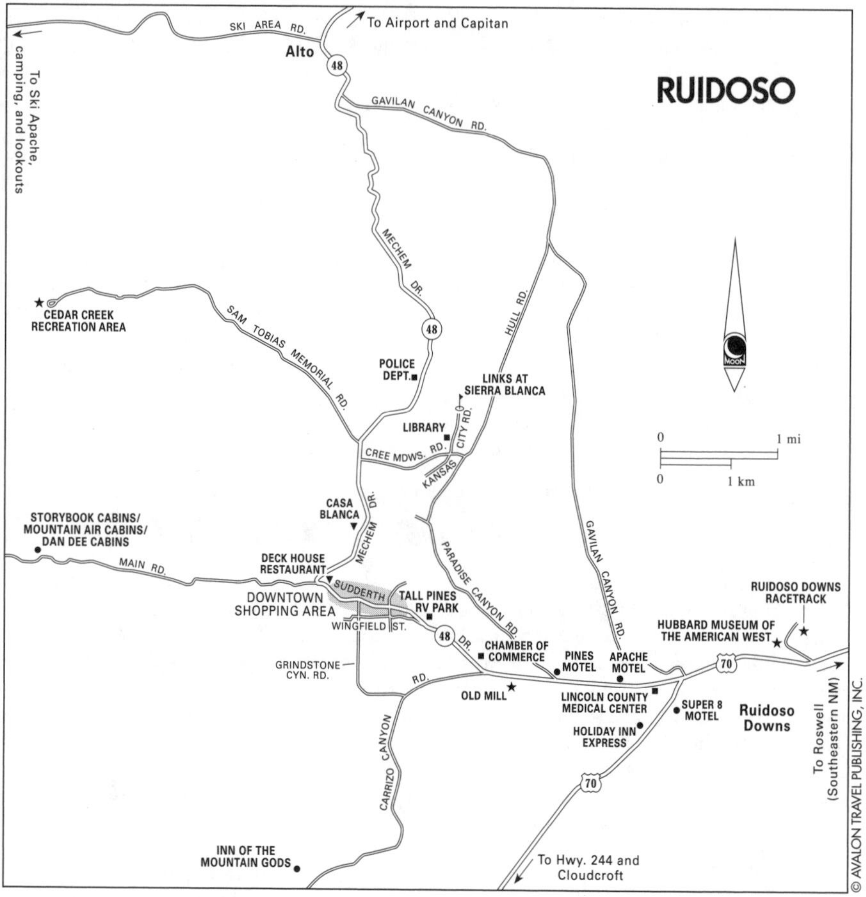

Ruidoso began to develop into the tourist mecca it is today—as horse racing in the area grew from friendly, neighborly contests into nationally known, big-money affairs held at the Ruidoso Downs Racetrack in Palo Verde, the small community just east of town. In 1946, when Palo Verde applied for a post office, enterprising horsemen, realizing the promotional possibilities of a racetrack with its own postmark, stipulated that the town's name be changed to Ruidoso Downs. Since then, summers have drawn bettors from throughout the country to the All-American Quarter Horse Futurity, a race with one of the biggest purses in the country.

In 1957, the Forest Service designated White Mountain Park (on Sierra Blanca) a winter snowplay area and in 1960 leased land on the mountain to the Sierra Blanca Corporation for a ski area. By the mid-1980s, Ski Apache, to which its name was changed, had become one of the most popular ski resorts in the Southwest, attracting nearly 300,000 skiers a season. Ruidoso had become a bona fide year-round playground.

SIGHTS

Old Mill

The original Dowlin's Mill, for which the town was

first named, has also been a post office and roadhouse, accommodating (at different times) Billy the Kid and General John "Blackjack" Pershing, who chased Pancho Villa back into Mexico after his raid on Columbus, New Mexico, in 1916 (see the special topic Pancho Villa in the Southwestern New Mexico chapter). Today, the mill, in downtown Ruidoso on Sudderth Drive just east of the chamber of commerce, houses a small curio shop.

Sierra Blanca

Take Ski Area Road west off Highway 48 and wind your way up through the aspens and evergreens to one of the most spectacular lookouts in the state. The road is steep and curvy, and the going is slow, but the view from 10,000 feet above sea level is well worth the drive.

Monjeau Lookout

Originally a wooden tower built in the 1930s and now made of solid rock, Monjeau is used as a fire lookout in the summer. Climb to the top (10,356 feet) for a look at the White and Sacramento Mountains, as well as the foothills rolling toward the valley. Take Highway 48 about a mile north of Ski Area Road and watch for the sign to the lookout.

Inn of the Mountain Gods

Even if you're not wealthy enough to stay here, or fortunate enough to be attending a conference or convention, stop in and have a look around. The monstrous complex sprawls over several acres of pristine forest and meadow and overlooks a small mountain lake, with tepees set up on the shore, plus tennis courts, swimming pools, stables, and a golf course—all in as beautiful a setting as you can imagine. Inside, you'll find a huge lobby with a fireplace and piano bar, as well as a gift shop and restaurant. The inn is owned and operated by the enterprising Mescalero Apaches, employing a good number of the tribe's people. Take Carrizo Creek Road south from Sudderth Drive. (See Accommodations, below, for rates.)

LOUISE FOOTE

Mule deer sometimes wander into the Ruidoso area.

Hubbard Museum of the American West

Just east of downtown Ruidoso at Ruidoso Downs, this relatively new (1996) museum specializes in exhibits relating to the horse and its role in American history, including Native American, Mexican, and U.S. saddles; carriages; surreys; a Conestoga wagon; and a completely restored (and gorgeous) 12-passenger stagecoach from 1866. The texts accompanying all displays here are in both English and Spanish. In addition, there's an impressive collection of equine-related art, with pieces by Remington, Russell, and others. The gift shop has everything from quality art to trinkety souvenirs, including books and T-shirts. Be sure to take a few minutes to watch the video "Whirlwind of Change," which examines the impact the horse has had on North America. Admission is $6 for adults, $5 for seniors and kids nine to 18. The museum is open daily 10 A.M.–5 P.M. Phone 505/378-4142 for more information.

RECREATION

Ruidoso is a recreation-lover's paradise, all year-round. Whether your bent is camping, golfing, fishing, snow skiing, or just about anything else that keeps the heart healthy and the spirit happy, you'll find lots here to satisfy.

Golf

From spring until late fall, when snow turns the greens to white, Ruidoso's golf courses attract drivers and putters of every persuasion. The area's newest course and one of the nicest around is **Links at Sierra Blanca,** 505/258-5300 or 800/

8-LINKS-1 (800/854-6571). Named in a *Golf Digest* article as one of the country's best new public courses, the Links opened in the summer of 1991 on the site of the old airport. **Alto Lakes Golf and Country Club,** 505/336-4231, and **Cree Meadows Country Club,** 505/257-9186, are both private clubs, open to members and guests only. Greens fees at the **Inn of the Mountain Gods,** 505/257-5141, ext. 7444, are about $20 for nine holes, $30 for 18 holes; fees for nonguests are slightly higher.

Fishing and Hunting

Ruidoso-area lakes and streams are open year-round, and they're stocked regularly with rainbow, cutthroat, brook, and brown trout. Waters on Mescalero Apache land require special permits. Southwest hunters stalk the White Mountains for deer, bear, elk, and wild turkey. For information and restrictions, check your local sporting goods store, or contact the **New Mexico Game and Fish Department,** 1 Wildlife Way, Santa Fe, NM 87507, phone 505/476-8000, or visit the website: www.gmfsh.state.nm.us. For information about hunting and fishing on the Mescalero Reservation, phone the **Mescalero Tribal Game and Fish Office** at 505/671-4427.

Skiing and Snowboarding

Ski Apache, 16 miles from downtown Ruidoso, offers some of the finest Alpine skiing in the Southwest. Eight chairlifts serve 40 trails: 25 percent beginner, 35 percent intermediate, and 40 percent advanced. Ski Apache is open 8:30 A.M.–4 P.M. daily. For ticket prices, current snow conditions, and other information, visit the website: www.skiapache.com/snowrept.htm.

For retail and rental equipment in town, check out **Wild West Ski Shop,** 1408 Mechem, 505/258-3131.

LOUISE FOOTE

Black bears live in the White Mountain backcountry.

Bicycling

The roads winding through the Ruidoso-area mountains will challenge the fittest cyclist. For a real test, take Ski Area Road up Sierra Blanca Lookout for one of the finest vistas in all of New Mexico. With Sierra Blanca towering behind you at 12,003 feet, you look north to the Capitan and Jicarilla Mountains and east toward the hills that roll down to Roswell. Allow plenty of time to stop and rest, especially if you've come up from sea level, as this is one steep mother and the air is thin: the lookout is just shy of 10,000 feet.

Ruidoso has also jumped on the mountain-bike bandwagon, and many of the roads and trails in the area are perfect for this new sport. For information and rentals, stop by the **Wild West Ski Shop,** 1408 Mechem, 505/258-3131.

White Mountain Wilderness

This rugged forest area between Sierra Blanca and Nogal Peak north of Ruidoso lures day-hikers and backpackers to the tall pines of Lincoln National Forest. For maps and more information, check the Smokey Bear Ranger Station on Mechem Drive, or phone 505/257-4095.

Cedar Creek Recreation Area

Lots of greenery here, and the hiking trails through the pines and cedar rejuvenate the tired spirit. No overnight camping, but pit toilets and plenty of picnic tables are available. Take Cedar Creek Road off Mechem/Highway 48 just north of Cree Meadows Drive.

PRACTICALITIES

Accommodations

Ruidoso's lodging varies from the many inexpensive motels along the main drags to condos

SKI APACHE

According to Mescalero Apache emergence myths, all life began on 12,003-foot Sierra Blanca, a towering peak north of Ruidoso in the northwest corner of the Mescalero Reservation. In addition, the mountain is the home of Ussen, an Apache god, who looks down on the 400,000-acre reservation from his mountain.

In May 1960, the Forest Service granted to the Sierra Blanca Corporation, headed by Roswellian Robert O. Anderson, a 30-year lease to build and operate a ski area on one of the formidable flanks of Sierra Blanca. A 1,700-foot gondola was constructed, and by the 1962–63 ski season, the resort was open for business and that year attracted 25,000 skiers. In the fall of 1963, however, the Mescaleros bought the ski resort for $1.25 million hoping to create jobs for the Apaches living on the reservation. It wasn't long before attendance figures at Sierra Blanca began to climb, and by 1984–85, the year the resort's name was changed to Ski Apache, the annual attendance was approaching 300,000.

Today, Ski Apache attracts downhillers from throughout the Southwest, particularly West Texas, with eight chairlifts, a surface lift, and the old gondola delivering skiers to the 40-plus runs and trails. And in case snowfall is lacking, Ski Apache has installed a huge snowmaking system that can pump a million gallons of water—frozen into snow—out over the trails in the course of a single evening.

Ski Apache hosts weekly NASTAR races, as well as the annual Texas cup, where Apache's out-of-state regulars vie for the title of best Lone Star skier. In addition, Ski Apache has a special program for disabled skiers, with facilities and instruction for both the blind and the physically disabled.

For more information, contact Ski Apache, P.O. Box 220, Ruidoso, NM 88345, 505/336-4356, or call the Ruidoso Chamber of Commerce at 505/257-7395. For rates and snow conditions, visit the website: skiapache.com.

COURTESY OF SKI APACHE/RIKER DAVIS

shredding through the trees at Ski Apache

tucked into the woods, from private rental cabins and homes to the lavish and sprawling Inn of the Mountain Gods. And although there doesn't appear to be any shortage of lodging, it's wise to make reservations well ahead of time, particularly on winter weekends during ski season and summer weekends during racing season (rates may be slightly higher those times, as well). Ruidoso's website has extensive listings of accommodations in the area, as well as links to those properties' sites. Check out the website: www.ruidoso.net.

Motels: $50–100

The **Apache Motel** at 344 Sudderth, 505/257-2986, is a down-homey little place where some rooms have kitchenettes. Just up the road at 620 Sudderth, with the same owners, is the **Pines Motel,** 505/257-4334. There's a **Super 8 Motel** at 100 Cliff Dr., 505/378-8180, and a **Holiday Inn Express** at 400 W. Hwy. 70, 505/257-3736.

Lodges and Inns: $100–150

If you'd like something a little fancier (and pricier), try the **Inn of the Mountain Gods,** 505/257-5141 or 800/545-9011. This spectacular lakeside resort complex and convention center (worth a visit even if you're staying down the road in cheaper digs) offers tennis, golfing, sailing, swimming, boating, cycling, fishing, horseback riding, saunas, trap and skeet shooting, and even archery. The inn also offers tennis, golf, and honeymoon package deals. For more information and complete rates, write Inn of the Mountain Gods, P.O. Box 269, Mescalero, NM 88340, or visit the website: www.innofthemountaingods.com.

Another Ruidoso classic is **Canyon Creek Lodge,** 505/257-9131 or 800/227-1224, built in 1874 and listed on the National Register of Historic Places (and formerly called the Carrozo Lodge). The inn offers renovated rooms appointed with 19th-century furnishings, as well as modern condo units.

High Country Lodge is right on the road to Ski Apache, 505/336-4321, and offers two-bedroom cabins with fireplaces, kitchens, outdoor barbecue grills, tennis courts, and an indoor pool.

Cabins

You'll also find abundant private cabins and homes for rent scattered throughout the Ruidoso hills, including several on the historic and picturesque Upper Canyon Road. Most have fireplaces and kitchens and offer ski and other vacation packages. **Story Book Cabins,** 505/257-2115, are individual log cabins that can accommodate up to 12. **Mountain Air Cabins,** 505/257-5600, has several funky little 1930s-vintage homes with fireplaces and kitchens. **Dan Dee Cabins,** 505/257-2165, offers studio-type cabins for two as well as three-bedroom cabins, which sleep seven. A cabin at any of the above will run $100–150 per night.

Bed-and-Breakfast

The Ruidoso area can also satisfy the bed-and-breakfast crowd. **Monjeau Shadows Country Inn,** 505/336-4191, tucked away in the pines near Alto just off Highway 48 between Nogal and Ruidoso, has large rooms with fireplaces. Rates start at around $100. Write Monjeau Shadows, Bonito Route, Nogal, NM 88341.

Camping and RVing

The piney woods and mountain meadows around Ruidoso seclude some of the most beautiful campgrounds in the state. **Skyline Campground** is on a lush hillside at the foot of Sierra Blanca. Tenters are charged $8 (for two), and RVs are $14 for complete hookups (also for two); each additional person pays another $.50. Skyline has flush toilets, showers, and a playground for the kids. Take Ski Area Road north of town and follow the signs. A couple of miles past Skyline is **Oak Grove Campground,** a free national forest facility with pit toilets but no showers. An absolutely gorgeous little campground, Oak Grove's tucked away in the trees, and the individual sites are nicely secluded.

The most primitive of the campgrounds in the area is **Eagle Creek Campground,** also just off Ski Area Road. Several unimproved sites are scattered along a narrow gravel road (not recommended for large RVs) that parallels Eagle Creek as it trickles down the hillside. Sites have rings for fires and flat areas for tents, but no tables, toilets, or water. Watch for the sign along Ski Area Road.

Tall Pines RV Park, 1800 Sudderth, 505/257-5233, although right on Ruidoso's main drag, is quiet and about as secluded as you can get right in town. **Blue Spruce RV Park** is also very close to the center of town (on Highway 48 three miles from the junction with Highway 70), 505/257-7993.

Food

Ruidoso's got restaurants to satisfy all hungers. Whether you're craving fast food or prefer to sit down at elegant white linen in true European tradition, you won't leave town unsatisfied. One of the best places for breakfast and lunch in Ruidoso, and a favorite among locals, is the **Deck House Restaurant** at the corner of Sudderth and Mechem, 505/257-3496. The Deck House bakes fresh bread daily, uses fresh chiles from the Mesilla Valley, and specializes in Indian cornbread, burritos, and chimichangas. Lunches run about $6–10. With the excellent food the Deck House serves, the anomalous dining room is a bonus: a screened-in deck overlooking the creek is garnished with geraniums and begonias everywhere there's not a table or chair.

Another good call for breakfast is the **Lincoln County Grill,** 2717 Sudderth, 505/257-7669, where you can get traditional American breakfasts or specials with a Southwestern flair (such as a "Lincoln County breakfast burrito") for $3–8. The restaurant also serves lunch and dinner—burgers, salads, chili, catfish, chicken-fried steak—for $5–10. I had the marinated chicken salad, one of the best I've had. Open daily 6 A.M.–9 P.M.

For good Mexican food, try **Casa Blanca,** 501 Mechem Dr., 505/257-2495, which serves excellent food at reasonable prices and is very popular with the young crowd as an after-ski and summer-evening hangout. Happy "hour" is daily 2–6 P.M., and you can hear live music (acoustic guitars, bluegrass, etc.) Friday and Saturday nights—outdoor on the patio if weather permits. Open daily for lunch and dinner.

The place to go for that special occasion, though, or when the boss or folks are buying, is **La Lorraine** at 2523 Sudderth, 505/257-2954. Open for lunch and dinner daily except Sunday. Try the "soupe du canard" or chicken and pasta salads, rack of lamb, scallops, or fillets. The house dessert specialty is a praline soufflé.

Finally, if you're looking for something a little different, try the **Flying J Ranch,** 505/336-4330, where meals are served Western-style, as if you just stepped in off the range. For $17, $9 for kids 4–11 (2002 prices), you get sliced beef, baked potato, "cowboy beans," biscuits, applesauce, and, best of all, the stage show, featuring the country music of the Flying J Wranglers. Doors open at 6 P.M., and the dinner bell rings at 7:30. Be sure to call for reservations though: the mess hall holds 400, and you want to make sure the ranch saves you some grub. Open Monday–Saturday Memorial Day through Labor Day, and Saturdays in September. Phone, or visit the website: www.flyingjranch.com for information, reservations, or directions.

Entertainment

Folks come to Ruidoso to enjoy themselves, and you won't find the sidewalks rolling up at sundown as in other New Mexico towns of similar size. Of course, Ruidoso's major entertainment feature is the horse racing. The season, which runs early May through Labor Day, attracts bettors and equine lovers from throughout the Southwest—particularly Texas—who come to bet on the thoroughbreds and quarter horses. Post time is 1 P.M., and the grandstand opens at 11 A.M. Parking is $1 per car, and general admission is $2. For reserved seating information, phone 505/378-4140 or 800/622-6023. The 24-hour Ruidoso Downs Racing Hotline number is 505/378-4081. To get to **Ruidoso Downs Racetrack,** take Highway 70 east to the village of Ruidoso Downs and watch for the signs.

Ruidoso also claims a number of popular nightspots, for those who've got race winnings to spend (or for those who want to forget they just never could make sense of that racing form). The following clubs feature live music, and some have dancing; phone for current listings and schedules: **Coyote Cantina,** at the corner of Eagle and Sudderth, 505/257-7522 (country and rock, with a 1,000-square-foot dance floor; **Win, Place, and Show,** 2516 Sudderth, 505/257-9982 (country dancing); and **Inn of the Mountain Gods,** 505/257-5141.

If you're looking for something a little tamer, check out the schedule for the **Spencer Center for the Performing Arts,** 505/336-4800 or 888/818-7872. This new complex (1997) features a wide variety of shows, from jazz piano and Russian folk music to western and contemporary drama to children's theater. Recent shows include *Forever Plaid* and *Man of La Mancha.* Visit the website at www.spencertheater.com for more information.

Annual Events

Ruidoso's annual chamber of commerce-sponsored **Ruidoso Arts Festival** draws artisans from throughout the West and buyers and admirers from southeastern New Mexico and West Texas. Usually in late July, the fair runs three days and features a wide variety of quality work, including jewelry, sculpture, painting, woodcarving, and hand-painted clothing, and you can watch many of the artists at work in their booths. Other annual events in Ruidoso include the **Mescalero Apache Ceremonial and Rodeo** in early July, with Indian dances and traditional games, as well as a cross-country run; fall festivities focus on the turning of the leaves. Contact the Ruidoso Chamber of Commerce for more information and specific dates.

Shopping

Ruidoso's Sudderth and Mechem Drives (Highway 48 through town) are lined with galleries and gift shops—from trinket and last-minute-something-for-Aunt-Jenny stores to high-quality shops specializing in original work by some of the Southwest's best-known painters and sculptors. You can pick up everything from sand-paintings, dream-catchers, and three-foot bronze Kokopellis to pottery, prints, and paintings. In past editions of this book, I've gone to great lengths to specify galleries that I thought were of particular interest, only to have them shut down or change hands before the book was on the shelves. My advice, then, is simply to allow yourself a half day or so to wander through midtown Ruidoso checking out the various shops.

Information and Services

The folks at the Ruidoso Valley **Chamber of Commerce** are extremely friendly and helpful. For more information about the Ruidoso area, write to P.O. Box 698, Ruidoso, NM 88355, or phone 800/253-2255. Check out the chamber's website at www.ruidoso.net, and email questions to ruidoso@zianet.com.

When you're in town, be sure to stop by the chamber's offices at 720 Sudderth for complete listings of events and attractions in the area. Pick up a copy of the *Official Vacation Guide,* which includes a section *en Español.* You'd also be wise during your stay to pick up copies of the ***Ruidoso News,*** the town's daily, available in racks around town. Of particular interest to visitors is Friday's "Weekend Edition," which includes a supplement outlining things to do in the area.

Ruidoso's new **public library** is off Cree Meadows near the corner of Hull (next to the Ruidoso Convention Center), 505/257-4335.

Lincoln County Medical Center is at 211 Sudderth (near the junction of Highway 70), 505/257-7381. Both the Ruidoso Police Department, 505/257-7365, and the New Mexico state police, 505/257-9111, are at 421 Wingfield, just off Sudderth.

Transportation

There is no commercial air service to Ruidoso, although private planes can land at Sierra Blanca Regional Airport, 505/336-8111. **Mesa Air,** 800/MESA-AIR (800/637-2247), flies from Albuquerque into both Roswell and Alamogordo. **Shuttles Ruidoso,** 505/336-1683, offers bus and van service to the museums, Ski Apache, Inn of the Mountain Gods, and nearby casinos.

CAPITAN

As you wind along Highway 48 between Ruidoso and Capitan, through the tall pines and firs of Lincoln National Forest, you pass through the tiny mountain communities of Alto and Angus. Once a rugged unpaved "shortcut" between the two towns, the road has been used by hunters and anglers for decades. Only in recent years—it's now paved and quite passable—has it been an alternative for tourists. Then you drop into the foothills and finally onto the valley floor and into Capitan, home to Smokey Bear Historical State Park.

Of course, every red-blooded American's heard of Smokey Bear, but not everyone knows the story. The people of Capitan do, though, and they like to tell it: In May 1950, a five-month-old bear cub was found in the smoldering Capitan Mountains, in which a 17,000-acre forest fire had been raging for five days. Firefighters named the bear "Hot Foot Teddy" and flew him to Santa

Fe, where his wounds were dressed and he was renamed "Smokey." Two months later, after an unsuccessful attempt to return him to the wild, Smokey was flown to Washington, D.C., where he was given a suite at the Washington Zoo and appeared over the years in parades and circuses and on television, becoming an unwitting symbol of forest-fire prevention. In 1958, President Eisenhower presented to the town of Capitan a "Smokey Oscar for Conservation."

Smokey stayed in Washington for the next 26 years, receiving visitors and answering his fan mail (letters written directly to Smokey, at his Washington D.C. zip, 20252, all get personal replies—signed with a paw print). Meanwhile, his "Only YOU Can Prevent Forest Fires" media blitz sharply increased national awareness of forest fires and decreased their occurrence by half. In fact, this advertising campaign, funded strictly by donations, has become one of the most successful in history; the Forest Service estimates it's saved the country more than $27 billion.

In 1976, the town of Capitan, without any outside funding, constructed the park and a museum. When Smokey died in November of that year, he was flown back to his hometown to be buried. His gravesite is behind the museum. Smokey Junior (no relation) inherited Smokey's Washington duties.

History

In Capitan, nonbear history takes a back seat to old Smokey, although the town does trace its heritage to the 1880s, when a number of mines were being worked in the nearby hills and a network of back roads connected the various settlements. Known as "Gray" until the turn of the last century, Capitan took its name in 1900 from Capitan Peak, a 10,083-foot mountain northeast of town, and served as post office for several of the mining towns in the area. By 1905, however, most of the mines and settlements had been abandoned, save for Capitan, which survived and continued to serve the area's farmers and ranchers, as well as outdoor enthusiasts, who often passed through Capitan en route to Ruidoso.

Also of historical importance to the area was Fort Stanton, built in 1855 to provide protection for settlers from White Mountain and Mescalero Apaches. In 1861, the fort, actually more of a stockade, was destroyed by Confederate troops from Texas. In 1868, the fort was rebuilt two miles north of its original site. Now about three miles south of Highway 380, between Capitan and Lincoln, Fort Stanton was abandoned by the military in 1896. Since then, it has served as a hospital for tuberculosis patients, as a sanatorium, and as a school for the mentally disabled.

Smokey Bear Historical State Park

In the center of town on Highway 380, this little park has a visitors center that shows films on the hour about Smokey's life and forest preservation. An interpretive nature trail takes visitors to Smokey's gravesite, and a gift shop sells Smokey souvenirs. The park, on the town's main drag at 118 Smokey Bear Blvd., is open daily 9 A.M.–5 P.M.

© STEPHEN METZGER

Smokey greets visitors at Smokey Bear Park.

Entrance fee is $1, $.50 for kids 7–12. For more information, phone 505/354-2748.

Accommodations and Food

There's not much here, although the **Smokey Bear Motel,** next to the park, 505/354-2253, has nice, clean rooms, with doubles running about $50. **Smokey Bear Restaurant,** 505/354-2257, open daily 6:30 A.M.–8 P.M., specializes in—what else?—Smokey Bear Burgers.

Annual Events

Every July 4, Capitan hosts the **Smokey Bear Stampede,** with a parade, barbecue, Western dance, and rodeo.

Information

For more information about Capitan or Smokey Bear State Park, write **Capitan Chamber of Commerce,** P.O. Box 441, Capitan, NM 88316, or call 505/354-2273. You can call the park directly at 505/354-2748.

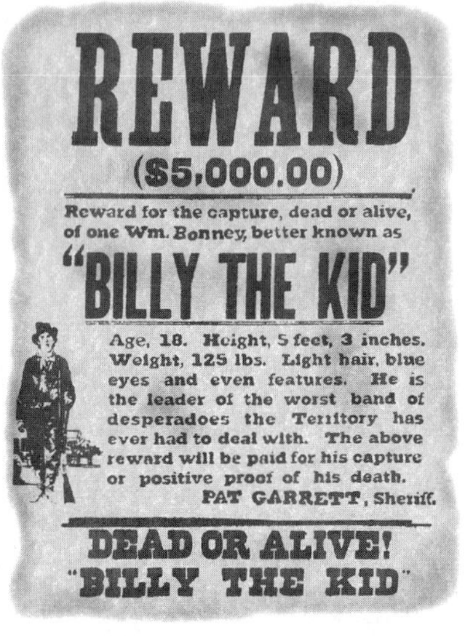

Garrett finally got his man on July 14, 1881.

LINCOLN

Apache warriors, Billy the Kid, Pat Garrett, the Lincoln County War, Kit Carson, John Chisum, and Susan McSween (also known as "The Cattle Queen of New Mexico")—the story of Lincoln County reads like a history of New Mexico in miniature. Indeed, the town of Lincoln is the epicenter of a 10-square-mile National Historic Landmark. Thanks to the hard work of the Lincoln County Heritage Trust, the Old Lincoln Memorial Commission, and the Museum of New Mexico, which have gone to great lengths to maintain the old town's historical integrity and keep schlocky tourism away, Lincoln today is one of the best places to see New Mexico as it really was when Billy the Kid rode the streets and Apaches roamed the nearby hills.

History

Lincoln was first settled in the late 1840s by farmers of Spanish descent who built stone fortresses to guard against Apache raids. Originally Las Placitas del Rio Bonito (Little Plazas on the Pretty River), the town's name was changed to Lincoln in 1869, when it was designated the seat of Lincoln County. In the late 1870s, an intense rivalry grew between two of the town's leading merchants, John Tunstall and L. G. Murphy, and their allies. In 1878, Tunstall was gunned down. Supporters of the two men squared off, and townspeople quickly proclaimed their loyalties. Among those loyal to Tunstall was one of his cowboys, who'd witnessed the killing. His name: William Bonney, or Billy the Kid. "The Kid" vowed to avenge Tunstall's death by killing all those involved, and the bloody 12-month Lincoln County War ensued, climaxing in a five-day gun battle in July 1878, with details of the battle receiving press as far away as the East Coast.

The final casualty in the five-day battle, which ended July 19, was cattle baron Alexander McSween, whose wife, Suzie, inherited his estate and went on to become "The Cattle Queen of New Mexico."

The governor of New Mexico Territory, Lew Wallace, declared amnesty for all involved in the war, and Billy the Kid submitted to arrest. He then testified but escaped house arrest after learning that the U.S. attorney was going to prosecute regardless of the governor's promise of a pardon. Troops stationed at nearby Fort Stanton, the black "Buffalo Soldiers" of the 9th Cavalry, tried to maintain calm, but as often as not inflamed passions.

In November, Pat Garrett was elected sheriff of Lincoln County and within two months had arrested Billy the Kid, who escaped again three months later. Garrett caught up with Billy again near Fort Sumner, fatally shooting him in a bedroom of the home of Pete Maxwell. Governor Wallace, meanwhile, went on to complete the novel *Ben Hur,* which he'd been working on during the final phase of the Lincoln County War.

By 1900, Lincoln had become a thriving and peaceful community of nearly 1,000 and had established itself as a trading center for farmers throughout the Rio Bonito Valley. In 1900, however, hard times came to Lincoln when the seat of Lincoln County (at the time covering roughly a quarter of New Mexico Territory) was moved and the town's population fell to about 60. Those who stayed, though, kept the old buildings from falling into total disrepair, while Lincoln sat waiting to be rediscovered by historians. Today, the 40 or so buildings in Lincoln are owned (in about equal proportions) by the Lincoln County Historical Trust, the State of New Mexico, and private holders.

Lincoln County State Monument

Comprising a large part of the little town of Lincoln, this newly designated state monument includes John Tunstall's store, which has been preserved and is itself now a museum; the courthouse, originally L. G. Murphy's store; Lincoln's country doctor's house and office; the site of the Old Lincoln Hotel (now the Wortley Hotel, built in 1936 and until recently operating as a hotel and restaurant); and El Torreon, the rock fortress built by early Spanish settlers. Start at the **Lincoln County Historical Center,** where a short video and exhibits of Apache, Spanish, and Anglo clothing, tools, and weapons, as well as uniforms and weapons of the Buffalo Soldiers, provide an overview of the area's history. The historical center is open daily 9 A.M.–6 P.M. (9 A.M.–5 P.M. in winter), and guided tours of the courthouse are given two to three times daily. Admission is $6 and includes admission to all the buildings on the tour.

Accommodations and Food

Lincoln County Heritage Trust is uninterested in becoming a gimmicky tourist center, so you won't find fast-food and motel franchises here. In fact, as a "living historical museum," Lincoln isn't much different from what it was in the 1880s—except you'll find docents instead of gunfighters as you wander the streets. The **Casa de Patrón,** P.O. Box 27, Lincoln, NM 88335, 505/653-4676 or 800/524-5202, is a bed-and-breakfast in an adobe building listed on the National Register of Historic Places. Named for builder Juan Patrón, who was killed in the Lincoln County War, the inn, opened in 1988, has already earned a solid reputation for its wonderful hospitality and intimate sense of history, earning write-ups in national publications varying from *America's Little Hotels and Inns* to *Recommended Country Inns of the Southwest.* Rates run $100–150. The **Ellis Store and Co. Bed and Breakfast,** 505/653-4609 or 800/653-6460, has period-decorated rooms in an adobe dating from 1850—said to be a haunt of Billy the Kid himself. In addition to the rooms in the main building—some of which share a bath—there's an outbuilding for larger groups. Rates are $100–150.

BOB RACE

Annual Events

Old Lincoln Days are held the first full Friday–Sunday weekend in August, with a parade, folk pageant, and living-history demonstrations. Write or phone the Lincoln Country Heritage Trust or Lincoln County State Monument for more information.

Information

For more details on the town of Lincoln, contact **Lincoln County Heritage Trust,** P.O. Box 98, Lincoln, NM 88338, 505/653-4372, or **Lincoln County State Monument,** P.O. Box 36, Lincoln, NM 88338, 505/653-4372.

Southeastern New Mexico

Introduction

Mornings in southeastern New Mexico are infused with a vague but glorious sense of possibility, spawned by the openness of the land, its hugeness, the feeling that you're all alone here, with lots of room to spread your wings and push your personal ceilings to the heavens. Mornings turn to afternoons, though, and slowly the day begins to close in around you. The heat, the glaring sun, the sweat on your brow and your back—by midafternoon you begin to feel small and somehow confined. Instead of feeling as if you could drive forever, you're ready to pull over for a nap.

At sunset, the mood shifts again. The pavement begins to cool, and there's a new depth to the sky. You breathe easier. And then the night, the deep and starry night that evokes the maddened, vertiginous spirit of Van Gogh, Dylan Thomas, or some restless visionary in a Springsteen ballad. At night the enormity of the land's soul changes somehow, becoming nearly as fearsome as it is full of possibility, and you find yourself looking back over your shoulder, catching sharp breaths, and wondering about the grievous and desolate angels that haunt the desert highways.

It's no wonder, then, that these southeast plains were the breeding grounds for the naive yet groundbreaking rock 'n' roll of Buddy Holly, as well as the mysteriously soulful supplications of Roy Orbison. In the late 1950s and early '60s, Holly and Orbison, and scores of other young musicians, drove earnestly—often all through the night—across the desert to Clovis, New Mexico, where, in the darkness on the edge of town, they recorded their flames,

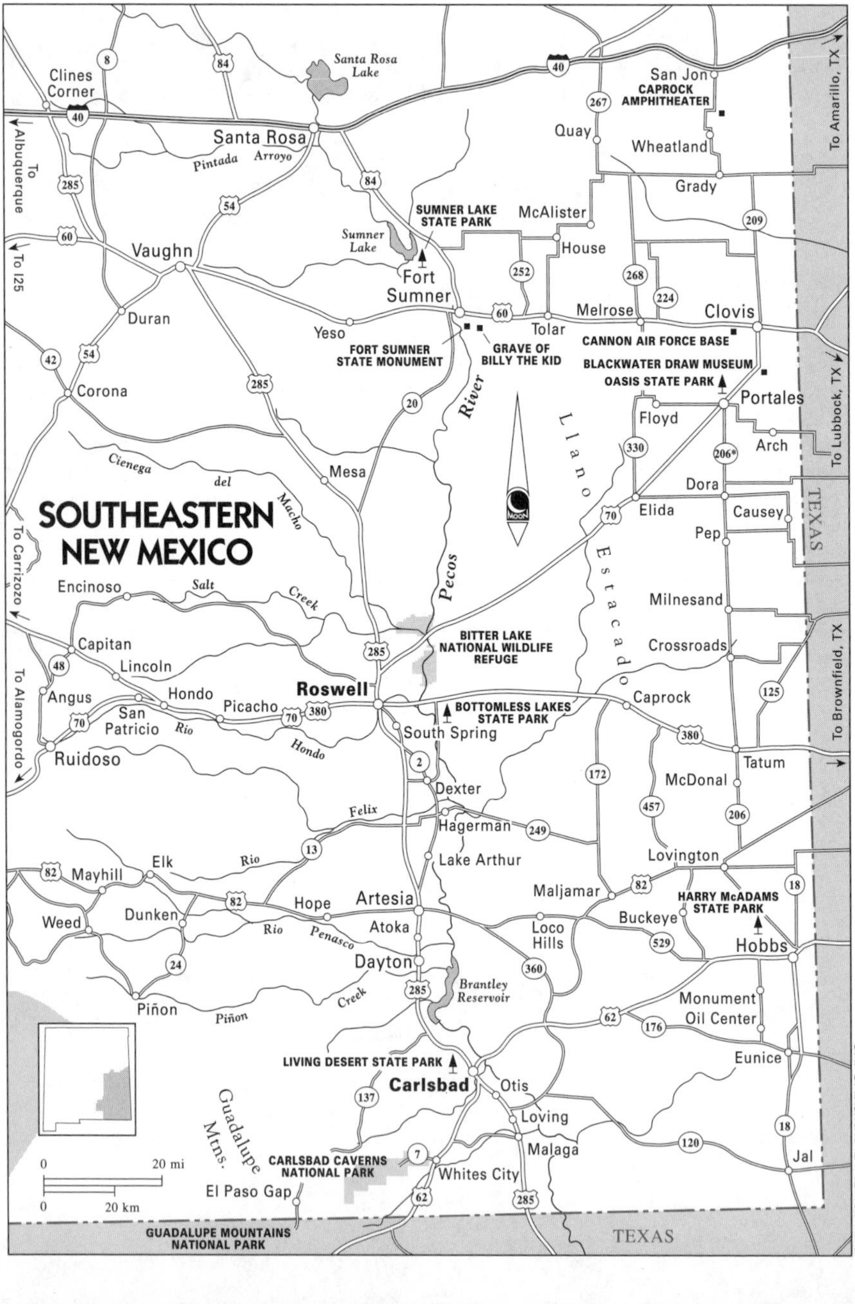

SOUTHEASTERN NEW MEXICO
Santa Rosa Lake
Clines Corner
Santa Rosa
Pintada Arroyo
To Albuquerque
To 125
Vaughn
Sumner Lake
SUMNER LAKE STATE PARK
Fort Sumner
McAlister
House
Quay
San Jon
CAPROCK AMPHITHEATER
Wheatland
Grady
To Amarillo, TX
Duran
Yeso
FORT SUMNER STATE MONUMENT
GRAVE OF BILLY THE KID
Tolar
Melrose
Clovis
CANNON AIR FORCE BASE
BLACKWATER DRAW MUSEUM
OASIS STATE PARK
Portales
Floyd
Arch
To Lubbock, TX
Corona
Cienega del Macho
Mesa
Pecos River
Llano Estacado
Dora
Elida
Causey
Pep
TEXAS
To Carrizozo
Encinoso
Salt Creek
Milnesand
Crossroads
BITTER LAKE NATIONAL WILDLIFE REFUGE
Capitan
Lincoln
Angus
Hondo
Roswell
Picacho
San Patricio
Rio Hondo
Ruidoso
To Alamogordo
BOTTOMLESS LAKES STATE PARK
South Spring
Caprock
To Brownfield, TX
Tatum
McDonal
Dexter
Felix
Hagerman
Lake Arthur
Lovington
Elk
Rio
Mayhill
Maljamar
HARRY McADAMS STATE PARK
Hope
Artesia
Dunken
Weed
Rio Penasco
Atoka
Loco Hills
Buckeye
Hobbs
Dayton
Brantley Reservoir
Piñon
Piñon Creek
Monument
Oil Center
Eunice
LIVING DESERT STATE PARK
Carlsbad
Otis
Loving
Guadalupe Mtns.
Malaga
Jal
CARLSBAD CAVERNS NATIONAL PARK
Whites City
El Paso Gap
0 20 mi
0 20 km
GUADALUPE MOUNTAINS NATIONAL PARK
TEXAS

furies, and passions—songs that would change forever the face of modern music.

Southeastern New Mexico is a flat and dry land, with high skies and wide horizons. It's a lonesome country, too, sparsely populated, with two-lane highways seeming to unfurl forever across the oil and cattle country of Curry, Lea, and Roosevelt Counties, the cotton and alfalfa fields of De Baca, Chaves, and Eddy Counties, and down through the Pecos River Valley, through Roswell, Artesia, and Carlsbad.

Especially in the far eastern part of this section of the state, about the only way to tell you're not in Texas is that the highways and roads are generally better across the border. Otherwise, things are pretty much the same on both sides of the border: oil rigs silhouette the sky, pumpjacks methodically and tirelessly draw oil from the ground, cattle graze in fields so huge it'll take two of you to see the other side, and folks speak in Dwight Yoakam drawls from the rolled-down windows of Texas-plated Caddies and Chevy pickups.

And then comes the night, the deep and starry night that evokes the maddened, vertiginous spirit of Van Gogh, Dylan Thomas, or some restless visionary in a Springsteen ballad.

The plains that dominate southeastern New Mexico are called the **Llano Estacado** (Staked or Stockaded Plain). Running 400 miles north to south, from Fort Sumner to Pecos, Texas, and 150 miles east to west, from West Texas to the Pecos River, the plains cover an area of 60,000 square miles. The origin of the name is uncertain, although some claim the stakes are actually the stalks of yucca, which stand tall over the flat desert. Others claim Comanche Indians drove stakes into the ground to mark trails in the otherwise indistinguishable landscape. A less apocryphal possibility is that the plains were once described as "stockaded," in reference to the fortified appearance of distant escarpments. At any rate, the land is so barren that it was described by a soldier passing through in 1849 as:

> *boundless as the ocean. Not a tree, shrub, or any other object, either animate or inanimate, relieved the monotony of the prospect; it was a vast illimitable expanse of desert prairie—the dread 'Llano Estacado' of New Mexico; or, in other words, the great Sahara of North America.*

Unlike in the Rio Grande Valley to the west and the mountains to the northwest, where Native Americans settled and lived for centuries before the white men came, southeastern New Mexico saw only nomadic bands of indigenous peoples, who came to the barren plains to hunt the buffalo, and then moved on to more fertile and sympathetic land. As early as 10,000 years ago, descendants of the earliest arrivals from Asia were hunting mastodon, bison, mammoth, and antelope on the plains of what is now southeastern New Mexico. The Blackwater Draw, a gravel pit near Clovis, where early hunters ambushed their prey, has proved an immensely rich archaeological lode, supplying eager anthropologists with evidence—particularly the famous "Clovis points"—of the first New Mexicans. Blackwater Draw Museum, just off Highway 70 between Clovis and Portales, is a combination lab and museum that displays the points, as well as bones of the animals on which the points were used.

In the 17th and 18th centuries, the Llano Estacado was Comanche country. Though various bands of Comanches roamed eastern New Mexico as far west as Taos and Santa Fe—mingling and warring with the Pueblo Indians—they pretty much had the plains to themselves until the late 19th century, when cowboys driving cattle from Texas to Colorado needed at least semipermanent stopovers.

The Goodnight-Loving and Chisum Trails were the major arteries of the Southwest, as men drove the lowing herds up to the Pecos River Valley and on to Denver. Roswell, on the Pecos River, was originally a cow town, founded in the early 1880s by ranchers moving north and west from Texas. Southeastern New Mexico is also where the infamous Billy the Kid made his last

HIGHLIGHTS

Bottomless Lakes State Park: camping, hiking, boating, swimming, and fishing

Carlsbad Caverns National Park: sight-seeing and hiking

Fort Sumner: museums, Billy the Kid's grave and various historical artifacts (and trinkets)

Roswell Museum and Art Center: historic and contemporary art and sculpture, and the Robert H. Goddard Collection of early rocketry

stand. He was killed just outside Fort Sumner in July 1881.

Two major discoveries put southeastern New Mexico on the national map. The first, right around the turn of the 20th century, was Carlsbad Caverns (actually, local Indians had known of the cave for hundreds of years), subsequently designated a national park in 1930. The second, and more fortuitous for southeastern New Mexicans, was oil in the Hobbs area in the late 1920s. As the "black gold" rose to the earth's surface, fortune seekers from around the country descended on Hobbs, establishing raucous communities of saloons and banks, brothels and tents.

Like most boomtowns, Hobbs busted within a few short years, and by the early 1930s, when the price of oil dropped from $1.05 to $.10 a barrel, three-quarters of the community had headed on. The area remained loyal to oil, though, and the economies of Hobbs and Lovington are still dominated by oil-related industry.

Meanwhile, Carlsbad Caverns continues to attract visitors from throughout the world. Truly one of the most bizarre and wondrous places on earth, this huge cave, millions of years old, invites both casual and serious spelunkers to explore its depths. You can either walk from the cave's mouth, via lighted trails, to its floor, or take an elevator straight down from the visitors center. You can also take a guided tour of the unappointed hollows of recently discovered Slaughter Canyon Cave.

Carlsbad has also been in the limelight lately for its underground salt beds. The federal Waste Isolation Pilot Plant calls for the burying of nuclear waste—much of it from the labs at Los Alamos—deep beneath the earth's surface. Though the myopic favor WIPP for its guarantee of much-needed jobs for southeastern New Mexicans, the project brings with it a number of serious problems, not the least of which is transporting the waste safely from around the country to its destination near Carlsbad.

Still, southeastern New Mexico remains largely as it's been through the years, as Indians, cowboys, oilers, and tourists have come and gone. Though much of the Llano Estacado is now irrigated with water from the Pecos River and from deep underground tables, and fields of cotton and alfalfa sprawl across the plains, the land is still dry and desolate—indeed a "vast, illimitable expanse."

Roswell

Roswell is a small town in the Northern Hemisphere of the planet Earth. It's surrounded by vast expanses of flat, completely undeveloped plateau land, where quadrupeds of the bovine species far outnumber their bipedal humanoid counterparts. If you're looking for a place to view the Earth without being seen yourself, you could hardly pick a better spot. Just be careful not to crash, as it appears the vehicle of another vacationing family did back in 1947. Surprisingly, there's still some debate among Earthlings as to whether this crash actually occurred, as some Earthlings in fact still trust the United States government, which has attempted to convince its people that the vehicle was instead a "weather balloon." I'm sure, had the Blorn family completed its mission and landed in Santa Fe, they'd never have even been noticed.

But seriously, folks . . .

Roswell (pop. 50,000; elev. 3,565 feet) is the largest community in southeastern New Mexico, and at the junction of two major New Mexico arteries (Highway 285 running north-south from Albuquerque to Carlsbad and beyond, and Highway 380 running east-west, from West Texas to Carrizozo and San Antonio), Roswell is a regular stopover for tourists and truckers on their way to other places. In addition, as a commercial hub for much of the southeastern part of New Mexico, Roswell also attracts farmers, ranchers, and business folk from the surrounding communities of Hobbs, Clovis, Vaughn, Carlsbad, and Artesia.

It also attracts UFO junkies. The International UFO Museum and Research Center draws travelers from all over, well, the world, who come to learn more about the alleged crash of an alien spaceship near Roswell on July 7, 1947. In fact, the town has capitalized on the renewed interest and publicity that the crash has generated—including an episode on TV's *Unsolved Mysteries* and a major motion picture, *Roswell,* which convincingly recounts the story of the crash and purported government cover-up. The familiar over-sized triangular head of the aliens appears on Roswell coffee cups and lapel pins. I half expected to see "Grandma and Grandpa visited the planet Earth and all I got was this lousy T-shirt."

When I last visited Roswell, a small piece of metal from the alleged crash had recently been found near the "impact site." After having been identified as an unfamiliar alloy of copper and silver, the once-cylindrical fragment was under constant video surveillance at the sheriff's office. I was told by a docent at the UFO museum that Los Alamos Labs had offered to examine it, but needed four days to do so. Scowling, he said:

> ***Yeah, right, we're going to turn it over to the government for four days. Can you imagine what we'd get back?***

He then told me that he had asked the sheriff what he'd do if the CIA demanded it. The sheriff told him that they'd have to arrest him first. (The piece of metal was later positively identified as a scrap from a St. George, Utah, jewelry studio.)

History

Roswell was a stopover town well before 1947. During the 1860s and '70s, cowboys moving cattle up the Chisum and Goodnight-Loving Trails between Texas and Colorado, as well as folks riding the train between Amarillo and Carlsbad, would lay over in Roswell. The name Roswell comes from Van C. Smith, one of the town's first businessmen and visionaries, who named it in honor of his father. In 1891, the Fort Worth Military University opened a branch here, although in 1893 the school's name was changed to the New Mexico Military Institute. Also in 1891, a huge artesian well was discovered under what is now downtown Roswell, securing the area's future as an important agriculture center.

Agriculture was Roswell's primary economic base through most of the first half of the 20th century. But in the 1940s and '50s the economy diversified when the U.S. government established the Roswell Army Flying School, which in 1948 was officially designated Walker Air Force Base (named for Brigadier General Kenneth

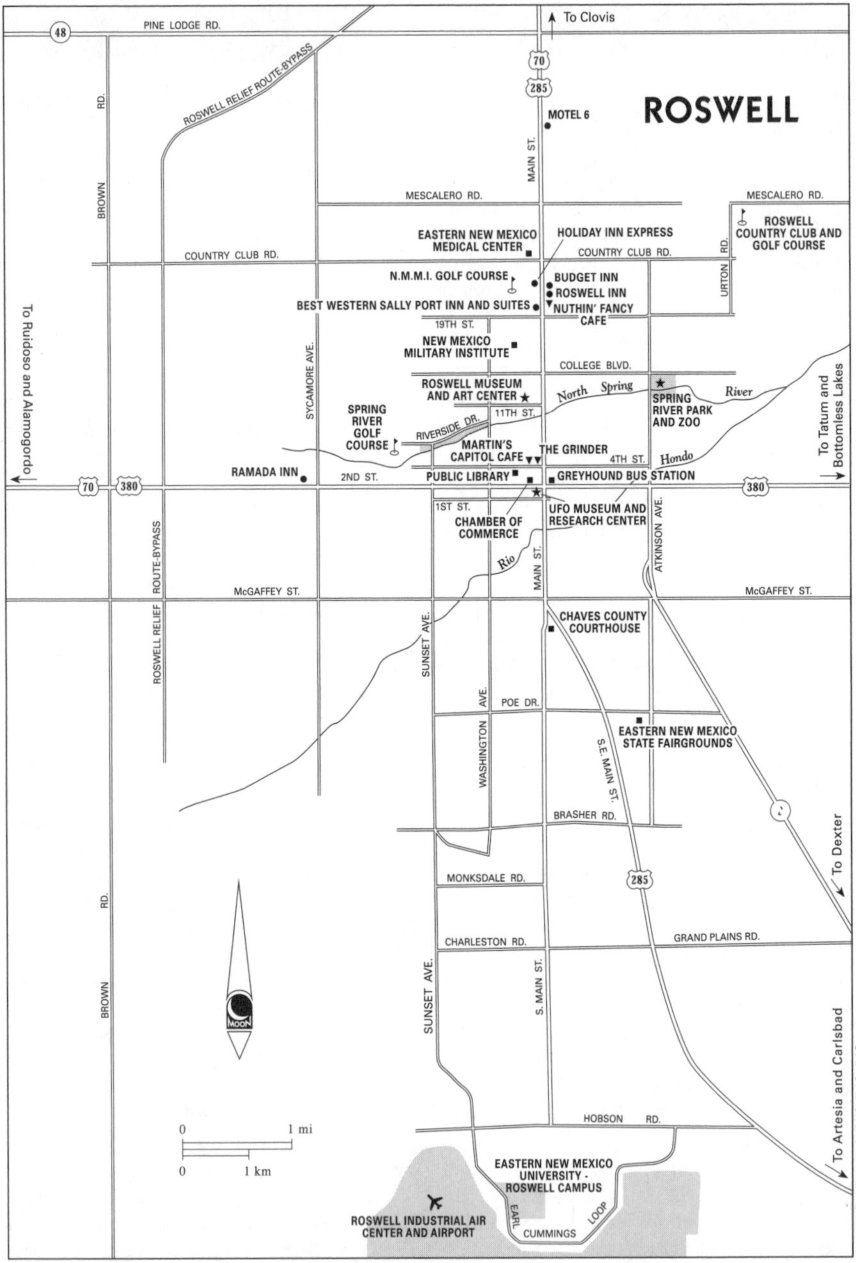
ROSWELL
To Clovis
PINE LODGE RD.
48
70
285
ROSWELL RELIEF ROUTE-BYPASS
BROWN RD.
MOTEL 6
MAIN ST.
MESCALERO RD.
EASTERN NEW MEXICO MEDICAL CENTER
HOLIDAY INN EXPRESS
ROSWELL COUNTRY CLUB AND GOLF COURSE
COUNTRY CLUB RD.
URTON RD.
N.M.M.I. GOLF COURSE
BUDGET INN
ROSWELL INN
BEST WESTERN SALLY PORT INN AND SUITES
NUTHIN' FANCY CAFE
19TH ST.
NEW MEXICO MILITARY INSTITUTE
COLLEGE BLVD.
ROSWELL MUSEUM AND ART CENTER
North Spring River
SPRING RIVER PARK AND ZOO
SPRING RIVER GOLF COURSE
11TH ST.
RIVERSIDE DR.
MARTIN'S CAPITOL CAFE
THE GRINDER
4TH ST.
Hondo
SYCAMORE AVE.
To Ruidoso and Alamogordo
To Tatum and Bottomless Lakes
RAMADA INN
2ND ST.
PUBLIC LIBRARY
GREYHOUND BUS STATION
380
1ST ST.
CHAMBER OF COMMERCE
UFO MUSEUM AND RESEARCH CENTER
ATKINSON AVE.
Rio
McGAFFEY ST.
ROSWELL RELIEF ROUTE-BYPASS
SUNSET AVE.
CHAVES COUNTY COURTHOUSE
WASHINGTON AVE.
POE DR.
EASTERN NEW MEXICO STATE FAIRGROUNDS
S.E. MAIN ST.
BRASHER RD.
To Dexter
MONKSDALE RD.
CHARLESTON RD.
GRAND PLAINS RD.
S. MAIN ST.
MOON
HOBSON RD.
0 1 mi
0 1 km
EASTERN NEW MEXICO UNIVERSITY - ROSWELL CAMPUS
EARL CUMMINGS LOOP
ROSWELL INDUSTRIAL AIR CENTER AND AIRPORT
To Artesia and Carlsbad

SOUTHEASTERN NM

Walker, of Cerrillos, New Mexico, who lost his life in the South Pacific during World War II). Eventually, nearly half of Roswell's workforce depended either directly or indirectly on Walker, so when the base was suddenly shut down in 1967, the town was thrown into a temporary panic, and 5,000 Roswellites fled for greener pastures; by 1970, the population had fallen from 50,000 to 33,000. In a short time, though, Roswell completely recovered from the loss, renovating some of the old base's buildings and putting them to use as office complexes, a hospital, homes, and a branch of Eastern New Mexico University.

SIGHTS

International UFO Museum and Research Center

Capturing perfectly, if inadvertently, both the seriousness and silliness of the UFO phenomenon, this intriguing little museum right downtown is definitely worth a stop, even if you're just passing through—New Mexico is rife with art and history museums, but you're not going to see anything like this anywhere else in your travels.

COURTESY OF NEW MEXICO DEPARTMENT OF TOURISM/DAN MONAGHAN

UFO Museum in Roswell

The focus of this city-run museum is the alleged UFO crash of July 7, 1947, which was written up in papers around the world before the United States government had time to report the official story. When the "official" report came out, it stated that what had fallen to earth here was an Air Force weather balloon. Among the displays here are replicas of the original newspaper accounts dating from both before and after the government's intervention; official statements and documents by locals who were involved (including the coroner, who was called in the middle of the night and asked if he had any four-foot hermetically sealed caskets); photos of UFOs from around the world; and two large video-viewing rooms, one regularly playing the story of the Roswell crash. A large library and research center holds out-of-print UFO-related books, documents by reputable scientists and military personnel testifying to the legitimacy of the crash, and clippings from newspaper and magazine accounts of the Roswell crash and other sightings and incidents. There's also a gift shop, with T-shirts, coffee cups, books, and reproductions of newspaper accounts and some of the scientific documentation.

The museum, at 114 N. Main, is open daily 9 A.M.–5 P.M. Admission is free, though donations—gladly accepted—go toward further research and acquisitions, and further efforts to fully and finally debunk the alleged government cover-up. For more information, write P.O. Box 2221, Roswell, NM 88202, or phone 505/625-9495.

Roswell Museum and Art Center

This is an eclectic little center in a stylishly modern building just off Main Street. Typifying New Mexico in the way it embraces both ancient history and modern technology, the museum displays a huge array of art and artifacts. First built in 1937 as a WPA project, the center today is 16 times its original size, with 17 galleries, eight offices, a gift/book store, work areas, and classrooms. The museum includes the Southwestern Collection of Paintings, Prints, and Sculpture, with works by Georgia O'Keeffe, Stuart Davis, John Marin, and others; the Rogers Aston Collection of American Indian and Western Art, including about 2,000 pieces (from Native American quillwork to Spanish armor and Western firearms) documenting the history of the Southwest; the Peter Hurd Collection, work by the Roswell-born landscape and portrait painter which depicts the mystery and magic of the Southwest; and the Native American and Hispanic Collection, including stunning pieces of 20th-century Indian pottery. Perhaps the most interesting, though, if only because it's so different from the Indian and other Southwestern art typically found in New Mexico museums, is the Robert H. Goddard Collection. In March 1926, Goddard launched the world's first liquid-fuel rocket. This wing of the museum includes an exact replica of the shop in which Goddard worked for the 12 years he was in Roswell, as well as engine parts, rocket assemblies, nose cones, and photos of the early experiments. Also on display is the space suit that Silver City, New Mexico, astronaut Harrison H. Schmidt wore on the moon.

The Roswell Museum and Art Center is open Monday–Saturday 9 A.M.–5 P.M., Sunday and holidays 1–5 P.M. Tours can be arranged on weekdays by special appointment. Admission is free, donations encouraged.

For more information, write Roswell Museum and Art Center, 100 W. 11th St., Roswell, NM 88201, or phone 505/624-6744.

Bottomless Lakes State Park

Named for the seven sinkholes scattered around the park's rambling acreage, Bottomless Lakes offers fishing, swimming, camping, windsurfing, and hiking. The lakes were formed when underground caverns collapsed and filled with rainwater. Though thought to be "bottomless" by 19th-century cowboys, they actually range 17–90 feet in depth. They also vary greatly in size: Devil's Inkwell, for example, is fewer than 100 feet across, while Lea Lake (the only one where swimming is allowed) covers roughly 13 acres and offers a sandy beach and boat rentals. Cottonwood Lake, one of the first you come to after the park's entrance, features a visitors center that explains the area's geography, as well as a nature trail leading to a view of Mirror Lake and Lake in the Making, a "sinkhole in progress." Two of the lakes are too alkaline for fish, while four others are stocked regularly with rainbow trout.

Camping is permitted throughout Bottomless Lakes State Park, although you should check in at the visitors center for any restrictions. If you prefer a structured campground, continue south on Highway 409 to Lea Lake, where you'll find campsites with hookups and a small concession-operated store and restaurant. Day use is $4 per car, and camping is $8 ($12 with hookups). To get to Bottomless Lakes State Park, take Highway 380 10 miles east from Roswell, turn right on Highway 409, and follow the signs. For information, phone 505/624-6058.

Bitter Lake National Wildlife Refuge

Occupying nearly 25,000 acres of marshy grassland 10 miles northeast of Roswell, this refuge provides excellent opportunities to view migrating ducks, geese, and sandhill cranes, especially in late fall and winter. An eight-mile self-guided auto tour through the refuge's south section has a number of viewing points and picnic areas, and a map of the area is available from the Bitter Lake headquarters. Take Highway 380 east or 70 north from Roswell and watch for the signs. To make sure the birds are "in," phone ahead, 505/622-6755.

Spring River Park and Zoo

If you take a fancy to seeing pathetic-looking wild animals (llamas, foxes, bobcats, etc.) in too-small cages, pacing angrily under hot desert skies, check out the Spring River Zoo. Otherwise, you might just enjoy a leisurely picnic at the adjoining park, where there's a kids' playground and large lawns. Park and zoo hours are daily 10 A.M.–sundown.

PRACTICALITIES

Accommodations

Roswell offers the visitor or passer-through a broad range of lodging possibilities, from quick-crash-

and-hit-the-road highwayside motels to modern hotels with spacious lobbies and room service. You'll find most of the nicer digs along Highway 285 (North Main Street), while the cheaper places tend to be along Highway 70/380 (which turns into 2nd Street) on the west side of town. One of the west side's newer and cleaner places is the **Ramada Inn,** 2803 W. 2nd, 505/623-9440 ($50–100). Large, clean rooms are also available at good rates at the **Best Western Sally Port Inn and Suites** just north of New Mexico Military Institute at 2000 N. Main, 505/622-6430 or 800/528-1234 ($50–100), and at the **Holiday Inn Express,** 2300 N. Main, 505/627-9900. Both $50–100. You'll find the least expensive rooms in town at the **Budget Inn,** 2101 N. Main St., 505/623-6050, and the **Motel 6,** 3307 N. Main, 505/625-6666. Both under $50.

Food

If I lived in Roswell, I'd eat at **Martin's Capitol Cafe,** 110 W. 4th, 505/624-2111, at least once a week. This is excellent (and hot!) Mexican and New Mexican food at very reasonable prices. Entrées—tamales, enchiladas, etc.—are $5–8. Open Monday–Saturday 6 A.M.–8:30 P.M. The **Nuthin' Fancy Cafe,** 2103 N. Main, 505/623-4098, serves breakfast, lunch, and dinner with lots of homemade dishes—soups, breads, pies—and entrées in the $7–10 range. Open daily at 6 A.M., closing weeknights at 9 P.M., weekends at 9:30 P.M. You'll also find lots of small *mama-y-papa* cafés around town serving authentic and inexpensive Mexican food.

Standard hub-town franchises here include **Denny's,** at both 200 and 2200 N. Main; **Cattle Baron,** 12th and Main; **Golden Corral Steak House,** 1415 W. 2nd; and a number of others. In addition, the **Sally Port Inn** has a dining room serving breakfast, lunch, and dinner.

For a caffeine jolt, check out **The Grinder,** 104 W. 4th, 505/623-2997, or 4501 N. Main, 505/622-3897, where you can get iced and regular espresso drinks and other gourmet coffees.

Recreation

In addition to the picnicking, fishing, hiking, camping, bird-watching, and windsurfing at Spring River Park, Bottomless Lakes State Park, and Bitter Lake National Wildlife Refuge (see Sights, above), Roswell has three golf courses: **Roswell Country Club and Golf Course,** north of town on Country Club Road East, 505/622-3410; **Spring River Golf Course** at 1612 W. 8th St., 505/622-9506; and the course at **New Mexico Military Institute** (phone 505/622-6250 for the school's main office). You'll also find a number of **tennis courts** in Roswell, including public courts at Cahoon Park on West 8th Street and at Spring River Park on East 12th.

Annual Events

The **UFO Encounter Festival,** July 4 weekend, offers tours of the "impact site," planetarium shows, and an "Alien Chase" fun run, as well as booths with crafts and "UFO information." The **Eastern New Mexico State Fair,** oldest fair in the state (dating to 1892), is held every September at the Eastern New Mexico State Fairgrounds on Southeast Main Street (on your left heading down Highway 285 toward Carlsbad). The fair features agriculture displays, arts and crafts, rodeos, and food booths. In November, Roswell hosts the **Wool Bowl,** the national junior college championship football game.

Information and Services

For further information about Chaves County and the Roswell area, write the **chamber of commerce** at Drawer 70B, Roswell, NM 88201, or phone 505/624-6870. The chamber's offices are at 131 W. 2nd Street. The Roswell **public library** is at 301 Pennsylvania St. (between West 3rd and West 4th), 505/622-7101.

Eastern New Mexico Medical Center, 405 W. Country Club Rd., 505/622-8170, is a full-scale medical facility. Phone the Roswell Police Department at 505/624-6770 and the state police in Roswell at 505/622-7200.

Transportation

Mesa Air, 800/MESA-AIR (800/637-2247), offers passenger service to Roswell from Albuquerque and Dallas. Roswell's airport is south of town at Roswell Industrial Air Center. Bus service to Roswell is available from **Texas, New Mexico, and Oklahoma Coaches,** 505/622-2510, under contract with Greyhound.

Artesia

About 10 miles south of Roswell, Highway 285 forks, with an alternative route, Highway 2, arcing over a little closer to the Pecos River paralleling the main highway for about 35 miles. Either way, it's pretty desolate country—flat prairieland and cotton fields, broken by an occasional hillock or farmhouse. On Highway 2, or Alternative 285, are the farming towns of Dexter and Hagerman. The Dexter Fish Hatchery in Dexter breeds and studies rare and endangered species of fish. Visitors are welcome.

Named for the huge underground water table and the artesian wells first drilled in the early part of the 20th century, Artesia (pop. 13,000) is a small oil and agricultural community in the heart of the Pecos River Valley, about midway between Roswell and Carlsbad. Though the underground water in the area gives the town its name, Artesia relies for its economic health on the underground oil in the area: the oil industry employs more than twice as many people as the town's second-largest employer, Artesia Public Schools. The other major Artesian concern, agriculture, also keeps the town bustling, the principal crops being cotton (6,000 bales a year), alfalfa (180,000 tons a year), and pecans (250,000 pounds a year). In addition, 65,000 Artesia-raised cattle find their ways to various meat counters each year.

The Abo Underground School in Artesia is a civil defense shelter, as well as a grade school. In case of nuclear attack, it purportedly will shelter 500 students and as many as 2,000 Artesia adults. Last I heard, Mickey Rooney, the Atomic Kid himself, was stumbling radiantly across the prairie looking to enroll in classes.

History

The first white settler in the Artesia area was Union soldier John F. Truitt, who named his homestead Blake's Spring. Later part of the Chisum cattle holding, Truitt's place became known as South Chisum Camp, and in the summer of 1880, the camp employed the notorious outlaw Billy the Kid.

By 1894, when the Pecos Valley Railroad was completed, the community's name had been changed to Miller's Siding; it was changed again a couple of years later when John Chisum's niece married Baldwin Stegman, and they named their new town—now complete with a post office—Stegman. In a short time, though, the area's vast underground water resources had been discovered, and the name was again changed, this time, and finally, to Artesia. In November 1903, the Artesia Townsite and the Artesia Improvement companies combined forces and drilled an 830-foot-deep well—at the time the deepest in the world—and water, always in short supply in New Mexico, flowed freely over the area's prairieland. During the next three years, Artesia grew into a substantial farming community, as 1,200 settlers—attracted by the newfound irrigation—put down stakes in the area.

In 1923, a different kind of natural resource was discovered beneath the Artesia earth: oil. Although today, regions to the east of Artesia—around Hobbs and Lovington, particularly—are larger contributors to New Mexico's overall oil production, the state's very first oil-producing well was drilled in Artesia in 1924.

Historical Museum and Art Center

Look for displays of rocks and minerals, early medical tools, local Indian artifacts, and other vestiges of local history in this small museum occupying a restored home at 505 W. Richardson, 505/748-2390. Hours are Tuesday–Saturday 8 A.M.–5 P.M. Admission is free. An art center in the house next door displays work by Southwestern artists.

Accommodations and Food

The **Pecos Inn Best Western,** 2209 W. Main St., 505/748-3324, has clean and spacious rooms ($50–100). Its dining room is open for breakfast, lunch, and dinner, with dinner entrées running $6–15. **La Fonda,** 210 W. Main, 505/746-9377, serves Mexican lunches and dinners for $5–10.

Information and Services

For more information on the Artesia area, contact the Artesia **Chamber of Commerce,** P.O. Box 99, Artesia, NM 88211-0099, 505/746-2744. The Artesia **public library** is at 306 W. Richardson St., 505/746-4252.

Artesia General Hospital is at 702 N. 13th St., 505/748-3333. Guadalupe Medical Center is 36 miles south in Carlsbad, 505/887-6633. The nonemergency number for both the Artesia Police Department and the New Mexico state police in Artesia is 505/746-2703.

Transportation

Mesa Air, 800/MESA-AIR (800/637-2247), flies into both Roswell and Carlsbad.

Carlsbad

The drive down Highway 285 from Albuquerque, through Roswell, Artesia, and on to Carlsbad (pop. 25,000; elev. 3,100 feet), is long and dry; in the summer, temperatures regularly soar into the 90s. As you barrel along, the desert monotony disturbed only by occasional railroad towns, a few cattle, junipers and piñon in the north and mesquite and yucca in the south, it's difficult to imagine that the entire area was once deep beneath the ocean's surface—teeming with the sea's vital organisms. Carlsbad, too, deep in the southeastern corner of New Mexico, is mostly dry today (receiving a scant 12.4 inches of rainfall annually), save for the meandering Pecos River—which rolls south on the east side of town—and a few small reservoirs.

But just 28 miles out of town, stunning evidence of the area's prehistoric relationship with vast amounts of water awaits the casual spelunker. Carlsbad Caverns, one of the most remarkable and geologically important cavern sites in the world, plummets deep into the earth's crust, allowing visitors to view the mystery and splendor of water-caused erosion and buildup. Were it not

Don't hesitate to explore downtown Carlsbad while you're in the area visiting the caverns.

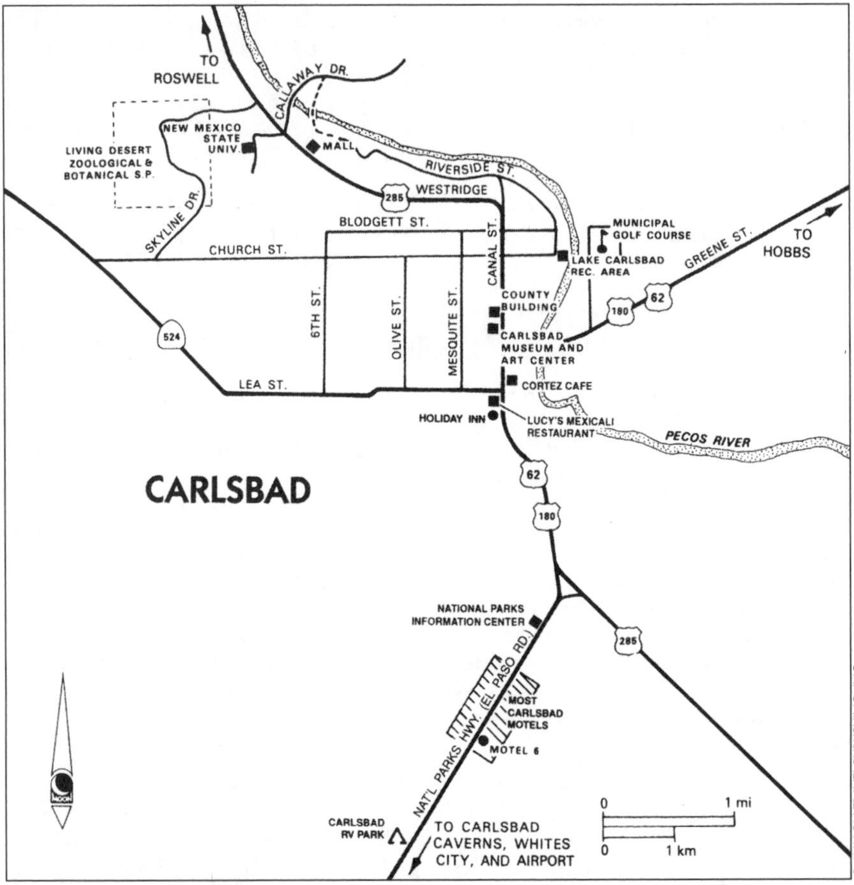

for the caverns, Carlsbad would be little more than just another small eastern New Mexico plains town important only to those who farm, ranch, and mine in the area, and to the small academic community of New Mexico State University.

Lately, though, Carlsbad has come into the public eye for a reason other than the caverns: The United States Department of Energy plans to bury low- and intermediate-level nuclear waste (much of it from the labs at Los Alamos) in the salt beds beneath the Carlsbad ground. The WIPP, or Waste Isolation Pilot Plant, has been a divisive issue for New Mexicans, who are typically both environmentally sensitive as well as hungry for economic development. According to an impact study done by New Mexico State University and Los Alamos National Laboratory (not exactly an objective observer), WIPP added millions of dollars to the New Mexico economy in the late 1980s, mostly in the form of wages and salaries, materials and services, capital equipment, and construction. In addition, WIPP directly created more than 1,000 jobs for New Mexicans (though in 1993 some of those were lost as a result of Department of Energy rulings). But at what cost? Opponents to WIPP claim that though the salt beds may in fact be the best way to deal with nuclear waste, transporting it south to the Carlsbad area is immensely dangerous, especially as the route from Los Alamos passes directly through several highly populated areas, despite a Santa Fe bypass.

Carlsbad, meanwhile, continues along the course it set for itself in the days before nuclear waste was a problem: the potash mines continue to operate, and farmers still plant, irrigate, cut, and reap the alfalfa that rolls across the Carlsbad-area flatlands.

And Carlsbad Caverns continues to attract tourists. About 700,000 people visit Carlsbad Caverns each year. From all corners of the globe, travelers put up with the barren desert drive to experience one of the earth's most intriguing natural wonders.

History

During the late 19th and early 20th centuries, Carlsbad was cowboy country in the true American tradition. Cattle were driven through the area by the thousands—most often west from Texas up to northern New Mexico and Colorado, and even into Wyoming and Montana. Eddy, as the town was originally known, was named for two local ranchers, John and Charles Eddy. In 1898, the town's name was changed to Carlsbad, after Karlsbad, Bohemia, whose pure mineral water was rivaled by that of a spring northwest of town. The Eddy County courthouse in Carlsbad, built in 1891 and rebuilt in 1939, is still standing, its entrances adorned with the cattle brands of local early-20th-century ranchers.

It wasn't until the 1920s that Carlsbad truly made its mark on the map. It was then that stories of a huge cave in the nearby hills began to attract national attention. It's uncertain who the first white person to see the cavern was, but in 1883 a 12-year-old boy was lowered into the cave by his father. According to some stories, two years later, on an early summer evening, two cowboys were looking for stray cattle when they saw bats flying out of a huge hole in the ground. On October 25, 1923, Calvin Coolidge proclaimed that hole Carlsbad Cave National Monument, and it has been an immensely and deservedly popular tourist attraction and site of geologic field study ever since.

The **Carlsbad Museum and Art Center** in downtown Carlsbad displays Indian and prehistoric artifacts, including bones from early New World camels, mammoths, and horses. Also exhibited are local crafts. Open Monday–Saturday 10 A.M.–5 P.M., on Fox Street, one block west of Canal Street. For more information, call 505/887-0276.

CARLSBAD CAVERNS NATIONAL PARK

Two hundred and fifty million years ago, during the Permian period, the mountains against which Carlsbad is nestled were a giant underwater reef—which geologists have dubbed Capitan Reef. Over the years, the ocean receded and the nearby Guadalupe Mountains were uplifted from the basin floor. Fractures, filled with a mixture of briny and fresh water, developed in the reef, and sulfurous gases, which seeped up from deep inside the earth, began to dissolve the limestone. Meanwhile, water remained in the resulting honeycombs, and over time, the reef was buried under gypsum and salt deposits.

Somewhere between two million and four million years ago, the earth heaved, and massive uplifts tilted to the west what had already been higher ground and pushed the old reef—by now the air-filled Guadalupe Ridge—back up above the valley floor.

Over the years, water percolating down through the giant chambers has created strikingly bizarre and fantastic formations. Limestone and calcite deposits appear at times lunar, at times like something out of Grimm's Fairy Tales. Stalagmites tower 60 feet from the cavern's floor. Stalactites hang from the ceiling, some massive and broadly conical, others narrow and long, like icicles, distorted and twisting. Huge boulders rest precipitously where they fell—four million years ago. One chamber, the Big Room (750 feet under the visitors center) is 1,800 feet long and 255 feet high.

Although the earliest explorers of the cave were Indians—faded pictographs appear at the cave's mouth, and mescal cooking pits are scattered nearby—they didn't venture in very far,

© STEPHEN METZGER

Hikers at Natural Entrance begin winding down into the cave.

mostly because of the huge drop-off immediately past the opening. Once the cave was discovered by local settlers and word of its existence—and the bats'—began to spread, people figured there might be a way to make some money here. In 1903, a claim was filed for the cave's guano (bat dung, which is rich in nitrates and very effective as a fertilizer). For the first fifth of the century, guano was brought out of the caves in mine cars and then sent to Southern California, where farmers were beginning to plant huge groves of citrus trees. Unfortunately, transportation costs were quite high, and the operations weren't, as we say today, cost-effective. In fact, the guano was so rich that en route—baked by the Southwestern sun—it often would spontaneously combust.

The Carlsbad Caverns bats (sounds like a baseball team . . .) don't venture very far into the cave, so early exploration was limited: miners went to where the guano was and no farther. One of the miners, though, James Larkin White, who had been a cowboy in the area and had first entered the cave in 1898, was so fascinated with the cave that he spent his spare time exploring it on his own. Alone with just a lantern, he'd venture into its recesses, returning with fascinating stories of what he'd seen. By 1922, the commissioner of the General Land Office, William Spry, was convinced White's stories were legitimate, and he assigned Mineral Examiner Robert Holley to investigate the cave as a possible national monument. Holley's report reads in part:

> ***I enter upon this task with a feeling of temerity as I am wholly conscious of the feebleness of my efforts to convey in words the deep conflicting emotions, the feeling of fear and awe, and the desire for an inspired understanding of the Divine Creator's work that presents to the human eye such a complex aggregate of natural wonders in such a limited space.***

The park drew international attention after the January 1924 edition of *National Geographic* ran photos and a story on the cave's exploration by geologist Dr. Willis T. Lee. In 1930, President Herbert Hoover declared Carlsbad Caverns a national park.

The first visitors to the park were lowered into one of the two "mine shafts" in a large bucket and explored the cave on wooden stairways. Modern visitors can either wander the paved trail down into the cave or take an elevator straight down from the visitors center. Whichever way you enter, exit from the cave is by elevator. Small CD players can be rented for a nominal fee and provide an audio tour of the cavern.

Exploring the Cave

Two self-guided tours of Carlsbad Caverns are offered, the Natural Entrance Tour and the Big Room Tour; both end up at the underground lunch room near the Big Room. The Natural Entrance Tour begins at the visitors center and enters the cave through the main entrance—the same gaping hole from which the bats depart on summer evenings. The trail is paved, but steep in places. It wanders by a number of stunning formations, including Whale's Mouth, Iceberg Rock, and the Boneyard. The Big Room Tour begins with a 750-foot descent in an elevator to the cave's floor, where a circuitous but mostly flat 1.25-mile trail explores the Big Room. Along the Big Room trail are the 42-foot-high Twin Domes, the 62-foot-high Giant Dome in the Hall of Giants, and the Bottomless Pit, now known to be 140 feet deep. The temperature inside the caves remains a constant 56°F. Rangers wander the trails, answering questions and giving periodic informal lectures.

Both tours cost $6 for adults and $3 for children ages six to 15. Children under six are free when accompanied by an adult. Separate, ranger-guided tours of King's Palace, Queen's Chamber, the Papoose Room, the Green Lake Room, Hall of the White Giant, and other nearby caves are available for an additional $8–20. The visitors center opens daily at 8 A.M. Tours begin at 8:30 A.M. The last Natural Entrance Tour begins at 3:30 P.M. (2 P.M. winter), and the last Big Room Tour begins at 5 P.M. (3:30 P.M. winter). The last elevator from the Big Room to the visitors center is at 6:30 P.M. (4:55 P.M. in winter), and the visitors center closes at 7 P.M. (5:30 P.M. winter). The park is open every day except December 25.

Wear sturdy and comfortable walking shoes, and bring a light sweater for the cool temperature.

The visitors center offers air-conditioned pet kennels. For more information, phone 505/785-2232 or 800/967-CAVE (800/967-2283), or write Carlsbad Caverns National Park, 3225 National Parks Hwy., Carlsbad, NM 88220. You can also get information from the Carlsbad Chamber of Commerce at 505/887-6516 or 800/221-1224.

Bat Flights

Every summer evening, just around sundown, hundreds of thousands of bats leave the cave mouth in a cloudy hurricane. They're hungry

THE CARLSBAD BATS

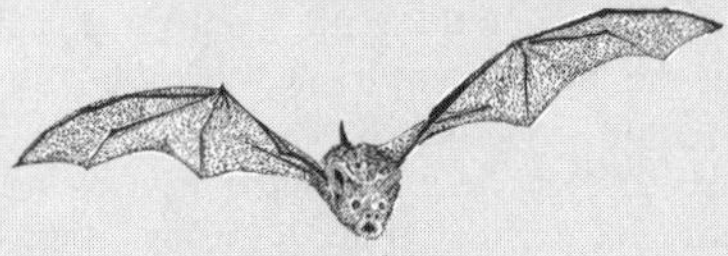

LOUISE FOOTE

The bats in Carlsbad Caverns are migratory Mexican free-tail bats; they spend their summers in New Mexico, then head back across the border in winter. The adult Mexican free-tail weighs about half an ounce and has an 11-inch wingspread. The Carlsbad bats spend their days about a half mile inside the cave—not on the tour route—hanging in close bunches from the ceiling, 30–80 feet above the cave floor.

It is thought that the Carlsbad bat colony once numbered in the millions, but the use of pesticides in the bats' hunting grounds has severely lessened their numbers. The current Carlsbad colony probably numbers about 300,000 individuals, and the ban on some of the more harmful pesticides should pave the way to a healthier and larger population.

The bats usually arrive in late April or early May and stay until October or November. Young are born in the spring, and by midsummer they are joining their folks on sorties.

The bats leave in a group, spiraling up out of the cave's mouth; the pitch is too steep for them to fly straight out. As many as 5,000 bats leave the cave each minute, looking something like a swirling cloud that disperses as it rises above the amphitheater and the surrounding grounds.

and going hunting, insects in the area being their sole food source. A stone and concrete amphitheater has been built at the cave's entrance, and visitors sit and listen to a ranger lecture while awaiting the nightly flight. The bats are on no identifiable schedule, and no one knows what determines exactly when they leave. They've been known to leave as late as midnight, and not at all. It's usually between 7:30 and 8:30 P.M., though, and rangers "guestimate" each night's flight time by the previous three or four. The lecture begins around sunset. Admission is free. One of the real thrills of a Carlsbad visit, the bat flights are particularly exciting for the kids in the audience. Phone the chamber of commerce or the caverns' offices for specific times.

Slaughter Canyon Cave

More hardy and adventurous visitors can tour Slaughter Canyon Cave, formerly called New Cave. This cave was discovered in 1937 and is not appointed with electricity and paved walkways. A half-mile walk takes you to the entrance, and rangers lead 25-member groups inside. Visitors must provide their own transportation to the parking lot, approximately 23 miles from the Carlsbad Caverns visitors center. Slaughter Canyon Cave is open only weekends during the winter and daily Memorial Day through mid-August. Tour cost is $15; children under six are not permitted. Allow about three hours, wear sturdy shoes, and bring a flashlight and water. Tour departure times are scheduled from the cave entrance, not the parking lot. Reservations are mandatory; call 800/967-CAVE (800/967-2283). To get to the Slaughter Canyon Cave parking lot, turn off Highway 62/180 five miles southwest of White's City.

White's City

This small town at the entrance to Carlsbad Caverns National Park is 20 miles from the town of Carlsbad and was founded in 1927 by Charley White, no relation to early cave explorer Jim White. Today it's a touristy and gimmicky souvenir stop, comprising an information center; gift shop specializing in cave and Indian mementos; museum with antique dolls, guns, and barbed wire; grocery store and post office; Fast Jack's Restaurant; and the Velvet Garter Saloon and Restaurant. There's also an RV park and the White's City Best Western Motel. Summer weeknights, melodrama is offered at Granny's Opera House.

Living Desert State Park

In many ways, this would be the perfect place to begin a visit to southern New Mexico. Living Desert State Park, on the hillside overlooking the expansive Pecos Valley, offers a fascinating introduction to life in the desert, particularly the Chihuahuan Desert, which ranges from Mexico up into Texas and southeastern New Mexico.

Self-guided trails lead through sand dunes and cactus, arroyos and juniper, and extensive wildlife exhibits. Marked by identifying plaques, the plants and animals are mostly from the area, although there is also a "Succulents of the World" exhibit, with cacti from Mexico, Bolivia, Madagascar, and South Africa.

Among the many types of plants displayed in a natural setting are furniture cholla, cowtongue, prickly-pear cactus, yucca, acacia, sotol, and agave. Rattlesnakes, king and gopher snakes, desert skinks, eagles, hawks, ravens, javelinas (collared peccary), pronghorn, bison, and even a gray wolf occupy the pens and cages along the path.

The park is actually a rehabilitation center as well as a zoo, some of the animals having been either injured or found sick. Injured animals are nursed back to health and sometimes—if it is determined they can survive on their own—returned to the wild.

The Living Desert State Park is open daily 8 A.M.–8 P.M. (last entry at 6:30 P.M.) Memorial Day–Labor Day, and 9 A.M.–5 P.M. (last entry at 3:30 P.M.) the rest of the year. Admission is $4 for adults, $2 for kids 7–12; kids six and under are admitted free. Organized groups of 20 or more pay $2 per person.

For more information, call 505/887-5516 or write Living Desert State Park, P.O. Box 100, Carlsbad, NM 88220-0100.

PRACTICALITIES

Accommodations

Motels in Carlsbad vary from the run-down-looking and very inexpensive ($20 a night for a single) to upscale Best Westerns and a Holiday Inn. A number of major economy chains fall somewhere in between. Most are on the main drag through town, or just southwest of town on National Parks Highway (El Paso Road).

Under $50

Lodging in this price range includes basic no-frills rooms at the **Carlsbad Inn,** 2019 S. Canal, 505/887-1171, and at the **Motel 6,** 3824 National Parks Hwy., 505/885-0011.

$50–100

The **Best Western Stevens Inn,** 1829 S. Canal, 505/887-2851, offers large clean rooms and a nice swimming pool, dining room, and lounge. The **Holiday Inn** is downtown at 601 S. Canal, 505/885-8500.

South of town, on the road to Carlsbad Caverns, you'll find a dozen or so motels offering doubles in the same range, including **Days Inn,** 3910 National Parks Hwy., 505/887-8800; **Quality Inn,** 3706 National Parks Hwy., 505/887-2861; and the **Continental Inn,** 3820 National Parks Hwy., 505/887-0341. If you want to stay nearer the park (it's 28 miles from Carlsbad to the Carlsbad Caverns visitors center), try the **Cavern Inn Best Western** at the park entrance, 505/785-2291 or 800/CAVERNS (800/228-3767).

Camping

Carlsbad RV Park and Campground, 4301 National Parks Hwy., 505/885-6333, has full hookups, lawns for tents, and a pool. Rates start at about $25, with discounts to AAA members, Good Sam Club, and senior citizens.

Food

A longtime local (and personal) favorite Carlsbad establishment is **Lucy's Mexicali Restaurant,** 701 S. Canal, 505/887-7714, where a large menu offers Mexican entrées for $4–8, as well as steaks and other American dishes. The **Cortez Cafe,** down the street at 506 S. Canal, 505/885-4747, is also very good, though decidedly lower profile. Inside the Holiday Inn at 601 S. Canal are the upscale **Ventana's Restaurant,** serving steaks and seafood, and **Phoenix Bar and Grill,** where you can get burgers, sandwiches, and salads; phone 505/885-8500.

The Flume Room, 1829 S. Canal, 505/887-2851, at the Best Western Stevens Inn is also good, serving Mexican dishes, seafood, pastas, and salads.

You'll also find all the fast-food and franchise restaurants, including McDonald's, Arby's, Denny's, Burger King, and a Golden Corral.

In White's City, **Cactus Jack's** self-service restaurant is open for breakfast, lunch, and dinner, serving Belgian waffles, *huevos rancheros,* burgers, and fajitas. It also serves 32 flavors of homemade ice cream, as well as homemade pies. The **Velvet Garter Saloon and Restaurant,** 505/785-2291, serves steaks, seafood, Mexican dinners, fried chicken, hamburgers, and cocktails.

Recreation

You can escape the summer heat at **Lake Carlsbad Recreation Area** at the east end of Church Street. Lake Carlsbad is a product of a dam across the Pecos River in Carlsbad, and sunbathers, water-skiers, and swimmers find the area an ideal spot to pass lazy summer afternoons. Also on Lake Carlsbad is the 18-hole **Carlsbad Municipal Golf Course.** Phone 505/885-5444 for rates and tee times.

Twelve miles north of town is **Brantley Lake State Park,** which offers water-skiing, camping, fishing, swimming, and hiking. A visitors center details the area's history, including the 1988 construction of the dam, and also provides interpretive literature on local wildlife and geography. Fees are $3 per vehicle for day use, $6 for camping, and $11 for RV camping with hookups. For information, phone 505/457-2384.

Information and Services

The Carlsbad **Chamber of Commerce and Visitors Bureau** is at 302 S. Canal St., 505/887-6516 or 800/221-1224, website: www.chamber.caverns.com. For extensive information on the caverns, visit the park service website: www.nps.gov/cave/home.htm. The **National Parks Information Center** is just outside downtown Carlsbad on the way to the park at 3225 National Parks Hwy., 505/885-8884.

Carlsbad Medical Center is at 2430 W. Pierce, 505/887-4100. The number for the Carlsbad Police Department is 505/885-2111. The number for the Eddy County sheriff is 505/887-7551.

Transportation

Mesa Air, 800/MESA-AIR (800/637-2247), flies into Carlsbad. The Carlsbad **bus depot** is downtown at 1000 S. Canyon, 505/887-1108.

Hobbs

It's pretty much a straight shot from Carlsbad over to Hobbs (pop. 29,000; elev. 3,625 feet), 70 miles over barren desert underlaid with rich deposits of potash and oil. About halfway, you cross from Eddy into Lea County, a dry, sprawling land that evokes westbound wagon trains and dusty cattle drives—miles of Texas longhorns lowing loudly and stubbornly under relentless summer suns. Lea County is literally about as close to Texas as you can get, nestled in New Mexico's interior corner formed by the pouting lower lip of West Texas that juts clear to El Paso. Nowhere in Lea County are you farther than 50 miles from the Texas border. In fact, if you were to walk a straight line from Lubbock to El Paso, you would pass just north of Hobbs.

The Hobbs area is figuratively about as close as you can get to Texas as well. This is a landscape dotted with pumpjacks drawing oil from beneath the earth's surface, of drilling rigs silhouetted against the bleak sky, of cattle and sheep grazing on the flat prairie, of Texas accents and license plates, ranchers and rodeoers, and of transplanted Texans who've all but forgotten they've moved.

History

Hobbs, in fact, was founded by a footloose Texan. According to *New Mexico, a New Guide*

© STEPHEN METZGER

A rest stop a couple of miles east of Hobbs welcomes travelers coming in from Texas.

to the Colorful State (see Suggested Reading), James Hobbs moved across the border in 1907 and built a dugout home and school, at what is now the corner of 1st and Texas Streets. Soon after, a store and post office were constructed, and small businesses—a broom-making enterprise and a molasses mill—set up shop. Then in 1928, the Midwest Oil Company discovered "black gold" in the Hobbs underground, and the town went berserk. Folks flocked to the area by the thousands, and entire towns were dismantled and moved to Hobbs. Knowles, once the largest town in Lea County, was taken apart plank by plank and relocated to Hobbs. Tent communities sprouted overnight. By 1930, more than 12,000 fortune-seekers had come to Hobbs hoping to cash in on the area's natural wealth.

At its peak—and in the middle of Prohibition—Hobbs was a wild and rowdy town, its brothels and taverns, domino parlors and pool halls operating virtually round the clock.

Then the bottom dropped out of the oil market. The price for a barrel went from $1.05 to $.10, and the fickle oilers packed up—both their belongings and their buildings—and moved on. Hobbs, as quickly as it had boomed, withered back to a quiet, dusty prairie town.

Throughout the next few years, a handful of loyal Hobbsians worked at rebuilding the community; improved oil-drilling technology returned the industry to the area in the mid-1930s, and some of the early wells are still in operation. Today, as you approach Hobbs on Highway 180 from the west, as the pumpjacks and drilling rigs of the countryside make way for the machine shops and supply stores of town, you're impressed immediately with the number of Hobbs businesses that rely for their very survival on the area's still-strong oil industry.

In 1942, an air base was built just east of Hobbs, and though the base was closed shortly after the war, it remains partially active. Now known as Hobbs Industrial Air Park, it's used by Lea County Airport. In 1983, the World Soaring Championships were held at Hobbs. In fact, so ideal are Hobbs's temperatures and wind patterns that Hobbs Industrial Air Park is now home to the Hobbs Soaring Society, the National Soaring Foundation, and the Soaring Society of America. The Lea County Airport just west of town on Highway 62 houses the New Mexico wing of the Confederate Air Force.

Hobbs is also home to two small colleges, New Mexico Junior College and the College of the Southwest. The latter is a private school with roughly 300 students, many of whom study liberal arts in preparation for teaching careers.

SIGHTS

Lea County Cowboy Hall of Fame and Western Heritage Center

Housed in a separate building on the New Mexico Junior College campus, the Cowboy Hall of Fame commemorates the area's founders and important cattlemen. Displays include plaques honoring all Cowboy Hall of Famers; early settlers' quilts, cookware, furniture, and carriages; area wildlife; and the Lea County rodeo awards. A recent addition is the early man/Native American exhibit. Also on display—oddly—are the personal effects of prominent local ranchers and cowboys—boots, wallets, belts, pocketknives, Bibles, even eyeglasses. The museum and college are on the northern outskirts of Hobbs, just off Highway 18. They're open Monday–Friday 8 A.M.–5 P.M. and Saturday and Sunday 1–5 P.M. For more information, contact **Lea County Cowboy Hall of Fame,** 5317 Lovington Hwy., Hobbs, NM 88240, 505/392-1275.

New Mexico Wing, Confederate Air Force

The New Mexico branch of the Confederate Air Force Museum (one of 80 such museums in the country) is in an old hangar at the Lea County Airport and provides sanctuary to old discarded airplanes and airplane engines, though some of the craft are still operational. Among the displays are a Stinson L-5, a 1943 German jeep, and a Beechcraft C-45. Offering the ultimate in self-guided tours, the museum may not even have an attendant present during your visit. For guided tours, contact the Hobbs Chamber of Commerce. Take Highway 62 west from Hobbs

© STEPHEN METZGER

vintage aircraft on display at the Confederate Air Force Museum

and watch for the signs. Admission is free, although donations are accepted.

Thelma A. Webber Southwest Heritage Room

The College of the Southwest has a small collection of local-interest pieces: prehistoric Indian pottery, early settler relics, and oil-field artifacts. In the Scarborough Memorial Library, the display is open during the school year Monday–Thursday 8 A.M.–9 P.M., Friday 8 A.M.–5 P.M. Hours vary during the summer. Admission is free. Phone 505/392-6561, ext. 315 for more information.

PRACTICALITIES

Accommodations

Most of the motels in Hobbs are on Broadway and Marland Streets on the south side of town. You can't go wrong at the **Howard Johnson,** 501 N. Marler, 505/397-3251; the **TraveLodge,** 1301 E. Broadway, 505/393-4101; or the **Days Inn** at 211 N. Marland, 505/397-6541. All are right around $50 for two. The **Holiday Inn Express,** 3610 N. Lovington, 505/392-8777, is one of the newer motels in town, with doubles running $50–100.

Food

For Chinese food, try the **Peking Restaurant** at 2404 N. Grimes, 505/392-2411. The local **Cattle Baron** is at 1930 N. Grimes, 505/393-2800. You'll have no trouble finding burger, pizza, and other fast-food restaurants.

Recreation

You'll find **Ocotillo Park Golf Course** a couple of miles north of town on Highway 18, 505/392-9297. The local area offers a variety of small-game hunting—quail, dove, prairie chicken, and rabbit; pronghorn wander the grasslands within a half hour of town.

Information and Services

The Hobbs **Chamber of Commerce,** 505/397-3202 or 800/658-6291, is at 400 N. Marland. The Hobbs **public library,** 505/397-2451, is at 509 N. Shipp.

Lea Regional Hospital is just north of town on Highway 18, 505/392-6581. The number for the Hobbs Police Department is 505/397-2431.

Transportation

Mesa Air, 800/MESA-AIR (800/637-2247), is the only airline offering passenger service to

Hobbs. **Greyhound** stops at the Hobbs bus terminal, 400 S. Turner.

TO LOVINGTON

Highway 18 angles northwest out of Hobbs toward Lovington, the 22-mile drive taking the traveler across more cattle and oil country. Just outside Hobbs, you'll pass a small state park with camping facilities, and then about halfway to Lovington, you'll pass through Humble City.

Harry McAdams State Park

Named for a World War II combat flier who after the war was assigned to Hobbs Army Field (now the Hobbs Industrial Air Park), this 35-acre park offers excellent picnicking to weary travelers. You'll find rolling lawns, a small lake (no fishing, swimming, or wading), picnic tables, 15 RV sites, and restrooms with hot showers. Cost for day use is $3, overnight is $7, and overnight with hookups is $11. Take Highway 18 north out of Hobbs approximately two miles.

Lovington

Lovington (pop. 9,300), like much of the Llano Estacado, is actually more West Texas than it is New Mexico. Flat and barren, the landscape outside the small towns is broken only by small herds of cattle and by pumpjacks working to draw the black stuff from beneath the earth's dry and stubborn crust. Indeed, as in most eastern New Mexico towns, the oil and gas industries are by leaps and bounds Lovington's largest employers. Lea County, of which Lovington sits smack in the middle, accounts for 71 percent of the crude oil produced in New Mexico and 28.8 percent of the natural gas. The county's crop (principally cotton and alfalfa) and livestock production is 5 percent of the state's total.

History

Although the area around Lovington—particularly just to the north—was at one time home to nomadic tribes of prehistoric hunters, the land was largely unsettled until the turn of the 20th century, when E. M. and J. W. Caudle came to the area from Seminole, Texas, 40 miles southeast. By 1907, the Love brothers, Robert and Jim, had also emigrated from Texas, Jim deeding part of his homestead for the town site of Lovington. In 1917, Lea County was formed from parts of Chaves and Eddy Counties, and Lovington was designated the county seat.

Primarily a cattle and farming center, Lovington experienced a minor face change in 1928, when small deposits of oil were discovered nearby. In 1950, the large Denton pool was discovered nine miles northeast of Lovington, and in a short time 92 wells had been dug and were working round the clock to help bring a bit of prosperity to Lea County. Since the 1950s, both oil and gas have had tremendous impact on Lea County and Lovington's economy. In the face of modern-day Lovington, one can see clearly its heritage: Texas forefathers, ranching and agriculture, and oil and gas.

Lea County Historical Museum

Rooms in this small museum in the old Plaza Hotel near the downtown plaza are decorated with relics and mementos from early settlers, from buggies to cookware. The museum is open Monday–Friday 1–5 P.M. Admission is $.50.

PRACTICALITIES

Accommodations

You'll find doubles at about $50 at the **Lovington Inn,** 1600 W. Avenue D, 505/396-5346, and the **Western Inn** at 2212 S. Main, 505/396-3635, has doubles priced at $50 or less. Camping is available at **Harry McAdams State Park** just outside Hobbs for $10 per campsite, plus $4 for hook-ups.

Recreation

Chaparral Lake and Park (South Commercial Drive) offers fishing, tennis, basketball, volleyball, a playground, and a one-mile jogging path. Hunters stalk quail, dove, prairie chicken, rabbit, and pronghorn on the plains of the Lovington area.

Annual Events

The **Fourth of July Celebration** is in Chaparral Park, with the "World's Greatest Lizard Race." The last weekend in November draws out-of-towners to Lovington's Main Street for the **Electric Light Parade**—lighted floats and cars heralding the holidays.

Information and Services

The Lovington **Chamber of Commerce** is at 201 S. Main St., 505/396-5311; write P.O. Box 1347, Lovington, NM 88260. The Lovington **public library** is at 100 W. Central Ave., 505/396-3144 or 505/396-6900.

Lea Regional Hospital is on the Hobbs-Lovington Highway in Hobbs, 505/396-4195 or 505/392-6581. The Lovington Police Department is at 213 S. Love, 505/396-2811.

Transportation

Mesa Air, 800/MESA-AIR (800/637-2247), has passenger service to Hobbs 22 miles to the southeast. The Lovington bus station, 913 S. Main St., 505/396-4501, is serviced by **Greyhound.**

TO PORTALES

Imagine a gorgeous waterfall plummeting 500 feet off a mountain cliff into a pool of clear water. Imagine lush vegetation, cool breezes, and balmy evenings. Now keep that image in mind as you drive across this barren stretch of desert because out here you won't see anything like that. You will see, though, the junction with Highway 380 at Tatum, the most exciting part of this 90-mile stretch of highway, as well as the thriving metropolises of Highway and Pep. Perhaps it's just as well you're driving.

Portales

Portales (pop. 12,280; elev. 4,010 feet) is a small college and farming town on Highway 70 about 20 miles from the Texas border. Home to Eastern New Mexico University (just under 4,000 students), Portales is also a hub for area ranchers and farmers; the primary crop is peanuts, but also important are wheat, corn, and potatoes.

History

Portales, "twin city" of Clovis, 20 miles northeast, began as a railroad town around the turn of the last century and in 1903 was designated the seat of newly formed Roosevelt County. In 1934, work on Eastern New Mexico Junior College was completed and classes begun; by 1955, the school had become the four-year Eastern New Mexico University and is today, along with agriculture, a mainstay of Portales's stable economy.

Early settlers arrived in the Portales area shortly after the Homestead Act of 1862. Deep water tables and low average rainfalls, though, made it difficult to hang on, and Portales didn't truly develop into a strong agricultural center until after World War II, when deep-water wells were first drilled here. This made the irrigation of wheat, sorghum, corn, soybeans, cotton, and peanuts possible, and made life much more tolerable for the region's livestock ranchers, who today account for more than $30 million of Portales's income. Roosevelt County produces 50 percent of all the Valencia peanuts grown in the

United States and ships 30 million pounds out of the county annually.

SIGHTS

Eastern New Mexico University

The third-largest university in the state and the largest single employer of Portaleans (more than 500), ENMU is also an important cultural contributor to the town. Its 3,700 students (from throughout the United States and the world), graduate programs, museums, library, and year-round activities combine to provide an otherwise predominantly agricultural community with a taste of life outside irrigation and harvest concerns. The college's principal areas of study are business, education, technology, fine and liberal arts, and sciences.

Roosevelt County Historical Museum

Across the lawn from ENMU's Tudor-style administration building, this two-story museum was established in 1940 to preserve the area's rich prehistoric-through-pioneer heritage. Exhibits include displays from the Blackwater Draw archaeological site, Kiowa and Comanche spear points and tools, and scores of relics from the days of early settlers: traps, branding irons, ox yokes, barbed wire, flags, medical tools, an Edison phonograph and cylinder dictaphones, quilts, saddles, toys, and clocks. The museum sponsors a lecture series each year, as well as various art shows and seminars. Hours are Monday–Friday 8 A.M.–5 P.M., Saturday 10 A.M.–4 P.M., and Sunday 1–4 P.M.Closed on weekends in the summer. For hours and information, phone 505/562-2592.

Jack Williamson Science Fiction Collection

Though eastern New Mexico may seem an unlikely place for a decent belles lettres collection, this symposium should delight bibliophiles and sci-fi fans alike. Williamson is an ENMU professor emeritus and author who has published 45 novels and more than 150 short stories. Among the major awards Williamson has received is the Hugo Award for his autobiography, *Wonder's Child: My Life in Science Fiction.* The collection houses the original manuscripts and foreign-language editions of Williamson's books, manuscripts by other well-known science-fiction

SOUTHEASTERN NM

© STEPHEN METZGER

administration building at Eastern New Mexico University

writers, and Williamson's correspondence with writers such as Ray Bradbury, Robert Heinlein, and others. The Jack Williamson Science Fiction Collection is in the Golden Library on the ENMU campus. For more information, call 505/562-2635.

PRACTICALITIES

Accommodations

Sands Motel, 1130 W. 1st St., 505/356-4424 or 800/956-4424, and the **Super 8,** 1805 W. 2nd (Highway 70 West), 505/356-8518, have doubles for under $50. The **Morning Star Bed and Breakfast,** 620 W. 2nd, 505/356-2994, offers five rooms in a 1930s-vintage two-story adobe that was formerly a doctor's home and clinic. Doubles go for $50 per night, with a continental breakfast.

Food

The **Wagon Wheel Cafe,** 521 W. 17th St., 505/356-5036, serves excellent homemade food in a down-home atmosphere. Specialties include fried catfish and Mexican food. The **Cattle Baron Steak and Seafood Restaurant,** 1600 S. Ave. D, 505/356-5587, is great for steak, fish, chicken, salad bar, etc.

Annual Events

The **Peanut Valley Festival,** begun in 1973, is held on the campus of Eastern New Mexico University in October and runs three days. In addition to the "Peanut Olympics" (events include peanut races—contestants push peanuts with their noses—and the peanut toss), the festival features a talent show, health fair, live music and other entertainment, and a variety of arts and crafts, from painting and pottery to jewelry and woodwork; artisans present scheduled how-to demonstrations throughout the festival. For more information, write Peanut Valley Festival, Portales, NM 88130.

Other annual Portales events include **Heritage Rodeo Days** (mid-June) and the **Roosevelt County Fair** (mid-August). For exact dates and more information, contact the Roosevelt County/Portales Chamber of Commerce.

Information and Services

The Portales **Chamber of Commerce** is at 200 E. 7th, 505/356-8541. The Portales **public library** is at 218 S. Ave. B, 505/356-3940. For general information on **Eastern New Mexico University,** call 505/562-1011.

The Portales Police Department is at 1700 N. Boston, 505/356-4404.

Transportation

Greyhound has passenger service to Portales. The Portales bus depot is at 215 E. 2nd St., 505/356-6914. **Mesa Air,** 800/MESA-AIR (800/637-2247), flies into Clovis, 20 miles northeast of Portales.

TO CLOVIS

Oasis State Park

Out on the sandy New Mexico desert between Portales and Clovis, this 196-acre park is quite aptly named. Though much of it sprawls over the wind-blown dunes, shade trees and a four-acre lake provide welcome respite from the barren wasteland. A popular picnic site since 1902, when settler William Taylor planted cedar, locust, and chinaberry trees on the land, it was given official state park status in 1961 (until then locals called it Taylor's Grove). You'll find both picnicking and camping facilities, including 13 RV sites and restrooms with hot showers. Cost is $4 for day use, $8 for overnight camping, and $12 for electrical hookups. Oasis State Park is seven miles north of Portales on Highway 467.

Blackwater Draw Museum

On Highway 70 about midway between Portales and Clovis, the Blackwater is a combination research and study laboratory and museum. On display are dioramas, timelines, and Clovis points and bones from the nearby Blackwater Draw archaeological site, where discoveries in the early 1930s blew then-current anthropological theories about the New World out of the water, so to speak. Until Blackwater, anthropologists had the first humans coming to North America across the Bering Straits not much earlier than the time of Jesus; Clovis points in mammoth skeletons at Blackwater, though, offered proof positive they'd been here at least 9,000 years before Jesus was even a twinkle in the Big Guy's eye. You can also view a number of short films. Outside you'll find picnic tables under shade-providing shelters.

Hours are Monday–Saturday 10 A.M.–5 P.M. and Sunday noon–5 P.M. Memorial Day through Labor Day; closed Monday the rest of the year. The $2 admission fee will also get you into the excavation site down the road (open Memorial Day through Labor Day only); a map is provided. Phone 505/562-2202 (museum) or 505/356-5235 (excavation site) for more information.

Clovis

The year is 1958. Not much is happening in eastern New Mexico—wheat's grown and harvested, cattle are raised and slaughtered, and teenagers, like teenagers everywhere, are dreaming of getting out. But in the little town of Clovis—just a cow pie's toss from the Texas border—big things are going down. In a small recording studio on the edge of town, a lone engineer, a bass player, a drummer, and a bespectacled guitarist/singer/songwriter are modestly laying down the roots of a brand-new sound—a sound that will redefine contemporary music, a sound that will turn some dreams into realities and make other realities more bearable, a sound that will ultimately play a huge role in the country's history.

Though Buddy Holly and the Crickets were from Lubbock, Texas, they drove across the border to Norman Petty's studio here in Clovis to record such innovative and influential tunes as "Peggy Sue," "Maybe Baby," and "That'll Be the Day." Locals love to tell about Holly and friends sitting in a Cadillac in the parking lot of the studio, doo-wah-dooing in harmony while they waited for Petty to open the doors.

Petty was Holly's manager, arranger, and recording engineer, and an accomplished musician himself. After Holly died in 1959, Norman Petty Studios, in an inauspicious little building at 1313 W. 7th St., continued its operations. Besides Holly, Petty "discovered" Roy Orbison, Buddy

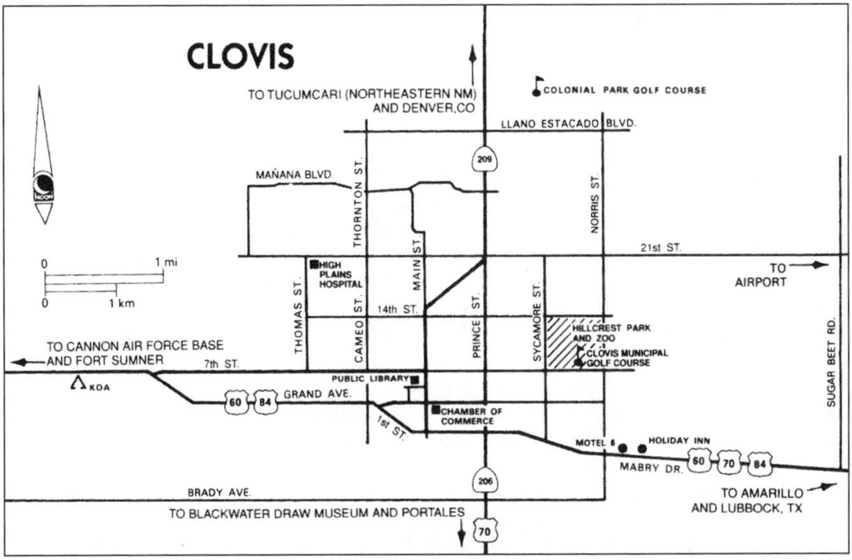

Knox ("Party Doll"), Roger Williams, and a number of other artists. He gave many struggling musicians their first breaks, polishing their rough edges into a marketable sound.

Petty died in 1984, but his wife, Vi, continued to manage the business. In 1986, a celebration honored both Petty and Holly, and the now-annual Clovis Music Festival was born. The festival attracts fans of vintage rock from around the country, who come to tour the studios—since moved into fancier digs downtown—and hear the music that Petty brought to the world.

History

Originally called Riley's Switch, Clovis was little more than a handful of shacks on the Santa Fe Railway line until shortly after the turn of the last century, when railroad officials decided to make the town the official division point on the newly established Belòn Cut-off. The daughter of a railroad official chose the name Clovis, after the King of the Franks, who converted to Christianity in A.D. 486. The railroad is still an important part of the Clovis community, employing more than 375 workers at the Santa Fe switching yard and roundhouse, the hub out of which spoke the Vaughn, Roswell, Amarillo, and Lubbock lines.

Though the high plains around Clovis, unlike many New Mexico regions to the north and east, aren't known for any specific and long-term Indian settlements, the area has been of supreme interest to archaeologists and students of prehistory. Clovis points, early spear points discovered near town, have helped establish the approximate dates of early man's first entrance into the Americas across the Bering Straits: Until Clovis Man and Sandia Man (whose artifacts were found in a cave near Albuquerque) were discovered, most archaeologists thought the first Americans arrived as recently as 2,000 years ago. We know now, though, that nomadic early Americans were hunting mastodon, bison, and saber-toothed tiger in what is now eastern New Mexico as early as 10,000 years ago.

Surrounded by the sprawling Llano Estacado, Clovis (pop. 33,000) is still primarily an agricultural and ranching community. Curry County, of which Clovis is the county seat, produces more wheat, grain, sorghum, and sugar beets than any other county in New Mexico. Alfalfa and corn are also important to the local economy. Annually, Curry County takes in $160 million in agriculture-based revenues. Since 1935, public livestock auctions have been held weekly, and horse sales are held every Monday (Clovis is the largest horse and mule market in the United States).

Cannon Air Force Base, six miles west of Clovis on Highway 60/84, is by far the largest employer in town; more than 10 percent of Clovis's population is employed in some capacity—either military or civilian—at Cannon. Before gaining military status during World War II, Portair Field—and later, Clovis Municipal Airport—was a transfer station for early transcontinental flights. As the Clovis Army Air Base in the '40s, the facility housed B-17s, B-24s, and B-29s, and since 1959 Cannon Air Force Base has been home to the 27th Tactical Fighter Wing of the U.S. Air Force. Today, the 27th TFW trains with F-111 fighter-bombers, which the Air Force considers among its most advanced aircraft.

Norman Petty Studios

Tours of this historic recording studio (see above) are available by appointment only. Phone 505/356-6422. For an online tour or more information, visit website: www.angelfire.com/mn/pdp/pettytour.

Hillcrest Park Zoo

This small zoo, near downtown in Hillcrest Park, includes more than 200 species of birds and animals, as well as an infirmary open for tours (Friday at 2 P.M.). Special presentations and slide shows include "Predators of New Mexico," "Reptiles and Amphibians," and "Poisonous Animals." Memorial Day through Labor Day, zoo hours are Tuesday–Sunday 9 A.M.–5 P.M. The rest of the year, the zoo closes at 4 P.M. Admission is $1 for adults; seniors and kids under six are admitted without charge. For more information, phone the Clovis Parks Department at 505/769-7873.

Clovis Train Depot Model Train Museum

This museum, housed in Clovis's restored Atchison, Topeka, & Santa Fe depot (built in 1907), features both artifacts and documents from railroading's history, as well as working model trains. The museum, at 211 W. 1st St., is open for one-hour guided tours daily noon–5 P.M. June through August and Wednesday–Sunday the rest of the year (closed in February and September). Admission is $4 for adults and $2 for seniors and kids 5–15. For more information, phone 505/762-0066.

PRACTICALITIES

Accommodations

Clovis's "motel row" is on Mabry Drive (Highways 60/70/84) on the east side of town. The following all offer good clean rooms: **Best Western La Vista Inn,** 1516 Mabry, 505/762-3808 (around $50); **Holiday Inn,** 2700 Mabry, 505/762-4491 ($50–100); and **Comfort Inn,** 1616 Mabry, 505/762-4591 ($50–100). RV camping is available at **Campground of Clovis,** 4707 W. 7th St., 505/763-6360.

Food

Clovis is home to several very good Mexican restaurants, including **Juanito's,** 1608 Mabry, 505/762-7822, and **Leal's,** 3100 Mabry, 505/763-4075. For steak and seafood, try the longtime local favorite **Poor Boy's Steakhouse,** 2115 N. Prince, 505/763-5222, open seven days a week. There's also a **K-Bob's,** 1600 Mabry, 505/763-4443, and a **Red Lobster,** 2601 N. Prince, 505/762-0355.

Recreation

Clovis Municipal Golf Course (18 holes; weekend greens fees are about $10) is on the grounds of Hillcrest Park on Norris Street, 505/762-0249, and the private **Colonial Park Country Club Golf Course** (18 holes; weekend green fees $13) is just north of town on Highway 209, 505/762-4775. Hillcrest Park also offers swimming, tennis, and picnicking.

Annual Events

Clovis Pioneer Days and Balloon Festival, the first weekend in June, includes a rodeo with competitors from throughout the Southwest. There's also a parade, dance, and chili cook-off, as well as the balloon liftoff, with as many as 25 balloons rising skyward. The **Curry County Fair,** in late summer at the fairgrounds on the corner of Brady and Norris on the southeast side of town, is the largest in the state, with agricultural displays, livestock exhibits, and tractor pulls. Also in late summer, the **Norman and Vi Petty Music Festival** attracts Buddy Holly and Norman Petty fans to the historic Norman Petty recording studios (see above). The **Clovis Cattle Festival** is in October, also at the fairgrounds. For more information, contact the Clovis Chamber of Commerce.

Information and Services

Contact the Clovis **Chamber of Commerce** at 215 N. Main, Clovis, NM 88101, 505/763-3535 or 800/261-7656. The **public library** is at 7th and Main, 505/769-1973.

Clovis's High Plains Hospital is on the west side of town at 2100 N. Thomas, 505/769-2141—emergency service with physician on duty 24 hours a day. The Clovis Police Department is at 217 W. 4th; call 505/769-1921 (911 for emergencies).

Transportation

Mesa Air, 800/MESA-AIR (800/637-2247), has passenger service between Clovis and Albuquerque. **Greyhound** stops in Clovis at the New Mexico Transportation Company office (505/762-4584) at 2nd and Pile Streets.

TO FORT SUMNER

The 60-mile shot west from Clovis to Fort Sumner is about as visually stimulating as the rest of the Llano Estacado. You pass through a handful of blink-and-you'll-miss-it towns, including St. Vrain (named for the Taos mountain man and Indian agent, Ceran St. Vrain), Melrose, Tolar, and Taiban. Watch for roadside fruit and vegetable stands as you approach Melrose; when it's hot and dry, not much tastes better than a tall glass of cold cherry cider.

Fort Sumner

The seat of De Baca County, Fort Sumner (pop. 1,300; elev. 4,030 feet), on the Pecos River out on the endless plain an hour and a half west of the Texas border, is classic New Mexico: rich in history, rife with museums and a state monument, and replete with trinkets and schlock. ("Step right up, folks. See the two-headed calf.") This is the New Mexico of Billy the Kid, Pat Garrett, Kit Carson, and gunfights, and of Indian treaties, betrayals, and massacres.

With such a colorful past on which to draw, it's no wonder Fort Sumner's economy relies so heavily on tourism, although agriculture, chiefly alfalfa, apples, and melons, also contributes to the area's economic health.

History

The town of Fort Sumner is actually the civilian settlement of the nearby Fort Sumner military installation, whose dubious history dates to the 1860s, when it marked the end of the infamous Navajo Long Walk. Colonel Kit Carson, scout, trapper, and Indian-fighter, was ordered in 1862 by Brigadier General James H. Carleton, commander of the Department of New Mexico, to "round up" the uncooperative Navajos; it seems the Indians were "out of hand." The Navajos, of course, were not particularly taken with the idea of being rounded up, and they resisted. On June 20, 1863, the deadline for their surrender, Carson and a regiment of New Mexico volunteers, including some Utes, enemies of the Navajo, began a "war" against them, burning hogans and crops and slaughtering cattle and horses. In 1863, Carson and his men killed 300 Navajos, and by February 1864 had run them ragged, trapping them in Canyon de Chelly.

Finally, 3,000 Navajos were indeed rounded up and forced to walk the 300 miles from Fort Wingate, near Gallup, to Fort Sumner. There they were penned in with a smaller group of Apaches at the Bosque Redondo Reservation in a government experiment to "concentrate" the Indians and teach them to be self-sufficient. Ultimately, the experiment failed, in large part because of the parched, hardened, and un-

© STEPHEN METZGER

the Billy the Kid Museum on the main drag in Fort Sumner

© STEPHEN METZGER

The Kid's gravestone was stolen so many times, a cage was built to protect it.

farmable land around Fort Sumner. In 1868, the Navajos were granted the reservation in northwestern New Mexico and eastern Arizona they now occupy. Finally, in 1870, Lucien Maxwell bought the fort from the U.S. government and added it to his already huge tract of land, at one time the largest privately owned piece of property in the country.

And what of Billy the Kid and Pat Garrett? After the Lincoln County War of 1878, "the Kid" was a fugitive in New Mexico, though some historians claim he was a good man and simply a victim of a corrupt political and legal system. Still, by 1881, Billy the Kid was wanted for several Lincoln County War murders and for escaping from Lincoln County jail. Garrett, sheriff of Lincoln County at the time, followed Billy northeast to the Fort Sumner area, where Billy had friends. On July 14, 1881, Garrett entered the home of Pete Maxwell, son of Lucien, and shot Billy dead. The Kid was 21. Legend has it he had killed 21 men.

(In addition to the debate over whether Billy was "bad" or "good," there is also speculation that Garrett never actually even killed him, that Billy wasn't in the Maxwell house at the time and that he later moved to West Texas, where he lived, keeping his profile low, well into the middle of the 20th century. Skeptics scoff, but others rub their hands in delight over the ambiguities of history. . . .)

SIGHTS

Fort Sumner State Monument

A state monument since 1968, old Fort Sumner is listed on the National Register of Historic Places. Displays and rangers at the visitors center detail the fort's history and contribution to the settling of the West. Living-history presentations are offered weekends by the monument rangers. The monument is four miles east of Fort Sumner (Highway 60) and three miles south, on Billy the Kid Road. Watch for the signs. Open daily 8:30 A.M.–5 P.M. Cost is $1. For more information, call 505/355-2573.

Billy the Kid Museum

This place is two parts artifacts of legitimate historical interest and one part gimmick. The museum, on Fort Sumner's main drag, features a self-guided tour through a mind-bogglingly huge display of everything from branding irons, firearms, and ox yokes to flatware, stoves, turn-of-the-20th-century carriages and Model Ts. Other items include personal belongings of Edwin Vose Sumner (the Civil War general for whom the town was named) and a rifle, chaps, and spurs once owned by Billy the Kid. You also walk right past the jail cell where the Kid supposedly did time. Open daily 8:30 A.M.–5 P.M.; May 16–October 14 Sunday hours are 11 A.M.–5 P.M. Entrance fee is $4; for kids six to 11 it's $2. Phone 505/355-2380.

Old Fort Sumner Museum

Just a few miles southeast of the town of Fort Sumner, this museum displays artifacts and documents from the old fort, as well as a variety of early pioneer tools, guns, domestic ware, and historical photos. A series of paintings along the walls depicts the major events of Billy the Kid's life, Native Americans are represented by Kiowa and Apache cradleboards and moccasins, and a two-headed calf debates with itself in the corner. A gift shop sells postcards and trinkety stuff: beaded Indian belts and reproductions of Billy the Kid's wanted posters. Open daily 8:30 A.M.–6 P.M. Entrance fee is $3. Phone 505/355-2942 for more information.

Billy the Kid's Grave

In the military cemetery behind the museum, enclosed in an iron cage, are the graves of Billy the Kid and two of his "pals." Apparently, the cage is necessary, as the headstone has had a habit of disappearing over the years, even turning up once in Southern California.

Sumner Lake State Park

Occupying 11,000 acres of Sumner Lake (formed by the 3,000-foot-long Alamogordo Dam across the Pecos River) and the surrounding lowlands, this is the fourth-largest state park in New Mexico. The lake is a popular recreation spot, offering boating, water-skiing, swimming, and fishing (Sumner is stocked with bluegill, pike, catfish, black bass, and crappie). You'll also find tennis courts, a playground, and camping facilities for both tenters and RVers. Entrance fee is $4 per vehicle and $8 for camping ($12 with hookups). Take Highway 84 10 miles north, then Highway 203 six miles west to Sumner Lake. Phone 505/355-2541 for more information.

Bosque Redondo Park

Named for the reservation where 7,000 Navajos and Mescalero Apaches were interned after their Long Walk from Fort Wingate near Gallup, this small park has picnicking and overnight camping facilities, as well as fishing for catfish, bass, and trout (no hookups).

PRACTICALITIES

Accommodations

You don't have a whole lot to choose from here, but if you don't feel like driving on to Albuquerque (160 miles) or to Clovis (if you're heading east), you will find lodging available. The **Billy the Kid Country Inn,** 1704 E. Fort Sumner Ave., 505/355-7414; the **Coronado Motel,** 309 W. Sumner Ave., 505/355-2466; and the **Super 8** at 1707 E. Sumner, 505/355-7888, all have good clean rooms. All $50 or less for two.

Food

A good choice for breakfast is **Sprout's Café,** 1701 E. Sumner, 505/355-7278. **Fred's Restaurant and Lounge,** 1408 E. Sumner, 505/355-7500, is open for Mexican and American lunch

BOB RACE

and dinner Tuesday–Saturday, while the **Dariland,** just down the street at 1304 E. Sumner, offers standard fast-food fare.

Recreation

Locals head for Lake Sumner when the weather gets warm, for the fishing, boating, water-skiing, swimming, and camping. Both bow and rifle hunters stalk the Fort Sumner plains for deer and pronghorn.

Annual Events

Old Fort Days, running five days in early June, includes cook-outs, shoot-outs, Indian dancing, living-history demonstrations, a Billy the Kid Tombstone Foot Race (participants must carry a large stone over a 25-yard course), a rodeo, western dance, and parade. For more information, contact the Fort Sumner Chamber of Commerce at 505/355-7705.

Information and Services

For more information on the Fort Sumner area, write the **chamber of commerce** at P.O. Box 28, Fort Sumner, NM 88119, or call 505/355-7705.

De Baca General Hospital, 505/355-2414, is at 500 N. 10th Street. The De Baca County sheriff is at 514 Ave. C, 505/355-2405. The New Mexico state police can be reached in Clovis at 505/763-3426 or Portales at 505/356-5139.

Northeastern New Mexico

Introduction

As you drive across northeastern New Mexico, don't be surprised if you find yourself thinking about Wells Fargo commercials, little houses on the prairie, and electric horsemen. This is the West of our national mythology, too often imprinted only through the magic of celluloid or Sony. And though Hollywood's interpretation of the Old West is often severely distorted, it's based to a large degree on a profound reality—reflected under the harsh skies of northeastern New Mexico. Here is where the plains met the mountains, the Cheyennes met the Apaches, westbound settlers met their greatest obstacles, and hard ambition and determination often met dismal failure and death. As well, though, it is where that ambition met success, where a unique American spirit—part Spanish, part Indian, and part Anglo—was born of a necessity to survive. Here, the Santa Fe Trail dropped out of Kansas and Colorado, cutting a southwest-bound swath from the corner of New Mexico to the bustling capital, and wagon ruts—100 years old—are still visible in the prairie hardpan.

The land itself is ancient. Sixty-five million years ago in the far northeastern corner of New Mexico, where Union County butts up against Texas, Oklahoma, and Colorado, a large inland sea lapped against a marshy shore, and dinosaurs sloshed through lush, prehistoric gardens. Later, when the water had receded, the land was a veritable cauldron of subterranean fury, with volcanoes spewing steam and molten lava from the earth's bowels. Today, hundreds of

Fort Union National Monument, where Kit Carson and the New Mexico volunteers were based during the 1860s

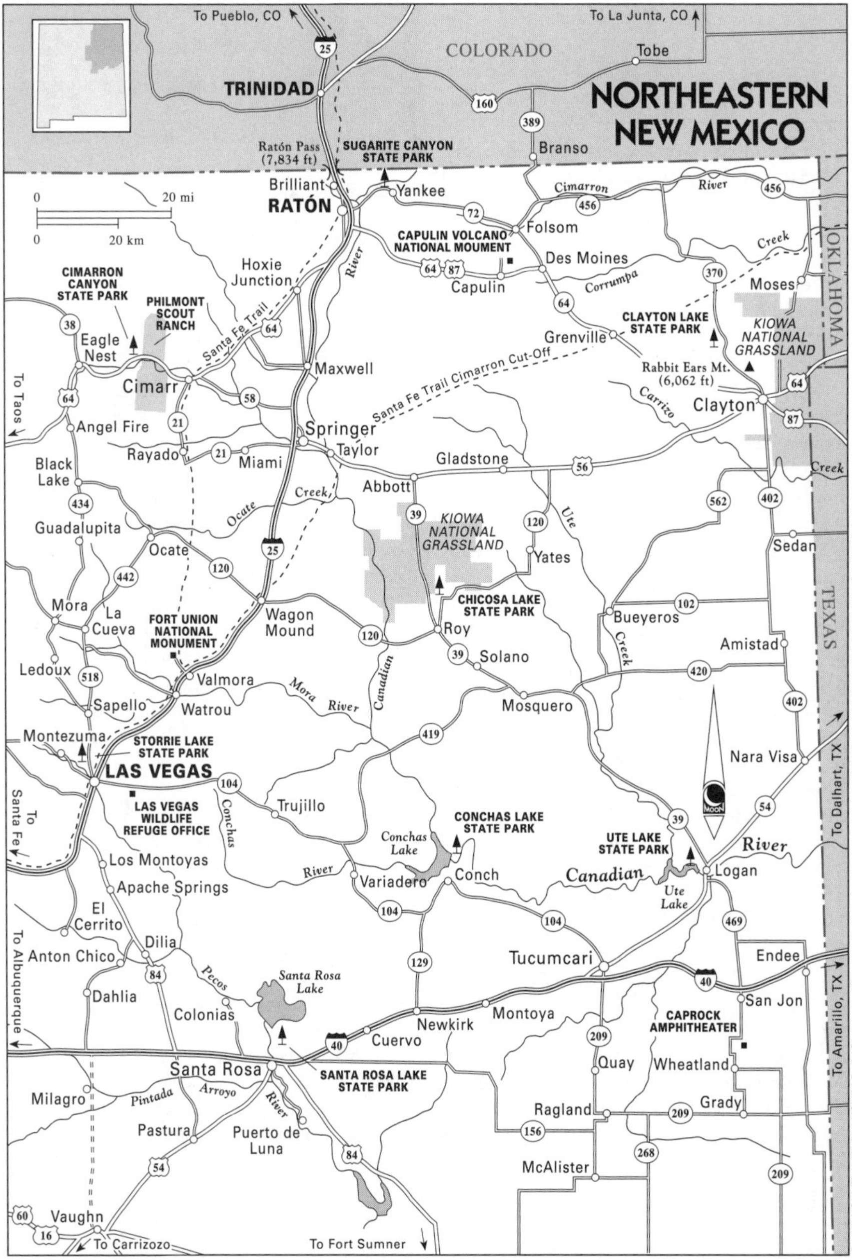

NORTHEASTERN NM

dormant volcanoes dot the plains from Clayton to Cimarron.

The land is also rich in history. Ten thousand years ago, descendants of some of the earliest immigrants from Asia roamed these plains hunting mastodons, woolly mammoths, and other animals now long extinct. The discovery of Folsom Man in 1925 set back by more than 8,000 years the date anthropologists believed the Bering Land Bridge was crossed and the North American continent inhabited.

Just a half century after Columbus "discovered" America, Spanish conquistador Francisco Vásquez de Coronado pushed his way through this part of New Mexico, looking for the fabled Seven Cities of Cibola. By then, the Apaches, along with the Navajos, who settled on the other side of the southern Rockies, had arrived from the north, and by the 18th century, when the Spanish colonizers began establishing settlements in the outlying areas of Santa Fe, the Indians had a homeland to protect.

The Indians didn't discriminate between the Spanish settlers and the Anglos, who began to appear from the east in the mid-19th century, and northeastern New Mexico was the site of hundreds of skirmishes and several major confrontations between natives and newcomers. As more and more supply wagons passed down through Ratón, Las Vegas, and Santa Fe, the Indians became more and more threatened and angry. Fort Union was built just north of Las Vegas in 1851 to protect travelers on both the main route and the Cimarron Cut-off of the Santa Fe Trail. Still the battles continued, with losses sustained by both sides.

The Indians were no match for the Iron Horse, though. By the late 19th century, the railroad had opened up the West, and the Indians, sadly, were pretty much licked. Some found refuge and solace on reservations. Some tried to make it in the white society. Still others wandered in an emotional and cultural limbo, their identities and senses of self lost somewhere between the two worlds.

HIGHLIGHTS

Cimarron: history, museums, fishing, camping, hiking

Fort Union National Monument: museum, sight-seeing

Las Vegas: historical tours, hiking, hot-springing, camping

Ratón: historical tours, horse racing, hiking, camping

From the late 19th to the mid-20th centuries, northeastern New Mexico depended largely on its rangeland—sheep and cattle grazed on the prairies, and wool and beef were shipped to points throughout the West. By the 1970s, the area had begun to open up to tourism. State parks were established on reservoirs that had long been used only for irrigation; motels were built to accommodate the increasing number of motorists; old Santa Fe Trail hotels were refurbished, and Victorian homes turned into bed-and-breakfasts; cross-country ski trails were cut into the forests, and lakes and rivers stocked with trout. By the late 1980s, some of northeastern New Mexico was already getting crowded. The gorgeous campgrounds along the Cimarron River between Cimarron and Eagle Nest are packed in the summer, antennae from RVs poking up into the pines and No Vacancy signs appearing regularly at Ratón motels.

Still, this is a wonderful and often-overlooked part of New Mexico. Don't be put off by the barrenness of the countryside flanking the highways. Get off the main routes and do some exploring. Imagine what it was like in the past, when dinosaurs trudged through the swampland, Folsom Man hunted mastodons, the Cheyenne followed the buffalo, and the Santa Fe Trail was the main artery of the Southwest's lifeblood.

Santa Rosa

Imagine driving along I-40 east of Albuquerque, trying to stay awake by playing license-plate bingo or "I Spy." The scenery is about the flattest, the drabbest, the driest, the least interesting you've ever seen. You're daydreaming of piney mountain forests or tropical beaches with cool offshore breezes. Suddenly a van passes you with a Divers Do It Deeper bumper sticker and New Mexico plates. What? Oh, probably just some nut who spent his vacation in Mazatlán or Kaua'i.

But then a station wagon passes, too, its backseat piled high with tanks and wet suits. You rub your eyes. You've been in the desert too long. You decide to pull off the freeway and get something to eat, maybe even a cold one.

But wait. The van and station wagon are pulling off here too. What is this? Martinique?

Well, no, but given that you're smack dab in the middle of some of the driest country on the continent, it's the next best thing. You're in Santa Rosa, New Mexico—home of Blue Hole, where divers from throughout the Southwest come to play *Sea Hunt* and make Lloyd Bridges proud.

Santa Rosa (pop. 2,250; elev. 4,600 feet), at the junction of Highway 54 and I-40, is the first decent-sized town you'll come to as you head east out of Albuquerque. Billing itself "The City of Natural Lakes" and situated on the banks of the Pecos River, Santa Rosa is a true oasis in the desert—either a convenient and amiable little pit stop or a place to head when you want to get down.

History

Originally settled in the 1860s by Spanish ranchers and farmers, Santa Rosa took its name in 1879 from a chapel built in town (then called Agua Negra Chiquita—Little Black Water) in honor of Santa Rosa de Lima, a Catholic saint. The railway arrived in the 1880s and with it an influx of railroad workers, several small shops and businesses, and the town's designation as seat of Guadalupe County. Although Santa Rosa's railroad-related prosperity was short-lived, the town attracted travelers and tourists from the late 1920s, when Route 66 was completed, until the 1970s, when I-40 bypassed the old motels and businesses.

Today, travelers come to Santa Rosa for the fishing, boating, and swimming afforded by the many nearby lakes and streams, as well as, of course, for the diving in Blue Hole.

SIGHTS

Blue Hole

Really. Folks come from all over the place to dive here. From as far away as Texas. Kansas. Virginia. Sometimes as many as 200 at a time. Sixty feet across at the surface and 81 feet deep, Blue Hole's water is kept amazingly clear (and the temperature a constant 61°F) by the subterranean river flowing through it at a rate of 3,000 gallons per minute. Divers at the bottom can see people peering down at them from the banks.

And they're not the only ones the divers see eyeing them. Catfish, goldfish, crawdads, and various species of snails and plantlife inhabit Blue Hole's depths and steep walls. The banks up top, meanwhile, are often inhabited by sunbathers and kids jumping off the 15-foot-high rocks into the cold water. The city has done an excellent job of making the hole accessible to swimmers of all levels and degrees of bravado: the banks of roughly half the circle have been paved, with steps built down into the pool, while across the water, low crags entice amateur platform divers, many of whom spend long minutes talking themselves into leaping, and then hold their noses as they drop, like Greg Louganis doing a Curly Howard impression.

Divers at Blue Hole must obtain permits from the Santa Rosa Police Department, in the city hall building on 5th Street just south of the chamber of commerce. Air and equipment are available at a small **Santa Rosa Dive Center** next to the hole, 505/472-3370. For more information, contact the dive shop or the Santa Rosa Chamber of Commerce.

Blue Hole is less than a mile from downtown

Some dive, some jump into Blue Hole in Santa Rosa.

Santa Rosa. Take 5th Street from Will Rogers Drive, and then Lake Drive east to Blue Hole Road.

Park Lake

This city-maintained park is midway between downtown Santa Rosa and Blue Hole. No camping is allowed, but you can swim, picnic, play tennis, shag flies at the baseball field, and clean up afterward at the hot showers. The park is open daily from dawn to dusk.

Santa Rosa Lake State Park

Santa Rosa Lake was built by the U.S. Army Corps of Engineers in 1980 to provide water storage as well as flood control for the Pecos River. Fish have thrived in the reservoir (particularly walleye pike, which are gillnetted and used as spawners in other waters throughout the state), and the park has quickly become popular with anglers, water-skiers, campers, and hikers.

The main campground, Rocky Point, has more than 40 sites with hookups and water, and the restrooms are equipped with flush toilets and showers. A smaller and less-developed area, Juniper Park, has boat ramps, picnic tables, and a restroom with flush toilets. Only Rocky Point has shelters, and if it's a hot day you'll want one, 'cause there's not much but low brush out here—which provides very little natural shade. Several hiking trails wander out into the piñon, juniper, and cholla.

A paved road winds through the hills overlooking the lake, across the dam to the Corps of Engineers' office and a small visitors center, where you'll find displays of the lake's fish—in addition to walleye pike, the reservoir is stocked with crappie and bass—and information on hydraulic engineering and flood control.

Entrance fee to the park is $4, and camping is $8 ($12 with hookups). Some sites provide wheelchair access, and a scenic/nature trail is specially designed for wheelchairs. To get to Santa Rosa Lake State Park, take the west Santa Rosa exit from I-40, and then 2nd Street north to Eddy Avenue; follow the signs seven miles to the lake.

For more information, write Park Manager, Santa Rosa Lake, P.O. Box 345, Santa Rosa, NM 88435, or phone 505/472-3110 or 800/451-2541.

PRACTICALITIES

Accommodations

Santa Rosa has a large number of motel rooms, though it'd still be wise to have a reservation waiting for you, especially if you're going to be getting in much after 5 P.M. or so. Most of the lodging is on Will Rogers Drive, the old Route 66 through town. You'll find a **Motel 6,** 3400 E. Will Rogers, 505/472-3045 (under $50), and a **Super 8 Motel,** 1201 Will Rogers Dr., 505/472-5388 (around $50). A bit nicer are the **Santa Rosa Inn Best Western,** 3022 W. Will Rogers, 505/472-5877, the **Adobe Inn Best Western Inn,** at I-40 and Highway 66, 505/472-3466, and a **Holiday Inn Express,** 3300 Will Rogers, 505/472-5411 (all $50–100).

Camping and RVing

Santa Rosa has two campgrounds in addition to Santa Rosa State Park (see above). The **KOA,** on the east end of town at 2136 Will Rogers Dr., 505/472-3126, charges about $25 for sites with basic hookups (extra charge for cable TV) and $20 for tent sites (both rates for two people).

Free camping is available at **Janes-Wallace Memorial Park** on the southeast end of town. Take 3rd Street south from Parker Avenue.

Food

A popular Santa Rosa refueling spot—not only for locals but informed passers-through—is **Joseph's Restaurant,** downtown at 865 Will Rogers Dr., 505/472-3361. Mexican food is the specialty, but you can also get standard American fare (eggs, burgers, and steaks). Lunches run $4–8 and dinners $6–14. Another local favorite for good, cheap Mexican food is **Comet Drive-In,** also downtown at 239 Parker Avenue.

Recreation

In addition to Blue Hole and Park Lake, Santa Rosa Lake north of town lures anglers, water-skiers, sunbathers, and those just wanting to cool off on a hot afternoon, and the hills and canyons around the lake abound in hiking trails. In addition, the Pecos River offers fishing for channel catfish, and El Rito Creek is stocked year-round with rainbow trout. Nearby areas are open to deer, pronghorn, dove, quail, and waterfowl hunting (for more information, stop in at the visitors center at Santa Rosa Lake State Park).

The **Santa Rosa Golf Club,** 505/472-3949, is a nine-hole course open to public play.

Annual Events

Santa Rosa Days in late May feature a parade, arts and crafts show, and fishing derby. A softball tournament and barbecue complement the city's **Fourth of July** fireworks at Park Lake.

Information and Services

For more information about the Santa Rosa area, contact the **Santa Rosa Tourist Information Center** at the Santa Rosa Chamber of Commerce,

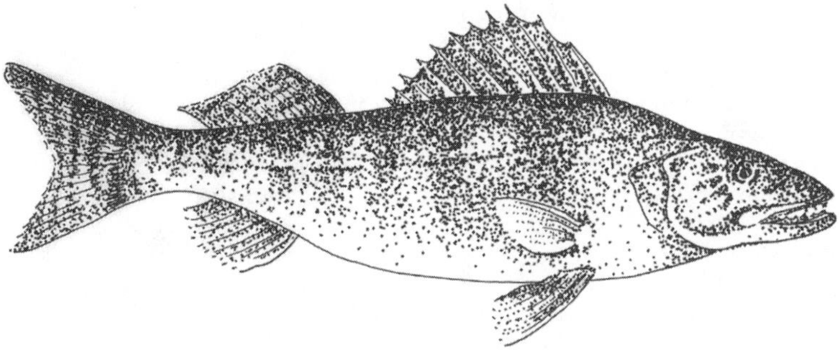

BOB RACE

Walleye pike thrive in the waters of Santa Rosa.

486 Parker Ave., Santa Rosa, NM 88435, 505/472-3763. Stop in at the visitors center there, at the corner of Will Rogers and 5th.

Guadalupe County Hospital is a small (18-bed) facility at 535 Lake Dr., 505/472-3417. Phone the Santa Rosa Police Department at 505/472-3605, and the state police at 505/472-3388.

Transportation

Santa Rosa has a small municipal airport for private planes. The closest passenger service is in Albuquerque (115 miles) or Clovis (105 miles); call **Mesa Air** at 800/MESA-AIR (800/637-2247). The Santa Rosa **Greyhound** bus depot is at 500 W. Coronado, 505/472-5720.

Tucumcari and Vicinity

About midway between Albuquerque and Amarillo, Tucumcari (pop. 7,000; elev. 4,085 feet) is a sight for the sore eyes of tired truckers and hungry tourists. With a roughly even parking meter-to-motel ratio, Tucumcari posts billboards that line I-40 for hundreds of miles in both directions, suggesting "Tucumcari Tonight," and claiming it's the city of 1,500 motel rooms. Makes sense, too. After all, this is one of the most traveled routes in North America. The Joads passed this way, and so did Woody Guthrie—and hundreds of others looking to get their kicks (on old Route 66).

After all, this is one of the most traveled routes in North America. The Joads passed this way, and so did Woody Guthrie—and hundreds of others looking to get their kicks (on old Route 66).

NORTHEASTERN NM

Coming into Tucumcari at night, you might be deceived. Compared with the barren and darkened desert that surrounds the town, Tucumcari's main drag—lined with bright neon signs—looks like downtown Las Vegas. It's still an awfully small town, though, with little more than the obligatory historical museum (operated by the "Tucumcari Historical Research Institute") and a couple of nearby lakes to keep travelers from packing up early and heading on down the road. In fact, so little goes on in Tucumcari, you'll find local sports on page three of the town's biweekly.

History

The plains around Tucumcari were home to nomadic Folsom hunters as early as 10,000 B.C. Prehistoric hunters ambushed mastodon, antelope, and other game that came to water at Tucumcari Lake northeast of town. Much later, the Comanches and Apaches hunted these plains for buffalo, and in the late 19th century, the Goodnight and Loving cattle drives passed through, often stopping here for rest and water.

Tucumcari wasn't founded until 1901, when railroad workers built it as a construction base for the Rock Island's main line. Named for Tucumcari Mountain, a mound south of town—and one of the Tucumcari plains' few topographical features—the town was originally known as "Six-Shooter Siding," in honor of the proverbial law of the West, which reigned supreme in these parts. In 1908, the town was given its current appellation, although no one is certain exactly where the mountain itself got its name. One theory is that Tucumcari is Comanche for Signal Peak, and that the mountain was used to send smoke signals. Another possibility is that the name comes from a bizarre Apache legend, part Shakespeare, part *F Troop:* A dying chief, Wautonomah, summoned two of his finest braves—Tonapah and Tocom—and asked them to decide between themselves who would become chief and husband of Kari, Wautonomah's daughter. Kari, who loved Tocom, watched the ensuing battle between her two suitors, and after Tonapah killed Tocom she in turn stabbed and killed Tonapah and then herself. Her father, dying Chief Wautonomah, arriving on the scene, cried out, "Tocom-Kari," just before plunging a knife into his own heart.

Between the 1930s and 1960s, Tucumcari was

an important stop for tired Route 66 travelers. To Tucumcari's dismay, though, the new interstate, built in the early '70s, bypassed the old route and most of the town's merchants—for decades dependent for their very survival on the business of passers-through. Not to be undone by the capriciousness of federal highway builders, though, Tucumcari sprang back, aggressively marketing itself, and today boasts a relatively healthy economy thanks to the tourists and truckers passing through.

SIGHTS

Tucumcari Historical Museum

This is one of those classic small-town historical museums composed mostly of collections donated by area residents—which explains the *bizarre* array of items: whale vertebrae, old saddles, barbed-wire displays, mammoth teeth, worn cowboy boots, gems and minerals, Folsom spear points, petrified wood, a pre-1900 windmill, a chuck wagon, and a "petrified dinosaur scale."

The museum is at 416 S. Adams and is open in the summer (June 2 through Labor Day) Monday–Saturday 9 A.M.–6 P.M., and the rest of the year Tuesday–Saturday 9 A.M.–5 P.M. For more information, phone 505/461-4201. Admission is $2 for adults and $.50 for children.

Mesalands Dinosaur Museum

This new museum (fall 1999), developed by Tucumcari's Mesa Technical College, houses exhibits and teaching facilities in a 17,000-square-foot building. Many of the displays feature discoveries from the surrounding area, which was a major dinosaur stomping grounds during the Triassic period. Also included are a children's science hall, hands-on exhibits, and classes in geology and paleontology.

The museum is at 222 E. Laughlin Street. March 15–October 15 the museum is open Tuesday–Saturday noon–8 P.M. The rest of the year, it's open Tuesday–Saturday noonP.M.–5 P.M. Admission is $5 for adults, with discounts for kids and seniors. Phone 505/461-4413 for more information.

Ladd S. Gordon Wildlife Area

The city has set aside 770 acres east of town as a wildlife refuge. Visitors can drive or hike out into the marshland to view migrating ducks and geese and the occasional bald or golden eagle. Watch for the signs on the east end of Tucumcari Boulevard (old Route 66).

Conchas Lake State Park

An immensely popular boating and fishing area, Conchas Lake was filled in 1939 after the construction of the 1,250-foot-long Conchas Dam. The lake is stocked with walleye pike, black bass, channel catfish, and several varieties of sunfish. One of the most developed state parks in New Mexico, Conchas has an airstrip, nine-hole golf course, marina (with rental boats), launching ramps, and more than 150 campsites.

Because most of the lake's shoreline is privately owned, lake access is pretty much restricted to the state park properties, including three separate campgrounds. Day use is $3, and overnight camping is $8 ($12 with hookups). A small general store stocks basic camping and fishing gear, as well as picnic supplies and groceries.

In addition, **The Lodge,** 505/868-2988, in the village of Conchas Park, has rooms overlooking the lake starting at $50 and a dining room serving breakfast, lunch, and dinner. Take 1st Street north from downtown Tucumcari, then Highway 104 northwest about 30 miles.

PRACTICALITIES

Accommodations

Tucumcari accommodates the budget of just about every type of traveler. The least expensive consistently reliable rooms are probably at **Blue Swallow Motel,** 815 E. Tucumcari Blvd., 505/461-9849, a classic Route 66 motel on the National Register of Historic Places (around $50). The **Discovery Motor Inn Best Western,** 200 E. Estrella, 505/461-4884, and the **Pow Wow Inn Best Western,** 801 W. Tucumcari, 505/461-0500, both have clean, good-sized rooms ($50–100), as does the **Holiday Inn** on the east end of town (3716 E. Tucumcari, Exit 335 from I-40), 505/461-3780 ($50–100). The Tucumcari Chamber of Commerce will gladly send you a brochure with a complete listing of the town's lodging options.

Camping and RVing

The Tucumcari **KOA,** 505/461-1841, has shaded sites with hookups for $20–28. You'll also find camping at nearby **Ute Lake State Park** (see Vicinity of Tucumcari, following) and **Conchas Lake State Park** (see above).

Food

Surprisingly, given the humongous number of motels in Tucumcari, there's not as much grub as you might expect. The **Pow Wow Grill,** 801 W. Tucumcari, 505/461-2587, serves three meals a day, seven days a week. Fare includes standard American breakfasts, breakfast burritos, sandwiches, steaks, and seafood. The Pow Wow also has live music regularly and is probably one of the few places in the area where you can get an espresso or *latte.* Steak, seafood, and chicken dinner entrées are $10–18, including salad bar; New Mexican food entrées run $8–14. **Del's,** 1202 E. Tucumcari Blvd., 505/461-1740, is a classic Route 66 diner, serving steaks, burgers, and some seafood and Mexican dishes—very reasonably priced. Tucumcari also satisfies the fast-foodies with its McDonald's, Blake's, Sonic, and Tastee Freez.

Recreation

Boating, water-skiing, and fishing are popular summertime activities at both Conchas and Ute Lakes (see Vicinity of Tucumcari, following). In addition, the areas around Tucumcari offer prime pronghorn, deer, duck, and upland game hunting, especially for grouse, pheasant, and quail. Tucumcari's nine-hole **municipal golf course** is just west of town and open every day but Monday—no tee-time reservations required (phone 505/461-1849 for more information). For a break from the heat, stop by the **municipal swimming pool** at 5th Street and Tucumcari Boulevard.

Annual Events

The **Quay County Fair** in mid-August features livestock exhibits, arts and crafts, rides, and food.

Information and Services

For specific information about the Tucumcari area, contact the **chamber of commerce,** Drawer E, Tucumcari, NM 88401, 505/461-1694, or stop by the office at 404 W. Tucumcari Boulevard. Also helpful is the chamber's website: www.tucumcarinm.com. The Tucumcari **library** is at 602 S. 2nd St., 505/461-0295. The **Readmore Bookstore,** 505/461-3108, stocks a wide array of books and magazines.

Dr. Dan C. Trigg Memorial Hospital is at 301 E. Miel de Luna (just off I-40; take Exit 332), 505/461-0141. Phone the Tucumcari Police Department at 505/461-2160 and the state police at 505/461-3300.

Transportation

Passenger bus service is provided to Tucumcari by **Greyhound,** 505/461-1350.

VICINITY OF TUCUMCARI

San Jon

This small town about midway between Tucumcari and the Texas border has a couple of gas stations and a small municipal park, with restrooms and free overnight parking.

Ute Lake State Park

Another favorite boating and fishing spot of Tucumcarians, as well as of West Texans driving over from the border 20 miles east, Ute Lake is stocked with northern and walleye pike, black bass, catfish, and sunfish. The state maintains three separate camping facilities at Ute Lake, although only North Area has hot showers and flush toilets; all three have boat ramps, shelters, and picnic tables. The main office/visitors center also has modern restrooms with hot showers. Camping is $8, $12 with hookups. Rental boats are available.

Ute Dam was built across the Canadian River in 1963 and named for Ute Creek, one of the Canadian's tributaries. The 2,000-foot dam is more than 120 feet high, and the spillway is 840 feet long. Take Highway 54 northeast about 25 miles from Tucumcari.

TO CLAYTON

Stay on Highway 54 northeast of Ute Lake, and then turn north on Highway 402 (old Highway 18) at Nara Visa. From there, it's another 60 miles to Clayton. Don't expect much in the way of scenery out here. This is flat grasslands, and it's easy to get a little excited at the sight of a hillock or even a distant mesa. If you keep your eyes peeled, however, you might catch sight of various wildlife, including coyotes, pronghorn, deer, eagles, hawks, and other small birds and animals.

Clayton and Vicinity

Clayton (pop. 2,500; elev. 5.050 feet) has two claims to fame: First, it bills itself as being in the "heart of dinosaur country." Okay. Don't forget, though, that it's been at least several decades since those critters were around, and chances are pretty slim you'll see a stegosaurus romping across the plain or a flock of pterodactyls darkening the sky. What you can see, though, are the footprints they left behind (see Clayton Lake State Park, following). Second, Clayton is the "CO_2 Capital of the World." What that means is that Union County, of which Clayton is the county seat, is home to Rio Bravo Carbon Dioxide Field, one of the largest CO_2 deposits in the world. A half mile below the rolling grasslands of the county, a layer of sandstone has trapped an estimated 10 trillion cubic feet of 99 percent-pure carbon dioxide. The oil companies have put this supply to good use. During the 1970s, as the country was realizing its oil resources weren't inexhaustible, the oil companies began injecting carbon dioxide into mature fields, increasing by 20 percent the amount of oil that could be recovered. With eastern New Mexico so rich in petroleum, the area relies heavily on Clayton's gases.

Other industries important to the Clayton and Union County areas are ranching and farming, with sheep, cattle, corn, wheat, alfalfa, potatoes, and sorghum among the leading products.

NORTHEASTERN NM

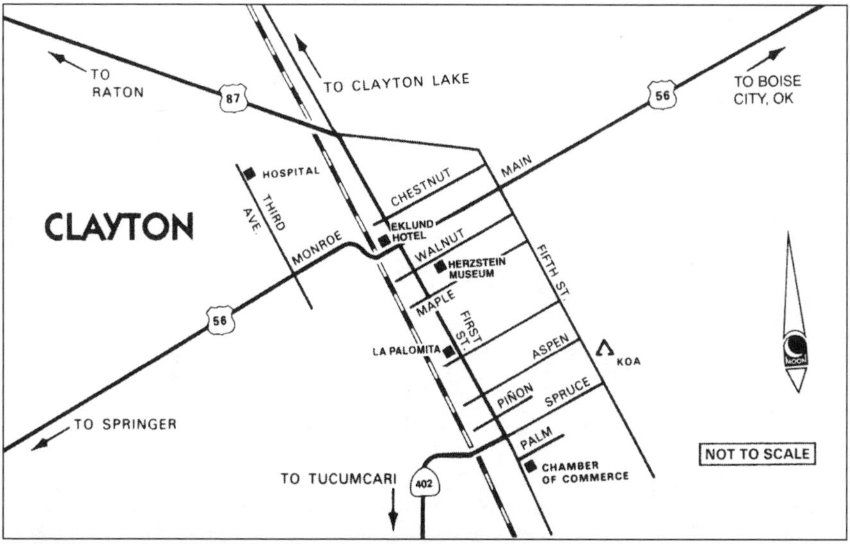

History

The Clayton-area plains were home to Indian hunters for thousands of years before Coronado passed through the area in 1540 looking for his illusory golden cities. During the 18th century, the plains were the site of many bloody battles between Comanche warriors and Spanish settlers. The confrontations continued well into the 19th century as Anglos began to settle the Southwest. Many battles were fought along the Cimarron Cutoff of the Santa Fe Trail, which branched off from the main route near Fort Dodge, Kansas, and dropped into Oklahoma, passing just north of Clayton.

The town of Clayton was founded in 1887, when the Colorado and Southern Pacific Railroad built a small camp at a site where cowboys had long rested and watered cattle. During the 1890s, several small stores and businesses opened in Clayton, and in 1892 John C. Hill built the Eklund Hotel, advertised as "the only first-class hotel between Trinidad and Fort Worth." Clayton was designated seat of Union County in 1895 and in 1901 hosted the public hanging (and inadvertent decapitation) and burying of notorious outlaw Thomas "Black Jack" Ketchum. Clayton has remained a major cattle and farming region.

SIGHTS

Clayton Lake State Park

This small lake (170 acres) 12 miles north of Clayton is the result of a dam built on Cieneguilla Creek in 1955. Perfect for swimming, the lake has a juniper-dotted shoreline with a number of sandy beaches, as well as rocky cliffs for jumping and diving. As with most of the state's waterside parks, you'll find camping, fishing (for walleye pike, trout, catfish, and bass), boating, and hiking here, but Clayton Lake offers also something different. It's situated on an ancient shoreline that 100 million years ago extended from the Gulf of Mexico to Canada, and at one time dinosaurs roamed the marshy flats. In 1982, rain washed away dirt from a large area near the dam—exposed by dam construction seven years earlier—and more than 500 dinosaur tracks were discovered.

Clayton Lake is situated on an ancient shoreline that 100 million years ago extended from the Gulf of Mexico to Canada, and at one time dinosaurs roamed the marshy flats. In 1982, rain washed away dirt from a large area near the dam and more than 500 dinosaur tracks were discovered.

A short trail leads along the lakeshore and over the dam to the tracks, where you'll find a small exhibit with drawings and descriptions of the different dinosaurs once prevalent here. From there, a wooden walkway wanders out among the tracks themselves. Standing there looking at these huge footprints, while an outboard motor drones in the distance, sucking up processed petroleum, you're reminded of the proverbial human paradox: our incontestable kinship with the earth and our collective disregard for its course.

Day use at Clayton State Park is $4, and overnight camping is $8. Take Highway 370 north from downtown Clayton.

Herzstein Memorial Museum

This small historical museum at the corner of South 2nd and Walnut in downtown Clayton is housed in the historic First Methodist Church, built in 1919. On display are 19th-century firearms, antique furniture, historical photos (including the macabre series of Black Jack Ketchum's hanging), and reproductions of dinosaur tracks from Clayton Lake.

The museum is open Tuesday–Saturday 1 P.M.–5 P.M. Admission is free. For information or to schedule a private tour phone 505/374-2977.

Rabbit Ears Mountains

The twin volcanic peaks you see to the north of Clayton were supposedly named for Cheyenne Indian Chief Orejas de Conejo (Rabbit Ears). An important landmark for Santa Fe Trail travelers during the 19th century, the mountains also provided shelter for Indians, who routinely attacked the increasing number of westbound coaches and wagon trains.

Clayton Historical Park

This small city park just off North 3rd Street is perfect for a picnic and to let the kids blow off some steam. If the swings and jungle gym aren't enough, turn them loose on the dinosaurs—friendly to most preteen *Homo sapiens.*

Kiowa National Grassland

Spread along 40 miles of the border east of town is one unit of the four-unit, 263,964-acre Kiowa National Grassland. (For more information see Springer to Las Vegas, following.)

PRACTICALITIES

Accommodations

There are only a half dozen motels in Clayton, so you can't be picky here. For around $50, you can get a room at the **Holiday Motel** on Highway 87 North, 505/374-2558, or the **Super 8,** at 1425 S. Hwy. 87, 505/374-8127. Doubles at the **Best Western Kokopelli Lodge,** 702 S. 1st St., 505/374-2589, run $50–100. The Clayton **KOA,** 903 S. 5th St., 505/374-9508, has both RV and tent sites; call for rates.

Food

For breakfast try the **Hi Ho Cafe,** 1201 S. 1st, 505/374-9515, where you can order standard American fare or New Mexican specials, including breakfast burritos—$4–10.

The **Eklund Dining Room and Saloon,** 15 Main St., 505/374-2551, built in 1892, also serves dinners. Beautifully restored, the hotel features an ornate dining room with high ceilings and chandeliers and the feel of the Old West. The menu includes Mexican dinners; steak, chicken, and seafood entrées; and children's plates. Open daily for lunch ($6–12) and dinner ($8–20).

Recreation

Boating, fishing, swimming, and hiking are available at **Clayton Lake State Park** (see Sights, above). The plains around Clayton are popular with upland game hunters, and the **Clayton Municipal Golf Course** (505/374-9957) is open to public play.

Annual Events

Clayton sponsors a rodeo on the **Fourth of July,** and the **Union County Fair** in late August features livestock and agricultural exhibits, food, and crafts. In late spring, the town hosts **Dinosaur Days,** with games, food booths, and guided tours of Clayton Lake State Park. The **Clayton Arts Festival** takes place the first weekend in October and draws sculptors and painters from many western states. Call the chamber for exact dates and more information.

Information and Services

The **chamber of commerce,** 1103 S. 1st St., 505/374-9253 or 800/390-7858, will happily fill your arms with brochures and other literature on Clayton and Clayton-area attractions and practicalities. Visit its website at www.claytonnewmexico.org. The Clayton **public library,** 505/374-9423, has a small collection of books on the area.

Clayton's Union County Medical Center is at 315 N. 3rd Ave., 505/374-8313. The Clayton Police Department is at 112 N. Front St., 505/374-2504. The state police are in the same building and can be reached at 505/374-2473.

CLAYTON TO RATÓN

The 85-mile drive from Clayton to Ratón is mostly uneventful, a flat stretch of highway (Highway 64/87) that drifts along the high plains, gradually rising from the seemingly endless grasslands to the pine and piñon forests east of Ratón, and finally to the southern end of the Rocky Mountains towering blue in the distance. About midway, you'll come to the tiny town of Des Moines, not much more than a gas station and a couple of small mom-and-pop cafés. The area will be of interest, though, both to geology and history buffs, as the road passes next to Capulin Volcano and near where the earliest evidence of human occupation in the United States was found.

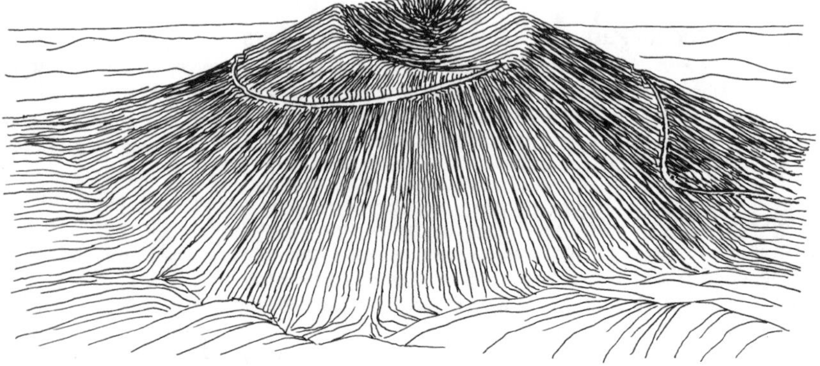

BOB RACE

Drive to the top of Capulin Volcano, then hike down into the crater.

Capulin Volcano National Monument

A 1,000-foot-high mountain rising steep and green from the brown grassy flatlands, Capulin is the cinder cone of a volcano that erupted as recently as 10,000 years ago. Visitors can drive up the side of the volcano and actually hike down inside. Start at the visitors center at the base of the mountain's northern flank. Besides exhibits of the area's flora and wildlife (from chokecherries to porcupines), the center continually shows a 10-minute film explaining volcanic activity—some of the footage of eruptions is absolutely stunning. From there, take the narrow two-lane road that winds up the side of the mountain to a parking lot and trailheads just below the summit (8,182 feet above sea level). Crater Rim Trail climbs gradually another mile along the crater's ridge, circling back to the parking lot. On a clear day, you can see Colorado, Kansas, Oklahoma, and, if you really want to, Texas (just kiddin', pardner!). A shorter, quarter-mile trail drops into the crater itself.

Capulin National Monument is open Labor Day through Memorial Day, 8 A.M.–4 P.M., and in summer 7:30 A.M.–6:30 P.M. Admission is $5 per car. The visitors center is three miles from Highway 87, and the summit is another two miles. You can't miss the signs on the main highway. Phone 505/278-2201.

Capulin

Just south of Capulin Volcano, this is another classic blink-and-you'll-miss-it town with minimal services—a gas station, Mt. Capulin General Store, and **Capulin Camp,** where RV sites are $12 with hookups and tent sites are $7 (hot showers included)—not the kind of place you'd want to stay very long, but if you need to pull off the road, there's not much else around.

Folsom

In 1925, a cowboy named George McJunkin was riding along an arroyo near Folsom when he noticed some odd-looking bones protruding from the earth. He stopped, dug them up, and found with them a handful of flint spearheads one to three inches long.

There was a difference, though, between McJunkin's spear points and others found in the area up until then: The bones found with them were from animals extinct for 10,000 years. The delicately made flint spear points had been used to kill mammoths, mastodons, elephants, four-toed horses, and giant ground sloths. The anthropology and archaeology of the Western Hemisphere, which had long believed the earliest occupation to have been not much before the year A.D. 1, was turned on its ear.

As news of the find spread, scientists descended on the little town of Folsom, which until McJunkin's discovery had been known for little more than the surrounding plains and the cattle that grazed there. Now we know that these early people were second only to Sandia Man in arriving in New Mexico, and that both were the ancestors of Indians who eventually continued their migration—begun long before, when they crossed the Bering Strait—into South America, where they would establish the most advanced prehistoric civilizations in the hemisphere. Folsom Man, as we call those who stayed behind, roamed the plains of North America from northeastern Colorado to southeastern New Mexico, and has played an important part in shaping modern anthropological theory.

On Main Street in the tiny town of Folsom, **Folsom Museum,** open summers only, displays spear points and fossils more than 12,000 years old. Open daily 10 A.M.–5 P.M. Memorial Day through Labor Day and by appointment the rest of the year. Admission is $1 for adults, $.50 for kids six to 12. Take Highway 325 about 10 miles north from Capulin or Des Moines. The museum is on Main Street. For more information, phone 505/278-3616, or write Folsom Museum, Main Street, Folsom, NM 88419.

Ratón

Nestled against the southeastern foothills of the Rocky Mountains, Ratón (pop. 7,400; elev. 6,600 feet), the seat of Colfax County, is a small and colorful town loaded with Victorian charm and surrounded by some of the best outdoor recreation areas in the Southwest. Popular among West Texans who come here in the summer to bet the ponies, and situated along the main routes between Texas and some of the best winter snow skiing in the country, Ratón is well equipped year-round to accommodate the traveler. And those who take the time to explore this little town—from its brick and stone historical district to Sugarite Canyon State Park—will find the slow pace relaxing and pine forests restorative.

History

Ratón owes its founding to its location at the foot of Ratón Pass, the most difficult section of the old Santa Fe Trail. In 1866, Richens Lacy ("Uncle Dick") Wootten built a 27-mile road over the pass, erected a toll gate, and charged every settler, outlaw, and soldier who passed through. Shortly after Wootten's road was complete, the U.S. government established a livestock forage station on Willow Creek (now Ratón Creek), just south of the pass, and the site became a popular resting spot between Wootten's gate and the Canadian River to the south. In 1871, a rancher from Colorado moved to Willow Creek and dug the town's first well to water his cattle; in 1879, the railroad passed through, with a station at Otero, a construction camp five miles south. A year later, the Atchison, Topeka, & Santa Fe Railroad, looking to build a repair shop closer to the pass, moved its buildings north and changed the name of Willow Springs to Ratón. Within a year, Ratón's population was approaching 3,000.

Through the early 20th century, the railroad and coal mining were the mainstays of Ratón's economy, while the past 30 years or so have seen tremendous growth in the area's tourism industry, with skiing, fishing, and horse racing among the primary draws. Today, Ratón still manages both to maintain its frontier-town feel and greet the traveler with every modern convenience—from motels to medical care.

SIGHTS

Sugarite Canyon State Park

This is one of the newest state parks in the state, as well as one of the prettiest. A narrow pine- and aspen-lined road winds eight miles up into Sugarite Canyon, ending at Sugarite Ski Basin. The park actually begins just a few miles up the road and continues north, eventually spilling over into Colorado. Lake Maloya, a small alpine reservoir that reflects the green mountains and deep sky, is popular among anglers, and four-pound trout have been pulled from its waters.

The park has two separate campgrounds, each with beautiful sites. Check out **Sodapocket Area,** a mile off the main road, where meadows of summer wildflowers meet towering palisades. Camping (once the snow melts) is $8, and day use is $4. Take Highway 72 (Sugarite Avenue) from Highway 85/87 on the north end of town and follow the signs.

Ratón Pass

Interstate 25 north of Ratón follows roughly the same route as the old Santa Fe Trail. Take the short, eight-mile drive to the 7,834-foot summit and try to imagine pushing wagon trains and building a railroad through these mountains.

Historical Tour

This self-guided walking tour begins at the old Santa Fe depot, where as many as 60 trains a day once passed by. Other buildings on the tour include the Shuler Theatre, home to old Ratón's opera house, fire station, and city offices; the old Seaburg European Hotel, at one time the state's largest; the Palace Hotel, restored to its original Victorian elegance; and the Swastika Hotel, built in 1929 and decorated with the Indian symbols of good luck (during World War II, for obvious reasons, the name was changed to the Yucca Hotel and the swastikas painted over). The tour includes nearly 30 buildings. For a map, stop in at the visitors information center, 100 Clayton Rd., or the Ratón Museum.

Ratón Museum

This small storefront museum downtown at 218 1st St. displays old farming equipment and other artifacts of historical and anthropological interest, as well as records of the original 19th-century settlers. Memorial Day through Labor Day, the museum is open Tuesday–Saturday 9 A.M.–5 P.M.; the rest of the year it's open Wednesday–Saturday 10 A.M.–4 P.M. Phone 505/445-8979 for information.

PRACTICALITIES

Accommodations

Although Ratón has a full range of lodging possibilities, it's a good idea to make reservations at least a week or so ahead of time, especially on weekends during the summer, when most rooms are spoken for by pony bettors. The **Best Western Sands Motel,** 300 Clayton Hwy. (Highway 87/64 East), 505/445-2737, is a good choice with doubles running $50–100. There's also a new **Holiday Inn Express,** 101 Card, 505/445-1500 ($50–100).

The Ratón **KOA** is right in town at 1330 S. 2nd St., 505/445-3488. Sites with complete hookups go for $20.

For a complete listing of Raton lodging, check out the chamber's visitor-information page at website: www.ratonchamber.com/visinfo/lodging.htm.

Food

A good place for breakfast is **Papa's Sweet Shop** at 1201 S. 2nd St., 505/445-9811. Specialties include French toast (made from homemade bread) and fresh fruit. For Italian food, try the **Capri Restaurant,** 304 Clayton Hwy., 505/445-9755. A local favorite, **K-Bob's Steakhouse,** is at 1228 2nd, 505/445-2548.

Recreation

Located where the plains meet the southern Rockies, Ratón is an outdoor lover's paradise. Fish, camp, hike, hunt, ski, or golf—even the most committed urbanophile would be tempted to swap Gucci loafers for hiking boots and step off the sidewalk. For starters, check out **Sugarite Canyon State Park** (see Sights, above), where there's peace and quiet among the pines and aspens, and the fishing is some of the best around. You'll also find excellent fishing southwest of Ratón in the Cimarron River and at Eagle Nest Lake, while hunters stalk the Ratón-area forests and plains for deer, pronghorn, quail, and grouse.

For information and regulations, phone the Ratón office of the **New Mexico Game and Fish Department** at 505/445-2311.

Downhill and cross-country skiers will delight in Sugarite Canyon. For the Nordic skier, dozens of trails wander into the forests and meadows, while **Sugarite Ski Basin** has a poma and chairlift for beginning and intermediate Alpine skiers. Take Highway 72 through town, and follow the signs to Sugarite Canyon State Park.

One of Ratón's most popular summer pastimes, among locals and out-of-towners, is horse racing. The downs at **La Mesa Park** on the town's south side feature quarter-horse and thoroughbred racing on weekends and holidays, May–September. For information, phone La Mesa Race Track, 505/445-2301, or write La Mesa Park, Ratón, NM 87740.

The nine-hole **Ratón municipal golf course** on Gardner Road, 505/445-8113, is open to the public.

Annual Events

The **Ratón Rodeo Association** sponsors a rodeo and parade in early June, while the local Jaycees hold theirs in mid-July. Several events are held annually at Sugarite Canyon State Park, including an **ice-fishing derby** in early February, a **yacht race** in August, and a **mountain-bike race** in September. Phone the chamber for exact dates or more information.

Information and Services

A **tourist information and welcome center** sits at the junction of Highways 85 and 87 (100 Clayton Hwy.). If the maps and literature on Ratón-area attractions don't answer all your questions, the friendly and knowledgeable employees will. Write the Ratón Chamber of Commerce at P.O. Box 1211, Ratón, NM 87740, or phone 505/445-3689 or 800/638-6161. The chamber's website: www.ratonchamber.com. The Ratón **public library** is at 244 Clark Ave., 505/445-9711.

Miners' Colfax Medical Center, 505/445-3661, is operated by the State of New Mexico and has a 24-hour emergency room. Take South 2nd to York Canyon Road and turn left on Hospital Drive. The office of the Ratón Police Department is at 224 Savage, 505/445-2704. Phone the state police in Ratón at 505/445-5571.

Transportation

Both **Greyhound,** 505/445-9071, and **Amtrak,** 800/872-7245, offer passenger service to Ratón. Amtrak's Southwest Chief passes through here westbound for Flagstaff and Los Angeles, and eastbound for Kansas City and Chicago. The bus depot is at the junction of I-25 and Highway 64/87, and Amtrak is in the old Santa Fe train depot downtown near the corner of 1st Street and Apache.

RATÓN TO CIMARRON

The 50-mile stretch of Highway 64 between Ratón and Cimarron crosses the plains and flirts with the southern edge of the Rocky Mountains. As you drive along, imagine yourself a westbound settler, fleeing the relatively cramped and populous East Coast. Look at the huge sky, the empty land that seems to stretch to forever. Think of the wagon trains, Conestogas filled with a family's only possessions. Imagine the spirits of the pioneers, pictures of the promised land painted radiant in their dauntless dreams.

Cimarron and Vicinity

Cimarron (pop. 1,000; elev. 6,430 feet) holds a special place in the hearts of many lovers of New Mexico, from history buffs to Boy Scouts. It's a tiny town, with the gentle Cimarron River running through it, and though there are only a handful of paved streets, there are also 14 historical markers noting Cimarron's contributions to the past.

Pulling into Cimarron, even for the first time, you immediately sense something different about this town, something that makes it stand out from the hundreds of other Southwestern towns its size. In part, it's the countryside. Absolutely gorgeous. Nestled in a tiny pocket of the southern Rockies and surrounded by thick pine forests and rolling green hills, Cimarron will take your breath away, and then quickly replace it with a gloriously rejuvenating mountain breeze. In part, too, it's the town's history, so crucial to the settling of the West—through the years Cimarron has attracted such figures as Lew Wallace, Buffalo Bill Cody, Annie Oakley, Kit Carson, Zane Grey, and Frederic Remington. And finally, it's Cimarron's proximity to some of the most varied and wondrous country in the Southwest—the vast butte-and volcano-dotted plains to the east, Cimarron Canyon, Eagle Nest, Red River, and Taos to the west. Cimarron is both a destination and a gateway, a town that feels as much like home as it does a threshold.

History

Though Cimarron (Spanish for Wild or Untamed) was most likely named after the wild horses and sheep early settlers found in the area, the appellation applies perhaps even more appropriately to the town's *people* in its early days. Once a wild and woolly hub of activity and a principal stop on the Santa Fe Trail, Cimarron was notorious throughout the West for its rowdy cowboys, impassioned politics, and 15 saloons.

The town's history dates to 1841, when a petition was filed for the Beaubein and Miranda Land Grant, and ranchers working the land needed a central gathering place. Soon a post office was established, and by 1849, Lucien Maxwell

Travelers have been staying at the St. James since the early 1870s.

had married Beaubein's daughter and was living on the property. When Beaubein died in 1864, Maxwell inherited his father-in-law's share of the land, and by 1865 he had bought off the other partners. The Maxwell Land Grant, as the property came to be known, was at the time the largest piece of private property in the country, covering 1,714,765 acres, an area three times the size of Rhode Island. The house Maxwell built in Cimarron took up an entire city block and included a dance hall and billiard room.

Lucien Maxwell was an enterprising sort, not one to put all his eggs in one basket. Among his ventures were banking, mining, and beef and sheep ranching, the latter in which he was partners with Buffalo Bill Cody from 1860 to 1862. Though the Cody-Maxwell sheep business didn't do as well as some of Maxwell's other businesses, another of Cody's Cimarron-based enterprises did: it was here that Buffalo Bill organized his Wild West Shows, and later often spent Christmases at the St. James Hotel, throwing lavish parties for the children of the area.

From 1872 to 1882, Cimarron was the seat of Colfax County, although its governmental status did nothing to quell the town's rowdies. The St. James Hotel, built as a saloon in 1873, was a common meeting place for ranchers, trappers, traders, and gunmen, and it was the site of 26 killings in just a few short years. A Las Vegas, New Mexico, newspaper once reported, "Everything is quiet in Cimarron. Nobody has been killed for three days."

In 1880, when the Atchison, Topeka, & Santa Fe Railroad built its repair shop in Ratón, and that town began to grow, things slowed down in Cimarron. In 1882, the seat of Colfax County was transferred to Springer (later to Ratón), further inviting hard times to town. The economy picked up again in 1905, though, when the St. Louis, Rocky Mountain and Pacific Railroad built a branch line to Cimarron. Shortly, a "New Town" was established, with newer homes and buildings springing up on the north side of the river, and in the 1930s much of Old Town was destroyed by fire.

In 1941, a new dimension was added to the Cimarron area. That year Waite Phillips donated 127,395 acres of land just a few miles south of town to the Boy Scouts of America. Through the years, the ranch—and its vast wilderness—has hosted more than half a million Boy Scouts (see Philmont Scout Ranch, following). The St. James Hotel was completely restored in 1985, and today, as in the late 19th century, it is the jewel of Cimarron, once again a popular gathering place.

SIGHTS

St. James Hotel

Built in 1873 by Henri Lambert, personal chef to both President Lincoln and General Ulysses S. Grant, the St. James has history oozing from every wall and nook and cranny. Buffalo Bill planned his Wild West Show here; gunman Clay Allison danced on the bar; early New Mexico governor Lew Wallace wrote part of *Ben Hur* and Zane Grey wrote *Fighting Caravans* here; and 26 murders have been committed in the hotel's rooms, hallways, and saloon.

During the restoration, completed in 1985, early hotel registers were discovered, so it's known who stayed where. Today, the rooms, each distinctly decorated, some with original furniture, are named for early boarders. Take a walk upstairs and peek into the Buffalo Bill Room, and imagine Annie Oakley sneaking down the hall from her room to spend the night with Mr. Cody, as she is rumored to have done.

For more information, call 505/376-2664 or 800/748-2694, or write the St. James Hotel, Rt. 1, Box 2, Cimarron, NM 87714.

Old Aztec Mill Museum

An old mill houses four stories of eclectic but well-displayed and annotated exhibits: Native American tools, weapons, pottery; Maxwell Land Grant paperwork and documents; antique surgical equipment; old photos, musical instruments, and a barber chair; place settings and silver from the original St. James Hotel.

The museum is across the street from the St. James and is open June–August, Monday–Saturday 9 A.M.–4:30 P.M. and Sunday 1–5 P.M.; in May and September, the museum is open Saturday 9 A.M.–4:30 P.M. and Sunday 1–5 P.M.

Admission is $2, $1 for senior citizens and Boy Scouts. For more information, phone 505/376-2913.

Walking Tour

Local boosters have mapped out a fascinating historical walking tour of Cimarron. Sites include many structures built between 1854 and 1874, including the home of Lucien Maxwell, the old Cimarron jail, a hardware store and livery stable, and the St. James Hotel. Annotated maps are available from the Cimarron Welcome Center at the corner of Highway 64 and Lincoln or by writing or phoning the Cimarron Chamber of Commerce.

Philmont Scout Ranch

This huge ranch is owned by the Boy Scouts of America and is the largest "campground" in the world, annually hosting more than 25,000 Scouts. The spread includes the elaborate **Villa Philmonte** ranch home, built by oil magnate Waite Phillips between 1922 and 1927. Modeled after buildings Phillips and his wife saw on their frequent Mediterranean cruises, and decorated mostly with furniture they bought in Europe, Villa Philmonte is a sprawling hacienda with bear-and cougar-skin rugs, a 16-person dining table with chairs of hand-tooled Moroccan leather, a custom-made piano, and a shower with seven separate showerheads (no way to hog the water in there!).

Tours of the villa are offered daily during June, July, and August, and run every half hour 8–11 A.M. and 1–4:30 P.M. Tours cost $4 and can be scheduled at the Philmont Museum or by calling 505/376-2281.

The **Philmont Museum** includes the library of Ernest Thompson Seton, naturalist, writer, sculptor, and painter. His 3,000 paintings—of birds, rabbits, buffalo, etc.—are displayed on a rotating basis, and you also read about Thompson's role as a leader in exterminating wolves from the area (thank you very much, Ernie). One of the highlights is a photo of Thompson—hard at work—with the delightfully ambiguous caption, "Ernest Thompson Seton mounting a great blue heron." The library is open 8 A.M.–5 P.M. daily in summer, and weekends only September–May. Admission is free.

To get to Villa Philmonte, take Highway 21 four miles south of Cimarron. For more information, phone 505/376-2281.

Boy Scout tents at the Philmont Scout Ranch, near Cimarron

© STEPHEN METZGER

the Valle Vidal sky near Cimarron

Also part of the Philmont Scout Ranch is the **Kit Carson Museum,** an interpretive history museum run by Philmont staffers, who dress in 19th-century garb and live on the premises. Visitors are led from room to room by tour guides, who pass you along from one to the next: The first guide, dressed and equipped as a blacksmith, gives you a historical overview while working his fire, bellows, hammer, and anvil. You then are led through the living quarters, kitchen, military room and armory, and finally out into the central plaza, where you're free to continue wandering on your own. Along the way, you learn a lot about life in late 19th-century New Mexico, although not much about Carson himself. Guides are young and very knowledgeable, and they clearly enjoy their work. Be sure to ask about the linseed oil and oxblood floors.

The Kit Carson museum is open daily 8 A.M.–5 P.M. mid-June through early August. Admission is free. Take Highway 21 10 miles south of Cimarron.

If you're interested in learning more about the Philmont Scout Ranch, visit the website: www.philmont.com.

Valle Vidal

This recently designated section of the Carson National Forest is without doubt one of the most spectacular regions in the Southwest. A very rough and rocky road wanders 40 miles into towering pines, groves of shimmering aspens, and sprawling meadows, where elk and cattle graze amid the wildflowers and tall, gently waving grasses. McCrystal Creek Campground, about 30 miles in, is an isolated and wonderfully peaceful area with a handful of free campsites (drinking water, pit toilets). Valle Vidal is closed May 1–June 30 every year to allow the elk herd to calve without human spectators. Take Highway 64 four miles east of Cimarron, and watch for the turnoff on your left. Make sure you've got a decent spare tire, as chances are slim you'll run across many other motorists (if any at all).

PRACTICALITIES

Accommodations

Anyone with even a moderate interest in history will find it fascinating to stay at the **St. James Hotel,** 505/376-2664. Built in 1873 and restored in 1985, the St. James offers the traveler the luxury of a first-class hotel and the feeling of the true Old West. Stay in the same rooms where celebrities of the past slept—Buffalo Bill, Annie Oakley, Jesse James, Zane Grey, Wyatt Earp. Rates run $100–150. In addition, the St. James's hotel annex has conventional motel-type rooms, $50–100. Be sure to call for reservations, especially if you plan to stay on Tuesday and Wednesday nights in summer (these are turnover nights for Philmont, and the place is likely to be packed with Boy Scouts and Scout Masters).

Casa de Gavilan, 505/376-2246, is a bed-and-breakfast in a turn-of-the-20th-century pueblo-style adobe home. The Gavilan also has a unique history: former owners include Waite Phillips, and Zane Grey set his novel *Knights of the Range* here. The four rooms run $75–100 each (for two; each additional person pays $10). For more information, phone, write P.O. Box 518, Cimarron, NM 87714, or check the website: www.casadelgavilan.com.

The **Cimarron Inn and RV Park,** a block south of the St. James, 505/376-2724, has doubles starting at about $35.

Camping

You'll find several state park and national forest campgrounds along Highway 64 between Cimarron and Eagle Nest.

Food

The **St. James Hotel,** 505/374-2664, has an elegant dining room, as well as a more casual diner-type restaurant, the latter serving three meals a day: standard American breakfasts are $4–7, sandwiches and burgers run $5–8, and dinner specials (salads, pastas, chicken, steak, and Mexican plates) are $7–12. The main dining room serves steak, chicken, seafood, and pasta dinners for $10–22.

Entertainment

Cimarron isn't exactly the nightlife capital of the Southwest, although the **Kit Carson Lounge** on Highway 64 has an excellent jukebox, pool tables, live music on weekends, and a reputation for getting *rowdy* at night. The bar at the St. James is a cozy little place to chat with the locals.

Shopping

Not a whole lot here in the way of gift shops and galleries either (part of what makes it so attractive), although the **Cimarron Art Gallery** on North 9th Street, 505/376-2614, sells Native American and Western art—from oil paintings to weavings—and has an old-fashioned soda fountain serving ice-cream cones and snacks.

Recreation

The vans stuffed with fishing, climbing, and backpacking gear indicate what kind of country this is. If Hemingway had been born in the Southwest, we might be reading stories about northern New Mexico instead of about upper Michigan. The Cimarron River, between Cimarron and Eagle Nest, offers excellent **trout fishing,** although you need to get away from the areas near the campgrounds—generally fished out or at best home to little more than recent hatchery releases. For **hiking,** you won't find more beautiful country than the Valle Vidal, northeast of Cimarron, and Cimarron Canyon has several marked hiking and backpacking trails ranging from three to 14 miles long. For a map of the area's hiking trails, contact the Cimarron Chamber of Commerce.

The Cimarron mountains are also home to elk, deer, bear, wild turkey, and other game. Contact the **New Mexico Department of Game and Fish** in Ratón at 505/445-2311.

Cimarron Canyon State Park on Highway 64 west of Cimarron is a popular rock-climbing area, with palisades of crenellated granite jutting above the treetops.

If you're just passing through Cimarron, you can join the guests in the **pool** at the St. James Hotel for $1.50.

Annual Events

Memorial Day, Cimarron celebrates **Western Weekend** with a juried art show and local merchants dressed in 19th-century garb. On the **Fourth of July** the area's cowboys get together for a rodeo, with team roping, fireworks, and a parade.

Information and Services

For more information on the Cimarron area,

contact the Cimarron **Chamber of Commerce,** P.O. Box 604, Cimarron, NM 87714, or phone 505/376-2614. In town, stop by the Cimarron Welcome Center at the corner of Highway 64 and Lincoln, where you can pick up maps and brochures highlighting area attractions.

The closest medical facility is Colfax General Hospital at 615 Prospect Ave. in Springer, about 25 miles southeast on Highway 58 and I-25, 505/483-2443. The Cimarron Police Department is at 9th and Jefferson, 505/376-2351.

Transportation

Both **Amtrak** (the Southwest Chief) and **Greyhound** have passenger service to Ratón, about 50 miles northeast, where you can rent cars.

WEST OF CIMARRON

The drive from Cimarron to Eagle Nest, about 25 miles west, is one of the prettiest in the state. The road winds along the Cimarron River, through a narrow canyon of tall pines and towering palisades. Along the way are several campgrounds, with tent and RV sites.

Cimarron Canyon State Park

This is part of the stunningly beautiful 33,000-acre Colin Neblett Wildlife Area, and it gets *packed.* Three campgrounds—Maverick, Tolby Creek, and Ponderosa—are right on the river and offer excellent access to the water. Be forewarned, though—fish get big for a reason: they elude fishermen. You'll have to get away from the easy-access areas if you want to hook into anything much bigger than a large pencil.

A little farther on, Palisades Picnic Area offers tables and shade at the foot of huge cliffs. The campgrounds are all right along the highway—you can't miss 'em. Day use is $4; overnight camping is $8, $12 with hookups. For more information, phone Cimarron Canyon State Park at 505/377-6271.

CIMARRON TO SPRINGER

To get back on I-25 from Cimarron, you can either head south on Highway 21 through Rayado and Miami or take Highway 58 east. Either way, you've got an easy drive through rolling hills and grasslands. The advantage of taking Highway 21 is that you'll pass both the Philmont Boy Scout Ranch and the Kit Carson Museum (see Sights, above). Highway 58, a more direct route, passes the old town of Maxwell, which during the late 19th century was the shipping center for the Maxwell Land and Irrigation Company.

Springer to Las Vegas

SPRINGER AND VICINITY

Springer (pop. 1,300; elev. 5,810 feet) was founded in 1879 when the Santa Fe Railroad was built through the area. Named for the prominent Springer brothers, Charles, a Cimarron rancher, and Frank, a Maxwell Land Grant lawyer, the town was the seat of Colfax County from 1882 until 1897, by which time Ratón had become a much more important commercial center and the county government moved north. Today Springer is home to the State Reform School for Boys.

The Santa Fe Trail Museum is in the old county courthouse on the main drag (614 Main) through town. Typical of New Mexico historical museums, this one houses a huge array of items, ranging in importance from Springer High School's senior class photos and assorted pieces that look as if they were hauled out of Aunt Minnie's basement to legitimately interesting artifacts, such as the only electric chair ever used in New Mexico (which might be less disturbing without the mannequin seated in it). You can also climb up into the tower where the gallows were housed, view a Santa Fe Trail–era covered wagon, and pore over historical newspaper clippings (many from World War II). Admission to the museum is $1 for adults, $.50 for kids. Memorial Day through Labor Day, it's open Monday–Saturday 9 A.M.–4 P.M. Open irregularly the rest of the year.

DORSEY MANSION

Built between 1878 and 1886 by U.S. Senator Stephen W. Dorsey of Arkansas, this huge house is unlike anything you'll see on the New Mexico plains. Two stories high and built of hewn oiled logs and sandstone, the mansion originally included a crenellated tower, lavishly decorated interior, indoor plumbing, carbide-gas lighting, a billiard room, and museum. Outside was a pool with three separate islands—one with a gazebo—a rose garden spelling out the name "Helen Dorsey" (the senator's wife), and a greenhouse.

In addition to Dorsey's involvement in national politics, he also dabbled in railroad investments and other businesses, many of which had dubious reputations. By 1892, Dorsey had left New Mexico. In his wake were angry business partners, bad debts, and charges of mail fraud.

For the next 80 years, the mansion was at various times a tuberculosis sanatorium, post office, general store, and private residence. In 1972, the mansion was listed on the National Register of Historic Places, and in 1976 it was declared a State Monument.

In recent years Dorsey Mansion has been mostly restored, and today its caretakers give tours of the house, by appointment only, daily noon–4 P.M. Dorsey Mansion is about 30 miles northeast of Springer. Take Highway 56 about 25 miles east, then go 12 miles north on the dirt road. Admission is $3 for adults, $1 for kids under 12 (with a $5 per party minimum). Hours are Monday–Saturday 10 A.M.–4 P.M. and Sunday 1 P.M.–5 P.M., but you should call ahead to make reservations and to check on road conditions.

For more information, write Dorsey Mansion Ranch, HCR 62, Box 42, Chico Route, Ratón, NM 87740. The phone number is 505/375-2222. You can also get information at the website: www.dorseymansion.com.

BOB RACE

You can get more information on the museum and on Springer from the Springer **Chamber of Commerce,** 812 3rd St., Springer, NM 87747, 505/483-2998.

Kiowa National Grassland

Kiowa National Grassland is part of a four-unit, 263,954-acre grasslands-restoration project administered by Cibola National Forest for the U.S. Department of Agriculture. The Kiowa, along with Rita Blanca, McClellan Creek, and Black Kettle National Grasslands (in Texas and Oklahoma), was farmed in the late 19th and early 20th centuries, though during the Dust Bowl the topsoil blew away, rendering the land virtually useless. The grassland was reclaimed by the Soil Conservation Service in 1938 and then transferred to the Forest Service in 1953. Today, the once-dusty plains sites are irrigated and green, the pastures providing protected watersheds and erosion control and encouraging the return of native wildlife.

New Mexico's Kiowa National Grassland consists of two separate units, one occupying the land between Clayton and the state borders (Texas and Oklahoma), and the other sprawling southeast of Springer along the Canadian River east to **Chicosa Lake State Park** and beyond. Among the recreational activities available are fishing, hiking, swimming, boating, camping, and hunting. Wildlife includes mule deer, pronghorn, bears, Barbary sheep (introduced from their native Africa), wild turkeys, pheasant, ducks, and geese.

To get to the Canadian River unit from Springer, take Highway 56 east from town 20 miles to Abbott, then turn south on Highway 39. (Or take Highway 120 east from Wagon Mound to Roy, then turn north on Highway 39.)

Write or phone for more information: Kiowa and Rita Blanca National Grasslands, 714 Main St., Clayton, NM 88415, 505/374-9652; or Chicosa Lake State Park, General Delivery, Roy, NM 87743, 505/485-2424.

SOUTH OF SPRINGER

I-25 continues south from Springer to Las Vegas and eventually around the south end of the Sangre de Cristo Mountains up into Santa Fe. It's a pretty straight shot, the freeway excellent and the scenery spectacular—the plains roll away to the east, while the southern Rocky Mountains loom omnipresent to the west. The 75-mile drive can be broken up by a couple of historically interesting stops.

Wagon Mound

The Cimarron Cut-off rejoined the main Santa Fe Trail near Wagon Mound, and the area around the little town, originally called Santa Clara, has a colorful and important history. In 1850, an eastbound party of Santa Feans, including a prominent doctor and his family, was attacked by Indians. The doctor, as well as 11 others in the party, were killed, and his wife, son, and nurse kidnapped. A group was sent from Santa Fe to recapture the prisoners, although after a battle with the Indians, the posse found the doctor's wife, propped against a willow tree, recently dead of arrow wounds, and the son and nurse were never found.

As the area was settled, however, Wagon Mound became a central trading post, and well into the mid-20th century was a shipping point for wool, sheep, and cattle. During the early part of the 20th century, Wagon Mound was also prominent for its annual pinto bean harvest. In 1910, the town held its first "Bean Day," and the annual September celebration (with a street carnival, parade, and 10K run) remains one of Wagon Mound's big events, although beans haven't been produced in the area for many years.

Fort Union National Monument

The stark red ruins of Fort Union rise ghostlike above the sprawling western grasslands. Those who grew up watching Saturday-afternoon Westerns will recall the archetypal images: Plains Indians on horseback, advancing in long lines, hundreds abreast; the U.S. Cavalry riding purposefully to meet them; lone trappers and traders, fur-clad and heading west on their own, existential terms; and the inevitable cliché—whooping Indians firing carbines and flaming arrows at peaceful settlers, their wagons drawn into a circle, the menfolk firing Colts and Winchesters while the women and children huddle inside the flimsy canvas.

But Fort Union's the real McCoy. Built in 1851 to protect Santa Fe Trail travelers, as well as to supply the area's smaller forts and provide a base for troop movements, Fort Union was the headquarters for the Ninth Military Department. During the 1860s, when Kit Carson and the New Mexico Volunteers were based here, the fort employed more than 1,000 carpenters, wagon builders, and other workers, and the Army store did $3,000 in business a day.

Today, visitors can walk out among the crumbling walls of the old fort, abandoned in 1890. A visitors center has artifacts recovered from the ruins, as well as reproductions of artillery, photos of the fort in its heyday, and "talking displays" that explain the fort's and the area's history. Fort Union National Monument is open to the public Memorial Day through Labor Day 8 A.M.–6 P.M., closing at 5 P.M. the rest of the year. Admission is $4 per vehicle. Take the Watrous exit from I-25 and follow the signs seven miles. For more information, phone 505/425-8025.

Las Vegas

This is one of New Mexico's relatively undiscovered jewels. A small town of about 16,500 in the forested foothills of the Sangre de Cristo Mountains, Las Vegas (pop. 15,000; elev. 6,415 feet) reflects much of what is grand about New Mexico: the history, the outdoors, the polycultural population, the arts, and the kick-back pace—without the crowds and the spoilage that have been wreaked upon some of the state's other towns.

Las Vegas (The Meadows) is a town of hardworking people, of trees, hilly streets, antique shops, galleries, and stately homes—from Spanish-style casitas to elegant Victorians, constant reminders of a glorious, if sometimes schizophrenic and outrageously rowdy, past. Las Vegas is also home to the restored Plaza Hotel, which stoically dominates the northwest corner of the town's central plaza, as it has since it was built in 1882. Unfortunately, the past few decades have not been all that kind to Las Vegas, and some of the plaza area looks rather run-down, with several of the old storefronts boarded up. In just the last few years, however, there has been what amounts to a sort of small-scale renaissance: many of the buildings on Bridge Street, just north of the plaza, are being converted to bookstores, galleries, and coffee shops. Locals hope the restoration will continue, yet pray they don't lose their town to upscale boutiques.

HISTORY

Originally known as Nuestra Señora de los Dolores de Las Vegas (Our Lady of Sorrows of the Meadows), Las Vegas dates to 1821, when Luis María C. de Baca petitioned the Mexican government to grant him some land on which he and his 17 sons could raise sheep. Ideally situated where the plains met the Rockies, and on the shores of the Gallinas River, the area was perfect except for one thing: the land was already occupied—by Indians, primarily Comanches, who didn't want their land taken from them. De Baca was given the grant in 1823, although the Comanches kept him from occupying all but a small section of it.

In 1833, another land grant was given to a different group of Spanish ranchers, this time contingent upon the building of a central plaza, where settlers could meet and defend themselves against raiding tribes. Meanwhile, travel on the Santa Fe Trail was increasing, and the newly built plaza became a trading center for overland wagon trains. In 1846, General Kearny arrived, claimed the land for the United States, and made Las Vegas a military headquarters until Fort Union was built five years later.

Las Vegas remained a primarily Spanish town until the Atchison, Topeka, & Santa Fe Railroad came in 1879, at which time New Town, or East Las Vegas, was built, in effect creating two Las

Vegases (the original became known as West Las Vegas). Soon this was the most important settlement in the state, both a prominent commercial center and gathering place, as well as a crucial unloading spot for Santa Fe Railroad–borne goods. With the town's new prosperity, though, came problems—some of the Southwest's most infamous outlaws and troublemakers, among them Scar-Face Charlie, the Durango Kid, Flapjack Bill, Stuttering Tom, Little Jack the Cutter, and Tommy the Poet. By 1882, the townspeople had become so outraged with the rowdiness and shooting that they routinely used the windmill in the plaza for hangings.

After the turn of the 20th century, Las Vegas continued to be a depot and shipping center for Mora and San Miguel Counties, which remained prominent sheep- and cattle-raising areas. Today, Las Vegas relies largely on its recreational and historical resources (the community has more than 900 buildings on the Federal Register of Historic Places) to keep its economy thriving. Also contributing greatly to the town's vitality are Las Vegas schools (including New Mexico Highlands University), which employ more than 1,000 people, and Las Vegas Medical Center (formerly New Mexico State Hospital), a state-run medical and mental-health institution, which employs 900 more.

SIGHTS

Plaza Hotel

A distinctively elegant hotel built in 1882, the Plaza is one of the classic old inns of the West and is listed on the National Register of Historic Places. The building's restoration, 1982–83, was carefully researched, and the result is an accurate replication of the hotel during its heyday—when its guests included such luminaries as Billy the Kid, Doc Holliday, and Big Nose Kate. Stop in for a drink at the old bar, and imagine what it was like a century ago, when you could watch "necktie parties" through the windows.

Historical Tours

Las Vegas has outlined three specific self-guided walking tours of its historical streets and buildings. In addition to the central plaza area, you can wander the old railroad district and the Carnegie Park area, both east of the plaza. On the railroad

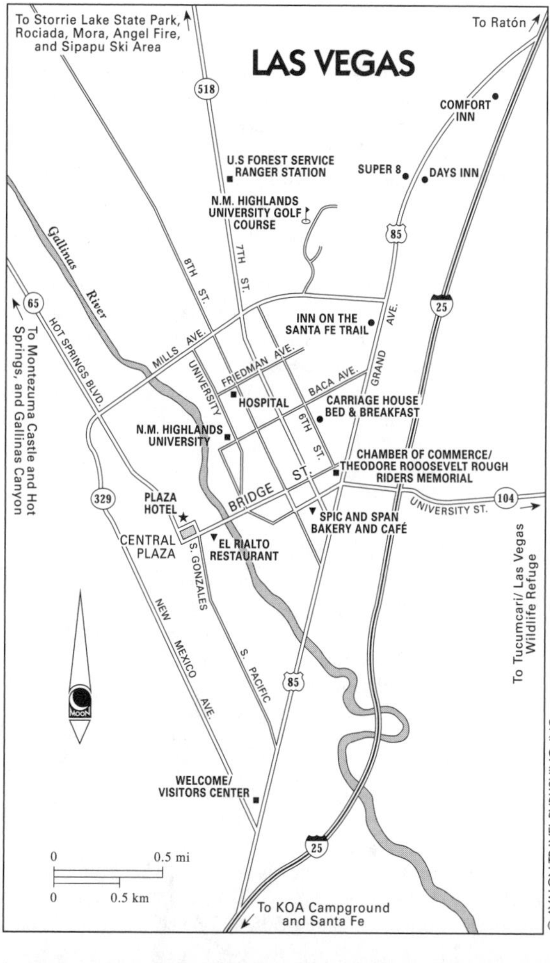

district tour, you'll view the Bank of Las Vegas, built in 1921, and the old City Hall, built in 1892. The Carnegie Park tour includes many of the town's old homes, built between 1882 and 1898, as well as the Carnegie Library, built in 1903 and modeled after Thomas Jefferson's Monticello.

For maps and details of Las Vegas historical tours, stop by the welcome center at the **chamber of commerce** at 727 Grand Ave., 505/425-8631 or 800/832-5947.

Theodore Roosevelt Rough Riders Memorial and City Museum

This small museum at 725 Grand Ave., in the same building as the chamber of commerce, commemorates the Rough Riders' campaign in the Spanish-American War of 1898 and houses an oddball collection of knickknacks and genuine historical articles. (More than 40 percent of Teddy's Rough Riders were from New Mexico, and many of them from Las Vegas. The first Rough Rider reunion was held in Las Vegas in 1899, and they were held here annually 1948–62.) In addition to military artifacts from the Cuba Campaign, the museum houses assorted relics from Las Vegas's history—including pioneer and Indian weapons, domestic items, and newspaper clippings of importance to the community. The museum is open daily 9 A.M.–noon and 1 P.M.–4 P.M. and by appointment; admission is free. For more information, phone 505/454-1401.

Las Vegas Wildlife Refuge

Home to prairie falcons, golden eagles, mule deer, and coyotes, as well as a stop on the routes of migrating sandhill cranes, long-billed curlews, geese, and ducks, these 18,000 acres just east of Las Vegas are open to the public for critter-watching, hiking, and a seven-mile driving tour. The acreage includes prairie, marsh, forest, and steep canyonlands, so be sure you have sturdy hiking gear; also be sure to carry water. Interpretive literature and hiking permits are available at the refuge office. To get to the refuge, take Highway 104 east from Grand Avenue and follow the sign six miles. The office is open Monday–Friday 8:30 A.M.–4 P.M. For more information, phone 505/425-3581.

HIGHWAY 65

Montezuma Hot Springs

This series of public hot springs, which according to legend was visited in the early 16th century by the Aztec chief Montezuma II and is said to have been used by local Indians for its curing powers, is five miles north of downtown Las Vegas. Shelters have been built around some of the pools, and some are lined with concrete; others are au naturel. A leisurely soak in the springs, free and unsupervised, is one of the best ways to wind up a day wandering around town or hiking or skiing in the nearby mountains. The tubs are drained and cleaned by United World College staffers. Take Hot Springs Boulevard/Highway 65 north from the central plaza.

Montezuma Castle

Soon after the Santa Fe Railroad came to Las Vegas, it bought a large parcel of land north of town—including Montezuma Hot Springs. The plan was to build a large hotel, develop the springs into a spa, and lure tourists from around the world. In 1882, the lavish three-story Montezuma Hotel was completed; two years later it burned to the ground. Almost immediately, a new hotel was built of red sandstone—as flameproof as possible. Completed in April of 1885, it was destroyed by fire in July of the same year.

The railroad owners, however, refused to let their ambitions cool and went about building still another hotel. Rising from the ashes of its predecessors, this one they dubbed the "Phoenix." Unfortunately, the resort complex was a financial embarrassment, losing money from the outset, and in 1903, the railroad finally gave up its interest in the property. During the next 70 years, the 77-room old stone hotel building across the road from Montezuma Hot Springs—Montezuma Castle, as it became known—changed hands a number of times, and was used for, among other things, a YMCA, Baptist college, and Jesuit seminary.

In 1981, the complex was bought by philanthropist Armand Hammer, who oversaw partial restoration and shortly thereafter opened **Armand Hammer United World College of the**

LOUISE FOOTE

Montezuma Castle

American West. The administrative offices and library occupy the renovated Stone Hotel. In 1998, the administration received a $45 million grant and has begun restoration on the complex. Classrooms, student housing, and other buildings are scattered around the 110-acre campus.

The college is one of the most fascinating and ambitious educational institutions in the world. Sprawling on its forested hillside, it is the unlikely gathering place for 200 teenagers from 70 countries, all studying together under a rigorous set of academic guidelines, with the added bonus of special wilderness activities as well as workshops aimed at promoting multicultural harmony. Although most of the school's students come to Montezuma from far corners of the globe—such as India and Nepal—others come from areas much closer: the first graduating class included two Pueblo Indian students, one from Zuñi and one from Acoma.

The two-year curriculum, roughly equivalent to the final year of high school and the first year of college, is designed to prepare students for university success. Based on the International Baccalaureate Degree, the diploma represents standards not only of academic excellence but of cross-cultural integration and understanding. The United World College also has campuses in Canada, Singapore, Swaziland, and Italy.

Each October, the school hosts **International Days,** to which the public is invited. Students share dishes from their home countries, perform dances, and open their classrooms to curious visitors.

Tours of the campus are offered by appointment; phone 505/454-4200.

Gallinas Canyon

Continue northwest on Highway 65 about six miles past Montezuma Castle and Hot Springs into one of the lushest and most beautifully forested canyons in the Southwest. The road hugs the cliffside along the river for several miles, then drops to a fertile valley and the small town of El Porvenir. A couple of miles up the road, you'll come to El Porvenir Forest Service campground, where several sites (with picnic tables, drinking water, and barbecue pits) are nestled among the firs and ferns of the canyon. Fee is $4 for overnight camping. Pit toilets only.

Storrie Lake State Park

Although water from the dam (built here in 1921) was originally intended for irrigation, the 1,100-acre reservoir—six miles north of Las Vegas on Highway 518—has become an immensely popular recreation spot since 1959, when it was given state park status. Recently, windsurfers have discovered Storrie Lake, whose flat and treeless surroundings at the base of the Sangre de Cristos make for consistently excellent winds. In addition, the lake is popular among anglers, the patient ones frequently pulling decent-sized rainbow and brown trout from the depths.

The state park offers sheltered campsites with RV hookups, flush toilets, hot showers, and a children's playground. Day use is $4, and camping is $8 ($11 with hookups).

PRACTICALITIES

Accommodations

The best way to experience Las Vegas is to spend the night downtown in the **Plaza Hotel** on the northwest corner of the old plaza, 505/425-3591. The rooms, though restored to their original Victorian simplicity, have all the modern conveniences—your color television, for example, may be hidden behind the doors of an antique armoire. Standard rooms run $50–100, suites $100–150.

Another excellent Las Vegas inn is **Carriage House Bed and Breakfast,** a century-old Victorian house four blocks from downtown at 925 6th St., 505/454-1784. Rooms run $50–100; view them at the website: www.newmexicocarriagehouse.com.

On the north end of town, you'll find a half dozen or so motels, including **The Inn on the Santa Fe Trail,** 505/425-6707, a **Super 8,** 505/425-5288, a **Comfort Inn,** 505/425-1100, and a **Days Inn** 505/425-1967. All are in the $50–100 range.

Camping and RVing

In addition to the camping north of town at Storrie Lake and Gallinas Canyon, the Las Vegas area offers an easy-access **KOA,** 505/454-0180, for those who don't want to venture too far from the freeway—take Exit 339 from I-25 just south of town. Campers also enjoy breakfast and dinner cookouts and tours to ghost towns and ruins.

Food

For hearty breakfast fare, try **Spic and Span Bakery and Cafe** right downtown at 713 Douglas, 505/426-1921. A classic small-town diner (each booth has a hat rack), this is where the local merchants meet over coffee and hotcakes before heading out into the day. Try Al's Special (ham, onion, cheese, chiles, and scrambled eggs) or some of the fresh-baked bread, cinnamon rolls, or éclairs. The Spic and Span is also open for lunch and dinner, with burgers, Mexican plates, and specials (spaghetti and meatballs). You can also get fresh-baked bread by the loaf.

A favorite for lunch is **El Rialto** at 141 Bridge St., 505/454-0037, which serves excellent Mexican plates (stuffed sopaipillas, burritos, enchiladas) Monday–Saturday 10:30 A.M.–9 P.M.

Adelia's Landmark Grill, the dining room at the Plaza Hotel, 505/425-3591, serves breakfast, lunch, and dinner, and a popular Sunday brunch. Breakfasts include eggs, hotcakes, and breakfast burritos. For lunch, try the fajitas or a Plaza Burger, with cheese, bacon, and green chiles. Complete Mexican, steak, and seafood dinners range $7–20.

Entertainment

One advantage of Las Vegas's location is its proximity to Santa Fe (64 miles) and the variety of music and clubs there. Locally, the lounge in the **Plaza Hotel,** 505/425-3591, often features live acoustic music, as do several of the coffee shops on Bridge Street.

Annual Events

Seems there's something going on in Las Vegas nearly every weekend—bluegrass festivals, arts and crafts shows, fairs, and fiestas. The Las Vegas *Visitor's Handbook,* available from the chamber of commerce, has a complete listing. The highlights? **Santa Fe Trail Heritage Days,** first weekend in May, with historic reenactment camps and period costumes; **Fourth of July** (parade, fireworks, and fishing and windsurfing regatta on Storrie Lake); and **San Miguel County Fair,** mid-August (classic county fair, with food, livestock, etc.).

Shopping

Las Vegas boasts a handful of interesting galleries and antique shops—particularly in the Bridge Street/plaza area—and you're generally more likely to find better prices here than in Santa Fe or Taos. I'm hesitant to list specific shops, however, as the area is in a state of flux, with a new gallery trying to make a go of it every few months. Advice: allow yourself an hour or so to browse around the Bridge Street shops, and keep your eye out for what look like new places.

Recreation

Las Vegas is surrounded by recreation possibilities—hiking, skiing, golfing, fishing, windsurfing, camping. For starters, head up into Gallinas Canyon, where you'll find El Porvenir Campground and numerous backcountry hiking trails into Carson National Forest. A local favorite, largely because of the spectacular view, is the eight-mile (round-trip) hike up to **Hermit's Peak** (the trailhead, near the campground, is well marked). Two other designated hiking trails branch from the Hermit's Peak Trail: **Dispensas Trail** (eight miles round-trip) and **Porvenir Canyon Trail** (at 28 miles round-trip more suited for backpacking). Take Hot Springs Boulevard out of town and continue about six miles past Montezuma Castle. For maps and information on hiking in Carson National Forest and the Las Vegas area, stop by the Forest Service district office at 1926 7th St., or phone 505/454-0560.

Gallinas Canyon is also popular for winter sports, with several designated **cross-country ski trails,** as well as a **skating pond** on the Gallinas River.

Downhill skiers can head up to **Sipapu Ski Area,** where two pomas and a triple chair service 865 vertical feet of beginner-to-advanced terrain. Take Highway 518 55 miles north of town. (For more information, phone 505/587-2240.) Taos, Angel Fire, and Red River ski areas are all fewer than 100 miles from Las Vegas.

Storrie Lake, just a few minutes north of town, is a favorite of windsurfers and anglers, and full camping facilities are available.

New Mexico Highlands University golf course is a public course off Mills Avenue on the northeast side of town, 505/425-7711. **Pendaries Golf and Country Club,** 505/425-6076), north of town in Rociada, is also open to the public. Pendaries also offers a swimming pool and tennis courts.

Information and Services

The Las Vegas **Chamber of Commerce,** 727 Grand Ave., 505/425-8631 or 800/832-5947, dispenses copious amounts of literature on the area, and the staff is friendly and knowledgeable. Useful information is also available at the chamber's website: www.lasvegasnm.net/visitor_information.htm.

One of the best places for information on historical Las Vegas and on the Southwest in general is **Los Artisanos Book Store,** 505/425-8331. You'll find a huge collection of used and rare books, with a special emphasis on books on Western Americana. Los Artisanos is on the central plaza, just a few doors down from the Plaza Hotel.

Las Vegas's full-care hospital, Northeastern Regional Hospital, is at 1235 8th St., 505/425-6751. The main office of the Las Vegas Police Department is at the corner of 6th and University, 505/425-7504. The state police office is at 1401 1st St.; call 505/425-6771.

Transportation

The closest air passenger service is in Santa Fe via **Mesa Air,** 800/MESA-AIR (800/637-2247). From there, you can take either **Amtrak,** 800/872-7245, or **Greyhound,** 505/425-8689, to Las Vegas.

LAS VEGAS TO ANGEL FIRE

Highway 518, the back road to Angel Fire and the Enchanted Circle, is a seldom-traveled beauty, winding up from the scrub oak into the firs and pines of Carson National Forest, much of the way following the gentle waters of Coyote Creek. The area is a favorite of local hunters, anglers, hikers, and campers, who realize it's not as likely to get as crowded as some of the better-known recreation areas in the state.

North-Central New Mexico

Introduction

When D. H. Lawrence wrote that visiting New Mexico was one of the greatest experiences he'd ever had, he was referring specifically to the north-central part of the state—to Santa Fe and Taos, the Sangre de Cristo and San Juan Mountains, the ancient Indian pueblos and the people who still live much as their ancestors did 1,000 years ago. He was talking about north-central New Mexico's soul, nearly palpable in its glorious connection to the people, the sky, and the land.

When Georgia O'Keeffe came to New Mexico, it was north-central New Mexico to which she was drawn—to two of the most colorful and curiously spellbinding spots in the Southwest: Taos and Abiquiu, the latter in which she lived and painted until the mid-1980s when she moved to Santa Fe because of failing health (she died in Santa Fe in 1986 at the age of 98). Translating the orange sculpted canyons, high desert, and moody skies to canvas, O'Keeffe worked in the seclusion of north-central New Mexico's seductive outback, and she was a key figure in attracting other painters to the area, as well as in helping nonartists see the natural canvases before them.

Many more have been drawn to this part of the country—both long before and well after Lawrence and O'Keeffe. In fact, although many of the area's people can trace their ancestry back hundreds of years, many more can remember arriving. "I just came to go skiing," you'll hear them say, or, "We were only going to stay in Santa Fe a week, but, well, we just couldn't leave."

It's no wonder. This is beautiful country, with a deep-rooted sense of history and a multicultural population sewn together like a great tapestry. Take a drive up into the mountains—the Jemez, Sangre de Cristos, or San Juans. Spend a morning

COURTESY OF NEW MEXICO DEPARTMENT OF TOURISM/JIM STEIN

HIGHLIGHTS

Back Road to Taos: mountain scenery, Spanish Colonial architecture, weaving shops

Bandelier National Monument: Indian ruins, hiking, and camping

Enchanted Circle: sight-seeing, fishing, camping, skiing

Jemez Mountains: camping, hiking, cross-country and downhill skiing

Pecos National Monument: Indian and mission ruins

Santa Fe: museums, galleries, gift shops, festivals, historical tours

Taos: museums, galleries, gift shops, historical tours

Taos Pueblo: 800-year-old home of Taos Indians

over cappuccino at a Santa Fe café and an afternoon exploring the capital's museums. Visit Taos Pueblo. Drive the Enchanted Circle. Take a week's vacation at Taos Ski Valley. You'll catch on; you'll see why folks stick around. Be careful, though. You just might find yourself looking through the want ads at real estate, or trying to explain to your parents why you're not coming home.

ALBUQUERQUE TO SANTA FE

Interstate 25 from Albuquerque to Santa Fe is probably the most traveled section of freeway in the state, with commuters, tourists, and truckers constantly buzzing up and down the 60-mile stretch between New Mexico's two most important cities. Paralleling the Rio Grande the first half of the way, the road passes through the reservations of several Pueblo tribes, which have relied for centuries on river water for their survival.

In terms of scenery, this isn't the most exciting road in the state, although the mountains flanking the freeway—the Sandias and the Sangre de Cristos to the east and the Jemez to the west—can sometimes provide a dramatic backdrop, especially when the lightning of a summer afternoon storm cracks the sky. There's not much to stop for along here, either. Once you've passed Bernalillo, and Coronado State Monument, you won't see much else until just outside the capital, where the southern Rockies loom before you and Santa Fe lies nestled against the lush foothills.

Visitors Information

Be sure to stop at the visitors information center just a few miles south of Santa Fe, where you can pick up maps, brochures, and other literature on various attractions in the area and throughout the state. The center is staffed with friendly Santa Feans, ready to answer any question you may have—about lodging, restaurants, galleries, camping, transportation, etc. The center also provides restrooms, and the parking lot is large enough to easily accommodate RVs.

Santa Fe

In Santa Fe (pop. 60,000; elev. 7,000 feet), the high desert meets the southern Rocky Mountains, centuries-old adobe churches stand next to blinking streetlights, and busy boulevards dead-end into sleepy plazas. Here, some of the finest art in the Southwest is sold beside some of the tackiest schlock, and about 70 vendors sell exquisite handmade jewelry on blankets on the sidewalk while white kids with nose rings, pierced eyebrows, and guitars sit in circles on the plaza lawns.

For generations Santa Fe has attracted artists, photographers, and writers, as well as those in search of physical and spiritual cures. More recently, it's lured gurus and New Age healers. So, too, does Santa Fe attract celebrities—Robert Redford, Amy Irving, Ali McGraw, Gene Hackman, Val Kilmer, Carol Burnett, and many others have spent time wandering the crooked streets of town and the nearby hills.

Even first-time visitors to Santa Fe will recognize immediately the town's draw and are

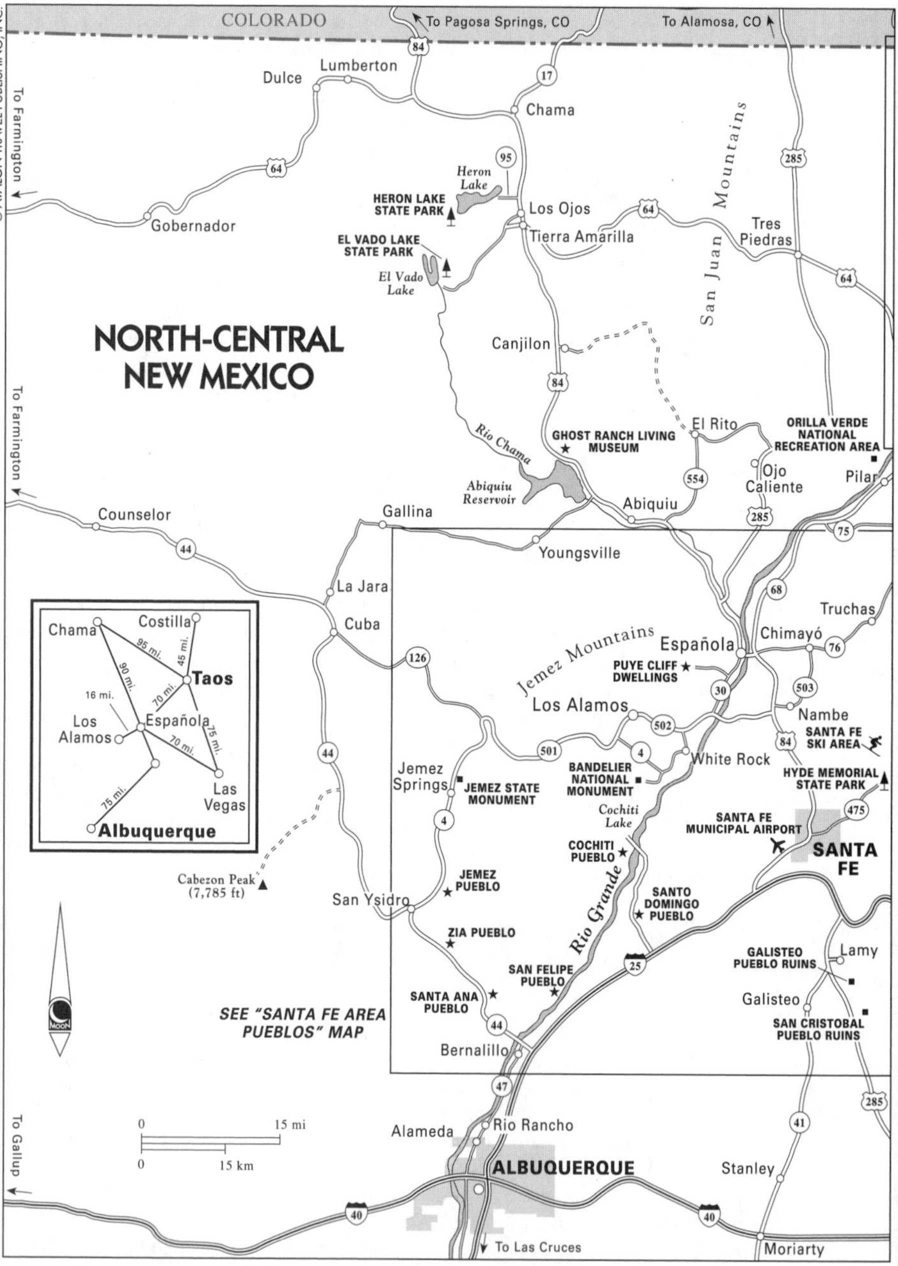
COLORADO
To Pagosa Springs, CO
To Alamosa, CO
NORTH-CENTRAL
NEW MEXICO
To Farmington
To Farmington
To Gallup
Dulce
Lumberton
Chama
Heron Lake
HERON LAKE STATE PARK
Los Ojos
Tierra Amarilla
Gobernador
EL VADO LAKE STATE PARK
El Vado Lake
San Juan Mountains
Tres Piedras
Canjilon
Rio Chama
GHOST RANCH LIVING MUSEUM
El Rito
ORILLA VERDE NATIONAL RECREATION AREA
Ojo Caliente
Pilar
Abiquiu Reservoir
Abiquiu
Counselor
Gallina
Youngsville
La Jara
Cuba
Truchas
Chimayó
Jemez Mountains
Española
PUYE CLIFF DWELLINGS
Los Alamos
Nambe
SANTA FE SKI AREA
White Rock
BANDELIER NATIONAL MONUMENT
Jemez Springs
JEMEZ STATE MONUMENT
HYDE MEMORIAL STATE PARK
SANTA FE MUNICIPAL AIRPORT
SANTA FE
Cochiti Lake
COCHITI PUEBLO
JEMEZ PUEBLO
Cabezon Peak (7,785 ft)
San Ysidro
SANTO DOMINGO PUEBLO
Rio Grande
ZIA PUEBLO
Lamy
GALISTEO PUEBLO RUINS
SAN FELIPE PUEBLO
SANTA ANA PUEBLO
Galisteo
SEE "SANTA FE AREA PUEBLOS" MAP
SAN CRISTOBAL PUEBLO RUINS
Bernalillo
Alameda
Rio Rancho
ALBUQUERQUE
Stanley
To Las Cruces
Moriarty
0 15 mi
0 15 km
Chama
Costilla
95 mi.
45 mi.
90 mi.
Taos
16 mi.
70 mi.
Los Alamos
Española
75 mi.
70 mi.
Las Vegas
75 mi.
Albuquerque
MOON

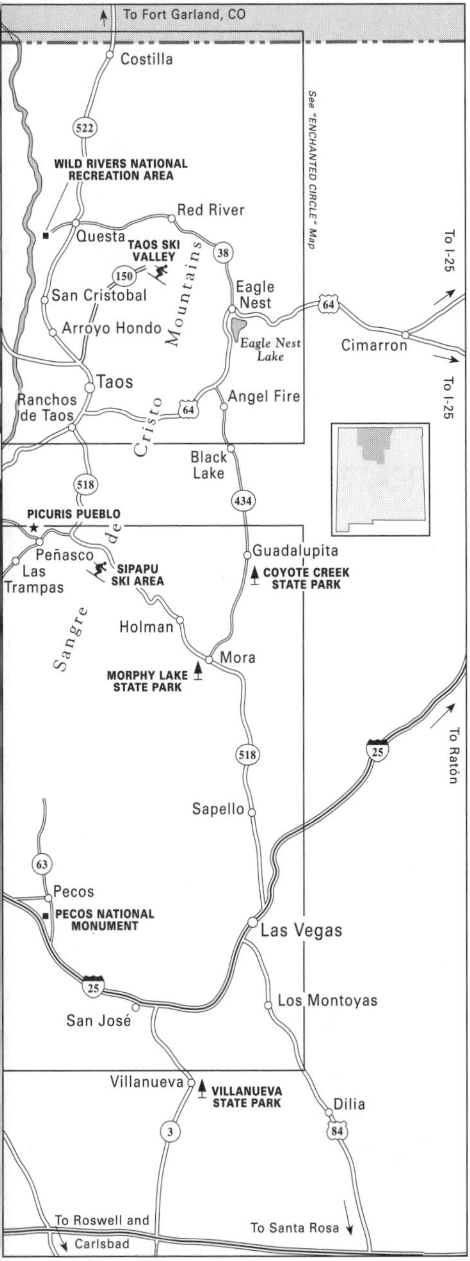

guaranteed to be smitten by its Old World charm and kick-back pace. The narrow streets are lined with sleepy adobe homes, squatting behind hand-carved wooden gates and half hidden by gnarled cottonwoods or softly hued hollyhocks. In summertime in the downtown plaza, Bermuda-shorted tourists, Doc Martined local teens, and upscale merchants mingle in a strange harmony under the benevolent high-desert sun. And in the winter, snow blankets the lawns and benches of city parks, softens the already-gentle adobe, and piles deep in the nearby mountains, making the area a haven for winter sports enthusiasts. In fact, Santa Fe's been called the Camelot of the Southwest, and with good reason. It's seductive, intoxicating, and magical. Once under the town's spell, you're likely to begin immediately making plans to come back, if not to stay at least to visit again, perhaps even to join the legions of travelers who return year in and year out—to their favorite galleries, bookstores, hotels, and restaurants, or to the annual Santa Fe Opera, one of the highlights of a New Mexico summer.

HISTORY

The oldest capital city in the country, Santa Fe was founded in 1607, more than a dozen years before the English pilgrims established Plymouth Colony. Don Pedro de Peralta, third governor of the new Spanish colony, Nuevo Mexico, built a small settlement here as the northernmost outpost in a series of forts and missions designed to convert the Pueblo Indians to Catholicism. Originally a simple adobe fortress and central plaza, La Villa Real de la Santa Fe de San Francisco de Asis, as the town was first known, was intended to provide protection for the Spanish missionaries and a headquarters for the province's political and military leaders; 60 of New Mexico's governors would eventually rule from the fortress, which became known as the Palace of the Governors.

By the mid-17th century, an estimated 14,000 Indians had been converted to Christianity, although many more preferred to maintain their non-Christian beliefs. The Spanish, infamously intolerant of those unwilling to convert, burned kivas and ceremonial objects and often flogged, hanged, and otherwise tortured Indians unwilling to accept the new religion. In August 1680, the Indians rebelled. Led by the San Juan Indian Medicine Man Popé, who had been flogged for practicing "witchcraft," the northern Pueblo tribes united to run the Spanish out. Beginning in the outlying areas, the Indians killed missionaries and settlers, burned farms and churches, then besieged Santa Fe.

Although the Spanish held out for several days, they eventually retreated, following the Rio Grande south to El Paso, picking up along the way converted Pueblo Indians. Meanwhile, the Palace of the Governors had been burned, and many important documents destroyed—to this day, some records of Santa Fe's early days are documented only in reports kept on file in Madrid, Spain. Once the Spanish were gone, the Indians moved into Santa Fe. Popé took up residence in the palace and demolished anything related, however remotely, to the Spanish and Catholicism—statues, crosses, and vineyards. Soon, though, bickering broke out among the various Pueblo tribes, and many of the Indians returned to their own pueblos—to Taos, San Juan, Santa Clara, and the others.

Indian occupation of Santa Fe lasted about 12 years. In 1691, the new governor, Don Diego de Vargas, armed with support from the Spanish crown, arrived in El Paso and began working his way north toward Santa Fe. Upon arriving, de Vargas took the Palace

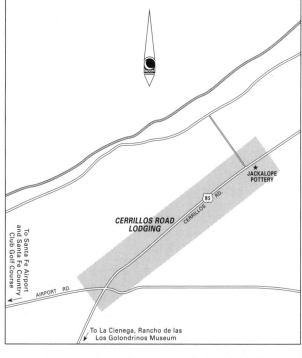

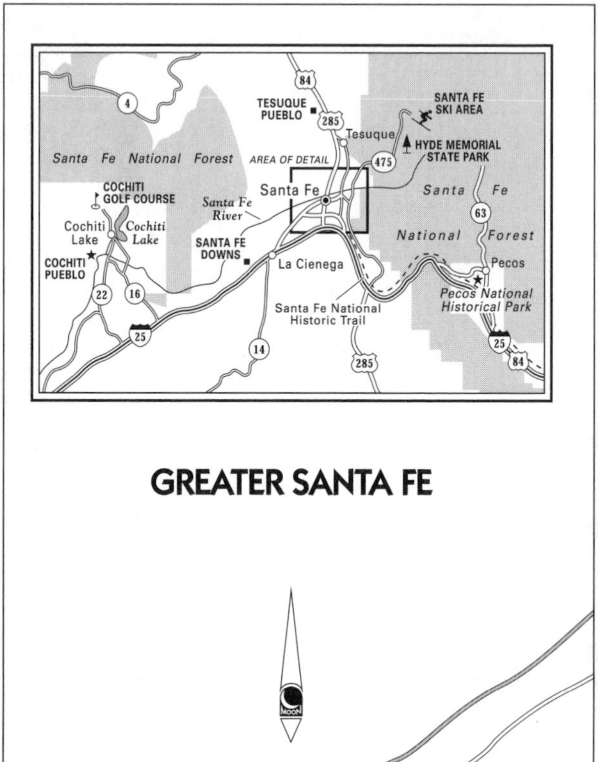

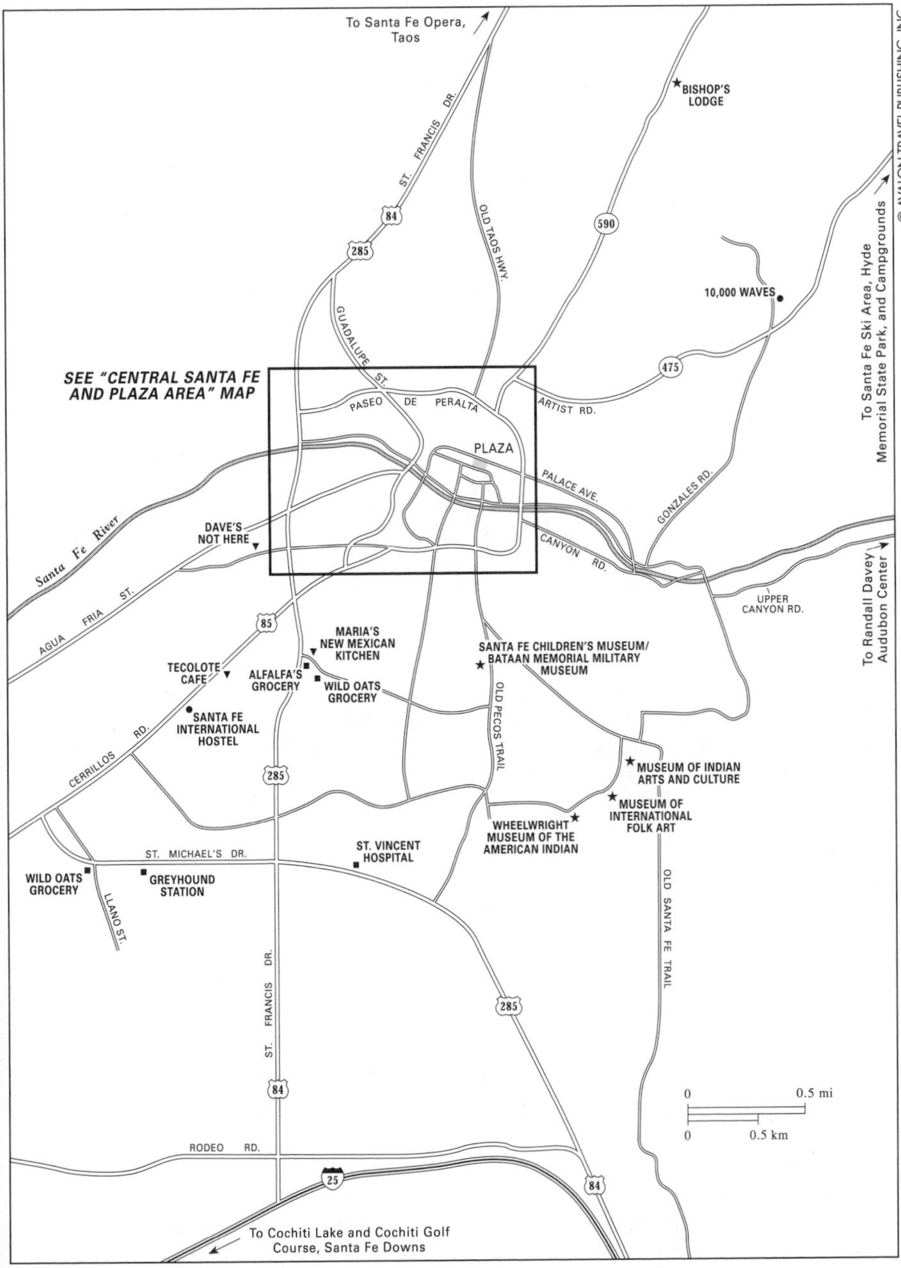
To Santa Fe Opera, Taos
BISHOP'S LODGE
ST. FRANCIS DR.
OLD TAOS HWY.
84
590
285
10,000 WAVES
GUADALUPE ST.
475
SEE "CENTRAL SANTA FE AND PLAZA AREA" MAP
PASEO DE PERALTA
ARTIST RD.
PLAZA
PALACE AVE.
GONZALES RD.
Santa Fe River
DAVE'S NOT HERE
CANYON RD.
UPPER CANYON RD.
AGUA FRIA ST.
85
MARIA'S NEW MEXICAN KITCHEN
SANTA FE CHILDREN'S MUSEUM/ BATAAN MEMORIAL MILITARY MUSEUM
TECOLOTE CAFE
ALFALFA'S GROCERY
WILD OATS GROCERY
OLD PECOS TRAIL
SANTA FE INTERNATIONAL HOSTEL
CERRILLOS RD.
MUSEUM OF INDIAN ARTS AND CULTURE
MUSEUM OF INTERNATIONAL FOLK ART
WHEELWRIGHT MUSEUM OF THE AMERICAN INDIAN
ST. MICHAEL'S DR.
ST. VINCENT HOSPITAL
WILD OATS GROCERY
GREYHOUND STATION
LLANO ST.
OLD SANTA FE TRAIL
ST. FRANCIS DR.
0 0.5 mi
0 0.5 km
RODEO RD.
25
To Cochiti Lake and Cochiti Golf Course, Santa Fe Downs
To Santa Fe Ski Area, Hyde Memorial State Park, and Campgrounds
To Randall Davey Audubon Center
© AVALON TRAVEL PUBLISHING, INC.

of the Governors by force, and afterward executed about 70 Indians and enslaved 400 others. By 1692, de Vargas had reconquered not only the capital but most of the surrounding pueblos as well, and the Pueblo Revolt, still considered the most organized and successful Indian uprising in the New World, was over.

For the next 100 years, the Spanish continued to occupy Santa Fe and rule New Mexico, discouraging as much as possible integration with the increasing number of American settlers arriving in the Southwest. In the winter of 1805–06, a small group of explorers, led by Zebulon Pike under orders from Thomas Jefferson, was caught trespassing along the headwaters of the Rio Grande and promptly arrested. Pike and his men were sent to Durango, Mexico, and later released.

Santa Fe has been called the Camelot of the Southwest, and with good reason. It's seductive, intoxicating, and magical.

In 1821, though, Mexico won its independence from Spain, and Santa Feans began to demand the goods that American traders were transporting across the continent. That same year, a group of Mexican soldiers encountered several Missourians trading with Plains Indians north and east of Santa Fe. The Americans followed the Mexicans back to Santa Fe, thus pioneering the Santa Fe Trail, and the capital was finally opened to trade from the east.

By midcentury, the United States, in attempting to realize its "manifest destiny," was marching toward the Pacific, and Santa Fe was right in its path, with General Stephen Kearny and his troops moving through the Southwest. Though New Mexico Governor Manuel Armijo had assembled 6,000 troops to ward off the approaching Americans, he fled to Chihuahua, Mexico, before any battle was ever fought; historians don't know whether he was bribed or if he simply realized that the stronger American forces guaranteed him certain defeat.

Kearny arrived in Santa Fe on August 18, 1846, claimed the territory for the United States, and named Charles Bent governor. In 1851, New Mexico was officially given territorial status. Meanwhile, the volume of trade—as well as the number of westbound settlers—was increasing over the Santa Fe Trail, and by 1849, a stage was running with some regularity from Independence, Missouri, to the capital of the new territory. The railroad's arrival in 1879, though, rang the trail's death knell, and by the mid-1880s the Iron Horse was steaming its way over Ratón Pass and down into Lamy, the railroad junction 20 miles south of the city.

When statehood finally came to New Mexico in 1912, the little capital celebrated in a big way.

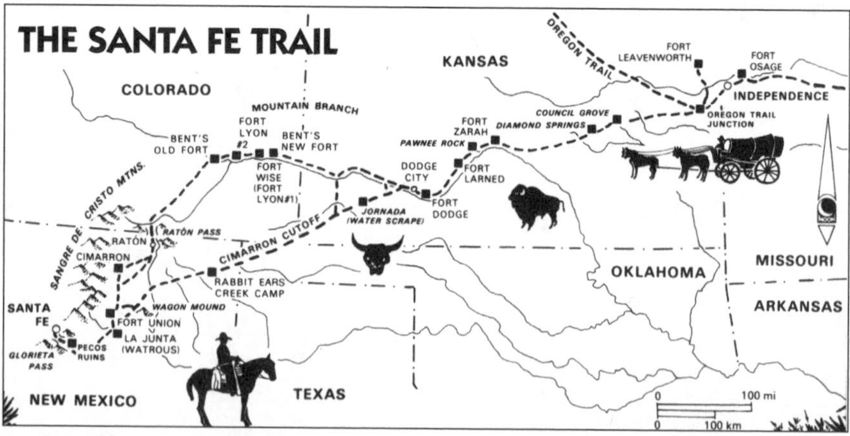

Santa Fe's plaza

A weeklong fiesta was followed by a sharp increase in construction, thanks to federal and state subsidies, and the people elected their first governor, William C. McDonald. The new state was a proud one, and from early on could boast of the artists and painters attracted by the rich landscapes and profound skies—Los Cinco Pintores (The Five Painters) was a group of impressionist-influenced artists who in 1921 banded together, vowing to make art more accessible to the area's working people.

A quarter-century after statehood, Santa Fe experienced another boom, when scientists and their families began moving to Los Alamos, 35 miles northwest. Though travel for the researchers was initially highly restricted, once the bomb had been dropped and World War II was over, people began filtering out of the high-security mountain community and looking to Santa Fe for housing, as well as for their shopping and entertainment needs.

Though Santa Fe today reflects its rich tricultural heritage—one to which Indians, Spaniards, and Anglos have all contributed—the Spanish influence dominates, from street names to food to architecture. As you wander the shops in the downtown plaza or explore Santa Fe's crooked backstreets, you realize that except for the cars and the pavement, not a whole lot has changed in three centuries. And city officials plan to keep it that way. New construction must meet strict building codes, and even the outlying franchise motels and restaurants—with their pueblo-style architecture and fake adobe—aren't as offensive to the eye as they are in many areas.

PLAZA AREA SIGHTS

La Fonda

One of the best places to begin a tour of the plaza area is the La Fonda Hotel. At the southeast corner of the plaza on San Francisco Street, this building dates from 1920, although the inn after which it was modeled was built much earlier; during the height of Santa Fe Trail trade, the inn was a gathering place for merchants, traders, trappers, soldiers, and politicians. La Fonda's lobby still serves as a central meeting place for travelers and locals, and an information desk provides maps and literature about Santa Fe. Though rooms no longer rent for $1 a day as they did in 1846 when General Stephen Kearny

THE SANTA FE TRAIL

The westward expansion of 19th-century America has become one of the centerpieces of our national mythology. The names—of people and places—sing down through our history and distill themselves into a common consciousness. Listen: Daniel Boone, Lewis and Clark, Jim Bridger, Jedediah Smith, John C. Frémont, John Sutter, Forts Laramie and Leavenworth, Dodge and Union, the Donner Pass, the Pony Express, and the Oregon Trail. Of course, a valid argument can be made that the cost of the birth of this new nation was the death of many others—entire tribes of Native Americans who got in the way were simply and systematically decimated. In fact, in our reckless rush to the riches of the West, we left in our wake a holocaust of horrible wounds and embarrassments. Still, though, we are inspired and humbled by the strong-willed men and women who left the East Coast and, traveling by foot and wagon through hostile landscapes, sought new lives in the West.

One of the most well-traveled roads west, an international trade route that has been celebrated in story, song, and film, was the Santa Fe Trail, a nearly 1,000-mile-long rutted dirt highway that ran from western Missouri southwest down into Santa Fe. At its peak in the mid-1860s, the Santa Fe Trail saw as many as 5,000 freight wagons a year, all of them loaded down with goods that could turn for their proprietors as much as $2,000 in profits.

In 1821, the same year that Missouri won statehood, Mexico won its independence from Spain. In Santa Fe, at the time home to about 6,000 people, there were great celebrations, as the new republic was now a much more likely candidate for participation in the burgeoning transcontinental trading. On September 1 of that year a group of traders, led by William Becknell, left Old Franklin, Missouri, to trade with Indians in the West. Along the way, Becknell's party ran into a group of Mexican soldiers who'd been exploring the area north of Santa Fe. Things were probably pretty tense at first, as apparently Becknell had illegally crossed into Mexico. However, instead of placing the trader under arrest, the soldiers convinced him to follow them back to Santa Fe, where he arrived on November 16 and quickly and easily sold his goods to the anxious and newly independent people; when he left to return to Missouri, his wagons were loaded with silver.

Recognizing the enormous trade potential in Santa Fe, and taking advantage of the new republic's attitude toward outsiders (the Spanish governors' policy had been one of isolationism, while the new Mexican government saw the advantages in trading with its booming neighbor to the north), Becknell quickly organized another expedition; this one would not end up in Santa Fe by chance, but by the quickest route. That route, which included the Mountain Branch north to Bent's Fort in Colorado (then dropped through Ratón and ran roughly parallel to what is now I-25) and the Cimarron Cut-off, was to become known as the Santa Fe Trail, and for the next 58 years it saw thousands of travelers.

In the 1840s and '50s, in response to increased Indian attacks, the U.S. Army built a number of forts along the trail, including Fort Union, the remains of which can be seen just north of Las Vegas. Until 1879, when the railroad arrived in New Mexico, the Santa Fe Trail continued to see great caravans of traders, soldiers, and settlers. In fact, traffic was so heavy on the trail that in some places wagon ruts, now well over 100 years old, can still be seen in the prairie hardpan.

Most bookstores in New Mexico stock a number of excellent books on the Santa Fe Trail. Among the best: *Along the Santa Fe Trail, On the Santa Fe Trail,* and *Following the Santa Fe Trail: A Guide for Modern Travelers* (all with texts by Marc Simmons), as well as two classics, *The Old Santa Fe Trail,* by Stanley Vestal (first published in 1939 by Houghton Mifflin), and *The Old Santa Fe Trail,* by Colonel Henry Inman (first published in 1916 by Crane and Company, and with an introduction by William F. "Buffalo Bill" Cody). The **Santa Fe Trail Center** publishes a quarterly newsletter and sponsors a wide array of educational activities and symposiums on the trail. Write the center at Rural Route 3, Larned, KS 67550, or phone 316/285-2054. You can also get information on the Santa Fe Trail from the Clayton, Ratón, Cimarron, and Las Vegas/San Miguel County chambers of commerce, the Santa Fe Convention and Visitors Bureau (see individual chapters for telephone numbers), and the New Mexico State Department of Tourism, 505/827-0291 or 800/545-2040.

© STEPHEN METZGER

the La Fonda Hotel on the Santa Fe plaza, once the end of the Santa Fe Trail

claimed New Mexico for the United States, you can still bunk down in the old hotel (see below).

Museum of New Mexico

This four-part museum complex includes the Palace of the Governors and the Museum of Fine Arts (both on the plaza), the Museum of Indian Arts and Culture, and the Museum of International Folk Art, a short drive from the plaza (see these last two under Other Santa Fe Sights, below). At any of them you can get a pass good at all four for $15 (kids 16 and under free). Admission to individual museums is $7, ($5 for New Mexico residents). The museum complex is open Tuesday–Sunday 10 A.M.–5 P.M., though the Palace of the Governors stays open free of charge Friday evening 5 P.M.–8 P.M. Sunday the Museum of New Mexico complex offers free admission to all venues to New Mexico residents.

For more information on the complex, visit the website: www.museumofnewmexico.org, where you can also get the schedules of special events and hours of docent-led tours. The phone number is 505/476-5060.

The **Palace of the Governors,** across the plaza from La Fonda, was built in 1610 and occupied through the years by Mexican soldiers, Indian insurgents, the American military, and Governor Lew Wallace, who wrote *Ben Hur* here. The various rooms in the palace, built around a large open courtyard, display items from throughout Santa Fe's history: precontact Indian pottery, Jemez pottery from 1300–1700, accounts of the Coronado expedition (published in 1556), a reconstructed 17th-century *carreta* (Spanish cart), maps of 18th-century Spanish America (including one showing California as an island), a horse-drawn hearse and chuck wagon from the mid-19th century, and the bindery and presses from the old print shop.

The Palace of the Governors also houses an extensive gift shop, with a huge selection of books on the Southwest, as well as Indian jewelry, rugs, and pottery. The store carries audio and videotapes of Pueblo Indian music and ceremonies.

The Palace of the Governors, on the north side of the plaza, is open Tuesday–Sunday 10 A.M.–5 P.M. Admission is $5, or $10 for a four-day pass good at all Museum of New Mexico museums; kids 16 and under admitted free. On

Sunday, admission is $1 for New Mexico residents. For more information, phone 505/476-5100.

The **Museum of Fine Arts** houses an excellent collection of Southwestern art displayed on a rotating basis. Specializing in traditional and 20th-century works, the museum exhibits many well-known New Mexican artists, including Georgia O'Keeffe and Peter Hurd. Though oil is the dominant medium among the museum's pieces, there's also some sculpture, as well as one room devoted to Spanish Revival furniture.

The Museum of Fine Arts is just west of the Palace of the Governors at 107 W. Palace Avenue. For information, phone 505/476-5072.

Cathedral of St. Francis of Assisi

From the Museum of Fine Arts, head one block east (in front of the Palace of the Governors) up Palace Avenue. The Cathedral of Saint Francis, near the corner of Palace and Cathedral Avenues, was built 1869–86 on the site of the original mission church, Our Lady of Assumption, which was built in 1610 and destroyed in the Pueblo Revolt 70 years later. Designed by Archbishop Jean Baptiste Lamy and a team of French architects, the Romanesque-style church stands in stark contrast to the pueblo-style buildings surrounding it. Bishop Lamy is buried beneath the main altar.

The Cathedral of Saint Francis is open daily 6 A.M.–6 P.M., and donations are gladly accepted. For more information, phone 505/982-5619.

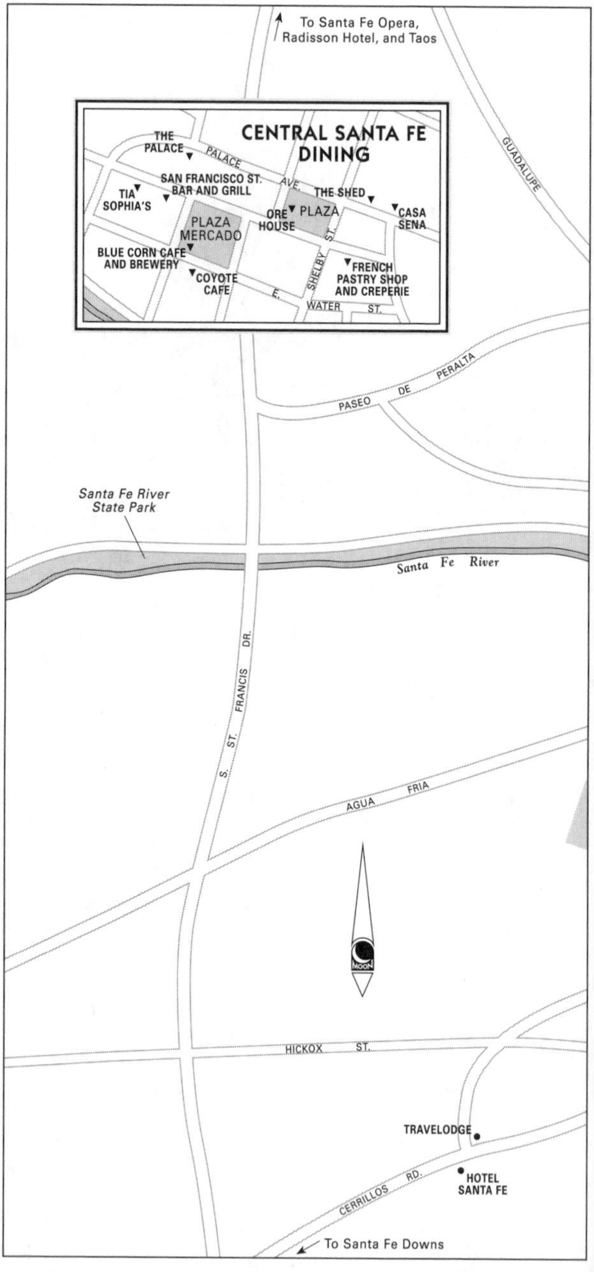

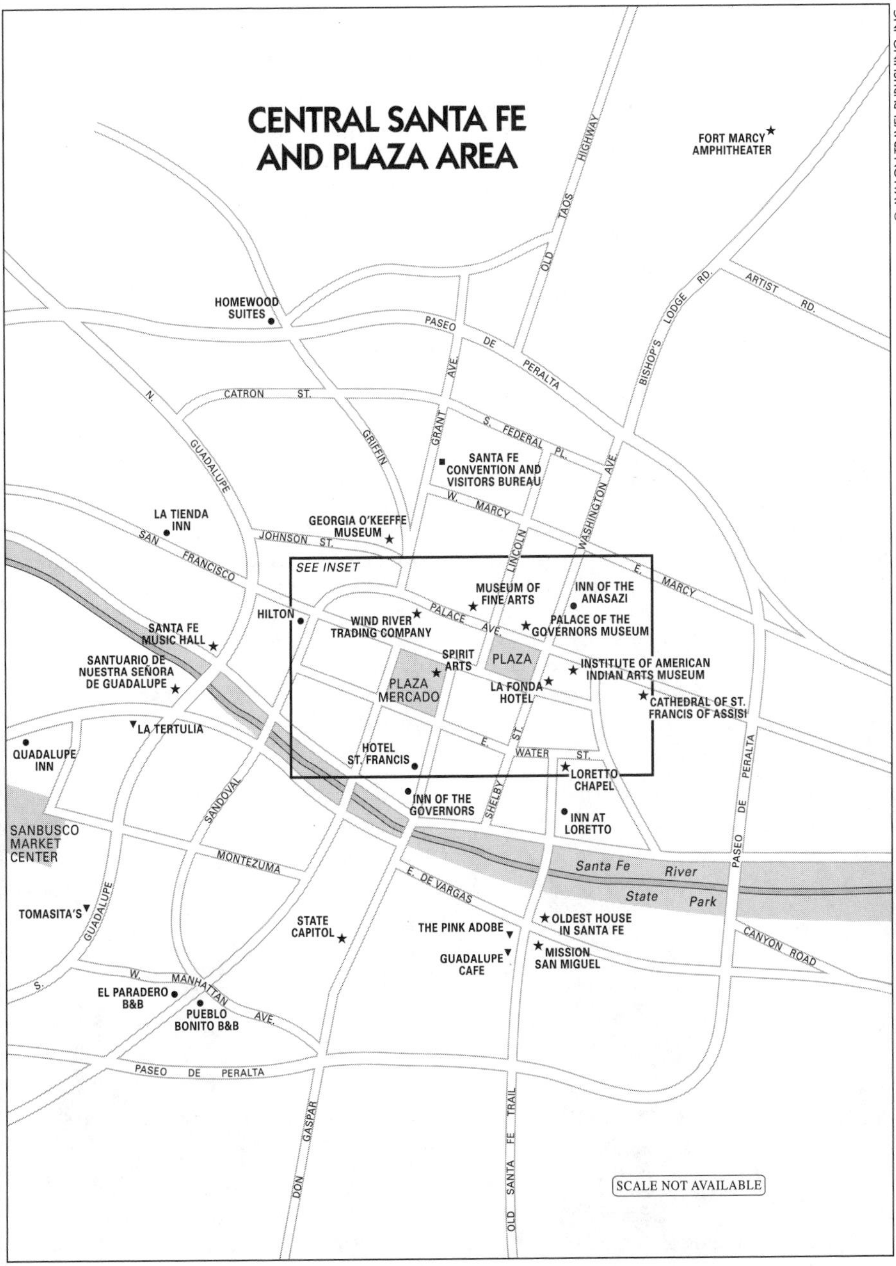

CENTRAL SANTA FE AND PLAZA AREA
FORT MARCY AMPHITHEATER
OLD TAOS HIGHWAY
ARTIST RD.
BISHOP'S LODGE RD.
HOMEWOOD SUITES
PASEO DE PERALTA
GRANT AVE.
CATRON ST.
N. GUADALUPE
GRIFFIN
S. FEDERAL PL.
SANTA FE CONVENTION AND VISITORS BUREAU
WASHINGTON AVE.
W. MARCY
LA TIENDA INN
GEORGIA O'KEEFFE MUSEUM
JOHNSON ST.
SAN FRANCISCO
LINCOLN
E. MARCY
SEE INSET
MUSEUM OF FINE ARTS
INN OF THE ANASAZI
HILTON
PALACE AVE.
WIND RIVER TRADING COMPANY
PALACE OF THE GOVERNORS MUSEUM
SANTA FE MUSIC HALL
SPIRIT ARTS
PLAZA
INSTITUTE OF AMERICAN INDIAN ARTS MUSEUM
SANTUARIO DE NUESTRA SEÑORA DE GUADALUPE
PLAZA MERCADO
LA FONDA HOTEL
CATHEDRAL OF ST. FRANCIS OF ASSISI
LA TERTULIA
QUADALUPE INN
HOTEL ST. FRANCIS
E. WATER ST.
SHELBY ST.
LORETTO CHAPEL
INN OF THE GOVERNORS
INN AT LORETTO
SANDOVAL
SANBUSCO MARKET CENTER
MONTEZUMA
Santa Fe River State Park
E. DE VARGAS
TOMASITA'S
GUADALUPE
STATE CAPITOL
THE PINK ADOBE
OLDEST HOUSE IN SANTA FE
CANYON ROAD
GUADALUPE CAFE
MISSION SAN MIGUEL
S.
W. MANHATTAN AVE.
EL PARADERO B&B
PUEBLO BONITO B&B
PASEO DE PERALTA
DON GASPAR
OLD SANTA FE TRAIL
SCALE NOT AVAILABLE

Institute of American Indian Arts Museum

Directly across Cathedral Avenue from the Cathedral of Saint Francis, the museum displays work by students at the Institute of American Indian Arts, where Native Americans work toward an Associate of Fine Arts degree. Although the exhibits rotate, you can usually count on seeing an excellent selection of beadwork, oil painting, and sculpture. Some of the student work is for sale. The museum, 108 Cathedral, 505/988-6211, is open daily 9 A.M.–5 P.M. and 10 A.M.–5 P.M. the rest of the year. Admission is $4; under 17 and students free. You can get more information at the website: www.iaiancad.org, or by phoning 505/983-8900.

Loretto Chapel

Modeled after Paris's Sainte Chapelle, the Loretto Chapel, 209 Old Santa Fe Trail, was built in 1878 for the Sisters of Loretto, six women whom Archbishop Lamy had brought with him to Santa Fe. Near the end of the chapel's construction the principal architect was killed by Lamy's nephew, John, who thought the builder had designs on his wife. Thus, building came to a halt and the Sisters of Loretto were left with a chapel without a staircase to the choir loft. According to legend, a series of novenas to St. Joseph was apparently answered by the appearance of an unknown carpenter, who built a staircase in six months using only a hammer, saw, and carpenter's square—and without nails or visible means of support. The stranger disappeared as soon as the job was done, and was neither paid, thanked, nor seen again by the sisters. His work has been called the "Miraculous Staircase" and is often attributed to St. Joseph.

The Loretto Chapel, also known as Our Lady of Light, is open Monday–Saturday 9 A.M.–9 P.M. and Sunday 10:30 A.M.–5 P.M. Admission is $2.50.

Mission San Miguel

Three blocks south of the plaza on Old Santa Fe Trail, this is the oldest mission in the United States and dates from Santa Fe's founding in 1610, although it was nearly destroyed during the Pueblo Revolt and rebuilt in 1710. Between 1710 and 1760, the chapel was used by the military, and in the late 19th century Archbishop Lamy's Christian Brothers, whose academy was next door, used the mission as their place of worship.

Inside, you'll find many examples of New Mexican religious art and Christian icons, in-

© STEPHEN METZGER

Mission San Miguel

cluding a statue of St. Michael from the 17th century and buffalo- and deer-hide paintings of Jesus. The bell on display in the anteroom was made in Spain in 1312 and brought to New Mexico in the 1800s.

The mission is open May–October, Monday–Saturday 9 A.M.–5 P.M., Sunday 1:30–4 P.M. Admission is $1. A small gift shop adjoins the chapel. For information, phone 505/983-3974.

"Oldest House in Santa Fe"

Just across the street from the Mission San Miguel, this tiny dirt-floored adobe "house" is enshrouded in myth and fancy—some claim the Spanish warrior whose remains were found here was killed by resident witches in the 17th century. No one knows for certain when it was actually built, though historians have certified that its vigas date from the early 1700s. It's a half block off Old Santa Fe Trail at 215 E. De Vargas. Donations accepted; open 11 A.M.–3 P.M. daily.

Santa Fe River State Park

This is an excellent place for a picnic or simply to rest awhile after a morning poking around the shops, galleries, and museums of Santa Fe. The 12-acre park was established in 1935 and features lush lawns and stone picnic tables along the north bank of the meandering Santa Fe River. Go two blocks south from the plaza.

OTHER SANTA FE SIGHTS

Santuario de Nuestra Señora de Guadalupe

This small chapel, probably built about 1796, was known during the 19th century as "the mission at the end of the [Santa Fe] trail." The church was abandoned in the mid-1960s, when a new chapel was built, although it was restored shortly thereafter, with ox blood rubbed into the walls to approximate the original coloration. Today, the chapel, four blocks west of the plaza at Guadalupe and Agua Fria, houses a small library and botanical garden and is used for concerts, lectures, and art exhibits. Hours are Monday–Saturday 9 A.M.–4 P.M. (Monday–Friday only in winter). Donations accepted.

State Capitol

Built in 1966 and remodeled to the tune of $34 million in 1992, the State Capitol building is modeled after a Zia sun sign, reflecting the circle of life. It features a huge rotunda with exhibits—on loan from the Museum of New Mexico—pertinent to the history of the state, as well as the Governor's Gallery, where work by local artists is displayed, and a gorgeously landscaped garden. The Capitol, at Paseo de Peralta and Old Santa Fe Trail, is open to visitors Monday–Saturday 8 A.M.–5 P.M., although the Governor's Gallery is closed Saturday. Tours are offered a couple of times a day. For tour times or more information, phone 505/986-4589.

Museum of Indian Arts and Culture

Another part of the Museum of New Mexico complex, this airy resource center and museum is in a huge and modern building on a hillside just off the Old Santa Fe Trail. The museum is divided into several smaller rooms off a central atrium.

The museum also houses a huge pottery and basketry collection, an exhibit of early and contemporary photographs of Southwestern Indians.

The Museum of Indian Arts and Culture is open Tuesday–Sunday 10 A.M.–5 P.M. Admission is $7; Museum of New Mexico passes are honored. Free gallery guidebooks are available at the main desk. Take Old Santa Fe Trail south from the plaza and turn right on Camino Lejo. For more information, phone 505/476-1250 or check out the website: www.miaclab.org.

Museum of International Folk Art

Next door to the Museum of Indian Arts and Culture, this is the fourth component in the Museum of New Mexico complex and one of the highlights of a visit to Santa Fe. Celebrating folk art from around the world, including work from more than 100 countries, the museum displays elaborate dioramas from 19th-century Europe, Chinese prints, embroidered Indian mandalas, toys from early-20th-century Germany, New Mexican quilts, Mexican masks, South American and African puppets, amulets, talismans, and a seemingly endless array of figurines and ceremonial clothing. A wonderland for kids, the museum is like a giant Christmas display window.

Be sure to pick up the free gallery guidebook that fully explains the various exhibits. The museum is open Tuesday–Sunday 10 A.M.–5 P.M., and admission is $7 (or use your Museum of New Mexico pass). For more information, phone 505/476-1200.

Georgia O'Keeffe Museum

The recently opened Georgia O'Keeffe Museum at 217 Johnson is home of the world's largest permanent collection of the artist's work. Easily the best-known New Mexico painter, O'Keeffe was also one of the most critically successful and will undoubtedly be remembered as one of the most original and influential painters of the 20th century.

The museum houses drawings, pastel paintings (oil and water), and sculptures spanning 1916–80; many of the paintings, particularly, have become nearly synonymous with New Mexico art and will be instantly recognizable. The museum also houses a gift shop, the O'Keeffe Cafe, and a small screening room showing a continually running film on O'Keeffe's life. Note: I'd highly recommend viewing the film before wandering through the museum; the film's overview will add immensely to your enjoyment and understanding of the art and artist. The museum is open Tuesday–Sunday 10 A.M.–5 P.M., and admission is $5. For more information, phone 505/995-0785, or visit the website: www.okeeffe-museum.org.

Wheelwright Museum of the American Indian

Next door to the Museum of International Folk

A short stroll from the plaza, the Georgia O'Keeffe Museum displays the artist's work from throughout her long career.

Art, the Wheelwright Museum is a privately owned museum with rotating exhibits that change about every four months. Among the displays are pottery, jewelry, rugs, basketry, and sandpaintings. Shaped like a Navajo hogan, with eight sides, its door facing east to greet the sun, the museum was first opened in 1937 to preserve the Navajo religion.

The **Case Trading Post** downstairs sells rugs, pottery, and baskets and has an extensive selection of books on Indians and Native Americana.

Summer hours are Monday–Saturday 10 A.M.–5 P.M., Sunday 1–5 P.M. During the winter, the museum is open Tuesday–Saturday 10 A.M.–5 P.M., Sunday 1–5 P.M. Admission is free, although a $2 donation is suggested. Take Old Santa Fe Trail south from the plaza to Camino Lejo. For more information, phone 505/982-4636, or check out the website: www.collectorsguide.com/sf/m001.html.

Randall Davey Audubon Center

Built on the site of a former sawmill, farm, and artist's home dating from the early 19th century, this nature center offers guided and self-led bird-watching tours and nature walks. The grounds are open daily from 8 A.M. to dusk, and the nature center and gift shop are open Monday–Friday 9 A.M.–5 P.M. and weekends 10 A.M.–4 P.M., with guided tours beginning Monday at 1 and 4 P.M. in summer only. The center is at 1800 Upper Canyon Road. For more information, phone 505/983-4609.

Canyon Road

No visit to Santa Fe is complete without a stroll or drive up Canyon Road. Originally a footpath used by 13th-century Indians traveling between the valley and Pecos Pueblo, and later by the Spanish conquistadors, the route follows the Santa Fe River through the gorgeous mountain pines of the lower Sangre de Cristos. During the early part of the 20th century, Canyon Road was the focus of Santa Fe's art colony, with painters and sculptors living and working in adobe homes dating from the 18th century.

Today, Canyon Road is made up primarily of galleries, private residences, and small restaurants, and is officially designated a "residential arts and crafts zone" by the city. Unfortunately, rents have skyrocketed in recent years, and only the most commercially successful artists can afford studios in the area.

In addition to the old homes along Canyon Road, **Cristo Rey Church** is of particular interest. Built in 1940 to commemorate the 500th anniversary of Coronado's expedition, the church houses one of New Mexico's best examples of Spanish Colonial art: an ornate *reredo* (altar screen), originally crafted in 1760, depicting God and a number of important saints. Two hundred thousand adobe bricks were used in the construction of Cristo Rey Church, all of them fabricated from the soil on the chapel site. The church is open to visitors, and there is no admission charge.

Bataan Memorial Military Museum

Right next door to the children's museum (1050 Old Pecos Trail), this museum commemorates New Mexico's role in wars around the world from the Spanish Conquest to the Gulf War. Special emphasis is on the 1,800 New Mexican members of the 200th Coast Artillery Regiment who suffered the horrors of the Bataan Death March and subsequent incarceration (900 of them returned). Particularly moving are letters from the War Department (including some from President Harry Truman and General Douglas MacArthur) to parents informing them of their sons' deaths, as well as postcards from American POWs to their families back home.

Included among the displays are weapons and uniforms from the last 400 years of battle, photos from the 20th-century wars, and a range of machinery, including Jeeps and two vintage Harley-Davidson motorcycles—one from 1917, the other from 1942. Hours are Tuesday–Friday 9 A.M.–4 P.M. and Saturday 9 A.M.–1 P.M. Admission is free. Phone 505/474-1670 for more information.

Santa Fe Children's Museum

This recently opened museum, 1050 Old Pecos Trail, features hands-on educational and adventure programs and displays designed for whole families. On Friday, local artists come to work with kids, and Sunday, scientists teach about fossils, rocketry, and other subjects. The museum is open Wednesday–Saturday 10 A.M.–5 P.M. and Sunday noon–5 P.M. Admission is $3 for kids under 12 and $4 for adults. Phone 505/989-8359 for more information. You can also get information at the museum's website: www.sfchildmuseum.org.

Bishop's Lodge

Jean Baptiste Lamy, bishop and archbishop of Santa Fe from 1853 until his death in 1888, built a retreat in Tesuque Canyon three miles north of the Loretto Chapel. Here, in the quiet of the canyon, among his orchards and gardens, and in the lodge itself—a chapel, a sleeping room, and a sitting room—Lamy could escape the demands of his office. He could also host visitors, which he often did: the Sisters of Loretto, clergy students, and nearby Pueblo Indians.

The property changed hands several times during the next century, with many well-known New Mexicans coming and going, both as employees and as guests. In the 1920s, New Mexico writer Erna Fergusson worked for a time at the lodge and at one time hosted a visit by her friend Willa Cather, author of *Death Comes for the Archbishop.*

Today, Bishop's Lodge serves as a hotel, retreat, and conference center (see below), its many adobe buildings sprawling at the foot of the original structure. A key to the chapel is available for asking at the front desk; donations are accepted. To get there, take Bishop's Lodge/Highway 590 north from town three miles and watch for the signs on your right. For more information, phone 505/983-6377 or 800/732-2240.

Rancho de Los Golondrinos Museum

About 15 miles south of central Santa Fe, near the tiny village of La Cienega, this restored Spanish Colonial ranch dates to the 1700s, when it was a stopping place on the El Camino Real. Several times throughout the year, historical reenactments take place, and visitors can view life as it was nearly three centuries ago. It's open to the public June–September 10 A.M.–4 P.M. Wednesday–Sunday it's open to groups, by appointment in April, May, and October. Admission is $4 for adults. To get there, take I-25 south to Exit 276. It's a good idea to call ahead, 505/471-2261.

Hyde Memorial State Park

The road from downtown Santa Fe up to Santa Fe Ski Basin winds steeply into the Sangre de Cristos, through thick forests of fir, pine, and spruce, and glades of shimmering aspens. Occasionally the road switches back just so, or a grove of trees gives way to a hillside meadow, and you'll find your breath nearly taken away by the view—long, sweeping vistas over treetops and through narrow canyons to the foothills and valley far below.

Hyde Park, deep in the most delicious part of the forest, offers camping and picnicking, as well as hiking and cross-country ski trails into the Santa Fe National Forest. Day use is $4, and camping is $8 ($11 with hookups). Take Artist Road north from town about seven miles. Phone 505/986-0283 for information and reservations.

ACCOMMODATIONS

Two types of lodging prevail in Santa Fe: the hotels downtown, and the motels along "Motel Row" (Cerrillos Road). Of course, if you stay downtown, you'll experience more of the Santa Fe lifestyle and be closer to the galleries, restaurants, and gift shops. But you'll pay for that. The motels out on Cerrillos Road offer rooms at significantly lower rates, and it's quite easy to get downtown from Cerrillos; the road heads virtually straight to the downtown plaza, and the Santa Fe Trails local bus system makes the run throughout the day. Remember, too, that summer is high season, and most places charge at least 25 percent more for rooms June–August. For assistance in finding lodging in Santa Fe, phone **Santa Fe Central Reservations** at 505/983-8200 or 800/776-7669. For a full range of lodging options, visit the website: santafe.org/Visiting_Santa_Fe/Lodging/index.html.

Under $50

Very little in this price range, as you'd expect, though if you want to rough it a bit you can get a bed at the **Santa Fe International Hostel,** 1412 Cerrillos, 505/988-1153. Rates for both dorm-style accommodations and for private rooms include use of the kitchen, and you can do your laundry for $1 a load. A **Motel 6,** 505/473-1380, is at 3007 Cerrillos.

$50–100

You'll find lots of suitable, if generic, lodging in Santa Fe in this price range, including many of the franchise inns south of town on Cerrillos Road. The following hotels and motels represent a small sampling of what's available: **La Quinta,** 4298 Cerrillos, 505/471-1142 or 800/531-5900; **Fairfield Inn,** 4150 Cerrillos, 505/474-4442; **Hampton Inn,** 3625 Cerrillos, 505/474-3900; and the **Holiday Inn Express,** 3470 Cerrillos, 505/474-4570. In addition, a little closer to downtown Santa Fe (just six blocks from the plaza) is the Santa Fe **TraveLodge,** 646 Cerrillos, 505/982-3551, where doubles start at about $90 but begin to sneak into the next price category.

$100–150

One of the most intriguing Santa Fe lodges, and one worth a visit even if you're staying elsewhere, is the **Hotel Santa Fe,** 1501 Paseo de Peralta (corner of Cerrillos), 505/982-1200. Property of the Picuris Pueblo Indian tribe, which holds 51 percent interest, this is one of the few hotels in the country owned by Native Americans. The hotel is distinctly decorated with Native American art, the grounds punctuated with sculpture, the lobby and rooms with paintings, prints, and weavings. (Note: though rooms start in this price range, suites go for as much as $450.)

The newly refurbished **Courtyard by Marriott,** 3347 Cerrillos, 505/473-2800, also offers a full restaurant and convention facilities. The **Holiday Inn,** 4048 Cerrillos, 505/473-4646, also has nice rooms in this price range.

Bed-and-Breakfasts: $100–150

Additionally, many of Santa Fe's bed-and-breakfasts—and there are, indeed, many—offer lodging in this price range. A few blocks from Santa Fe's downtown plaza is **El Pueblo Bonito Bed and Breakfast,** 138 W. Manhattan, 505/984-8001, website: www.bbonline.com/nm/pueblobonito/rooms.html. This 18-room inn is a long-standing favorite and has garnered many awards through the years.

El Paradero Bed and Breakfast Inn is just down the street at 220 W. Manhattan, 505/988-1177. Some of the 14 rooms offer private baths.

A reader writes to recommend **La Tienda Inn and Duran House,** 445-447 and 511 W. San Francisco, 505/989-8259, which he claims was the best place he stayed during his extended visit to New Mexico. The walled compound that comprises La Tienda has seven rooms, and the newly acquired and remodeled Duran House offers four more—all with private baths.

The **Guadalupe Inn,** 604 Agua Fria, 505/989-7422, website: www.guadalupeinn.com, is a discreet little inn with 12 rooms on an alleyway in the Guadalupe District, a 10-minute walk from the downtown plaza. Highlights include the green-chile-infused breakfasts: you can have them served over your breakfast burrito or, as Betsy did on three consecutive mornings, heaped in a bowl with a tortilla on the side. There's also fare for the less adventurous, including pancakes, scrambled eggs, or Shredded Wheat and bananas.

Just south of Santa Fe, in the tiny isolated village of La Cienega, is the newly built **Adobe Retreat Bed and Breakfast,** 505/474-7725. Just a mile from the Los Golondrinas Museum, this inn offers serenity in the softly rolling hills. For a brochure and more information, write 16 Amado Sueno, Santa Fe, NM 87505, or check out the website: www.newmex.com/adoberetreat.

Plaza Area: $150–200

If I wanted to stay right downtown, I'd probably check into the classy **Hotel St. Francis,** at 210 Don Gaspar, 505/983-5700. This is a gorgeously and classically appointed hotel, first built in the 1880s and remodeled a century later. While the low-end rooms here are affordable—and still quite nice—the upper-end suites go for as much as $400.

Plaza Area: $200 and Up

One of Santa Fe's oldest and most colorful hotels is **La Fonda,** 505/982-5511 or 800/523-5002, right on the downtown plaza at the "end of the Santa Fe Trail." La Fonda's lobby is decorated in wonderful Southwest tile and adobe, and the folks at the front desk happily dispense tourist information and maps to both guests and nonguests.

The **Hotel Loretto,** 210 Old Santa Fe Trail, 505/988-5531, just a block off the plaza, is a large and impressive building of ancient pueblo architecture offering convenience and class. The Santa Fe **Hilton,** 100 Sandoval, 505/988-2811, is also near the heart of the old town, just two blocks from the plaza.

Other recommended plaza-area hotels include the **Inn of the Anasazi,** 113 Washington Ave., 505/988-3030 or 800/688-8100, and the **Inn of the Governors,** 234 Don Gaspar, 505/982-4333 or 800/234-4534. Both have suites and rooms with fireplaces.

Farther Afield

Guests at **Bishop's Lodge,** 505/983-6377 or 800/732-2240, stay on property once owned by Santa Fe's archbishop Jean Baptiste Lamy, who built a small chapel/retreat here in the 1870s (see above). Isolated in Tesuque Canyon, Bishop's Lodge offers seclusion and privacy just three miles from the downtown plaza. Take Bishop's Lodge Road/Highway 590 north from Santa Fe and watch for the signs on your right. Doubles run $180–400 depending on season and amenities.

Camping and RVing

You'll find a number of excellent campgrounds within a short drive of downtown Santa Fe. **Black Canyon** Forest Service campground has nicely secluded sites set back among the aspens, firs, and junipers of Santa Fe National Forest. Camping is $6.50—drinking water and pit toilets. Take Artist Road (Highway 476) about seven miles north of the plaza. **Hyde Memorial State Park** (see above) abuts Black Canyon and has both tent and RV sites.

You'll also find a number of RV parks in the immediate Santa Fe area. In town, **Babbitt's RV Resort,** 3574 Cerrillos, 505/473-1949, offers clean, quiet sites with full hookups for about $25. About 10 miles north of town, **Rancheros de Santa Fe Camping Park,** 505/983-3482, has tent and RV camping, with sites scattered among the piñon and juniper. Take I-25 north to the Vaughn exit (Exit 290) and follow the signs one mile. A few miles north of Rancheros Park, **Santa Fe KOA,** 505/466-1419, also offers camping for tenters and RVers. Take Exit 294 or 290 and follow the signs.

FOOD

By the time you've been in Santa Fe 20 minutes you'll have realized that this is a very restaurant-oriented town, and the folks here quite food-focused. In fact, Santa Fe not only boasts a disproportionately large number of eating establishments per capita (there are about 200 restaurants), but the cuisine is so good and so distinctive that most decent-sized towns in the country have one or more restaurants featuring Santa Fe-style cooking, where meals begin with blue-corn tortilla chips and salsa or guacamole, fresh meat and seafood are grilled over mesquite or pecan-wood fires, the food is seasoned with Southwestern produce from green chiles to piñon nuts, and it's all washed down with a margarita or *cerveza.* In addition, Santa Fe cuisine has spiced up another industry: publishing. Check out the cookbook section of your local bookstore, and note the number of books devoted entirely to Southwestern cooking, with many of the recipes coming straight from Santa Fe restaurants. In fact, two of Santa Fe's best and most upscale restaurants have published cookbooks. The Coyote Cafe and the Pink Adobe both hawk books with their favorite recipes, complete with mouthwatering photos and menu suggestions. They're available at the restaurants and in bookstores in town (see below, as well as Suggested Reading). Following is a very brief sampling of Santa Fe's best restaurants. You'll have fun discovering your own, as you wander down backstreets and follow your nose to the sources of the delicious aromas.

For a complete listing of Santa Fe–area restaurants, visit website: santafe.org/Visiting_Santa_Fe/Restaurants/index.html.

Start Me Up

One of the best places to begin a day of wandering about Santa Fe is the **Tecolote Cafe,** 505/988-1362, a sprawling roadhouse-type restaurant at 1203 Cerrillos. Among the favorites are the breakfast burritos and blue-corn pancakes. Complete (read "huge") breakfasts run $4–8. Closed Monday. For espresso coffees and homemade pastries, muffins, and breads (multi-grain, green-chile, sourdough), it's tough to beat the **French Pastry Shop and Creperie,** 110 W. San Francisco, 505/963-6697.

Plaza-Area Favorites

You could eat at a different restaurant twice a day for weeks on end without ever leaving the two or three blocks that surround Santa Fe's downtown plaza. And most likely you'd be more than satisfied every time. Whenever I visit, I'm torn between stopping in at old standbys and visiting places I've never tried but that have been highly and frequently recommended. Such is life.

Herewith, then, a brief sampling; I can almost guarantee you won't go wanting.

One exclusively Santa Fe lunch experience is **The Shed** at 113 ½ E. Palace, just off the downtown plaza, 505/982-9030. You'll most likely have to wait for a table—as long as 30–45 minutes during the high tourist season—but it'll be worth it, especially since you can lounge in the brick-floored atrium or wander into the nearby galleries while you're waiting. The Shed is famous for its blue-corn tortillas, and the green chile, "shedburgers," burritos, and tacos are excellent. Prices run from about $3 for a cup of green chile to $6–8 for the burgers and Mexican plates. Daily dessert specials (cheesecake, mocha chocolate cake, pies, and sundaes) go for $2–3. Hours are 11 a.m.–2:30 p.m. daily.

Another excellent plaza-area restaurant is **Tia Sophia's** at 210 W. San Francisco, 505/983-9880, a favorite among local businessfolk and tourists alike. Open for breakfast and lunch 7 a.m.–2 p.m., this bustling little spot features breakfast burritos, green-chile stews, and blue-corn dishes. Closed Sunday.

The Blue Corn Cafe and Brewery, in the Plaza Mercado, 116 W. San Francisco (or enter from the other side of the complex at 133 Water St.), 505/984-1800, serves "tortillas and tequila" and other related lunch and dinner fare. Its excellent green-chile stew (hot!) is punctuated with both potatoes and posole (hominy), and the "brewery burgers" are delicious. To wash your grub down, choose from a huge variety of margaritas ($4–10), as well as a half-dozen house brews, or you can play it safe with iced tea and other saner concoctions.

A popular lunch and dinner stop right on the downtown plaza is the **Ore House,** 50 Lincoln, 505/983-8687, where burgers run about $7, burritos are $7–9, and seafood (trout and salmon) starts at about $8. The Ore House also prides itself on its desserts, sorbets, and cheesecakes, for about $5. It serves lunch and dinner daily.

For a quick beer, snack, lunch, or dinner cantina-style, try the **San Francisco Street Bar and Grill,** 110 W. San Francisco St., 505/982-2044. Appetizers—chips and salsa and fajitas—are $3–7, and meals, including salads, burgers, and steaks, run $6–15.

The Palace, 142 Palace Ave., 505/982-9891, is one of Santa Fe's continental-style restaurants, serving pasta, beef, and seafood dinners, with prices ranging $12–25. The lunch menu includes veal, prime rib, salads, and pastas. Prices range $8–15.

Chances are good you've heard of the **Coyote Cafe,** 132 Water St., 505/983-1615. The Coyote's owner, Mark Miller, has been very successful in promoting the restaurant and making it almost synonymous with Santa Fe–style cuisine, selling his *Coyote Cafe cookbook,* assorted spices, and kitchen and gourmet-cooking utensils. The restaurant is on the second floor of the building, and the window tables look down on narrow Water Street, which gives the place a distinctly Old World feel. The menu includes a wide range of grilled meats and seafood, as well as vegetarian dishes always prepared innovatively and deliciously. Main dinner courses run $18–28, lunches $8–16. Prix fixe dinners are offered for about $45. Note: reservations are required, and during the height of the tourist season should be made at least a couple of days in advance.

A less formal, more reasonably priced alternative to the Coyote Cafe's main dining room is its separate, open-air **Rooftop Cantina.** Order a margarita and a side of chips and watch the sunset paint the adobe walls of the surrounding buildings, or stick around for dinner—burritos, tamales, and specials for $7–10. The Rooftop Cantina is closed in the winter.

Another true Santa Fe tradition is **The Pink Adobe,** 406 Old Santa Fe Trail, 505/983-7712. The founder of the Pink Adobe, Rosalea Murphy, has been featured on the PBS series *Great Chefs of the West* and written up in both *Newsweek* and *Food and Wine* magazines. She claims as customers such celebrities as Robert Redford and Robert Duvall, and Sam Shepard and Jessica Lange were said to be "regulars" when they lived in Santa Fe. The Pink Adobe is in an airy 300-year-old adobe building, decorated with plants and Murphy's paintings, which hang on the 36-inch-thick walls. Dinners include both New Mexican and continental cuisine, and prices range from about $12 for chicken enchiladas to $24 for steak Dunigan (New York steak with green chiles). Appetizers, escargots to artichokes, are $6–10. Lunch prices are slightly lower, with salads running $6–9 and enchilada and tamale plates $8–12. Lunch is served Monday–Friday 11:30 a.m.–2:30 p.m. and dinner nightly 5:30–10 p.m. On opera nights, the Pink Adobe opens at 5 p.m. Like the Coyote Cafe, the Pink Adobe collects some of its best recipes in a cookbook, the *Pink Adobe Cookbook,* available at the restaurant and at bookstores throughout New Mexico.

Virtually next door to the Pink Adobe is the **Guadalupe Cafe,** 422 Old Santa Fe Trail, 505/982-9762. This busy little café serves breakfast, Saturday and Sunday brunch, lunch, and dinner, specializing in blue-corn tortilla dishes and other New Mexican fare, such as chicken chimichangas, crab enchiladas, and chalupas. Entrées run $7–12. Even on weekdays, though, the place gets crowded, so be prepared to wait—you'll be glad you did.

Guadalupe District

Just a few blocks from the plaza (easy walking distance) is the rejuvenated Guadalupe Historical District, where you'll find several excellent restaurants and gift shops and galleries to wander through as you walk off your meal. I personally would find a visit to Santa Fe incomplete without stopping in at **Tomasita's,** 500 Guadalupe, 505/983-5721. This is a crowded and noisy good-time cantina, where the margaritas flow like the laughter does, and families and courting couples will feel equally comfortable. Tomasita's serves daily specials—tamales, *flautas,* and *carne adovada*—for about $10, while everyday entrées, including several vegetarian dishes, run $5–10. Try a burrito, a stuffed sopaipilla, or the Mexican steak, and wash it down with a glass of sangria or a margarita. Got a big party? Even better: you can also get margaritas by the pitcher.

Another nearby favorite is **La Tertulia,** 416 Agua Fria, 505/988-2769, which offers a rare, only-in-Santa Fe dining experience and serves some of the best New Mexican food in town to boot. Converted from part of the Guadalupe Mission Church, La Tertulia's six dining rooms were at one time the individual rooms of the convent. The richly tiled floors and thick adobe walls reflect the building's history and make you feel as if you've just returned from patrol with a unit of 18th-century Mexican soldiers or ridden in on the Santa Fe Trail. *Carne adovada,* burritos, fajitas, and other New Mexican specialties run $10–16.

Two Local Favorites

For something a little different, try **Dave's Not Here,** 1115 Hickox, 505/983-7060. At this small and unpretentious diner, you're more likely to share a table with a local plumber or electrician than you are with a sculptor or camera-toting tourist, and the food is some of the best around. Excellent burgers, chimichangas, burritos, and salads (try the Greek salad) run about $4–7. It's open Monday–Saturday 11 A.M.–4 P.M.

Another local favorite, as well as one at the top of my personal list, is **Maria's New Mexican Kitchen,** 555 W. Cordova, 505/983-7929. Famous for its margaritas—serving more than 70 with 50 different kinds of tequila—Maria cooks up some of the best green-chile stew, fajitas, and burritos in the city. In addition, you can watch tortillas being made in a small glass booth toward the back of the restaurant. When I asked for a second flour tortilla to go with my stew, the waitress turned to the tortilla cook, who took one off the grill, wrapped it in a red napkin, and handed it to her, hot, fresh, and steaming. Dinners run $6–12.

Learn to Cook It Yourself

If you're at all interested in New Mexican cooking, be sure to check out the **Santa Fe School of Cooking,** 116 W. San Francisco, just off the plaza. Here you can choose from a variety of excellent courses offered by some of Santa Fe's top chefs. We were a little disappointed that we'd missed the course on traditional northern New Mexican dishes and settled for one the next day on tapas (typically, appetizer-type dishes from Spain). It turned out to be one of the highlights of our visit. The three-hour course focused on local organic ingredients, with equal amounts of history, humor, and culinary expertise. Plus we got to eat the food. (When classes are small, participants get to join in the fun—slicing, dicing, basting, and even tasting along the way.) Among the courses offered are "Contemporary Southwest," "Southwestern Breakfasts," and "Dessert Parties."

The "classroom" is on the third floor of the Plaza Mercado, and there are seats and tables enough for about 40 students; there were 16 in our class. Adjoining the classroom is the Santa Fe School of Cooking Market, where you can pick up a wide range of ingredients used in local cooking (very reasonable prices), as well as utensils, other kitchenware, and cookbooks. Courses run about $45–70 per person, with wine and beer additional. For a schedule and more information, phone 505/983-4511, or check out the website: www.santafeschoolofcooking.com/calen.html.

Dinner Theater

At least one Santa Fe restaurant offers theater and/or music as part of the dining experience. **Casa Sena,** 125 E. Palace, 505/988-9232, presents skits and music from a range of well-known shows and composers. The talented singers and dancers also serve your meal. Dinner, with drinks and tip, will cost $40–70 a person.

Grocery Stores

In addition to the standard supermarkets that you find in any town this size, Santa Fe has two **Wild Oats** and an **Alfalfa's** grocery store. Though decried by some as being overpriced and too "YUP"-scale, these stores have excellent selections of organic produce, juices, range-fed beef, and other healthful foods. Santa Fe's Wild Oats stores are at 1090 St. Francis, 505/983-5333, and 1708 Llano, 505/473-4943. They're open seven days a week and also have delis and salad bars. Alfalfa's is at 333 W. Cordova, 505/986-8667.

Santa Fe Area Farmer's Market

Every Saturday and Tuesday morning (7 A.M.–noon), from late April through early November, northern New Mexican farmers sell their produce in the railyard, near the train depot off Guadalupe Street. This is an excellent opportunity to choose from a huge range of fruits and vegetables, from the everyday to the exotic. Not only will you find spinach, cabbage, and chiles, but you'll also likely see bok choy, *mizuna,* and interesting varieties of cucumbers and onions, as well as local honey, dried flowers, and locally produced salsas and jams.

November through March, when there's a lot less produce available and the weather is not as accommodating, vendors set up Saturday morning 9 A.M.–1 P.M. at El Museo Cultural in the railyard. For more information, phone 505/983-4098.

ENTERTAINMENT

Santa Fe prides itself on keeping folks entertained, and whether your bent is theater, film, soft lounge music, opera, or a full-scale rock 'n' roll extravaganza, you'll find something to fill the evening hours here. Because of the vast possibilities, your best bet is to pick up a copy of Friday's *New Mexican* and check out the supplement *Pasatiempo,* which includes current listings of club acts, concerts, and movies. Another useful resource is *Bienvenidos, A Visitor's Guide to Northern New Mexico,* published annually by the *New Mexican* newspaper and available for $1 throughout the area. The guide includes complete listings of performing arts, as well as short reviews and

© KEN HOWARD

Santa Fe Opera

profiles of local musicians, dancers, and actors. The *Santa Fe Visitors Guide,* published each year by the convention and visitors bureau, also includes short descriptions of Santa Fe's various entertainment options. For a free copy, stop by the visitors center at 201 W. Marcy. Following is a partial listing of Santa Fe performing arts.

Santa Fe Opera

This is without doubt the highlight of Santa Fe's after-hours scene and one of the true joys of the city. Established in 1957, the opera runs from early July to late August every summer, and openings are marked by audiences as bizarrely bedecked as the casts, though the more conservative may opt for conventional tuxedos and gowns. The 2,000-seat amphitheater offers a chance to see big-name stars performing classical and modern opera under starry New Mexico skies. The new roof, added in 1998, features clear glass, and the summer of 1999 saw the addition of an electronic English libretto system (just in case you don't understand Italian).

Ticket prices range from about $30 for side seating Monday–Thursday to about $250 for orchestra seating on opening nights. Some standing-room tickets are also sold, at considerably reduced prices. Season tickets are also available.

The Santa Fe Opera is about seven miles north of town on Highway 84/285. For more information, or for current schedules, write Santa Fe Opera, P.O. Box 2408, Santa Fe, NM 87504-2408, or phone 505/986-5900 or 800/280-4654. Information is also available through the Santa Fe Convention and Visitors Bureau, P.O. Box 909, Santa Fe, NM 87504-0909; phone 800/777-CITY (800/777-2489).

Santa Fe Chamber Music Festival

This has been an immensely popular Santa Fe event since the early 1970s. Running mid-July to mid-August, the concert series includes lectures and seminars (on a wide range of musical genres) as well as special concerts geared especially for younger audiences (Tuesday-afternoon Youth Concerts). For tickets ($15–40) and information, write P.O. Box 853, Santa Fe, NM 87504-0853, or phone 505/983-2075 or 505/982-1890.

Santa Fe Playhouse

Established in the 1920s and the oldest theater group in New Mexico, this troupe performs one-acts, melodramas, musical comedy, and conventional stage productions. Tickets are about $12 for adults, with discounts for students and seniors. For more information, write 142 E. de Vargas St., P.O. Box 2084, Santa Fe, NM 87504, or phone 505/988-4262.

Shakespeare in Santa Fe

Offering performances on Friday–Sunday evenings in July and August in the Fort Marcy Amphitheater, this enthusiastic local company usually produces two of the Bard's plays each summer. Music begins at 6 P.M., plays at 7. Reserved and lawn seating are both available. For more information and prices, phone 505/982-2910.

Clubs

The city's main concert venue is the **Paulo Soleri Auditorium,** which hosts an annual summer concert series with big-name, large-crowd performers, from Dave Matthews to Big Head Todd and the Monsters. For information and tickets, phone 505/989-6318. The auditorium is at 1501 Cerrillos. In addition, many of the hotels near the plaza offer live music and dancing. Check out the Fiesta Lounge in **La Fonda** on the plaza, 505/982-5511, for live music and to pick up literature on what else is going on around town.

ANNUAL EVENTS

Santa Fe's polycultural heritage makes it a city of festivals, and you could plan a year in town around them (it's likely that some folks do). From the Spanish Market to the opera opening to the Indian Market, there's always something happening in Santa Fe. Check local papers for current listings.

Spanish Market

Held every summer in late July, the Spanish Market at the Palace of the Governors features more than 100 artists displaying and selling the folk art of their ancestors—embroidery, weaving, furniture, and *santos* (holy figures) carved and crafted from wood, tin, gold, silver, or straw. Admission is free.

The Contemporary Hispanic Market, also in the Palace of the Governors, runs concurrently with the Spanish Market and features about 40 artists; free.

For more information, contact the Spanish Colonial Arts Society, P.O. Box 1611, Santa Fe, NM 87501, 505/983-4038.

Indian Market

One of Santa Fe's most popular annual events, Indian Market packs the streets the third weekend in August with collectors from all over the world. After a juried competition, more than 1,000 of the Southwest's finest artists display their work—jewelry, drums, baskets, kachinas, pottery, sandpaintings, rugs—and sell to buyers smart enough to arrive early (dealing usually starts about sunup the first day). Note: this is one of Santa Fe's busiest times of the year, and you should book accommodations well in advance. For more information, phone 505/983-5220.

Fiesta de Santa Fe

First held in 1712 to commemorate the Spaniards' defeat of the Pueblo Revolt in 1692, the Fiesta de Santa Fe is held every Labor Day weekend and includes parades, arts and crafts displays and sales, and the ceremonial burning of Zozobra, the 40-foot-tall effigy of "Old Man Gloom." The fair attracts upward of 50,000 people to Santa Fe's plaza.

SHOPPING

Newcomers to Santa Fe are likely to be absolutely overwhelmed by the apparently countless number of art galleries, museums, and gift shops (actually, there are more than 130 galleries alone). Every corner you turn, it seems, more galleries and stunning window displays present themselves. From stylized alabaster sculpture to representational Western oil paintings, from Navajo turquoise and silver to neo-impressionism and functional art (Southwestern furniture), the galleries offer a mind-boggling array of gifts, souvenirs, and genuine art investments.

Most of Santa Fe's gift shops and galleries are centered around the plaza area, although others are sprinkled throughout town, particularly on Canyon and Cerrillos Roads. Just like anyplace else, the best way to make sure you get a good deal is to shop around. Don't buy the first bolo, print, rug, or vase that strikes your fancy; instead, check to see if it's in other shops as well, and compare prices. (Don't worry—chances are slim you've found the last one in town and that it'll be gone before you can get back.)

Sidewalk Vendors

You can find an excellent selection of rugs, handbags, jewelry, and other assorted wares without ever setting foot inside one of the shops. Every day as many as 70 different vendors spread blankets on the sidewalk under the portal of the Palace of the Governors and sell authentic handmade wares. New Mexico state law stipulates that the work must be genuine, and the vendors must be licensed; in addition, the vendors must be approved by a separate committee, and their work is checked daily. Prices are generally fixed, so

don't try to barter, but they're often better than in the stores. Remember, too, that although the scene may appear the perfect "photo opportunity," most of the vendors are of Native American descent and find having their pictures taken offensive; ask permission first.

Shops

Though it would be next to impossible to list all of Santa Fe's gift shops—and not all that useful, either, as half the fun is simply wandering aimlessly—a few are worth mentioning here. For one of the largest selections of Indian jewelry, pottery, and kachina dolls, check out **Wind River Trading Company,** a half block east of the plaza at 113 E. San Francisco. Wind River also sells pawned (used) Indian jewelry, including dozens of silver and turquoise Navajo watchbands. **Indian Trader West,** 204 W. San Francisco, has a good selection of Navajo baskets and rugs, as well as pottery from many of northern New Mexico's pueblos, while **Joshua Baer and Company,** 116 ½ E. Palace, 505/988-8944, features museum-quality Navajo rugs and other crafts and artwork. Also worth a visit is **Spirit Arts** at 108 Don Gaspar, a low-key shop specializing in antique artifacts from around the world: embroidered linen and quilts, vintage clothing, kimonos, even New Zealand fertility dolls.

For a delightful change of pace in the plaza area, stop in at **Bizarre Bazaar,** an African import shop at 277 Galisteo 505/988-3999. Proprietor and importer Mohamed Sharif has spent 25 years traveling to west Africa collecting a huge range of masks, rugs, jewelry, woodcarvings, sculpture, and beads, the result of which seems as much museum as retail shop. All work is authentic, and Sharif can explain its symbolic and/or cultural significance.

One of Santa Fe's most popular tourist stops is **Jackalope Pottery** at 2820 Cerrillos Rd., a sort of Santa Fe–style Pier 1. In addition to crafts from throughout New Mexico and the Southwest, you'll find lots of outdoor pottery, ironwork, and tiles, as well as T-shirts and other knickknacks and souvenirs.

TOURS

Several companies book tours of Santa Fe and the surrounding area. I was lucky enough to join local cultural historian, lecturer, and guide Alan Osborne on a tour through Tesuque Canyon, Española, and Picuris Pueblo, where we stopped for a fabulous lunch. You can arrange tours with Osborne by calling him at 505/466-2775. Osborne also leads walking tours of Santa Fe (and also teaches snowboarding at Santa Fe Ski Area). Call for prices. **Historic Walks of Santa Fe** is a long-standing tour company with an excellent reputation. The walks leave from inside the Plaza Galeria and the La Fonda Hotel. Rates are $10 for adults, kids 16 and under free. For reservations or more information phone 505/986-8388 or visit the website: www.historicwalksofsantafe.com.

Historian-led walking tours of the city are offered by **Aboot About Santa Fe Walks and Tours,** 505/988-2774 (from the Hotel St. Francis); **Afoot in Santa Fe Walking Tours,** 505/983-3701 (from the Hotel Loretto).

Fiesta Tours, 505/690-7068 or 505/473-2800, ext. 486, offers several daily 75-minute tours of 40 or so historical sites in Santa Fe. Rates are $7 for adults; kids under 12 pay $4. **Southwest Safaris,** 505/988-4246, offers one- to five-day tours throughout New Mexico, Colorado, Arizona, and Utah. Prices range about $300–1,700 and include travel, lodging, and food. **Gray Line,** 505/983-9491, offers three-hour city tours daily except Sunday; the driver will pick you up at your hotel or motel.

Offering a wide range of educational tours and seminars, **Recursos de Santa Fe** is a nonprofit educational foundation specializing in the natural history, art, literature, and cuisine of the Southwest, as well as of Mexico and Central and South America. Recursos works with highly respected faculty, and most fees include transportation and lodging. For more information, phone 505/982-9301, or write 826 Camino del Monte Rey A-3, Santa Fe, NM 87501. **Rojo Tours,** 505/983-8333, has a complete range, from walks of the plaza to tours of nearby pueblos and Indian ruins.

RECREATION

You don't have to look too closely at Santa Fe folk to see that they spend a lot of time outdoors. The darkened skin, the eyes full of life and laughter, the sinewy flesh—all reflect a love for the gorgeous countryside and a penchant for getting out in it. Situated in the pine-and piñon-covered foothills of the southern Rocky Mountains, Santa Fe is the Southwest's epicenter of outdoor activities. Whether your bag is skiing, windsurfing, cycling, camping, fishing, golf, or white-water rafting, you'll find plenty of it in the Santa Fe area.

Windsurfing

Santa Feans have taken to windsurfing with a passion. On summer days on I-25, you might be surprised at the number of cars you pass with boards strapped atop them. Most likely, they're heading west to Cochiti Lake or east to Storrie Lake, near Las Vegas. Cochiti Lake is a small reservoir on the Cochiti Indian Reservation on the Rio Grande. Immensely popular among boardsailers, thanks in part to the wind that whips across the north valley, Cochiti also has numerous campsites, although there's no shade (pit toilets only). A visitors center at the lake is open 8 A.M.–3:30 P.M. Take I-25 south from Santa Fe about 25 miles and watch for the sign for the exit. The lake is about 10 miles northwest of the freeway.

Storrie Lake is the most popular windsurfing lake in the state, with races and regattas held there regularly (see Las Vegas in the Northeastern New Mexico chapter). Take I-25 north from Santa Fe, then Highway 518 north from Las Vegas.

Cycling

Touring and mountain biking are both popular in Santa Fe. For a serious on-road workout, head up toward Hyde Park from Artist Road. This steep and winding two-laner will push to the max the heartbeats of even the most in-shape riders. And the view and mountain air once you get up out of town are unbeatable. Another favorite, longer but mostly flat, is the Turquoise Trail to Albuquerque. A little more than 70 miles one way, this back road rolls through the tiny towns of Cerrillos, Madrid, and Golden, and if you've got a good bike and a decent amount of stamina it's a great way to get out of town.

Santa Fe National Forest north and east of the city offers dozens of trails excellent for mountain biking, although you should check with rangers before heading out. Stop by Forest Service headquarters at 1220 St. Francis Dr., or phone 505/988-6940 for more information. You can also get information on mountain biking in the area, as well as rent bikes, from **Bike-n-Sport,** 1829 Cerrillos, 505/820-0809.

White-Water Rafting

More popular each year, with more and more companies offering excursions, white-water rafting is becoming a summer tradition in northern New Mexico. Several Santa Fe–based companies book trips of various lengths for paddlers of different levels of experience. Among them: **New Wave Rafting Company,** 107 Washington Ave., 505/984-1444 or 800/869-7238; **Santa Fe Rafting Company and Outfitters,** 1000 Cerrillos Rd., 505/988-4914 or 800/984-1444; **Santa Fe Detours,** based in the La Fonda Hotel on the plaza, 505/983-6565 or 800/338-6877; and **Known World Adventures,** 1303 Cerrillos (Wild River Sports), 800/983-7756.

Fishing

Santa Fe is the gateway to some of the best fishing in the state. The Rio Chama (which feeds into the Rio Grande just north of town), the Pecos River east of Santa Fe, and the many small streams of the Santa Fe National Forest attract anglers of all ages and degrees of seriousness—from bait plunkers to serious fly casters. For information on fishing in the Santa Fe area, contact the **New Mexico Department of Game and Fish**, 1 Wildlife Way, Santa Fe, NM 87507, 505/476-8000, website: www.gmfsh.state.nm.us.

For fly gear and information on fly-fishing, stop by the **High Desert Angler,** 435 S. Guadalupe, 505/988-7688.

Golf

Santa Feans and visitors have their choice of two public golf courses. **Santa Fe Country Club Golf Course** is at the southwest end of town on Airport Road, 505/471-0601. If you've got the time and want to get out of town a ways, try **Cochiti Golf Course,** 505/465-2239, overlooking the north valley, Cochiti Lake, and the gently sloping southern Rockies. It was recently listed among *Golf Digest's* top 25 public courses in the country. Take I-25 south to Exit 264. Go right (west) at Highway 16. Take 16 to the end, and then go right on Highway 22 (north). The golf course is at the end.

The new **Marty Sanchez Links de Santa Fe,** 505/438-5210, 15 minutes west of the plaza, offers both nine- and 18-hole courses in rolling hills overlooking the Jemez and Sangre de Cristo Mountains.

Skiing

In wintertime, Santa Feans head for the hills. Less than a half hour from the heart of the city, **Santa Fe Ski Area** has four chairlifts, four surface lifts, and a vertical drop of 1,650 feet (from its 12,000-foot peak). Although food, instruction, and rental equipment are available at the ski area, the closest lodging is in town. Take Artist Road and follow the signs.

The road to the ski area is steep and winding, though it's usually plowed and sanded; carry chains to be on the safe side. For more information, phone 505/982-4429, or write Santa Fe Ski Area, 1210 Luisa St., Suite 10, Santa Fe, NM 87501. For snow conditions, phone 505/983-9155.

Santa Fe is also close to several other ski areas,

© DEBORAH FLEIG 2002

pagodas at 10,000 Waves

both downhill and cross country. Taos, Red River, Sipapu, Angel Fire, and Pajarito are all near enough for one-day excursions.

Cross-country skiers will delight in the trails and backcountry skiing available in Santa Fe National Forest. Trails abound in the mountains to the northwest and northeast of town. For maps and information, stop by the ranger station at 1220 St. Francis Dr., or phone 505/984-9606.

And When Your Muscles Are Sore

Once you've sampled the wide range of recreational activities Santa Fe has to offer, or even if you've just spent time wandering the streets and shops, it'll be time to relax. For a unique and classy place to do so, check out **10,000 Waves,** a Japanese-style spa in the foothills just outside Santa Fe. Here, you can get everything from a basic whirlpool to a full-on, pull-out-the-stops treatment, complete with massages, facials, herbal wraps, aromatherapy, and other indulgences. My wife, much more experienced in the massage area than I, gave 10,000 Waves an unequivocal thumbs-up.

Prices range from $13 (unlimited time in the communal tub) to about $300 for a five-hour private treatment that includes a 90-minute massage. Limited lodging (four "Houses of the Moon") is also available. Phone for hours and to make reservations.

For a brochure and more information, write Box 10200, Santa Fe, NM 87504, or phone 505/982-9304.

INFORMATION AND SERVICES

Because Santa Fe's streets are so crowded with shops and galleries, and because the architecture is all so similar (some newcomers actually complain that "everything in Santa Fe looks just the same . . ."), it can be easy to get lost, or at least to forget where you parked your car. Fortunately, Santa Feans are very accommodating, and local boosters and businesses have gone to great lengths to help you find your way around town. A small **Tourist Information Center** on the plaza stocks a variety of maps and literature, and attendants can answer most questions. Hours are Monday–Saturday 9:30 A.M.–4:30 P.M.

The **International Visitors Center** is on the mezzanine at La Fonda Hotel, on the southeast corner of the plaza. La Fonda is another good place to pick up Santa Fe maps and literature. In addition, two magazines are especially useful: *Bienvenidos* (published annually by the *New Mexican* newspaper), a 150-plus-page guide to the area's history, galleries, restaurants, etc., and *Santa Fe Visitors Guide* (published, also annually, by the Santa Fe Convention and Visitors Bureau). Both are available at hotels and tourist centers around town. Bill and Cheryl Jamison's book, *An Insider's Guide to Santa Fe* (Boston: Harvard Common Press), features a complete look at the area's history and offers street-by-street tours of town—available at most bookstores.

The **Santa Fe Convention and Visitors Bureau,** 201 W. Marcy, 505/984-6760 or 800/777-2489, is also an excellent place to stop for literature and information. Internet users can also find its excellent website: www.santafe.org. The offices of the **New Mexico State Department of Tourism and Economic Development** are in Santa Fe in the Lamy Building at 491 Old Santa Fe Trail. Call 505/827-0291 or 800/545-2040.

On your way into town from Albuquerque, stop at the **visitors information center** just a few miles south of Santa Fe. Here you'll find maps, brochures, literature on various area and state attractions, restrooms, and a friendly staff ready to answer any question about lodging, restaurants, galleries, camping, transportation, etc.

The **Collected Works** bookstore, 208-B W. San Francisco, 505/988-4226, has lots of books on travel—local to international. For maps, as well as a large selection of new, used, and out-of-print books on New Mexico and the American West, check out **Dumont Maps and Books of the West,** 314 McKenzie St., 505/988-1076.

Santa Fe's St. Vincent Hospital is at 455 St. Michael's Dr., 505/983-3361. The Santa Fe Police Department is at 2515 Camino Entrada; phone 505/473-5000. Call the state police at 505/827-9000.

TRANSPORTATION

Mesa Air, 800/MESA-AIR (800/637-2247), provides passenger service to Santa Fe, and most major airlines fly into Albuquerque, an hour south of town. Shuttle service is provided by Sandia Shuttle Express, 505/982-4311 or 800/775-5696.

You'll find Santa Fe's **Greyhound** bus depot at 858 St. Michael's Dr., 505/471-0008 or 800/528-0447, and the **Amtrak** station is 14 miles south of town in Lamy, 800/421-8320. (Amtrak's Southwest Chief passes through here daily on its run between Chicago and Los Angeles.) **Lamy Shuttle and Tours** runs regular shuttle service between the train station and Santa Fe, 505/982-8829 or 800/317-4516.

The **Santa Fe Trails** bus system offers regular service throughout the city, with all routes ending near the plaza. Cost is $.50. For route information, phone 505/438-1464. Phone **Capital City Cab** at 505/438-0000.

Vicinity of Santa Fe

SOUTH OF SANTA FE

Before heading north to Ratón and into Colorado, I-25 drops due south out of Santa Fe, then meanders southeast until, finally, on the east side of the southern Rocky Mountains, it doglegs back up toward Las Vegas. Just south of Santa Fe on I-25 North, Highway 285 cuts down into the Galisteo Basin and then crosses I-40 on its way to Roswell and Carlsbad.

This is some of New Mexico's prettiest high-desert country. The green Rockies loom as a backdrop; the hills, their soft brown mottled with piñon and juniper, roll out to meet the sky, often dramatically punctuated with fast-forming thunderheads. About seven miles south on Highway 285, you'll see the little town of Lamy off to the east.

Lamy

Named for Archbishop Jean Baptiste Lamy, this village dates to the 1870s, when the Santa Fe Railroad Company, which was running a line from the Ratón Pass to Albuquerque, decided to build its station here instead of in Santa Fe, where the terrain was too steep for a main line. Santa Fe-bound railway passengers had to disembark in Lamy and take the shuttle (a separate rail line) into town.

A mile beyond Lamy, the highway forks, with 285 continuing to Clines Corners and Highway 41 beelining through the Galisteo Basin toward Moriarty. From the 13th to the 17th centuries, this area was home to two large populations of Tano-speaking Indians. San Cristobal Pueblo, with more than 2,000 rooms, was abandoned during the Pueblo Revolt and never reinhabited. Nearby Galisteo Pueblo, on the other hand, was also abandoned in the 1680s but resettled in the early 18th century. The pueblo was abandoned for good soon after, though, under pressure from raiding groups of Comanches.

Galisteo

Galisteo is a tiny little town whose Spanish heritage dates to the early 1700s. Except for the main drag (Highway 41), Galisteo's handful of streets are much the same as they've been for 2.5 centuries—unpaved, dusty, and lined with adobe walls, behind which squat quiet adobe homes, some nearly falling apart in disrepair, others having been "saved" and restored. The **Galisteo Inn,** 505/466-8200, is a small adobe lodge, beautifully appointed with Southwest furniture, paintings, and rugs. A secluded little hideaway, the inn would be a perfect place to rejuvenate the spirit after a long project at work or a particularly grueling semester of school. The huge, shady, grass front yard practically begs you to lie down and take a nap—or to plant a lawn chair and get lost in a 1,000-page novel full of intrigue and sex. Rooms range $125–200, and three-course prix fixe health-food dinners served Wednesday–Sunday are $36–45.

EAST OF SANTA FE

Interstate 25 continues east after the junction with Highway 285, through Apache Canyon, and then over the Glorieta Pass (7,400 feet), where one of the West's few Civil War battles took place. In March 1862, the Blue were moving south from Las Vegas and met the Gray, led by Brigadier General H. H. Sibley, who were coming up from Fort Bliss, Texas, through Santa Fe. The "Gettysburg of the West," as the battle has been called, ended on the second day, when Sibley retreated after his supplies were destroyed by two Union soldiers, who sneaked into his camp and torched them.

Pecos National Historic Park

Pecos is one of the oldest and most visually arresting of New Mexico's pueblo ruins, as well as one of the closest to a major freeway. About four miles north of I-25, Pecos—which consists of both pueblo and mission ruins—was first inhabited as early as the 9th century. Recently discovered pit houses are similar to the Anasazi architecture of the Four Corners area, suggesting

© STEPHEN METZGER

mission ruins at Pecos National Historic Park

that the first Pecos Indians arrived from the north and west. By the 13th century, the people—corn, bean, and squash farmers—were climbing out of their scattered pit homes and consolidating in a central area; by the middle of the 15th century, Pecos Pueblo stood five stories high and contained 660 rooms (some for storage, some for living quarters) and 22 kivas.

The Pecos Indians' first contact with outsiders was in 1540, when they met Coronado west of the pueblo and invited him to visit. Coronado sent Hernando de Alvarado and a small contingent of soldiers to Pecos, where Alvarado was told of riches on the plains to the east. Apparently, this was a ruse to lure the Spaniards away from the Rio Grande–area pueblos and out onto the harsh desert, where they might be unable to survive. By the summer of 1541, it was clear to Coronado that he wasn't going to find his fabled lost cities, and he returned to Mexico.

Fifty years later, another Spaniard, Gaspar Castano de Sosa, arrived at Pecos Pueblo after having followed the Pecos River from the south. Met with arrows and rocks, Castano and his small army (37 soldiers) attacked the pueblo and easily defeated the 500 Indians. Castano, keeping careful record of his occupation of the pueblo, described the dress of a typical Pecos woman:

> ***A blanket drawn in a knot at the shoulder and a sash the width of a palm at the waist . . . Over it are placed some other very gaily worked blanket or some turkey feather robe and many other curious things.***

In the early 17th century, the Franciscans, attempting not only to convert the pagans to Christianity but also to restructure their political and economic philosophies, founded the Misión de Nuestra Señora de los Angeles de Porciuncula. The mission consisted of the church, carpentry shops and tanneries, weaving rooms, and lands where sheep, goats, cattle, and horses—newly introduced by the Spanish—could graze. The church, which was 170 feet long and 90 feet wide, was considered one of the finest mission churches in the New World, a "splendid temple of distinguished workmanship and beauty," according to an address given in 1630 by Father Benavides.

In 1680, though, the Pecos Indians burned their church to the ground and drove the Spaniards off the pueblo. For 12 years, until they were reconquered by de Vargas, they tried to live as they had before their conquest. In the 18th century, Pecos Pueblo, like most of the pueblos on the western plains, was a victim of repeated Comanche raids. In addition, the Indians had begun to die off from diseases introduced by their European subjugators. By 1770, the village itself was dying out, and in 1838, the last 20 Pecos Indians abandoned their home to live at Jemez Pueblo on the other side of Santa Fe.

Pecos Pueblo was given National Monument status in 1965, thanks in part to the efforts of late actress Greer Garson and her husband, E. E. Fogelson, who owned much of the land nearby. Excavation was begun the following year, and in 1967 workers discovered the foundations of the old church, some of which, along with the pueblo itself, has been reconstructed to allow the visitor to imagine what life was like here in the 17th and 18th centuries.

A first-rate museum at the pueblo's visitors center chronicles the history of the pueblo and exhibits Indian pottery and Spanish coins and tools discovered on the site. A 10-minute film (narrated by Greer Garson) shown every half hour provides an excellent background to what happened here during the various phases of occupation and excavation. The gently sloping path through the ruins is about 1.25 miles long; be sure to pick up the interpretive trail guide at the visitors center before heading out.

To get to Pecos National Historic Park, take either the Glorieta or Rowe exit from I-25 and follow the signs to the park. Hours are 8 A.M.–6 P.M. Memorial Day through Labor Day, and 8 A.M.–5 P.M. the rest of the year. Admission is $3. Facilities are limited to a small picnic area near the parking lot. For more information about Pecos National Historic Park, write Drawer 11, Pecos, NM 87552, or phone 505/757-6414.

Pecos Wilderness Area

Highway 63 continues north from the town of Pecos into Santa Fe National Forest and eventually dead-ends in the Pecos Wilderness. One of the prettiest drives in the state, the road winds along the upper Pecos River through forests of pine, spruce, and aspen, which occasionally give way to sweet mountain meadows. A popular if tricky trout stream, the upper Pecos is a favorite of northern New Mexico anglers—hard-core fly casters and bait plunkers alike. A half-dozen riverside campgrounds—some with flush toilets and running water, some with only picnic tables and fire pits—provide cool and shady respites from the heat of the nearby desert. For maps and specific information on camping, backpacking, fishing, or sight-seeing in Santa Fe National Forest or Pecos Wilderness, contact Santa Fe National Forest, District Office, Pecos, NM 87552, 505/757-6121.

Villanueva State Park

From Pecos National Monument to Las Vegas is about a 40-mile drive, with I-25/Highway 84 following the route of the old Santa Fe Trail through the southeastern foothills of the Sangre de Cristo Mountains. Just east of San José, you can turn south on Highway 3, which follows the Pecos River and one of the routes of the 16th-century Spanish conquistadors, including Coronado and Sosa.

Named for nearby Villanueva, a tiny walled village built in 1808 as an outpost to protect local farmers from raiding Comanches, Villanueva State Park straddles the banks of the Pecos River and offers excellent camping, picnicking, fishing, and sight-seeing. A footbridge across the river provides access to both banks, and hiking trails meander through the grounds. The park is equipped with modern restrooms (with hot showers), running water, campsites with shelters, and a children's playground. Day use is $4, and camping is $8.

Morphy Lake State Park

Highway 518 shoots due north out of Las Vegas (see Las Vegas, in the Northeastern New Mexico chapter) to Mora and on to Taos through rolling foothills of pine, oak, and cottonwood. One of the most primitive and secluded parks in the state, Morphy Lake is just southwest of Mora on the edge of the Pecos Wilderness at an elevation of 7,840 feet. Best known for its fishing, the little lake after which the park is named is stocked regularly with rainbow trout, and its lack of easy access makes it a favorite among serious anglers—who know that hard work can often mean big fish.

Its water levels rising and lowering according to the amount of water pumped by the two irrigation companies that own it, the little reservoir varies 25–50 acres in surface area. Only rowboats are allowed on the lake. Pit toilets, picnic tables, and fire pits are scattered around the park. Day use is $4, and camping is $8.

To get to Morphy Lake State Park, take Highway 94 south from Mora to Ledoux. From there, a *rough* three-mile dirt road leads to the park. Note: backcountry veterans recommend the road for four-wheel-drive vehicles only.

Mora

As you drive through this quiet little town (pop. 4,000), try to imagine it as it was 100 years ago—an important commercial hub and trading center with thriving mills, stores, saloons, and hotels. Today, it's little more than a ghost of that time.

Established in 1835 on land granted to a party of 76 Mexican settlers, Mora was probably originally known as Lo de Santa Gertrudes de Mora—the "Lo" is thought to be a bastardization of *el ojo* (short for *el ojo del agua,* or the spring); *mora* means mulberry. Another possibility is that the name is derived from L'eau des Mortes, or Waters of the Dead, which the river through town was named by a French trapping party that discovered human bones along its banks. During its heyday in the late 19th century, Mora was famous for its violence and disreputable characters, many of whom trickled over from Las Vegas, another wild and woolly frontier town.

Today, Mora is the seat of Mora County, as well as an educational center: kids from the surrounding isolated farms and communities are bused to Mora's schools.

Mora to Taos

The **Cleveland Roller Mill Museum** two miles west of Mora displays the history of the Mora Valley, with special emphasis on wheat farming and the milling industry. Dating to the turn of the last century, the Cleveland Roller Mill was a two-story adobe mill with a 50-barrel daily capacity. The mill was placed on the National Register of Historic Places in 1979 and restored in the 1980s. The museum also houses an art co-op displaying the work of about 15 local artists. For hours and admission prices, phone 505/387-2645, or write P.O. Box 287, Cleveland, NM 87715.

The road from Mora to Taos winds for about 50 miles across Santa Fe National Forest and over the Sangre de Cristo Mountains, again some of the prettiest country in the Southwest. About 25 miles from Taos, you'll come to one of New Mexico's smaller ski resorts, **Sipapu.** Usually open from around Thanksgiving to Easter, Sipapu caters primarily to intermediate skiers, its one chairlift and two pomas servicing 18 trails over a 900-foot vertical drop. The resort has a small restaurant and snack bar, as well as a ski-rental shop and limited on-slope lodging. During the summer, the ski area is a popular disk-golf course. For more information, contact Sipapu Ski Area, P.O. Box 29, Vadito, NM 87579, 505/587-2240.

Coyote Creek State Park and Vicinity

Highway 434 cuts off 518 at Mora and winds north through Coyote Creek Canyon to Angel Fire. Though for decades this has been a favorite area of anglers and deer hunters, the canyon seems largely undiscovered by New Mexico travelers, and the meandering road is often nearly deserted.

My friend Jeff Everist, New Mexico fly fisherman and outdoorsman extraordinaire, calls this his favorite state park. Actually, Everist admits that there are better places to fish in the state—the San Juan River, for starters—but he likes the mountain scenery here, the fact that the park doesn't get a whole lot of traffic, and the wondrous fields of wildflowers that grace the canyon meadows from spring to fall.

Flanking the willow- and cottonwood-lined banks of Coyote Creek, this 80-acre park has pit toilets, picnic tables, and fire pits, and some of the campsites are sheltered (no hookups). Day use is $4, and camping is $8.

Just north of Coyote Creek State Park, on the north side of the little village of Guadalupita is **Sierra Bonita Cabins and RV Park,** where you can set up your RV in a site with full hookups or rent one of the cabins (about $70, which include linens and full kitchens; cabins sleep up to seven). Use of laundry and showers is included. For rates and more information, write P.O. Box 274, Guadalupita, NM 87722, or call 505/387-5508.

WEST OF SANTA FE

The Rio Grande passes about 20 miles west of Santa Fe, continuing its plateau-cleaving route south. Just west of the river, the valley floor rises to meet the foothills of the Jemez (HAY-mus) Mountains—a range of massive ridges, towering peaks, green mountain meadows, trickling trout streams, and an estimated 7,000 Indian ruins tucked under cliffsides and perched high on crumbling escarpments.

From Española, Highway 30 winds up the Pajarito Plateau into Los Alamos—where much of the work was done on the 1940s Manhattan Project. From there, it passes just north of Bandelier National Monument, which, along with Chaco Canyon, is one of the most important Indian ruins in the state. The road then joins Highway 4, which wanders through the pines and firs of the Jemez Mountains. Eventually the road drops out of the mountains, paralleling the Jemez River through the little town of Jemez Springs, past Jemez State Monument, and then through the Jemez Reservation, where weekend travelers are greeted by Indians making and selling frybread in tiny roadside shacks. Finally, at San Ysidro, the highway tees into Highway 44, where you can wander north to Farmington or continue south to Bernalillo and Albuquerque. The round-trip from Santa Fe to Santa Fe—via Los Alamos, San Ysidro, Bernalillo, and then I-25 back to the capital—is only about 150 miles, but you could easily spend several days exploring the sights along the way: the museums in Los Alamos, the Indian ruins, and the hiking trails and campgrounds scattered throughout the Jemez Mountains.

Los Alamos

Los Alamos (pop. 19,000; elev. 7,400 feet) is a bustling outdoor-oriented community northwest of Santa Fe. Though made famous by the top-secret government research that took place here in the 1940s and by the high-tech Los Alamos National Laboratories, Los Alamos today has largely left behind its reputation as the nation's "Atomic City."

A relatively well-to-do community, Los Alamos boasts one of the lowest unemployment rates in New Mexico, as well as the highest per-household annual income (over $50,000, due largely to high salaries paid to Loas Alamos National Labs scientists). In addition, the folks here have a true sense of civic pride, and the many community-oriented events tend to bring out the crowds. And when folks aren't out for an event, they're just plain out—jogging, hiking, mountain biking, skiing, Little Leaguing, or exploring any of the several nearby archaeological sites, such as Bandelier National Monument, which, along with Chaco Canyon, is one of the most important Indian ruins in the state.

HISTORY

Anasazi Indians occupied the Pajarito Plateau between A.D. 1150 and the 16th century, leaving thousands of ruins hidden in the rugged backcountry. Yet Los Alamos itself is a relative newcomer to New Mexico. In 1918, Detroit businessman Ashley Pond established the Los Alamos Ranch School, where boys studied the classics and enjoyed the immense recreational opportunities of the Jemez Mountains, particularly horseback riding. The school was successful for nearly 25 years, but closed its doors in 1943, thanks to the federal government's larger plans for the spot.

In the fall of 1942, General Leslie Groves and Robert Oppenheimer drove up through the Jemez Mountains from Albuquerque looking for a secluded site for the lab. They found it at Pond's school on the Pajarito Mesa, and shortly afterward the government took over Los Alamos Ranch School, using its buildings for housing and administrative offices. Scientists, many of whom knew little about the research they would be doing, were brought to the site from around the country, and work officially began at Los Alamos Scientific Laboratories in April 1943. For the next two years, completely unknown to all but the highest government officials, they engaged in a race with the Germans and other powers for the first atomic bomb. By summer 1945, after a series of setbacks and growing ambivalence among the workers about the project, the Americans had won. The world's first atomic bomb was ready to be tested. Just before dawn on July 16, at Trinity Site, 60 miles northwest of Alamogordo, the bomb was detonated from a tall tower. The flash, which could be seen from as far away as Santa Fe, Gallup, and El Paso, changed forever the course of the earth and the human race. Oppenheimer said later that the blinding light reminded him of the Hindu quotation, "I am become Death, destroyer of worlds."

Three weeks later, Hiroshima and Nagasaki were flattened, and Japan surrendered.

In 1957, Los Alamos became an "open city," with security controls considerably decreased. Five years later, President Kennedy signed a bill allowing for the ownership of private property in the area. Los Alamos has maintained its position as a leader in defense-industry research, working under contract with the University of California. The Bradbury Science Museum opened in 1993.

Ladders take Bandelier visitors to a ceremonial cave high on a cliffside.

SIGHTS

Bandelier National Monument

Bandelier is a 33,000-acre monument to the Anasazis who once thrived in these hills and canyons—leaving hundreds of ruins in their wake—as well as to Adolph Bandelier, the Swiss-American ethnologist who studied many Southwest pueblo ruins in the late 19th century. Established in 1916, the monument contains 70 miles of trails, which lead to ancient pueblos, cliff dwellings, a ceremonial cave, and backcountry National Park Service camping areas.

Most likely first occupied more than 2,000 years ago, the area around what is now Bandelier was probably settled in the mid-12th century, perhaps by Chaco Canyon refugees, who farmed beans, squash, and corn, and hunted deer, turkey, and rabbit. By the mid-16th century, the people of Bandelier were already beginning to leave, and by the early 1600s the pueblos were deserted, although some were inhabited briefly during the Pueblo Revolt.

Adolph Bandelier is credited with discovering the ruins in 1880, although he actually was shown them by a Cochiti Indian whom he followed up onto the Pajarito Plateau from the valley floor. In the early part of the 20th century, archaeologist Edgar Lee Hewet carried out excavations at Bandelier, leading early visitors through the ruins and running a field school on the site. In 1934 the Civilian Conservation Corps began work on a road into the main ruins, as well as on the buildings that today house the museum and visitors center. Congress declared 23,000 acres of the park a National Wilderness Area in 1977.

Bandelier is one of the most important and complex ruins sites in the Southwest, and if you've got even a mild interest in history or anthropology, you'd be crazy to pass it by. Stay a half day, or stay two weeks. Poke around the visitors center and wander up the 1.5-mile trail through Frijole Canyon, or strap on a backpack and explore the wilderness. Either way—or anywhere in between—you'll be amply rewarded for your efforts.

Entrance to Bandelier National Monument is $5 per person, or $10 per carload (good for seven days). Be sure to check the chalkboard at the visitors center, which lists each day's talks, tours, and evening campfire program. You can also pick up maps and brochures with detailed information about the various sites within the park. Next to the visitors center, a gift shop sells a wide range of souvenirs, including pottery from Acoma, Santa Clara, and Jemez Pueblos. For more information, phone 505/672-3861.

You'll find two campgrounds at Bandelier. **Juniper Campground** is open on a first-come first-served basis, and includes 94 sites ($10 a night, $5 for Golden Age pass-holders) that can accommodate tents or RVs. Juniper has flush toilets, running water, and an RV dump station, but no hookups. **Ponderosa** is a group campground with two large sites available by reservation (phone 505/672-3861); fee is $35 for each site. Public showers are available at the YMCA in Los Alamos (15th and Iris), which is open to the public daily. You can also get cleaned up at **Aquatic Park,** 2760 Canyon Rd., Los Alamos, 505/662-8170, where there are public showers and a pool.

To get to Bandelier National Monument, take Highway 501 six miles south from Los Alamos to the junction with Highway 4, and follow the signs to the park. Note: it's a good idea to get there early on weekends, as it gets crowded rather quickly.

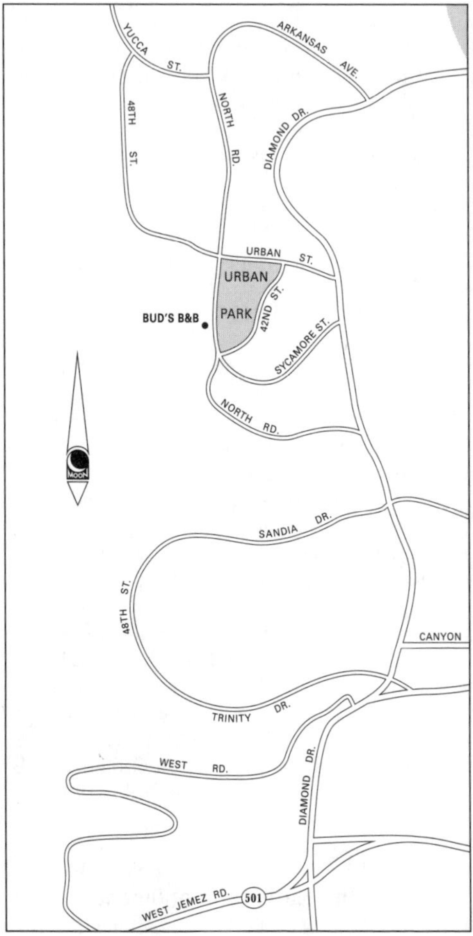

Tsankawi Ruins

Just a few miles from the main Bandelier ruins, Tsankawi is the remains of a pueblo community dating from the mid-12th to the late 16th century. Not for the timid or out of shape, Tsankawi is accessible by a rugged and sometimes-steep 1.5-mile self-guided tour that winds out on a high mesa past dozens of caves, petroglyphs, and observation sites; the marked trail corresponds with the map you pick up at the trailhead. As you wander the cliffside (be careful—sometimes the trail gets *very* close to steep drop-offs), you'll be following the same paths that have been used for centuries. In places it's worn two feet into the soft rock, and you have to walk carefully, placing one foot in front of the other inside the trough. In other places, you must take ladders (primitively built of unmilled logs to approximate those the Indians used) between the levels. You can also walk inside a 10- by 10-foot

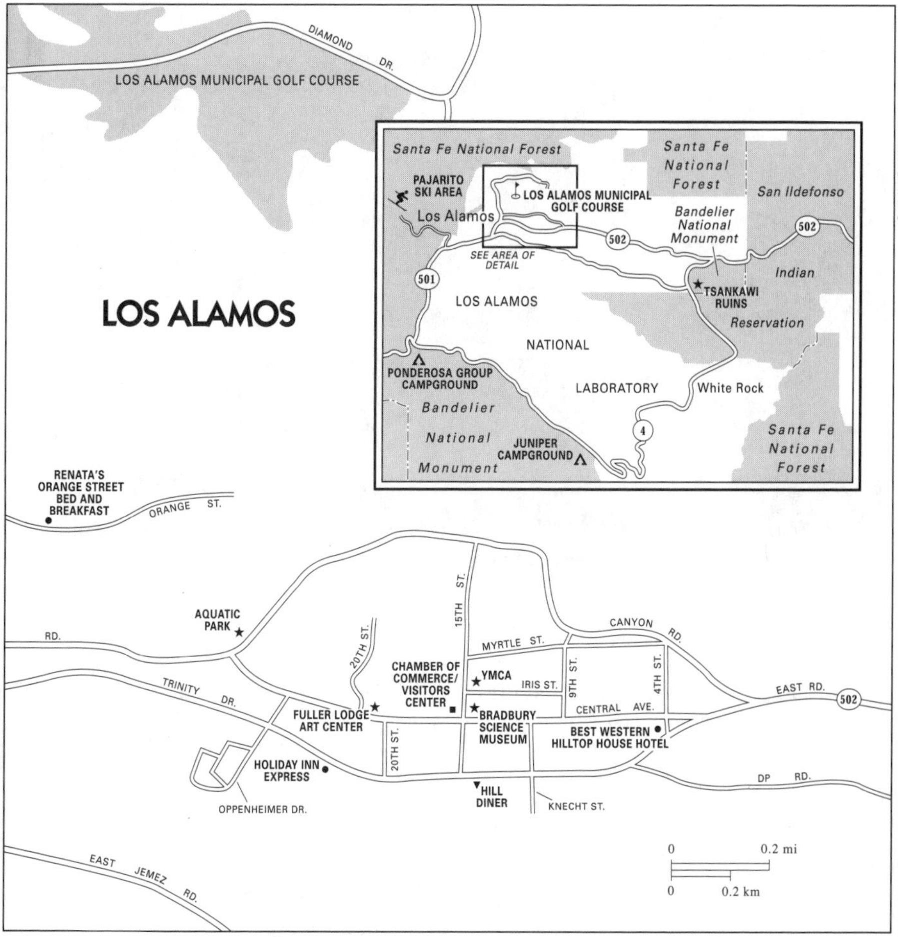

cave and note the blackened ceiling from centuries of smoky fires. An unexcavated pueblo ruin lies crumbling along the trail.

To get to Tsankawi, take Highway 4 north from the main Bandelier ruins. Watch for the trailhead and parking lot—little more than a highway pullout—on the west just past East Jemez Road, two miles north from White Rock.

Bradbury Science Museum

Named for the scientist Norris, not the writer Ray, the Bradbury Museum is a highlight of a visit to Los Alamos and a project in which the community takes great pride. The museum's main focus is an overview of the work taking place at Los Alamos National Laboratories, and exhibits include looks at the history of the Manhattan Project, as well as displays of the latest in laser, computer, geothermal, solar, nuclear, and other technologies, from health research to environmental studies.

Historical and informational films are shown continually. Hours are Tuesday–Friday 9 A.M.–5 P.M., Saturday–Monday 1–5 P.M. Admission is

© STEPHEN METZGER

Climb down into the kiva in the ceremonial cave.

free. The museum is downtown at 15th and Central. For more information, phone 505/667-4444.

Fuller Lodge Art Center and Museum

Originally the dining room and recreation hall for Los Alamos Ranch School and later for the Manhattan Project scientists, the large log building is now a National Historic Landmark. Take Central to 20th Street, and look for the sign on your right. The center displays work of northern New Mexico painters and sculptors, as well as occasional traveling exhibits, with work by nationally and internationally known artists. Hours are Monday–Saturday 10 A.M.–4 P.M. Admission is free. Phone 505/662-9331 for more information.

Also in Fuller Lodge is **Los Alamos Historical Museum.** Documenting the history of the Pajarito Plateau, with special emphasis on the Manhattan Project, this small museum displays Anasazi ax heads, needles, potsherds, and arrowheads, as well as various items from the days when Los Alamos was the "Secret City." Included are memos to and from Oppenheimer, photos of atomic testing and post-bomb Nagasaki, and copies of the leaflets the United States dropped, warning the Japanese about the bomb.

In addition, a small but well-stocked bookstore carries a variety of literature about Los Alamos and the Southwest, including maps of self-guided walking tours of town. Hours are Monday–Saturday 10 A.M.–4 P.M., Sunday 1–4 P.M. (opening half an hour earlier and later during daylight saving time). Admission is free, donations gladly accepted. For more information, phone 505/662-4493.

PRACTICALITIES

Accommodations

Most visitors to Los Alamos stay in either Santa Fe or Albuquerque, although the town does have a few lodging options.

$100–150

Try the **Best Western Hilltop House Hotel** at 400 Trinity (corner of Central), 505/662-2441, and the **Holiday Inn Express,** 2455 Trinity, 505/661-1110.

For bed-and-breakfast accommodations, check out **Renata's Orange Street Bed and Breakfast,** 3496 Orange St., 505/662-2651, with six rooms and three suites, or **Bud's Bed and Breakfast,**

1981 B North Rd., 505/662-4239. At Bud's you'll find a sauna, hot tub, greenhouse, and eight rooms, as well as an eccentrically hilarious proprietor. Bud lived in Berkeley in the '60s but finally found a home in Los Alamos when he found "everyone here's as neurotic as I am." Bud will also cook dinner.

Food

Not much to choose from here, but I had an excellent lunch at **Hill Diner,** 1315 Trinity, 505/662-9745. This very popular little place is open seven days a week for lunch and dinner (open daily 11 A.M.–9 P.M.). Specials include homemade soups and stews, and other all-American diner fare, including meatloaf, chicken-fried steak, and burgers. Entrées run $6–10.

There's also a restaurant at the **Best Western Hilltop House Hotel** at 400 Trinity (corner of Central), 505/662-2441—open seven days a week for breakfast, lunch, and dinner.

Annual Events

In August, the **County Arts and Crafts Festival** offers pottery, jewelry, woodwork, and fine art, as well as food booths and live music. At the **County Fair,** also in August, you can check out the wares of the local artisans and cooks, dance to a country band, and watch the clowns and cowboys at the rodeo.

Recreation

The Jemez Mountains provide Los Alamos with excellent recreational opportunities, particularly camping, hiking, bicycling, and cross-country skiing. Southwest of Los Alamos, Highway 4 winds though some of the prettiest parts of Santa Fe National Forest, and along the way you'll find several campgrounds and trailheads, all well marked. In the winter, the Los Alamos area attracts cross-country skiers from throughout the central state. Watch for the sign five miles east of town, where a road leads to Pajarito Ski Area and a handful of Nordic trails. (Note: this road is one steep mother; be sure to carry chains if the weather is at all iffy.) For more information on downhill and cross-country skiing in the Los Alamos area, contact **Los Alamos Ski Club,** P.O. Box 155, Los Alamos, NM 87544, 505/662-5725, or **Pajarito Ski Area,** 505/662-7669.

Urban Park, in one of the residential areas of Los Alamos, has nice lighted tennis courts, a handball backboard, basketball court, and kids' playground. Tee off at **Los Alamos municipal golf course,** 4250 Diamond Dr., 505/662-8139. A wooded public picnic area is in the residential section off Diamond Drive.

Information and Services

For more information on the Los Alamos area, stop in at the bookstore in the Los Alamos Historical Museum and at the Los Alamos **Chamber of Commerce,** 15th and Central. Both distribute helpful maps and literature on the area. Phone the chamber at 505/662-8105, or write P.O. Box 460, Los Alamos, NM 87544. For online information, check out the website: www.losalamos.com.

Otowi Station, 505/662-9589, is a bookstore and gift shop next door to the Bradbury Science Museum, specializing in educational and regional-interest books.

You'll find Los Alamos Medical Center at 3917 West Road. Phone 505/662-4201 for nonemergencies and 505/662-4325 for ambulance service. Phone the Los Alamos Police Department at 505/662-8222.

VICINITY OF LOS ALAMOS

Valle Grande

South of Los Alamos, Highway 4 climbs off the Pajarito Plateau and into the rugged Jemez Mountains. Here, the views are some of the most spectacular in the Southwest. The road winds through deep forests of towering ponderosa, past mountain meadows, serene with wildflowers and grazing cattle, and along the southern edge of the Valle Grande, a gigantic caldera formed when a series of volcanoes collapsed and the mountains—thought to have been 14,000 feet high—were sucked into the earth.

Today, the floor of the Valle Grande is at about 8,500 feet, and the rim 9,000. One of the largest measured craters on earth, the valley contains 176 square miles of grassy meadowland.

© STEPHEN METZGER

Valle Grande is a 176-square-mile caldera, an open crater, formed when a series of volcanoes collapsed and their 14,000-foot peaks were sucked into the earth.

Camping in the Jemez Mountains

The many campgrounds in the Jemez include tiny spots with just a few primitive sites to large developed areas with paved access roads, running water, and pit toilets. Beginning about five miles south of the Valle Grande is a series of national forest campgrounds—**Las Conchas, Jemez Falls,** and **Redondo.** Hiking trails abound in the area, and Jemez Creek, which meanders along the roadside, attracts trout fishermen not intent on trophy-sized fish.

La Cueva Campground, near the junction of Highway 126 and 4, has a scattering of tables and pit toilets along a quiet and shady stretch of Jemez Creek.

At **Jemez Canyon Overlook** a nature trail loops away from the small parking lot, and the various trees and shrubs in the area are identified. (You'll also find pit toilets here.) In addition, **Battleship Picnic Area,** near mile marker 23, is open for day use only and has barbecue pits and pit toilets. Note: no trailers or RVs longer than 16 feet allowed.

Soda Dam

Two miles north of Jemez Springs, this bizarre natural dam is the result of deposits from a carbonate spring that surfaces here. Three hundred feet long, 50 feet high, and 50 feet wide at the base, the dam looks like a Dali-inspired mushroom from an *Alice in Wonderland* set. Visitors can climb up inside the dam's caves and dip their toes into the cool pools of mineral water, deposits from which continue to change the shape of the dam.

Across the dam and up the hillside a couple of hundred feet is Jemez Cave, an archaeological treasure trove where ancient grinding stones and atlatls have been found, in addition to a 2,000-year-old mummified Indian boy wrapped in a blanket made of turkey feathers.

Jemez State Monument

These ruins are the original home of the Jemez Indians, who now live in a pueblo village about 20 miles south. A short trail leads out from the visitors center to the partially excavated pueblo and the Misión de San José church, built in 1622 by Fray Alonso de Luga, who came to the New World with Oñate in 1598. The remains of the mission, the labor for which was provided largely by Jemez women (the men thought such work disgraceful), provides excellent insights into Spanish Colonial architecture: the door of the church is 11 feet across, the nave 33 feet wide, and the church itself 110 feet long, suggesting 11 feet was a basic unit of measure.

De Luga's attempts to convert the Jemez, who called their village Giusewa, were met with hostility, although he did succeed in converting a handful of Indians. Some are buried in the church's *campo santo* (cemetery). He also managed, in his "quest for souls," to destroy the pueblo's kivas.

A visitors center at the monument explains the history and mythology of the Jemez people and has pottery dating from 1300, blankets of rabbit skin and turkey feathers, and other artifacts from the ruins.

Jemez State Monument is open daily 8:30 A.M.–5 P.M. Admission is $3 for adults 17 and older, 16 and younger free. For more information, phone 505/829-3530.

Jemez Springs

With a Zen center, a fishing-supply store, bathhouses, and a couple of Catholic retreats, all within shouting distance of pueblo ruins dating to the 14th century, Jemez Springs is a tiny resort town nestled inside the walls of the Jemez River canyon. Known as Hot Springs in the 19th century, Jemez Springs grew up as a farming village, though at one time it was the site of wild saloons and gambling houses. Today, things are much quieter here, the town's handful of small buildings hugging the shady roadside. A park with a nice lawn, swings, and tennis courts makes for a perfect picnic area.

Jemez Springs Bath House was built in the 1870s and added onto in 1940. Recognized as a State Historic Site, the spa offers hot mineral baths, therapeutic massage, and sweat wraps. There's also an outdoor tub you can use by the hour. Summer hours are 9 A.M.–9 P.M.; open 10 A.M.–7:30 P.M. the rest of the year. Reservations recommended, 505/829-3303.

The Jemez Mountains Inn, 505/829-3926, has rooms with kitchenettes that will sleep up to four. Rooms go for $80–120. The **Dancing Bear Bed and Breakfast,** 505/829-3336, is a small four-room inn and retreat on the Jemez River at the base of towering sandstone cliffs ($80–130).

A great place to stop for lunch in Jemez Springs is **Los Ojos Cafe,** 505/829-3076, a rowdy saloon-type restaurant decorated with dark woods and antlers. Very good Mexican food, as well as burgers and sandwiches. Open daily and serving prime rib Saturday nights.

Jemez Pueblo

Among the Pueblo tribes most resistant to Spanish conquest, the Towa-speaking Jemez continued to fight de Vargas even after the Pueblo Revolt. In 1696, the Spanish, along with allies from Zia Pueblo, attacked and defeated the Jemez, many of whom fled west to Navajo country. This led to a strong alliance between the two tribes, as well as many intermarriages. Many of the 2,000 Indians living on the reservation today are part Navajo.

On weekends, Jemez families cook and sell frybread in tiny roadside shacks made of scrap lumber. Indians and tourists alike stop to watch the dough sizzling in the hot oil and to pick up a loaf or two for the road. It's a delicious—if not particularly nutritious—snack for travelers heading up into the mountains.

San Ysidro

Highway 4 dead-ends into Highway 44 at San Ysidro, near the confluence of the Jemez and Salado Rivers. This tiny farming village dates from the late 17th century, when Juan Trujillo settled here. Primarily a crossroads town, San Ysidro provides motorists with a couple of gas stations, a package liquor store, and a burger-shakes-and-fries restaurant.

SAN YSIDRO TO FARMINGTON

At San Ysidro, you can either head north to the Four Corners area or turn south for Bernalillo and Albuquerque. Highway 44 north takes you up through Cuba, across the southwestern corner of the Jicarilla Apache Reservation, and over the energy-rich Colorado Plateau to Bloomfield and Farmington. The first part of this 140-mile trip

(San Ysidro to Bloomfield) is particularly scenic, with the road curving up along the west side of the Jemez Mountains and then onto the sagey high plateau, with juniper-dotted mesas and weathered sandstone cliffs.

Cabezon Peak

Dominating the western horizon from as far away as the hills of Albuquerque, Cabezon (Big-Headed) is a volcanic basalt "plug" rising 2,200 feet from the Rio Puerco Valley. A favorite of backcountry hikers, campers, and climbers, the Cabezon area has been home to Anasazis and 18th-century Spanish farmers and has recently fallen victim to overgrazing. **Holy Ghost Recreation Area** at the base of Cabezon offers camping, picnicking, and drinking water. To get there, watch for the sign 19 miles north of San Ysidro. A well-maintained dirt road leads to Cabezon, about 15 miles off the highway. For more information, call the BLM in Albuquerque, 505/761-4504.

Cuba

Forty miles north of San Ysidro, Cuba (pop. 600) was first settled in the late 18th century by Spanish land grantees. Originally known as Nacimiento, Cuba has been a farming and ranching center for nearly 200 years. Today, the town is a refueling stop for tourists and truckers and a gateway for hikers and backpackers heading into the San Pedro Wilderness Area and the Santa Fe National Forest in the mountains east of town.

Spread out along about two miles of highway, Cuba has a half dozen or so gas stations and cafés, as well as a couple of motels. You can get lodging at **The Cuban Lodge Hotel,** 505/289-3269, and **Del Prado Motel,** 505/289-3475 (both around $50).

El Bruno's Cantina, 505/289-9429, has an excellent reputation, drawing diners from miles around, and is open daily, serving northern New Mexican specials as well as American food, with dinners in the $8–12 range. Also good is **Bobby and Margie's Cuban Cafe,** where the truckers chow down and the highway patrol hangs out (always a good sign)—at the south end of town, serving good-sized breakfasts ($2.50-4.75) and lunches and dinners ($3–8).

SAN YSIDRO TO BERNALILLO

The 25-mile stretch of Highway 44 between San Ysidro and Bernalillo takes the traveler down from the arid southern edge of the Colorado Plateau into the lush Rio Grande Valley, from the relatively unpopulated Zia Indian Reservation to the busy northern reaches of Albuquerque. Along the way, you pass Zia and Santa Ana Pueblos, as well as the ruins of Kuaua Pueblo, where Coronado camped when he first marched up from Mexico in 1540 (see Coronado State Park and Monument in the Sights section of the Albuquerque chapter).

Zia Pueblo

From 1541 through the mid-17th century, the Zia people got along decently with Spanish missionaries, and after 1613, when Nuestra Señora de la Asunción Catholic church was built, they attended Mass faithfully. By the time of the Pueblo Revolt, however, relations were growing strained, and the Zias joined the other Pueblo tribes in the rebellion. In 1687, General de Posada, in an early attempt to reconquer the Indians, attacked Zia Pueblo, killing as many as 600 and taking another 70 prisoner. Perhaps with the memory of this bloody battle in their minds, the Zians were among the first to submit to de Vargas's reconquest five years later, going so far as to join with the Spanish in raids on other pueblos. This led to their being scorned by other tribes, and even today, 300 years later, the Zians are often looked down upon by some Indians for having so easily and completely submitted.

In addition, the harmony of the Zia tribe today is disturbed by internal conflict and factionalism. This, along with the tribe's notoriously dry and difficult-to-farm land, has made life hard for them. Barely 100 Zians live on the pueblo today, as compared to the 5,000 living here when Coronado arrived.

The Zia sun sign has been adopted as the state symbol, appearing on the flag (as well as on T-shirts, mugs, and baseball caps). Their pottery is highly regarded throughout the Southwest. The pueblo is open to the public during daylight hours only. Phone 505/867-3304 for more information.

© STEPHEN METZGER

Camel Rock, north of Santa Fe

Santa Ana Pueblo

In the 1940s, a revival of traditional Santa Ana pottery helped bring new life to a people on the edge of extinction. When Oñate arrived at Santa Ana (called Tamaja by these Keresan-speaking Indians), he found a thriving and friendly people. They quickly converted to Christianity, and though they took part in the Pueblo Revolt, by 1692 they were again allied with the Spanish. Their land, though, was dry and rocky and difficult to farm; by the early 1900s, the Santa Ana Indians had begun to migrate south toward the Rio Grande and more fertile land on which to plant their beans, corn, and squash. Known as Ranchitos de Santa Ana (or Santa Ana Pueblo Two), the little community became home to more and more Indians, and by the early 20th century, the original pueblo was all but deserted, maintained for ceremonial purposes only.

In recent years, however, many Santa Ana Indians have begun to move back onto the old pueblo and are taking a new pride in their heritage. Santa Ana artisans produce not only high-quality polychrome pottery but ornate wooden crosses inlaid with straw, as well as painted woodcarvings of dogs, horses, and other animals. Their work is available in quality gift stores in the Santa Fe and Albuquerque areas. For information on the pueblo, phone 505/867-3301. Santa Ana Pueblo is eight miles northwest of the junction of I-25 and Highway 44.

Santa Fe to Española

The main road from Santa Fe to Taos (Highway 285/84 to Española, Highway 68 thereafter) is 70 miles and takes about an hour and a half. At Española, the route rejoins the Rio Grande, and the fast ribbon of highway follows the river north, dipping in and out of the canyon and offering views of the brown water, until about 15 miles south of Taos, where it veers east of the river.

You can also take the back way. Winding up into the Sangre de Cristos and the Santa Fe National Forest—through Chimayó, Truchas, Las Trampas, and Vadito—this rural two-laner offers views of centuries-old Spanish farms, encounters with leather-skinned cowboys, and chances to see fifth-generation Mexican weavers at work in their tiny shops. If you've got any inkling to see the "real" New Mexico, this back road to Taos is the *only* way to go, although it'll take you at least an extra hour—and that's assuming you don't stop at all along the way.

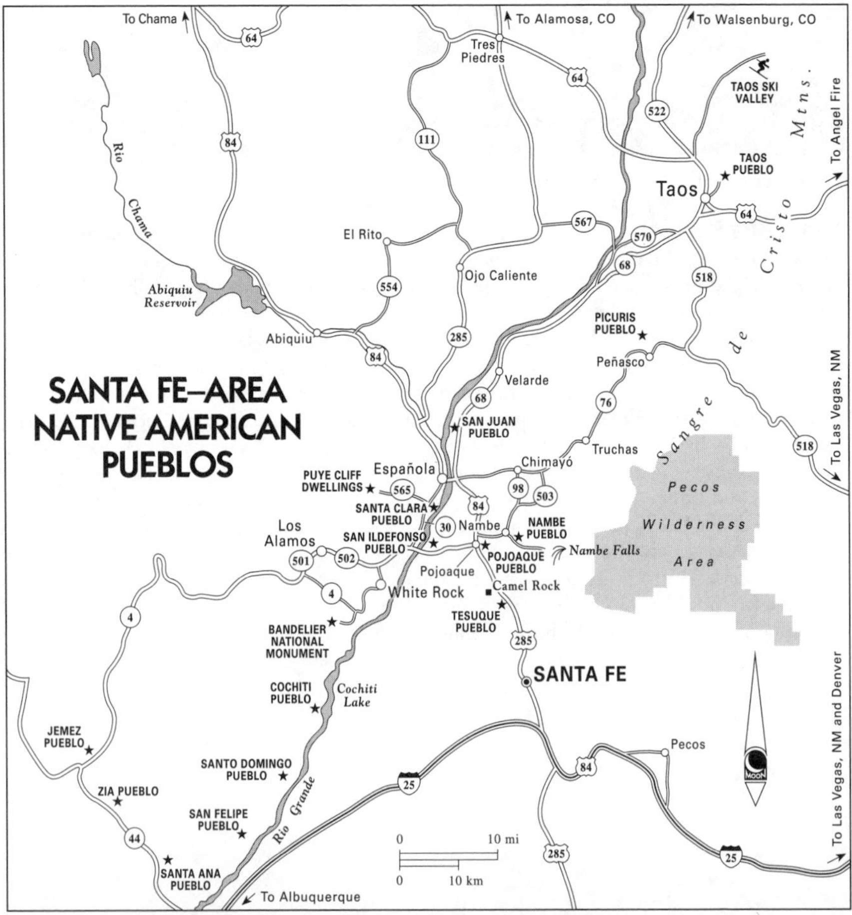

SIGHTS

Highway 285 climbs up out of the Santa Fe hills, past the Santa Fe Opera and Camel Rock, through the Tesuque, Pojoaque, Santa Clara, and San Ildefonso Indian Reservations, and then drops back down to the Rio Grande Valley and Española.

Tesuque Pueblo

About 10 miles north of Santa Fe on Highway 285, Tesuque (a Tewa word, pronounced "tu-SU-kee," meaning The Place Where the River Water Disappears into Sand) is one of the most traditional of the New Mexican pueblos. Partly because of its proximity to Santa Fe, Tesuque Pueblo played a seminal role in the Pueblo Revolt of 1680. Recent excavations show that the pueblo was inhabited as early as 1250.

Visitors are welcome on the pueblo, particularly November 12, Tesuque's annual **Feast Day.** Small fees are charged to sketch, shoot photos, or film videos. For more information, phone the Governor's Office at 505/983-2667, or write Pueblo of Tesuque, Rt. 5, Box 360-T, Santa Fe, NM 87501.

Visitors are also welcome, of course, at the new casino here. **Camel Rock Casino** is just across from the naturally eroded sandstone formation that has been rearing its head and acting as a landmark for centuries of travelers.

Duran's Pottery in the pueblo sells traditional Tesuque pottery and beadwork. Phone 505/983-7078 for hours of operation.

Camel Rock RV Park, near the exit to the pueblo, charges about $25 for full hookups, including hot showers; phone 505/455-2467 for information and reservations.

Pojoaque Pueblo

Five miles north of Tesuque, Pojoaque (po-WOK-ay) is another of the Tewa-speaking pueblos. Though the Pojoaque was partially resettled in 1706—after having been abandoned during the Pueblo Revolt—the pueblo has no central village. The **Pojoaque Pueblo Tourist Center** on the east side of the highway is staffed with very friendly and knowledgeable tribe members who, along with providing copious literature and maps, will answer any question you have about Pojoaque, other pueblos, or other northern New Mexico attractions. In addition, the center, open seven days a week, sells locally crafted pottery, sandpaintings, rugs, sculpture, kachinas, and other souvenirs. For more information, phone 505/455-3460. You can also write the **Pojoaque Pueblo Tourist Information Center,** Route 11, Box 21GS, Santa Fe, NM, 87501.

Nambe Pueblo

In the rolling valleyland at the foot of the Sangre de Cristos, with a gorgeous series of waterfalls, a lake, and quiet campground, Nambe dates from about 1300, although only a handful of the original buildings are still standing. Tribal members, of whom there are about 400, are reviving traditional weaving, beadwork, and pottery.

The Nambe Indians welcome visitors, and the pueblo's recreational area, with its camping and picnicking facilities, is especially conducive to visits by travelers passing through the area. On the **Fourth of July,** as well as Nambe Pueblo's **Feast Day** in October (in honor of St. Francis of Assisi), ceremonial dances are held at the pueblo, and the public is invited.

To get to Nambe Pueblo, go east on Highway 503 from Pojoaque (about eight miles south of Española on Highway 285) and follow the signs for about six miles. For more information, write Governor's Office, Pueblo of Nambe, Rt. 1, Box 117-BB, Santa Fe, NM 87501, or phone 505/455-2036.

Nambe Falls Recreational Area

In the rolling pine- and piñon-covered hills above the pueblo, this little recreation area offers fishing, lakeside picnicking, and a nicely shaded campground (porta-toilets only). In addition, those up for a short hike (10–15 minutes from the main picnic area) can view the three-part Nambe Falls, which, according to legend, are the tears of an Indian maiden weeping over her lost lover.

Picnicking fees are $4 per car, camping is $8 the first night and $5 a night thereafter, and a fishing permit is $5 ($3 for kids under 12). Season is November–March, and hours are

6 A.M.–9 P.M. (summer) and 7 A.M.–7 P.M. (winter). To get to the recreation site, follow the signs on Highway 503 southeast of Española. The lake is about three miles past the turnoff to the pueblo. For information, phone 505/455-2034.

San Ildefonso Pueblo

In the 1920s, potter Maria Martinez revived traditional San Ildefonso pottery, and her pots, with the black matte on black finishes, soon were among the most in-demand pieces of Indian pottery, highly prized among collectors around the world. Martinez, who became one of the most famous Native American artists, continued to produce her wares well into the 20th century, and her work is ranked with the highest-quality American Indian art. Descendants of Martinez carry on her tradition.

Known to San Ildefonsoans as Pox Oge, or Place Where Water Passes, the pueblo had its Christian name bestowed upon it by Oñate, in honor of a 7th-century Spanish archbishop. In 1675, Spaniards from Santa Fe arrested about 50 San Ildefonso Indians—charging them with witchery—and sold them as slaves. When de Vargas recaptured Santa Fe in 1692, ending the Pueblo Revolt, San Ildefonso was one of the last pueblos to surrender, finally submitting in 1694.

At the **San Ildefonso Visitors Center,** you can buy Indian pottery, paintings, and other crafts, arrange tours, and pick up postcards and souvenirs. Open in summer daily 8 A.M.–5 P.M. and in winter Monday–Friday 9 A.M.–4 P.M.; phone 505/455-3549 for more information.

San Ildefonso Pueblo Museum displays local art and photographs and demonstrates pottery-making methods and tribal history. Hours are Monday–Friday 8 A.M.–4 P.M., weekends 9 A.M.–5 P.M. (phone the visitors center to confirm hours).

San Ildefonso Pueblo is about six miles west of Highway 285 on Highway 503.

ESPAÑOLA

Española (pop. 9,000; elev. 5,590 feet) is a friendly little town serving as a hub for much of northern New Mexico. A relatively stable economy is due in large part to the ranching and farming of the fertile Española Valley, as well as to nearby Los Alamos Laboratories and the many tourist attractions in the area, particularly the Indian pueblos and ruins. Española provides goods and services to more than 60,000 folks in the surrounding area.

Puye Cliff Dwellings

These ruins, extending a mile along a cliffside on the Pajarito Plateau, are the remains of an Anasazi village inhabited from about 1100 to 1580. Open daily 8 A.M.–7 P.M., the ruins, on the Santa Clara Indian Reservation, are reached by a difficult walk, recommended for the hale and hearty only. Admission is $5, $4 for seniors and kids seven to 12 (includes camera permit; video or sketching permit $15 extra). Phone 505/753-7326 for more information.

From Española, take Highway 30 about five miles south, then Highway 5 west. The entrance is well marked. For more information, to book tours, or to double-check hours (always a good idea), phone 505/753-7326.

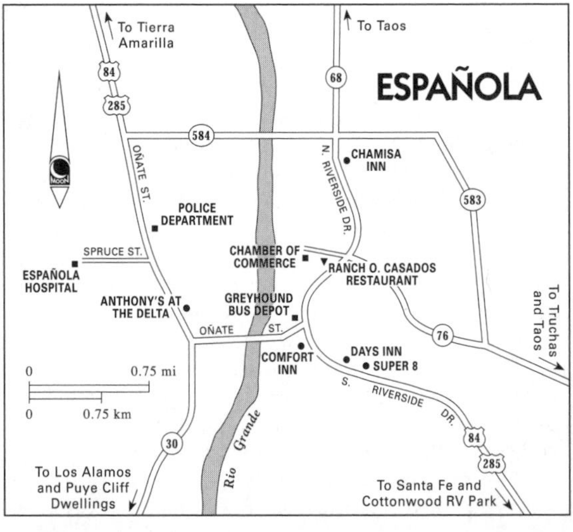

Important note: Puye has suffered inopportune closings from time to time. Call ahead to confirm that it is indeed open to the public.

Accommodations

You'll find a number of roadside mom-and-pop motels in Española, all of which offer rooms at bargain prices. In addition, the past several years have brought the construction of several larger motels, where you can get good, clean rooms at decent rates.

As you approach town from the south, you'll pass the **Super 8,** 811 S. Riverside Dr., 505/753-5374; **Days Inn,** 807 S. Riverside, 505/747-1242; and the **Comfort Inn,** 604 S. Riverside, 505/753-2419. All $50–100.

In addition, a number of bed-and-breakfasts offer more personalized accommodations. Two rooms are available at **Casa del Rio,** a small ranch on the Chama River. Write P.O. Box 92, Española, NM 87532, 505/753-2035. $100–150.

The **Inn of La Mesilla Bed and Breakfast,** 505/753-5363, is three miles south of Española and offers two rooms (private baths; about $100) with a hot tub and views of the Jemez Mountains.

Cottonwood RV Park, a half mile south of Española on Highway 285, has 38 sites with hookups, plus 50 tent sites. Phone 505/753-6608 for rates and more information.

Food

As a hub of ranching and farming activity in the area, Española claims its fair share of fast-food restaurants—the main drag through town is chockablock with burger huts, pizza parlors, and fried-chicken chains. When I'm passing through, I usually stop in at **Ranch O. Casados,** 411 N. Riverside, 505/753-2837. This comfy little not-much-to-look-at-from-the-outside diner is popular among locals and prides itself on its New Mexican specialties: excellent *chiles rellenos, carne adovada, flautas,* and chimichangas, made with homegrown red and green chiles and homemade blue-corn tortillas. Breakfasts run $3–8, lunches $6–10, and dinners $6–16.

Another long-standing Española-area restaurant with an excellent reputation is **Anthony's at the Delta,** 228 Oñate, 505/753-4511, which has been in the same family since 1949 and specializes in steaks and seafood. Entrées are in the $8–20 range.

Information and Services

At the Española **Chamber of Commerce,** 417 Big Rock Center (Riverside Drive), 505/753-2831, you'll find maps and literature on Española and the surrounding area.

The ***Rio Grande Sun,*** Española's newspaper, published every Thursday, includes listings of local happenings. The paper's main office, 238 N. Railroad, stocks a large selection of books on the Southwest—history, travel, and fiction.

Española Hospital is at 1010 Spruce St., 505/753-7111. Call the Española Police Department at 505/753-5555.

Española to Chama and Farmington

The 110-mile drive between Española and the Colorado border is one of the most visually arresting in the Southwest. Rising from Rio Grande Valley and into the high southern Rockies, the road takes you through the polychrome mesas of Georgia O'Keeffe country, through spacious mountain valleys, and into some of the most popular hunting, fishing, sailing, and cross-country skiing areas in the state.

SIGHTS

Ojo Caliente

About six miles north of Española, you can catch Highway 285 north for the town of Ojo Caliente, rich in history and tradition. According to Tewa myth, Ojo Caliente (idiomatic for Hot Springs) was the birthplace of their leader Poseyemu, and Apaches, Utes, and Comanches raided early Spanish settlers in the area. Among the early Americans passing through was Zebulon Pike, who wrote of the hot mineral baths. Ojo Caliente today is a favorite winter stopover among cross-country skiers, who find its waters perfect after a day exploring the snowy backcountry of Santa Fe or Carson National Forest.

Ojo Caliente Mineral Springs Resort offers a range of accommodations and spa treatments, from hot mineral baths (spring water to 113°F) to facials and therapeutic massage. Stay in the hotel or one of the cottages. Rates start at about $80 per person, which includes access to the springs and mineral-water swimming pool; most of the treatments are extra. Write P.O. Box 68, Ojo Caliente, NM 87549, or phone 505/583-2233 or 800/222-9162.

El Rito

This is a tiny artists' community on Highway 554 about 12 miles north of Abiquiu (though the turnoff is four miles south of Abiquiu on Highway 84). Many of its studios are open to the public. Several readers have recommended the restaurant **El Farolito,** 1212 Main St., 505/581-9509, whose chef has won numerous awards for his green-chile dishes.

Abiquiu

Even in New Mexico, where landscapes twist ghostlike and the earth's colors seem otherworldly, where farmers and artists and spiritualists spin gracefully around and among each other like a crystal's prismatic colors dancing on a bedroom window—even here, where you've come to expect it—Abiquiu is a little more intense. It's like all of New Mexico squeezed into a tiny stained-glass jar. Situated on the west bank of the Rio Chama, Abiquiu was built on the site of a Tewa pueblo ruin and settled in the early 18th century. In the late 1800s, the little village was a stop on the overland stage route to the new Spanish settlement on the Pacific coast—Los Angeles.

Abiquiu, about 50 miles north of Santa Fe, is best known today as the home of the late Georgia O'Keeffe, who fell in love with the scrubby red canyons and fertile river valley, and through her painting brought it to art lovers around the world. Tours of Georgia O'Keeffe's house can be arranged by calling 505/685-4539; reservations are required, and tours are booked months in advance.

Even in New Mexico, where landscapes twist ghostlike and the earth's colors seem otherworldly, Abiquiu is a little more intense. It's like all of New Mexico squeezed into a tiny stained-glass jar.

Abiquiu is also the site of the Dar Al-Islam mosque, an ornate mesa-top structure across the Rio Chama. Built in the early 1980s at a cost of $1,372,000, the mosque includes a 17,000-square-foot school and library complex, as well as elaborate prayer rooms and living quarters. The mosque, which sits on a 9,000-acre tract of land, was once home to more than 30 Muslim families from the United States, Egypt, Turkey, Syria,

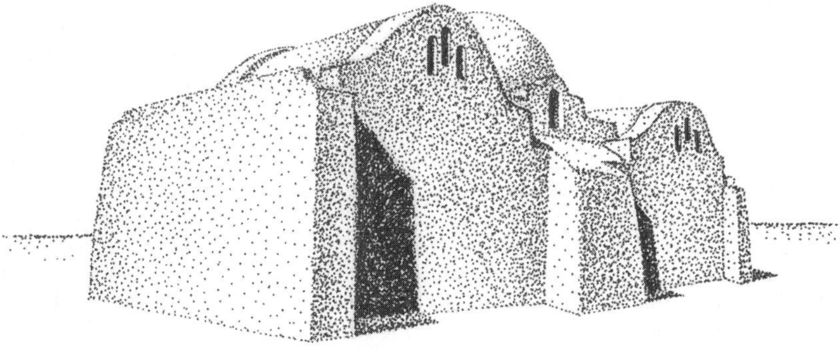

BOB RACE

Dar Al-Islam mosque in Abiquiu

Jordan, Great Britain, Holland, and Belgium. By the early 1990s, the school had closed and most of the families had moved away. Visitors are welcome. To get to Dar Al-Islam, turn right at the El Rito turnoff, then left over the bridge across the river. A three-mile dirt road takes you to the mosque.

Abiquiu Reservoir

About seven miles north of Abiquiu, you'll come to the turnoff to Abiquiu Dam and Reservoir. A popular fishing, swimming, and sailing spot, the lake has picnic tables, but no overnight camping is allowed.

Ghost Ranch Living Museum

Billing itself a "forest in miniature through animals' eyes," this zoo/nature museum at the north end of Abiquiu Reservoir is tailor-made for kids and school field trips. A "talking beaver" introduces the purpose of the museum, which is to provide a microcosmic view of natural New Mexico, and an illustrated guidebook leads you along the meandering pathway and explains the roles the different plants and animals play in the state's ecology. Meet Harriet the mountain lion, Hugo the badger, Bonnie and Clyde the raccoons, Thorny the porcupine, Kino and Kiki the Mexican wolves, and Frank, Minnie, and Rainbow the elk, as well as owls, eagles, and black bears. At the Beaver Museum, view a cutaway beaver dam and see stylized Indian paintings of beavers.

Ghost Ranch Living Museum, named for the spirits said to haunt the canyon, is open Tuesday–Sunday 8 A.M.–4:30 P.M. Admission is $3 for adults and $2 for seniors and students. Kids under 12 and school groups are admitted free. For more information, phone 505/685-4312.

Echo Amphitheater

You'll find a small national forest campground with pit toilets at this bizarre natural bowl in the orange and red cliffside a mile north of Ghost Ranch. Formed by water and wind carving away the soft rock, the amphitheater can be seen from the highway, although you can walk right into the bowl along a very short interpretive nature trail. Another short trail (a quarter mile) leads to a separate amphitheater "in the making," so you can get a better idea of how the larger one was formed. Camping is $4, and day use is free.

Tierra Amarilla

The capital of Rio Arriba County, Tierra Amarilla (Yellow Land) lies in a large valley against the northern slope of the San Juan Mountains. Home to Utes and Jicarilla Apaches in the 18th and 19th centuries (before they were moved to their present reservations in the 1870s), the area was also home to a number of Spanish farmers, who first moved to the valley in 1832 after Spain granted land here to Juan Martinez.

From Tierra Amarilla you can take Highway 64 east to Taos. The 80-mile drive winds over the gorgeously forested San Juan Mountains, through Tres Piedras, and down across the Rio Grande. Note: heavy snowfall usually keeps this route closed throughout the winter.

El Vado Lake State Park

In 1935, El Vado Dam was built across the Rio Chama, and what had once been one of the county's largest communities was submerged. Between 1904 and 1923, El Vado was a busy lumber and railroad town, with a school and opera house, churches, saloons, and bordellos. When logging fell off in the area, the New Mexico Lumber Company moved from El Vado to Dolores, Colorado, and the town was abandoned. Little is left to remind us today of the city at the bottom of the lake, save for a handful of headstones in the old cemetery at the reservoir's north end.

El Vado is a popular fishing, swimming, and boating lake, and the state park includes a campground with several scattered sites and flush toilets. Camping is $8 a night. The park is about 12 miles southwest of Tierra Amarilla. The road is well marked.

El Vado RV Park near the lake is open to members of the "Coast-to-Coast" club only.

Heron Lake State Park

This 4,000-acre state park completely surrounds Heron Lake, named for K.A. Heron, who actively promoted the building of Heron Dam across the Rio Chama. Completed in 1972, the 265-foot-high earth-filled dam plays a key role in the San Juan-Chama Diversion Project, which diverts water from tributaries of the San Juan to the upper Chama, where it is stored at Heron Lake.

A popular summer fishing and sailing lake (with regular fishing derbies and regattas), Heron is also a favorite of ice fishermen, those hardy souls who cut holes in a lake's winter crust and sit booted and mittened until a hungry fish happens by. Heron is known for its rainbow trout and kokanee salmon. Designated a "quiet" lake, Heron allows motorboats but limits them to trolling speed.

One of the more fully appointed state parks in the system, Heron provides a marina, a boat ramp, modern restrooms (with showers), hiking and cross-country ski trails, and a visitors center with exhibits explaining the area's and the lake's history. Camping facilities include sites with shelters and hookups. Overnight charge is $8, $12 for RV hookups.

Heron Lake is 11 miles northwest of Tierra Amarilla. Take Highway 84 north from town and turn west on Highway 95. For more information, phone 505/588-7470.

CHAMA

Best known as the departure point for the Cumbres and Toltec Scenic Railroad, Chama is a quiet little resort town about five miles south of the Colorado border. Just north of the junction of Highways 84 and 64, Chama also attracts outdoor lovers year-round—to the fishing, hunting, backcountry horseback riding, and especially cross-country skiing and snowmobiling.

Cumbres and Toltec Scenic Railroad

One of the state's most popular tourist attractions, the narrow-gauge railroad winds 64 miles through some of the most beautiful country in the Rocky Mountains—through tunnels and pristine vales, and across high trestles over deep mountain gorges. Crisscrossing the Colorado border several times, and finally winding up in Antonito, Colorado, the line is the sole survivor of what was once a vast network of railways connecting the mining camps scattered throughout the southern Rockies.

Several trips are offered Memorial Day to mid-October. You can go roundtrip from Chama to Osier, about a third of the way (six hours), for

$40; you can go all the way to Antonito and return by van (eight hours) for $60. Reservations are highly recommended. Write Cumbres and Toltec Scenic Railroad, P.O. Box 789, Chama, NM 87520, or phone 505/756-2151.

Accommodations

Chama, only 107 miles from Santa Fe, is a favorite summer and winter getaway for many northern New Mexicans, and you'll find a variety of lodging options, from RV parks to old hotels and newly built hunting lodges. Two of the newer lodges in town are the **Branding Iron Motel,** 1511 Main, 505/756-2162 or 800/446-2650, and the **Vista del Rio Lodge,** 505/756-2138, on the Chama River two miles south of downtown Chama (both $50–100). The **Little Creel Lodge,** 505/756-2382, caters especially to anglers, hunters, and skiers, and has individual cabins with or without kitchenettes, some with fireplaces. Doubles run $50–100. Also quite nice is **Elkhorn Lodge,** 505/756-2105, which offers small cabins (sleeping up to 10 and starting at about $100), as well as rooms in the lodge ($50–100) and RV sites with full hookups. At **Twin Rivers Trailer Park and Campground,** 505/756-2218, RV sites with full hookups are about $18.

Food

For good Mexican food in Chama, try **Vera's,** 505/756-2557, open daily 7:30 A.M.–9 P.M.; lunches run $5–7. At the **High Country Restaurant and Saloon,** right downtown across from the train depot, 505/756-2384, you can snatch a booth or belly up to the bar with the talkative locals and order a hot beef, barbecue chicken, or steak sandwich for $7–12. The High Country serves lunch and dinner 11 A.M.–10:30 P.M.

Events

Several annual events in the Chama Valley have recently begun to attract large crowds. The **Chile Classic** is a cross-country ski race held in February. Two routes (5K and 10K) follow the Cumbres and Toltec Railroad line. In recent years the event has attracted upward of 500 participants, competing not only for best time, but for best costume, oldest and youngest skier, and other awards. For more information, phone 505/268-4876. Also in February is the **Balloon and Snowmobile Festival,** a rare chance to see the wildly colorful hot-air balloons against a snowy winter backdrop. **Chama Days,** in August, features a rodeo and food and crafts booths.

Information

For more information on exploring the Chama Valley—or on events and lodging in the area—write the Chama Valley **Chamber of Commerce,** P.O. Box 306-A, Chama, NM 87520, or call 505/756-2306.

TO FARMINGTON

Highway 64 cuts through the top of northwestern New Mexico, across the lush Jicarilla Apache Reservation, and through an isolated adjunct of Carson National Forest. About 10 miles west of Chama, the road crosses the Continental Divide and then begins to wind slowly down onto the high desert of the Four Corners area. Not one of the most highly traveled routes in the state, this stretch of highway rolls through forested mountains thick with tall ponderosa pines and foothills studded with piñon, and then drops to the San Juan River, which cuts a ribbon of green across the rocky mesas and canyonlands east of Bloomfield.

Dulce

Situated on the east end of the 722,000-acre Jicarilla Apache Reservation about 30 miles west of Chama, Dulce (Sweet) is the hub of northern Apache commerce and education. Archaeological sites, including pit houses dating from A.D. 500, are scattered throughout the area, although the Anasazis who inhabited them were no relation to the Apache, who arrived from the northwest around the 13th century.

Little remains of the original Jicarilla culture, although tribal elders are attempting to revive some of the traditional crafts, including buckskin, beadwork, and basketry. For the most part, the Jicarilla economy relies for its stability on the sale of timber and on leasing reservation land for oil and natural-gas drilling, as well as on cattle and sheep ranching. The reservation is home to about 1,800 Indians.

The large **Best Western Jicarilla Inn,** 505/759-3663, is a convenient stopover for travelers, as well as for hunters and anglers plying the hills and waters of the reservation. $50–100.

For more information about hunting and fishing on the Jicarilla Apache Reservation, write Jicarilla Game and Fish Department, P.O. Box 546, Dulce, NM 87528, or phone 505/759-3255 or 505/759-3260.

Española to Taos—The Main Route

Highway 68 follows the Rio Grande about three-fourths of the way from Española to Taos, and if you're looking for the quickest route, this is it—an easy 40-mile drive. For centuries, this region has been farmland, cultivated first by Indians, then later by Spaniards and Mexicans. Recently, it has become an increasingly popular recreational area, especially among rafters, most of whom run the river with guides from the many companies offering white-water excursions.

San Juan Pueblo

Largest and northernmost of the remaining Tewa pueblos, San Juan was actually the first "capital" of New Mexico—so designated by Oñate upon his arrival here in 1598. San Juan was also the home of Pueblo Revolt leader Popé, though, and when conflict broke out between the Spanish and the Indians in 1692, San Juan played a key role.

Today, San Juan Pueblo is a quiet community taking pride in its revival of traditional crafts, including red pottery, wood and stone carvings, and weavings. In the pueblo's central plaza, the Catholic church stands beside two ancient kivas, perfectly symbolizing the "two worlds" in which modern Indians must live.

San Juan Indians invite tourism, and the **O'Ke Oweenge Arts and Crafts Cooperative** is an excellent place to see the exquisite work of this area's artisans. Turquoise and silver jewelry, pottery, and other wares are for sale. Hours are Monday–Saturday 9 A.M.–5 P.M. For more information, phone 505/852-2372.

San Juan Pueblo is one mile north of Española on Highway 68. Watch for the sign on the west side of the highway. Note: recording of any kind, including sketching and photography (still cameras, movie cameras, and camcorders) is allowed by permit only. For more information, phone 505/852-4400.

Pilar

About 30 miles north of Española, where the highway veers east of the Rio Grande, Pilar was a Jicarilla Apache farming community until 1694, when it was torched by de Vargas after the Pueblo Revolt. In 1795, 20 families were granted land here by New Mexico governor Fernando Chacon, contingent upon their living communally with the natives. The Spanish moved in, began to farm the land, and tried to ignore the Apache. But the Apaches, not taking kindly to their land being usurped, began a series of raids that lasted more than 50 years, until they were forced in the mid-1800s to sign a treaty and move to the newly established reservation between Chama and Farmington.

Orilla Verde National Recreation Area

In 1959, the State of New Mexico, hoping to curb development along the Rio Grande, officially gave state park status to the entire Rio Grande Gorge from the Colorado border to Velarde, 14 miles north of Española. Known to locals as "the box," the stretch of river was immensely popular among anglers and river-runners, although initially as a park it was on somewhat shaky legal footing: the state didn't own all of the land it was claiming. Nonetheless, the move halted development.

In 1968, the U.S. Congress passed the National Wild and Scenic Rivers Act, and the Rio Grande was one of the first rivers to come under protection. On May 13, 1970, the Rio Grande Wild and Scenic River was formally dedicated.

However, with this transference to federal property, the state lost "the box."

Rio Grande Gorge State Park was taken over by the BLM in the mid-1990s and renamed Orilla Verde National Recreation Area, today a small area flanking the river just north of Pilar. Several campgrounds scattered along the river's banks offer both sheltered and primitive campsites—with running water and pit toilets. The sites are nicely spaced to provide privacy, although there's very little natural shade. Day use is $3, primitive campsites are $6, and sites with shelters are $8. Watch for the signs on the west side of the highway near Pilar.

Rio Grande Gorge Hostel

At the turnoff to Orilla Verde Recreation Area, this hostel, 505/758-0090, is popular among rafters and other river rats. Bunks go for about $15 with a continental breakfast (discount with AYH card).

Española to Taos—The Back Road

Instead of remaining on Highway 68 out of Española and following the river, you can take the back way: Highway 76 to Highway 518 and then back onto 68 just a few miles south of town. Hands-down the best way to get to Taos from the south, this route will take you an hour longer—more if you stop along the way. And there are plenty of reasons to stop: to see the Santuario de Chimayó, to watch fifth-generation weavers working at handmade looms, or just to take in the breathtakingly beautiful scenery of the Sangre de Cristo Mountains and Santa Fe National Forest.

CHIMAYÓ

Chimayó, on the site of an ancient Tewa pueblo, is known throughout the Southwest for the Santuario de Nuestro Señor de Esquipulas and the Chapel of the Santo Niño, both of which are reputed to have great healing powers, as well as for its fine weavers, whose ancestors were brought over from Spain to help develop and promote the craft. It's also a prime farming area, with fruit—particularly apples— and chiles its most important products.

Marking the eastern boundary of the Province of New Mexico from 1598 to 1695, Chimayó takes its name from the Tewa word Tsimajo, for "superior-quality flaking stone," or obsidian. In 1805, certified master weavers Don Juan and Don Ignacio Balzán were imported from Spain on a six-year contract to teach weaving to Santa Fe youth. Not particularly enthralled with the capital, the brothers soon moved to Chimayó, and the town has been a weaving center ever since; by the mid-19th century, nearly 100 Chimayó families had weaving businesses. Today, you can stop in town and watch weavers working their characteristically complex patterns into rugs, shawls, blankets, and placemats. At **Trujillo's,** as well as at **Ortega's Weaving Shop,** for example (both are in town near the junction of Highway 76 and Highway 520), you can not only watch the artisans at work, but you can also get excellent prices on their quality products.

Santuario de Chimayó

Built 1813–16 by Don Bernardo Abeyta, this small church has attracted pilgrims and cure-seekers for nearly 200 years. According to one legend, Abeyta built the church on the site of his own curing from a deathly illness: After having been summoned there by a vision, Abeyta touched the ground and was immediately healed. When he laid the chapel's floor, he left a small hole so that people could continue to touch the sacred earth.

Another story deals with a crucifix that was buried at the *santuario* during the Pueblo Revolt. Shortly after the reconquest, it was dug up and ceremoniously carried to a church nine miles away. However, it promptly vanished, only to reappear inexplicably back at the *santuario.* Three times the crucifix was moved, and three times it appeared back in Chimayó.

Whatever the reality of the chapel, crutches, braces, and other symbols of thanks and healing

© STEPHEN METZGER

Santuario de Chimayó

have been left in the church and are testimony to the site's power.

Even for those not in search of the cure, the church is well worth a visit: the well-preserved building is an excellent example of Spanish pueblo architecture, from the choir loft to the cemetery in front. Heading north, watch on the right for the sign to the "Santuario."

Santo Niño

Although this chapel is privately owned, it is open to visitors. Touching the small statue of the Santo Niño Perdido (Lost Holy Child) reportedly will heal those sick in body or spirit. Notes and photos of those asking to be cured have been pinned to his robes.

Practicalities

Hacienda Rancho de Chimayó, 505/351-2222, is a bed-and-breakfast in a 100-year-old adobe home. The seven rooms are beautifully appointed with antiques and include private baths and views of the courtyard. Rooms run $100–150 (discounts offered November–March). Also in Chimayó is **Casa Escondida** bed-and-breakfast, 505/351-4805, on six acres with five rooms and three detached guesthouses ranging in price—$100–150.

Restaurante Rancho de Chimayó, 505/351-4444, is a favorite among northern New Mexicans as well as travelers lucky to have stumbled upon it. With dining rooms spread about a sprawling adobe home, as well as with outside seating, Rancho de Chimayó specializes in *flautas, carne adovada,* and sopaipillas. Dinners run $8–15. When the weather's nice, sit outside on the patio; when it's cooler, enjoy a fireside table in one of several small dining rooms. Open daily mid-May through mid-October and Tuesday–Sunday the rest of the year. Hours are 11:30 A.M.–9 P.M., with breakfast served weekends from 8:30-10:30.

TRUCHAS

Although Truchas (pop. 650) is a little hamlet where not much happens, big times came to town in late 1987. That's when Hollywood rolled in. Or, more precisely, that's when Robert Redford arrived, along with a crew of actors and extras, key grips and publicists, and a $10 million budget—to film *The Milagro Beanfield War.* Although the movie was originally slated to be shot down the road in Chimayó, the location was changed to Truchas after a group of Chimayoans protested that they didn't want the intrusion that would result from a major film company's setting up camp for several months of shooting.

The village you see in *The Milagro Beanfield War* probably isn't a whole lot different from the Truchas of the mid-18th century, then known as Nuestra Señora de Rosario de las Truchas (Our Lady of the Rosary of the Trout). The plaza, dusty roads, adobe houses, rickety fences, pigs, goats, and cattle—all have been part of Truchas since its founding. According to the WPA's *New Mexico, A Guide to the Colorful State* (see the Suggested Reading), the town is mentioned in a 1752 Spanish archive, although the first reference to anything actually happening here is in a document from 10 years later, when the people of Truchas (probably Indians) were "transferred" to the "Parish of Picuris." Ten years after that, in March 1772, records show that the people of Truchas requested from the New Mexico government "12 muskets and powder," to help fend off the invading Comanche. "Denied" is written across the memo.

Today, from its setting on a hillside high on the west flank of Sangre de Cristos (the town is almost 8,000 feet above sea level), Truchas commands a gorgeous and historically important view—south over the Chimayó and Española Valleys: the land of the Tewa Indians and their Spanish conquerors.

BOB RACE

LAS TRAMPAS

Las Trampas (The Traps), a small adobe-walled village about midway between Española and Taos, dates to 1751, when Spaniard Juan de Arguello was given a land grant and brought 12 families to the area to farm the fertile land. Of particular interest here is the old church, San José de Garcia, which has been recently restored and is one of the best examples in North America of Spanish missionary architecture.

The four-foot-thick adobe walls of this Catholic church, built in the mid-18th century and originally known as the Church of the Twelve Apostles, stand more than 30 feet tall and even from the nearby road seem imposing and severe. Placed on the National Register of Historic Places in the 1970s to protect it from impending highway construction, the church has long been a center of ceremonial activity in the area. The church has twin belfries: the lighter-toned Gracia bell was rung to celebrate Mass and to mourn the deaths of infants, and the heavier-toned Refugio was rung at Masses mourning the deaths of adults. Today the church stands quietly beside the road inviting the occasional passerby to venture through the gate into the weedy churchyard, or on into the building itself. Note: though the church is closed except during services, you can ask at the small store across the road to have it opened.

PICURIS PUEBLO

Picuris, the most isolated and remote of the New Mexico pueblos, wasn't discovered by the Spanish until 1591, 50 years after Coronado had invaded the Rio Grande–area villages. At that time, the pueblo was home to at least 2,000 Indians who lived in multistoried apartment-type buildings. Five years later, the pueblo was abandoned, as the Indians, no match for the Spanish and refusing to submit to them, fled to the east, where they lived among the Apaches for 10 years. Eventually, though, they returned to their pueblo,

THE PENITENTES

One of the most bizarre chapters in the history of New Mexico is the story of Los Hermanos Penitentes, or Los Hermanos de Luz (The Brothers of Light). Thought to be derived from Medieval European Christianity, Los Penitentes are a "secret order" of Spanish Christians whose members at one time practiced self-flagellation and carried out strange ceremonies in the Sangre de Cristo Mountains around Las Trampas, Vadido, and Taos.

Most prominent in the mountain villages of northern New Mexico, although they also practiced in southern Colorado and northern Mexico, the Penitentes "celebrated" Holy Week by sacrificing themselves in penance for their own sins, as well as those of the world. On hillsides and in mountain meadows, they beat their own backs with whips made of yucca, enacted Passion Plays to a frightening and disturbing degree of authenticity, and, reportedly, even crucified members of their group.

Although the Penitentes had the blessing of the Catholic Church for centuries, by the early 1800s, their rituals were seen as too extreme by most clerics. In 1828, they officially lost their clerical support, although they continued to perform ceremonies well into the 20th century. In 1948, the Catholic Church offered them its blessing and protection, contingent on the order's proceeding with "moderation."

Today, of course, although the order does claim active members, none of the extreme rituals are practiced. Hikers in the local mountains occasionally stumble across *moradas* (old huts where the Penitentes lived) and crosses marking the brothers' graves.

For further reading: Warren A. Beck's "The Penitentes," in *New Mexico, Past and Present: A Historical Reader,* Albuquerque, University of New Mexico Press, 1971; and Fray Angelico Chaves's "Penitentes of New Mexico," in *New Mexico Historical Review,* vol. XXXIX (April 1954).

and during the 18th century they joined forces with the Spanish against the Apaches, Comanches, and Utes.

Today, fewer than 150 people live at Picuris, although the tribe appears to be strong and proud, and tribal leaders are actively promoting tourism and education in hopes of revitalizing the pueblo. In addition, Picuris Pueblo owns 51 percent of the Hotel Santa Fe in Santa Fe, though several people I talked with at the pueblo seemed a bit removed from the deal. While they assumed the hotel was turning a profit, they seemed puzzled as to why some of it wasn't returning to the pueblo.

To get to Picuris Pueblo, go west on Highway 75 just before Peñasco and watch for the sign to Picuris.

Picuris Pueblo Museum displays and sells locally crafted pottery, weaving, and beadwork. For more information, write Picuris Pueblo Museum, P.O. Box 427, Peñasco, NM 87553, or phone 505/587-2957. **San Lorenzo de Picuris,** the pueblo's Catholic church, has been in continuous use since the late 1700s, when it was built to replace the 1621 original that was destroyed in the Pueblo Revolt.

Next door to the museum is the **Hidden Valley Restaurant,** serving about the best *carne adovada* I've ever tasted, as well as burritos, tamales, and other New Mexican food. Open for lunch—$5–10.

Pu-na and **Tu-Tah Lakes** are two small lakes at the pueblo and are stocked regularly with trout. Fishing permits, available at the museum, are $4 for non-Indian adults and $3 for kids. A handful of picnic tables and grills are provided for overnight camping. Check at the museum for rates.

For more information, contact Picuris Pueblo at Box 127, Peñasco, NM 87553, 505/587-2519, or visit the website: www.picurispueblo.com.

PEÑASCO

Peñasco, originally several smaller settlements, is a sprawling little village south of Picuris Pueblo. Founded in 1796, Peñasco until the mid-20th century was a thriving community and a com-

BOB RACE

mercial hub for ranchers and farmers working in the region. Today, Peñasco is more important as an educational center, as kids from the surrounding communities attend school here. Many of the village's older houses have been sold to out-of-towners as summer homes.

The **Carson National Forest ranger station,** just north of Peñasco, is a good place to stop for information on hiking, camping, and sight-seeing in the area. Trail and road maps are available; phone 505/587-2255.

RANCHOS DE TAOS

Not to be confused with the *town* of Taos or Taos Pueblo, Ranchos de Taos is thought to have been founded by Taos Indians who moved the few miles south looking for better fields to farm. Extending on both sides of the highway (Highway 68), Ranchos de Taos remains a farming community, quiet and low-key, without the profusion of the galleries, gift shops, and restaurants found up the road in Taos. The church here, **San Francisco de Asis,** was built about 1730 and is a favorite subject of local and visiting photographers, sketchers, and painters. Notable for its towering four-foot-thick walls, the church contains European and New Mexican paintings. Look for the church on the east side of the highway.

Taos

Taos is one of those magic little towns with which people fall instantly in love. Nestled on the Taos Plateau against the west flank of the Sangre de Cristos, Taos (pop. 6,200; elev. 6,695 feet) is a microcosm of all that's good about New Mexico: you'll find here an Indian pueblo at least 700 years old; Indian, Spanish, and Anglo cultures living and working in relative harmony; a thriving arts and literary community; a slow, kick-back lifestyle; and some of the best year-round recreational possibilities in the country, including snow skiing, rafting, fishing, camping, hiking, cycling, and just about anything else you can do outdoors.

Which is largely what's been attracting travelers for centuries. As early as the mid-1800s, Taos first started to lure painters and writers, drawn by the surreal landscapes—the sprawling plateau and distant mountain peaks, the sundering Rio Grande and dusty back roads leading to ancient pueblos and Spanish Colonial haciendas. This artists' colony survives today. The visitor can't help but be impressed by the town's disproportionate number of painters and writers, galleries and bookstores, shows and poetry readings. Of course, any town that lends such credence to its artists and literati is going to risk reduction to a certain degree of artsy-fartsiness and leather-elbow-patched pretentiousness, but it's all relatively heartfelt here—honest, and down to earth. In fact, some of the writers and painters most likely came to Taos, where you can touch the land and feel an intimate connection to its people, to *escape* those trappings.

Ultimately, a trip to New Mexico without at least a short stop in Taos is incomplete. But be forewarned: The place has grown up in the past few years, and some of the romance has been replaced by a degree of cynicism. You'll still find quality artwork and artists of supreme integrity, but you'll also find some pretty tacky stuff ("I Heart Taos" T-shirts and mugs in the gift shops) and an increasing number of marketing types capitalizing on the town's appeal to tourists.

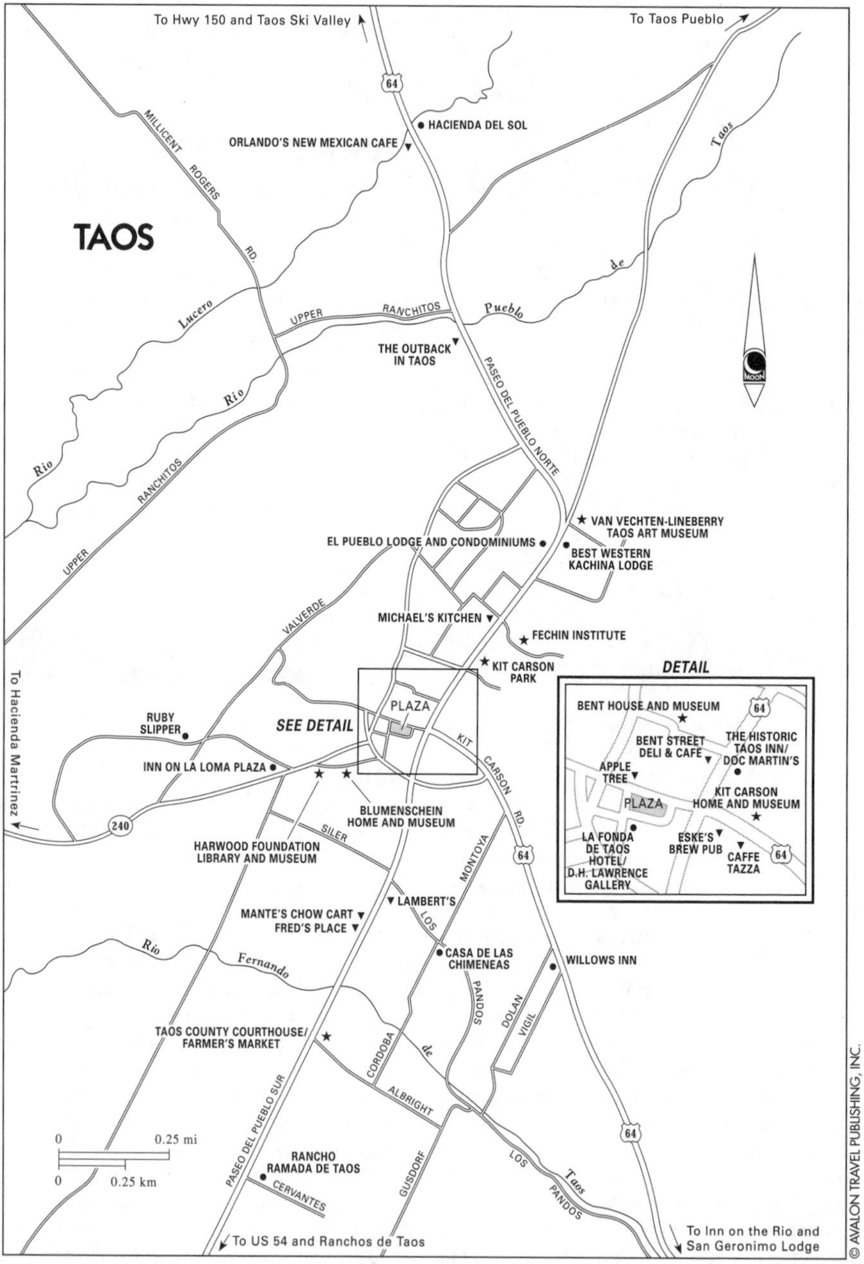
TAOS
To Hwy 150 and Taos Ski Valley
To Taos Pueblo
HACIENDA DEL SOL
ORLANDO'S NEW MEXICAN CAFE
MILLICENT ROGERS RD.
Rio Pueblo de Taos
Rio Lucero
UPPER RANCHITOS
THE OUTBACK IN TAOS
PASEO DEL PUEBLO NORTE
VAN VECHTEN-LINEBERRY TAOS ART MUSEUM
EL PUEBLO LODGE AND CONDOMINIUMS
BEST WESTERN KACHINA LODGE
VALVERDE
MICHAEL'S KITCHEN
FECHIN INSTITUTE
KIT CARSON PARK
To Hacienda Martrinez
RUBY SLIPPER
SEE DETAIL
PLAZA
KIT CARSON RD.
INN ON LA LOMA PLAZA
BLUMENSCHEIN HOME AND MUSEUM
HARWOOD FOUNDATION LIBRARY AND MUSEUM
SILER
MONTOYA
240
64
DETAIL
BENT HOUSE AND MUSEUM
BENT STREET DELI & CAFE
THE HISTORIC TAOS INN/ DOC MARTIN'S
APPLE TREE
KIT CARSON HOME AND MUSEUM
LA FONDA DE TAOS HOTEL/ D.H. LAWRENCE GALLERY
ESKE'S BREW PUB
CAFFE TAZZA
LAMBERT'S
MANTE'S CHOW CART
FRED'S PLACE
Rio Fernando de Taos
LOS PANDOS
CASA DE LAS CHIMENEAS
WILLOWS INN
DOLAN
VIGIL
TAOS COUNTY COURTHOUSE/ FARMER'S MARKET
CORDOBA
ALBRIGHT
PASEO DEL PUEBLO SUR
GUSDORF
RANCHO RAMADA DE TAOS
CERVANTES
0 0.25 mi
0 0.25 km
To US 54 and Ranchos de Taos
To Inn on the Rio and San Geronimo Lodge
© AVALON TRAVEL PUBLISHING, INC.

The classic adobe architecture and narrow streets of Taos put travelers in another time and another place, seemingly far away from the noise and clutter of modern times.

You'll also find crowds. On weekends in summer, the main drag through town is bumper-to-bumper with RVs and jam-packed station wagons from around the country, as well as with the red convertibles and foreign sports cars of Santa Feans and Albuquerqueans fleeing the cities.

HISTORY

According to Taos Indian legend, an eagle led their ancestors to the Taos Valley more than 800 years ago. A Tiwa-speaking people, the Taos Indians were living peacefully in their pueblo—one of the oldest continuously inhabited communities in the country—when the Spanish arrived in 1540 led by Hernando de Alvarado, from Coronado's expedition. Originally, the Indians were friendly, and when the Spanish started settling in the valley in the early 17th century, they were welcomed by the native inhabitants. Soon, though, the Spaniards' increasing numbers, as well as the frequency of marriages between Indians and Spanish, began to worry the Indians, and relations grew strained.

In 1617, Fray Pedro de Miranda built a church on the pueblo, one that would serve the Indians and Spanish alike. Before long, though, the conflict between the two groups had grown quite heated, and in 1631, Miranda and two Spanish soldiers were killed. Shortly thereafter, the Indians asked the Spanish to move "a league away" from their pueblo. Thus was born the present-day town of Taos, officially known as Fernando de Taos, perhaps named for Don Fernando de Chavez, a prominent settler.

As early as 1650, the Taos Indians were conspiring with other tribes to rebel against the Spanish. This revolt never got off the ground, though, apparently thanks to the Hopis' refusal to take part. But 30 years later, Popé, from San Juan Pueblo but based at Taos, led the Pueblo tribes in a rebellion that ran the Spanish out of New Mexico. The Pueblo Revolt lasted 12 years, and Taos wasn't reconquered until 1692, at which time it was again occupied by the Spanish.

For the next 75 years, the Indians and Spanish were forced into a mutually dependent relationship, as other tribes (Utes, Apaches, and Comanches) carried on a relentless series of raids on the pueblo and town. In 1760, after

© STEPHEN METZGER

downtown Taos in winter

one particularly brutal Comanche blitz, the town sent for reinforcements—soldiers from Santa Fe, who tracked the Comanches down and killed 400 of them but never recovered the 50 women and children the Indians were said to have kidnapped.

That pretty much put a stop to the raids on Taos, and by the beginning of the 1800s, the town had become a vital trade center for Plains and Pueblo Indians. Every summer, the various tribes held huge trade fairs, which by the early 19th century were attracting French trappers and Colonial-American mountain men. Corn and beans were traded for buffalo meat, horses, and cattle, which in turn were traded for beaver pelts, textiles, axes, and guns. Taos had become the busiest village in New Mexico. The annual trade fair became a "rendezvous," and participants took their drinking and socializing as seriously as their trading.

Among the mountain men who came to Taos in the early 19th century was Kit Carson, who in 1826 arrived as a teenager from Missouri. Three years later, Carson left on a trapping expedition, and for the rest of his life he was involved in various enterprises throughout the West—he guided trappers, fought Indians, assisted on John C. Frémont's expeditions, and helped round up the Navajos for the Long Walk. Although Carson spent little time actually in town, he married twice here, his first wife dying during childbirth. Toward the end of his life, he served as an Indian Agent based in Taos. Carson died in 1868, and his house is now the site of the Kit Carson Museum.

While Carson was off fighting Indians, a native New Mexican was trying to bring some sense of education and civilization to the province, particularly to Taos. Padre Antonio José Martinez, who was born in Abiquiu, came to Fernando de Taos in 1826 and worked most of his life for the church and for his people. Martinez established the first coed school in the Southwest and also brought to Taos the state's first printing press, on which he printed the newspaper *El Crepúsculo* (The Dawn). Unfortunately, Martinez and Archbishop Lamy didn't see eye to eye, and Martinez was defrocked in 1854. When Lamy ordered mandatory tithing of New Mexico Catholics, Martinez, who thought tithing should be voluntary, resisted and was promptly excommunicated. He died in the 1860s, never having given up the cloth, although his church was no longer officially recognized.

Fernando de Taos remained predominantly Spanish and peaceful—save for a couple of minor skirmishes—throughout the 19th century. In one significant uprising, a group of Taos Indians and Hispanics attacked and killed the first American governor of New Mexico, Charles Bent, at his family's house near the plaza. The counterattack by the U.S. government quickly subdued the opposition, killing 100, with only seven fatalities on its side.

Meanwhile, the town was already beginning to attract writers and artists. In 1845, Lewis H. Garrard arrived in Taos and published the story of his trip in *Wah-to-Yah, or the Taos Trail.* Three years later, painters E. M. and R. N. Kern arrived in town with Frémont, and the brothers, who immediately saw the potential for New Mexico landscapes to be put to canvas, were the forerunners of Taos's famous artists' colony, which peaked in the early 20th century.

In 1880, American artist Joseph Henry Sharp arrived in the Taos area and began a series of sketches. So enamored of the Southwest was Sharp that he sent word to two East Coast friends and fellow artists, Bert Phillips and Ernest Blumenschein, and the two were soon on their way west, painting as they traveled and planning eventually to journey as far as Mexico. En route, though, about 30 miles from Taos, a wheel from the pair's wagon broke, and Blumenschein, losing a coin toss, carried the wheel by horseback into Taos for repairs. Three days later he returned with the newly repaired wheel, but by that time he'd already discovered the magic of the Taos area. The two painters decided not to continue south and to stay instead with Sharp in Taos, where—along with Irving Couse—they founded the Taos Society of Artists. The group began sending its work east, and before long the New York art establishment was taking notice; soon East Coast collectors and buyers were regularly traveling to the tiny village of Taos to keep tabs on the important work being done there.

In 1917, Mabel Dodge, a prominent and wealthy East Coast patroness, arrived in Taos, and immediately her well-known friends began to follow. Among them: Andrew Dasburg, Georgia O'Keeffe, Ansel Adams, and John Marin. Some stayed only briefly; others, such as D. H. Lawrence, shared Dodge's enthusiasm for the area and stayed. Lawrence, who remained in Taos for two years and wrote a number of essays and fictional pieces here, is enshrined in the mountains above town. He wrote:

> ***I think the skyline of Taos the most beautiful of all I have ever seen in my travels around the world.***

Except for short trips, Dodge stayed in Taos the rest of her life, eventually marrying Tony Luhan (her fourth husband) from Taos Pueblo. Together they built a large hacienda on the north side of town, where her famous and influential friends stayed when in the area. During her lifetime she wrote 11 books. She is buried in town in Kit Carson Cemetery.

Today, Taos is a wondrous blend of artists and writers (some famous and successful, such as John Nichols, author of *The Milagro Beanfield War* and many other books, others unknown and struggling); Hispanics and Indians who trace their Taos lineage back several centuries; outdoor lovers, particularly white-water rafters and skiers; and many who simply came to visit and, like Phillips and Blumenschein, ended up staying—seduced by the Taos magic. Here, as in much of New Mexico, extremes meet, converge, and ultimately harmonize.

SIGHTS

The main attraction of Taos is the little town itself—the central plaza, the narrow, adobe-home-lined backstreets, the galleries and gift shops, the bookstores and museums. Small enough to walk from one end to the other in a matter of minutes, downtown Taos exemplifies Southwestern charm and is the perfect place to poke aimlessly about. The curious traveler afoot could hardly do better than to set out without direction and simply follow his nose through town. Still, you'll want to check out some specific sights near the plaza and on the outskirts of town.

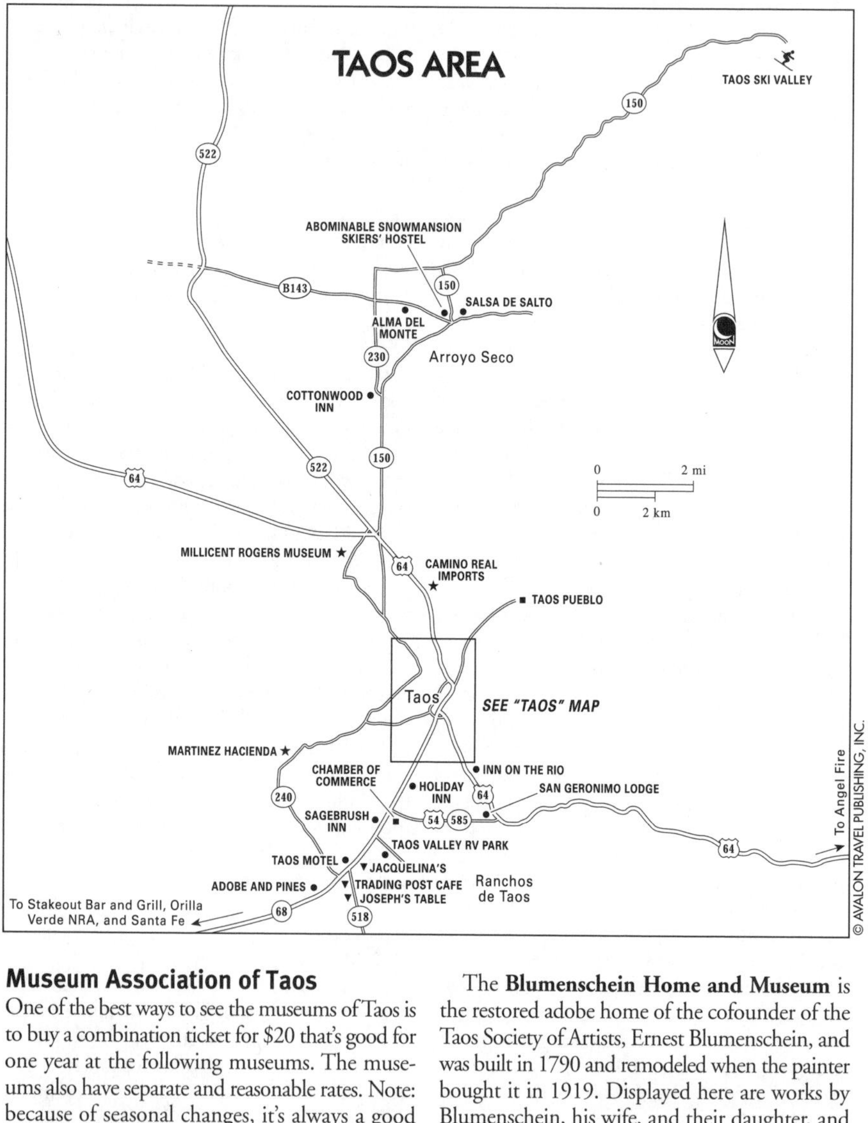

Museum Association of Taos

One of the best ways to see the museums of Taos is to buy a combination ticket for $20 that's good for one year at the following museums. The museums also have separate and reasonable rates. Note: because of seasonal changes, it's always a good idea to call ahead to confirm hours of operation

Hours of operation tend to change fairly frequently. I'd suggest calling ahead to double-check, especially if you're planning to visit early or late in the day, or on Saturday or Sunday, especially in winter.

The **Blumenschein Home and Museum** is the restored adobe home of the cofounder of the Taos Society of Artists, Ernest Blumenschein, and was built in 1790 and remodeled when the painter bought it in 1919. Displayed here are works by Blumenschein, his wife, and their daughter, and the rooms are furnished with the family's original antique furniture, European antiques and Spanish Colonial pieces. The house is two blocks west of the central plaza at 222 Ledoux St., 505/758-0330; open daily 9 A.M.–5 P.M. April–October, 11 A.M.–4 P.M. November–March.

Harwood Foundation Library and Museum, 238 Ledoux St., is a complex of adobe buildings, many of which date to Taos's Spanish Colonial days. The buildings house a fascinating and important cultural center that includes a museum, public library, and research center. Among the items of interest: a large collection of books by and about D. H. Lawrence and other Taoseños; artwork by early Taos painters; sculpture and paintings by Indian and contemporary Anglo artists; and Indian and Spanish carvings and religious icons. Hours are Tuesday–Saturday 10 A.M.–5 P.M. and Sunday noon–5 P.M. For more information, phone 505/758-3063.

The **Kit Carson Home and Museum** is in a 12-room adobe that dates from 1825 and was Carson's home 1843–68. On display is a huge variety of items from northern New Mexico's rambunctious 19th century—from saddles and firearms to clothing (Indian, Spanish, and "American") and domestic utensils and tools. The Kit Carson Museum is one block east of the plaza on Kit Carson Road. It's open daily 8 A.M.–6 P.M. April–October and 9 A.M.–5 P.M. November–March. For information, phone 505/758-0505.

La Hacienda de los Martinez, which was built in 1804 by Don Antonio Severino Martinez, is one of the few completely restored Spanish Colonial haciendas in the Southwest open to the public. Martinez was an early Taos *alcalde* (mayor) and prominent merchant. The home's 21 rooms, furnished to re-create the era, and the two large patios are enclosed within thick adobe walls, suggesting the dangers of living lavishly on the poor and lawless frontier. Take Highway 240 south two miles and watch for the signs. It's open daily 9 A.M.–5 P.M. April–October and 10 A.M.–4 P.M. November–March. For more information, phone 505/758-0505.

Millicent Rogers, a wealthy heiress to the Standard Oil fortune, came to Taos in 1947, and until she died in 1953 she amassed a huge collection of Indian and Spanish Colonial art. The **Millicent Rogers Museum** exhibits Rogers's personal collections, as well as work donated by friends and other patrons. Displayed are Zuñi and Hopi pottery from the 14th century; works by Maria Martinez, the famous San Ildefonso potter; Hispanic religious and domestic art; a diorama of a Navajo silversmith's shop; and a Spanish Colonial "death cart"—a skeleton with a bow and arrow riding in a wooden cart. There's also a large bookstore and gift shop selling prints, pottery, jewelry, rugs, and blankets. Take Highway 64 four miles north of town and turn west at the sign (crank a hard left just past the gas station; the road to the museum doubles back parallel to the highway). It's open daily 10 A.M.–5 P.M., closed Monday November–April. For more information, phone 505/758-2462.

The **Fechin Institute,** 227 Paseo del Pueblo Norte, 505/758-1710, is housed in an early-20th-century adobe on the National Register of Historic Places. The institute displays the art and collected Old World furniture of Russian immigrant Nicholai Fechin. Hours are Wednesday–Sunday 10 A.M.–5 P.M. April–October and 10 A.M.–2 P.M. November–March. The **Van Vechten-Lineberry Taos Art Museum,** 501 Paseo del Pueblo Norte, 505/758-2690, displays work of the more than 100 members of the Taos Society of Artists. Open Wednesday–Friday 11 A.M.–4 P.M. and Saturday–Sunday 1:30–4 P.M.

Other Taos Museums

The **Bent House and Museum,** one block north of the plaza at 117 Bent St., was the family home of New Mexico's first American governor, Charles Bent, who was killed here in an Indian and Hispanic uprising in 1847. Today, the building houses original furniture, Southwestern art, and a gift shop with books, prints, and Indian jewelry and pottery. It's open daily 10 A.M.–5 P.M.; admission $1. For more information, phone 505/758-2376.

The **D. H. Lawrence Gallery,** in a tiny room behind the main desk at **La Fonda de Taos Hotel,** displays a dozen or so paintings Lawrence did while in Taos. For die-hard Lawrence fans only, the strangely distorted nudes and lovers are a far cry from the characters he created in his fiction. You'll also find a handful of photos of and letters by Lawrence. Small admission fee.

Kit Carson Park

This small park just two blocks north of the plaza on Highway 68 is an ideal spot for a between-museums or after-a-morning-of-sight-seeing picnic. Surrounding Kit Carson Cemetery, where Carson, Mabel Dodge Luhan, and other Taos luminaries are buried, this quiet, shady park offers a welcome respite from the crowded gift shops and galleries. And if you feel like sticking around after your picnic, you can always shoot some hoops, play a set of tennis, choose sides for a softball game, or turn the kids loose in the playground. In the winter, a 17,000-square-foot ice-skating rink is open days and evenings (till 8 P.M.on weekdays and 10 P.M. on weekends); phone 505/758-4160 for more information.

Hours are 8 A.M.–8 P.M. in summer and 8 A.M.–5 P.M. in winter. Admission to the park is free.

Taos Pueblo

Together with Acoma Pueblo near Grants, Taos Pueblo is one of the most fascinating in the state and well worth going out of your way to visit. The northernmost of New Mexico's 19 pueblos, Taos—most likely inhabited for 800 years—is home to a thriving group of Tiwa-speaking Indians whose ancestors played integral roles in the Pueblo Revolt of 1680.

Taos Pueblo stands at the foot of the Sangre de Cristo Mountains. Wheeler Peak, the state's highest point at 13,161 feet, towers to the northeast and is sacred to the Taos Indians. The pueblo itself actually consists of two separate multistory apartment-type buildings typical of the structures that once dotted the banks of the Rio Grande between Taos and Albuquerque. Between the two buildings runs Pueblo Creek (also known as Rio Pueblo de Taos), and the two halves of the pueblo have been mildly rivalrous over the years; for centuries during the Feast of San Geronimo in late September, the two factions have run footraces, pitting the tribe's fastest runners against each other.

Recently, Taos Pueblo has begun an aggressive marketing campaign to attract tourists. Former Tourism Director Roy Bernal said:

> ***We want outsiders to see how we live so that a greater respect can grow between our cultures.***

Visitors to the pueblo can wander among the homes and Indians going about their daily chores as they have for centuries. Watch Indian women cooking bread in the large *hornos* (outdoor ovens),

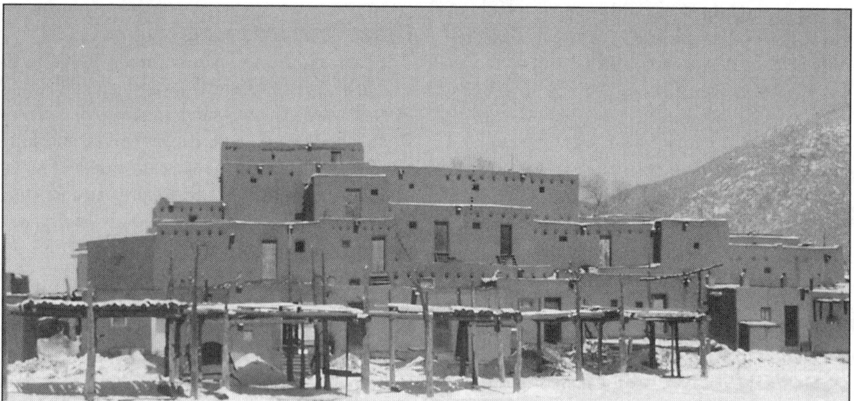

© STEPHEN METZGER

If the Taos Pueblo looks familiar, think Dennis Hopper and Peter Fonda: Easy Riders Billy and Captain America passed through on their way to New Orleans.

and step inside tiny curio shops where you can buy handcrafted jewelry and pottery or homemade bread and candy.

Taos Pueblo is a must for anyone traveling through Taos, but you should be aware of a few things: First, it gets crowded on summer weekends. Try to arrive early in the morning so you won't have to wait in line to park. (The best time to visit is winter, when the already-soft lines of the buildings are softened further by light blankets of snow and the pueblo is mostly empty of other tourists.) Second, these people *live* here and are allowing you to walk through their streets and neighborhoods. Imagine what it would be like if gawkers were walking past your doorways and windows year-round, and be respectful. "Do unto others . . . " Finally, there is an entrance fee ($10) as well as photography ($10), sketching ($10), and video-camera fees ($20). Remember, though, that because photography violates the beliefs of the Indians, no picture-taking is allowed on Feast Days, and you should ask permission before photographing individuals. Additionally, sometimes, as in the cases of funerals, the pueblo closes to the public altogether without notice.

Taos Pueblo is two miles north of the town of Taos. Take Highway 68 and watch for the sign on the east side of the road. For more information, write Taos Pueblo, Tourism Director, P.O. Box 1846, Taos, NM 87571, or phone 505/758-1028.

ACCOMMODATIONS

Places to bed down in Taos run the full gamut from bottom-of-the-barrel dives to classy hotels, condos, and quiet little bed-and-breakfasts, with rates ranging from $35 to well over $200 a night. Note: Prices will be higher during the summer and during ski season, which is Thanksgiving to Easter. Be sure to call ahead, both to double-check rates and, if you plan to visit during the high season, to make reservations.

For general information on Taos lodging, contact **Taos Central Reservations,** P.O. Box 1713, Taos, NM 87571, 800/821-2437 or 505/758-9767, website: taoswebb.com/plan/tcr.

Under $50

For clean, quiet, and inexpensive rooms, check out the **Taos Motel,** 505/758-2524 or 800/323-6009, three miles south of town on Highway 68.

The **Abominable Snowmansion Skiers' Hostel,** 505/776-8298, is in Arroyo Seco about midway between the town of Taos and Taos Ski Valley and is a popular hangout for young, on-the-road skiers. Dormitory-style lodging ($22) includes full breakfast; weather permitting, tents can be pitched outside. You can also get private rooms for about $50. The hostel also offers excellent group rates. Write P.O. Box 3721, Taos, NM 87571.

$50–100

About two miles south of town, at 1508 Paseo del Pueblo Sur, is the **Sagebrush Inn,** 505/758-2254 or 888/449-8267. You can get nice rooms here for under $100, though suites go for $150 and up. Restaurant and cozy after-ski lounge on site.

The **Ramada Inn de Taos,** 1.5 miles south of town, 505/758-2900 or 800/659-8267, has an indoor pool and gargantuan hot tub that are perfect for après-ski relaxing.

Just four blocks north of town is the **Best Western Kachina Lodge,** 415 Paseo del Pueblo Norte, 505/758-2275 or 800/522-4462. This faux adobe offers dependably clean and quiet rooms a short walk from the plaza. Larger rooms go for a bit more, up to $160.

$100–150

If you want to stay right in town, you'll pay a bit more, although being walking distance to some of the shops and museums is a definite bonus. **The Historic Taos Inn,** 125 Paseo del Pueblo Norte, 505/758-2233 or 800/TAOS-INN (800/826-7466), is an award-winning old adobe hotel in the heart of town. A popular watering hole and gathering place for locals and travelers alike, the Taos Inn is furnished with antiques and has a palpable air of Southwestern charm and dignity.

La Fonda de Taos, 505/758-2211 or 800/833-2211, is right on the plaza (108 S. Plaza), has a popular on-site restaurant, and overlooks central Taos.

Bed-and-Breakfasts: $100–150

The Taos area abounds in colorful and distinctive bed-and-breakfasts, many of them in historic homes and ranches and offering only-in-New Mexico lodging experiences. The **Taos Bed and Breakfast Inns** has more than a dozen members and can send you detailed descriptions of all of them as well as make reservations on line. Contact the organization at website: www.taos-bandb-inns.com.

As with Taos hotel and motel lodging, with bed-and-breakfasts you have your choice between in-town properties and those on the outskirts of town, many of the latter situated on the road between Taos and Taos Ski Valley and commanding stunning views of the mountains and sprawling Taos Plateau.

One mile north of the central plaza in Mabel Dodge Luhan's retreat is the **Hacienda del Sol,** 505/758-0287. Guests have included Frieda Lawrence and Georgia O'Keeffe. Write P.O. Box 177, Taos, NM 87571. Most of the 13 rooms go for under $150, though the larger suites run to about $250. Some have private hot tubs.

Another option is the **Inn on La Loma Plaza,** 315 Ranchitos Rd., 505/758-1717 or 800/530-3040, a walled hacienda that dates from 1800, when it served as part of the Spanish fortifications for adjacent La Loma Plaza. Some rooms have kitchenettes, and the larger rooms and suites top out at about $275.

Inn on the Rio is about two miles from Taos Plaza on East Kit Carson Road, 505/758-7199, just far enough away to offer a more rural retreat but still close enough for convenience. The inn provides free mountain bikes for guest use.

The **Willows Inn,** 505/758-2558 or 800/525-TAOS (800/525-8267), is an oasislike walled adobe compound just up Kit Carson Road from the plaza. The former home and studio of famous Taos artist E. Martin Hennings dates from the early part of the 20th century and is listed on the national and state historic registries. The five rooms are separate from the main house.

Bed-and-Breakfasts: $150 and Up

In town on the corner of Los Pandos and Cordoba, **Casa de las Chimeneas,** 505/758-4777, is a quiet little hacienda-style inn. Each of the four guest rooms has a bath, fireplace, and private entrance to the patio/garden, and the inn is decorated throughout in classic (and classy) New Mexico fashion. Breakfast specialties include blue-

Alma del Monte Bed-and-Breakfast, Taos

corn pancakes and *huevos rancheros* with green chile. Write P.O. Box 5303, Taos, NM 87571

Among the suggested bed-and-breakfasts outside town are the **Adobe and Pines Inn,** 505/751-0947 or 800/723-8267, which is just south of town at Mile Marker 41 in Ranchos de Taos and which has a reputation for warm hospitality and gourmet breakfasts. Write P.O. Box 837, Ranchos de Taos, NM 87557.

The **Alma del Monte,** in Arroyo Seco en route to Taos Ski Valley, 505/776-2721 or 800/273-7203, has gorgeously appointed rooms, part of the beautiful adobe and terra-cotta-tiled main house, each with its own whirlpool bathtub and outside access. Write P.O. Box 1434, Taos, NM 87571, or check the website: www.AlmaDelMonteB-B.com/spirit.

Just down the road from the Alma del Monte is the **Cottonwood Inn,** 505/776-5826 or 800/324-7120, with eight huge rooms in a remodeled two-story pueblo-style adobe built in the 1940s. One of the rooms has a whirlpool. Write State Rt. 230, HCR 74, Box 24609, El Prado-Taos, NM 87529.

The **Salsa de Salto,** 505/776-2422 or 800/530-3097, also en route to Taos Ski Valley, is a beautiful adobe-style house on a sprawling lot with breathtaking vistas of Mt. Wheeler and the Taos Plateau. Amenities include a tennis court, large pool, and hot tub.

The restored 1920s-era **San Geronimo Lodge,** 505/751-3776 or 800/894-4119, occupies 2.5 fruit-treed acres five miles east of Taos Plaza. Originally built as a home for socialite Clara Witt, the adobe lodge has served through the years as a popular gathering place and a venue for weddings, dances, and family reunions. Write 216M Paseo del Pueblo Norte, Suite 167, Taos, NM 87571.

Camping and RVing

If you're coming to Taos in the summer and want to spend some time outside and save some money on accommodations, you're in luck. The area is full of campgrounds. On the road to Taos Ski Valley (Highway 150), you'll find several small creekside spots with picnic tables and fire pits. **Lower Hondo** (pit toilets), **Cuchilla de Media** (running water), **Cuchilla,** and **Upper Cuchilla** are all free. Watch for the signs.

East of Taos, on Highway 64 to Angel Fire, you'll find **El Nogal, La Vinateria, Las Petacas,** and **Capulin** national forest campgrounds—all $4 and within 15 minutes of the plaza. For more information on camping in Carson National Forest, phone 505/758-6200.

South of Taos, you'll find good riverside camping at **Orilla Verde National Recreation Area.** To get there, drive south through Ranchos de Taos, then west on Highway 570.

At **Taos Valley RV Park,** south of town in Ranchos de Taos, 505/758-4469, sites with hookups are about $22, including showers. Turn east off Highway 68 onto Este Es Road at the Rio Grande Ace Hardware.

FOOD

Taos is one of the state's best towns for eating out, and the options vary from burrito wagons to high-class, linen-napkin-type, break-out-the-Visa-card dining establishments. Either way, or anyplace in between, you won't go hungry, and whether you're getting ready to head out for a day of exploring, skiing, or shopping, or whether you're relaxing afterward, you'll find a restaurant in Taos to satisfy. At least I always do—which is why I always manage to put on a few pounds whenever I pass through.

Start Me Up

One place guaranteed to get your Taos morning off to a grand start is **Michael's Kitchen,** on Paseo del Pueblo Norte, 505/758-4178. This extremely popular coffee shop and bakery serves a huge array of breakfasts, including pastries, banana breads, pancakes (nearly 20 different kinds), waffles, omelettes, steak and eggs, and *huevos rancheros.* Breakfast prices run $4–10. Michael's is also open for lunch and dinner, serving salads, burgers, and Mexican dishes. For a cappuccino or *caffe latte* jumpstart, stop by the **Bent Street Deli and Cafe,** across from the Bent Museum, 505/758-5787, where you can grab a fresh-baked bran muffin (or full breakfast) and read the morning paper while watching plaza folks—merchants and tourists alike—dosing on caffeine to better face the day. The deli also serves lunch and dinner; the deli specializes in exotic cheeses, while dinners include seafood, pastas, and salads ($8–16). Another good place for espressos and pastries is **Caffe Tazza,** at 122 Kit Carson across from the plaza, 505/758-8706.

Mexican and New Mexican Food

As in Santa Fe, most restaurants in Taos manage to find at least some room on their menus for Mexican and New Mexican food, or at least food with a Mexican or New Mexican twist—ever try green-chile pizza?

The locals are gonna have my hide for this—they don't want their secret out—but I gotta say it: The best food for the best price in town is at **Fred's Place,** 332 Paseo del Pueblo Sur, 505/758-0514. Here, heaping servings of burritos, tamales, and enchiladas—topped with delicious chile salsas—run all of $8 or $9 .Fred's is open for dinner only and closed Sunday. Plan to wait 15–20 minutes for a table, but plan to be glad you did.

Other places to find good Southwestern food are **Orlando's New Mexican Cafe,** 1114 Paseo del Pueblo Norte, 505/751-1450, and **Jacquelina's,** 1541 Paseo del Pueblo Sur, 505/751-0399.

For something good, quick, and entirely unfancy, try **Mante's Chow Cart,** 402 Paseo del Norte, 505/758-3632, where a delicious burrito will set you back two or three bucks and combo plates run $4–6. Mante's is open for breakfast, lunch, and dinner and also serves traditional American food, including pancakes, burgers, and fries.

But I'm Tired of Burritos!

A true Taos classic—pricey but worth it—is **Doc Martin's,** in the Taos Inn, 125 Paseo del Pueblo Norte, 505/758-1977. Here, you soak in the historic atmosphere and local color and dine on continental or traditional Southwestern cuisine, with entrées running $12–26. Lunch and dinner are served daily.

One of my favorites is the lively **Trading Post Cafe,** 4179 Hwy. 68, just south of town in Ranchos de Taos, 505/758-5089. Here you'll find a wide range of prices and types of food, from salads and pastas in the $8 range to roast duck, lamb chops, and fresh fish running to $22. The horseshoe-shaped bar wraps around the kitchen, and its high stools are perfect for watching the chefs in action, as well as the action in the dining room itself. Just down the road is **Joseph's Table,** 4167 Hwy. 68, 505/751-4512. This is a small, intimate restaurant (you have to walk through the kitchen to get to the dining room) with a daily-changing menu, often featuring lamb, beef, duck, vegetarian lasagna, and fish. Entrées run $14–26. It's open weekdays for lunch, Tuesday–Sunday for dinner. Another high-end restaurant popular among locals is **Lambert's,** 309 Paseo del Pueblo Sur, 505/758-1009, serving contemporary continental and American cuisine; entrées, including lasagna, lamb, and beef, are in the $10–22 range.

For excellent steaks and stunning dining-room vistas, try the **Stakeout Grill and Bar,** four miles south of Ranchos de Taos on Highway 68, 505/758-2042; pastas, salads, beef, and seafood dishes run about $15–25.

Right next to Taos plaza is the **Apple Tree Restaurant,** 123 Bent St., 505/758-1900, where curry, lamb, steaks, and New Mexican specials are $10–20. The Apple Tree, in an old home with several small dining rooms (some with only one table), offers an excellent Sunday brunch.

At **Eske's Brew Pub,** 106 de Gorges Ln., behind the parking lot at the corner of Kit Carson and Paseo del Pueblo Norte, 505/758-1517, you can sip a brewed-on-the-premises ale and listen to live music on the patio outside. The pub also serves salads, burgers, green-chile stew, and sandwiches. Dinners run $6–12.

For what many swear is the "best pizza in town," try **The Outback in Taos,** 505/758-3112, where you can also get sandwiches and choose from an excellent beer selection.

Farmers' Market

Beginning in midsummer and running through October, the Taos Farmers' Market offers locally grown fresh produce, most of it grown organically. Depending on the time of the season, you can pick up tomatoes, chiles, chokecherries, apples, apricots, potatoes, pickles, and fresh herbs. The market is in the parking lot of the Taos

County Courthouse complex in the 400 block of Paseo del Pueblo Sur. For more information, phone the Taos County Agricultural Extension office at 505/758-3982.

RECREATION

Though best known for its world-class Alpine ski resort less than a half hour from town, as well as for several others not much farther away, Taos is also the gateway to some of the finest fishing, hiking, cycling, and white-water rafting in the state. As soon as Taos Ski Valley shuts down its lifts, outdoor-loving Taoseños pack away their stretch pants and pull on their shorts—from late spring until Thanksgiving the warm mountain sun shines on Taos, and those who get outside to enjoy it inevitably feel just a little bit more alive.

Skiing

Mention the word Taos to any downhill skier in the country, and she'll immediately perk up her ears. Tell her you've skied the mountain's trees and steep chutes or that you've bashed the bumps on famous Al's Run, and you'll have earned her respect. Known throughout the ski world for its high percentage of advanced and expert skiing, Taos Ski Valley is simply one of the best ski resorts on the planet. Period.

© STEPHEN METZGER

Taos Ski Valley

Not to imply that Taos is strictly an advanced skier's mountain. It's not. Though 51 percent of the mountain is designated expert, there's plenty of beginner (24 percent) and intermediate skiing (25 percent) as well. In fact, one of the area's claims to fame is its "Learn-to-Ski-Better-Weeks," when skiers of all levels enjoy lessons every day of their stay. Talk to skiers who've been through the program, and you'll hear them praise it without reservation. They'll tell you it's why they return, year after year.

The brainchild of ski-industry legend and United States Ski Hall-of-Famer Ernie Blake, Taos Ski Valley sits at the end of a box canyon deep in the Sangre de Cristo Mountains and rises from its base at 9,207 feet to its 11,819-foot peak. Eleven lifts (including four quads and a triple) spoke out over the sprawling 1,094 acres of wide-open bowls, narrow trails, and gentle slopes. You could spend entire seasons exploring Taos Ski Valley. And if that's not enough, several other ski areas lie nearby, including Angel Fire and Red River, which have joined Taos Ski Valley in offering an interchangeable ski pass that also includes discounts at many of the local ski and sports shops. For information, contact the individual resorts at website taoswebb.com/ski3.

At the base of the lifts is a small alpine village with a handful of Old World-type lodges, as well as a few recently built condominium complexes. Keep in mind that lodging rates here vary widely based on season, with winter holidays being the most pricy. A couple of favorites among returning Taos skiers are **Thunderbird Lodge,** 505/776-2280 or 800/776-2279, and **Hotel St. Bernard,** 505/776-2251, both walking distance to the lifts. Both offer nightly rates as well as weeklong packages that include lift tickets, lessons, and meals. **Kandahar Condominiums,** 505/776-2226 or 800/756-2226, is the closest lodging to the lifts, and you can literally ski to your front door. Another favorite is **Austing Haus,** 505/776-2649 or 800/748-2932. Be forewarned: it's not cheap to set yourself up in one of these lodging-meal-skiing package deals (they start at about $700 per person), but you'd be hard-pressed to find a better ski week.

One of Taos Ski Valley's newer lodges is the **Inn at Snakedance,** 505/776-2277 or 800/322-9815, which opened in late 1993. The **Amizette Inn,** 1.5 miles down the road from the ski valley, 505/776-2451, offers rooms at slightly more affordable rates ($100–150).

Most of the lodges and hotels in Taos Ski Valley include meals in their package plans, and most skiers staying in the valley "eat in." With reservations, however, the restaurants at most of the lodges do serve meals to nonguests. In addition, if you do happen to find yourself still in the valley after a day of skiing (maybe, say, after lingering too long in the bar at the ski resort . . .), stop in at the Thunderbird Lodge, where on winter evenings in January you can round out your day in the lounge enjoying the music of the annual January Jazz Festival.

To get to Taos Ski Valley, take Highway 68 north through Taos and watch for a sign on your right. Shuttles run regularly between the Taos airport and Taos Ski Valley. Note: If you're driving, be sure to carry chains. Even when the streets are dry and clear in town, the road to the ski valley can be 10 inches deep in snow.

For more information, write Taos Ski Valley, Inc., Taos Ski Valley, NM 87525, or phone 505/776-2291. For information on lodging, phone 800/992-SNOW (800/992-7669; on-slope) or 800/821-8437 (in town). For snow conditions, phone 505/776-2961.

Hiking

You'll find plenty of excellent hiking in the mountains around Taos, particularly in Carson National Forest. For starters, head up the road to Taos Ski Valley. Several marked trails, including one to Wheeler Peak, begin at the roadside. Most of them are just below the ski area. For maps and information on degrees of difficulty, contact the national forest office in Taos at 505/758-6200. You'll also find lots of great hiking trails at Wild Rivers Recreation Area north of town.

In addition, **El Nogal Nature Trail** near the plaza is perfect for families. Take Kit Carson Road about two miles east and watch for the sign on the right.

Cycling

Cycling, both mountain biking and touring, is extremely popular in Taos. In-shape roadies will enjoy the winding 20-mile workout up to Taos Ski Valley (not to mention the cruise back down). Traffic is minimal, and the aspens, pines, and firs, as well as the creek trickling along the road, are a bonus. Mountain bikers will have field days on the dirt roads through the national forest (call the ranger's office for information and restrictions). For more information on cycling in Taos, stop by **Gearing Up,** 129 Paseo del Pueblo Sur, 505/751-0365.

Rafting

Rolling through the roiling white water of the Rio Grande is one of the most popular diversions among Taos visitors, and several companies offer a variety of trips—from short, half-day scenic floats to serious three-day expeditions. For information, prices, and reservations, call **Big River Raft Trips,** 505/758-9711; **Far Flung Adventures,** 505/758-2628 or 800/359-2627, website: www.farflung.com; **Los Rios River Runners,** 505/776-8854; **Native Suns Adventures,** 505/758-9342; or **New Wave Rafting Co.,** 505/984-1444 or 800/984-1444.

Riding

Several companies in the Taos area offer horseback riding—rentals as well as lessons and group rides. Among them are **Rio Grande Stables,** in Taos Ski Valley, 505/776-5913; and **Shadow Mountain Ranch,** 505/758-7732.

For an only-in-Taos experience, check out **Taos Indian Horse Ranch,** which offers rides on Taos Pueblo, otherwise off-limits to the public. In addition to individual and group rides, you can also take riding lessons and learn to work with draft horses. In the winter, you can take sleigh rides. Rates start at about $40 for 45-minute rides. For a full brochure, write P.O. Box 3019, Taos, NM 87571, or phone 505/758-3212 or 800/659-3210.

Fishing

Fly casters find the Taos-area streams ideal for tricking wily trout with a well-tied Royal Coachman or caddis fly. The Rio Hondo paralleling the road to Taos Ski Valley is a favorite, as is the Rio Fernando east of town on Highway 64. You can arrange Taos-area and other northern New Mexico fishing trips through **Los Rios Anglers,** 800/748-1707, or the **Willows Inn,** 505/758-2558 or 800/525-TAOS (800/525-8267). Costs for equipment, transportation, instruction, and inside tips on the "hot spots" usually start at about $150 per day for one person, with a second angler adding $50.

Summer Chairlift Rides

Summer visitors to Taos Ski Valley can see the area as skiers do in the winter: by chairlift. Ride to the top of the resort's Al's Run for views of the surrounding mountains and chances to see bighorn sheep, elk, deer, and other wildlife. Rates are about $12 for adults, discounts for kids 12 and under. For information, phone 505/776-2291.

OTHER PRACTICALITIES

Entertainment

If you're looking to hear some good live music, check out the lounge at the **Sagebrush Inn,** 505/758-2254. Chances are you'll get to hear one of Taos's hot country bands. In the winter, the fire's always roaring, and the hot brandies go down awfully nice. The lounges at the **Holiday Inn,** 505/758-4444, **Kachina Lodge,** 505/758-2275, and **Ramada Inn,** 505/758-2900, all offer live music, as does the **Adobe Bar** at the Historic Taos Inn, 505/758-2233; call for details. **Tim's Chile Connection,** on Ski Valley Road, 505/776-8787, also features live music—to go with its sangria, margaritas, and microbrews.

Taos bonus: Taos is home to singer/songwriter Michael Martin Murphey, who often performs for benefits and has played local lounges often through the years. Who knows? You might get lucky and hear a big-name act in a small-club setting.

Annual Events

In Taos, as in Santa Fe and Albuquerque, something's going on almost every weekend. For what's happening, pick up a copy of the *Taos News* (published every Thursday), which lists events, exhibits, and shows. Among the most popular annual events: **Taos Spring Arts Celebration,** a three-week extravaganza with art shows, gallery openings, poetry readings, storytelling, music and dancing, workshops and demonstrations (late May through mid-June); **Taos School of Music Summer Music Festival** (mid-June through early August); **Taos Fall Arts Celebration; Yuletide in Taos,** with special tours, luminarias, music, and other Christmas celebrations (December). In addition, Taos Pueblo hosts several annual festivals and other events, including **Turtle and Deer Dances** in January and a large **powwow** in July.

For more information, contact the Taos County Chamber of Commerce at 505/758-3873 or 800/732-8267.

Shopping

Taos is probably second only to Santa Fe in its per-capita number of gift shops and galleries. In the central plaza area, you'll find the usual range of New Mexico souvenirs and artwork—whether you're looking for a cheap memento or investment-quality sculpture, you'll find it here. Among Taos's locally crafted products are Indian blankets and other weavings, Indian drums and moccasins, paintings and sculpture, jewelry and furniture. A classic and inexpensive souvenir is a *ristra* (string of chiles), which will add color to your kitchen and flavor your cooking for a year or more. Most of the museums have gift shops where you can pick up souvenirs and knickknacks, as well as high-quality art. In addition, you should allow some time to stroll the shops on the plaza and on Bent Street (from cookware shops to bookstores to boutiques) and to take a stroll up Kit Carson Road, where small galleries and shops are scattered along the boardwalk, squeezed between plumbing-supply stores and dry cleaners—which makes them seem a little less tourist-targeted than those near the plaza.

Both north and south of town, you'll see a

number of "trading posts," where you can pick up gifts and souvenirs, from pottery (much of it imported from Mexico) and *ristras* to blankets, rugs, leather goods, T-shirts, and key chains. **Camino Real Imports,** 505/758-7999, about two miles north of the central plaza, is a fascinating place to wander through, if only to marvel at the amazing range of inventory—from woven rugs and throws to rubber tomahawks and your-name-here coffee mugs.

Information and Services

The Taos County **Chamber of Commerce,** 505/758-3873 or 800/732-TAOS (800/732-8267), operates a popular tourist stop and information center on the main drag at the south end of town (junction of Highways 68 and 64). Information is available on everything from Indian dances to ski resorts in the Taos area and throughout northern New Mexico, and you can also book sight-seeing tours. In addition, you'll find an information booth on the plaza with maps, brochures, and transportation schedules. Hours are Monday–Saturday 10 A.M.–4:30 P.M. For online information, visit the website: www.taoschamber.com.

For one of the area's best selections of books on the Southwest and American Indians, check out **Moby Dickens Bookshop,** 23 Bent St., 505/758-3050, and **Taos Bookshop,** 114 Kit Carson Rd., 505/758-3733. For tips and advice on hiking, cross-country skiing, and other recreation, stop in at **Taos Mountain Outfitters,** 114 S. Plaza (on Taos Plaza).

Taos's full-service hospital, Holy Cross Hospital, is south of the plaza at 1397 Weimer Rd. (east side of road), 505/758-8883. Call the Taos Police Department at 505/758-2216, the state police in Taos at 505/758-8878, and the Taos County sheriff at 505/758-3361.

Transportation

Commercial passenger airline service to Taos is limited to winter only, with **Rio Grande Air** offering two flights per day on weekends; the airline offers charter service the rest of the year. In addition, several local companies offer ground transportation between Taos and the international airport in Albuquerque. Among them: **Twin Hearts Express,** 505/751-1201, and **Faust's Transportation,** 505/758-3410. Twin Hearts and Faust's also offer tours and shuttles to Taos-area attractions, including Taos Ski Valley, Red River, and Angel Fire.

Greyhound and **Texas, New Mexico, and Oklahoma Coaches** offer bus service to Taos; phone 505/758-1144 for schedules and information.

Note: Although you can get to Taos by plane or bus, you're probably not going to want to be here without your own rig—the town's just too spread out. If you're coming in from out of the area, I'd recommend renting a car in Albuquerque. You'll have much more freedom, not only to explore Taos itself, but the surrounding countryside as well.

Hertz, 505/758-1668 or 800/654-3131, and **Dollar,** 505/758-3500, both offer local car rental.

The Enchanted Circle

The Enchanted Circle is an 85-mile loop that takes you into the mountains east of Taos, past Angel Fire, along the west shore of Eagle Nest Lake, over the gorgeous 9,854-foot Red River Pass, down into the resort town of Red River, past New Mexico's shrine to one of its favorite authors, D. H. Lawrence, and back onto the Taos Plateau. Circling 13,161-foot Wheeler Peak, the highest point in New Mexico, and encompassing the Taos Indian Reservation, the route rewards you with stunning mountain scenery, broad vistas of distant valleys, and gateways to some of the finest recreation areas in the state, including three Alpine ski resorts.

ANGEL FIRE

Angel Fire is a resort complex about 25 miles east of Taos. Built in 1966, originally as a ski area, the resort has recently begun to court the summer outdoor crowd as well, with a golf course, large tennis facilities, and a small lake

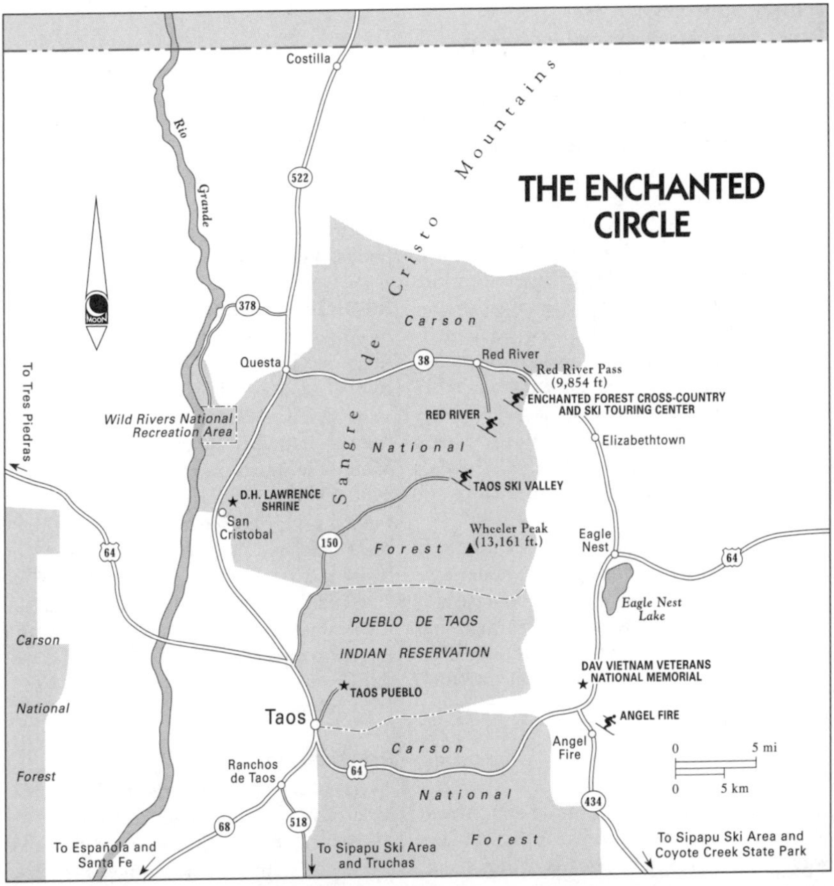

for fishing. The resort caters largely to area property owners, and real estate is as big a business here as skiing.

The first few years of Angel Fire's existence were tough, with the resort going in and out of bankruptcy several times. However, in 1995, an investment group from Texas bought the resort and nearly immediately pledged $40 million in upgrades and improvements. One of the first was a high-speed detachable quad chair—the Chile Express—at the ski area, first opened in the winter of 1996–97. Other plans include more lifts and trails, as well as improved lodging and other base facilities.

BOB RACE

Winter Sports

Aimed primarily at beginning and intermediate skiers, Angel Fire's quad chair and four double chairs, plus a surface lift, service a 2,050-foot vertical drop, and many of the long, gently sloping trails lead literally to the edge of town—some of the condos offer ski-in/ski-out convenience. In addition, Angel Fire aggressively courts snowboarders, with a specifically designated snowboard park as well as many annual snowboard races and other events. Angel Fire offers ski and snowboarding lessons (with a special program aimed at youngsters), equipment rental and sales, day care, and NASTAR and pro racing. You can also rent equipment at a number of shops in town, including **Bumps!,** 40 N. Angel Fire Rd., 505/377-3490; **Mountain Sports,** 3405 Centro Plaza, Hwy. 434, 505/377-3490; and **Ski Tech,** in the Village Center on North Angel Fire Road, 505/377-3213.

Angel Fire also participates in the Enchanted Circle Ski Pass, an interchangeable, money-saving lift ticket good also at Taos and Red River.

Angel Fire's **Nordic Center,** at the Angel Fire Country Club, has beginner and intermediate trails and offers lessons and equipment rental. All-day trail passes are about $10, and lessons start at about $30 (three-hour group lesson).

Also at the base of the ski area is a small tubing hill open evenings only (lighted).

Finally, Angel Fire hosts the annual "World Shovel Race Championships" each February, when participants sit on shovels with the handles protruding through their legs. Racers have been clocked at faster than 60 mph. Events include fastest, fastest modified shovel, and "wackiest shovel."

For more information on skiing Angel Fire, write Drawer B, Angel Fire, NM 87710; or for information, central reservations, or snow reports, phone 800/633-7463.

Summer in Angel Fire

In summer, you'll find an 18-hole golf course at Angel Fire, in addition to well-maintained tennis courts (use of which is $8 an hour). Nearby is some of the best mountain biking in the state; you can rent bikes and get tips on local trails at **Mountain Sports** on Highway 434, 505/377-3490. Other summer recreation includes whitewater rafting, horseback riding, and hot-air ballooning, and sight-seeing from the ski area's chairlifts. For information phone 800/633-7463.

In addition, Angel Fire hosts the annual **Music from Angel Fire** classical music festival (mid-August to early September). Ticket and schedule information is available at 505/377-3233 or 505/758-4667.

Practicalities

There's plenty of lodging at Angel Fire, although it's largely limited to condos and property management companies. The largest and closest lodging to the slopes is at the **Angel Fire Resort**

Hotel, 505/377-6401 or 800/633-7463, literally at the base of the lifts—ski packages available. For a complete listing check out the website: www.angelfireresort.com.

Zebadiah's Restaurant in Angel Fire, 505/377-6358, has a soup-and-salad bar and serves burgers, sandwiches, steaks, chicken, and Mexican food for lunch and dinner daily 11 A.M.–9 P.M. and breakfast 7–10 A.M. **The Early Bird Café and Bakery,** in the village at 3420 Hwy. 434, 505/377-3992, is a little deli-bakery-ice-cream counter that serves breakfast and lunch daily except Tuesday. **Aldo's,** 505/377-6401, next to the base chairlift, serves salads, soups, pastas, New Mexican food, and steaks in the $8–22 range.

Angel Fire Information

For more information on Angel Fire lodging, restaurants, and activities, write the Angel Fire **Chamber of Commerce,** P.O. Box 547, Angel Fire, NM 87710, or call 505/377-6353 or 800/446-8117. You can also get online information at website: www.angelfireresort.com.

VIETNAM VETERANS NATIONAL MEMORIAL

In sharp contrast to the golf carts and slick condos at Angel Fire, the Disabled American Veterans memorial to American GIs killed in Vietnam stands stark and strong on a hillside across the valley. The less said here the better, probably, as your visit is subject to your experience with the war. Suffice it to say that the memorial, built by a grieving father to a son killed overseas, will bring lumps to the throats of the most hardened cynics and tears to the eyes of the rest—no matter which side of the conflict you stood (or stand) on. Simply not to be missed. It's open daily 8 A.M.–5 P.M. No admission charge. For information, write P.O. Box 608, Angel Fire, NM 87710, or phone 505/377-6900.

EAGLE NEST

Charles Springer built Eagle Nest Dam in the Moreno Valley in 1916 at the head of Cimarron Canyon, and the town of Eagle Nest (pop. 200) was established in 1920 (although it was originally called Therma and changed to Eagle Nest in 1935). The 78,800-acre privately owned lake provides irrigation for farmlands as far as 50 miles east, and it is immensely popular for trout fishing, with tournaments and competitions held throughout the year. Lately, Eagle Nest has become a favorite of local windsurfers, and in the winter the area is popular for cross-country skiing, showshoeing, ice fishing, and snowmobiling. Several RV campgrounds and tourist cabins dot the shoreline.

Practicalities

You can get motel-type lodging in Eagle Nest at the **Laguna Vista Lodge,** 51 Therma, 505/377-6522, **Cottonwood Lodge,** 51 Therma, 505/377-6522, while the **Moore Rest Inn,** 715 East Hwy. 64, 505/377-6813, and the **Cottonwood Inn,** 124 East Therma, 505/377-3382, offer large suites and apartments for groups and longer stays. All $50–100.

Golden Eagle RV Park, 505/377-6188, has full hookups and showers for about $20.

Laguna Vista Restaurant, 505/377-6522, serves huge burgers for $7–9 and Mexican plates for $8–12; there's also a small salad bar.

For more information on Eagle Nest, write the **chamber of commerce,** P.O. Box 322, Eagle Nest, NM 87718, or phone 505/377-2420.

Elizabethtown

As you drive up out of the Moreno Valley toward Red River Pass, watch on the left for the crumbling remains of Elizabethtown. Founded in 1865, the town at one time had five stores, two hotels, a half dozen saloons, and several dance halls. E-town, as it was known, was destroyed by fire in 1903. Today, a few stone walls stand above the valley floor, in summer a colorful riot of wildflowers, in winter a quiet snowscape.

RED RIVER

The steep descent down Red River Pass into the town of Red River (pop. 400; elev. 8,750 feet) is marked by spectacularly dramatic scenery—

ANSWERS TO THE NEW MEXICO QUIZ

Following are the answers to the quiz that appears in the On the Road chapter.

1) Though archaeologists speculate that people may have passed through the area as early as 20,000 years ago, there is conclusive evidence they were here at least 8,000 years ago.
2) "Anasazi" is a Navajo word that translates to Enemies of Our Ancestors (not The Ancient Ones, as some sources claim).
3) The Anasazi pueblos had been abandoned by the end of the 13th century. No one knows for certain why they left. Some of the theories: the Athapascan Indians (Navajo and Apache) arrived and ran them out; a severe drought drove them to greener pastures; disease decimated the people; the pueblos became overcrowded; the people overfarmed and exhausted the land. It's generally accepted that the Anasazi were the ancestors of the modern-day Pueblo tribes, including the Hopi of Arizona.
4) A kiva is a round, underground (or partly underground) adjunct to a pueblo used for ceremonial gatherings and symbolic of the womb of the earth.
5) Mimbres pottery is unique in that when a piece was no longer used, it was ceremoniously "killed" by breaking a hole in its base.
6) Though the first Spanish probably passed through what is now New Mexico sometime in the early 1530s, the first explorers didn't arrive until 1539. Francisco Vásquez de Coronado led the first army to New Mexico in 1540. The first Spanish were looking for gold and for pagans, whom they would convert to Christianity.
7) Santa Fe was founded in the winter of 1607.
8) In 1680, the Pueblo Indians ran the Spanish out of Santa Fe and occupied the city for 12 years.
9) New Mexico was under Mexican rule for 27 years, from 1821, when Mexico won its independence from Spain, until 1848, when the United States and Mexico signed the Treaty of Guadalupe Hidalgo.
10) In March of 1864, the U.S. Army forced a large group of "uncooperative" Indians, mostly Navajo, to walk 300 miles from Fort Wingate, near Gallup, to Bosque Redondo, near Fort Sumner, where 8,000 were imprisoned.
11) Fort Union was built in 1851 to protect travelers on the Santa Fe Trail.
12) New Mexico was admitted to the Union on January 6, 1912.
13) The world's first atomic bomb was detonated near Alamogordo on July 16, 1945.
14) New Mexico is the fifth-largest state, behind Alaska, Texas, California, and Montana.
15) New Mexico's highest point is 13,161-foot Mt. Wheeler, near Taos; the lowest point is 2,840 feet, in the southeastern desert, near the Texas border.
16) The Sandia Mountains begin on the northeastern city limits of Albuquerque. Their highest point is 10,678 feet above sea level. Though perhaps apocryphal, one story has it that when the Spanish arrived in the area, they thought that the squash the Indians were growing was watermelon, sandia in Spanish.
17) The headwaters of the Rio Grande are in the Colorado Rockies.
18) Mexico's Chihuahua and Sonora Deserts both sprawl over into southern New Mexico.
19) Grant, Harding, Lincoln, McKinley, Roosevelt.

20) Roughly a million and a half people live in New Mexico; a third of them live in the Albuquerque area.
21) In addition to the 19 pueblos, there are two Apache reservations and parts of the Ute and Navajo reservations in New Mexico.
22) The Pueblo people speak five distinct languages.
23) James Coburn and Kris Kristofferson played the leads in *Pat Garrett and Billy the Kid.* Bob Dylan had a small part and contributed "Knockin' on Heaven's Door" to the score.
24) In the early 20th century, Maria Martinez, of San Ildefonso Pueblo, watched archaeologists unearth fragments of her ancestors' work. At a young age she began to duplicate it and ultimately became one of the Southwest's preeminent potters.
25) Albuquerque author Tony Hillerman has written a series of whodunits whose detectives are Navajo Indians. The books are exhaustively researched and impeccably precise in their details, and they have earned Hillerman the Navajo Tribe's Special Friend Award.
26) D. H. Lawrence lived on Kiowa Ranch, outside Taos.
27) Georgia O'Keeffe lived a large part of her life in Abiquiu, where the landscapes informed and inspired her work.
28) You can stay in the Ronald Reagan Room at the El Rancho Hotel in Gallup.
29) In Taos and Santa Fe.
30) Santa Rosa's Blue Hole is famous statewide for diving.
31) Madame Butterfly, from the Puccini opera, would most likely be encountered in Santa Fe, at the world-famous Santa Fe Opera, which performs every summer.
32) Carlsbad Caverns in the southern part of the state attracts 700,000 visitors annually.
33) Peanuts.
34) Acoma Pueblo sits atop a 357-foot-high mesa, whose steep walls at one time served to protect the tribe from invaders.
35) The Atomic Energy Museum is in Albuquerque near Old Town, where it awaits its new building at Balloon Fiesta Park; it had spent 32 years at Kirtland Air Force Base.
36) The roadrunner.
37) New Mexico's best chile peppers are grown in the far southern part of the state in the area around Las Cruces and Hatch. The best time to buy them is in the fall, beginning in early September.

What Your Score Means

1–4 wrong: *Muy bueno.* You're a bona fide New Mexico expert. Roast up some Hatch chiles and pour yourself a margarita.

5–8 wrong: You're well on your way to expertise. Take a balloon ride over Albuquerque and spend the next 12 Sundays in bed reading the *Albuquerque Journal, New Mexico Magazine, Moon Handbooks New Mexico,* and all the Tony Hillerman and John Nichols you can get your hands on.

9–12 wrong: Well, you've still got a ways to go. If I were your teacher I'd recommend holding you back.

13 or more wrong: Downright shameful. Go directly to Texas. Do not pass Ruidoso.

mountainside groves of aspens, pines, and spruces mixed together to form a mottled blanket of deep green. Used as a recreation site since the late 19th century, when miners from Elizabethtown came over the hill to the cool waters of the river, the little year-round resort town of Red River caters to skiers, anglers, sightseers, and hikers venturing into the Carson National Forest and the Sangre de Cristo Mountains.

Skiing

Red River Ski Area, built in 1958, is the town's main draw, though cross-country skiing and backcountry snowmobile touring are becoming increasingly popular, as are various summer activities, from mountain biking to four-wheeling to fishing. The ski resort has six chairlifts, including four doubles and two triples, and about two-thirds of the 57 runs are designated beginner to intermediate. On-mountain facilities include children's and adults' ski schools, snowmaking, and equipment rental and sales. For more information on skiing Red River, write P.O. Box 900, Red River, NM 87558, or phone 505/754-2223.

Three and a half miles east of Red River, **Enchanted Forest Cross-Country and Ski Touring Center** offers 35 kilometers of ski trails and 11 kilometers of snowshoeing trails on 1,200 acres of varied terrain, 90 percent of which is groomed regularly. This highly regarded Nordic ski area also provides ski rentals and lessons (skating, ski-mountaineering, and Telemarking). Write P.O. Box 521, Red River, NM 87558, or phone 505/754-2374 for more information.

Other Red River Attractions

When the snow melts and the slopes shut down, you'll still find a lot to do in Red River. In fact, you can take summer scenic tours on the ski area's chairlifts. Carson National Forest offers excellent hiking opportunities, with trails wandering throughout the Red River area (the chamber of commerce will supply you with maps of the nearby trails). For information on fishing in the Red River area, pick up a chamber-published *Fishing Guide,* which will lead you to nearby streams and high lakes. **New Mexico Adventure Company,** 505/754-2437, has two offices in town (one in the Lifts West hotel lobby, the other on the main drag in town) and can set you up with a variety of activities—white-water trips, jeep tours, mountain-bike rentals, and hot-air balloon rides. Check out the company's website: www.redriver1.com.

Several of Red River's hotels and lounges feature live music, and the Red River Inn stages melodrama throughout the summer. Phone 505/754-2930 for information and/or reservations.

Practicalities

Red River offers more than two dozen different lodges, motels, and condo complexes from which to choose, and there's really not a loser among them. Writing the **Red River Chamber of Commerce,** P.O. Box 870, Red River, NM 87558, will get you a copy of the resort's visitors guide, which has complete descriptions and photos of the various accommodations; phone 800/348-6444. You can also get a complete list with individual lodge descriptions at website: redrivernm.com.

A particularly nice choice is **Riverside Lodge and Cabins,** 505/754-2252 or 800/432-9999, where you'll find both motel-type rooms and individual cabins (both with kitchenettes), as well as a nice kids' play area; the Riverside is right downtown, walking distance to the shops and other attractions. Also nice and within walking distance of the center of town is **Arrowhead Ski Lodge,** 505/754-2255; the Arrowhead also has apartments with kitchenettes, some of which sleep up to eight people. The **Ponderosa Lodge,** 200 W. Main, 505/754-2988 or 800/336-7787, offers nice rooms, some with kitchens. Motel rooms at all three run $50–100, and suites, cabins, and rooms with kitchenettes $75–150.

Lifts West Condominium and Resort Hotel, 201 W. Main, 505/754-2778 or 800/221-1859, is the area's largest hotel, with motel rooms and apartment-type units, as well a ski shop (with rentals), restaurant, heated pool, and two spas. Rates vary widely, depending on amenities, package options, and season

At **Roadrunner RV Campground** just outside of town, 505/754-2286, sites with full hookups start at about $30 a night or $575 a month.

A popular chow house is **Texas Red's Steak-**

house and Saloon, 111 E. Main, 505/754-2964, where the steaks ($12–20) are legendary, and you can add your own touch to the casual decor by tossing your peanut shells on the floor. The **Redwood Cafe,** 210 E. Main, 505/754-2951, serves very good Mexican and American breakfasts ($3–8) and burgers, sandwiches, and Mexican plates, as well as barbecued ribs, sausage, and chicken, for lunch and dinner ($6–12).

When you get to Red River, be sure to stop by the chamber of commerce visitors center on the north side of the street. You'll find a huge array of literature on lodging, eating, and recreation in the Red River area.

Questa

West of Red River, Highway 38 winds through the lush Red River Canyon, then dead-ends into Highway 522 at Questa, where you'll head south to complete the Enchanted Circle loop. A farming community dating from the early 1800s, Questa (Hill or Slope) has been a molybdenum mining center since the first part of the 20th century—driving through will reveal the environmental havoc that mining has wreaked on the region.

TO COSTILLA

At Questa, you can leave the Enchanted Circle and head up Highway 522 to Costilla on the Colorado border, about 15 miles north. With 10,000-foot Ute Peak and the upper Rio Grande to the west and the Sangre de Cristo Mountains to the east, this road passes through some of New Mexico's most breathtaking scenery.

Wild Rivers National Recreation Area

Three miles north of Questa, Highway 378 circles back south down into the Rio Grande Gorge, where a recently established recreation area invites visitors. During the summer, the visitors center offers guided nature hikes every Saturday and Sunday at 10 A.M. and campfire programs Saturday evenings at 8:30 P.M.. Camping is $6 a night (running water and pit toilets, but no hookups). For information, phone the BLM at 505/758-8851.

SOUTH TO TAOS

D. H. Lawrence Shrine

On the east side of Highway 522 near San Cristobal, as you drop back onto the Taos Plateau, look for the sign to the D. H. Lawrence Shrine and Ranch. A six-mile dirt road winds up the side of Lobo Mountain to the ranch, where Lawrence and his wife, Frieda, spent a couple of years in the 1920s. Originally known as Kiowa Ranch, the property, which commands a stunning view of the Taos Plateau and upper Rio Grande Valley, today belongs to the University of New Mexico.

A short trail leads from the parking lot in front of the ranch house to a small shrine housing what are reputedly Lawrence's ashes (some biographers claim they're elsewhere) and French documents certifying his death. (Lawrence died in France in 1930, but Frieda had his remains shipped back to his beloved New Mexico.) Be sure to sign the guest book, and spend a few minutes perusing its back pages. People have come from around the world, and their messages of thanks to Lawrence—many with references to specific books and characters—are inspiring.

Resources

Glossary

abierto: Spanish for "open." If you see this on the door of a Mexican restaurant, there's at least a better-than-even chance the food'll be authentic—and good.

Anasazi: Navajo word describing the ancient settlers (about A.D. 1–1300) of the Four Corners and Rio Grande River Valley areas. Though the word is commonly translated as The Ancient Ones, many scholars insist the word is actually from "anaa," which means war, enemy, or discord, and "zaja," for ancestors—thus Anasazi, or Enemies of Our Ancestors.

bolo: Indian string tie, or "cowboy" tie, often decorated with a silver-and-turquoise slide

cantina: usually a small Mexican or New Mexican restaurant and bar, where folks come to talk and be with friends as much as to eat and drink

cerveza: beer. Highly recommended for washing down everything from chips and salsa to green-chile stew and tamales.

flan: baked caramel custard

frijoles: beans

frybread: large, flat floury bread often cooked over open fires and sold for a buck or so at roadside stands on New Mexico pueblos, particularly in the northern part of the state. Though the bread is associated with New Mexico Native Americans, it is not truly a "native" food at all; in fact, it developed after lard and other "staples" were introduced by the U.S. government in the late 19th century.

horno: beehive-shaped outdoor oven used by Spanish and Pueblo cooks, particularly for breads

huevos: eggs

kachina: usually refers to the Indians' kachina dolls, although in different contexts, kachinas are also thunderheads, spirits, and human dancers

kiva: round, underground, or at least partly underground, adjunct to an Indian pueblo, used for ceremonial gatherings and symbolic of the "womb of the Mother Earth"

llano: Spanish for "plain." You'll run across this a lot. "Llano Estacado," in eastern New Mexico, for example, means Staked Plain, and "Llano Seco" means Dry Plain.

luminaria: lanterns made from candles burning inside paper bags; a tradition in New Mexico at Christmastime, when hundreds line the streets of towns and pueblos. Known in northern New Mexico as *farolitos.*

menudo: tripe, which Mexicans claim is the ultimate hangover cure. "Menudo served daily" scribbled on a New Mexico restaurant's window or menu usually indicates quality and authenticity.

petroglyphs: ancient line carvings on rocks or cave walls, usually representing gods, people, animals, crops, or weather

pictographs: ancient paintings on rocks or cave walls

pueblo: 1) an apartment-type village built by ancient Southwest Indians; 2) "modern" Indian village or community; 3) (usually capitalized) an Indian of the ancient or modern pueblos

reservation: federally owned tract of land set aside for Indians, usually with its own sets of laws and regulations

ristras: the strings of chiles you see hanging from the vigas of adobe homes

rooster pull: an Indian game in which a rooster becomes the unwitting object of a tug-of-war competition between teams of players on horseback

sipapu: the symbolic hole in the center of a kiva, through which spirits pass between this world and the one on the "other side"

sopaipilla: a deep-fried, pillow-shaped, pastry-like dessert often served with honey: tear it open and squirt the honey inside. A perfect (and filling!) finale to any of the classic New Mexican or Mexican dinners, particularly a hot bowl of green-chile stew

tamale: spicy beef, chicken, or pork filling in a thick cornmeal-bread casing, usually wrapped in cornhusks and steamed

tortilla: thin, flat, crepelike cake made from corn or flour, the basis of many Mexican and New Mexican dishes

vigas: round, exposed beams jutting from the sides of adobe (and fake adobe) buildings

Suggested Reading

In 1987, when I first started seriously researching this book, there weren't all that many others to recommend. The last few years, however, have seen an explosion of books about the state, nearly all of them interesting and valuable to at least some degree. Shelves in New Mexico bookstores are packed with books on the state's history, culture, ecology, economy, and everything else imaginable, from hiking and mountain biking to cooking and bed-and-breakfasting. It would be impossible to list them all. I'd suggest, then, taking a look at the list I have assembled here—these are all top-notch publications—but allowing yourself plenty of time to browse in the bookstores you come across on your trip.

A word on out-of-print books: You'll notice that some of the books I've listed are out of print. Not to worry. Among the many parts of our lives that the Internet has changed is the availability of books. Rare and out-of-print titles are now just a website away, and they're often not as expensive as you might think. Unless you're looking for a signed first edition of *For Whom the Bell Tolls,* or something along those lines, out-of-print books are generally quite reasonable. My favorite site is **Bibliofind.com,** which was recently taken over by **Amazon.com.** Go to Bibliofind's website and type in the title and/or author you're looking for, and you'll get a list of books, with descriptions, conditions (VG = very good, for example), prices, and availability. Books are usually delivered within a couple of days of your ordering them. You can also go straight to Amazon.com, which now also includes out-of-print titles with information on how to get them.

History

Alberts, Don E. *Balloons and Bombers, Aviation in Albuquerque (1882–1945).* Albuquerque: Albuquerque Museum, 1988.

Baxter, John O. *Las Carneradas: Sheep Trade in New Mexico, 1700–1860.* Albuquerque: University of New Mexico Press, 1988. An exhaustive and rather academic study of the role of sheep in New Mexico, beginning with their use as a food staple for early Spanish explorers.

Beck, Warren A. *New Mexico, A History of Four Centuries.* Norman, OK: University of Oklahoma Press, 1971 (fourth printing). Exhaustive treatment of New Mexico's past, beginning with discussion of geology and working through the state's natives, Spanish invasion and rule, Indian wars, ranching and farming, and industry and transportation. One of the best histories available, although its publication date (1962) precludes examination of the state's modern technology, particularly the increased contracting in the computer field and the defense industry.

Bolton, Herbert. *Coronado: Knight of Pueblos and Plains.* New York: Whittlesey House (Division of McGraw-Hill Book Co., Inc.), and Albuquerque: University of New Mexico Press, 1949. Exhaustively researched account of Coronado's 16th-century expedition from Mexico through the Southwest. Winner of the Whittlesey House Southwestern Fellowship Award.

Duffus, R. L. *The Santa Fe Trail.* New York: Tudor Publishing Company, 1934. If you read this with the sophisticated demands of the 1990s, you're likely to think it somewhat melodramatic and overwritten, but if you allow yourself to sink into the past a bit, you'll find the prose lively and entertaining—and Duffus's coverage of the historic trail is fact-filled and fascinating. Maps and historical illustrations and photos.

Dumark, Judith Boyce, ed. *Essays in Twentieth-Century New Mexico History.* Albuquerque: University of New Mexico Press, 1994. Mostly academic look at issues of historical, social, and economical interest to the state.

Ellis, Richard N., ed. *New Mexico, Past and Present: A Historical Reader.* Albuquerque: University of New Mexico Press, 1971. This collection of scholarly essays, many originally from journals and historical reviews, discusses New Mexico from Spanish contact through the atomic bomb and modern-day Hispanic activism.

Fergusson, Erna. *New Mexico, A Pageant of Three Peoples.* Albuquerque: University of New Mexico Press, 1964. A wonderfully written and witty account of New Mexico's founding and of its three major cultures. The book is somewhat dated (1951) and out of print, but if you can lay your hands on a copy, you'll have a priceless resource.

Fergusson, Harvey. *Rio Grande.* New York: Alfred A. Knopf, 1936. A discussion of the Rio Grande's place in New Mexico's history, by one of the state's foremost men of letters.

Fierman, Floyd S. *Roots and Boots: From Crypto-Jew in New Spain to Community Leader in the Southwest.* Hoboken, NJ: KATV Publishing House, Inc., 1988. During the Spanish Inquisition, a large number of Jews fled Europe and were exiled to the New World, particularly what's now the American Southwest. New Mexico has a good-sized population of the descendants of that exodus. Fierman's book (along with *Roots and Boots'* forerunner, *Guts and Ruts,* 1985) tells their story, from their arrival, through their status as a "secret society," to modern times and their relative acceptance by non-Jews.

Gonzalez, Nancy L. *The Spanish-Americans of New Mexico: A Heritage of Pride.* Albuquerque: University of New Mexico Press, 1969. A somewhat academic study of New Mexico's people of Spanish descent, and a testimonial to their contributions.

Horgan, Paul. *Great River: The Rio Grande in North American History.* New York: Holt, Rinehart and Winston, 1968. A comprehensive and very readable account of four cultures—Indian, Spanish, Mexican, and Anglo—that have alternately clashed and coexisted in New Mexico.

Kadlec, Robert F., ed. *They "Knew" Billy the Kid.* Santa Fe: Ancient City Press, 1988. A collection of archival and well-annotated recollections by folks who claimed to have known the Kid. Kadlec's commentary helps readers discern between the authentic and the imaginary.

Lister, Florence, and Robert Lister. *Those Who Came Before.* Tucson: University of Arizona Press, 1983. A fascinating study of the Indians who lived in or passed through the Southwest, including Arizona, Colorado, New Mexico, and Utah. The Anasazi, Mogollon, and Hohokam cultures are examined in depth, as are the later Pueblo peoples. Beautiful color and black-and-white photos.

Murphy, Lawrence R. *Philmont: A History of New Mexico's Cimarron Country.* Albuquerque: University of New Mexico Press, 1972. Traces the history of this area (centered around Cimarron) from the days of prehistoric cave dwellers through the development of the Philmont Boy Scout Ranch in the 1940s and '50s.

Pearson, Jim Berry. *The Maxwell Land Grant.* Norman, OK: University of Oklahoma Press, 1961. A detailed look at the largest land grant in United States history.

Riley, Glenda. *Women and Indians on the Frontier, 1825–1915.* Albuquerque: University of New Mexico Press, 1985. A refreshingly unique look at the settling of the West. Riley argues that women were less likely to prejudge the natives than were men, and that women both greatly contributed to and were significantly liberated by westward expansion.

Roberts, Calvin A., and Susan A. Roberts. *New Mexico.* Albuquerque: University of New Mexico Press, 1988. An exhaustive history of the state, unique for its attention to lesser-known contributors and personalities and fresh angles on characters and stories already well known. Chock-full of facts, dates, and details.

Silverberg, Robert. *The Pueblo Revolt.* New York: Weybright and Talley, 1970. A look at the events leading to the famous 1680 revolt (beginning with Coronado's expedition in 1540), the 12 years of rebellion, and the aftermath.

Simmons, Marc. *Murder on the Santa Fe Trail: An International Incident, 1843.* El Paso: Texas Western Press, 1988. A true story of good guys, bad guys, politics, and murder.

Szasz, Ferenc Morton. *The Day the Sun Rose Twice.* Albuquerque: University of New Mexico Press, 1984. The history of Trinity Site, including looks at the wartime mood of the American defense industry, modern physics, and the personal dynamics of the scientists working at Los Alamos.

Udall, Stewart L. *To the Inland Empire: Coronado and Our Spanish Legacy.* Garden City, NY: Doubleday and Company, Inc., 1988. The former Arizona congressman looks at the 1540 expedition of Coronado, including events leading up to it and its repercussions.

Wilson, John P. *Merchants, Guns and Money: The Story of Lincoln County and its Wars.* Santa Fe: Museum of New Mexico Press, 1988. Probably the most complete history of Lincoln County yet published, this book traces the history of the area from the early 1850s to the present, focusing on the motivation for the area's development and problems: money.

Description and Travel

Abbey, Edward. *Desert Solitaire: A Season in the Wilderness.* New York: Ballantine Books (through arrangement with McGraw-Hill Book Co.), 1968. Abbey's notes and observations as a May-to-September Park Service ranger, spent in virtual solitude in the Southwest desert (actually Arches National Monument in southeast Utah). Some of the most poetic, emotional, and inspiring writing to come out of the area.

Alden, Peter, ed. *National Audubon Field Guide to Western States: Arizona, New Mexico, Nevada, and Utah.* New York: Knopf, 1999. Everything you need to know to identify critters, plants, stars, and anything you see outside in New Mexico.

Brandi, John. *That Back Road In.* Berkeley: Wingbow Press, 1985. A collection of Southwestern poetry, based in large part on Brandi's wanderings through the Four Corners area.

Calvin, Ross. *Sky Determines.* Albuquerque: University of New Mexico Press, 1948. A thorough and readable treatise on the influence of the climate—and the sky—on New Mexico's history and culture. First published in 1934. Ernie Pyle called it the "Southwestern Bible."

Chilton, Lance, et al. *New Mexico: A New Guide to the Colorful State.* Albuquerque: University of New Mexico Press, 1984. Indispensable to the New Mexicophile, this is the most complete and well-written general guide to the state (actually an updated Work Projects Administration book—see below), although the sheer size and weight of this tome make it difficult to carry around. The authors look at the history of the state, as well as the geology, flora and fauna, people, religion, architecture, etc. The book is organized around 18 short tours. No practicalities.

Christiansen, Paige W., and Frank E. Kottlowski, eds. *Mosaic of New Mexico's Scenery, Rocks, and History.* Socorro: State Bureau of Mines and Mineral Resources, New Mexico Institute of Mining and Technology, 1972. An eclectic assortment of articles, the subjects of which vary from early Indians and Spanish settlers to frontier forts, from fishing spots and state parks to rocks and exotic plants.

Chronic, Halka. *Roadside Geology of New Mexico.* Missoula: Mountain Press Publishing Company, 1987. Route-by-route discussions of New Mexico's geology—caprock, lava flows, and alluvial plains. Includes special section on national parks and monuments.

Eppele, David L., ed. *Desert in Bloom: Flora and Cacti of the Desert Southwest.* Bisbee, AZ: Arizona Cactus and Succulent Research, 1987. Short reference work (32 pages, with as many photos).

Evans, Harry. *50 Hikes in New Mexico.* Pico Rivera, CA: Gem Guides Book Company, 1987. Detailed descriptions—lengths, difficulty ratings, necessities—of hikes around New Mexico, including maps.

Jamison, Bill, and Cheryl Jamison. *Insider's Guide to Santa Fe.* Harvard Common Press, 1990. Very thorough and readable guide to the city, including history, attractions, events, and practicalities. Excellent descriptions of historical sites and buildings.

Lekson, Stephen H. *Great Pueblo Architecture of Chaco Canyon New Mexico.* Albuquerque: National Park Service, U.S. Department of the Interior, 1984. Profound case study of Chaco. Very academic and not really readable for the layperson. However, photos, maps, charts, and diagrams are interesting.

Lummis, Charles F. *The Land of Poco Tiempo.* Albuquerque: University of New Mexico Press, 1952. This classic book of the Southwest, first published in 1893, looks at the people and landscape of New Mexico through the eyes of a writer who first saw the area while *walking* from Cincinnati to Los Angeles.

Matthews, Kay. *Hiking Trails in the Sandia and Manzano Mountains.* Albuquerque: Heritage Associates, Inc., 1991. Detailed discussions of trails in the Sandias and the Manzanos. Includes geology, preparation (what to wear and bring), what to do in emergencies, maps, and a short section on cross-country ski trails.

Mays, Buddy. *Guide to Western Wildlife.* San Francisco: Chronicle Books, 1988. Pocket-sized guide to the huge variety of critters out West.

Morrill, Claire. *A Taos Mosaic: Portrait of a New Mexico Village.* Albuquerque: University of New Mexico Press, 1973. An intimate look at the folks who have peopled this storied village over the years. Black-and-white photos by Laura Gilpin.

Murray, John A. *The Gila Wilderness, A Hiking Guide.* Albuquerque: University of New Mexico Press, 1992. An extremely detailed look at the Gila area—including maps, charts, and photos—this is both a hiker's guidebook and a home library reference work, with lots of useful, fascinating facts about the area's history, both natural and human.

Nichols, John. *If Mountains Die: A New Mexico Memoir.* New York: Alfred A. Knopf, 1979. Photography by William Davis. In 1969, Nichols *(The Sterile Cuckoo, The Milagro Beanfield War)* moved to the Taos Valley to escape the craziness of New York City. He writes here about his experiences with the land and the elements, and about the struggle he and his neighbors face to protect that land from "overcrowding and human greed." Sixty-five beautiful color photos.

Norwood, Vera, and Janice Monk, eds. *The Desert Is No Lady: Southwestern Landscapes in Women's Writing and Art.* New Haven: Yale University Press, 1988. A widely varied collection of essays on Anglo, Hispanic, and Indian woman writers, photographers, and painters.

Santa Fe Group of the Sierra Club. *Day Hikes in the Santa Fe Area.* Santa Fe: National Education Association Press, 1981. Various short hikes around Santa Fe, with difficulty ratings, driving directions and times, lengths, hiking time, and seasonal considerations. Also includes maps.

Ungnade, Herbert E. *Guide to the New Mexico Mountains.* Albuquerque: University of New Mexico Press, 1972. Detailed descriptions of the mountains and ranges throughout the state. Includes mountaineering history, hiking trails, maps, and photos.

Varney, Phillip (with foreword by Tony Hillerman). *New Mexico's Best Ghost Towns.* Albuquerque: University of New Mexico Press, 1987. A town-by-town look at dozens of the state's historic towns. Photos and maps, with tours and trip suggestions.

Works Progress Administration. *New Mexico: A Guide to the Colorful State.* New York: Hastings House Publishers, Inc., 1953 (fourth printing). From the classic WPA guidebook series, this book is most useful when discussing the state's history (pre-1950 or so, of course). Now out of print, the book is usually available only in libraries and from rare-book dealers. (Also of interest to collectors: in good condition, the book sells for quite a bit more than even a top-notch, up-to-date guide would.)

Politics and Government

Brown, F. Lee, and Helen M. Ingram. *Water and Poverty in the Southwest.* Tucson: University of Arizona Press, 1988. A scholarly look at the problems caused by the Southwest's proverbial lack of water supplies and its early irrigation methods, with special attention to the Hispanic population of the upper Rio Grande Valley.

Chavez, John R. *The Lost Land, The Chicano Image of the Southwest.* Albuquerque: University of New Mexico Press, 1985. An emotional study of New Mexico's Chicanos and their land, with special attention to their loss of a collective social and historical memory through their physical and spiritual displacement at the hands of Anglos.

Clark, Ira G. *Water in New Mexico: A History of Management and Use.* Albuquerque: University of New Mexico Press, 1987. Huge and exhaustive study of the politics of water in the state, from the Anasazi through the Spanish conquerors, statehood, dam construction, and Indian water rights.

deBuys, William. *Enchantment and Exploitation: The Life and Hard Times of a New Mexico Mountain Range.* Albuquerque: University of New Mexico Press, 1985. Director of the Carolina Nature Conservancy, deBuys looks at the history of the civilization of the Sangre de Cristo Mountains, drawing attention to the people and land that have been damaged along the way.

Eaton, David J., and John Michael Anderson. *The State of the Rio Grande/Rio Bravo.* Tucson: University of Arizona Press, 1987. A reference work useful to geographers, government agencies, and hard-core data hounds.

McCutcheon, Chuck. *Nuclear Reactions: The Politics of Opening a Radioactive Disposal Site.* Albuquerque: University of New Mexico Press, 2002. An in-depth look at the problems posed by our nation's dependence on nuclear energy and where to dispose of its waste—looking particularly at the Carlsbad area.

Prucha, Francis Paul. *The Great Father: The United States Government and the American Indian.* Lincoln: University of Nebraska Press, 1984. This 1,300-page, two-volume set is one of the definitive reference works on the delicate and often stormy relationship between Native Americans and those who subdued them.

Shroyer, Jo Ann. *The Secret Mesa: Inside Los Alamos National Laboratory.* Indianapolis, IN: John Wiley and Sons, 1997. A thorough and often times disturbing look at the role Los Alamos has played in the development of world nuclear culture.

Native Americana

Batkin, Jonathan. *Pottery of the Pueblos of New Mexico—1700–1840.* Colorado Springs: Colorado Springs Fine Arts Center, 1987. Beautiful oversized book with lots of black-and-white and color photos. Examines separately the pottery of each pueblo and traces the history of the craft.

Bennett, Noel (photography by John Running). *Halo of the Sun: Stories Told and Retold.* Flagstaff: Northland Press, 1988. Using Navajo as a sort of metaphor, Bennett looks at the common threads running through Navajo culture and society.

Bruchac, Joseph. *Survival This Way: Interviews with American Indian Poets.* Tucson: University of Arizona Press, 1988. Interviews with Joy Harjo, N. Scott Momaday, Simon Ortíz, and 18 others.

Cushing, Frank Hamilton. *The Mythic World of the Zuñi.* Albuquerque: University of New Mexico Press, 1988. A collection of 25 ancient Zuñi myths, reported more than 100 years ago in the "oral tradition." Handsomely illustrated by Barton Wright.

Cushing, Frank Hamilton. *Zuñi Fetishes.* Las Vegas, NV: KC Publications, 1987. Scholarly look at a huge array of fetishes dating to pre-Columbian times. Includes photos and translations of Zuñi "prayers."

Dedra, Don. *Navajo Rugs: How to Find, Evaluate, Buy and Care for Them.* Flagstaff: Northland Press, 1975 (sixth printing, 1988). Scores of interpretive photos and illustrations, as well as photos of Navajo weavers, accompany the text.

Dodge, Robert K., and Joseph B. McCullough, eds. *Voices from Wah'kon-Tah.* New York: International Publishers, Inc., 1976. A widely varied collection of contemporary Native American poetry, uneven in quality but always evocative, stirring, and often disturbing. Contributors include such well-known Indian writers as Paula Gunn Allen, N. Scott Momaday, Simon Ortíz, Marnie Walsh, and James Welsh. Excellent introduction by Vine Deloria Jr.

Fergusson, Erna. *Dancing Gods: Indian Dances of New Mexico.* Albuquerque: University of New Mexico Press, 1931 (fourth printing, 1988). Lively discussions of dances and mythology of Hopi, Zuñi, and Rio Grande Pueblo Indians. Good illustrations of dancers and costumes.

Hartman, Russell P. (Photographs by Stephen Trimble, forward by Clara Lee Tanner.) *Navajo Pottery, Traditions and Innovations.* Flagstaff: Northland Press, 1988. Fascinating look at Navajo pottery, from its origins and history through the current revival.

Iverson, Peter. *The Navajo Nation.* Albuquerque: University of New Mexico Press, 1984. In-depth study of the structure and politics of the Navajo, with all proceeds from the book going to the Nation.

Kraul, Edward Garcia, and Judith Beaty, eds. *The Weeping Woman: Encounters with La Llorana.* Santa Fe: The Word Process, 1988. A collection that examines the myth of *la Llorana,* the mysterious woman who weeps throughout Hispanic legend and folklore.

Marriott, Alice, and Carol K. Rachlin, eds. *American Indian Mythology.* New York: New American Library, 1968. One of the best collections available of Native American myths, including many by Southwestern tribes. Meet

Coyote, Grandmother Spider, the War Twins, and many others, and watch for the huge differences *and* fascinating parallels between Native American and Judeo-Christian mythology. Introduction alone is almost worth the price of admission.

Murphy, James E., and Sharon M. *Let My People Know.* Norman, OK: University of Oklahoma Press, 1981. Scholarly study of Native American journalism, from confiscated presses of mid-19th century to modern Indian journals and newspapers.

Neihardt, John G. *Black Elk Speaks.* New York: Washington Square Press, 1959. Told to Neihardt by the Sioux warrior and medicine man, the story recounts Black Elk's youth on the plains, his Vision, the coming of the white man, and the Battle of Wounded Knee. Though not about New Mexico or Southwestern Indians, the book offers a unique insight into Native American life in the late 19th century. A painful yet important book.

Olson, James S., and Raymond Wilson. *Native Americans in the 20th Century.* Chicago: University of Illinois Press, 1984. A somewhat academic but highly readable account of the forces working against the 20th-century American Indian. The authors look at past government attempts at "helping" the Indians, from Compensation to Termination and Relocation, as well as at Native American responses—passive resistance to militancy. Excellent historical and contemporary photos.

Sando, Joe E. *Nee Hemish.* Albuquerque: University of New Mexico Press, 1982. Humanistic history of Jemez Pueblo written by a Jemez Indian. Covers ancient times to modern land squabbles. Includes photos as well as drawings of the pueblo.

Witt, Shirley Hill, and Stan Steiner, eds. *The Way, An Anthology of Native American Literature.* New York: Alfred A. Knopf, Inc., 1972. Wonderfully eclectic collection of songs, poetry, oratory, mythology, and contemporary journalism by Native Americans. Includes poetry by Simon Ortíz and N. Scott Momaday, oratory by Tecumseh, and Geronimo's surrender speech to General Crook.

Wroth, William. *Weaving and Colcha from the Hispanic Southwest: Authentic Designs.* Santa Fe: Ancient City Press, 1986. A collection of the original Indian designs on which much of New Mexico's traditional furniture, weaving, and leatherwork are based.

Fiction

Abbey, Edward. *The Monkey Wrench Gang.* New York: Avon Books, 1976. The founding father of modern environmentalism tackles the money-hungry bureaucrats wrecking the Southwest's deserts and rivers.

Anaya, Rudolfo A. *Bless Me, Ultima.* Berkeley: Tonatiuh-Quinto Sol International, 1986. Set on the llanos (plains) near Santa Rosa, New Mexico, this is the story of a young boy torn between Catholicism and older, more mystical beliefs and powers. Written in a poetical and moving prose, a prize-winning novel and a great read.

Bandelier, Adolph. *The Delight Makers.* San Diego: Harcourt, Brace, Jovanovich, 1971. Fictionalized account of life among the ancient Pueblo Indians—graceful blend of scientific fact, archaeology, and story.

Cather, Willa. *Death Comes for the Archbishop.* New York: Alfred A. Knopf, 1955. Story of Catholic missionaries in mid-19th century New Mexico. Vivid descriptions of landscape and culture, although with a clear pro-Spanish bias.

Chavez, Fray Angelico. *The Short Stories of Fray Angelico Chavez.* Albuquerque: University of New Mexico Press, 1988. Collection of Chavez's 60 years of short fiction.

Hillerman, Tony. *Dance Hall of the Dead; Skinwalkers; The Ghostway; The Dark Wind; People of Darkness; Listening Woman; The Fly on the Wall; The Blessing Way; A Thief of Time; Talking God; Coyote Waits; Sacred Clowns; et al.* Most available in Avon paperback. Hillerman's murder mysteries, which take place in Zuñi Pueblo and on the Navajo Reservation, are universally acclaimed for their authenticity and brilliant depictions of the Southwest. Readers trying to unravel the crimes along with Detective Jim Chee and Lieutenant Joe Leaphorn learn intimate and fascinating details about Indian culture.

L'Amour, Louis. *Haunted Mesa.* New York: Bantam Books, 1988. Certainly a far cry from the finely crafted work of Tony Hillerman and the profoundly literary tales of Leslie Marmon Silko, L'Amour's novels are hurriedly written (he cranked out more than 100 novels in his lifetime) action-filled page-turners. *Haunted Mesa* deals with the Anasazis' "other world," using their puzzling 13th-century disappearance as a basis for a modern-day mystery. Readers patient enough to put up with the roughness of the prose and the caricatures masquerading as characters will learn some odds and ends about the Four Corners area's earliest home builders. A good plane-trip read.

Momaday, N. Scott. *House Made of Dawn.* New York: Perennial Library, 1977. A young Jemez Indian attempts to return to the traditions of his pueblo after fighting in World War II. Beautifully written by one of the great Native American novelists and poets, the story draws on the mythology, vision, and spirit of the Pueblo Indians.

Nichols, John. *The Milagro Beanfield War.* New York: Ballantine Books, 1976. A good-guy-versus-bad-guy (bean growers vs. developers) story, told with unending magic and charm. Robert Redford directed the wonderful 1988 movie of the same title. Nichols's trilogy is completed with *The Magic Journey* and *Nirvana Blues.*

Ondaatje, Michael. *The Collected Works of Billy the Kid.* New York and London: Penguin Books, 1984. Bizarre montage of fact, fiction, poetry, personal recollections, and photos. One of the best, if most stylistically experimental, books about the Kid.

Seton, Anya. *The Turquoise.* London: Hodder and Stoughton, 1976. Historical romance set partially in New Mexico in the mid- to late-19th century. Not great literature, but the first few chapters give a good flavor of life in Santa Fe and along the Santa Fe Trail during the 1860s. Written by the daughter of Ernest Thompson Seton, founder of the Boy Scouts.

Silko, Leslie Marmon. *Ceremony.* New York: Viking Press, 1977. Powerful story of the spiritual healing of a Navajo war veteran. Blends Indian mythology and storytelling with conventional fictional devices. A must-read for anyone interested in Southwestern Indians, especially in their literature.

Snodgrass, Melinda M., ed. *A Very Large Array: New Mexico's Science Fiction and Fantasy.* Albuquerque: University of New Mexico Press, 1988. An anthology of science fiction and fantasy by New Mexican writers, both native and transplanted, including Jack Williamson, George R. R. Martin, Suzy McKee Charnas, and Stephen R. Donaldson.

Biography

Branch, Louis Leon. *Los Bilitos: The Story of Billy the Kid.* New York: Carlton Press, 1980. Based on a rediscovered manuscript written by Charles F. Rudolph, one of Pat Garrett's posse. Includes letters by the Kid to Governor Wallace.

Cowart, Jack, and Juan Hamilton. *Georgia O'Keeffe: Art and Letters.* Boston: New York Graphic Society Books/Little, Brown, and Company, 1988. Reproductions of O'Keeffe's art, as well as letters to husband Alfred Stieglitz, Mabel Dodge Luhan, and Eleanor Roosevelt (asking her to support the Equal Rights Amendment). Also included are essays by Jack Cowart, curator of 20th-century art at the National Gallery of Art, and Juan Hamilton, O'Keeffe's assistant in her later years.

Greenberg, Henry, and Georgia Greenberg. *Carl Gorman's World.* Albuquerque: University of New Mexico Press, 1985. The complex and at times painful life story of Carl Gorman, one in a long line of famous and influential Gorman artists (Carl is father to R. C.).

Lange, Charles, et al., eds. *The Southwestern Journals of Adolph F. Bandelier.* Albuquerque: University of New Mexico Press, 1986 (Volume IV). Widely assorted notes and annotations (from discussions of his profession to comments on Santa Fe's breweries) by one of New Mexico's early archaeologists and intellectuals.

Waters, Frank. *To Possess the Land: A Biography of Arthur Rochford Manby.* Chicago: The Swallow Press, Inc., 1973. A chronicle of "the West's greatest unsolved mystery": the unexplained death of Manby, whose strange obsession to rule a 100,000-acre land grant near Taos led him to create "a secret society, which terrorized whole towns and villages."

Art and Photography

Callaway, Nicholas, ed. *Georgia O'Keeffe: One Hundred Flowers.* New York: Alfred A. Knopf, in association with Callaway Editions, 1988. Large collection of O'Keeffe's work, both recognizable pieces as well as lesser-known ones.

Caplin, Harvey. *Enchanted Land, New Mexico.* Albuquerque: Bank Securities Inc. in collaboration with Calvin Horn Publisher, Inc., 1973. Caplin captures the state's color and moods, people and villages, in wondrous black-and-white photos.

D'Emilio, Sandra, and Suzan Campbell. *Spirit and Vision: Images of Ranchos de Taos Church.* Santa Fe: Museum of New Mexico Press, 1987. Nearly 100 black-and-white and color plates of the church by the numerous painters and photographers it has captivated.

Johnson, Byron A., and Robert K. Dauner. *Early Albuquerque: A Photographic History, 1870–1918.* Albuquerque: Albuquerque Journal, City of Albuquerque, and Albuquerque Museum, 1981. A fascinating collection of photos of the streets, the buildings, and the people of old Albuquerque, although this book is now out of print and difficult to find.

Muench, David. *New Mexico.* Portland, OR: Graphic Arts Center Publishing, 1974. This portfolio-sized coffee-table-style book, with warm and informative text by Tony Hillerman, features stunning photos of the state in all its glory by one of the country's preeminent landscape photographers.

Myers, Joan, with text by Marc Simmons. *Along the Santa Fe Trail.* Albuquerque: University of New Mexico Press, 1986. Two-part look at the Santa Fe Trail: Myers's stark black-and-white photos and Simmons's narrative, in which he retraces the old trail himself and recounts its history along the way.

Shapiro, Michael Edward, and Peter H. Hassrick (with other contributors). *Frederic Remington: The Masterworks.* New York: Harry N. Abrams, Inc., 1988. An impressively large study of both the work and the man, who helped define Western art and gave many Americans their only view of late-19th-century cowboys, soldiers, Indians, and mountain men.

Trimble, Stephen. *Talking with the Clay: The Art of Pueblo Pottery.* Santa Fe: School of American Research Press, 1987. Photos and discussions of the pots and the people who make them.

Warren, Nancy Hunter. *Villages of Hispanic New Mexico.* Santa Fe: School of American Research, 1988. A compelling look at New Mexico's small settlements, with emphasis on the Catholic Church (and churches).

Language

Cobos, Ruben. *A Dictionary of New Mexican and Southern Colorado Spanish.* Santa Fe: Museum of New Mexico Press, 1983. Many Southwesterners of Spanish descent still speak a Spanish much like that of 16th- and 17th-century Spaniards. This fascinating dictionary gives the background of the phenomenon and translates Spanish words unlikely to be encountered outside small rural pockets of New Mexico and southern Colorado.

Smith, Cornelius C. *A Southwestern Vocabulary: The Words They Used.* Glendale, CA: Arthur H. Clark, Co., 1984. More than 500 words brought to New Mexico by its various settlers and passers-through: Spanish, Anglo, Indian, and U.S. military.

Cookbooks

Cameron, Sheila MacNiven. *The Best from New Mexico Kitchens* and *More of the Best from New Mexico Kitchens.* Santa Fe: New Mexico Magazine, 1978 and 1983. Scores of excellent recipes—sourdough flapjacks to chile stews.

Fergusson, Erna. *Mexican Cookbook.* Albuquerque: University of New Mexico Press, 1945. Southwest dishes, from chile stews to tortillas to *melococha* (molasses candy), by one of New Mexico's best-loved writers.

McKee, Gwen and Barbara Moseley, eds. *The Best of the Best from New Mexico: Selected Recipes from New Mexico's Favorite Cookbooks.* Brandon, MS: Quail Ridge Press, 1999. From *carne adovado* to green-chile stew to breakfast burritos, it's all here.

Miller, Mark. *Coyote Cafe.* Berkeley: Ten Speed Press, 1989. A cookbook and much more, this gorgeously illustrated collection of recipes from Santa Fe's Coyote Cafe includes background information on Southwestern cuisine and cooking, as well as excerpts from Native American mythology (see "How Coyote Brought the Chiles"). Recipes range from the simple to the elegant, from commonplace to exotic. Special sections on cocktails and sauces.

Murphy, Rosalea. *The Pink Adobe Cookbook.* New York: Dell Publishing Company, 1988. Recipes and menus from Santa Fe's famous Pink Adobe restaurant, including salsas, "Dobeburgers," and French pie. Murphy has been featured on the PBS series *Great Chefs of the West.*

Odds and Ends

Campbell, Walter S. *The Book Lover's Southwest.* Norman, OK: University of Oklahoma Press, 1955. Though dated, probably the most thorough bibliography available. Annotated, with chapters on Biography and Autobiography, Description and Interpretation, Drama, Folklore, History, Humor, Juvenile, Satire, Science Fiction, and more.

Chew, Joe. *Storms above the Desert: Atmospheric Research in New Mexico, 1935–1985.* Albuquerque: University of New Mexico Press, 1988. A witty account of the history of Langmuir Laboratory for Atmospheric Research's thunderstorm research (at New Mexico Technical Institute in Socorro). Partly sanctioned by the Historical Society of New Mexico.

Hillerman, Tony, ed. *The Spell of New Mexico.* Albuquerque: University of New Mexico Press, 1984. A widely varied collection of essays by well-known authors—both native New Mexicans and "outsiders." Contributors include D. H. Lawrence, Carl Jung, Mary Austin, Oliver La Farge, and Winfield Townley Scott, among others. One of the best literary companions for New Mexicans and visitors alike.

Peacock, Doug. *Grizzly Years: In Search of the American Wilderness.* New York: Henry Holt and Company, 1990. A first-person account by the West's preeminent desert rat and rabble-rouser (as well as the model for George Hayduke, the hero in Ed Abbey's *The Monkey Wrench Gang*), *Grizzly Years* is the story of Peacock's quest for wild bears and American backcountry. The journey is also a personal purging, beginning with Peacock's return from Vietnam in 1968 (complete with numerous and disturbing flashbacks to the jungle) and taking him deep into the solitude of the Rockies and his own soul. A painful but important book.

Stegner, Wallace. *The American West as Living Space.* Ann Arbor: University of Michigan Press, 1987. Stegner shares his insights and offers (as usual) intriguing analyses of why folks live in and love the West.

Taylor, Lonn, and Dessa Bokidas (photography by Mary Peck and Jim Bones). *New Mexican Furniture, 1600–1940.* Santa Fe: Museum of New Mexico Press, 1988. A handsomely illustrated look at Southwestern furniture, from the early Spanish woodworkers through the "antimodernist" Spanish Colonial Revival. Of particular interest is the historical framework in which the story of the furniture is told.

Magazines

New Mexico Magazine. Invaluable magazine for the serious New Mexicophile. Profiles, travel features spotlighting out-of-the-way places around the state, regular "Sundial" of events, and the tongue-in-cheek "One of Our Fifty is Missing," which looks at outsiders' weird perceptions of New Mexico. Also publishes the annual *Vacation Guide,* an excellent overview of things to do and see in the state. Subscription information: New Mexico Magazine, Subscription Dept., P.O. Box 409, Mt. Morris, IL 61054, 800/435-0715, website: nmmagazine.com.

The Santa Fean. Monthly magazine focusing on Santa Fe living and particularly the arts scene there. Beautifully laid out, albeit heavy on the slick-ad side, the magazine lists local lodgings and gallery showings and openings, and includes a Santa Fe–area calendar. Write 1440-A Saint Francis Dr., Santa Fe, NM 87501, or call 505/983-8914, website: www.santafean.com.

Newspapers

Albuquerque Journal. Daily morning paper (locally owned), distributed throughout the state. Large Sunday edition. Regular "Trends" and "New Mexico" sections of special interest to tourists and travelers, as well as "Indian Country Events" in Sunday's paper. Write 7777 Jefferson NE, Albuquerque, NM 87103, or call 505/823-4400, website: www.abqjournal.com.

Albuquerque Tribune. Afternoon newspaper, daily except Sunday (Scripps Howard paper). Write 7777 Jefferson NE, Albuquerque, NM 87103, or call 505/823-4400, website: www.abqtrib.com.

Daily Lobo. Newspaper of the University of New Mexico. Stories about university and international matters (some wire stories). Good source for what's happening on the music and arts scene. Free at various locations around Albuquerque; website: www.dailylobo.com.

El Paso Times. Daily out of El Paso, Texas, but distributed widely in southern New Mexico. "New Mexico" section focuses on the state's news. Phone number for circulation: 505/526-5444 (in Las Cruces) or 800/351-1677, website: www.elpasotimes.com.

Las Cruces Sun-News. Daily of Las Cruces and Mesilla, although the *El Paso Times* appears to be the town's more widely read paper. Write P.O. Box 1749, Las Cruces, NM 88004, or call 505/523-4581, website: www.lcsun-news.com.

The New Mexican. Daily paper of Santa Fe and northern New Mexico (Gannett publication). Listings of events, galleries, and music. Profiles of Santa Fe-area celebrities. Write 202 Marcy Rd., Santa Fe, NM, 87501, or call 505/983-3303, website: www.sfnewmexican.com.

The Taos News. Small-town weekly (covers local softball games, residents' anniversaries, etc.) lists happenings in the Taos area and keeps residents up to date on nearby resorts and reservations, galleries and concerts. Comes out every Thursday. Call 505/758-2241 or write P.O. Box U, Taos, NM 87571, website: www.taosnews.com.

Internet Resources

General New Mexico Tourist Information

New Mexico Department of Tourism
www.newmexico.org

This is a good place to begin, whether you want to order a hard-copy brochure of a New Mexico vacation guide or to explore the many links—to everything from museums and backroads to accommodations and dining.

Regional Tourist Information

The websites of most of the following towns and cities offer specifics on lodging, dining, sight-seeing, and relocation information, in addition to links to other helpful online resources.

Alamogordo Chamber of Commerce
www.alamogordo.com

Albuquerque Convention and Visitors Bureau
www.itsatrip.org

Angel Fire
angelfirechamber.org

Carlsbad
www.chamber.caverns.com

Cloudcroft
cloudcroft.com

Farmington
www.farmingtonnm.org

Gallup
www.gallupnm.org

Grants
www.grants.org

Las Cruces
lascrucescvb.org

Las Vegas
lasvegas.net

Navajoland Tourism Office
www.newmexico.org/culture/res_navajo.html

Red River
redrivernm.com

Roswell
roswellnm.org

Ruidoso
www.ruidoso.net

Santa Fe
santafe.org

Silver City
silvercity.org

Taos
taosvacationguide.com

Transportation

Albuquerque International Airport
www.cabq.gov/airport

Flight information, ground transportation, lodging, dining, car rental, maps, parking, and lots more.

Amtrak
www.amtrak.com

Schedules, routes, ticketing, specials and promotions, and general planning information.

Road Conditions
www.nmshtd.state.nm.us/roadadv

Information on road construction, closures, weather, and other travel alerts.

Outdoors and Sports

New Mexico State Parks
www.emnrd.state.nm.us/nmparks

Tours of parks, reservations, calendars of events, and volunteer and employment opportunities.

New Mexico Department of Game and Fish
www.gmfsh.state.nm.us

Information on hunting and fishing, including licensing and special restrictions and registrations.

Hiking and Biking in New Mexico
www.newmexico.org/outdoors

Thorough state-funded site not only to hiking and biking but to horseback riding, camping, kayaking, and winter sports.

International Mountain Biking Association
www.imba.com

An excellent website, with links to local chapters and clubs.

Ski New Mexico
skinewmexico.com

Information on all the ski and snowboard resorts in the state, including cross-country areas, as well as links to lodging, dining, and other nearby attractions, plus snow reports.

Accommodations

Hosteling International-American Youth Hostels
www.hiayh.com

The complete source for information about hosteling in New Mexico and around the world.

International Bed and Breakfast Pages
www.ibbp.com

This website provides information on inns with ratings from other travelers.

New Mexico Bed and Breakfast Association
www.nmbba.org

Probably the most thorough guide to the bed-and-breakfasts of the state, listed regionally and by city, with maps and links to individual inns.

Index

Archaeological Sites

Native Americans (Indians)

Events and Festivals

Museums and Exhibits

O

Pueblos

QR

S

UV

Unusual Claims to Fame

WXYZ

Acknowledgments

A lot of good people helped me put this book together, and many have stayed with me as it's gone into six editions. Thank you. Thanks, too, to all the readers who took the time to write and point out misteaks, tyops, and ommis ions, as well as to the many friends, old and new, who suggested a back road, offered a couch to crash on, let me pick their brains over espressos or microbrews, or feigned interest as I passed around photos of my family back in California.

Also, thanks to all the chambers of commerce and convention and visitors centers that have provided direction, inspiration, and in many cases lodging. For assistance with maps, I'd especially like to thank Chris Faivre in Las Cruces, Jessica Chaves in Roswell, Tanya Amento in Albuquerque, and Ed Jungbluth in Gallup.

Most of all, though, I'm grateful for the support of my family—Betsy, Hannah, and Gina. Twenty thousand roads I went down, down, down, and they all led me straight back home to you.

U.S. ~ Metric Conversion

1 inch	=	2.54 centimeters (cm)
1 foot	=	.304 meters (m)
1 yard	=	0.914 meters
1 mile	=	1.6093 kilometers (km)
1 km	=	.6214 miles
1 fathom	=	1.8288 m
1 chain	=	20.1168 m
1 furlong	=	201.168 m
1 acre	=	.4047 hectares
1 sq km	=	100 hectares
1 sq mile	=	2.59 square km
1 ounce	=	28.35 grams
1 pound	=	.4536 kilograms
1 short ton	=	.90718 metric ton
1 short ton	=	2000 pounds
1 long ton	=	1.016 metric tons
1 long ton	=	2240 pounds
1 metric ton	=	1000 kilograms
1 quart	=	.94635 liters
1 US gallon	=	3.7854 liters
1 Imperial gallon	=	4.5459 liters
1 nautical mile	=	1.852 km

To compute celsius temperatures, subtract 32 from Fahrenheit and divide by 1.8. To go the other way, multiply celsius by 1.8 and add 32.

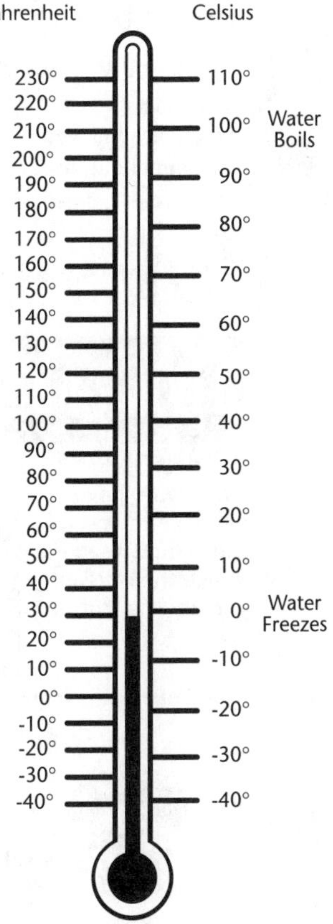

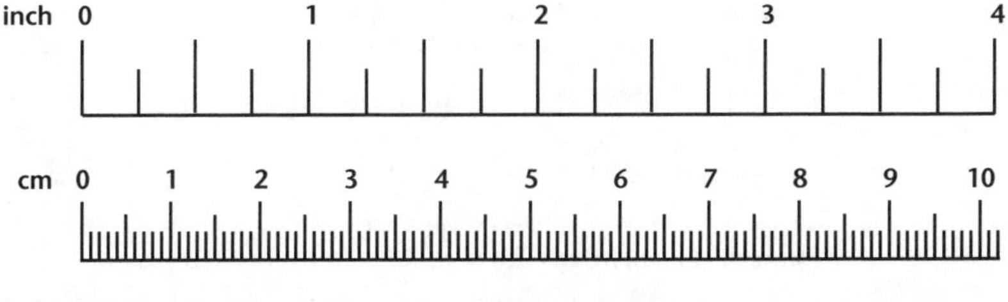

ALSO FROM

AVALON TRAVEL PUBLISHING

www.travelmatters.com

MOON METRO
UNFOLD THE CITY

Map-based Moon Metro unfolds each city neighborhood by neighborhood, with insider recommendations on the best spots to eat, sleep, shop, and explore.

www.moon.com

Rick Steves

More *Savvy*. More *Surprising*. More *Fun*.

As the #1 authority on European travel, Rick gives you inside information on what to visit, where to stay, and how to get there—economically and hassle-free.

www.ricksteves.com

LIVING ABROAD

DREAM. PLAN. MAKE IT HAPPEN.

With authors who have made the move themselves, these guides show readers how to make their dream of living in another country a reality.

www.livingabroadin.com

ROAD TRIP USA

OPEN ROAD. ENDLESS POSSIBILITIES.

See what the interstates have left behind. **ROAD TRIP USA** takes you off the beaten path, onto classic blacktop, and into the soul of America.

www.roadtripusa.com

THE DOG LOVER'S COMPANION

The Inside Scoop on Where to Take Your Dog

A special breed of guidebook for travelers and residents who don't want to leave their canine pals behind.

www.dogloverscompanion.com

FOGHORN OUTDOORS®

YOUR ADVENTURE STARTS HERE

Foghorn authors are recreation experts who provide readers with the most up-to-date information on enjoying the outdoors.

www.foghorn.com

AVAILABLE AT BOOKSTORES AND THROUGH ONLINE BOOKSELLERS